DATE DUE

BRODART, CO.   Cat. No. 23-221

UNITED STATES COURT OF APPEALS
FOR THE DISTRICT OF COLUMBIA CIRCUIT

Division for the Purpose of
Appointing Independent Counsel
Division No. 86–6

FINAL REPORT OF THE INDEPENDENT COUNSEL FOR IRAN/CONTRA MATTERS

Volume III:
Comments and Materials Submitted by Individuals and Their Attorneys
Responding to Volume I of the Final Report

LAWRENCE E. WALSH
Independent Counsel

December 3, 1993
Washington, D.C.

DATE DUE

OCT 2 1994	
FEB 1 0 2001	

UNITED STATES COURT OF APPEALS
FOR THE DISTRICT OF COLUMBIA CIRCUIT

Division for the Purpose of
Appointing Independent Counsel
Division No. 86–6

FINAL REPORT OF THE INDEPENDENT COUNSEL FOR IRAN/CONTRA MATTERS

Volume III:
Comments and Materials Submitted by Individuals and Their Attorneys
Responding to Volume I of the Final Report

LAWRENCE E. WALSH
Independent Counsel

December 3, 1993
Washington, D.C.

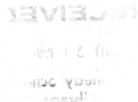

For sale by the U.S. Government Printing Office
Superintendent of Documents, Mail Stop: SSOP, Washington, DC 20402-9328
ISBN 0-16-043009-7

REPORTS OF INDEPENDENT COUNSEL

On August 5, 1993, the Office of Independent Counsel for Iran/contra Matters submitted a three-volume report to the United States Court of Appeals for the District of Columbia Circuit, Division for the Purpose of Appointing Independent Counsel:

1. Volume I: Investigations and Prosecutions
2. Volume II: Indictments, Plea Agreements, Interim Reports to the Congress, and Administrative Matters and a third classified volume that remains under seal.

On December 3, 1993, the Court ordered that the *Final Report of Independent Counsel* be released to the public subject to the completion of an appendix, containing comments and materials submitted by individuals and their attorneys responding to Volume I of the *Final Report* pursuant to 28 U.S.C. §594, and the filing of the completed report, with the exception of any deletions required by law or further order of the Court. These comments and materials are compiled in Volume III.

The materials from Independent Counsel's investigations that are not contained in the *Final Report* have been deposited with the National Archives. Materials are also held, some under seal, in the United States District Courts for the Districts of Columbia and Maryland and the Eastern District of Virginia and in the United States Courts of Appeals for the District of Columbia and Fourth Circuits.

Contents

Volume I

Volume II

Volume III

United States Court of Appeals
For the District of Columbia Circuit

FILED DEC 0 3 1993

RON GARVIN
CLERK

UNITED STATES COURT OF APPEALS
FOR THE DISTRICT OF COLUMBIA CIRCUIT
Division for the Purpose of
Appointing Independent Counsels

Ethics in Government Act of 1978, as Amended

In re: Oliver L. North, et al.   Division No. 86-6
       (Emergency Motion of
       Society of Professional
       Journalists, et al.)

Before: Sentelle, *Presiding*, Butzner and Sneed, *Senior Circuit*
    Judges

ORDER

This matter came on to be heard and was heard on the Motion of
the Society of Professional Journalists, the Reporters Committee
for Freedom of the Press, and the National Security Archive
requesting the full disclosure of the Final Report of Independent
Counsel Lawrence E. Walsh inclusive of all comments submitted
pursuant to 28 U.S.C. § 594(h)(2). It appears to the Court for
reasons more fully set forth in the memorandum filed
simultaneously herewith that the motion should be in large part
allowed. It is therefore

ORDERED, ADJUDGED, and DECREED that: (1) the Final Report
of the Independent Counsel, inclusive of an appendix containing
all comments or factual information submitted by any individual
pursuant to 28 U.S.C. § 594, shall be released to the public upon

1

the completion of the appendix and the filing of the completed report; (2) this release is subject to any deletions required by law or further order of this Court; and (3) this order does not release the classified appendix to the Report.

For the Court this _____3^RD_____ day of _December_, 1993.

Per Curiam
For the Court:

Ron Garvin

Ron Garvin, Clerk

MEMORANDUM

Two journalistic associations and another non-profit research institute (collectively "movants") have moved the Court for the release of the Final Report of Independent Counsel Lawrence E. Walsh submitted to the Court pursuant to 28 U.S.C. § 594(h)(1)(B) in the above-captioned matter (the "Iran/Contra Investigation"). As the movants note, the Court is empowered by law to "release to the Congress, the public, or any appropriate person," all or part of reports, such as Walsh's, setting forth the work of an independent counsel as "the court considers appropriate." 28 U.S.C. § 594(h)(2). As the movants note, the Iran/Contra Investigation has been the occasion of massive media coverage and public debate. The Court not only "considers [it] appropriate," but in the public interest that as full a disclosure as possible be made of the Final Report of the Independent Counsel herein. Therefore, the Court is granting the disclosure sought by the movants, subject only to slight delay and such deletions as may be required by law.

As to the delay, Congress in 28 U.S.C. § 594(h)(2) has empowered the Court to make "any portion of a final report ... available to any individual named in such report for the purposes of receiving within a time limit set by the division of the court any comments or factual information that such individual may submit." In this case, the Court has exercised that power, first by granting to all individuals named in the Report a period of time from the original filing of the Report in August until

October 3, 1993, to make comments and thereafter by extending that period by order to December 3, 1993. Congress has further empowered the Division to require that "[s]uch comments and factual information, in whole or in part, ... be included as an appendix to such final report." *Id.* The Court has heretofore ordered such inclusion. The Independent Counsel has remained active for the purpose of completing the further required filing of the Report inclusive of this appendix. As the period for comment does not lapse until December 3, and as the publication of the Report inclusive of the appendix will require additional time on the part of the Independent Counsel, it will not be physically possible to release the Report inclusive of the comments for some short period of time after December 3, 1993. The Court notes that it has denied all requests for further extensions of the comment deadline beyond December 3.

As it appears to the Court from the framework of the statute that Congress contemplated the protection of the reputational and other interests of persons named in the Report by the inclusion of a statutory appendix as a part of the Final Report, the congressional goal would be in part thwarted if the Final Report were given general release before the appendix. For that reason, we have incorporated in the order of release the slight delay occasioned by the creation of the appendix. Upon the completion of that task, the Report will be released.

We do note that the possibility exists that either Rule 6(e) of the Federal Rules of Criminal Procedure or some other statutory mandate may require limited deletions from the Final Report before its general release. We anticipate that these deletions, if any, will be minor. In this connection, we further note that a classified appendix exists to the original Final Report of the Independent Counsel and expressly specify that the release of that classified appendix is not contemplated in our order.

Reporting Requirements
Statute and Legislative History

Independent Counsel Walsh was appointed pursuant to the Ethics in Government Act of 1982. The 1982 requirement for a Final Report and its release by the Court is found at 28 U.S.C. §595 (b)(2)(3), published in the "Historical and Statutory Notes" following 28 U.S.C.A. §595 (West 1993 Supp.). A reprint of these subsections follows. The 1978 legislative history for the reporting requirement is also included. In the preceding Order, the Court cites to 28 U.S.C. §594(h) (1987) which reenacted these provisions after Walsh's appointment.

28 § 589a

then the Attorney General shall include in such report a recommendation regarding the manner in which the fees payable under section 1930(a) of title 28, United States Code, may be modified to cause the annual amount deposited in the Fund to more closely approximate the annual amount expended from the Fund.

(e) There are authorized to be appropriated to the Fund for any fiscal year such sums as may be necessary to supplement amounts deposited under subsection (b) for the purposes specified in subsection (a).

(f) For the purpose of recovering the cost of services of the United States Trustee System, there shall be deposited as offsetting collections to the appropriation "United States Trustee System Fund", to remain available until expended, the following—

(1) 16.7 per centum of the fees collected under section 1930(a)(3) of this title;

(2) 40 per centum of the fees collected under section 1930(a)(6) of this title.

(Added Pub.L. 99–554, Title I, § 115(a), Oct. 27, 1986, 100 Stat. 3094, and amended Pub.L. 101–162, Title IV, § 406(c), Nov. 21, 1989, 103 Stat. 1016; Pub.L. 102–140, Title I, § 111(b), (c), Oct. 28, 1991, 105 Stat. 795.)

HISTORICAL AND STATUTORY NOTES

1991 Amendment

Subsec. (b)(2). Pub.L. 102–140, § 111(b)(1), substituted "50 per centum" for "three-fifths".

Subsec. (b)(5). Pub.L. 102–140, § 111(b)(2), substituted "60 per centum" for "all".

Subsec. (f). Pub.L. 102–140, § 111(c), added subsec. (f).

1989 Amendment

Subsec. (b)(1). Pub.L. 101–162, § 406(c), substituted "one-fourth" for "one-third".

Effective Date of 1991 Amendment

Section 111 of Pub.L. 102–140 provided in part that the amendment of this section and section

1930 of this title are effective 60 days after the date of the enactment of Pub.L. 102–140, which was approved Oct. 28, 1991.

Effective Date

Enactment by Pub.L. 99–554 effective 30 days after Oct. 27, 1986, except as otherwise provided for, see section 302(a) of Pub.L. 99–554, set out as a note under section 581 of this title.

Legislative History

For legislative history and purpose of Pub.L. 99–554, see 1986 U.S.Code Cong. and Adm.News, p. 5227.

CHAPTER 40—INDEPENDENT COUNSEL

HISTORICAL AND STATUTORY NOTES

1987 Amendment

Pub.L. 100–191, § 2, Dec. 15, 1987, 101 Stat. 1293, in item 592 substituted "Preliminary investigation and application for appointment of an independent counsel" for "Application for appointment of a independent counsel", in item 594 substituted "an independent counsel" for "a independent counsel", in item 595 substituted "Congressional oversight" for "Reporting and congressional oversight", in item 596 substituted "an independent counsel" for "a independent counsel", in item 598 substituted "Severability" for

"Termination of effect of chapter", and added item 599.

1986 Amendment

Pub.L. 99–554, Title I, § 144(g)(1), Oct. 27, 1986, 100 Stat. 3097, substituted "40" for "39" in chapter heading.

1983 Amendment

Pub.L. 97–409, § 2(a)(1)(A), Jan. 3, 1983, 96 Stat. 2039, substituted "independent counsel" for "special prosecutor" in the chapter heading and in items 592, 594, and 596 of the analysis.

LAW REVIEW COMMENTARIES

Constitutional rationale for the independent counsel law. Donald J. Simon, 25 Am.Crim. L.Rev. 229 (1987).

Constitutionality of the independent counsel statute. Simon Lazarus and Jane E. Larson, 25 Am.Crim.L.Rev. 187 (1987).

fully and completely a description of the work of the independent counsel, including the disposition of all cases brought, and the reasons for not prosecuting any matter within the prosecutorial jurisdiction of such independent counsel which were not prosecuted, with the division of the court authorized to release to the Congress, the public, or to any appropriate person, such portions of a report made under this subsection as the division deems appropriate under such orders appropriate to protect the rights of any individual named in such report and to prevent undue interference with any pending prosecution.

Subsec. (c). Pub.L. 100–191 added a subsec. (c) heading and, in text, re-enacted existing provisions without change but for the addition of language requiring that the information which the independent counsel receives be received by the independent counsel's as part of the independent counsel's activities in carrying out the independent counsel's responsibilities under this chapter.

Subsec. (d). Pub.L. 100–191 struck out subsec. (d) and transferred its content to subsec. (a)(1) of this section.

Subsec. (e). Pub.L. 100–191 struck out subsec. (e), which had provided that a majority of majority party members or a majority of all nonmajority party members of the Committee on the Judiciary of either House of the Congress could request in writing that the Attorney General apply for the appointment of an independent counsel, that not later than thirty days after the receipt of such a request, or not later than fifteen days after the completion of a preliminary investigation of the matter with respect to which the request was made, whichever was later, the Attorney General had to provide written notification of any action the Attorney General had taken in response to such request and, if no application had been made to the division of the court, why such application had not been made, and that such written notification was to be provided to the committee on which the persons making the request served.

1983 Amendment

Subsec. (a). Pub.L. 97–409, § 2(a)(1)(A), substituted "independent counsel" for "special prosecutor" wherever appearing.

Subsec. (b)(1). Pub.L. 97–409, § 2(a)(1)(A), substituted "independent counsel" for "special prosecutor".

Pub.L. 97–409, § 2(a)(1)(B), substituted "independent counsel's" for "special prosecutor's".

Subsecs. (b)(2), (c), (d), (e). Pub.L. 97–409, § 2(a)(1)(A), substituted "independent counsel" for "special prosecutor" wherever appearing.

Effective Date of 1987 Amendment

This section, as amended by Pub.L. 100–191 and as set out in text above, to take effect on Dec. 15, 1987, and to apply only to new independent counsel proceedings and to new independent counsels coming into existence on and after Dec. 15, 1987, see section 6 of Pub.L. 100–191, set out as a note under section 591 of this title. For applicability to previously initiated proceedings still pending on Dec. 15, 1987, see note above.

Effective Date

Section effective Oct. 26, 1978, except for specific information received by the Attorney General pursuant to section 591 of this title based on determinations made by the Attorney General respecting such information, see section 604 of Pub.L. 95–521, set out as a note under section 591 of this title.

Proceedings Pending on December 15, 1987

Section 6(b) of Pub.L. 100–191, set out as a note under section 591 of this title, provided that, with respect to previously initiated independent counsel proceedings still pending on Dec. 15, 1987, this section, in its pre-Pub.L.100–191 form and in lieu of its text as amended by Pub.L. 100–191, shall continue to apply to such pending proceedings until such proceedings are terminated in accordance with this chapter.

Prior to amendment by Pub.L. 100–191, this section read as follows:

"§ 595. Reporting and congressional oversight

"(a) A [1] independent counsel appointed under this chapter may make public from time to time, and shall send to the Congress statements or reports on the activities of such independent counsel. These statements and reports shall contain such information as such independent counsel deems appropriate.

"(b)(1) In addition to any reports made under subsection (a) of this section, and before the termination of a [2] independent counsel's office under section 596(b) of this title, such independent counsel shall submit to the division of the court a report under this subsection.

"(2) A report under this subsection shall set forth fully and completely a description of the work of the independent counsel, including the disposition of all cases brought, and the reasons for not prosecuting any matter within the prosecutorial jurisdiction of such independent counsel which was not prosecuted.

"(3) The division of the court may release to the Congress, the public, or to any appropriate person, such portions of a report made under this subsection as the division deems appropriate. The division of the court shall make such orders as are appropriate to protect the rights of any individual named in such report and to prevent undue interference with any pending prosecution. The division of the court may make any portion of a report under this section available to any individual named in such report for the purposes of receiving within a time limit set by the division of the court any comments or factual information that such individual may submit. Such comments and factual information, in whole or in part, may in the discretion of such division be included as an appendix to such report.

"(c) A [1] independent counsel shall advise the House of Representatives of any substantial and credible information which such independent counsel receives that may constitute grounds for an impeachment. Nothing in this chapter or section 49 of this title shall prevent the Congress or either House thereof from obtaining information in the course of an impeachment proceeding.

"(d) The appropriate committees of the Congress shall have oversight jurisdiction with respect to the official conduct of any independent counsel appointed under this chapter, and such independent counsel shall have the duty to cooperate with the exercise of such oversight jurisdiction.

UNITED STATES CODE

Congressional and Administrative News

95th Congress—Second Session

1978

Convened January 19, 1978
Adjourned October 15, 1978

Volume 4

LEGISLATIVE HISTORY

ST. PAUL, MINN.

WEST PUBLISHING CO.

LEGISLATIVE HISTORY
P.L. 95–521

ETHICS IN GOVERNMENT ACT OF 1978

P.L. 95–521, see page 92 Stat. 1824

Senate Report (Governmental Affairs Committee) No. 95–170,
Mar. 16, 1977 [To accompany S. 555]

Senate Report (Judiciary Committee) No. 95–273, June 15, 1977
[To accompany S. 555]

House Report (Judiciary Committee) No. 95–800, Nov. 2, 1977
[To accompany H.R. 1]

House Report (Post Office and Civil Service Committee)
No. 95–642(I), Sept. 28, 1977 [To accompany H.R. 6954]

House Report (Armed Services Committee) No. 95–642(II),
Oct. 17, 1977 [To accompany H.R. 6954]

House Report (Judiciary Committee) No. 95–1307,
June 19, 1978 [To accompany H.R. 9705]

House Conference Report No. 95–1756, Oct. 11, 1978
[To accompany S. 555]

Cong. Record Vol. 123 (1977)

Cong. Record Vol. 124 (1978)

DATES OF CONSIDERATION AND PASSAGE

Senate June 27, 1977; October 7, 1978

House September 27, October 12, 1978

The Senate bill was passed in lieu of the House bill. The Senate
Reports (this page, p. 4376) and the House Conference
Report (p. 4381) are set out.

SENATE REPORT NO. 95–170
[page III]

CONTENTS

ETHICS IN GOVERNMENT ACT
P.L. 95–521

SENATE REPORT NO. 95–170
[page 1]

The Committee on Governmental Affairs, to which was referred the bill (S. 555) to establish certain Federal agencies, effect certain reorganizations of the Federal Government, to implement certain reforms in the operation of the Federal Government and to preserve and promote the integrity of public officials and institutions, and for other purposes, having considered the same, reports favorably thereon with an amendment in the nature of a substitute, and recommends that the bill as amended do pass.

I.—PURPOSE OF LEGISLATION

The purpose of this legislation is to preserve and promote the accountability and integrity of public officials and of the institutions of the Federal Government and to invigorate the Constitutional separation of powers between the three branches of Government.

Title I of the bill establishes a stand-by mechanism for the appointment of a temporary special prosecutor when needed and establishes an Office of Government Crimes within the Department of Justice.

Title II of the bill establishes an Office of Congressional Legal Counsel to represent the vital interests of Congress in matters before the courts.

Title III of the bill requires the public disclosure of the financial interests of high-level officers and employees of the Federal Government.

Title IV of the bill establishes an Office of Government Ethics within the Civil Service Commission.

Title V of the bill sets forth certain restrictions on the post employment activities of officers and employees of the Executive Branch of the Federal Government.

[page 70]

enforcement of criminal laws, the special prosecutor will seriously consider those policies and have a legitimate reason for departing therefrom if it is necessary or desirable to do so.

It is important to note that the Committee is not intending to unalterably tie a special prosecutor to following the written policies of the Department of Justice respecting the enforcement of criminal law. The Committee sought to find a concise statement of what those policies were and was not able to do so. While the U.S. Attorneys' Manual may contain many or most of these policies, they are mixed in with large amounts of other material in that manual. In spite of that fact, the Committee felt it was desirable to give the special prosecutor the general direction contained in subsection (f) so that, to the extent possible, a special prosecutor will apply the same policies in conducting the investigation that the Department of Justice would apply.

SECTION 595—REPORTING AND CONGRESSIONAL OVERSIGHT

Subsection (a) of section 595 simply authorizes the special prosecutor appointed under this chapter to make public or send to Congress any statements or reports on his activities as special prosecutor as he deems appropriate. No reports are required by this section. In determining what statements, reports or information to make public, the special prosecutor will, of course, be bound by the cannons of ethics of the legal profession and the basic principles of our criminal justice system which protect the rights of the innocent.

Subsection (b) provides for the filing of a mandatory final report in addition to any reports or statements a special prosecutor may choose to make under subsection (c). This mandatory final report is considered by the Committee to be very important to ensure the accountability of a special prosecutor. The Committee is well aware of the enormous power and responsibility which a special prosecutor has because of all the protections provided in this chapter to make sure that the special prosecutor is independent. This final report will provide a detailed document to permit the evaluation of the performance of a special prosecutor at an appropriate time.

The report required by subsection (b) must be submitted by each special prosecutor to the division of the court at the conclusion of such special prosecutor duties. Paragraph (2) provides that that report must set forth a full and complete description of the work of the special prosecutor, including the disposition of all cases brought and the reasons for not prosecuting any matter within the prosecutorial jurisdiction of the special prosecutor. This report must be in sufficient detail to allow a determination of whether the special prosecutor's investigation was thoroughly and fairly completed.

One of the serious problems with the appointment of a truly independent special prosecutor is that there is no one supervising the activities of the special prosecutor. Inherent in such a situation is the possibility of a runaway prosecutor or a special prosecutor who does not bring the prosecutions which should be brought. While this report will not necessarily be contemporaneously reviewed by the Department of Justice, the court, the public or Congress, this will be a

ETHICS IN GOVERNMENT ACT
P.L. 95–521
[page 71]

detailed and official record of the activities of the special prosecutor which may be reviewed and analyzed at the appropriate time.

Paragraph (3) provides that the division of the court may release portions of the report to Congress, the public, or to any appropriate person, but that the Court may not comment on the content of the report. Again, this latter proviso was added to make it perfectly clear that it is not the responsibility of the court to supervise or judge the conduct of a special prosecutor or the exercise of the special prosecutor's prosecutorial discretion. The division of the court is directed to make such orders as appropriate to protect the rights of any individual named in the report and to prevent undue interference with any pending prosecution. The division of the court is also authorized to make any portion of the report available to any individual named in the report for the purpose of receiving within a time limit set by the division of the court any comments or factual information the individual may submit. The comments and factual information submitted, in whole or in part, may, in the discretion of the court, be included as an appendix to the report.

Thus, the handling of the report, its release and the opportunity for rebuttal are within the control and discretion of the court. The Committee feels that there may be situations where the release of the report or parts of the report would not prejudice the rights of any individual or prejudice any ongoing prosecution and could be public at the time it is submitted or soon thereafter. Experience has shown that a special prosecutor who is very well respected in the legal community often is willing to make information equivalent to what would be contained in such a report public in the form of memoirs or other writings within a few short years of serving as special prosecutor. The Committee strongly feels that this type of detailed information about the activities of the office of special prosecutor should be recorded and preserved and made available to the public and the Congress when the court deems appropriate.

Subsection (c) authorizes the special prosecutor to advise the House of Representatives of any substantial and credible information which the special prosecutor receives that may constitute grounds for impeachment of the President, Vice President, or a justice or judge of the United States. This provision is permissive because the Committee did not want to imply that such a special prosecutor would be the final judge of what information should be turned over for an impeachment investigation or be the judge of what constituted an impeachable offense. For that reason also, the last sentence of subsection (c) provides that nothing in the new chapter 39 created by this title, or section 49 added to title 28 by this statue, should be interpreted to prevent the Congress or either House thereof from obtaining information in the course of an impeachment investigation.

Subsection (c) simply gives the special prosecutor, who has information which he wants to turn over to the House of Representatives because it involves potentially impeachable offenses against the individuals names in this subsection, the authority to so turn over that information.

This section should in no way be interpreted as identifying individuals who are not subject to criminal prosecution prior to being im-

Elliott Abrams

ELLIOTT ABRAMS
1015 18TH STREET, N.W., SUITE 200
WASHINGTON, D.C. 20036
202-223-7770 · FAX 202-223-8537

RECEIVED

DEC 0 2 1993

CLERK OF THE UNITED
STATES COURT OF APPEALS

December 2, 1993

Mr. Ron Garvin
Clerk,
United States Court of Appeals
District of Columbia Circuit
United States Courthouse
Washington, DC 20001

Dear Mr. Garvin:

Pursuant to your notice to me dated August 9, 1993, and the extension of time to December 3, 1993 for the submission of comments or factual information responding to the Final Report of Independent Counsel Lawrence Walsh, please find attached my submission. I hope it will be included as an appendix to the Final Report.

Thank you.

Sincerely yours,

Elliott Abrams

COMMENT ON INDEPENDENT COUNSEL'S FINAL REPORT
by Elliott Abrams

In 1989 the American Bar Association's Criminal Justice Section suggested amending the "Ethics in Government Act" to eliminate entirely, on grounds of elementary fairness, the publication of Independent Counsels' final reports. The ABA reasoned that anything an Independent Counsel had to say should be said in court papers, not in conclusory statements that may be unfair to those mentioned. This Report, insofar as I was permitted to review the passages related to me, certainly proves that the ABA was right.

First, the Report makes selective use of facts to justify its own actions rather than presenting a full and accurate picture. One example involving me may suffice. The Report claims that I was familiar with the finances of the Col. North's contra resupply efforts, which included the regular use of foreign bank accounts to transfer funds to contra groups. Seeking to provide "evidence" to support this conclusion, the Report states that during a lunch with Adm. Poindexter he and I "discussed possible methods of transferring the funds" to be solicited from Brunei. This seems to sustain the Report's conclusion unless one is familiar with the full record, which reveals that in fact Poindexter had been careful to divulge nothing to me about contra finances. Indeed, as the Independent Counsel well knows, Poindexter recounted in a prof note to North that he had asked me about Brunei during the lunch but "never letting on that we had access to accounts." A fair report would have included that line, which reveals North and Poindexter deliberately keeping me in the dark and undercuts the Report's efforts to draw opposite conclusions. But the OIC's Report omits the line.

Second, the Report is filled with assertions of fact that are baseless or best highly debatable. To take but one of the many available examples, the Report states that I "falsely denied" knowing some information about Felix Rodriguez. I denied in 1986 and throughout the OIC investigation and deny today knowing what the OIC imputes to me about Rodriguez's activities on behalf of the contras, and was never charged with any such knowledge. There are no findings of facts, pleas, or admissions on my part related to Rodriguez. There is no documentary or testimonial evidence sustaining the Independent Counsel's allegation that I knew all about Rodriguez's activities, which is presumably why I was never charged with such knowledge or with "falsely denying" it. What then is the basis of the OIC's statement in this regard? It is the presentation of unsupported opinion as fact.

Third, the Report unsurprisingly fails to comment on the timing of the OIC's move against me. The OIC would have it that it is mere coincidence that, after deciding not to prosecute me, the office moved swiftly against me in the immediate aftermath of the reversal of the conviction of Col. North. It helps to understand the case if the reader sees the chronology: after losing its conviction of North, and faced with the near certainty of losing that of Poindexter, the OIC then picked up my case again.

Which, finally, raises squarely the matter of prosecutorial discretion. Reading the sections of the Report made available to me, I was amazed at the pattern of decision-making regarding whom to prosecute. Simply put, there seems to have been no <u>law</u> involved at all. At least two persons were said to have made false statements to the OIC and failed lie detector tests, but were not prosecuted. Others were said to have willfully misled Congress, prepared false testimony, misled the OIC, or willfully withheld information from Congress, but none of these were prosecuted. Decisions as to whom to prosecute seem at times to have been whimsical, but it is clear that where law is absent, the door is open to political and personal biases. This is what I believe motivated the OIC in my case.

None of this would have come as a surprise to some wiser, and fairer, prosecutors such as the late Supreme Court Justice Robert Jackson, who while Attorney General of the United States said the following to a meeting of federal prosecutors:

> Law enforcement is not automatic. It isn't blind. One of the greatest difficulties of the position of prosecutor is that he must pick his cases, because no prosecutor can ever investigate all of the cases in which he receives complaints....If the prosecutor is obliged to choose his cases, it follows that he can choose his defendants. Therein is the most dangerous power of the prosecutor: that he will pick people that he thinks he should get, rather than cases that need to be prosecuted. With the law books filled with a great assortment of crimes, a prosecutor stands a fair chance of finding at least a technical violation of some act on the part of almost anyone...it is not a question of discovering the commission of a crime...it is a question of picking the man and then...pin[ning] some offense on him. It is in this realm... that the greatest danger of abuse of prosecuting power lies. It is here that law enforcement becomes personal...." (Robert Jackson, "The Federal Prosecutor," Address Delivered at the Second Annual Conference of United States Attorneys, April 1, 1940)

This Report reveals that that "greatest danger" of which Justice Jackson spoke was not avoided here, and that law enforcement did indeed become personal in this Independent Counsel's office.

Richard L. Armitage

United States Court of Appeals
For the District of Columbia Circuit

FILED DEC 0 2 1993

RON GARVIN
CLERK

UNITED STATES COURT OF APPEALS
FOR THE DISTRICT OF COLUMBIA CIRCUIT

Division for the Purpose of
Appointing Independent Counsels

Ethics in Government Act of 1978, as Amended

In re: Oliver L. North, et al.   Division No. 86-6

SUBMISSION OF RICHARD L. ARMITAGE

UNDER SEAL

Pursuant to this Court's <u>Per Curiam</u> Order (filed August 5, 1993 and 28 U.S.C. Sec. 594(h)(2), Richard L. Armitage, by counsel, respectfully submits the attached comments and factual information for inclusion in the Appendix to the Office of Independent Counsel's Final Report. To the degree that those portions of the Final Report which relate to Mr. Armitage (<u>i.e.</u>, those portions made available for review to the undersigned counsel by the Clerk of Court, Mr. Ron Gavin) are made public by the Court, we request that the enclosed materials be included in the Appendix to the Final Report.

Included in this submission is a Statement of Richard L. Armitage dated December 3, 1993 (four pages), Affidavit of Richard Secord dated November 24, 1993 (two pages), and the Affidavit of Lincoln P. Bloomfield, Jr., dated November 26, 1993 (two pages).

Accompanying this submission is a Motion for Filing Under Seal.

Respectfully submitted this 2nd day of December, 1993.

JOSEPH M. JONES, ESQ.
SCHWALB, DONNENFELD, BRAY
    & SILBERT
A Professional Corporation
Suite 300 East
1025 Thomas Jefferson Street, NW
Washington, D.C. 20007
(202) 965-7910

Counsel for Richard L. Armitage

STATEMENT OF RICHARD L. ARMITAGE

DECEMBER 3, 1993

I categorically and unequivocally deny that I violated any law in the course of my service as Assistant Secretary of Defense for International Security Affairs, or subsequently in relation to the investigations of the Iran-Contra matter. To the contrary, I cooperated fully with all the investigations, including those by the Congress, the Tower Commission and the Office of Independent Counsel. My attorney received expressions of praise and appreciation on numerous occasions from the staff of the Independent Counsel for my exceptional and unending cooperation.

Furthermore, I protest the action of the Independent Counsel in characterizing me as guilty of any wrongdoing in this matter. There is nothing in the judicial system of the United States which ever permits a prosecutor to label as a criminal someone who has not been charged. When the government does charge someone, that person is entitled to a fair hearing to respond to the government's charges; that is the essence of due process. By venturing outside these fundamental boundaries of our legal system, the Independent Counsel has fashioned theories into conclusions which would not have survived an open search for the truth.

The following examples will suffice to illustrate why, in truth, the Independent Counsel chose not to bring an indictment or even classify me as a "target" during its six-year investigation:

--   I was the Department of Defense official who handled, among other things, policy regarding U.S. arms sales to Asia, Africa, Latin America and the Middle East, including Israel. In that capacity, I had periodic contact with the Director-General of the Israeli Ministry of Defense, General Meron. In December 1985, I was actively engaged in learning about the proposed transfer of U.S. weapons to Iran, and kept the Secretary of Defense informed of what I learned. Our Department's strong and often voiced opposition to the idea was, in the end, unpersuasive to the President, and the activity was authorized by a Presidential Finding and carried out thereafter. The Independent Counsel has erroneously confused my activities concerning prospective transfers of arms with the actual transfer of arms by Israel to Iran in late 1985, an activity in which I was not involved.

Richard L. Armitage   page 2

Graphic evidence of the Independent Counsel's misstatements in this regard is provided by the Final Report's false characterization of a meeting between me and Richard Secord in the December 1985 - January 1986 time frame. The Independent Counsel suggests that General Secord and I talked about recent arms sales to Iran or the need to resupply Israel for its earlier shipments to Iran. General Secord's enclosed affidavit makes it clear that <u>no</u> such discussions took place, and that our meeting had focused solely on General Secord's attempt (ultimately unsuccessful) to persuade me to support a prospective program. General Secord's affidavit also completely refutes the Independent Counsel's assertion that Secord had suggested to General Meron that I was involved in or knowledgeable of the prior sales or resupply issue.

--   Indeed, the notation in Oliver North's notes of a November 18, 1986 telephone conversation with me, to wit, "Call from Arm - lawyers - Israeli shipments - did we know - When did we promise to replenish," makes evident my lack of knowledge concerning the Israeli shipments. I was calling Lieutenant Colonel North because of a query I had received from the Department of Defense General Counsel. Had this information already been known to me, I would not have queried North.

--   Regarding the "Special Project Re Iran" memorandum, I told the Office of the Independent Counsel that I could have obtained it on any of three different occasions: it is possible that I received it from Oliver North in December 1985 and it is possible that I received it as the program was being carried out in 1986. However, it is most likely, in my judgment, that I received it later in 1986, around the time that the Iran-Contra matter was publicly disclosed. I would suggest that if I had any exposure to this memorandum prior to November 1986, it would have been in the form of an oral presentation by Oliver North.

--   Any and all questions regarding the turning over of documents in my possession or the possession of the organization I headed in the Department of Defense should begin with a clear understanding of my role in this process. Upon the announcement by President Reagan in late 1986 of the Iran arms transfers and the diversion of funds to the Contras, I enlisted a reputable official of my organization to move into my front office complex as a Special Assistant and work with the Department's Office of the General Counsel to ensure that my organization responded fully and appropriately to the various authorities investigating the Iran-Contra affair -- a total of eight separate investigations. I granted this Special Assistant, Mr. Lincoln P. Bloomfield, Jr., full and unconditional access to my own files and to the files of the organization, as well as a full and unconditional mandate to send forward any and all materials responsive to the requests. I exercised absolutely no control, restraint or influence whatsoever on the nature, substance or timing of my organization's responses to these investigatory requests, other than mandating that the work be done properly and expeditiously.

Moreover, all requests for documents came to my organization from the Department of Defense Office of the General Counsel; and it was to the Office of the General Counsel that my organization provided responsive documents. The documents, and the dates when these documents were provided by my organization to the Office of the General Counsel, were meticulously recorded and made a matter of record. Neither I nor anyone in my organization can speak to the timing, or the process, by which the General Counsel's office may subsequently have forwarded these documents to the Independent Counsel or to other investigative bodies. The enclosed affidavit of Lincoln P. Bloomfield, Jr. addresses the document production process, and makes clear that the Independent Counsel is in error in attributing to me, by implication at least, a role in the document production process which, quite simply, I did not have.

The "Final Report" of the Office of Independent Counsel represents an assault on the foundations of Anglo-American jurisprudence. Rather than indicting and bringing to trial those whom he speculates may have acted illegally in connection with the Iran-Contra affair, the Independent Counsel has instead established himself as judge and jury. Having reached private, nonjudicial verdicts of "guilty" concerning those he whom he dares not indict, the Independent Counsel seeks now to dispatch his intended victims to the gallows of public condemnation.

Richard L. Armitage   page 4

A close reading of the report will lead any fair-minded person to the conclusion that it is a sophomoric term-paper built on self-serving assumptions, suppositions and implications. Anyone reading this litany of allegations would do well to bear in mind two questions: if any or all of the essay were true, then why were the malefactors not brought to trial? Why would any prosecutor, armed with so seemingly persuasive a case, content himself with an extralegal hit-and-run attack?

The Independent Counsel himself tries to anticipate these questions with the following assertions: his "resources" were too limited; and his "evidence" did not reach the threshold of proof beyond a reasonable doubt.

If the Independent Counsel lacked adequate resources, one of two things is called for: a redefinition of the word "adequate," or an audit. Every prosecutors' office in the United States operates with fewer resources than this Independent Counsel; yet none has ever issued a report on those it wanted to charge but did not. The fact that something in excess of $34,000,000 has been expended by the Office of Independent Counsel is in the public domain. If this sum was inadequate to bring to justice those who the Independent Counsel believes broke the law, then how and for what purposes were the taxpayers' funds spent?

It is, however, the admission that the so-called "evidence" was inadequate to merit a trial that is so self-damning. If the Independent Counsel had no faith in his "case," what in the world would a jury have made of it? More to the point, since when is the absence of credible evidence a mere detail, a minor inconvenience? Under our system of law the burden of proof is on the government. If the government has no case, then it has no business condemning citizens either inside or outside of the courtroom. In this abysmal episode, a rogue agent of the government has issued such a condemnation without even attempting to make a legal case.

In the end the issue is fairness. Americans will not long remember the details of the stale apologia, the ill-tempered catalogue of allegations and excuses issued by the Office of Independent Counsel. Yet neither will they soon forget that in the history of our democracy we have, from time-to-time, endured demagogues who thrived on unsubstantiated accusations and gloried in the destruction of reputations. Invariably, they have run afoul of the fundamental demands of fair play built into the way we conduct our public business.

One of the essential elements of the American legal system, a cardinal rule of every prosecutor, is articulated in an expression well-known to anyone raised in this country: "Put up or shut up." The Independent Counsel has done neither. That is why this report will, upon complete examination and in the fullness of time, be seen to reflect more the lapsed standards and impure motivations of its authors than the public stewardship of its intended victims. And although this attempt to harm my standing as a public servant and a citizen is a burden to me, I will be sustained by a clarity of conscience that the authors of this report may themselves come to envy.

AFFIDAVIT OF RICHARD SECORD

I, Richard Secord, being duly sworn, depose and say as follows:

1.   Reference has been made to a purported meeting between me, LTC North and Menachem Meron, then Director-General of the Israeli Ministry of Defense, on or about December 2, 1985, at which, it has been suggested, I told Meron that then-Assistant Secretary of Defense Richard L. Armitage was the Department of Defense's point of contact on the issue of resupplying weapons Israel had previously transferred to Iran.

I did not tell Meron, or anyone, that Mr. Armitage was involved in, or even knowledgeable of, the resupply issue. Mr. Armitage was the responsible policy official regarding normal arms sales to countries worldwide, including Israel. The resupply issue, however, was part of a compartmented program outside the Defense Department, and I did not believe or have any reason to believe that Mr. Armitage was a participant in or had knowledge of the compartmented program.

My view on this matter was formed through discussions I had held in Israel in November, 1985, in which Israeli officials involved in the Iran program, including Director-General Meron, insisted that Mr. MacFarlane of the NSC had pledged that the U.S. would resupply the TOW weapons Israeli had provided to Iran. Knowing, from my long official experience in security assistance matters, of no legal mechanism by which the resupply could be accomplished, I expressed strong skepticism to the Israeli officials that Mr. MacFarlane had indeed made such a pledge. Upon my return to the United States, I learned that, in fact, Mr. MacFarlane had made such a pledge. Throughout all of these discussions I was aware of no involvement in or knowledge of the issue on the part of Mr. Armitage.

2.   Reference is made to a meeting I held with Assistant Secretary Armitage in the December 1985 - January 1986 timeframe. Although scheduling logs apparently refer to two meetings, I recall meeting Mr. Armitage once, and would suggest that the two scheduling entries refer to the same meeting, postponed but not so noted in the schedule.

My purpose in calling on Mr. Armitage was to discuss the so-called "Iran initiative," a U.S. program under discussion at that time which was authorized by the January 17, 1986 Presidential Finding and carried out thereafter using weapons provided by the Department of Defense to the CIA. I did not discuss with Mr. Armitage the resupply of arms to Israel under the above-mentioned compartmented program, because (to repeat) I did not believe or have any reason to believe that Mr. Armitage was a participant in or had knowledge of the compartmented program.

Richard Secord   p. 2

My objective in meeting with Mr. Armitage was to persuade him -- and through him, hopefully Secretary Weinberger -- to cease the Department of Defense's opposition to the proposed Iran initiative. The arms transfers to Iran in that initiative, which I discussed with Mr. Armitage, were entirely prospective, and were to be accomplished legally. As I have testified, I was not successful in changing Mr. Armitage's position in opposition to the U.S. initiative.

[signature]
Richard Secord

SUBSCRIBED AND SWORN TO before me, a Notary Public in and for the County of Fairfax, this 24th day of November, 1993

[signature]
NOTARY PUBLIC

My Commission Expires: _Dec 31 1996_

Affidavit of Lincoln P. Bloomfield, Jr.

I, Lincoln P. Bloomfield, Jr., being duly sworn, depose and say as follows:

In late 1986, I was asked by Richard L. Armitage, then the Assistant Secretary of Defense for International Security Affairs, to serve as Special Assistant to the Assistant Secretary for the initial purpose, among other duties, of overseeing the International Security Affairs organization's responses to requests for documentary information in its possession emanating from investigations of the Iran-Contra matter. I served in the position of Special Assistant for approximately two years beginning in December 1986.

My understanding of the task at hand, from all my contacts with Assistant Secretary Armitage, was that the International Security Affairs organization (hereafter "ISA"), and the Defense Department as a whole, were to respond fully, forthrightly, properly and expeditiously to the authorities investigating this matter, including (eventually) the FBI, the Senate Select Committee on Intelligence, the the Tower Commission, the General Accounting Office, the Army Inspector General, the House Armed Services Committee, the House and Senate Select Iran-Contra Committees and, of course, the Independent Counsel. ISA was tasked by, and responded to, the Department of Defense Office of the General Counsel.

Assistant Secretary Armitage granted me full, unconditional and continual access to the files of the ISA organization, including the files he kept in his office, which I reviewed completely numerous times so as to be able to attest to a complete search. In every single instance when I had any question about whether a document or documents were responsive to an Iran-Contra investigation request from the General Counsel's office, I provided the material to the Office of the General Counsel, requested and received a ruling from that organization, and acted in accordance with that ruling. Assistant Secretary Armitage played no role whatsoever in determining what materials I would forward from ISA to the Office of the General Counsel; the discretion was entirely my own, guided by the Department's legal authorities and backed by unlimited access to ISA materials and a mandate from the Assistant Secretary to respond to these requests fully, appropriately and expeditiously. This I did to the best of my ability.

All of the responsive materials I provided to the Office of the General Counsel I forwarded under the cover of a memorandum, signed by me, detailing the precise materials forwarded and the request to which the materials were responsive, and dated as of the day the material went forward from ISA to the Office of the General Counsel. I have no knowledge of the process by

Lincoln P. Bloomfield, Jr. 2

which the Department of Defense Office of the General Counsel turned over
materials received from ISA or any other office of the Department of Defense
to the various Iran-Contra investigative authorities, including the contents or
timing of such. I am aware of no involvement by any official of the ISA
organization in decisions or actions of the Office of the General Counsel
regarding its turning over of responsive DoD materials to the investigative
authorities.

Lincoln P. Bloomfield Jr
Lincoln P. Bloomfield, Jr

SUBSCRIBED AND SWORN TO before me, a Notary Public in and
for the County of Arlington, this 26th day of November, 1993

Maria T. Chiles
Notary Public

My Commission Expires: Feb 28, 1997

United States Court of Appeals
For the District of Columbia Circuit

UNITED STATES COURT OF APPEALS
FOR THE DISTRICT OF COLUMBIA CIRCUIT
FILED DEC 0 2 1993

Division for the Purpose of
Appointing Independent Counsels
RON GARVIN
CLERK

Ethics in Government Act of 1978, as Amended

In re: Oliver L. North, et al.   Division No. 86-6

MOTION FOR FILING UNDER SEAL
─────────────────────────────

Richard L. Armitage, by counsel, hereby requests that the accompanying submission of comments and factual information to the Final Report of the Office of Independent Counsel be filed and remain under seal (per the Court's Per Curiam Order of August 5, 1993) unless and until this Court determines which portions of the Final Report are to be made public. To the degree that this Court makes public those portions of the Final Report which related to Mr. Armitage (and thus were made available to the undersigned counsel by the Clerk of Court), it is requested that this submission be included in the Appendix of the Final Report.

This submission consists of a Statement of Richard L. Armitage dated December 3, 1993 (four pages), Affidavit of Richard Secord dated November 24, 1993 (two pages), and the Affidavit of Lincoln P. Bloomfield, Jr., dated November 26, 1993 (two pages).

A proposed Order is attached.

Respectfully submitted this 2nd day of December, 1993.

JOSEPH M. JONES, ESQ.
SCHWALB, DONNENFELD, BRAY
   & SILBERT
A Professional Corporation
Suite 300 East
1025 Thomas Jefferson Street, NW
Washington, D.C. 20007
(202) 965-7910

Counsel for Richard L. Armitage

United States Court of Appeals
For the District of Columbia Circuit

**UNITED STATES COURT OF APPEALS
FOR THE DISTRICT OF COLUMBIA CIRCUIT**

FILED DEC 0 2 1993

**Division for the Purpose of
Appointing Independent Counsels**

RON GARVIN
CLERK

Ethics in Government Act of 1978, as Amended

In re: Oliver L. North, et al.   Division No. 86-6

ORDER
TO FILE UNDER SEAL

Upon motion of Richard L. Armitage, the Court hereby grants his motion to file under seal his submission of comments and factual information to the Final Report of the Office of Independent Counsel be filed and shall remain under seal (per the Court's <u>Per Curiam</u> Order of August 5, 1993) unless and until this Court determines which portions of the Final Report is to be made public.

Entered this ____ day of _____, 1993.

_____
United States District Judge

Conformed copies furnished to:

JOSEPH M. JONES, ESQ.
Schwalb, Donnenfeld, Bray & Silbert
1025 Thomas Jefferson Street, N.W.
Suite 300 East
Washington, D.C. 20007

Counsel for Richard L. Armitage

Former President George H. W. Bush

KING & SPALDING

1730 PENNSYLVANIA AVENUE, N.W.
WASHINGTON, DC
20006-4706

———

202/737-0500
FACSIMILE: 202/626-3737

<table>
<tr><td>191 PEACHTREE STREET
ATLANTA, GEORGIA 30303-1763
TELEPHONE: 404/572-4600
TELEX: 54-2917 KINGSPALD ATL
FACSIMILE: 404/572-5100</td><td>December 1, 1993</td><td>120 WEST 45TH STREET
NEW YORK, NY 10036-4003
TELEPHONE: 212/556-2100
FACSIMILE: 212/556-2222</td></tr>
</table>

RECEIVED

DEC 0 2 1993

CLERK OF THE UNITED
STATES COURT OF APPEALS

The Honorable David Bryan Sentelle
Special Division
United States Court of Appeals
  for the District of Columbia Circuit
333 Constitution Avenue, N.W.
Washington, D.C. 20001

Re: <u>Former President George H.W. Bush</u>

Dear Judge Sentelle:

On behalf of my client, former President George H.W. Bush, I respectfully request that the enclosed "Response To Independent Counsel Report On Iran-Contra" be included as an appendix to Independent Counsel Lawrence E. Walsh's sealed report, as allowed under 28 U.S.C. 594(h)(2). (For your convenience, I have enclosed three copies of the Response.) We very much appreciate your consideration of our request.

Best regards.

Sincerely,

Griffin B. Bell

cc: Honorable George H.W. Bush
     J. Sedwick Sollers III, Esq.

/wkm

KING & SPALDING

1730 PENNSYLVANIA AVENUE, N.W.
WASHINGTON, DC
20006-4706

202/737-0500
FACSIMILE: 202/626-3737

191 PEACHTREE STREET
ATLANTA, GEORGIA 30303-1763
TELEPHONE: 404/572-4600
TELEX: 54-2917 KINGSPALD ATL
FACSIMILE: 404/572-5100

United States Court of Appeals
For the District of Columbia Circuit

FILED DEC 0 2 1993

RON GARVIN
CLERK

120 WEST 45TH STREET
NEW YORK, NY 10036-4003
TELEPHONE: 212/556-2100
FACSIMILE: 212/556-2222

RESPONSE TO INDEPENDENT
COUNSEL REPORT ON IRAN–CONTRA

GRIFFIN B. BELL
J. SEDWICK SOLLERS III

INTRODUCTION

The investigation conducted by the Office of Independent Counsel ("OIC") under Judge Lawrence Walsh has largely been an inquiry into a political dispute between a Republican Administration and a Democratic Congress over foreign policy. OIC has spent over six years and $40 million trying to give a criminal hue to the serious constitutional struggle over separation of powers between the Congress and the Executive in the foreign policy area. While the Report speculates that laws were broken by certain Administration officials other than President Bush, the real thrust of its conclusions relate to purported contravention of government <u>policy</u>. The Independent Counsel's authorizing legislation did not contemplate the investigation of such policy differences.

Congress has used the Independent Counsel statute as a tool for inserting itself into foreign policy, which is reserved under the Constitution to the Executive. An attempt to criminalize public policy differences jeopardizes any President's ability to govern. By seeking to craft criminal violations from a political foreign policy dispute, OIC was cast in a biased position from the beginning. Notwithstanding this inherent bias, however, the Report does not and cannot dispute that:

(1)   President Bush was unaware of the contra
       diversion as he has always maintained;

(2)   President Bush told the truth in both his 1988
       deposition to the OIC, which subsequently he
       released to the public, and in his 1987 FBI
       interview; and

(3)   President Bush never violated any criminal
       statute.

       Furthermore, despite statements or inferences in the

Report to the contrary:

(1)   President Bush issued the pardons of Caspar Weinberger
       and others because he believed it was the right and
       courageous thing to do. He was not concerned about the
       upcoming trials nor that he might be called as a witness
       by the defense.

(2)   President Bush completely cooperated with OIC's
       investigation. As the Report even states, he told his
       staff to "give them [OIC] everything."

(3)   President Bush had no idea that his personal, political
       thoughts, dictated well after the events of Iran-contra,
       were responsive to any OIC document requests until a
       member of his staff discovered them in a safe and
       reviewed them in late September 1992. President Bush
       immediately directed that the diary be turned over to
       White House Counsel Boyden Gray for his review, which
       was done. Mr. Gray subsequently produced the diary to
       OIC in December.

(4)   President Bush's diary was exculpatory and would have
       had no material effect on the investigation had it been
       produced sooner. The Report acknowledges that the
       contents of the diary did not justify a reopening of the
       investigation.

(5)   President Bush, through King & Spalding, provided OIC
       with thousands of additional documents in 1993 that
       related generally to Iran-contra, even though OIC had
       declared months earlier that the investigation was
       finished.

(6)   President Bush would have agreed to a final interview/
      deposition under reasonable conditions. OIC refused to
      negotiate and decided to simply declare in its Report
      that the President was uncooperative.

I. IRAN ARMS SALE

°   President Bush has always acknowledged that he was aware

        that arms were sold to Iran. The Report offers nothing

        new on this issue.

°   On December 3, 1986, then Vice-President Bush told the

        American public about his knowledge of the Iran arms

        initiative immediately after the story broke:

>   I was aware of our Iran initiative and I
>   support the President's decision. I was not
>   aware of and I oppose any diversion of funds,
>   any ransom payments, or any circumvention of
>   the will of the Congress, the law or the
>   United States of America.

        Speech to American Enterprise Institute ("AEI")

        (Attachment 1).

        This statement was accurate, and the Report offers no

        evidence to the contrary. Inexplicably, however, the

        Report contends that President Bush's public statements

        conflicted with his deposition testimony and FBI

        interview, all of which reflected his knowledge of the

        Iran arms sales. The Report is simply wrong.

°   Most importantly, President Bush did not believe there
      was anything illegal about the arms sale to Iran. In
      fact, after six years of investigation and expenditures
      of $40 million, OIC remains unsure whether any laws were
      violated by the arms sale. As the Report acknowledges,
      the Reagan Administration Justice Department issued an
      opinion that the shipments of U.S. weapons to Iran <u>did</u>
      <u>not violate the law</u>. President Bush was never advised
      by anyone that the Iran arms shipments were illegal.

II.   <u>CONTRA DIVERSION</u>

°   President Bush was unaware of the contra diversion until
      the news of the diversion broke publicly in November
      1986. The Report confirms this fact.

°   Moreover, the Report found that there was an effort to
      keep then Vice-President Bush and his staff in the dark
      about the entire resupply effort:.

          There was no credible evidence obtained that
          the Vice-President or any member of his staff
          directly or actively participated in the
          contra resupply effort that existed during the
          Boland Amendment prohibition on military aid
          to the contras. To the contrary, the OVP's
          staff was largely excluded from RIG meetings
          when contra matters were discussed and during
          which North openly discussed operational
          details of his contra efforts.

III. **THE PARDONS**

°   OIC contends that defense counsel for Caspar Weinberger
    indicated their intent to call President Bush as a
    witness. In fact, President Bush was never subpoenaed
    or included on any witness list.

°   The sole allusion to the possibility that Secretary
    Weinberger's counsel might attempt to call President
    Bush occurred two weeks before the Weinberger trial was
    to commence in a pre-trial conference during which
    numerous matters were discussed. The possibility that
    President Bush would actually be called to testify was
    always remote. Furthermore, there was little chance that
    President Bush would actually be required to testify
    even if called. Secretary Weinberger's counsel did not
    give any notice to the White House of an intent to call
    President Bush nor was it likely that counsel could have
    made the required showing that President Bush would
    provide any testimony that could not have been obtained
    through other means. The slim possibility that he could
    be called as a witness was not a factor in issuing the
    pardons.

IV.   PRESIDENT BUSH'S DIARY

°   President Bush issued the pardons of Caspar Weinberger
      and others on December 24, 1992.

°   That evening, Judge Walsh publicly proclaimed President
      Bush to be a "subject" of his investigation on ABC's
      Nightline for allegedly failing to produce earlier a
      personal diary of primarily political thoughts. The
      public pronouncement constituted a remarkable departure
      from prevailing prosecutorial standards of conduct.
      Judge Walsh then began a new investigation into the
      timing of the production of the Bush diary, <u>a diary that
      was exculpatory</u> and contained information that would
      have helped, not hurt, President Bush's reelection
      chances.

°   At the time of Judge Walsh's proclamation, OIC had
      already reviewed the diary and was aware of its
      personal, political nature. As OIC later stated in its
      Report, the Bush diary did not warrant a reopening of
      the investigation.

° As the Report also acknowledges, "Bush's notes[1] themselves proved not as significant" as others. In fact, the diary was made <u>after</u> the events of Iran-contra and corroborated his lack of knowledge as events were uncovered.

° The Report implies that President Bush was aware that his diary dictation was responsive to OIC's document requests and purposefully did not produce the material. In support, the Report cites a 1987 Bush diary entry that indicates surprise at Secretary Shultz' production of his personal, contemporaneous notes dictated immediately following meetings with President Reagan. Contrary to the Report's implication, President Bush never believed that his random, personal dictation on a variety of issues, contemporaneous only with the aftermath and not the events of Iran-contra, was responsive to any OIC document request until September 1992 when his staff reviewed the diary. President Bush <u>was</u> concerned, however, that by keeping their own, sometimes unreliable notes of confidential communications with the President, cabinet members could

---

[1] The Report apparently uses "diary" and "notes" interchangeably. President Bush's chron files were repeatedly referenced as his "diary" both by his own staff and OIC.

have a chilling effect upon the ability of the Executive

to benefit from frank and candid discussions. Hence,

the passage in his diary relating to Secretary Shultz'

notes.

º   The bottom line is that President Bush turned over all

of his responsive documents on Iran-contra.

V.   PRESIDENT BUSH'S COOPERATION

º   Completely at odds with the Report's implication of

willful withholding of documents is the following

passage in the Report:

> Related to the issue of the diary was the
> production of the chron files. When the Iran/
> contra document request was circulated, <u>Bush
> instructed [Suzie] Peake to "just give them
> everything</u>." (Emphasis added.)

º   The Report fails to acknowledge that Peake was one of

the people who typed the dictated diary. If President

Bush was trying to withhold the diary, he never would

have given Peake such an instruction. Furthermore, none

of the other staff members who had knowledge of

President Bush's diary dictation, Don Rhodes, Jack

Steel, and Betty Green, believed that the diary was

responsive to OIC's document requests.

o   The Report does acknowledge that when the diary was discovered in a personal safe by Patty Presock in late September 1992, President Bush, who was in the middle of the campaign, immediately stated: "let's call Boyden and he can sort it out." Mr. Gray subsequently reviewed and turned over the diary to OIC. President Bush's policy was always to provide OIC whatever material it requested.

A.   <u>1993 Document Production</u>

o   The Report contends that in 1993 King & Spalding adopted a "very narrow approach to the OIC document request, allowing production of only those materials that related to the production of the diary." The report asserts that King & Spalding claimed that all other documents requested were protected by the attorney-client privilege. Again, OIC's position is contrary to the facts.

o   By letter dated January 27, 1993 (Attachment 2), King & Spalding informed OIC as follows:

> Although it is our understanding that the [OIC is] investigating the delay in the production of President Bush's November/December 1986 dictation transcripts, consistent with your

request <u>we will nevertheless provide you non-
privileged documents which related generally
to Iran-contra</u> (emphasis added).

° In accordance with our representation, King & Spalding
   reviewed 111 boxes of files stored at the National
   Archives and produced approximately 6,500 pages of non-
   privileged documents related to Iran-contra and
   unrelated to the diary production issue. King &
   Spalding also produced all documents, regardless of
   privilege, related to the diary production.

° OIC lawyers originally directed King & Spalding to
   review 400 boxes of documents stored at the Bush
   Presidential Materials Project in College Station, Texas
   but later backed off once they realized the breadth of
   their request. (<u>See</u> letter dated February 22, 1993,
   Attachment 3). King & Spalding subsequently produced
   326 pages of documents from College Station relating to
   the diary production issue.

° Finally, King & Spalding also produced President Bush's
   "chron" files to OIC in their entirety, constituting in
   excess of 29,000 pages of documents. (The chron files
   had been made available to OIC prior to then Vice-
   President Bush's deposition in 1988.) Only a total of
   14 documents were withheld because of attorney-client

privilege.   President Bush never asserted, as would be his right, executive privilege over any documents.

B.   Interview of George Bush

°   President Bush fully cooperated with the OIC investigation. He voluntarily gave a 5 hour videotaped deposition to OIC lawyers in 1988 covering the entire subject of Iran-contra. In addition, he was interviewed at length by the FBI. In all respects, he was truthful and candid -- the Report never contends otherwise.

°   The Report, however, contends that the investigation of President Bush was somehow incomplete, citing OIC's inability to question President Bush further in 1993. As is evident by the following chronology, OIC had effectively finished its investigation in September 1992 and absent the issuance of the pardons would never have sought another deposition of President Bush.

°   In the summer of 1992, OIC indicated to the White House that it might seek additional information from President Bush in the form of interrogatories. Later in the summer, OIC postponed until after the election any request for additional information.

°   In September 1992, OIC reported to the special D.C.
Court of Appeals panel (the "Special Panel") that the
investigation was complete, barring unforeseen
developments at the upcoming Weinberger and Claridge
trials. The Report's admission that OIC had concluded
its investigation is inconsistent with any need or even
desire on the part of OIC to interview President Bush
again on the substance of Iran-contra.

°   After the election, OIC remained silent regarding the
notion of obtaining additional information from
President Bush through interrogatories.

°   OIC did not renew its request for responses to
interrogatories even after the White House informed OIC
on December 11, 1992 about the discovery of President
Bush's personal dictation.

°   It was the issuance of the pardons on December 24, 1992
that triggered OIC's deposition request to President
Bush and the general reopening of the investigation.

°   In its Report, OIC misstated the negotiations, or lack
thereof, surrounding a possible second Bush deposition
in 1993. The following are the facts.

° First, <u>Judge Walsh turned down Griffin Bell's offer to have Judge Walsh conduct President Bush's deposition</u>. Judge Walsh stated that he was too busy preparing the Report and that it would be necessary for his deputy, Craig Gillen, to conduct the deposition.

° In addition to Judge Walsh's refusal to conduct the deposition, OIC refused to consider any reasonable limitations on the deposition, including the following specific proposals:

(1) That the deposition be conducted in Houston or any location other than OIC's office in D.C.

(2) That there be some general understanding of the time to be devoted to the deposition. OIC would not even commit to finishing in one day.

(3) That there be an agreement as to the scope of the questioning. We would have considered favorably a request to explore new Iran/contra material or issues, in addition to the questions surrounding production of the diary. OIC made no counter-proposal.

(4) That the inquiry be conducted, as originally contemplated, through interrogatories.

(5) That there be some assurances concerning the purpose of the inquiry and OIC's intent.

<u>See</u> letter dated February 24, 1992, Attachment 4.

° OIC never discussed with King & Spalding lawyers any one of these proposals, as King & Spalding fully expected OIC would. Mr. Gillen's response in his February 26,

1993 letter (Attachment 5) was that "further negotiation
was pointless." In fact, OIC refused to negotiate on
any points.

°   If OIC believed that President Bush had important
    additional information as the Report suggests, OIC would
    have negotiated over the terms of a voluntary
    deposition. If President Bush remained an "important
    witness," despite having already submitted to a lengthy
    deposition and FBI interview, OIC would have issued a
    grand jury subpoena. OIC's excuse for not doing so, the
    absence of an "appropriate likelihood of a criminal
    prosecution," misstates the standard for issuance of a
    grand jury subpoena to a witness.

VI.   REMAINING QUESTIONS FOR PRESIDENT BUSH

°   The Report lists seven areas of inquiry that OIC would
    have covered with President Bush had another deposition
    occurred in 1993. Any deposition would have been
    cumulative of the previous wide-ranging deposition and
    FBI interview conducted of President Bush.

°   Three months before the pardons issued, OIC represented
    to the Special Panel that the investigation was
    finished. Thereafter, no circumstances changed that

warranted another deposition of President Bush.
Certainly, the diary produced in December 1992 did not
warrant an additional deposition on the substance of
Iran-contra. OIC's own Report stated "They [the
diaries] did not justify re-opening the investigation."

° President Bush's knowledge of Iran-contra has been
explored to exhaustion, beginning with his December 3,
1986 speech to AEI, continuing with his 5 hour
deposition by OIC, his FBI interview and countless press
conferences and inquiries. OIC's suggestion that the
investigation of President Bush was "regrettably
incomplete" is nonsense.

-15-

ATTACHMENT – 1

THE VICE PRESIDENT
OFFICE OF THE PRESS SECRETARY

91000021

FOR RELEASE   CONTACT: 202/456-6772
Wednesday, December 3, 1986

REMARKS AS DELIVERED BY
VICE PRESIDENT GEORGE BUSH
AMERICAN ENTERPRISE INSTITUTE'S
PUBLIC POLICY LUNCHEON
WASHINGTON, D.C.
WEDNESDAY, DECEMBER 3, 1986

Mr. President, at the outset of these remarks, let me just pay my respects to you and thank you for all you do for this wonderful institution, AEI, an institution for which I have so much respect. I'm delighted to see you. Bob Melott, too.

And, of course, I was invited sometime ago by Paul McCracken to come here, and I hope that you'll all be interested in the topic that Paul asked me to address: "Special Drawing Rights, the Snake and its Effect on Disintermediation."

I am delighted to be at this AEI forum. You couldn't have scheduled a better time to discuss public policy. A great many citizens currently are troubled about recent revelations, and I'm grateful for this chance to address some of those concerns of the American people.

There's been much criticism and confusion in recent weeks over the Administration's, our, policies regarding Iran. I understand the skepticism of the American people. The result, as you all know, according to these opinion surveys, is that the Administration's credibility has been hurt. This is especially painful to the President and to me as well. After all, we're in the White House because of the trust that the American people placed in us.

We must restore that trust and so today I'd like to discuss some of the basic concerns that the American people rightfully have about our policy toward Iran -- questions of why we tried to open channels, open channels with a regime that all of us Americans despise; questions of how we can have a policy of not sending arms to Iran and then seemingly do just the opposite; and questions about the operation of the National Security Council staff.

- more -

2

Let me start with a basic concern. Why did we open a
dialogue with Iran?

Here was a country that deeply humiliated the United States
by kidnapping our diplomats, burning our flag. We still have
vivid memories of blindfolded Americans being paraded around our
own Embassy in there in Tehran. There is in the hearts of the
American people an understandable animosity -- a hatred really --
to Khomeini's Iran. I feel that way myself, to be very honest
with you, and so does the President who has been vilified time
and time again by Iran's radical leaders; we're told that most
Iranians feel the same way about us, the country that they call
the Great Satan.

So why have anything to do with them? I'm sorry I didn't
bring a map, but if you look at a map, Iran is all that stands
between the Soviets and the Gulf oil states. It's all that
stands between the Soviets and a warm water port. Either a
disintegrating Iran or an overly powerful Iran could threaten the
stability of the entire Middle East, and especially those
moderate Arab states -- our friends whose stability and
independence are absolutely vital to the national security of the
United States. We may not like the current Iranian regime, and
I've said we don't, but it would be irresponsible to ignore its
geopolitical and strategic importance.

That doesn't mean we should simply appease any Iranian
regime. It does mean, however, that we can't ignore this looming
transition that will soon take place in Iran. Khomeini will pass
from the scene. A successor regime will take power, and we must
be positioned to serve America's interests, and indeed the
interests of the entire free world.

Apart from the strategic reasons, humanitarian concern about
American hostages in Lebanon provided another reason to open a
channel to Iran. The Iranians themselves are not holding our
hostages, but we believe they have influence over those who do
hold some of our hostages.

But let me add something very important. In spite of our
bitter feelings toward Iran's leadership, we would've tried to
begin a dialogue with Iran whether we had hostages in Lebanon or
not. In fact, for three years prior to the first hostage
kidnappings, this Administration attempted to find reliable --
hopefully moderate -- Iranian channels through which to conduct a
responsible dialogue.

And more recently we've been receiving intelligence that
pragmatic elements within Iran were beginning to appreciate
certain sobering realities. To the east in Afghanistan, we
estimate 115,000 Soviet troops are committing atrocities on

- more -

Iran's Islamic brothers. To the north, 26 Soviet divisions, right there on Iran's border for whatever opportunities might arise.

To the west, Iran is engaged in a war of unbelievably horrible human dimensions, war with Iraq -- 12-year old kids, 14-year old kids, pressed into service, and then ground up in combat. And at home, Iran is teetering on the economic brink right there in its own front yard, 40 percent unemployment rate. Many Iranian leaders understand that their own survival, and certainly the rebuilding of their economy, may depend on normalizing ties with their neighbors and with the Western world.

So, we for our reasons and certain elements in Iran for their reasons -- in spite of this mutual hatred -- began a tentative, probing dialogue -- which brings us to another question.

How can the United States Government have a policy against countries sending arms to Iran and then turn around and itself send arms? I know the American people simply do not understand this.

When we started talking to the Iranians, both sides were deeply suspicious of each other. And remain so, I might say. Those Iranians who were taking enormous personal risks by just talking to us felt that they needed a signal that their risks were worth it. We were told the signal they required, and we gave them that signal by selling a limited amount of arms -- about one-tenth of one percent of the arms that have supplied by other countries.

Likewise, we needed proof of Iranian seriousness. We required signs of a cessation of Iranian use of terrorism and help in gaining the release of our hostages in Lebanon. And we did see certain positive signs, we have seen them. They opposed, for example, the Pan American hijacking in Karachi and immediately after, they denied landing rights. They interceded with the TWA hijackers in Beirut. And, of course, three hostages once held in Lebanon by the Islamic Jihad are today with their families here in the United States of America.

And I, perhaps President Ford will agree with this, but when you are President, any American held captive against his will anywhere in the world is like your own son or daughter. I know that's the way our President feels about it. But you must remain true to your principles. And I can tell you the President is absolutely convinced that he did not swap arms for hostages.

Still the question remains of how the Administration could violate its own policy of not selling arms to Iran. Simple human

- more -

hope explains it perhaps better than anything else. The
President hoped that we could open a channel that would serve the
interests of the United States and of our allies in a variety of
ways. Call it leadership; given 20-20 hindsight, call it a
mistaken tactic if you want to; it was risky, but potentially of
long-term value.

The shaping of the Iranian policy involved difficult
choices. As complex as the public debate on the issue would be,
the matter was further clouded by the way in which the
President's goals were executed, specifically allegations about
certain activities of the National Security Council staff.

Clearly mistakes were made.

Our policy of conducting a dialogue with Iran, which was
legitimate and arguable, has become entangled with the separate
matter of this NSC investigation.

A week ago Monday afternoon the President learned of
possible improprieties. A week ago Monday. On Tuesday, he
disclosed the problem to the public and instructed the Attorney
General to go forward with a full investigation. On Wednesday,
he created a bipartisan commission, outstanding individuals, to
review the role of the NSC staff and make recommendations for the
future. And just yesterday, he moved to appoint, have the court
appoint an independent counsel to ensure a full accounting for
any possible wrongdoing.

The President pledged full cooperation with the United
States Congress, urging it to consolidate and expedite its
inquiries. Yesterday he also named Frank Carlucci, a seasoned
professional with broad experience, so well known to many people
here, to serve as his national security advisor. Now this is
fast action in anybody's book.

These are actions I fully support and which I believe the
American people will judge commendable.

The President has moved swiftly, strongly, but let me add
this. I'm convinced that he will take whatever additional steps
may be necessary to get things back on track and get our foreign
policy moving forward.

As the elected representatives of all the people, the
President and the Vice President, he and I have a duty to
preserve the public trust and uphold the laws of this country.
We take that duty very, very seriously.

I'd like to say something about my role in all of this. I
was aware of our Iran initiative and I support the President's

- more -

5

decision. I was not aware of and I oppose any diversion of
funds, any ransom payments, or any circumvention of the will of
the Congress, the law of the United States of America. As the
various investigations proceed, I have this to say -- let the
chips fall where they may. We want the truth. The President
wants it. I want it. And the American people have a fundamental
right to it.

And if the truth hurts, so be it. We've got to take our
lumps and move ahead.

Politics do not matter; personalities do not matter; those
who haven't served the President well don't matter. What matters
is the United States of America.

And we musn't allow our foreign policy to become paralyzed
by distraction.

There can be no denying that our credibility has been
damaged by this entire episode and its aftermath.

We have a critical role to play internationally and I intend
to help the President tackle the challenges that lie before us in
the last two years of this Administration: Putting U.S.-Soviet
relations on a new footing; pursuing a breakthrough in arms
reduction; building on the potential that I saw so clearly just
this past summer for making new strides for peace between Israel
and its Arab neighbors; working to end apartheid and creating a
more hopeful future for all Africans; solidifying the remarkable
changes taking place in Asia; combatting international terrorism
in close conjunction with our allies; and, of course, fostering
the development of democracy in Central America.

And let me add, the freedom of the people of Central America
should not, must not, be held hostage to actions unrelated to
them. This nation's support of those who are fighting for
democracy in Nicaragua should stand on its own merits, not hang
upon events related to Iran. The Marxist-Leninist regime in
Managua must not benefit from the errors of some people in
Washington, D.C.

Our Administration has a duty to follow a foreign policy
that reflects the values of its citizens. This sounds simple;
and yet it is often, as so many of you here know, a very complex
matter. It's not easy translating general values into specific
foreign policy programs. And this is why there's always so much
internal debate over our nation's role in world affairs -- from
Iran to arms reduction.

- more -

The Reagan Administration has two years left in which to pursue our particular vision of how America's foreign policy should fit America's values. There's one thing, however, on which critics and supporters would agree -- U.S. foreign policy must move forward. The U.S. has obligations as leaders of the free world. It has opportunities and responsibilities unmatched by any other country to bring stability to the world.

And we must move forward with the trust of the American people. To the extent that that trust has been damaged it must be repaired, and only the truth can repair that. Our government rules not by force or intimidation, but by earning the confidence and respect of the American people.

Our duty must be to uphold that confidence and restore that respect.

Sometimes true bipartisanship is called for and, in my view, now is such a time. And I have been very pleased that Republicans and Democrats alike have pledged to help get the facts out and move on.

A storm is now raging, but when the full truth is known -- and it will be; and when the American people come to understand that this strong and honest President moves swiftly to correct what might have been wrong, then a forgiving American people -- in spite of their misgivings about Iran and weapons and diverted funds -- will say, "Our President told the truth. He took action. Let's go forward together."

‡ ‡ ‡

ATTACHMENT – 2

KING & SPALDING

1730 PENNSYLVANIA AVENUE N.W.
WASHINGTON, DC
20006-4706
———
202/737-0500
TELECOPIER: 202/626-3737

191 PEACHTREE STREET
ATLANTA, GEORGIA 30303-1763
TELEPHONE: 404/572-4600
TELEX: 54-2917 KINGSPALD ATL
TELECOPIER: 404/572-5100

January 27, 1993

745 FIFTH AVENUE
NEW YORK, NY 10151
TELEPHONE: 212/758-8700
TELECOPIER: 212/593-3673

Craig A. Gillen, Esq.
Deputy Independent Counsel
Office of Independent Counsel
Suite 701 West
555 13th Street, N.W.
Washington, D.C. 20004

RE: Bush Presidential Documents

Dear Mr. Gillen:

I want to make absolutely clear the procedures King & Spalding is following to respond to your document request dated January 22, 1993 relating to White House Counsel documents now retained at the National Archives. I also want to ensure that we have no misunderstanding concerning the documents we will be voluntarily producing.

As an initial matter, I want to emphasize the enormity of our task. We now believe we will be required to review over 100 boxes of documents page by page. Once we determine which documents are responsive and are not privileged, the National Archives insists that a copy be made for your team to review.

With regard to our procedures, a team consisting of three King & Spalding lawyers and a paralegal is currently reviewing the boxes sent to the National Archives by the various counsel named in your letter. It is my understanding that these boxes generally contain George Bush Presidential documents.

Our lawyers are reviewing the documents for relevancy and privilege. You have asked for any documents that relate to any aspect of the Iran-Contra matter, which obviously is extremely broad. Although it was our understanding that you are investigating the delay in the production of President Bush's November/December 1986 dictation transcripts, consistent with your request we will nevertheless provide you non-privileged documents which relate generally to Iran-Contra.

Craig A. Gillen, Esq.
January 27, 1993
Page 2

We will also make available to you documents, under a
non-waiver agreement, that pertain to the delay in turning over
the 1986 tapes/transcripts that were the subject of Judge Walsh's
public allegations of misconduct on the part of President Bush.
As you are aware, King & Spalding prepared a report on this issue
and to the extent that a document is relevant to the subject
matter of the report, it will be produced.

With regard to the bulk of the documents, which are
subject to the attorney/client privilege and/or work product
doctrine, we will provide you with an index of privileged
documents. As I stated to you on the phone previously, we do not
intend to enter into any agreements to waive the attorney/client
privilege or work product doctrine.

If you have any questions about our procedures or the
nature of our production, please give me a call.

Sincerely,

J. Sedwick Sollers III

/md
cc: Judge Griffin B. Bell

ATTACHMENT – 3

KING & SPALDING

1730 PENNSYLVANIA AVENUE, N.W.
WASHINGTON, DC
20006-4706

——————

202/737-0500
TELECOPIER: 202/626-3737

191 PEACHTREE STREET
ATLANTA, GEORGIA 30303-1763
TELEPHONE: 404/572-4600
TELEX: 54-2917 KINGSPALD ATL
TELECOPIER: 404/572-5100

745 FIFTH AVENUE
NEW YORK, NY 10151
TELEPHONE: 212/758-8700
TELECOPIER: 212/593-3673

February 22, 1993

VIA TELECOPIER

Jeffrey S. Harleston, Esquire
Associate Independent Counsel
Office of Independent Counsel
Suite 701 West
555 13th Street, N.W.
Washington, D.C. 20004

Dear Mr. Harleston:

I am responding to your letter of February 18, 1993, and
to Sam Wilkins' letter of February 19, 1993, both of which were
addressed to my associate, Jim Snyder.

With regard to Mr. Wilkins' letter, we believe that he
mischaracterizes when we had agreed to produce the privilege list
for the Archives document production. We received your request to
review over 100 boxes of documents stored at the Archives on
January 22, 1993. We agreed to review the documents and provide
you with a privilege list as quickly as possible. As you are
aware, this project was far more complicated than either of our
offices had initially anticipated. We have kept you informed at
all stages of the production and have provided to you responsive
documents on a rolling basis. As we already have informed your
office, we are willing to produce the privilege list to you today.

Mr. Wilkins also expressed concern that there may be a delay
in your investigation in order for the Justice Department to
ensure that our attorneys and support staff have obtained the
necessary security clearances. He implies that King & Spalding
may somehow be responsible for this delay. This, of course, is
not the case.

Jeffrey S. Harleston, Esquire
February 22, 1993
Page 2

     As you are aware, our attorneys initially were provided
valid, temporary security clearances in order to accommodate your
desire to review President Bush's "Chron" files as quickly as
possible. Following completion of the Chron file project, your
office made additional requests that our attorneys review over 100
boxes of documents stored at the National Archives and now an
additional 400 boxes of material stored at the Bush Presidential
Library.

     Given the continuing nature of your requests, the Justice
Department believes it would be more appropriate that our
attorneys receive permanent, rather than temporary security
clearances. It is your office's expanding requests to review
additional records, not any lack of diligence on the part of King
& Spalding, that has resulted in the need for our personnel to
receive permanent security clearances.

     We presently are coordinating with the Justice Department and
will request that the Justice Department grant the necessary
security clearances as quickly as possible. It remains our
intention to comply to the fullest extent with the procedures for
handling classified documents.

     In regard to your letter, I first take issue with your ill-
considered characterization of the document production as
"glacial". Your overbroad document request pertaining to over one
hundred boxes of documents that you well knew contained almost
exclusively attorney-privilege material is the source of the
problem, not our review procedures. The fact that your office
waited until the last few days of the Bush Administration, after
most of these documents were boxed and sent to storage, to place
anyone on notice concerning your possible interest in counsel's
files created a logistical nightmare. The shotgun approach that
has been taken by your office in demanding the production of
predominantly privileged documents from six years of White House
Counsel files renders our task virtually impossible.

     Your characterization is even more absurd given the
extraordinary cooperation you have been provided by both President
Bush and numerous federal agencies. In order to respond as
quickly as possible to your request we have sought and obtained a
special waiver of standard review procedures for classified
documents from the Defense Department, the National Security
Agency, the Central Intelligence Agency, and the State Department.

Jeffrey S. Harleston, Esquire
February 22, 1993
Page 3

        In addition, we have received unlimited cooperation from the
National Archives, which detailed staff full-time to the project
and authorized overtime to ensure that the project would be
completed as soon as possible.

        You are now requesting that our attorneys conduct an
additional document review of nearly 400 boxes of documents stored
at the Bush Presidential Library in Texas. This equates to an
estimated 800,000 pages/documents. Once again, you have
emphasized that time is of the essence, yet you have made no
attempt to limit the scope of your request either by time-period
or subject matter. On the contrary, you have vastly expanded the
scope of your request to include files of additional individuals.

        In your January 23 request you asked to review the files of
seven attorneys who worked in the Office of White House Counsel
whose files had been sent for storage at the National Archives in
Washington, D.C. In your most recent request you have asked to
review the files of the following additional individuals: Dean
McGrath, Michael J. Austrue, Pat Bryan, Nelson Lund, McLane
Layton, Fred Nelson, Arnold Intrafer, Jay Bybee, Jeffrey
Holmstead, Gene Schaerr, M.B. Riordan, Greg Walden, Patti
Arronsen, Lauren Reynolds, Don Rhodes, Amy Schwartz, Robert T.
Swanson, Mr. Hollinger, Tom Collamore, Mr. Porter, Francine Burns,
as well as a box marked pardon material and a box marked
"miscellaneous."

        We estimate that it would take several months to review the
files you have requested. As you are well aware, during this time
period, attorneys from both our offices would be required to
commute to and live at College Station, Texas. The incredible
expense of such an undertaking clearly is unwarranted given that
limited relevance of these documents. If you had viewed these
documents as critical to your investigation, you could have
requested to review them sometime during the past six years when
the boxes were housed in Washington.

        Accordingly, unless we can narrow the scope of your request
by agreement, we do not intend to embark on a multi-month review
of the 400 boxes of privileged counsel's files in Texas. You have
every opportunity to interview the witnesses relating to what we
understood to be the remaining area of your inquiry, the
production of the November-December 1986 Bush diary transcripts,
and we have already provided you the critical documents. We
believe the rest of this exercise is no more than a fishing
expedition.

Jeffrey S. Harleston, Esquire
February 22, 1993
Page 4

    As always, we look forward to cooperating with you in your
investigation of this matter. Please feel free to call me once
you have reviewed this letter.

                    Sincerely,

                    J. Sedwick Sollers III
                       by JCS

                    J. Sedwick Sollers III

cc: Judge Griffin B. Bell

ATTACHMENT – 4

KING & SPALDING

1730 PENNSYLVANIA AVENUE, N.W.
WASHINGTON, DC
20006-4706

———

202/737-0500
TELECOPIER: 202/626-3737

191 PEACHTREE STREET
ATLANTA, GEORGIA 30303-1763
TELEPHONE: 404/572-4600
TELEX: 54-2917 KINGSPALD ATL
TELECOPIER: 404/572-5100

745 FIFTH AVENUE
NEW YORK, NY 10151
TELEPHONE: 212/758-8700
TELECOPIER: 212/593-3673

February 24, 1993

VIA TELECOPIER

Craig A. Gillen, Esquire
Deputy Independent Counsel
Office of Independent Counsel
Suite 701 West
555 13th Street, N.W.
Washington, D.C. 20004

Dear Mr. Gillen:

        I am responding to your letter dated February 23, 1993,
in which you formalized your request, made by telephone to me on
February 9, to take another deposition of former President Bush.
In January, you mentioned that it was your intent to seek a
deposition or "recorded interview" of former President Bush, but
we did not discuss specifics at that time.

        I was unaware until yesterday that the Office of
Independent Counsel ("OIC") had made a request to take another
deposition of former President Bush prior to our conversation in
January. It was my understanding that your Office intended only
to seek responses to some interrogatories from former President
Bush.

        The following is my understanding of the parameters of
your request for another deposition of former President Bush to be
taken during the week of March 15:

        First, you would conduct the interview.

February 24, 1993
Page 2

Second, you would not agree to any limitation of the scope of the questions beyond a general, "free ranging" inquiry concerning Iran-Contra. It is your intent to explore Iran-Contra from the beginning, notwithstanding the opportunity previously afforded the OIC to take then Vice President Bush's videotaped deposition for five hours in January 1988.

Third, you would not agree to any limitation as to the time to be devoted to the deposition. Although you hope to finish in one day, you would not rule out additional sessions.

Fourth, you would not consider issuing interrogatories in lieu of the deposition.

Fifth, you would not consider conducting the deposition in Houston or at any other location except for your office.

Finally, you would provide no assurances concerning the purpose of your inquiry and your intentions with regard to our client.

We are unable to accept the terms of your proposed deposition. As we have stated previously, we are cooperating fully with what we understood to be the scope of your continued inquiry -- the reason(s) that former President Bush's dictated diary transcript was not produced sooner than December 1992. We believe that any inquiry beyond that scope is cumulative, redundant and at this late date in your investigation wholly inappropriate. Such a broad based inquiry, without limitation, is inconsistent with our understanding that the OIC investigation into Iran-Contra is concluding.

Let's discuss this matter after you have reviewed this letter.

Sincerely,

J. Sedwick Sollers III
by JCS

J. Sedwick Sollers III

cc: Judge Griffin B. Bell

ATTACHMENT – 5

OFFICE OF INDEPENDENT COUNSEL
SUITE 701 WEST
555 THIRTEENTH STREET, N.W.
WASHINGTON, D.C. 20004
(202) 383-8940

February 26, 1993

BY FACSIMILE

Mr. J. Sedwick Sollers III, Esq.
King & Spalding
1730 Pennsylvania Avenue, N.W.
Washington, D.C. 20006

Dear Mr. Sollers:

        This will acknowledge your response to my February
23, 1993 letter memorializing our oral requests for a
substantive Iran-Contra deposition of former President George
Bush.

        Your six reasons for refusing to agree to a
voluntary deposition of President Bush are self-serving and a
disappointment. Any responsible deposition of President Bush
would have to include an inquiry into the important new
material uncovered since his last deposition. Your
insistence on an artificial limitation on the scope of the
deposition is unacceptable and renders further negotiation
pointless.

                                Sincerely,

                                Craig A. Gillen
                                Deputy Independent Counsel

Duane R. Clarridge

DUANE R. CLARRIDGE
532 CALLE DE LA PAZ
ESCONDIDO, CALIFORNIA 92029

11 September 1993

Dear Sirs:

I appreciated the opportunity to read the Walsh report as it pertains to me and below please find my comments:

Sticks and stones may break my bones, but the pitiful, feeble evidence of my alleged crimes presented in the Walsh report will <u>never</u> hurt me.

From my point of view, I certainly hope you will not seal this document, for it illustrates, even without my counter arguments, what frivolous, shallowly based indictments Walsh et al brought against me. Thus, the motivation of this man Walsh, who is known to be besotted with egotistical greed, must be vengeance — I would not curtsy to his request to turn state "snitch" and denied him another undeserved "scalp" of his tenure.

I will deal with Walsh's allegations in the fullness of time and on my own terms. At that time, may he recall from the here and now or from the

2.

grave that what goes around, comes
around.
    To be judged without a trial (unfortunately)
by a man who, as acting attorney General
pointed out in 1960 to the then Secretary
of STaTe and the Director of CIA "that
there was some point at which you
simply had to circumvent the law and
that what was important was that the
INS be given a plausible basis for doing
So" is, if nothing else, shabby justice
by an unworthy judge.

                    I remain,

                        Sincerely

                    Duane Clarridge

Thomas G. Clines

Clerk of the Court   December 1, 1993
United States Court of Appeals
District of Columbia Circuit

RE: Independent Counsel, Lawrence Walsh's Final Report

Dear Mr. Ron Garvin,

I have read fragments of the Independent Counsel's Final Report that pertain to my actions during Iran/Contra; and I understand that I have a right to respond to his allegations. His report is not always accurate or complete and it requires further clarification.

The report is correct in stating that Iran/Contra was not a "Rogue" operation - that it was conceived and condoned by two presidents of the United States and that a cover-up took place that resulted in many of us being "scapegoats." When it became evident that Mr. Casper Weinburger would face a trial on charges of lying, President Bush pardoned six key officials - but left some of us "out in the cold." I will not rest until we are vindicated.

Much of the report, however, contains "Facts" that are self-serving, distorted or incorrect in an effort to vilify key people. I feel compelled to respond because this seven year "witchhunt" destroyed or severely damaged many reputations. All Iran/Contra participants are highly decorated patriots who have served this great country in combat all of our adult lives. History demands that our actions during Iran/Contra be completely and accurately understood.

I was imprisoned a year because of an overzealous, vindictive Independent Counsel who has operated for seven years with no supervision. I recognize that a naive jury, confused by the trial tactics of the Independent Counsel, found me guilty; but I remain convinced of my innocence. I appealed my case to the U.S. Supreme Court expending all the funds in my possession in doing so. The charges against me; underreporting income and failing to declare foreign financial accounts are untrue. I admitted I made a mistake on my original 1985 tax return; filed when I was overworked in securing the release of American hostages and assisting the Contra's in forcing the communist government of Nicaragua to have free elections; but in 1987, prior to the Independent Council showing any interest in my taxes I amended my 1985 return correcting my mistake.

The Independent Counsel, himself, has been investigated for misconduct relating to his actions during Iran/Contra i.e. evading taxes, falsifying vouchers, losing secret documents, etc. I understand that he did pay a fine to the District of Columbia to avoid charges being filed against him. Over seventy members of the U.S. Congress also signed a letter addressed to the Honorable William Barr, U.S. Attorney General on August 6, 1992, requesting a Department of Justice inquiry into his conduct.

I'll now list the Independent Counsels specific allegations and the facts as they pertain to my role:

ALLEGATION

Page 157: In 1984, SSI, a corporation that Clines owned pleaded guilty to theft of Government Property and paid the fine of $100,000.00 with money from Secord.

FACT

"The $100,000 was paid on behalf of SSI to SETTLE CERTAIN <u>CIVIL</u> CLAIMS, i.e. certain <u>OVERCHARGES FOR FREIGHT</u>, which allegations Mr. Clines <u>DENIES</u>" in order to pay the SSI fine Mr. Clines borrowed $33,000 from his friend, Gen. Secord and repaid him later with interest.

On <u>Page 161</u> the Iran/Contra states that Clines' acquaintance with the owner of Defex, Portugal enabled Secord to work directly with that company.

This is a <u>FALSE STATEMENT</u>. Mr. Clines did not know the owner of Defex, Portugal until Gen. Secord introduces him in 1985.

On <u>Page 174</u> the Independent Counsel states that in the Spring of 1986
Secord and Clines and <u>others vacationed</u>
at a German Weight-Reduction <u>SPA</u> using $4,600 from Korel and Clines profit accounts.

This is another example of the Independent Counsel taking liberty with the facts. Secord and I alone went to the clinic [Not Spa] for health reasons. It was no <u>vacation</u>. He also fails to mention that Mr. Hakim stated that he was going to pay for this visit. [see page 636 of Clines Trial Transcript "A.H. asked me [Zucher] to arrange everything with the clinic as he wants to settle the invoice for them."]

One <u>Page 175</u> the Independent Counsel states that Secord was not charged with giving false information on his IRS form because the Swiss Financial Records available should not be used in a tax case, under the provisions of the Treaty through which the records were obtained.

The use of swiss financial records by the Independent Counsel in Clines' trial was not <u>LEGAL</u>. The <u>TREATY</u> under which the Independent Counsel obtained the financial records of the enterprise from Switzerland <u>explicitly provides that the records cannot be used in the prosecution of tax crimes</u>.

On <u>Page 180</u> the I/C states that Hakim was guilty of possible tax crimes but records must come from some source other than pursuant to Treaty.

In an egregious act of prosecutorial misconduct the Independent Counsel utilized Swiss Records he had received from Albert Hakim, regarding an entirely <u>unrelated</u> matter, [an agreement signed by Hakim] to convict Clines. The Independent Counsel, repackaged the Swiss Records given him by Hakim and sent them to Mr. Gossin of the Swiss Federal Office of Police Matters for retransmittal to William Zucher, who under a grant of immunity had to cooperate with the Independent Counsel.

Next the Independent Counsel directed Albert Hakim, under the Civil Agreement he had signed with the I/C, to demand the Swiss Records from Zucher.

Zucher complied and the Swiss Records were given by Hakim to an FBI Agent assigned to the Independent Counsel for their use at Clines' trial.

The Postmark on the Package demonstrates that the Swiss Records were sent from the Independent Counsels office to the Swiss Government - to Zucher - to Hakim and back to the Independent Counsel [This package was never even opened on its journey from the Independent Counsel's office to Switzerland and back to the Independent Counsel's office. [Albert Hakim has the postmarks to prove this.] These Swiss Records were actually received from the Swiss government under the treaty for an unrelated case and it was a violation of the "Swiss Treaty" to use these records in a tax case. The Swiss were furious about this action.

On Page 181 the Independent Counsel states that Mr. Clines trial was held in Maryland as Mr. Clines' accountant filed his tax forms in Maryland.

In fact, the tax forms were filed in Virginia by Mr. Clines [the accountant mailed them to Mr. Clines, in Virginia, for signature], the Independent Counsel desperately wanted to try Mr. Clines in a venue outside of Virginia and/or Washington, D.C.

On Page 181 the Independent Counsel states that Mr. Clines earned $468,431 in 1985 and reported only $265,000.

Mr. Clines was unable to determine the precise amount of his Gross income in 1985 when he filed his original return as he was very actively engaged in freeing the American Hostages in Iran and in keeping the Contras alive. He reported his Net Income [funds he brought into the USA and did not utilize for expenses].

In 1987, prior to the Independent Counsel expressing any interest in his taxes, Mr. Clines filed an amended return for 1985 that the Independent Counsel received prior to trial [the amended return reported earnings of $486,490], higher than even the Independent Counsel stated. Mr. Clines declared earning a total of $889,003 from Iran/Contra on his 1985 and 1986 returns and the Independent Counsel stated he earned only $882,954 - hardly an action that would be taken by a person trying to avoid declaring his income.

On <u>Page 182</u> the Independent Counsel states that Mr. Clines decided on an assumed name when he signed a fiduciary agreement with CSF.

The transcript at trial of Mr. Clines [page 356] clearly shows that Mr. Zucher <u>Decided</u> on the assumed name - not Mr. Clines. Furthermore, Mr. Clines had another page attached to the fiduciary document stating that his son would receive the funds in the event of his demise. <u>THIS DOCUMENT WAS SIGNED IN TRUE NAME - AND AT TRIAL WAS DETACHED FROM THE FIDUCIARY AGREEMENT; A DISTORTION OF THE FACTS</u>.

On <u>Page 183</u> he admitted that the answer on his income tax return stating that he did not have a foreign account was "incorrect". [I/C cited Page #1305 of my trial transcript dated 9/14/90].

Page #1305 of Clines' transcript pertained to a foreign account in 1986. Only during trial discovery in 1990 did Mr. Clines realize that he had received interest on this fiduciary account [Account was opened on 18 September 1986 and closed on 10 December 1986]. The funds had been kept by the owner of Defex, Portugal without Mr. Clines' knowledge. I readily admitted that the box on my income tax return for 1986 that asks if I had any foreign financial accounts should/would have been checked "yes" in 1987 rather than "no", if I had known interest was received. At no time did I receive a statement pertaining to the C-Tea account from CSF - so I had no idea of this interest.

In closing, I can only say that I am a real political victim of the Independent Counsel's desperate search for convictions to justify his $40 million, 7 year prosecutorial odyssey. It is therefore absolutely essential that my remedial comments above be made a part of the official report.

Sincerely,

Thomas G. Clines

In closing, I can only say that I am a real political victim of the Independent Counsel's desperate search for convictions to justify his $40 million, 7 year prosecutorial odyssey. It is therefore absolutely essential that my remedial comments above be made a part of the official report.

Sincerely,

Thomas G. Clines

Charles J. Cooper

SHAW, PITTMAN, POTTS & TROWBRIDGE

A PARTNERSHIP INCLUDING PROFESSIONAL CORPORATIONS

2300 N STREET, N.W.
WASHINGTON, D.C. 20037-1128
(202) 663-8000
FACSIMILE
(202) 663-8007

1501 FARM CREDIT DRIVE
McLEAN, VIRGINIA 22102-5004

201 LIBERTY STREET, S.W.
LEESBURG, VIRGINIA 22075-2721

CHARLES J. COOPER
(202) 663-8257

September 16, 1993

Ron Garvin
Clerk of the Court
U.S. Court of Appeals for the
  District of Columbia Circuit
United States Courthouse
333 Constitution Avenue, NW
Washington, DC 20001

Re: Division No. 86-6; Final Report of
    Independent Counsel Lawrence Walsh

Dear Mr. Garvin:

Independent Counsel Walsh's Final Report in the Iran-Contra matter contains a factual statement that conflicts with my current memory of the relevant events. The statement is made twice, once at page 541 and again on page 542. In footnotes 170 and 181 my grand jury testimony is cited as support for these statements. I should like to review the cited excerpt from my grand jury testimony to assist me in determining the statement's accuracy, and thus in determining whether to submit a comment to the Court.

Sincerely,

Charles J. Cooper

CJC:lam
0134:212cjc.93

SHAW, PITTMAN, POTTS & TROWBRIDGE

A PARTNERSHIP INCLUDING PROFESSIONAL CORPORATIONS

2300 N STREET, N.W.
WASHINGTON, D.C. 20037-1128
(202) 663-8000
FACSIMILE
(202) 663-8007

1501 FARM CREDIT DRIVE
McLEAN, VIRGINIA 22102-5004

201 LIBERTY STREET, S.W.
LEESBURG, VIRGINIA 22075-2721

CHARLES J. COOPER
(202) 663-8257

December 3, 1993

United States Court of Appeals
For the District of Columbia Circuit

FILED DEC 0 3 1993

RON GARVIN
CLERK

Ron H. Garvin
Clerk of the Court
U.S. Court of Appeals for
  the District of Columbia Circuit
333 Constitution Avenue, N.W.
U.S. Courthouse, Fifth Floor
Washington, D.C. 20001

Re: In re Oliver L. North, et al.
Division No. 86-6

Dear Mr. Garvin:

While I have been permitted to review only 25 or so pages of
Mr. Walsh's voluminous report, even this scanty sampling betrays
the essential nature of the report, and thus of the purpose of
its principal authors. Far from a dispassionate, balanced, and
careful recitation of the facts and evidence unearthed by
Mr. Walsh in his interminable and costly investigation,
Mr. Walsh's report is a tendentious polemic, manipulating some
facts and inventing others in a determined effort to portray
President Reagan and his principal national security advisors as
lawless, or at least indifferent to the law. He may even suggest, in pages that I have not been permitted to review but which
have nonetheless been discussed in newspaper accounts of
Mr. Walsh's report, that these public servants, led by Attorney
General Meese, conspired to conceal the nature and extent of
President Reagan's contemporaneous knowledge of the arms transfers to Iran in 1985. Not only is Mr. Walsh's portrayal not
true, it is an inversion of the truth. In short, Mr. Walsh's
report is a political document, and is thus a fitting denouement
to his investigation, which was actuated by Attorney General
Meese to discover and prosecute any criminal wrongdoing that may
have occurred in connection with the Iranian arms initiative, but
was transmogrified by Mr. Walsh into a political jihad.

I have neither the time nor the inclination to record here
the many thoughts that crowded my mind in reading the few pages
of Mr. Walsh's report to which I have been provided access. But
I must correct one of his errors, for I suspect that it plays at

SHAW, PITTMAN, POTTS & TROWBRIDGE
A PARTNERSHIP INCLUDING PROFESSIONAL CORPORATIONS

Ron H. Garvin
December 3, 1993
Page 2

least a corroborating role in assertions made, I suspect, on
pages of the report that I have not been permitted to see. In
two places the report states that I became convinced during the
fact-finding effort led by Attorney General Meese during the
weekend of November 21-23, 1986, that "Shultz was telling the
truth and that the President knew of, and may have approved, the
pre-Finding shipments" of arms to Iran. See Report at pp. 541,
542. To be sure, I became convinced during the weekend fact-
finding effort that Secretary Shultz was telling the truth -- and
that Mr. McFarlane and Lt. Col. North accordingly were not -- on
the issue that inspired our weekend mission in the first place;
namely, whether anyone in the United States government knew that
there were hawk missiles, rather than oil-drilling equipment, on
the CIA proprietary aircraft sent to Iran in November of 1985.
It became clear to me from interviews conducted during that weekend that Secretary Shultz, as well as Mr. McFarlane and Lt. Col.
North, had contemporaneous knowledge that the aircraft were
delivering arms rather than oil-drilling equipment. It was not
at all clear to me then, however, that President Reagan knew in
November 1985 that anything was being transferred to Iran by the
United States, let alone that Hawk missiles were being transferred in CIA proprietary aircraft.

Sincerely,

Charles J. Cooper

0134:270cjc.93

Edwin G. Corr

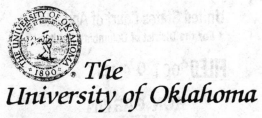

**The
University of Oklahoma**

DEPARTMENT OF POLITICAL SCIENCE
455 West Lindsey Street. Room 304
Norman. Oklahoma 73019-0535
(405) 325-6622

RECEIVED,

OCT 0 4 1993

CLERK OF THE UNITED
STATES COURT OF APPEALS

Ambassador Edwin G. Corr
Professor of Political Science
Occupant of the Henry Bellmon
Chair in Public Service

October 1, 1993

Ron Garvin, Clerk
U.S. Court of Appeals
District of Columbia Circuit
Washington, D.C. 20001-2866

Dear Mr. Garvin:

Attached are my comments on those portions of the
Final Report of the Independent Counsel that I was
permitted to review. I am submitting the comments to you
in order that they may be included as an appendix to the
Final Report.

Thank you for your courtesy when I reviewed the
Report in your office. With best wishes,

Sincerely,

Edwin H Corr

Edwin G. Corr

EGC:dlb

Attachments

Comments of Edwin G. Corr on those Portions that Refer to Him in
the Independent Counsel's Final Report on the Iran-Contra Affair

In accordance with the letter to me of August 9, 1993 from Ron Garvin, Clerk of the U.S. Court of Appeals of the District of Columbia Circuit, I am submitting comments and factual information that I want to be included as an appendix to the Final Report of the Independent Counsel (IC). My comments, of course, are limited to those selected parts of the Final Report that I was allowed to examine in Mr. Garvin's office in the U.S. Court of Appeals on September 2, 1993.

My comments are divided into four parts:

1. Comments on the IC's erroneous determination that I intentionally presented false testimony, as alleged in Chapter 26 of the IC Report, beginning on page 393.

2. Comments on other parts of the IC Report where I am mentioned or discussed.

3. Comments on the allegation that I withheld documents.

4. Comments on the IC's decision not to prosecute me.

Edwin H. Corr
Edwin G. Corr
October 1, 1993

Comments on the Independent Counsel's Erroneous Determination that I Intentionally Presented False Testimony

The Independent Counsel (IC) does not determine in his Final Report that I broke the law with respect to the Boland Amendments. The IC's explicitly stated conclusion is that I presented false testimony, and that the IC had sufficient evidence to prosecute me successfully. I did not intentionally present false testimony (that is, knowingly lie) to any of the investigating bodies of the Iran-Contra affair, including the IC and the IC attorneys, either in voluntary meetings with them or when I was before the Grand Jury. I do not believe that the evidence presented by the IC in its Final Report substantiates his erroneous conclusion; and I do not believe that the IC's argument would be convincing to the unbiased, discriminating reader, nor would it have been to a jury, had the IC chosen to prosecute me.

The IC's erroneous determination that I lied focuses almost entirely on a meeting I had with General Richard V. Secord on April 20, 1986 in my office in the American Embassy in San Salvador, and whether Lt. Col. Oliver North was also present in that meeting. My best recollection was, and is, that Lt. Col. North was not present in the meeting, that the meeting was primarily a "courtesy call" on me by General Secord, and that little of consequence was discussed. I recall nothing about that meeting that at the time would have given me knowledge of illegal involvement of the U.S. government in providing assistance to the Contras. Even were North in the meeting, it would not establish that there was conversation in the meeting that involved me in any illegal activities, nor establish that I <u>knowingly</u> lied that North was not in the meeting, since my best memory of that meeting is that he was not a participant.

The IC purports to present "evidence" from statements by General Secord, Lt. Col. North, Col. James Steele, former DCM David Dlouhy, and myself to establish that I intentionally lied. When Secord made his courtesy call on me I did <u>not</u> know he directed the private operation, only that he was an active private supporter of the U.S. government policy in Central America and of the Contra cause. According to the IC, General Secord himself stated that I provided the private operation nothing more than moral support. Secord did claim, however, according to the IC, that he, Steele, and North were present in the April 20, 1986 meeting, and that I expressed interest in an earlier meeting with General Juan Bustillo, the Commander of the Salvadoran Air Force who was key to achieving the U.S. government's major objectives in El Salvador. I naturally would have been interested in Bustillo. This would not establish that Secord and I talked of anything that would have revealed to me any illegal U.S. involvement with the private operation to support the Contras.

Lt. Col. Oliver North's testimony to the IC was that he did <u>not</u> recall meeting with me in the Embassy on April 20, 1986, but he did remember bringing Secord to the Embassy for an "introduction" meeting with me.

Colonel Jim Steele's testimony of 1986, 1987, and later with the IC varied, but, according to the IC, was finally that both Secord and North met with me in the April 20, 1986 meeting.

David Dlouhy's initial testimony, according to the IC Report, was that he heard while he was in El Salvador on temporary duty at the time of the April 20 meeting that I had met briefly at the airport (not in my office) with North. The IC itself subsequently discredited Dlouhy's testimony by showing that he had direct knowledge only of events from April 16-19, 1986, and that anything else was hearsay, or his confusion with later events.

I do not believe that North was in the April 20, 1986 meeting. I recall that Steele brought Secord to my office for a courtesy call and remained briefly before excusing himself. I suspect that Steele left my office to talk with North or to take him somewhere. I do not recall knowing that North was in El Salvador on that date, and did not, in my recollection, learn he had been in El Salvador on April 20, 1986 until investigations had begun on the Iran-Contra affair after the downing of the Hazenfus flight on October 5, 1986.

By the time of questioning by the IC, I was unable to recall with clarity and preciseness the details and content of many events, meetings, and conversations. A number of years had passed. I did not know prior to the beginning of the investigations much of what the IC erroneously presumed I had known earlier. But because of the intense interest of the IC in the April 20, 1986 meeting, I have occasionally wondered if my own mind might have somehow reconstructed who was present at the April 20, 1986 meeting and what was discussed. Until I was permitted to read portions of the

IC Final Report referring to me, I did not know what others giving testimony to the IC were saying about me. Having now had the opportunity to read selected parts of the IC Final Report, I am even more inclined to trust my own recollection of the meeting. And, even if that recollection could be wrong, I am certain that I did not intentionally lie to the Grand Jury.

The IC attempts to use alleged statements by me to Senator Christopher Dodd and Jon Wiant and my Country Team notes of April 21, 1986 to show that I had lied about matters, and therefore had lied about whether North was or was not in the April 20, 1986 meeting. The IC says Dodd said I denied to him knowing about the Contra supply activity. I told Dodd that I knew of <u>no</u> U.S. government <u>illegal</u> support for the Contras, which was the truth, not that I had not known about the existence of the private operation. Everyone had known about the private supply effort. It was in the newspapers. Dodd's statement does not show I was lying, and is irrelevant to the April 20, 1986 meeting.

The IC claims that Jon Wiant told the IC in a January 1987 conversation that I was scared and concerned I might be in trouble for things <u>others</u> had done at Ilopango. Ambassador Morris Busby, the President's Special Negotiator for Central America, visited El Salvador in January 1987. Jon Wiant, a friend and professional colleague, was a member of his delegation. Iran-Contra was much in the news and investigation of the matter had begun. There were some news articles falsely suggesting that I had been illegally involved with the private effort out of Ilopango to aid the

Contras. I expressed concern to my friend Jon that something illegal could have occurred at Ilopango without my having known about it. I do not recall specifically talking about Walker and Abrams, but I am sure I did not say they told me everything was okay at Ilopango. The pattern would have been for them to ask me what was occurring at Ilopango, not I them. If I did say to Jon that someone had told me the U.S. government's relations with the Nicaraguan Resistence and the private organization were "okay," it was most likely based on a conversation I had with Lt. Col. North. I had asked him if his meetings with the Nicaraguan Resistence were legal and he responded that a White House attorney had so advised him. My assumption, as I have repeatedly stated, was his role was that of a liaison and of being knowledgeable about the Nicaraguan Resistence's activities. My conversation with Jon Wiant, as I am confident he would affirm, was to say that I had done nothing wrong and had been unaware of any U.S. official's possible wrong-doing. The IC unsuccessfully attempts to show by providing a single excerpt from Jon's testimony that I lied or covered up, which his testimony does <u>not</u> show.

Finally, as supposed proof of my illegal involvement and lying, the IC cites my April 21, 1986 preparation notes for a Country Team meeting in which I was to remind the key officers of the Embassy that I was the "action officer for the Nicaraguan Democratic Resistence." The use of this State Department terminology was in keeping with my consistent efforts to ensure that I nor U.S. government personnel under my direction did

6

anything illegal to support the Contras. In early September 1985, after my arrival in El Salvador in August, my then Deputy Chief of Mission (David Passage) informed me that representatives from the Contra groups had made approaches to Embassy personnel. I made very clear to Passage that we should avoid such contacts because of the Boland amendment. Based on my personal notes, but not on explicit memory, I evidently discussed the question of such contacts with Assistant Secretary Elliott Abrams at the Chiefs of Mission Conference in Panama, September 8-10, 1985. I know that I returned from that meeting to re-affirm my policy of limiting contacts. My policy was that I be kept informed of any significant chance encounters or conversations. I recall repeatedly using the instructions with my staff that no one should do anything that was, or could be construed to be, "advising, directing, or providing materiel support to the Contras." I stressed that any questions on this matter should be directed to me.

I personally followed the changing legal guidance from the Department of State Legal Office on what U.S. government employees could and could not do with the Contras. I left the over-all coordination of the NHAO program and liaison with the Nicaraguan Resistence to Washington (as were my instructions), involving myself and my people only in directed tasks, such as counting items (e.g. shoes) being turned over to the Nicaraguan Resistance. I asked Colonel Steele that he keep me informed about any of the private organization's activities that might impact on the Embassy's efforts to carry out U.S. policy in El Salvador, while cautioning him to be careful not to step over the line into advising and directing, and being especially careful not to permit any U.S. government materiel provided to El Salvador be passed to the Contras. It was these actions and my often reiterated policy on contacts with the Contras that I was referring to when I said I was the action officer on the Nicaraguan Democratic Resistence. It shows my diligence to stay within the law, and it does not show that I was aware of any U.S. officials being outside the law.

The IC refuses to accept the fact that prior to the beginning of the investigations, I regarded the private supply effort to the Contras as a non-U.S. government operation, for which my chief responsibility was to assure that U.S. government employees under my direction did not become illegally involved. My major and almost totally consuming work was to support Salvadoran democrats in their efforts to defeat the guerrillas, consolidate democracy, reduce human rights abuses, and create economic development and justice.

I am certain that I did all possible to keep persons under my direction and myself from breaking the law. And, I am certain that I did not know of any acts which I considered illegal by U.S. government officials to support the Contras prior to the beginning of investigations after the October 5, 1986 downing of the Hazenfus flight.

The Reagan Administration had made clear its support for the Nicaraguan Democratic Resistence. The U.S. government did not discourage private support as long as that support did not violate

8

U.S. law. The U.S. government acknowledged that Embassy personnel had contact with private citizens who may have engaged in Contra supply activities. There was nothing illegal or improper about such contacts. They were inevitable at Ilopango Air Base. My main concern about the private operation at Ilopango was to know enough about happenings there to be sure they did not adversely affect U.S. goals in El Salvador, for which I was responsible, and to be sure that U.S. employees under my direction did not violate U.S. law. This was what I tried to do.

Comments on Other Parts of the IC Report
where I am Mentioned or Discussed

1.   On page 8 the IC says that I was one of the persons who helped keep Felix Rodriguez in place at Ilopango Airport.

The reason I encouraged Felix to remain in El Salvador was because of the important contribution he was making toward the achievement of U.S. goals in El Salvador, and had nothing to do with Felix's role in support of the private supply effort. Felix introduced to the Salvadoran military the "lightening tactical concept" for the combined use of helicopters and ground troops against the FMLN guerrillas, which helped change the balance in the war. He helped keep the Salvadoran military from carrying out coups against the elected civilian government, and he helped improve Salvadoran military attitudes and comportment on human rights. I was unaware of Felix's "formal" role in the private effort to supply the Contras. I regarded him as working for General Bustillo to coordinate matters with the Americans, both official and those in the private operation.

2. On page 30 the IC states that I, along with others, "falsely denied details of their knowledge" of the Iran-Contra affair.

As stated earlier, this is false. The IC was committed to the idea that there was a conspiracy among U.S. officials to deny knowledge of illegal involvement of the U.S. government in the private resupply operation. I was not part of any such conspiracy, and I doubt that it existed. After seven years it is unlikely that had such a conspiracy existed it would not have come <u>clearly</u> to light.

Knowledge that a private supply effort existed was commonplace. Stories had been written in newspapers about the private effort. A plane delivering arms to Ilopango for the private group in February 1985 had been forced to jettison arms all along the Pan American highway. One of the private group's planes flew into a mountain in El Salvador on another occasion. These events were reported in the press. My officers working at Ilopango informed me of the private operation there. The private effort was not a secret. Who was running it was, and, wisely or unwisely, was not something I tried to discover.

The situation and discussion of the matter was further complicated by the fact that there had been legal and public U.S.

government efforts to help supply the Contras. At times it was legal to provide lethal and humanitarian aid. At times it was legal to provide humanitarian aid only. At times there was an in-between situation in which humanitarian aid plus communications gear, and, then later, humanitarian aid plus communications equipment and intelligence could be legally provided. And, there were also periods in which no aid could be legally supplied.

The questions to me from the media, and, indeed, from the U.S. government, after the downing of the Hazenfus plane on October 5, 1986, about my knowledge of the private effort were interpreted by me to refer to my knowledge of <u>illegal</u> U.S. government assistance. I assumed (correctly, I think) that the persons asking the questions assumed that I knew what was public knowledge, i.e. that a private effort existed. I was aware of it, and, there had been contacts between my officers working at Ilopango and members of the private organization.

While I used the words that there was "no connection" between the Embassy and the private group, it was obvious in the context of the events being discussed that I was referring to there being <u>no</u> <u>illegal</u> <u>connection</u>. This was demonstrated by the fact that at a press conference with a large number of reporters, one (and only one) of the reporters misinterpreted my remarks concerning Max Gomez (alias Felix Rodriguez) to be a denial that I knew Felix. When that one reporter's story ran in the <u>Washington</u> <u>Post</u>, I had my Public Affairs Counselor immediately communicate with the reporter to clarify that I did know Felix, and that my remarks were meant to confirm this (as evidently understood by all other reporters), not to deny it. This, I submit, shows I was trying not to lie about any knowledge I had. My response that the Embassy had no connection with the private group was an effort to say I had no knowledge of <u>illegal</u> activity on the part of the U.S. government, which I did not have at that time.

3. On pages 41 and 42 the IC discusses the relationship between Steele and me. Steele told the IC he "believed" he told me about a lethal cargo flight in April, 1986. I do not doubt this. As I said in my testimony, Steele told me of a couple such specific flights, either before or after their execution. However, I did not even know the magnitude of the number of such flights made from Ilopango (which was only about a dozen) until finding out during sessions with investigators; and I in no way, explicitly or implicitly, gave authorization for any such flights. It was not within my authority or capacity to do so for a Salvadoran airbase nor for a private American organization.

Steele said he informed Corr "of everything that wasn't below his noise level." That excluded information that Lt. Col. North was actually involved in the private organization's operations. In retrospect, I gave Col. Steele an impossible task: to keep me informed sufficiently about the private operation so that we could be sure it did not jeopardize the achievement of the U.S. goals we were responsible for in El Salvador, and <u>not</u> to do anything that could be construed as directing, advising or providing materiel

12

support for the Contras. I fear that his participation in some meetings for the purpose of monitoring and keeping informed were later erroneously interpreted (in terms of Steele's and the Embassy's motive) as something more sinister than monitoring.

Steele told the IC that both he and I were aware that North was working "very closely" with the Contra resupply operation. As naive as I may seem to the IC, I well knew that North worked closely with the Contras, but believed that his role was one of close liaison with the Contras, a promoter of U.S. private support for the Contras (but not a director or decision-maker in the operations of the private effort, nor a direct recipient of private sector funds for the Contras), and an encourager to U.S. government officials that the Congress would ultimately endorse U.S. aid for the Contras. As stated earlier, I even asked North if he was sure his activities were legal, and he assured me that the attorney for the Intelligence Review Board had told him that they were. I accepted this.

Steele said I was in a "damage control mode" after the Hazenfus plane shootdown. Of course I was. That was my job. But, I was not intentionally lying, and I was not covering up any illegal U.S. actions regarding the private Contra resupply operation, because at that point I did not know of any; and had I, I would not have lied about the subject. I was insistent with my staff that we could not lie.

4.   On page 42 the IC states that a note I made about an October

14, 1986 telephone conversation shows that Elliott Abrams and I discussed Felix Rodriguez and his role in the private resupply effort. The IC says that by that date I was "fully aware of Rodriguez' role."

It is natural that Elliott and I spoke of Felix Rodriguez. He had been mentioned by Hazenfus in radio interviews from Nicaragua as having been a U.S. government employee engaged in the Contra resupply operation. Contrary to what the IC report alleges, I was not yet "fully aware" of all Rodriguez' roles. I did not yet know of North having asked Rodriguez in a September 1985 letter to work with the private effort. I was to learn of that later from investigators. I still saw Rodriguez as working for Bustillo (not as a member of the private group). In addition to serving as an adviser and combat pilot in the Salvadoran Air Force, I regarded Felix to be a liaison and coordinator for Bustillo with the private group and also with the American Embassy.

I am sure, although I do not remember explicitly, that I told Elliott on October 14, 1986 I had no information of Rodriguez being a part of any U.S. government operation. That was my best information at the time. That was the information Abrams had from me about Rodriguez when Abrams gave testimony to a Congressional Committee that afternoon.

5. On pages 265 and 266, the IC states that Steele and I were concerned about coordination of NHAO with the Salvadoran Air Force for the delivery of humanitarian aid authorized by Congress.

Bustillo wanted to deal with Rodriguez and/or Steele rather than CIA officers. This was true.

Bustillo, who was a key actor in achieving the objectives for which we were striving in El Salvador

                                                                          I
see nothing sinister about that, only good management. Neither do I see anything remiss about my note of February 5, 1986 saying we must attain better "coordination among the Front Office, Steele, Felix and UNO/FDR." This was related to the legally authorized NHAO program, and nothing more than another attempt to improve management of the legal humanitarian effort.

6.   The IC misrepresents on page 377 the situation at Ilopango airport on December 30, 1985 when he alleges that "Walker, North, Corr, Steele, among others, represented U.S. in meeting with Bustillo. Rodriguez was present." As my testimony to the IC stated, there were several meetings simultaneously among different persons at the Ilopango airport that day. There may have been one meeting of all the persons listed by the IC with Bustillo. I am not sure. There were others in which Bill Walker and I were not present "representing the U.S.," and there may have been others with Bustillo in which not all North, Steele and Rodriguez were present simultaneously. I am sure that I took part in no meetings on that day in which the delivery of lethal supplies was discussed.

15

My focus for the day was on legally authorized humanitarian assistance.

7.   The IC on page 378 cites a telephone conversation I had with Walker in which he expressed concern about Gomez (Felix Rodriguez) checking everything with North and disrupting the NHAO operation, and that I should impress on Fears that we cannot proceed in this "fouled up manner." The IC cites this as evidence of my knowledge of illegal U.S. government involvement in the Contra supply effort. Placed in the context of the situation at the time and the fact that I was unaware of the true nature of North's involvement with the private operation, Bill Walker was merely impressing on me to impress upon Fears the need to have a line drawn between legal U.S. government assistance efforts and private efforts.

8.   On page 381, the IC refers to a note I made of points to discuss with Abrams at the September 8-10, 1985 Chiefs of Mission meeting in Panama. Among these were: "3) Contras - 3 contacts; FDN talk w/Steele (NO); 4) Rodriguez; 5) Ollie North conversation - S. Front." The IC report says that I bracketed the three items and put "√'s" by the ones discussed. Again, the IC attempts to imply something the facts do not sustain.

I do not, as I told the IC, specifically recall the details of my conversation with Elliott at this conference. I do not doubt discussing these points but they do not indicate that Elliott and I were discussing any illegal actions by the U.S. government nor plotting to utilize Felix Rodriguez in the private effort to supply the Contras. We continued in the Embassy to limit contacts with the Nicaraguan Democratic Resistence, leaving liaison with the Contras to Washington. I did not know of Rodriguez' agreement to work with the private organization, as distinct from working for Bustillo, which was my consistent view of his role. And, there continued to be a view within the U.S. government (one also held strongly by the Salvadoran government) that the opening of a southern front by Eden Pastor would be desirable, but the U.S. government continued to limit contact with Pastor because of concerns about his possible links to drug traffickers. These facts substantiate, I think, that any discussion of the three points in my notes were related chiefly to the achievement of U.S. objectives in El Salvador, and not to the Contra effort, as the IC tries to imply.

9. On page 381 the IC refers to my telephone conversation with Abrams' note of October 8, 1986 about the downing of the Hazenfus plane on October 5, 1986. The content of the note supports my testimony that I did not have detailed information about the private operation at Ilopango. I was citing to Abrams the telegraphic reports from Managua of what the Sandinistas and Hazenfus were saying, _not_ drawing on my own personal knowledge. Elliott's comment that North was out of the U.S., would return that evening, and Elliott would try to get information from him, further shows my and Elliott's lack of knowledge about private operations

at Ilopango.

I talked with Elliott about the Salvadoran role and Bustillo saying the Government of El Salvador would deny any involvement. Elliott and I "brain-stormed" on the impact of such a Salvadoran position on U.S. interests. This was exactly what the Assistant Secretary and the Ambassador should have been doing. My comment that leaks would be inevitable referred to leaks about the Salvadoran military's cooperation with the private organization at Ilopango possibly without explicit Duarte clearance, not U.S. government involvement. We were continuously trying to promote cooperative Salvadoran civilian-military relations in a way that the civilians were increasingly stronger vis a vis the military and the military was not challenging civilian authority. Relations between Bustillo and Duarte were always a little tense, and I did not want Bustillo's support for the private organization to disrupt the democratic consolidation we sought in El Salvador. The notes refer to legitimate, appropriate matters, not illegal matters.

10. The IC's discussion of my alleged comments in the August 10, 1986 meeting in Don Gregg's office on pages 387-88 say that I expressed concern about the transition from the private operation to a possibly Congressionally approved CIA operation, about equipment being taken from the Contras by the private organization, the need to resupply the southern front, and about the Bustillo/Rodriguez relationship. Although I do not recall precisely what I said in that meeting, I know that if I addressed these matters it

18

was to relate General Bustillo's concerns about them. During the weeks immediately preceding the meeting, Bustillo had made clear his worries about these matters to Steele and to me. My statement of Bustillo's concerns were just that, not that of someone involved in the private operation, but as the Ambassador who wanted to maintain a productive legal relationship with Bustillo who was a key player in El Salvador for which I was responsible.

As the IC Report points out, I expressed my view that I did not believe that either the CIA or Col. Steele could, under then existing law, perform the role that Rodriguez had carried out as Bustillo's liaison to the private organization. It was my view, and still is, that Rodriguez was a private citizen lawfully engaged in providing (on behalf of Bustillo and from his own experience) advice and support to the private organization. I had told Steele and other Embassy personnel that they should not cross the line into providing advice, direction or materiel support to the private effort. The Commander in Chief of the United States Southern Command, based on conversations we had, also cautioned Steele that he nor his officers could cross the line.

Having Steele or the CIA assume the function of liaison between Bustillo and the private operation that Rodriguez was carrying out would have, in my view, inevitably led to activity that would have been unlawful. Consequently, the opinion that the IC says I expressed at the August 12, 1986 meeting are fully consistent with the importance I attached to staying within the bounds of existing law and my consistent effort to assure that I and people under my direction did so.

Finally, I sought to protect my relationships with both Bustillo and Rodriguez, who were influential actors in El Salvador. I suggested that should Congress change the law (which the Administration advocated) and it become legal to use Steele or the CIA, it should be done in a manner so as not to offend Rodriguez, nor Bustillo (because of their friendship). Rodriguez had done a great job in advancing U.S. goals with the Salvadoran military. The views I expressed in the August 12, 1986 meeting were consistent with my perception that Rodriguez was working for Bustillo as a liaison to the Americans, not of him as a member of the private organization, of which I was unaware, and which Rodriguez and Bustillo strongly criticized.

11. On page 392, the IC says Corr's notes, among other persons' notes, showed Abrams' knowledge of North's activities. I cannot speak for other persons' notes. My notes certainly show mention of Rodriguez in my conversations with Abrams, but they do _not_ show Abrams' knowledge that Rodriguez had been enlisted by North as a part of the private organization, since I did not know that myself. Neither could they contain comments indicating illegal activities by North because I was unaware of such activities.

12. The IC says on page 493 that I praised Rodriguez to Vice President Bush on May 1, 1986, and said I wanted Rodriguez to stay in El Salvador. That was because of the contribution he was making

to improve the Salvadoran military's operational effectiveness against the Salvadoran guerrillas and to making the Salvadoran military, especially Bustillo, more committed to democratic rule and human rights. That was reason enough. It had absolutely nothing to do with any role he had in support of the Contras, as the IC evidently would have the reader infer.

Comments on the Allegation that I "Withheld" Documents

The Independent Counsel states that I withheld documents, and, implicitly, relevant information, from Iran-Contra investigators and the Independent Counsel. This statement is false.

The Sandinistas downed the Hazenfus flight on the night of October 5, 1986. Radio Havana announced the downing on the afternoon of October 6. I began reading telegrams and news reports out of Managua. I began obtaining information from my staff. On the morning of October 7, I started conversations with Salvadoran officials, and I talked with Washington. The purpose was to gain and exchange information, and to assess the impact of the incident on U.S.-Salvadoran relations. Felix Rodriguez was not in El Salvador at this time, and officers on my staff did not talk with him.

At noon on October 10, 1986, San Salvador was hit by a catastrophic earthquake that killed over 1800 persons, immediately created between 250,000 to 300,000 homeless, and destroyed much of the city, including government buildings and the Embassy in which we were working. Rubble, water damage from the buildings' ruptured fire prevention sprinkling system, and danger of the remaining, standing, unstable Embassy structure falling (in a situation of continuing shocks) made it impossible to enter parts of the destroyed Embassy building to recover papers for a couple months. Some papers were never recovered. My immediate highest priority was keeping the Salvadoran government functioning in the midst of natural catastrophe and civil war, to assure the safety and welfare of Americans, to oversee disaster relief, and to perform all my other duties, including attention to the mounting Iran-Contra affair.

I received on December 3, 1986 a cable from the Executive Secretary and the Legal Adviser of the Department of State requesting information about all papers in the Embassy that related to arms transfers to Iran, the release of American hostages involving arms as an inducement, and transfer of funds from Iran arms transactions to the Nicaraguan Resistence. Also requested was information about materials in the Embassy about specific individuals relating to these subjects. My telegraphic reply was fully responsive to the request, and was based upon a search of all Mission records recovered from the earthquake-damaged building. The Embassy was not requested to submit documents at that time but to report on pertinent documents held and to assure their safe-keeping.

On December 19, 1986 I replied fully and at length by cable to a specific inquiry from the Senate Select Committee on Intelligence. On April 1, 1987 I interviewed at Homestead Air Force Base in Florida with Federal Bureau of Investigation (FBI) agents assigned to the Independent Counsel, and separately with other FBI agents on behalf of the Senate and House Select Committees. I gave a lengthy sworn deposition in Washington to the Senate Select Committee on Secret Military Assistance to Iran and Nicaraguan Opposition on April 30, 1987. To prepare for that deposition I had gone through my personal files to select all items I thought might be pertinent to the investigation. The examiner, Mr. Terry A. Smiljanvich, asked that I "consider" providing the Select Committee the opportunity to review those papers. I discussed the matter with a State Department Attorney, and I submitted those notes and papers to the Select Committee via the State Department Legal Office.

Officials of the Walsh Commission travelled to El Salvador to meet with me on February 5, 1988. The meeting lasted one hour and forty minutes, and, as always, I tried to the best of my ability to respond to all questions.

Over two years later, on October 19, 1990, the Department of State informed me by telephone that the Independent Counsel wanted to talk with me as a potential witness. On November 13, 1990 John Barrett of the Independent Counsel called me to say the Independent Counsel would like to see me. He called me again on December 3, 1990. On January 9 and 10, 1991, while I had travelled to Washington for other business, I voluntarily took time from a

packed schedule for lengthy meetings in Washington at the IC
offices with IC attorneys. The IC informed me I was a "subject" of
the Grand Jury's investigation. Most of the questions the IC
attorneys asked me were related to the substantial number of
personal notes of conversations I had voluntarily provided the
Senate Select Committee. It was clear that the Independent Counsel
was working on a theory that there had been a large conspiracy to
cover up information, and that the IC erroneously thought I was
part of such a conspiracy.

The Independent Counsel again informed me by letter dated
March 26, 1991 that I was a subject of the Grand Jury
investigation. I received a subpoena dated March 28, 1991 to
appear before the Grand Jury, commanding me to bring with me
documents or objects which the subpoena described. This
description included such items as "all handwritten notes and
copies of handwritten notes created by you during the period July
1, 1985 through July 1, 1987;" and "all other written, printed,
audiotaped or videotaped material, and all copies thereof, to, from
or concerning the following" lengthy list of people. I discussed
the subpoena with Stan Mortenson, the very able attorney that I had
engaged. My common sense, perhaps erroneously, told me that
despite the IC's language I need not include things irrelevant to
or already available to the Iran-Contra investigators, e.g. notes
on the repair of the earthquake-damaged Embassy, Christmas cards,
published books from my library, published testimony of persons
before the Select Senate Committee, etc.

On April 8, 1991 I requested by telephone to the Department of State Legal Office that it provide me copies of the documents I had given it to give to the Senate Select Committee, so that I could submit them to the Independent Counsel. I spoke to the Legal Office again on April 11, 1991. A lawyer there told me that the Legal Office was having difficulty locating copies of the papers I had provided, and, furthermore, might not be able to give them to me because there was a legal question as to whether the papers belong to me or the Department of State. I sent a letter dated April 23, 1991 to the State Department Legal Office again asking for copies of the documents I had provided the Legal Office to give to the Select Committee.

At my first session with the Grand Jury on April 26, 1991, I produced notes and documents, both those I had obtained from the Department of State Legal Office and additional ones from a further cursory review of my personal papers. I fully explained that I did not bring every note, document, and publication, but had brought those related to the Iran-Contra affair under the broadest interpretation of that term. Associate Prosecutor Greg Guillen asked me if I had brought stenographer-type notebooks in which I had taken notes at Chiefs of Mission meetings and while on consultations in Washington, and notebooks covering my briefings prior to my travel to post to serve as Ambassador. I replied that I had not, but I had reviewed them, though I could not be certain I had found all pertinent notations. I told Guillen I had been unsuccessful in finding my appointment calendars for prior to the

October 10, 1986 earthquake, which I presumed were destroyed, and
that I had not located my calendars for after that date, though I
had thought they were among my personal papers. Guillen told me
that my secretary had provided the IC her schedule books for my
appointments during the time stipulated by the IC. To this I
replied "Good!" I was not trying to hide anything, and I pointed
out the difficulty of complying with the very broad and, in many
respects, vague description of items requested.

Prior to my second appearance before the Grand Jury on May 29,
1991, I produced additional documents for the Independent Counsel
that were voluminous in the number of pages but had not many pages
or notations relevant to the Iran-Contra affair. The additional
submission was based on a thorough review of all my papers and took
into account Guillen's questioning during the first session and
subsequent conversations between my attorney and the IC. Some of
the papers on El Salvador that I found had been mis-located with my
Bolivian papers during my move from San Salvador to Oklahoma, and
I therefore had not found them in my review of documents prior to
the first Grand Jury session. The IC says that I had withheld my
calendars but later submitted them. I believe that the
appointments book I later submitted with this second tranche of
papers was for 1988, not for the earlier period that had been
stipulated by the IC in its subpoena, and for which the IC had
obtained the appointments book kept for me by my secretary. My
superb attorney also had to vet the additional papers through the
Department of State before he could give them to the IC.

The statement of the Independent Counsel on page 393 that I "withheld documents requested by the Independent Counsel" is, I think an unfair one, and bespeaks a motive to smear my character rather than present a correct statement of facts. The above record indicates that I supplied the documents requested insofar as I was able to in light of the nature of the Independent Counsel's requests.

The Independent Counsel's Decision Not to Prosecute Me

The Independent Counsel asserts he had determined he could prove beyond a reasonable doubt that my testimony was false about the April 20, 1986 meeting, specifically about who was present; and, I suppose, about what was discussed in the meeting. As I have attempted to show earlier in this memorandum, I do not believe the IC could have done so, and even if it were concluded by a jury that North had been in the meeting (and I still think he was not), the IC would have had to establish that I intentionally presented false testimony, which I know that I did not. The IC would not have been able to convince a jury that I <u>deliberately</u> lied, and thereby committed perjury.

The IC says he decided not to prosecute me because the IC had recently obtained from Elliott Abrams a guilty plea to misdemeanors, had brought indictments against Clair George and Dewey Clarridge, and had acquired Casper Weinberger's and highly

27

relevant Department of State notes. The logic and force of the IC's reasoning escapes me. The IC was charged with prosecuting those he believed he could show broke the law. He sought plea-bargaining arrangements and lesser charges against some persons under investigation because he feared he could not prosecute them successfully on a greater charge, or, to obtain their cooperation or testimony in prosecution of other targets. I did not fall into either of these categories.

I wish to note that in meetings with the IC on January 9 and 10, 1991 and by letter of April 26, 1991 the IC informed me that I was a "subject" of the investigation. This was defined by the IC in his letter to me as "a person whose conduct is within the scope of the Grand Jury's investigation," and was distinct from that of a "target," defined by the IC as "a person as to whom the prosecutor or the Grand Jury has substantial evidence linking him/her to the commission of a crime and who, in the judgement of the prosecutor, is a putative defendant." The IC never informed me at any time that he had changed my status from "subject" to "target," although the IC seemed to treat me as if I were a "target" from January 1991. Because the IC never changed my status, one might assume that the IC did not reach the conclusion he had sufficient grounds to indict me, or the IC seemingly was ignoring normal procedures and, perhaps, regulations.

There is a generally held strong opinion that the IC particularly in 1991 and 1992 wanted convictions to offset the negative views increasingly being expressed about the IC, especially his expenditures of taxpayers' money with limited results. The IC does not claim that he had evidence to show I had violated the Boland Amendments or other pertinent laws on aiding the Contras. He claims he had sufficient evidence to convict me of perjury. I believe that had the IC been confident of that he would have indicted me. My attorney made clear to the IC that I did not believe I had broken the law and that I would not plea bargain under any circumstance. The IC, in my opinion, did not attempt to prosecute me because he did not want to risk further tarnishing the growing IC image of incompetence and few successful prosecutions.

To close, I state my strong belief that public servants must obey our nation's laws and that they should be held accountable when they do not. Yet, I believe that a more humane and effective way must be found to achieve this than those manifested by the IC's procedures, attitudes, expenditures, and results. The costs to me personally, to my family, to my reputation, and of my time and money have been great. They also have been great for my supremely competent, humane, and generous attorney. The legal fees were in the range of $30,000.00, and I still have not paid the bill in full. I am deeply appreciative to Stan Mortenson, my attorney, to my family, and to my friends, whose support and prayers were invaluable in helping me through this ordeal.

Louis Dupart

DAN GLICKMAN, KANSAS, CHAIRMAN

BILL RICHARDSON, NEW MEXICO
NORMAN D. DICKS, WASHINGTON
JULIAN C DIXON, CALIFORNIA
ROBERT G. TORRICELLI, NEW JERSEY
RONALD D COLEMAN, TEXAS
DAVID E. SKAGGS, COLORADO
JAMES H. BILBRAY, NEVADA
NANCY PELOSI, CALIFORNIA
GREG LAUGHLIN, TEXAS
ROBERT E. (BUD) CRAMER, JR., ALABAMA
JACK REED, RHODE ISLAND

LARRY COMBEST, TEXAS
DOUG BEREUTER, NEBRASKA
ROBERT K. DORNAN, CALIFORNIA
C.W BILL YOUNG, FLORIDA
GEORGE W. GEKAS, PENNSYLVANIA
JAMES V. HANSEN, UTAH
JERRY LEWIS, CALIFORNIA

RICHARD A. GEPHARDT, MISSOURI, EX OFFICIO
ROBERT H MICHEL ILLINOIS EX OFFICIO

U.S. HOUSE OF REPRESENTATIVES

PERMANENT SELECT COMMITTEE
ON INTELLIGENCE
WASHINGTON, DC 20515-6415

ROOM H-405, U.S. CAPITOL
(202) 225-4121

MICHAEL W SHEEHY, CHIEF COUNSEL
STEPHEN D NELSON, MINORITY COUNSEL

September 28, 1993

Mr. Ron Garvin
Clerk
United States Court of Appeals
District of Columbia Circuit
Washington, D.C. 20001-2866

Dear Mr. Garvin:

On Friday, September 17, 1993, I read sections of the final report prepared by Judge Lawrence Walsh regarding the Iran-Contra affair, which pertained to me. These sections comprised pages 235 through 238 and pages 275 through 278. I found the two sections to be very comprehensive and, based on my personal knowledge, well-documented through either ample explanation in the text or further illumination via footnotes.

In Chapter 19, page 275, beginning with the sentence "By July 10, 1986, ..." I believe that the text needs further amplification as follows in order to make it accurate. Following the sentence, "By July 10, 1986, the arrangements were complete and reported to CATF." Adding here:

"Louis Dupart, the Task Force Compliance Officer and a lawyer, decided that the plan took the CIA too close to the line drawn by the Boland Amendment restrictions on contra aid. Dupart had harbored growing reservations about the level of CIA involvement with the proposed communicator at Ilopango. But, it was the intimate CIA involvement in funding and placing of the communicator at Ilopango compounded by the recent passage by the House of Representatives of the $100 million Nicaraguan Resistance legislation that led him to approach Fiers with concerns about the legality of the proposed endeavor."

-2-

Resume the existing text in Judge Walsh's report as follows: "Dupart persuaded Fiers that the move was politically and legally risky..."

Chapter 19, page 277, the sentence begins, "...the Hasenfus crash unleashed chaos in the Task Force." This is inaccurate. The Hasenfus crash unleashed a frenzy of activity in the Central American Task Force. At <u>no</u> time during my tenure at the Central American Task Force from June of 1985 through May of 1988, was the Task Force ever in chaos. Alan Fiers had a careful and steady hand on the helm of the Task Force throughout his tenure there. Other than those issues about which he was not fully informed and which Fiers discussed in both his public testimony and presumably with Judge Walsh's staff, Alan Fiers exercised precise control and direction over the Task Force. Thus, I think that the word "chaos" should be changed to "frenzy."

These conclude my comments on Judge Walsh's report. Thank you for giving me the opportunity to read it and submit my written comments.

Sincerely,

Louis H. Dupart
Senior Counsel

Robert C. Dutton

To: Ron Garvin   November 29, 1993
       Clerk of the United States Court of Appeals

From: Mr. Robert C. Dutton

Subject: Final Report of the Independent Counsel

Sir:

   I have read those sections of the subject report which are
purportedly the only ones having to do with me and am concerned.
The many instances of misstatement of fact and the use of
innuendo cause me to believe that Mr. Walsh is trying to rewrite
history to make it fit concepts he was never able to prove in a
court of law.
   The following are my specific comments:
(1) Page 30: The I.C. states that Mr. Secord was under the control
             of Lt. Col. North.
    Comment: Mr. Secord did not operate under North's control.
             Secord ran the operations that I was involved in
             with North providing the political and intelligence
             support where necessary.
(2) Page 30: The I.C. implies that the Boland Amendment applied
             to our activities.
    Comment: The I.C. well knows that this amendment applied only
             to U.S. Government appropriated funds and therefore
             had no bearing on our activities. This is a prime
             example of the I.C. ignoring fact in order to taint
             the activity with illegality.
(3) Page 59: States that North directed Secord to purchase the
             aircraft.
    Comment: Secord had the money and the authority to purchase
             the aircraft, not North.
(4) Page 60: States that North frequently gave me orders ref.
             specific operations.
    Comment: As I frequently testified, North did not give me
             operational directions, Secord did.
(5) Page 60: States that the resupply operation trained Contra
             forces in the use of explosives.
    Comment: In all of my readings and contacts with the resupply
             forces, this is the first I have ever heard of this
             and it would run counter to instructions I received
             and passed on to the resupply force.
(6) Page 66: The I.C. refers to the operation as "illicit".
    Comment: That our operation was unlawful is a fact that Mr.
             Walsh was never able to prove in a court of law yet
             he feels free to call it unlawful in his report. The
             operation was a legal covert action taken on behalf
             of and with the support of the U.S. Government. To
             brand those of us who supported the government
             "outlaws" is slanderous. Unsubstantiated allegations
             and insinuations such as this should not be allowed
             to be part of the report.

(7) Page 66:The report states that the CIA looked on our resupply
             operation unfavorably.
     Comment:In September 1986, after the resupply operation had
             become successful, it was reported to me that the
             CIA looked favorably on the operation and felt it was
             the most cost effective way to continue the air
             support to the Contras.
(8) Page 167:The report indicates that the $60,000 death benefit
             for the two crewmen killed in Nicaragua was not paid
             either because we lied to the families or we just
             didn't care about our people.
     Comment:The I.C. knows perfectly well that the funds that
             were to be used to pay this benefit have been tied up
             in the Swiss system, by him, since the operation
             closed down. This total disregard for the facts in
             order to present a false picture that fits what Mr.
             Walsh would like to, but the courts would not let,
             sell is precisely what is wrong with much of this
             report.
(9) Page 494:The report states that North accompanied Rodriguez
             and I to the Vice Presidents offices.
     Comment: This is totally inaccurate, North did not accompany
             us.
(10) Page 494:The report states that North or Earl was present
             when I met Watson in the V.P.'s office and that I
             was introduced as,"our man for resupply".
     Comment: Not only is this inaccurate in that neither North
             nor Earl were present when I met Watson but it also
             presents an interesting dilemma. If I could be
             introduced to Watson in this manner then he must
             have been aware of the Contra support flights
             months earlier than he admitted to in court.
             Additionally, his boss Don Gregg must have also
             been aware.
     One more concern that I have is the fact that I was given
nothing to read relating to my involvement with the last two
shipments into Iran and my part in the release of David Jacobson.
It is possible that these events were not part of the report but
I would find that strange in that these were activities where our
network was dealing directly with the Israeli government in the
one case and with the U.S. Embassy in Lebanon in the other.
     In summary, since I have seen so little of the report it is
difficult for me to generalize; however, if on a percentage basis
the rest of the report is as contaminated with misstatement of
fact, innuendo and possible omissions of events then I would
request a serious review and rewrite before it becomes history.

Sincerely,

Robert C. Dutton

Lt. Col. Robert L. Earl, Ret.

United States Court of Appeals
For the District of Columbia Circuit

FILED DEC 0 1 1993

RON GARVIN
CLERK

UNITED STATES COURT OF APPEALS
FOR THE DISTRICT OF COLUMBIA CIRCUIT

IN RE: OLIVER L. NORTH, et al.   Division No. 86-6
            (LT. COL. ROBERT L. EARL, Ret.)

RE: Comments on OIC Report on Behalf of Lt. Col. Robert L. Earl. Ret.

Dear Ron Garvin, Esq.:

The report of the Iran-Contra Office of Independent Counsel (OIC) is a report from Judge Walsh
to his superiors on the six-year prosecution, and his **personal opinions** on criminality. The
report should remain under seal. It should not be released to the public where it will tend to be
seen as some sort of final, authoritative report on Iran-Contra or the alleged facts appearing in
it.

It was Congress' role to make the facts and political implications known to the American people.
Congress performed that role.

It was the OIC's role to prosecute any individuals accused of being guilty of wrongdoing. The
OIC did that.

It would be inappropriate for the OIC to go beyond his prosecution role and present a personal
political assessment of Iran-Contra to the American people - thereby infringing on Congress'
role.

The inappropriateness of public release of this document is specifically attested to by the damage

1

that would result to at least thirty-one (31) named individuals that would be publicly branded as wrongdoers by virtue of a chapter being dedicated to each of them. (This has the appearance of vindictiveness and revenge - getting back at people that Judge Walsh thinks "escaped" punishment). The OIC report makes allegations that if true should have been prosecuted, and yet were not. If not true, they should not be published to besmirch persons unfairly.

The document has an unfair, biased view of events. Only one interpretation of events is made, viewed from the perspective of the OIC's interpretation that individuals committed <u>crimes</u>. (In our system of justice, a judge and jury make this determination, not an Independent Counsel).

For example, the report makes no mention of covert operations as a legitimate United States Government (USG) activity (at least in the thirty-five (35) pages of "relevant" material that I was provided). An understanding of USG covert operations is absolutely essential to an understanding of what people were doing and their motivations for doing them.

"Closing down" covert operations, when their existence is known and the persons are compromised, is never addressed. Nor are "cover stories", as alternative explanations of covert operations which are used to maintain reasonable secrecy of sensitive USG endeavors, explained or even mentioned. Half explanations without a balanced factual viewpoint and full perspective of events make the OIC report not good writing, much less a legal document of credibility. It is transparently one-sided in the pronouncements of judgements on the facts it chose to disclose.

The report gratuitously presents the "case" it claims it would have made on Count One had the charge not been dropped. Why should the OIC be allowed to "try" his case (again) in a different forum when he was unable to in the proper forum - a court of law? (This, again, smacks of vindictiveness and revenge). This approach seeks to rewrite history, a long discredited practice, and one that should not be followed here.

Sloppy assignations by the OIC report of blame/guilt/wrongdoing that encompass all involved were overly speculative without properly identifying parties (such noted instances as "... and others"). A broad brush stroke of smearing public servants indiscriminately does not reflect positively on the merits for truth finding in the legal system. The Washington Post did an article recently on Judge Walsh, where his legal staff attorneys stated they had trouble stopping him from prosecuting persons doing their routine security documents review job, because he felt they were too slow, or in doing their routine public service were somehow obstructing his moves.

Because the report is not a balanced and fair discussion of the events and national security strictures of Iran-Contra - but instead is a polemical defense of six years of government-funded investigative and prosecutorial activities - the report should remain under seal. The public interest will not be served by releasing publicly for broadcast news display the biased political self-justification and "sour grapes" of a frustrated prosecutor.

It is a private and personal defense counsel opinion that there was insufficient result for the astronomical millions of tax dollars spent, and this report by the OIC contains lots of self-serving, self-justification efforts.

The more important reasons for sealing the OIC report are the lives and efforts of human beings still laboring in the fields of intelligence gathering for and in the government, and in foreign countries, and the obviously secret nature of their on-going work. The Earl notes so often cited by the OIC themselves, in text and footnotes of the report, have to still be (even in the report) censored and marked "Classified information withheld" (top secret). (I.e., see Earl notes, in text on page 497 in Chapter 29 of OIC report). Yet that does not protect against a foreign intelligence service, hostile to our own, using the focusing context of the published report and using the data surrounding it in context with other chapters, and putting the notes back together. Real, legitimate reasons exist (and will continue in the foreseeable future) to save lives of American agents in place from reckless endangerment and needless sacrifice. Human intelligence assets are still operational and in place, and the report of Judge Walsh (while entertaining reading) could potentially cause irreparable harm by putting the puzzle together for other "public readers". The value of such contents of the report do not outweigh the clear risks. There is an alternative source of data in the vast public record and court history of this six- year

3

process, and that is sufficient to answer the public and press needs.

According to press reports, a lawsuit by various press organizations, the National Security Archive, etc. argues that the report should be made public because many of the Iran-Contra figures are "public" figures and have written books with their versions of Iran-Contra events. My client is <u>not</u> a public figure, has no desire to become one, has not written an Iran-Contra book and has no intention of doing so. He and many others cited in Judge Walsh's report seek to maintain their privacy. Please do not let Judge Walsh invade that privacy again.

Respectfully submitted this 30th day of November,

By Dennis Dean Kirk, Esq.
Counsel to
Lt. Col. Robert L. Earl, Ret.

Joseph F. Fernandez

SEYFARTH, SHAW, FAIRWEATHER & GERALDSON
ATTORNEYS AT LAW

55 EAST MONROE STREET · SUITE 4200
CHICAGO, IL 60603-5803
(312) 346-8000
FAX (312) 269-8869

ONE CENTURY PLAZA · SUITE 3300
2029 CENTURY PARK EAST
LOS ANGELES, CA 90067-3063
(310) 277-7200
FAX (310) 201-5219

767 THIRD AVENUE
NEW YORK, NY 10017-2013
(212) 715-9000
FAX (212) 752-3116

101 CALIFORNIA STREET · SUITE 2900
SAN FRANCISCO, CA 94111-5858
(415) 397-2823
FAX (415) 397-8549

770 L STREET · SUITE 1150
SACRAMENTO, CA 95814-3325
(916) 446-3970
FAX (916) 446-4214

815 CONNECTICUT AVENUE, N.W.
WASHINGTON, D.C. 20006-4004

(202) 463-2400
FAX (202) 828-5393

WRITER'S DIRECT DIAL ~~UNDER SEAL~~

(202) _____

December 3, 1993

INTERNATIONAL

AVENUE LOUISE 500, BOÎTE 8
1050 BRUSSELS, BELGIUM
TELEPHONE (32) (2) 647.60.25
FAX (32) (2) 640.70.71

AFFILIATE FIRMS

MATHEWS, DINSDALE & CLARK
TORONTO, CANADA

MATRAY, MATRAY et HALLET
BRUSSELS AND LIEGE, BELGIUM
COLOGNE, GERMANY

United States Court of Appeals
For the District of Columbia Circuit

FILED DEC 0 3 1993

RON GARVIN
CLERK

By Hand

Mr. Ron H. Garvin
Clerk
United States Court of Appeals
  for the District of Columbia Circuit
333 Constitution Avenue, N.W.
United States Courthouse
Fifth Floor
Washington, D.C. 20001-2866

   Re: In re: Oliver L. North, et al.,
    Division No. 86-6

Dear Mr. Garvin:

   Enclosed for filing in the captioned matter, please
find the original and four copies of the Comments of Joseph F.
Fernandez on the Final Report of Independent Counsel
Lawrence E. Walsh. We understand that the Comments will be
filed under seal.

   Thank you for your assistance in this matter. Should
you have any questions, please do not hesitate to contact me.

       Sincerely,

       SEYFARTH, SHAW, FAIRWEATHER
         && GERALDSON

     By _Thomas E. Wilson_

TEW/bvj
Enclosure
4060f

United States Court of Appeals
For the District of Columbia Circuit

UNITED STATES COURT OF APPEALS
FOR THE DISTRICT OF COLUMBIA CIRCUIT

FILED DEC 0 3 1993

Division for the Purpose of
Appointing Independent Counsels

RON GARVIN
CLERK

Ethics in Government Act of 1978, as Amended

In re: Oliver L. North, <u>et al</u>.   Division No. 86-6

Before: Sentelle, <u>Presiding</u>, Butzner and Sneed, <u>Senior Circuit</u>
         <u>Judges</u>

<u>UNDER SEAL</u>

COMMENTS OF JOSEPH F. FERNANDEZ ON FINAL
<u>REPORT OF INDEPENDENT COUNSEL LAWRENCE E. WALSH</u>

Joseph F. Fernandez, through his undersigned counsel,

respectfully submits the following comments on those portions

of the Final Report of Independent Counsel Lawrence E. Walsh

which are relevant to Mr. Fernandez. Mr. Fernandez requests

that these Comments be included as an Appendix to the Final

Report.

<u>INTRODUCTION</u>

<u>Preliminary Statement</u>

The Independent Counsel's Final Report (the "Report")

presents a highly distorted picture of the activities of

Joseph F. Fernandez while he served as the CIA Chief of Station

("COS") in San Jose, Costa Rica from 1984 to 1987. The Report

also puts forth a seriously misleading description of the

circumstances surrounding the Independent Counsel's efforts to

- 2 -

prosecute Fernandez, first in the District of Columbia in 1988 and later in the Eastern District of Virginia in 1989.

The portions of the Report which purport to summarize the role played by Fernandez in the Iran-Contra affair portray Fernandez as a rogue CIA officer on a frolic and detour of his own, violating the Boland Amendment with abandon, disobeying the orders of his CIA superiors, taking instructions from Lt. Col. Oliver L. North in derogation of clearly articulated CIA policies and, finally, intentionally lying to investigators from the Tower Commission and the CIA's Office of Inspector General ("IG") in order to cover up his misconduct in office.

These allegations are completely untrue -- and the proof of their lack of truth is contained in those portions of the Report which summarize the activities of Fernandez's CIA superiors, especially Alan Fiers, Chief of the CIA's Central American Task Force ("CATF"), and Clair George, CIA's Deputy Director for Operations ("DDO").

None of Fernandez's activities while he was COS in Costa Rica violated the Boland Amendment. The Fiers/George portions of the Report make it clear that CIA Headquarters was fully aware of Fernandez's dealings with North and the Contras during the relevant period, including his perfectly legal efforts to facilitate the resupply of the Contras through the sharing of information with the "private benefactors" who were making deliveries to the Contras of military supplies at a time

- 3 -

when the Boland Amendment prevented CIA from providing those
supplies under the auspices of the United States Government.

Throughout 1985, and continuing into the spring and
summer of 1986, when most of the activities for which Fernandez
has been criticized took place, the Reagan Administration was
engaged in a desperate political effort to persuade Congress to
re-initiate military funding for the Contras. That effort was
politically delicate and deeply contentious. Fernandez's CIA
superiors knew full well that the Contras were being resupplied
with military equipment during the period of the Boland
proscriptions by a network of private citizens which came to be
known as the "private benefactors." They also knew that
network was being overseen on behalf of the Reagan
Administration by Oliver North, who was then serving as a staff
member of President Reagan's National Security Council.

When questioned about the identity of the "private
benefactors" by members of Congress, many of whom were
profoundly antagonistic toward President Reagan's Central
America policy, those senior CIA officials, including George
and Fiers, professed ignorance. The leadership at CIA
understood very clearly that, if the "private benefactors" were
ever identified, such information would inevitably lead to
North and to the disclosure that, during the pendency of the
Boland restrictions, the Reagan Administration had been
secretly orchestrating the military resupply of the Contras

- 4 -

despite Congressional efforts to curtail that policy. The
disclosure of that information would no doubt result in a
political eruption which might derail President Reagan's
political efforts to do away with the Boland restrictions. It
also could be expected to encourage wider Congressional
opposition to President Reagan's Central America policy.

Understandably, no CIA official was anxious to be
identified as the individual who caused the Reagan policy
towards the Contras to run on the rocks. As a consequence,
even though they well knew that Fernandez and other CIA
officials in Central America were having as part of their
official duties to have direct dealings with North and the
"private benefactor" resupply network, CIA Headquarters
personnel withheld that information from Congress.

On October 5, 1986, the Contra resupply flight
carrying Eugene Hasenfus was shot down by the Sandinistas.
Congressional inquiries and other investigations began
promptly. In January 1987, Fernandez was interviewed by
investigators from the Tower Commission and the CIA's IG
Office. During those interviews, Fernandez frankly admitted
having had extensive dealings with North and with the "private
benefactor" resupply network. Unbeknownst to Fernandez, such
information was precisely what his CIA superiors, including
Fiers and George, had chosen not disclosed to Congress.

- 5 -

Fiers, George and other senior Reagan Administration officials professed "shock" at "learning for the first time" that Fernandez had for more than a year worked closely with North and various representatives of the "private benefactor" network to facilitate the military resupply of the Contras. When Fernandez asserted that his superiors were fully aware of his activities, he was branded a liar and, in essence, thrown overboard in a misguided effort to limit the damage being done by the ever-widening stain of the Iran-Contra scandal. The reality is that Fernandez's CIA superiors knew a great deal more than Fernandez knew about North's extensive world-wide activities, the identities of the "private benefactors," and the nature and extent of their activities both in Central America and elsewhere in the world.

Fernandez was a classic scapegoat. Despite the overwhelming evidence that his superiors knew full well what Fernandez was doing -- much of which, ironically, is summarized in the portions of the Report relating to Fiers and George -- the Independent Counsel nevertheless continued to pursue Fernandez for allegedly lying to Tower Commission and IG investigators in untranscribed, informal interviews ostensibly in order to cover up what the evidence which was then available to the Independent Counsel clearly indicated his superiors already knew.

- 6 -

The Report states that the Independent Counsel "decided to go forward with a case against Fernandez in hopes of eventually using Fernandez as a witness." Report at Ch. 20, Pg. 284, n.4. The Independent Counsel did not need to prosecute Fernandez in order to secure his cooperation. From the outset, Fernandez <u>wanted</u> to cooperate with the Independent Counsel, just as he had previously cooperated with the Tower Commission and with Congress in the form of more than twenty hours of detailed, transcribed testimony.

Because of the highly charged atmosphere at the time, and the Independent Counsel's manifest animosity towards him and towards the CIA in general, Fernandez sought immunity before telling the Independent Counsel what he knew. The Independent Counsel was furious at Fernandez's request, on the advice of counsel, that he be provided with immunity before making himself available to the Independent Counsel. The Independent Counsel accused Fernandez of flatly refusing "to cooperate" (<u>i.e.</u>, waive his Fifth Amendment privilege). Thereafter, the Independent Counsel brought the full weight of the United States Government to bear against Fernandez in two mean-spirited attempts to prosecute him. In the process, the Independent Counsel violated the mandate of the Ethics in Government Act by ignoring the Attorney General's regulations under the Classified Information Procedures Act ("CIPA"), needlessly expended vast resources of the United States

- 7 -

Government, forced Fernandez to incur huge legal fees in his

defense, and unnecessarily delayed his own investigation for

three long years.[1]

Section-by-Section Summary

Part I of these Comments shows that Fernandez did not

violate the Boland Amendment. That section also summarizes the

numerous inaccuracies in the Independent Counsel's version of

the facts relating to Fernandez's activities.

Part II reflects the internally inconsistencies in the

Report. The portions of the Report which discuss Fernandez

portray him as acting alone and contrary to the orders of his

superiors. The portions of the Report which address the

activities of his superiors, Fiers and George, paint a very

---

[1] Neither of the two indictments the Independent Counsel
     secured against Fernandez charged him with personal
     venality or official corruption. Rather, Fernandez was
     charged only with a series of false statements and
     obstruction of justice based on those statements. None of
     the false statements charged against Fernandez were
     transcribed.

     Importantly, Fernandez testified three times where
     transcripts were created -- before the Tower Commission,
     before Congress, and before the grand jury after the
     Independent Counsel granted him immunity. On each of those
     three occasions, Fernandez told in greater detail the same
     story he had told the CIA IG and the Tower Commission
     investigators. Had Fernandez lied during his three
     transcribed appearances, he was susceptible to prosecution
     for perjury. The reality is that Fernandez has never been
     accused by anyone, including the Independent Counsel, of
     having made a false statement where there exists a
     transcript which reflects the question asked and the answer
     given.

- 8 -

different picture of Fernandez. Those portions of the Report make clear that Fiers and George were fully aware of Fernandez's Contra-related activities and intentionally dissembled about that knowledge in order to protect themselves.[2]

Part III addresses the Independent Counsel's prosecutions of Fernandez. Contrary to the Independent Counsel's suggestions, the second Fernandez prosecution was not dismissed because the Attorney General deliberately thwarted the prosecution by refusing to allow the release of information that was already publicly known. The Independent Counsel's prosecution of Fernandez was flawed from its inception because, prior to indicting Fernandez, the Independent Counsel failed to balance the potential damage a Fernandez prosecution would do to the national security against the other federal interests that would be served by proceeding with such a prosecution. The Independent Counsel's failure to perform the balancing required by CIPA was a clear violation of the Ethics in Government Act.

---

[2] The Report even reveals that Fiers, George and then Chief of the Latin American Division concocted a fictitious meeting on November 10, 1986 at which George and Fiers supposedly learned for the first time the details of Fernandez's extensive dealings with the "private benefactors" in aid of the Contras. The ostensible purpose of this bogus meeting was to cover up the fact that George had not told Congress during hearings on October 10 and 14, 1986 what in fact he then knew about Fernandez's "private benefactor" Contra activities. Report at Ch. 17, Pg. 237-38.

- 9 -

Part IV highlights the numerous obstacles -- apart
from the classified information problems -- which confronted
the Independent Counsel in his wrong-headed and ill-fated
efforts to prosecute Fernandez. In particular, the Independent
Counsel faced serious problems under Kastigar v. United States,
406 U.S. 441 (1972). As a consequence, it is plain that,
especially in light of the decision of the United States Court
of Appeals for the D.C. Circuit in United States v. North, 910
F.2d 843 (D.C. Cir. 1990), the Independent Counsel could never
have satisfied the government's "heavy burden" under Kastigar
to show that none of its evidence was derived directly or
indirectly from Fernandez's immunized testimony. Kastigar,
supra, 406 U.S. at 461.

COMMENTS

I.   CONTRARY TO THE INDEPENDENT COUNSEL'S REPORT,
        FERNANDEZ DID NOT VIOLATE THE BOLAND AMENDMENT.

        A.   Description of the Boland Amendments Which Were
                in Effect During 1985 and 1986.

Whether Fernandez's activities with respect to the
Contras and the "private benefactors" were proper can only be
assessed in the context of a correct understanding of the

- 10 -

Boland Amendments which were in effect during the relevant
period, 1985 and 1986.[3/]

The various Boland Amendments were appropriations
measures designed to circumscribe the authority of CIA (and
other enumerated agencies of the United States Government) to
provide _military_ assistance to the Nicaraguan Contras in their
guerilla war against the Nicaraguan Sandinista regime. The
Boland Amendments _never_ restricted CIA's dealings with the
Contras for the purpose of gathering intelligence, the CIA's
principal function. The Boland Amendments also _never_ limited
the activities of the CIA in support of the Contras _political_
infrastructure. The _only_ limitations the Boland Amendments
placed upon the CIA related to providing assistance in support
of the Contras' _military_ activities.

From October 1984 to August 1985, the Boland Amendment
prohibited CIA from giving any military assistance to the
Contras. The 1985 Boland restrictions disallowed military aid
to the Contras up to and including sharing intelligence which
might help the Contras conduct resupply activities. Throughout
the period, however, CIA was in close contacts with the Contras
for purposes of gathering intelligence with respect to Contra
activities and for purposes of supporting Contra political
activities.

3/ For a summary of the various provisions of law which
    comprised the Boland Amendments which were in effect during
    1985 and 1986, see _United States v North_, 708 F. Supp. 375,
    377 n.1 (D.D.C. 1988).

- 11 -

In late 1985, Congress changed the Boland Amendment to provide the Contras with $27 million in humanitarian aid and $3 million in communications assistance designed to assure that Contra supplies could be safely delivered. The responsibilities of the CIA were also adjusted in order to accommodate the new regimen. Specifically, during 1986, CIA was <u>required</u> by the Boland Amendment (i) to monitor the delivery of the humanitarian aid for the Contras to make sure that those supplies were going where Congress intended, and (ii) to provide information and advice to the Contras in order to assure the secure delivery of both humanitarian <u>and</u> military supplies. Under Boland as it was in effect in 1986, the limitations on CIA with respect to military aid to the Contras were <u>very</u> <u>narrow</u> -- specifically, CIA could not use any appropriated funds to provide the Contras with <u>lethal</u> assistance; CIA also could not supply the Contras with information or advice in support of <u>specific military operations</u>, as distinguished from general resupply activities.[4]

4/   The 1986 Boland restrictions are summarized in a series of opinions rendered by the CIA General Counsel. Those opinions are classified and, as such, are no longer available to Fernandez's counsel. The conclusions reached in those opinions were disseminated by CIA Headquarters to the affected CIA stations by cable. Despite the fact that the precise nature of the Boland Amendment restrictions is crucial to the Independent Counsel's conclusions, the Report gives no indication the Independent Counsel ever completely understood the limited applications of the Boland restrictions, especially in 1986.

- 12 -

The Independent Counsel never charged Fernandez with violating the Boland Amendment. The Report, however, alleges that Fernandez "deliberately violated the Boland restraints." Report at Part VI, Pg. 200. The Independent Counsel claims that Fernandez violated the Boland Amendment in three respects: "by [(i)] his efforts to facilitate construction of a clandestine airstrip in Costa Rica for contra resupply, [(ii)] his promises to Contra leaders of military supplies, and [(iii)] his role in carrying out those promises." Report at Part III, Pg. 67. All of these allegations are incorrect; none of Fernandez's activities violated the various versions of the Boland Amendment in effect during the relevant period.[5]

> **B. Fernandez's Monitoring Of The Construction Of An Airstrip In Costa Rica Did Not Violate The Boland Amendment.**

Costa Rica is a neutral country. In late 1985, the Costa Rican government had a serious political problem. The lack of resupply of the forces of Contra leader Eden Pastora since mid-1984 as a result of the Boland restrictions had caused those forces to seek the relative safety of northern

---

[5] The Independent Counsel further alleges that Fernandez violated the Boland Amendment "on instructions from North." Report at Part III, Pg. 67. CIA's responsibilities in Costa Rica caused Fernandez (and Ambassador Lewis Tambs, for that matter) to be in constant contact with North. North, however, was never in Fernandez's chain of command. As such, North was never in any position to "instruct" Fernandez to do anything, and he never did.

- 13 -

Costa Rica. Armed bands of Contras were causing unrest among
the Costa Rican population and were drawing Sandinista raiding
parties into Costa Rica in pursuit of the Contras. Both the
Costa Rican and United States Governments believed that Costa
Rican security interests made it imperative that the Contras be
induced to leave Costa Rica by venturing back inside southern
Nicaragua.

In August 1985, Ambassador Lewis Tambs secretly
secured the concurrence of the Costa Rican government to permit
the establishment of clandestine Contra resupply bases inside
Costa Rica. It was hoped that such facilities would eventually
facilitate the resupply of the Contras thereby making it
possible to persuade the Contras to leave Costa Rica. In the
meantime, such facilities might prove useful in the event the
Sandinistas were to invade Costa Rica. United States
Government funds could not be used to construct such facilities
because of the Boland restrictions. Eventually, the "private
benefactors" came up with the money to improve a remote
airstrip in northwestern Costa Rica for Contra resupply. The
airstrip site was selected by a senior Costa Rican
official. [6]

---

[6] The Costa Rican Administration of President Alberto Monge
     concluded that Contra resupply bases were vital to getting
     Contra forces to leave Costa Rica, thereby reducing the
     risk to Costa Rica from Nicaragua. Long before Fernandez

                              (Footnote Continued on Next Page)

- 14 -

Fernandez reported the decision by the Costa Rican government to permit Contra resupply bases in Costa Rica to CIA Headquarters on or about August 13, 1985. On August 17, 1985, in an "Eyes Only" cable from Fiers, CIA Headquarters instructed Fernandez to monitor those activities as part of his intelligence functions. Fernandez followed those instructions precisely; he later monitored the activities relating to the airstrip, nothing more.

The Report inaccurately describes Fernandez's activities with respect to the Costa Rican airstrip and creates the misimpression that Fernandez was actively involved in the planning and construction of the airstrip. The Report states

---

6/ (Footnote Continued from Previous Page)

was ever indicted, Ambassador Lewis Tambs explained the Costa Rican concern to the Independent Counsel and the Costa Rican's perception of the importance of the airstrip as a necessary evil which would help provide for Costa Rican security interests. On August 10, 1988, eight months before Fernandez was indicted for the second time, the Independent Counsel notified Fernandez by letter that Independent Counsel representatives had been informed by a very senior Costa Rican official that he -- not Fernandez or anyone else -- had selected the site for the airstrip and that the site was also intended for use as a training facility for the Costa Rican civil guard. Despite the uncontroverted evidence available to the Independent Counsel, he nevertheless charged repeatedly that Fernandez had lied when he told the CIA IG investigator that "a project to build an airstrip in northern Costa Rica in 1985 was an initiative of the Costa Rican government to be used for training activities by Costa Rican forces in preparation for a possible Nicaraguan invasion of Costa Rica." District of Columbia Indictment at Count Five (Attachment A); Alexandria Indictment at Count Two (Attachment B).

- 15 -

that Fernandez participated in "the planning and construction of an airstrip in Costa Rica to serve the contra resupply operation . . .." Report at Ch. 20, Pg. 283. See also Report at Ch. 20 at Pgs. 284-85 ("beginning in August 1985, Fernandez assisted North, Secord and others in building a refueling airstrip at Santa Elena in remote northwest Costa Rica that was designed to facilitate aerial resupply of the contras"); Report at Ch. 20, Pg. 285 ("throughout the first nine months of 1986, Fernandez worked closely with Rafael Quintero, North and Secord's representative in Central America, . . . in building the airstrip . . ."). In actuality, Fernandez at no time participated in the planning or construction of the airstrip; he merely monitored its progress in fulfillment of his duties as an intelligence officer.

In addition, several of the airstrip-related activities attributed to Fernandez in the Report are simply inaccurate. The Report states that, during the fall of 1985, Fernandez met with William Haskell (a "private benefactor" representative), and that Fernandez "traveled to the airstrip site with Haskell and provided assistance to Haskell's efforts." Report at Ch. 20, Pg. 285. This statement is completely wrong. Fernandez never traveled to the airstrip site with Haskell; nor did Fernandez provide any assistance to Haskell's efforts. When Haskell came to Costa Rica to negotiate for the purchase or lease of property for the

- 16 -

airstrip, Fernandez met with Haskell in order to be kept
apprised of the status of the negotiations. He did nothing to
facilitate or further those discussions in any way.

The Report further states that, in January 1986,
Fernandez traveled with Quintero to inspect the site for the
airstrip and that "after this trip, Fernandez modified the
layout of the airstrip to accommodate the swampy terrain."
Report at Ch. 20, Pg. 285 (footnote omitted). This allegation
is also inaccurate. Fernandez did not travel to the airstrip
with Quintero. The only occasion on which Fernandez visited
the airstrip was in September 1985 with Robert Owen, not
Quintero. On another occasion, Fernandez traveled with
Quintero to a near-by site; Fernandez went along on the trip
solely to fulfill his responsibilities as an intelligence
officer.

The statement that Fernandez "modified the layout of
the airstrip to accommodate the swampy terrain" is nothing
short of absurd. Id. Fernandez was a foreign intelligence
officer, not a paramilitary officer. He had no training in the
military arts. He also was not an engineer. As a consequence,
he would have had no clue how to accomplish what the Report
says he did. Moreover, in fact, the airstrip never was
modified to "accommodate swampy terrain"; in June 1986, an
ammunition ladened "private benefactor" resupply flight got
stuck in the mud on the airstrip for several hours before the

- 17 -

"private benefactors" were able to dig it out. Fernandez
learned of the stuck airplane only after the fact; he had no
involvement in the incident.

        The Report's conclusion that Fernandez violated the
Boland Amendment by facilitating the construction of the
airstrip is based upon a completely erroneous account of
Fernandez activities in that regard. He did nothing improper
by keeping informed of the status of the construction of the
airstrip -- something which he was required to do as an
intelligence officer and had been expressly instructed to do by
his superiors.

        **B.   Fernandez Did Not Violate The Boland Amendment By
                 <u>Promising The Contra Leaders Military Supplies.</u>**

        The Report inaccurately alleges that Fernandez induced
the Contra leaders to take up the struggle against the
Sandinistas by promising them lethal and non-lethal
supplies.[7] Report at Ch. 20, Pg. 284. As Fernandez told
the grand jury, he never promised the Contras anything which he
was not sure he could deliver. Fernandez's credibility with
the Contras was vital to his ability to do his job. Thus, it
would have been counter-productive for Fernandez to promise the

---

[7] Significantly, Boland was an appropriations measure. The
     only way it could be violated was for Fernandez to have
     expended United States Government funds in derogation of
     Boland's restrictions. Promising to do something that
     would be prohibited by Boland would never by itself rise to
     the level of "violating" Boland.

- 18 -

Contras that he would secure for them lethal supplies in violation of the Boland Amendment when Fernandez had no ability to make that happen.

The portions of the Report addressing Alan Fiers's activities make clear that Fiers directed Fernandez to persuade the Contra military leaders to leave Pastora and join UNO. Report at Ch. 19, Pg. 270. The Report further states that Fiers himself "encouraged CIA officers and others to lead the NACs [non-aligned Contra commanders] to believe that Fiers would do whatever was possible under the law to support them if they left Pastora." Report at Ch. 19, Pg. 271. The Independent Counsel's suggestion that Fernandez promised the NACs more than his boss promised them is simply not credible.

D.   Fernandez's Communications To Facilitate Contra
        Resupply In 1986 Were Expressly Permitted By The
        Boland Amendment.

The Independent Counsel's claim that Fernandez violated the Boland Amendment by facilitating the delivery of lethal supplies to the Contras is based upon a fundamental misconception of the Boland restrictions. The Independent Counsel's assertions are predicated on the erroneous contention that the Boland Amendment prohibited all types of United States Government support to the Contras. As noted previously, even the strictest version of the Boland Amendment -- the one that was in effect in 1985 -- permitted political support of the

- 19 -

Contras; it merely forbade the use of appropriated funds to support Contra <u>military</u> operations.

When viewed properly, Fernandez's passing of information designed to ensure the safe operation of Contra resupply flights was <u>required</u> by the Boland Amendment which was in effect in 1986, not prohibited by it.[8/]

II.   THE INDEPENDENT COUNSEL'S REPORT IS INTERNALLY INCONSISTENT.

The portions of the Report which address Fernandez's conduct portray Fernandez as acting alone and contrary to the orders of his superiors. The sections of the Report which relate to Alan Fiers and Clair George make clear that they were aware of and approved Fernandez's activities.

The Report's chapter on Fernandez states that Fernandez urged Contra leaders to take up the struggle against the Sandinistas and "induced them by promising lethal and non-lethal supplies." Report at 20, Pg. 285. No mention is made in this portion of the Report of CIA Headquarters or

---

8/   The Independent Counsel also overstates the extent of Fernandez's activities in coordinating the resupply flights. The Report states that, "[d]uring the first nine months of 1986, Fernandez spent considerable time coordinating the resupply of weapons and ammunition to the Contras along the southern front." Report at Ch. 20, Pg. 286. Even if that were true, it would <u>not</u> have been illegal. Be that as it may, Fernandez testified repeatedly that the amount of time he spent trying to facilitate Contra resupply was very small, perhaps as little as 1% of his time.

- 20 -

Fiers.   The chapter on Fiers, however, makes clear that
Fernandez pursued his efforts to persuade the Southern Front
Contra commanders to join UNO "under Fiers' supervision and
kept CIA headquarters informed of his progress." Report at
Ch. 19, Pg. 270 (emphasis supplied).

         Similarly, in its discussion of Fernandez's activities
in coordinating the resupply flights, the chapter on Fernandez
nowhere mentions the role played by and knowledge of CIA
Headquarters in this activities. In fact, CIA Headquarters
provided Fernandez with the flight vector and "hostile risk"
information which Fernandez passed on to the "private
benefactor" pilots through Quintero. Additionally, Fernandez
reported to CIA Headquarters on each successful delivery of
lethal material. As the chapter on Fiers discloses, "Fiers
approved specific activities that facilitated the [private]
network's operations." Report at Ch. 19, Pg. 264. Indeed,
"[o]n one occasion, Fiers encouraged the network to drop
supplies to [the Southern Front Contras]. Id. at 264. See
also id. at 269-70 ("In one instance, . . . Fiers encouraged
and perhaps directed a lethal 'private benefactor' mission to
forces that had been promised lethal aid by the CIA.")(emphasis
supplied).

         The chapter on Fiers further describes his very active
role in insuring that "private benefactor" lethal supplies were
delivered to the Southern Front Contras:

- 21 -

> On March 15, 1986, Fiers <u>directed</u>
> Fernandez and other CIA personnel in
> Central America to assist a drop of
> lethal supplies by UNO/FDN to the
> NACs. . . .
>
> By this cable, Fiers instructed
> Fernandez and other CIA personnel in
> Central America not only to encourage
> an FDN drop to the NACs, <u>but to make
> sure that it happened.</u>

Report at Ch. 19, Pg. 272 (emphasis supplied)(footnote

omitted). In addition, Fiers sent the following cable: "[I]t

is more <u>crucial</u> than ever that we maintain our commitment to

the NAC's and that the required drop be made at the <u>absolutely</u>

<u>first possible opportunity</u>.'" Report at Ch. 29, Pg. 273

(emphasis supplied). In light of the powerful evidence showing

Fiers's very active role in ensuring the delivery of lethal

supplies to the Southern Front Contras, it is simply

disingenuous for the Independent Counsel to suggest that

Fernandez acted without the knowledge and approval of his

superiors in connection with the very flights which Fiers

directed Fernandez and other CIA personnel to facilitate.

The chapter on Fernandez further states that

"Fernandez . . . disregarded explicit warnings from his

superiors. Report at Part VI, Pg. 200. Nowhere does the

report reveal, however, what those explicit warnings might have

been. In reality, Fernandez's CIA superiors never provided

such "explicit warnings." The chapter on Fiers reveals that

Fiers "knew as early as May 1986 that Fernandez had passed

- 22 -

information directly to the 'private benefactors.'" Report at
Ch. 19, Pg. 275-76. Fiers learned of this information after
Fernandez had told the Chief of the Latin American Division in
April 1986, among other things, that "he was passing
intelligence directly to the private benefactors to facilitate
the delivery of supplies, including guns and ammunition, to the
southern front" and that "he communicated with the private
benefactors by 'communications gear' used in connection with
the telephone and manufactured by TRW [a so-called KL-43]. .
.." Report at Ch. 19, Pg. 275.

The chapter on Fiers also explains that Fiers
subsequently rejected a plan to place a UNO/South communicator
at Ilopango in order to eliminate the need for Fernandez to
have direct communications with the "private benefactors."
Report at Ch. 19, Pg. 275. After approving the plan in May
1986, Fiers reversed himself and scotched it without
explanation by cable in July 1986. Fiers's decision to
withdraw his approval for placing a Nicaraguan in El Salvador
to get Fernandez "out of the loop" left Fernandez with the
responsibility under Boland to facilitate the resupply of the
Contras with no way to do it without having direct contact with
the "private benefactors." While the Report at Ch. 19,
Pg. 275, indicates that Fiers assured the Chief of the Latin
American Division that the Contras would place the communicator
in Ilopango without CIA assistance, the Report fails to

- 23 -

indicate how Fiers imagined that was going to happen. In the
meantime, Fernandez received no guidance from anyone. He was
simply left to sort things out on his own as best he could.[9/]

The Report is also internally inconsistent with
respect to Fernandez's superiors' knowledge of his
communications with Oliver North. At one place, the Report
states that Fernandez "minimized and concealed from his
superiors at the CIA the true nature of his contacts with North
and North's private representatives." Report at Part III,
Pg. 59. At the same time, the chapter on Fiers states that,
during 1986, "Fiers admitted that he knew that North and
Fernandez talked often about the Contras." Report at Ch. 19,
Pg. 279.[10/] In addition, the Report states that Fernandez

9/   After Fiers had ordered the stand-down on the communicator,
     CIA Headquarters continued to provide flight vector
     information for the "private benefactor" flights and
     Fernandez continued to report to CIA Headquarters on the
     successful drops of lethal material to the Contras. As
     Fiers knew that there was no UNO South communicator at
     Ilopango, the only reasonable conclusion he could have
     drawn was that Fernandez was still passing the information
     directly to the "private benefactors" himself. At no time
     thereafter did Fiers tell Fernandez to stop; he also never
     questioned his activities.

10/ In light of Fiers's knowledge of Fernandez's communications
     with North and the "private benefactors," there would have
     been no reason for Fernandez to have taken "steps to erase
     records of his relationship with North and Quintero," as
     the Independent Counsel alleges he did. Report at Ch. 20,
     Pg. 287. Fernandez merely instructed a U.S. Embassy
     employee, Eva Groening, to segregate the relevant telephone
     records for safekeeping and to prevent access to those

                    (Footnote Continued on Next Page)

- 24 -

told the Chief of the Latin American Division in April 1986,
among other things, that North had introduced him to the
"private benefactors." Report at Ch. 19, Pg. 275.

   Evidence that Fernandez's CIA superiors had knowledge
of and encouraged Fernandez's Contra-related activities --
which the Independent Counsel ignores in his discussions of
Fernandez -- is crucial to understanding Fernandez's activities
and the Independent Counsel's case against him. The
Independent Counsel's theory was that Fernandez lied to the CIA
IG and the Tower Commission investigators in order to hide
activities, which violated the Boland Amendment, and about
which his superiors were ignorant.   As the Fourth Circuit
recognized in the second <u>Fernandez</u> appeal, "The demonstration
of widespread CIA involvement in the resupply operation, if
successful, would be crucial to Fernandez's defense that he did
not lie to or mislead the Tower Commission about his knowledge
of North's role in the operation, or about his knowledge of the
type of supplies he assisted in delivering to the Contras in
1986. It would also go to whether Fernandez possessed the
requisite criminal intent to make the allegedly false
statements, since numerous persons throughout the CIA were

_____

<u>10</u>/ (Footnote Continued from Previous Page)

  records by foreign nationals. Moreover, the fact that the
  telephone records revealed hundreds of calls between
  Fernandez and North is hardly surprising; as part of their
  jobs, North and Fernandez discussed political issues
  concerning the Contras frequently.

- 25 -

deeply involved in the project which he purportedly
misrepresented." <u>United States v. Fernandez</u>, 913 F.2d 148, 160
(4th Cir. 1990).

The portions of the Report addressing Fernandez's
activities are incomplete and misleading because they omit
crucial information concerning the knowledge and approval of
Fernandez's CIA superiors of the very activities about which
Fernandez is alleged to have had a motive to lie.

III.   THE INDEPENDENT COUNSEL TOTALLY MISCHARACTERIZED THE
         REASONS FOR THE DISMISSAL OF THE FERNANDEZ PROSECUTION
         <u>UNDER THE CLASSIFIED INFORMATION PROCEDURES ACT.</u>

When discussing the Fernandez case, the Independent
Counsel repeatedly urges his theory that the Attorney General
deliberately withheld from disclosure information that was
publicly known in order to put an end to the Fernandez
prosecution. In that way, the Report suggests the Bush
Administration avoided having CIA officials implicated in
Contra-related activities. <u>See</u>, <u>e.g.</u>, Report at Ch. 20, Pg.
292-93. The Independent Counsel's theory has no merit.

The real reason for the dismissal of the Fernandez
case was the Independent Counsel's failure <u>pre-indictment</u> to
balance the possible harm to national security which
prosecution of the case would bring about against the interests
that would be served by prosecuting Fernandez, as the Ethics in
Government Act required him to do. Further, the Independent

- 26 -

Counsel scornfully trivializes the harm which would have resulted from the disclosure of the classified information which was destined to be revealed during the course of the Fernandez trial.

The Report itself acknowledges that "[t]he indictment of Fernandez represented the first time that a CIA chief of station had been charged with crimes committed in the course of his duties as a CIA officer." Report at Ch. 20, Pg. 283. It should have come as no surprise, therefore, that prosecution of the case was going to cause the disclosure of highly sensitive classified information. Despite those transparent realities, the Independent Counsel made no attempt to follow the Attorney General's Guidelines for Prosecutions Involving Classified Information, Attachment C hereto, notwithstanding the statutory requirement that an Independent Counsel abide by Justice Department policy except in those rare situations where it is not possible to do so. See 28 U.S.C. § 594(f); Morrison v. Olson, 487 U.S. 654, 696 (1988). The Attorney General's CIPA Guidelines, at 2, required the Independent Counsel, prior to pursuing a prosecution which might reveal classified information, to "determine whether the need to protect against the disclosure of the classified information outweighs other federal interest that would be served by proceeding with the prosecution." Further, the Guidelines make clear that "it is the responsibility of the [Independent Counsel], in

- 27 -

consultation with the agency or agencies whose classified
information is involved, to identify and assess these competing
interests so that a reasoned decision may be made with respect
to continuing the investigation or prosecution." Id. See also
Guidelines at 3-4.

    If the Independent Counsel had followed the Attorney
General's Guidelines, the Fernandez indictments would never
have been sought. The first-ever § 6(e) Affidavit which
ultimately was filed in this case demonstrates that if the
Independent Counsel had consulted with the intelligence
agencies, as he was obligated to do under the Guidelines and
the Ethics in Government Act, he would have had to conclude
that proceeding with the prosecution of Fernandez would result
in undue harm to national security. Had the Independent
Counsel played by the rules under which the law required him to
operate, needless expenditure of valuable resources would have
been avoided and Fernandez would have been spared the agony and
expense of suffering through two ill-fated prosecutions.[11]

11/ The Independent Counsel compounded the expense and delay
    associated with prosecuting Fernandez by first indicting
    Fernandez in the District of Columbia. There, the
    Independent Counsel persuaded the grand jury to return an
    indictment where venue was lacking for four of the five
    counts. The delay that resulted was in no way the fault of
    Fernandez. Fernandez filed his motions to dismiss the
    malignant counts in accordance with the district court's
    instructions. Moreover, the Independent Counsel created
    the problem in the first instance by bringing the

               (Footnote Continued on Next Page)

- 28 -

Further, the Independent Counsel's claim that the
Attorney General precluded a trial of Fernandez solely to
protect the "location of two well-known CIA stations" is
plainly wrong. Report at Ch. 20, Pg. 292. As the Attorney
General's office informed Congress, Judge Hilton's CIPA order
permitted disclosure of not only the locations of CIA
facilities, "but also the activities of and details about those
facilities." Letter from Assistant Attorney General W. Lee
Rawls to Hon. Anthony C. Beilenson (Oct. 24, 1990) (hereinafter
"Rawls letter"), Attachment E, at 3. Moreover, the Attorney
General's decision that it could not permit release of the
information needed for the Fernandez prosecution was
precipitated by the Independent Counsel's own request that the
court conduct the CIPA pretrial proceedings according to
categories of information, as opposed to specific information

_____

11/ (Footnote Continued from Previous Page)

prosecution in the District of Columbia. Importantly, the
one count as to which venue did exist in the District of
Columbia -- the conspiracy count -- could have been brought
in the Eastern District of Virginia. Ironically, when the
Independent Counsel had Fernandez reindicted in Virginia,
he chose not to bring the conspiracy count and to prosecute
Fernandez on false statement and obstruction alone.

The District of Columbia indictment was abusive and
unnecessary. Further, as Chief Judge Aubrey E. Robinson
noted after Fernandez moved to dismiss four counts on venue
grounds, by cross-moving to dismiss the entire District of
Columbia indictment, the Independent Counsel conveniently
avoided having to comply with Judge Robinson's order that
the Independent Counsel provide discovery to the defense
pursuant to United States v. Kastigar. See Attachment D.

- 29 -

items. Id. at 2-3. See also Letter from James S. Reynolds to
Hon. Claude M. Hilton (Oct. 12, 1990), Attachment F.

In addition, the Report wrongly claims that "[t]he
intelligence agencies' submission to the Attorney General were
not specific enough to rebut" the fact that the location of the
two CIA stations was well known. Report at Ch. 20, Pg. 292.
The declarations submitted by the agencies in an effort to
avoid disclosure of some of the most sensitive information
involved in the case were detailed and thoroughly supported.
Further, "[t]he potentially serious damage to national security
which could result from the disclosure of the two categories of
information [the location of particular CIA facilities and
essential details of three highly sensitive classified
programs] [was] exacerbated by the prospect for additional
disclosures at trial. In the words of one senior official, the
damage could be 'devastating.'" Rawls letter at 6.

Moreover, the Independent Counsel's suggestion that
the case could have gone forward on a reduced number of counts
without the release of the information concerning the programs
-- which Judge Hilton found were relevant to explain
Fernandez's involvement with the Costa Rican airstrip -- is
erroneous. As the Report acknowledges, Judge Hilton ruled that
the classified information concerning the programs had
relevance beyond the charges relating to the airstrip. Report
at Ch. 20, Pg. 292. The Fourth Circuit concurred in this

- 30 -

ruling, pointing out that the Independent Counsel conceded that "it would still need to introduce evidence demonstrating Fernandez's involvement in the airstrip project" in order to prove the remaining counts. United States v. Fernandez, 913 F.2d at 159.

In further attempting to lay blame for the dismissal of the Fernandez case on the Attorney General, the Independent Counsel incorrectly states that the Attorney General declined the Independent Counsel's invitation to reconsider his decision to file a § 6(e) Affidavit after the Fourth Circuit affirmed the dismissal of the case. Report at Ch. 20, Pg. 292. To the contrary, the Attorney General "undertook a full and thorough reconsideration of his prior invocation of CIPA § 6(e)." Rawls letter at 1-2. (See also Rawls letter at 4-5 for a description of the reconsideration process.) In particular, the Attorney General's reevaluation "considered the views previously expressed by the Independent Counsel concerning the appropriateness of invoking section 6(e)." Id. at 4.

A review of the relevant facts makes clear that the Attorney General did absolutely nothing improper in filing a § 6(e) Affidavit in this case and was merely acting in accordance with his "constitutionally-based power to protect information important to national security." Appeal of United States by Attorney General, 887 F.2d 465, 470 (4th Cir. 1989)(quoting Department of the Navy v. Egan, 108 S. Ct. 818,

- 31 -

824 (1988)). <u>See</u> <u>also</u> <u>id.</u> at 471 (the Ethics in Government Act "plainly does not affect the Attorney General's authority to protect information important to national security by filing a section 6(e) affidavit").

The Independent Counsel's real complaint is that it does not believe that the authority to protect national security information should rest with the Attorney General in cases prosecuted by an Independent Counsel. The Independent Counsel's position ignores the fact that an alternative procedure might raise constitutional concerns. <u>See</u> <u>id</u>. More to the point here, it is irrelevant that the current process may not have met with the Independent Counsel's approval; the process mandated by CIPA is <u>the</u> <u>law</u> and the Independent Counsel was obliged to follow it in the Fernandez case whether he agreed with it or not.

III.   THE REPORT OVERSTATES THE STRENGTH OF THE FERNANDEZ
         CASE AND THE LIKELIHOOD OF A SUCCESSFUL PROSECUTION.

As the Attorney General recognized, the Independent Counsel's case against Fernandez was "a relatively weak one which would not have been brought had Fernandez been willing to cooperate with the investigation." Rawls letter at 5. The Report characterizes the Attorney General's assessment of the Fernandez case as an "uninformed assessment of the merits of the prosecution." Report at Ch. 20, Pg. 292. The reality is that, apart from the classified information problems, there

- 32 -

were a number of factors which made it extremely unlikely that Fernandez would ever be prosecuted successfully. Those factors included problems of satisfying the Government's "heavy burden" under Kastigar v. United States and proof problems with respect to the specific false statements alleged. 12/

A.   Kastigar Problems

The Independent Counsel's claim that "Judge Hilton had little difficulty in disposing of Fernandez's Kastigar challenge." Report at Ch. 20, Pg. 288. That is not true. Judge Hilton did hold that further discovery and a pretrial Kastigar hearing were not necessary. Nevertheless, he also ordered that trial witnesses, prior to their testimony, would be thoroughly questioned "to make sure that their answers to questions are based solely on their own personal knowledge and recollection of the events in question . . .." Order (July 10, 1989) at 7, Attachment G.

Two of the government's most crucial witnesses slated to testify at the Fernandez trial were Leonard Cole Black, a

---

12/ The Independent Counsel further argues that "the Attorney General must have known that Fernandez admitted to the Select Committees that he had lied to both the Tower Commission and the CIA's Inspector General." Report at Ch. 20, Pgs. 292-93. In fact, Fernandez did not admit that he ever intentionally lied to anyone. What he told the Select Committees was that he had initially not told investigators all he knew because he was operating under restrictive guidelines that he understood had been worked out by the DDO, i.e., the questioning would be limited to the resupply flights.

CIA IG officer to whom Fernandez allegedly made the statements

implicated in Counts I and II of the Virginia indictment, and

Louis Dupart, who during the relevant period had been the

Compliance Officer for the CIA's CATF and was intimately

familiar with many of the facts necessary for the government to

make even a prima facie case at trial.

In two statements which were provided to the Fernandez

defense, Mr. Black stated that, prior to any substantive

discussions about Fernandez, he had informed Independent

Counsel attorneys on more than one occasion that (i) he had

reviewed extensively portions of printed records of the

Iran/Contra Select Committee hearings; (ii) his knowledge of

Fernandez's activities and the entire Iran-Contra matter "was a

continuum"; and (iii) that he "could not as a practical matter

-- and would not as a matter of principle -- accept

responsibility" for distinguishing between information derived

from immunized testimony and information derived from

non-immunized sources. Statement of Mr. Leonard Cole Black, at

1-2, Attachment H. See also Supplemental Statement of

Mr. Leonard Cole Black, Attachment I. Without Black's

testimony, at least two of the counts against Fernandez --

fully one-half of the indictment -- would have had to have been

dismissed.

Insofar as concerns Louis Dupart, the Independent

Counsel was well aware that Dupart had carefully reviewed and

- 34 -

annotated a transcript of Fernandez's immunized Congressional
testimony. Affidavit of Nancy D. Grundman, ¶5 , Attachment J.
As a result, Dupart expressed the belief to counsel for
Fernandez that "it would have been impossible for his mental
impression of the events relating to the Iran/Contra affair,
including Mr. Fernandez's alleged involvement, not to have been
influenced by the Congressional hearings, including Mr.
Fernandez's compelled testimony." Id., ¶ 7. In addition,
Dupart made his annotated transcript available to any CIA
personnel who wished to see it. Id., ¶5. Hence, it is likely
that other CIA witnesses whom the Independent Counsel intended
to call at trial would have been tainted by Fernandez's
immunized testimony and, as a consequence, would have been
unable to testify at trial.[13]

Hence, the Independent Counsel's position that
Kastigar posed no problem for its prosecution of Fernandez is
incorrect. To the contrary, it would have been virtually
impossible for the Independent Counsel to present a case
against Fernandez which would not have violated Fernandez's
Fifth Amendment rights.

---

[13] The Independent Counsel's assertion that because
Fernandez's immunized testimony was given in executive
session, "dissemination of his immunized therefore was much
more limited and therefore posed less of a problem for the
trial judge," Report at Ch. 20, Pg. 288 n.32, ignores the
fact that many CIA witnesses on whose testimony the
Independent Counsel's case against Fernandez would have
depended were thoroughly exposed to Fernandez's immunized
testimony.

- 35 -

B.   Underline: False Statement Proof Problems.

All of the false statements alleged in the indictment
were based upon statements made in informal interviews. As
such, there were no transcripts to support the alleged false
statements, making proof of precisely the questions asked and
the answers given impossible. Further, the Independent Counsel
could prove no motive for Fernandez to have lied. As
demonstrated above, Fernandez had engaged in no illegal
activity in connection with the Contras and his CIA superiors
were well aware of and approved of his Contra resupply
efforts. In addition, the evidence simply did not support the
Independent Counsel's false statement allegations against
Fernandez.

1.   False Statements Relating to the Costa Rican
Airstrip.

Count Two of the Alexandria indictment alleged that
Fernandez falsely told CIA's Inspector General's office "that a
project to build an airstrip in northern Costa Rica in 1985 was
an initiative of the Costa Rican government;" and "that the
airstrip was to be used for training activities by Costa Rican
forces in preparation for a possible Nicaraguan invasion of
Costa Rica." Alexandria Indictment, Attachment B. See also
Report at Ch. 20, Pg. 286 (describing Fernandez's alleged
statement that "the purpose of the airstrip was to provide

- 36 -

defensive support to Costa Rica in the event of an invasion by
Nicaragua" as "a cover story").

The testimony of former United States Ambassador to
Costa Rica Lewis Tambs before the Iran/Contra Select Committees
demonstrates that the foregoing alleged false statements were
in fact true. Tambs provided extensive testimony concerning
the Costa Rican Government's fear of a Nicaraguan invasion and
Costa Rica's desire to have the Contras move out of Costa Rica
into Nicaragua. Transcript of Testimony of Lewis A. Tambs
("Tr.") at 373-74. Tambs further testified that the Costa
Ricans were interested in two things: (i) getting the Contras
out of Costa Rica into Nicaragua, and (ii) "having an airfield
by which an inter-American defense force could arrive and
protect them from a possible invasion."[14] Tr. at 374.

According to Tambs, discussions with the Costa Rican
government "yielded an airfield which could be used for
reinforcement and resupply if there was an invasion from
Nicaragua. At the same time, the airfield would be used for
refueling and for emergency purposes of private aircraft which
would be used to supply the Nicaraguan Democratic Resistance,

---

14/ Importantly, as stated previously, by letter dated
August 10, 1988, the Independent Counsel informed Fernandez
that a senior Costa Rican official had told Independent
Counsel representatives that he had selected the site for
the airstrip and that he intended to use the location to
train members of the Costa Rican civil guard. See n. 6,
supra.

- 37 -

which obviously would have to move inside Nicaragua to be resupplied there . . . ." Tr. at 375.[15/]

Tambs's testimony makes clear that the Costa Rican airstrip served a dual purpose, one of which was to assist Costa Rica in defending against a Nicaraguan invasion.[16/] Significantly, the Independent Counsel never accused Ambassador Tambs of being a liar. Yet, for making statements which were completely in line with Ambassador Tambs's testimony, Fernandez's was indicted, not once, but twice. Not surprisingly, Ambassador Tambs was not named on the list of witnesses the government intended to call against Fernandez at trial.

_____

15/   The Independent Counsel asserts at one point that an airstrip built to provide defensive support to Costa Rica in the event of an invasion by Nicaragua "would have been redundant since the U.S. Army's Southern Command maintained its own airport, with a paved airstrip, only one hour's drive from Santa Elena." Report at Ch. 20, Pg. 286.

      This claim is remarkable nonsense. Costa Rica is a neutral country and, as such, the U.S. Army's Southern Command has never maintained a paved airstrip there. While the Report is not entirely clear, in this statement, the Independent Counsel might have been referring to the commercial airstrip near the Costa Rican town of Liberia. That airstrip is located right on Highway 1. As such, it was not easily defensible in the event of a Sandinista invasion of Costa Rica and was totally unsuited for clandestine Contra resupply activities.

16/   Tambs provided similar testimony in a 244 page deposition given to the Independent Counsel in early May 1987. Despite the fact that the deposition completely exculpated Fernandez, the Independent Counsel withheld the transcript from Fernandez until Judge Hilton ordered it turned over.

- 38 -

2.   **False Statements Relating To The Contra Resupply Operation.**

Counts Three and Four of the Alexandria indictment were predicated on allegations that Fernandez falsely stated to the Tower Commission investigators (i) "that [he] did not know for a fact that Oliver L. North had been involved in assisting the resupply of the Contras"; and (ii) "that [he] did not know that the supplies [he] assisted in delivering to the Contras in September 1986 contained weapons and ammunition." Attachment B.   In fact, Fernandez never made those statements.

With respect to the alleged statement that he did not know for a fact that North was involved in the resupply operation, the Tower Commission investigators' own notes directly contradicted the alleged statement.   Those notes stated that Fernandez told the investigators that "over the span of many conversations with North, [he] came to the conclusion that North **was** connected with the suppliers of arms to the Contras" (emphasis supplied).

The Independent Counsel would have had an equally difficult time of proving that Fernandez lied about the lethal nature of the September 1986 deliveries to the Contras.   In early 1986, there were two kinds of flights making resupply drops to the Contras -- humanitarian aid flights funded by the Nicaraguan Humanitarian Assistance Office ("NHAO") of the U.S. Department of State, and military resupply flights funded by

- 39 -

the "private benefactors." By June 30, 1986, all the

humanitarian aid had been purchased and delivered; there were

no NHAO flights inside Nicaragua after June 30, 1986. The

flights addressed in Fernandez's alleged statement occurred in

September 1986. Since there were no NHAO humanitarian aid

flights after June 1986, the September flights had to have been

deliveries of lethal supplies, and no one knew that better than

Fernandez.

Moreover, Fernandez made official reports of the

September 1986 flights to CIA Headquarters. Those reports

reflected that lethal material was delivered. It is highly

implausible that Fernandez would have lied to investigators

about well-documented facts which he himself had reported to

CIA, especially when he knew that his reports would be made

available to Iran-Contra investigators. It is also highly

unlikely that Fernandez would have lied about conduct which he

firmly understood to have been perfectly legal. [17]

17/ Fernandez's alleged statement to Tower Commission
    investigator Brian Bruh that "[he, Bruh] had [Fernandez]
    and his career is ruined," Report at Ch. 20, Pg. 288 n.29,
    is not evidence that Fernandez had previously lied to
    Bruh. In January 1987, Fernandez well knew that Oliver
    North was "radioactive" inside Washington. Fernandez
    further knew that if there were to be produced written
    documentation of Fernandez's dealing with North, that
    relationship, in the prevailing climate, could be made to
    appear improper, even though Fernandez's dealings with
    North had been perfectly legal and appropriate. When Bruh
    confronted Fernandez with KL-43 messages, several of which
    Fernandez himself had sent to North, Fernandez knew that he
    was going to be tarred with the same brush as North and
    that, as a result, his career was in ruins.

- 40 -

CONCLUSION

Contrary to the picture painted by the Report,
Joseph F. Fernandez was victimized at every step of the
Iran-Contra process. He was betrayed by his superiors and then
persecuted by Independent Counsel Walsh who was unhappy because
Fernandez would not, in essence, waive his Fifth Amendment
privilege. After two attempted prosecutions of Fernandez
failed, Independent Counsel Walsh did what he could have done
all along: he immunized Fernandez, put him in the grand jury
and Fernandez told the truth.[18/] The prosecution of
Joseph F. Fernandez was a vendetta by Walsh and was completely
unnecessary. Moreover, the unprecedented CIPA § 6(e) Affidavit

---

18/ The Report makes clear that the evidence of the level of
knowledge that Fernandez's superiors had regarding North
and the activities of the "private benefactor" resupply
network was amply reflected in CIA cables and other
documents. As a result, the Independent Counsel never
needed access to Fernandez in order to learn the facts
which ultimately provided the basis for false statement
charges against Fiers and George. In this connection, it
is important to note that the Independent Counsel did not
call Fernandez as a witness against George during his
trial.

- 41 -

filed by the Attorney General was a direct result of the

Independent Counsel's refusal to comply with the Ethics in

Government Act.

Respectfully submitted,

Thomas E. Wilson

SEYFARTH, SHAW, FAIRWEATHER
& GERALDSON
Suite 500
815 Connecticut Ave., N.W.
Washington, D.C. 20006-4004
(202) 463-2400

Counsel for Joseph F.
Fernandez

Dated: December 3, 1993

TAB – A

UNITED STATES DISTRICT COURT
FOR THE DISTRICT OF COLUMBIA

Holding a Criminal Term

Grand Jury Sworn in on January 28, 1987

UNITED STATES OF AMERICA	:	Criminal No.
v.	:	
	:	Grand Jury Original
JOSEPH F. FERNANDEZ,	:	
Defendant.	:	Violations:
	:	18 U.S.C. § 371;
	:	18 U.S.C. § 1001;
	:	18 U.S.C. § 1505.
	:	
	:	(Conspiracy; False
	:	Statements; Obstruction
	:	of Proceedings)

I N D I C T M E N T

COUNT ONE

(Conspiracy)

The Grand Jury charges:

INTRODUCTION

1. At all times relevant to this Indictment, the Central
Intelligence Agency ("CIA") was the principal United States
Government agency responsible for the collection of foreign
intelligence and the conduct of covert and foreign intelligence
operations.

2.   At all times relevant to this Indictment, the
National Security Council ("NSC") was a government entity whose
function was to advise the President on the integration of
domestic, foreign and military policies relating to the
national security, to facilitate cooperation among the military
services and other departments and agencies of the government
in matters involving the national security, and to review,
guide and direct foreign intelligence activities and covert
actions.

3.   At all times relevant to this Indictment,
intelligence activities undertaken by the United States were
subject to the restrictions and limitations contained in
Executive Order 12333, promulgated by the President on December
4, 1981, which, in part, prohibited any United States
Government agency, except the CIA, from conducting covert
actions without a determination by the President that the
agency other than the CIA was more likely to achieve a
particular objective. On January 18, 1985, the President
signed National Security Decision Directive 159, which required
that the President specifically approve by a written finding
all covert actions undertaken by any United States Government
agency or entity.

4.   At all times relevant to this Indictment, the
Contras, also known as the Nicaraguan democratic resistance,
were military insurgents engaged in military and paramilitary
operations in Nicaragua. In many instances, these operations

occurred near the borders of Costa Rica and Honduras,
Nicaragua's neighboring countries to the south and north
respectively.

5.   From in or about December 1981 to on or about October
11, 1984, the United States Government, acting principally
through the CIA, pursuant to written presidential findings,
provided the Contras with financial support, arms and military
equipment, as well as supervision, instruction, tactical and
other advice, coordination, intelligence and direction.

6.   On October 12, 1984, Public Law 98-473 was enacted
and expressly prohibited funds available to the CIA, as well as
certain other agencies and entities of the United States, from
being obligated or expended in support of military or
paramilitary operations in Nicaragua, stating in relevant part:

> During fiscal year 1985, no funds available to
> the Central Intelligence Agency, the Department
> of Defense, or any other agency or entity of the
> United States involved in intelligence
> activities may be obligated or expended for the
> purpose or which would have the effect of
> supporting, directly or indirectly, military or
> paramilitary operations in Nicaragua by any
> nation, group, organization, movement, or
> individual.

This provision of law was commonly known as the Boland
Amendment. On October 19, 1984, staff members of the CIA's
Central American Task Force informed CIA personnel stationed in
Central America by cable that the Boland Amendment "clearly
end[ed] U.S. support for the war in Nicaragua" and prohibited
"any expenditure, including those from accounts for salaries
and all support costs" for the purpose of such support.

7.   On August 12, 1985, Congress modified the Boland Amendment by approving $27 million for humanitarian assistance to the Contras and permitting the United States Government to exchange information with the Contras.

8.   On December 4, 1985, Congress passed modified restrictions on Contra aid for fiscal year 1986.   This legislation authorized the provision of $3 million for communication equipment and communication training for the Contras.   In addition, it allowed United States Government employees to provide "advice" to the Contras on the "effective delivery and distribution of materiel."   Congress, however, retained the prohibition upon the CIA and other agencies or entities involved in intelligence activities from engaging in activities "that amount[ed] to participation in the planning or execution of military or paramilitary operations in Nicaragua by the Nicaraguan democratic resistance, or to participation in logistics activities integral to such operations."   In November 1985, in anticipation of this legislation, staff members of the CIA's Central American Task Force informed CIA personnel stationed in Central America by cable of this restriction. This prohibition remained in force until October 18, 1986, when Congress authorized the CIA to provide military aid to the Contras.

THE DEFENDANT

9.   At all times relevant to this Indictment, the
defendant JOSEPH F. FERNANDEZ was an employee of the CIA,
serving as the senior CIA officer in Costa Rica. As the senior
CIA officer, the defendant FERNANDEZ had immediate control over
and responsibility for all CIA operations in Costa Rica. The
defendant FERNANDEZ reported to and received supervision from
the Chief of the CIA's Central American Task Force, who was
stationed at CIA headquarters in Langley, Virginia.

THE CONSPIRACY AND ITS OBJECTS

10.   From the late spring or early summer of 1985 up to
and including at least January 1987, in the District of
Columbia and elsewhere, the defendant JOSEPH F. FERNANDEZ,
together with others known and unknown to the Grand Jury,
unlawfully, willfully and knowingly did combine, conspire,
confederate and agree together and with each other:

(a) to defraud the United States by impeding, impairing,
defeating and obstructing the lawful governmental functions of
the United States, including compliance with legal and
administrative restrictions governing the conduct of military
activities and covert actions and congressional control of
appropriations and exercise of oversight for such activities,
by deceitfully and without legal authorization organizing,
directing and concealing a program to continue logistical and
other support for military and paramilitary operations in

-5-

Nicaragua by the Contras, at a time when the prohibitions of
the Boland Amendment and other legal and administrative
restrictions on the execution of covert actions were in effect;

(b) to commit offenses against the United States,
including:

(1) Violations of Title 18, United States Code,
Section 1505, Obstructing an Inquiry Being Conducted By The
President's Special Review Board (the "Tower Commission"), as
alleged in Count Two of this Indictment;

(2) Violations of Title 18, United States Code,
Section 1001, Making False and Misleading Statements to
Government Agencies, to wit, the Tower Commission and the CIA's
Office of Inspector General, as alleged in Counts Three through
Five of this Indictment.

THE BACKGROUND OF THE CONSPIRACY

11. In order to continue activities in support of the
Contras and to conceal those activities following the enactment
of the Boland Amendment in October 1984, members of the
conspiracy enlisted and utilized private individuals to provide
lethal military weapons and supplies to the Contras.

12. In the middle of 1985, members of the conspiracy
established a clandestine supply network to support military
and paramilitary operations in Nicaragua by the Contras. To
promote these operations, members of the conspiracy purchased
aircraft, recruited and employed pilots, crews and other

-6-

individuals, and arranged for the use of a military airfield
and warehouse in a Central American country. They concealed
their role in creating and maintaining this operation by, among
other things, instructing the individuals they had recruited
not to reveal the participation of specific members of the
conspiracy in these activities and not to disclose the use of
intervening corporate entities. The network of individuals
working under the direction of certain members of the
conspiracy came to be known as the "private benefactors."

THE MEANS OF THE CONSPIRACY

13. In the middle of 1985 and thereafter, in order
further to assist the Contras in Nicaragua, the defendant
JOSEPH F. FERNANDEZ worked in coordination with his co-
conspirators in establishing a clandestine supply network to
support military and paramilitary operations in Nicaragua by
the Contras and, among other things, undertook to enable the
Contras to engage in military operations in southern Nicaragua
(the "Southern Front").

14. In August 1985, the defendant JOSEPH F. FERNANDEZ met
on several occasions in Costa Rica with an associate of a co-
conspirator and discussed various strategies to accomplish the
formation of a Southern Front, including the resumption of
combat by Contra forces in southern Nicaragua and the
construction of an airstrip in northern Costa Rica.

15.   In August 1985, the defendant JOSEPH F. FERNANDEZ undertook to locate a site for and begin construction of a clandestine airstrip in northern Costa Rica that could be used to assist the resupply of lethal military supplies to the Contras.

16.   In the late summer or early fall of 1985, members of the conspiracy, in coordination with the defendant JOSEPH F. FERNANDEZ and others, and to conceal their participation in these activities, enlisted an individual and utilized Udall Research Corp., a Panamanian corporation, to acquire land in northwest Costa Rica for construction of an airstrip to be used for the delivery of lethal military supplies to the Southern Front.   Throughout the fall of 1985, the defendant JOSEPH F. FERNANDEZ met regularly with this individual in order to coordinate the construction of the airstrip.

17.   In the fall of 1985 and the winter of 1985-86, while the airstrip was being built, the defendant JOSEPH F. FERNANDEZ took additional steps to strengthen the military capabilities of the Contras along the Southern Front.   By promising Contra leaders that he would support them with military supplies, the defendant FERNANDEZ caused Contra forces inside Costa Rica to return to Nicaragua and continue fighting the Sandinista forces.

18.   Beginning in January 1986, in order to ensure the secrecy of the communications between the defendant JOSEPH F. FERNANDEZ and others within the private benefactor network, a

member of the conspiracy obtained a number of secure
communication devices from a United States Government agency.
In January or February 1986, one of these secure communication
devices was delivered to the defendant FERNANDEZ.

19.   Between January and early April 1986, the defendant
JOSEPH F. FERNANDEZ and his co-conspirators, in coordination
with private benefactors, made attempts to deliver military
supplies to the Contra forces then located along the Southern
Front.   In connection with these attempts, the defendant
FERNANDEZ identified the location of Contra forces that were
prepared to receive an air drop of supplies, and notified those
forces of the date and time of delivery.

20.   On or about April 11-12, 1986, the defendant JOSEPH
F. FERNANDEZ, along with his co-conspirators, caused the
successful aerial delivery of lethal military supplies to
Contra forces. Following this successful air drop, the
defendant FERNANDEZ sent a secure message to a co-conspirator
in which the defendant FERNANDEZ described his plans for
expansion of the Southern Front military forces.

21.   Between the middle of April and September 1986, the
defendant JOSEPH F. FERNANDEZ, along with his co-conspirators,
continued to direct the delivery of lethal military supplies to
the Contras in southern Nicaragua. On approximately eight
occasions during this period, Contra forces received deliveries
of weapons and ammunition based upon the defendant FERNANDEZ's

designation of the locations where and the troops to whom the
lethal military supplies were to be dropped.

22.   In June 1986, in order to conceal the secret resupply
operation being directed by the defendant JOSEPH F. FERNANDEZ
and his co-conspirators, a co-conspirator sent a secure
communication to the defendant FERNANDEZ advising him of steps
being taken to shield the defendant FERNANDEZ and his co-
conspirator from being held responsible for directing the
resupply operation in the event that the operation became
exposed.

23.   In late September 1986, to conceal and cover up the
conspirators' illegal activities, the defendant JOSEPH F.
FERNANDEZ made a false and misleading statement to an employee
of the CIA's Central American Task Force when the defendant
FERNANDEZ was questioned about the CIA's role in the
construction and operation of the airstrip in northern Costa
Rica.

24.   In November and December 1986, following the shooting
down in October 1986 of an aircraft that was attempting to drop
supplies to the Contras in Nicaragua, the defendant JOSEPH F.
FERNANDEZ was directed by an attorney assigned to the CIA's
Central American Task Force to document any involvement the
defendant FERNANDEZ had with the private benefactor network and
the lethal resupply of the Contras. The defendant FERNANDEZ,
to conceal and cover up the conspirators' illegal activities,

submitted incomplete and unresponsive cables to officers of the CIA's Central American Task Force.

25.   In January 1987, to conceal and cover up the conspirators' illegal activities, the defendant JOSEPH F. FERNANDEZ made false and misleading statements to a member of the CIA's Office of Inspector General concerning, among other things, the nature of the defendant FERNANDEZ's involvement in the construction of the airstrip in northern Costa Rica, the extent of the defendant FERNANDEZ's contacts with members of the conspiracy, and the extent of the defendant FERNANDEZ's involvement in assisting the lethal resupply of the Contras.

26.   In January 1987, to conceal and cover up the conspirators' illegal activities, the defendant JOSEPH F. FERNANDEZ made false and misleading statements to investigators conducting a fact-finding inquiry on behalf of the Tower Commission concerning, among other things, the role of a member of the conspiracy in assisting the lethal resupply of the Contras as well as the defendant FERNANDEZ's own role in supporting the Contras.

OVERT ACTS

27.   The following overt acts, among others, were knowingly committed and caused to be committed, in the District of Columbia and elsewhere, by the defendant JOSEPH F. FERNANDEZ and his co-conspirators in furtherance of the conspiracy and to effect the objects thereof:

(1)   On June 28, 1985, in Miami, Florida, Oliver L.
North and Richard V. Secord met with, among others, Adolfo
Calero, a Contra leader, and Enrique Bermudez, the Contras'
military commander.

(2)   In August 1985, in Costa Rica, the defendant
JOSEPH F. FERNANDEZ met with, among others, Robert W. Owen, an
associate of Oliver L. North, to discuss the construction of an
airstrip and other means to support the Contras.

(3)   In August 1985, in Costa Rica, the defendant
JOSEPH F. FERNANDEZ directed CIA officers to survey and select
a site for the construction of an airstrip to support the
lethal resupply of the Contras.

(4)   In September 1985, in Vienna, Virginia, Oliver
L. North and Richard V. Secord met with William Haskell, a/k/a
"Robert Olmsted."

(5)   In October 1985, Oliver L. North and Richard V.
Secord caused William Haskell, a/k/a "Robert Olmsted," to meet
with the defendant JOSEPH F. FERNANDEZ in San Jose, Costa Rica.

(6)   In or about late 1985, in Costa Rica, the
defendant JOSEPH F. FERNANDEZ directed a CIA officer to meet
with and train members of the Contras.

(7)   In January 1986, in Costa Rica, the defendant
JOSEPH F. FERNANDEZ met with Rafael Quintero, an associate of
Oliver L. North and Richard V. Secord.

(8)   Beginning in January 1986, in the District of
Columbia, Oliver L. North obtained certain secure communication

devices belonging to an intelligence agency of the United States Government.

(9) In or about January or February 1986, in Costa Rica, the defendant JOSEPH F. FERNANDEZ travelled with Rafael Quintero and others to inspect the site of the airstrip being built in northern Costa Rica.

(10) In or about January or February 1986, in Costa Rica, the defendant JOSEPH F. FERNANDEZ received from Rafael Quintero a secure communication device that had been obtained by Oliver L. North.

(11) In the spring of 1986, in Costa Rica, the defendant JOSEPH F. FERNANDEZ directed a CIA officer to meet with and train members of the Contras.

(12) In March 1986, in the District of Columbia, the defendant JOSEPH F. FERNANDEZ met with Richard V. Secord, Rafael Quintero and others to discuss the airstrip in northern Costa Rica.

(13) On or about April 11-12, 1986, in Costa Rica, the defendant JOSEPH F. FERNANDEZ assisted Oliver L. North, Richard V. Secord and others in the delivery of weapons and supplies to the Contras' Southern Front.

(14) Between the spring and fall of 1986, in Costa Rica and elsewhere, the defendant JOSEPH F. FERNANDEZ sent to and received from Oliver L. North and Rafael Quintero by a secure communication device numerous messages concerning the lethal resupply of the Contras.

(15) Between June and September 1986, in Costa Rica and elsewhere, the defendant JOSEPH F. FERNANDEZ, together with members of the conspiracy, directed the delivery of approximately eight shipments of weapons and supplies to the Contras' Southern Front.

(16) In late September 1986, in Langley, Virginia, the defendant JOSEPH F. FERNANDEZ made a false and misleading statement to a staff member of the CIA's Central American Task Force regarding the airstrip in northern Costa Rica.

(17) In or about November and December 1986, in Costa Rica and elsewhere, the defendant JOSEPH F. FERNANDEZ sent cables to officers of the CIA's Central American Task Force.

(18) In January 1987, in Langley, Virginia, the defendant JOSEPH F. FERNANDEZ made false and misleading statements to a member of the CIA's Office of Inspector General.

(19) In January 1987, in Langley, Virginia, the defendant JOSEPH F. FERNANDEZ made false and misleading statements to investigators conducting a fact-finding inquiry on behalf of the Tower Commission.

(Violation of Title 18, United States Code, Section 371.)

COUNT TWO

(Obstruction of the Tower Commission)

The Grand Jury further charges:

1.   Paragraphs 1 through 27 of Count One of this Indictment are repeated, realleged and incorporated by reference herein as if fully set forth in this Count.

2.   On or about January 21, 1987, in the Eastern District of Virginia, the defendant JOSEPH F. FERNANDEZ unlawfully, willfully and knowingly did corruptly influence, obstruct and impede and endeavor to influence, obstruct and impede the due and proper administration of the law under which a pending proceeding was being had before a department and agency of the United States, to wit, the Tower Commission's conduct of a fact-finding inquiry on behalf of the President, by making false, fictitious, fraudulent and misleading statements and representations to investigators of the Tower Commission, all for the purpose of concealing and causing to be concealed material facts.

(Violation of Title 18, United States Code, Section 1505.)

COUNT THREE

(False Statement to the Tower Commission)

The Grand Jury further charges:

1. Paragraphs 1 through 27 of Count One of this
Indictment are repeated, realleged and incorporated by
reference herein as if fully set forth in this Count.

2. On or about January 21, 1987, in the Eastern District
of Virginia, the defendant JOSEPH F. FERNANDEZ unlawfully,
willfully and knowingly did make and cause to be made a
material false, fictitious and fraudulent statement to a
department and agency of the United States, to wit, the Tower
Commission, in a matter within its jurisdiction, to wit, the
examination of the role of the NSC staff in national security
operations, as follows: that the defendant FERNANDEZ did not
know for a fact that Oliver L. North had been involved in
assisting the resupply of the Contras.

3. That statement and representation was false,
fictitious and fraudulent because in truth and in fact, as the
defendant JOSEPH F. FERNANDEZ then and there well knew and
believed, among other things, Oliver L. North had been involved
in assisting the resupply of the Contras.

(Violation of Title 18, United States Code, Section 1001.)

COUNT FOUR

(False Statement to the Tower Commission)

The Grand Jury further charges:

1. Paragraphs 1 through 27 of Count One of this Indictment are repeated, realleged and incorporated by reference herein as if fully set forth in this Count.

2. On or about January 21, 1987, in the Eastern District of Virginia, the defendant JOSEPH F. FERNANDEZ unlawfully, willfully and knowingly did make and cause to be made a material false, fictitious and fraudulent statement to a department and agency of the United States, to wit, the Tower Commission, in a matter within its jurisdiction, to wit, the examination of the role of the NSC staff in national security operations, as follows: that the defendant FERNANDEZ did not know that the supplies the defendant FERNANDEZ assisted in delivering to the Contras in September 1986 contained weapons and ammunition.

3. That statement and representation was false, fictitious and fraudulent because in truth and in fact, as the defendant JOSEPH F. FERNANDEZ then and there well knew and believed, among other things, the supplies that the defendant FERNANDEZ helped deliver to the Contras in September 1986 contained weapons and ammunition.

(Violation of Title 18, United States Code, Section 1001.)

-17-

<u>COUNT FIVE</u>

(False Statement to the CIA's Office of Inspector General)

The Grand Jury further charges:

1.   Paragraphs 1 through 27 of Count One of this Indictment are repeated, realleged and incorporated by reference herein as if fully set forth in this Count.

2.   On or about January 11, 1987, in the Eastern District of Virginia, the defendant JOSEPH F. FERNANDEZ unlawfully, willfully and knowingly did make and cause to be made a material false, fictitious and fraudulent statement to a department and agency of the United States, to wit, the CIA's Office of Inspector General, in a matter within its jurisdiction, to wit, the investigation of unlawful and unauthorized CIA support for military and paramilitary operations in Nicaragua by the Contras, as follows: that a project to build an airstrip in northern Costa Rica in 1985 was an initiative of the Costa Rican government to be used for training activities by Costa Rican forces in preparation for a possible Nicaraguan invasion of Costa Rica.

3.   That statement and representation was false, fictitious and fraudulent because in truth and in fact, as the defendant JOSEPH F. FERNANDEZ then and there well knew and believed, among other things, the project to build an airstrip in northern Costa Rica was not an initiative of the Costa Rican government, but rather was an initiative of the defendant

-18-

FERNANDEZ and his co-conspirators, among others, designed to facilitate the resupply of the Contras.

(Violation of Title 18, United States Code, Section 1001.)

A TRUE BILL:

_____
FOREPERSON

_____
LAWRENCE E. WALSH
INDEPENDENT COUNSEL

TAB-B

IN THE UNITED STATES DISTRICT COURT FOR THE

EASTERN DISTRICT OF VIRGINIA

Alexandria Division

UNITED STATES OF AMERICA	)	CRIMINAL NO.
	)	
v.	)	VIOLATIONS:
	)	
JOSEPH F. FERNANDEZ	)	18 USC 1505
	)	Obstruction of
	)	Proceedings
	)	(Counts 1 and 3)
	)	
	)	18 USC 1001
	)	False Statements
	)	(Counts 2 and 4)

INDICTMENT

APRIL 1989 TERM - At Alexandria

COUNT ONE

THE GRAND JURY CHARGES THAT:

INTRODUCTION

1.   At all times relevant to this Indictment, the
Central Intelligence Agency ("CIA") was the principal United
States Government agency responsible for the collection of
foreign intelligence and the conduct of covert action and
foreign intelligence operations.

2.   At all times relevant to this Indictment, the
defendant JOSEPH F. FERNANDEZ was an employee of the CIA,
serving as the chief of station in Costa Rica. As the CIA
chief of station, the defendant FERNANDEZ had immediate
control over and responsibility for all CIA operations in
Costa Rica. The defendant FERNANDEZ reported to and received

supervision from the Chief of the CIA's Central American Task Force, who was stationed at CIA headquarters in Langley, Virginia.

3.   At all times relevant to this Indictment, the National Security Council ("NSC") was a government entity established by the National Security Act of 1947, whose statutory members were the President of the United States, the Vice President, the Secretary of State and the Secretary of Defense. At all times relevant to this Indictment, other officials were also members of the NSC by appointment of the President. The function of the NSC was to advise the President on the integration of domestic, foreign and military policies relating to the national security, to facilitate cooperation among the military services and other departments and agencies of the government in matters involving the national security, and to review, guide and direct foreign intelligence and covert action activities.

4.   At all times relevant to this Indictment, the Contras, also known as the Nicaraguan democratic resistance, were military insurgents engaged in military and paramilitary operations in Nicaragua. In many instances, these operations occurred near the borders of Costa Rica and Honduras, Nicaragua's neighboring countries to the south and north, respectively.

5.   From in or about December 1981 to on or about October 11, 1984, the United States Government, acting

principally through the CIA, pursuant to written presidential findings, provided the Contras with financial support, arms and military equipment, as well as supervision, instruction, tactical and other advice, coordination, intelligence and direction.

6.   On October 12, 1984, Public Law 98-473 was enacted and expressly prohibited funds, including salaries, available to the CIA as well as certain other agencies and entities of the United States, from being obligated or expended in support of military or paramilitary operations in Nicaragua. This provision of law was commonly known as the Boland Amendment.

7.   On August 12 and December 4, 1985, Congress adopted modifications to the Boland Amendment that authorized the provision of humanitarian aid to the Contras, including communications equipment and communication training, and allowed United States government employees to exchange information with the Contras, including "advice" on the "effective delivery and distribution of materiel." At all times between October 12, 1984 and October 17, 1986, however, the CIA was prohibited from spending funds (including funds for salaries and transportation) for activities that "amount[ed] to participation in the planning or execution of military or paramilitary operations in Nicaragua by the Nicaraguan democratic resistance, or to participation in logistics activities integral to such operations." As of

October 18, 1986, Congress again authorized the CIA to provide military aid to the Contras.

8.   At no time during the period October 12, 1984 through October 17, 1986, was any member of the NSC staff authorized by a presidential finding to undertake any covert or special activities with respect to Nicaragua, including any of the covert or special activities previously undertaken by the CIA. At all times during this period, Oliver L. North was a member of the NSC staff.

9.   On October 6, 1986, a plane carrying lethal supplies for delivery to the Contras was shot down over Nicaragua. The sole survivor of this incident was an American citizen named Eugene Hasenfus.

10.   In early November 1986, reports appeared in the foreign and domestic press that the United States Government had participated in the shipment of arms to Iran.

11.   On November 25, 1986, the Attorney General of the United States announced that proceeds from the arms transfers to Iran may have been diverted to assist the Contras.

12.   In late November 1986, the CIA's Office of Inspector General began an investigation into possible unlawful and unauthorized CIA support for military and paramilitary operations in Nicaragua by the Contras.

13.   On January 11, January 24 and February 2, 1987, the defendant JOSEPH F. FERNANDEZ met with an investigator working for the CIA's Office of Inspector General at CIA

Headquarters, Langley, Virginia, to answer questions with respect to that Office's inquiry.

14. From on or about January 11, 1987 to March 1, 1987, in Fairfax County, within the Eastern District of Virginia, the defendant JOSEPH F. FERNANDEZ unlawfully, willfully and knowingly did corruptly influence, obstruct and impede and endeavor to influence, obstruct and impede the due and proper administration of the law under which a pending proceeding was being had before a department and agency of the United States, to wit, the conduct of an investigation by the CIA's Office of Inspector General into possible unlawful and unauthorized CIA support for military and paramilitary operations in Nicaragua by the Contras, by making false, fictitious, fraudulent and misleading statements and representations to an inspector of the CIA's Office of Inspector General, including false statements more fully set forth in Count Two of this Indictment, for the purpose of concealing and causing to be concealed material facts.

(Violation of Title 18, United States Code, Section 1505.)

COUNT TWO

THE GRAND JURY FURTHER CHARGES THAT:

15. Paragraphs 1 through 13 of Count One of this Indictment are repeated, realleged and incorporated by reference herein as if fully set forth in this Count.

16. On or about January 11, 1987, in Fairfax County, within the Eastern District of Virginia, the defendant JOSEPH F. FERNANDEZ unlawfully, willfully and knowingly did make and cause to be made material false, fictitious and fraudulent statements to a department and agency of the United States, to wit, the CIA's Office of Inspector General, in a matter within its jurisdiction, to wit, an investigation into possible unlawful and unauthorized CIA support for military and paramilitary operations in Nicaragua by the Contras, as follows: that a project to build an airstrip in northern Costa Rica in 1985 was an initiative of the Costa Rican government; that the airstrip was to be used for training activities by Costa Rican forces in preparation for a possible Nicaraguan invasion of Costa Rica; and that the defendant FERNANDEZ's only contacts with Rafael Quintero were on the occasions of resupply flights.

17. Those statements and representations were false, fictitious and fraudulent because in truth and in fact, as the defendant JOSEPH F. FERNANDEZ then and there well knew

and believed, among other things, the project to build an
airstrip in northern Costa Rica was an initiative of the
defendant FERNANDEZ and others; the airstrip was designed to
facilitate the resupply of the Contras; and the defendant
FERNANDEZ had numerous contacts with Rafael Quintero in
connection with matters other than the resupply flights,
including the construction of the airstrip in northern Costa
Rica.

(Violation of Title 18, United States Code, Section 1001.)

COUNT THREE

THE GRAND JURY FURTHER CHARGES THAT:

18. Paragraphs 1 through 11 of Count One of this Indictment are repeated, realleged and incorporated by reference herein as if fully set forth in this Count.

19. On December 1, 1986, the President established a Special Review Board, also known as "the Tower Commission," to examine the proper role of the National Security Council staff in national security operations, including the arms transfers to Iran. Among its areas of inquiry, the Tower Commission was authorized to examine all of the circumstances. surrounding the "Iran/Contra matter."

20. On January 21, 1987, the defendant JOSEPH F. FERNANDEZ met with investigators working for the Tower Commission at CIA Headquarters, Langley, Virginia, to answer questions with respect to the Tower Commission's inquiry. On January 28, 1987, the defendant FERNANDEZ testified before the Board of the Tower Commission.

21. From on or about January 21, 1987 to January 28, 1987, in Fairfax County, within the Eastern District of Virginia, the defendant JOSEPH F. FERNANDEZ unlawfully, willfully and knowingly did corruptly influence, obstruct and impede and endeavor to influence, obstruct and impede the due and proper administration of the law under which a pending

proceeding was being had before a department and agency of
the United States, to wit, the Tower Commission's conduct of
a fact-finding inquiry on behalf of the President, by making
false, fictitious, fraudulent and misleading statements and
representations to representatives of the Tower Commission,
including false statements more fully set forth in Count Four
of this Indictment, for the purpose of concealing and causing
to be concealed material facts.

(Violation of Title 18, United States Code, Section 1505.)

COUNT FOUR

THE GRAND JURY FURTHER CHARGES THAT:

22. Paragraphs 1 through 11 of Count One and paragraphs 19 and 20 of Count Three of this Indictment are repeated, realleged and incorporated by reference herein as if fully set forth in this Count.

23. On or about January 21, 1987, in Fairfax County, within the Eastern District of Virginia, the defendant JOSEPH F. FERNANDEZ unlawfully, willfully and knowingly did make and cause to be made material false, fictitious and fraudulent statements to a department and agency of the United States, to wit, the Tower Commission, in a matter within its jurisdiction, to wit, the examination of the role of the NSC staff in national security operations, as follows: that the defendant FERNANDEZ did not know for a fact that Oliver L. North had been involved in assisting the resupply of the Contras; and that the defendant FERNANDEZ did not know that the supplies the defendant FERNANDEZ assisted in delivering to the Contras in September 1986 contained weapons and ammunition.

24. Those statements and representations were false, fictitious and fraudulent because in truth and in fact, as the defendant JOSEPH F. FERNANDEZ then and there well knew and believed, among other things, Oliver L. North had been

-10-

involved in assisting the resupply of the Contras; and the
supplies that the defendant FERNANDEZ helped deliver to the
Contras in September 1986 contained weapons and ammunition.

(Violation of Title 18, United States Code, Section 1001.)

A TRUE BILL:

_____

LAWRENCE E. WALSH
INDEPENDENT COUNSEL

TAB – C

UNITED STATES DISTRICT COURT FOR THE DISTRICT OF COLUMBIA

UNITED STATES OF AMERICA   :

      v.   :   Crim. No. 88-0236

JOSEPH F. FERNANDEZ,   :

    Defendant.   :

FILED

AUG 1 9 1988

CLERK, U.S. DISTRICT COURT,
DISTRICT OF COLUMBIA

ORDER

    Upon consideration of the Defendant's Motion to Dismiss the Indictment for Violations of the Fifth Amendment and 18 U.S.C. § 6001 et seq. or, in the Alternative, to Dismiss Count Five of the Indictment and to Order Discovery and an Evidentiary Hearing, the Government's Opposition thereto, the Defendant's Reply and the arguments advanced at the hearing held on August 16, 1988, it is by the Court this ___ day of August, 1988,

    ORDERED, that the Government shall provide to the Defendant and the Court the following:

    1) Affidavit(s) detailing the independent source of each proposed trial witness who was interviewed after Defendant gave immunized testimony and each exhibit the government plans to introduce at trial, including the date each witness was interviewed, the substance of the witness' proposed testimony, any contact the witness had with Defendant's immunized testimony, the date each exhibit was first located and obtained, the date the government determined that such witness or exhibit would be useful at

EXHIBIT 1

-2-

trial, and the basis of the government's decision that such witness or exhibit would be useful at trial[1].

2) a list of all CIA personnel interviewed after the date Defendant gave immunized testimony, which list shall include the date of each interview and the basis of each interview;

3) any transcripts (other than grand jury transcripts), notes or memoranda prepared in connection with interviews referred to in the preceding paragraph;

4) the "Douglass file", to the extent said file contains references to Defendant's immunized testimony; and

5) the same or similar materials relied upon by the Court in United States v. Poindexter, Cr. No. 88-0080, (D.D.C. June 16, 1988)(Appendix), to the extent they were made available to the Defendants in that case and to the extent they relate to the investigation and testimony of Defendant Fernandez; and it is

FURTHER ORDERED, that in addition to the materials described above the government shall submit to the Court for in camera review the following:

1) affidavit(s) detailing the independent source

---

1. Although the Court expects that the government will construe this paragraph liberally to include witnesses and exhibits it is not yet sure it will introduce, the failure of the government to list a witness or exhibit will not preclude introduction of such witness' testimony or exhibit; instead, such witness' testimony or exhibit's admissibility will be determined during trial.

-3-

of any witness the government may introduce at trial who was not interviewed after the Defendant gave immunized testimony, including the date the witness was interviewed, the substance of the witness' proposed testimony, any contact the witness had with Defendant's immunized testimony, the date the government determined that such witness would be useful at trial, and the basis for the government's determination that such witness would be useful at trial;

2) the transcribed portions of the grand jury proceedings, including all testimony given and all grand jury exhibits;

3) an index of all subpoenas issued during the course of the investigations;

4) the same or similar materials relied upon the Court in <u>United States v. Poindexter</u>, <u>supra</u>, but which were not made available to those defendants and have not been made available to this Defendant pursuant to this Order and which relate to the investigation of this Defendant; and it is

FURTHER ORDERED, that any materials disclosed pursuant to this Order shall be filed and remain under seal pending further Order of this Court and Defendant shall treat the materials accordingly; and it is

FURTHER ORDERED, that the government shall submit the materials no later than September 22, 1988; and it is

FURTHER ORDERED, that the Defendant will have an

-4-

opportunity to submit materials in opposition, including affidavits, contesting the claim that the evidence the government proposes to use has been derived from sources wholly independent of Defendant's immunized testimony, and the date by which Defendant will have to submit his materials in opposition will be determined either by further written Order or in open Court at the next scheduled hearing in this matter; and it is

FURTHER ORDERED, that the Court reserves the right to disclose to the Defendant any information submitted to the Court <u>in camera</u>, and further reserves the right to conduct an evidentiary hearing pretrial, but it is the Court's expectation that the documentary submissions will allow the Court to determine preliminarily whether the trial should go forward, subject to any post-trial proceedings that may prove necessary; and it is

FURTHER ORDERED, that in light of the foregoing the Motion to Dismiss is DENIED without prejudice to renewal.

Aubrey E. Robinson, Jr.
Chief Judge

TAB – D

Office of the Attorney General
Washington, D. C. 20530

<u>ATTORNEY GENERAL'S GUIDELINES FOR</u>

<u>PROSECUTIONS INVOLVING CLASSIFIED INFORMATION</u>

1. Introduction

The determination of whether it is appropriate to decline prosecution of a violation of federal law is a matter within the discretion of the Executive Branch. It is the policy of the Department of Justice that where it is believed that a person has committed a federal offense and there is sufficient evidence to secure conviction, prosecution should be sought unless no substantial federal interest would be advanced by the prosecution or unless there are other substantial federal interests that would be served by declining prosecution.

This principle was among those articulated in the recently published "Principles of Federal Prosecution." [1] Paragraph 2 of Part B of the "Principles", which addresses the decision to decline prosecution, provides that:

> The attorney for the government should commence or
> recommend federal prosecution if he believes that the
> person's conduct constitutes a federal offense and that
> the admissible evidence will probably be sufficient to
> obtain and sustain a conviction, unless, in his judgment,
> prosecution should be declined because:
>
> (a) no substantial federal interest would be served
> by prosecution;

---

[1] The "Principles of Federal Prosecution," which apply to all federal prosecutions, were published by the Department of Justice in July 1980, and are set out in section 9-27.000 of the U.S. Attorneys' Manual.

EXHIBIT A

- 2 -

(b) the person is subject to effective prosecution
in another jurisdiction; or

(c) there exists an adequate non-criminal alternative
to prosecution.

However, in cases in which there is a possibility that classified
information may be revealed if the prosecution is pursued, an additional
consideration must be addressed in determining whether it is appropriate to
continue with the investigation or prosecution; that is, whether the need
to protect against the disclosure of the classified information outweighs
other federal interests that would be served by proceeding with the
prosecution. In such cases, therefore, it is the responsibility of the
Department of Justice, in consultation with the agency or agencies whose
classified information is involved, to identify and assess these competing
interests so that a reasoned decision may be made with respect to continuing
the investigation or prosecution.

The purpose of these guidelines is to identify those factors which
should be considered in determining whether to prosecute a violation of
federal law where it appears that there is a possibility that classified
information will be revealed if prosecution is pursued. While these
guidelines do not provide an exhaustive list of all factors which may
properly have a bearing on this determination, an attempt has been made to
enumerate those factors which are most important and are likely to arise
with some frequency.

2. Ceneral Provisions

a. Authority. These guidelines are issued pursuant to section 12(a)
of the Classified Information Procedures Act of 1980 (Pub. L. No. 96-456,
94 Stat. 2025), which provides in pertinent part that:

- 3 -

... the Attorney General shall issue guidelines
specifying the factors to be used by the Department
of Justice in rendering a decision whether to prosecute
a violation of Federal law in which, in the judgment of
the Attorney General, there is a possibility that
classified information will be revealed.

b. <u>Definitions</u>. As used in these guidelines--

(1) the term "classified information" means any information or
material that has been determined by the United States Government,
pursuant to an Executive order, statute, or regulation, to require
protection against unauthorized disclosure for reasons of national
security and any restricted data, as defined in paragraph r of section
11 of the Atomic Energy Act of 1954 (42 U.S.C. 2014(y)); and

(2) the term "national security" means the national defense
and foreign relations of the United States.

c. <u>Functions of the Attorney General</u>. The functions and duties of
the Attorney General under these guidelines may be exercised by the Deputy
Attorney General, Associate Attorney General, or an appropriate Assistant
Attorney General. However, the exercise of these functions and authorities
by an official other than the Attorney General shall in no way limit the
authority of the Attorney General to review, reverse, or amend any decision
made under these guidelines.

3. <u>Initiating or Declining Prosecution</u>

a. <u>Determination of the propriety of initiating or declining prosecution.</u>
Where, in the judgment of the Attorney General, it appears that the
prosecution of a violation of federal law may result in the disclosure of
classified information, the Attorney General shall determine whether the
potential damage to the national security that might result from such
disclosure outweighs other federal interests that would be served by the

- 4 -

prosecution of the offense. If it is determined, after review of all
relevant factors, that the potential damage to national security interests
posed in prosecuting such a case outweighs other federal interests in
proceeding with prosecution, prosecution of the offense may be declined.

In making this determination, the Attorney General shall assess all
relevant information and evidence, consult with and seek the advice of the
appropriate interested departments and agencies, and, whenever appropriate,
fully utilize the procedures set out in the Classified Information Procedures
Act of 1980 in order to assess more accurately the probability that
classified information would be disclosed if the case were prosecuted, and
the likely nature and extent of such disclosure.

b. Factors bearing on the decision to initiate or decline prosecution.

In rendering a decision whether to prosecute a violation of federal
law where there is a possibility that classified information may be
revealed, the following factors, among others, should be considered:

(1) The likelihood that classified information will be revealed
if the case is prosecuted. All relevant considerations bearing on
this issue should be weighed, including:

(a) whether it will be necessary for the government to
reveal classified information publicly in order to establish an
element of the offense;·

(b) whether the introduction of classified information
will be sought by the defendant as a means of establishing a
defense;

(c) whether the government will be required to disclose
classified information to the defendant under the Brady doctrine,
the Jencks Act, or in fulfillment of due process or other
requirements;

- 5 -

(d) the likelihood that, under the procedures of the
Classified Information Procedures Act, classified information
sought to be disclosed publicly by the defendant would be found
to be inadmissible, or the government would be permitted to use
a substitute for the disclosure of specific classified information;

(e) the number and nature of persons to whom disclosure
of classified information may be necessary, and the nature and
extent of protective measures that may be available to prevent
disclosure beyond authorized recipients; and

(f) whether the government's refusal to permit disclosure
of classified information would result in dismissal of the
indictment or a lesser sanction.

(2) The damage to the national security that might result if
the classified information is revealed. All relevant considerations
bearing on this issue should be weighed, including:

(a) the nature and extent of anticipated harm to the
foreign relations or national defense of the United States;

(b) the level of classification and sensitivity of the
information at issue;

(c) the extent of any previous unauthorized disclosure of
the information; and

(d) the likelihood that disclosure of classified
information in the course of the prosecution would confirm the
accuracy of classified information previously unsubstantiated.

- 6 -

(3) <u>The likelihood that the government would prevail if the case were prosecuted</u>. As in all federal prosecutions, in any case where proceeding with prosecution may result in disclosure of classified information, the likelihood of a successful prosecution based on the available evidence should be established.

(4) <u>The nature and importance of other federal interests that would be served by prosecution</u>. Although an assessment of the federal interests that would be served by prosecution is a consideration in the decision to prosecute any case, where proceeding with prosecution may result in the disclosure of classified information that would create a risk of damage to the national security, all relevant considerations bearing on this issue should be carefully weighed, including:

(a) the seriousness of the offense charged;

(b) the extent of the prospective defendant's involvement in the commission of the offense;

(c) the likely sentence that would be imposed if conviction were obtained;

(d) the likely deterrent effect of conviction; and

(e) the availability of adequate non-criminal alternatives to prosecution.

4. <u>Reservation</u>

a. <u>Relation to the authority of the Attorney General</u>. Nothing in these guidelines shall be construed to limit the authorities or responsibilities of the Attorney General under the Constitution or laws of the United States.

- 7 -

b. _Non-litigability._ The guidelines set forth herein are solely for
the purpose of internal Department of Justice guidance. They are not
intended to, do not, and may not be relied upon to create a right or
benefit, substantive or procedural, enforceable at law by any party to any
matter, civil or criminal.

5. _Term and Effective Date_

These guidelines shall become effective on June _10_, 1981, and shall
remain in effect until modified in writing by the Attorney General.

Issued this _10_ th day of June, 1981.

WILLIAM FRENCH SMITH
Attorney General

TAB – E

U.S. Department of Justice

Office of Legislative Affairs

Office of the Assistant Attorney General   Washington, D.C. 20530

OCT 2 4 1990

Honorable Anthony C. Beilenson
Chairman, Permanent Select Committee
   on Intelligence
House of Representatives
Washington, D.C. 20515

Dear Mr. Chairman:

Your Committee has oversight responsibility for the operation
of the Classified Information Procedures Act (CIPA), 18 U.S.C.
App. IV, § 13. In that capacity, you have expressed a continuing
interest in the CIPA aspects of <u>United States v. Joseph F.
Fernandez</u>, Crim. No. 89-150-A, Eastern District of Virginia, an
Ethics in Government Act prosecution brought by the Iran-Contra
Independent Counsel. As a result, I am writing to advise you of
recent developments under CIPA in the <u>Fernandez</u> case.

You will recall that on November 22, 1989, the Attorney
General filed a declaration under section 6(e) of CIPA precluding
the disclosure of two categories of classified information which
have been referred to generally as "programs" and "facilities."
The district court had ruled that the defendant could disclose
those categories of information at trial.

The Attorney General's declaration urged further judicial
examination of the rulings which had caused him to invoke
section 6(e). It was hoped that such examination would provide a
basis for accommodating both the defendant's rights and the
national security interests at stake, thereby allowing the
<u>Fernandez</u> case to be tried to conclusion. The declaration further
stated that, as expressly permitted by CIPA, the Attorney General
would reconsider his invocation of section 6(e) in light of a
resulting appellate court decision on the issue.

Following dismissal of the case, the Independent Counsel did
pursue an appeal. On September 6, 1990, the United States Court
of Appeals for the Fourth Circuit affirmed the district court
rulings. Copies of both the public, unclassified version of the
court of appeals opinion and the classified version are enclosed
for your information. Enclosures 1 and 2. As a result of the
appellate decision, the Attorney General proceeded with a thorough

2

reconsideration of his invocation of CIPA § 6(e). That process
culminated on October 12, 1990, with a notification to the district
court that the Attorney General had concluded that he had no
alternative but to continue his invocation of section 6(e).

The Attorney General's decision on reconsideration was
essentialy predetermined when the Independent Counsel agreed during
the pretrial CIPA proceedings to have classified information
evaluated by broad categories rather than on an item-by-item basis,
as required by CIPA. Section 6(a) of CIPA requires an evaluation
of "each item of classified information." The Independent
Counsel's tactical decision to have the district court evaluate
the potentially admissible information on a categorical basis
resulted in the court of appeals opinion that all the information
in two broad categories was relevant and admissible. Consequently,
the Attorney General was only allowed to decide whether to risk
admission of all of the classified information or continue to
invoke section 6(e). He could not selectively invoke section 6(e)
in such a way that would enable the prosecution to proceed with the
least possible damage to the national security. Because admission
of all of the classified information would seriously damage the
national security, the Attorney General had no choice but to
protect it in its entirety.

This Department sought to compel compliance with CIPA's
pretrial item-by-item review procedure as part of an appeal which
we filed in July 1989. The Independent Counsel opposed our
position concerning the inadequacy of the category approach to CIPA
both in his brief (IC Reply Brief at 20, n.13) and at oral argument
(Oral Argument Transcript at 10-13). The issue was not resolved
since the court of appeals ruled that, in the context of an Ethics
in Government Act case, only the Independent Counsel has authority
to pursue an appeal. <u>Appeal of the United States by the Attorney
General</u>, 887 F.2d 465 (4th Cir. 1989).

Subsequently, after the prosecution was dismissed by the trial
court, the Independent Counsel initiated his own appeal. In so
doing, he reversed his position, arguing that the district court
had erred in making "generalized" and "blanket" rulings which
failed to apply the CIPA procedures to each item of classified
information. IC's Opening Brief at 17, 34. However, the
Independent Counsel was not in a position to pursue this argument
effectively, since his own prosecutors had agreed to the district
court's use of the category approach to CIPA. Indeed, the court
of appeals noted that "it is incongruous for the [Independent
Counsel] to be complaining about the very CIPA process which it
urged on the court below." Unclassified Opinion at 19.

3

As a result of the Independent Counsel's tactical decision during the pretrial CIPA proceedings, the Attorney General was placed in the position of reconsidering the CIPA § 6(e) invocation in <u>Fernandez</u> without knowing the scope of the classified information that might be admitted at trial. This defeats the express purpose of CIPA to "permit the government to ascertain the potential damage to national security . . . before trial." S. Rep. 823, 96th Cong., 2d Sess. 1 (1980). Without item-by-item pretrial rulings, "the deck is stacked against proceeding" with the case because the Attorney General has no choice but to base his determination on <u>all</u> the classified information which <u>might</u> be disclosed at trial. <u>Id</u>. at 4.

Although the "programs category" is comprised of several programs, each of which has a myriad of classified details, the district court simply issued a generalized ruling that information in this category could be disclosed by the defendant at trial. The court deferred to trial any rulings concerning the degree of detail that would be permitted in such disclosures.

In contrast, the district court's ruling on the "facilities category" seemed to be somewhat more specific. According to the Independent Counsel, under this category the defendant could disclose only "the <u>existence</u> of [the facilities]." Memorandum to the Attorney General from Lawrence E. Walsh at 5 (July 18, 1989) (emphasis in original). Enclosure 3. That memorandum went on to state that the category did not include "operational details" about or "descriptions of any programs being run . . . at these facilities." <u>Id</u>. at 6. However, the court of appeals concluded that under this category the defendant could disclose not only the locations but also the activities of and details about those facilities. Unclassified Opinion at 28, 39. As with the program category, the degree of detail that would be permitted about the facilities would be determined during trial.

The "category" approach to CIPA conflicts sharply with the intent of the CIPA legislation. At best, this approach defines the general areas of classified information at issue, although it cannot even be relied on to accomplish that, as demonstrated by what has occurred with the facilities category. Under the category approach, all rulings concerning specific items of classified information are deferred to trial. In contrast, CIPA provides, in section 6(a), for a pretrial hearing at which the court is to "make all determinations concerning the use, relevance, or admissibility of classified information that would otherwise be made during trial." Such determinations are to be made "as to each item of classified information."

4

The Senate Report which constitutes the primary body of legislative history for CIPA makes clear that the pretrial procedures contained in section 6 are "the heart of the bill." S. Rep. 823, supra, at 7. Indeed, the Report specifies that the "purpose of the bill" is to "permit the government to ascertain the potential damage to national security of proceeding with a given prosecution before trial." Id. at 1. "Without a procedure for pretrial rulings on the disclosure of classified information, the deck is stacked against proceeding with cases because all of the sensitive items that might be disclosed at trial must be weighed in assessing whether the prosecution is sufficiently important to incur the national security risks" (emphasis added). Id. at 4.

Notwithstanding this problem, the Attorney General undertook a full and thorough reconsideration of his prior invocation of CIPA § 6(e). As part of that reconsideration, the Acting Assistant Attorney General in charge of the Criminal Division convened a meeting of the general counsel of the pertinent federal agencies to explore at length the potential for accommodating the interests of both national security and the Fernandez prosecution. Changes in circumstances since last November which might impact on the programs and facilities were examined. The Attorney General was advised of the results of that meeting and was provided detailed written evaluations prepared by CIA, NSA, and the State Department. Enclosures 4, 5, and 6. Thereafter, the Attorney General convened a meeting of the heads of the pertinent agencies, or their designated representatives, at which the national security implications of public disclosure were re-examined. Further, a summary was prepared of the key national security considerations. Enclosure 7, pp. 3-9.

The reconsideration process also considered the views previously expressed by the Independent Counsel concerning the appropriateness of invoking section 6(e). In July 1989, the "Independent Counsel requested that the Department of Justice file an affidavit under CIPA § 6(e) to block disclosure of classified information about the . . . programs." Opening Brief of Independent Counsel in Appeal of the United States by the Attorney General at 6 (July 27, 1989). Indeed, in his July 18, 1989, memorandum to the Attorney General, the Independent Counsel stated that his office "completely supported" the intelligence agency concerns for protection of the programs. Memorandum to the Attorney General from Lawrence E. Walsh, supra, at 4, n.1. While that same memorandum urged that section 6(e) not be invoked as to the facilities, that recommendation was based on the express understanding that it was only the "existence" of the facilities which would be disclosed at trial and not any information concerning "operational details" about or "descriptions of any

5

programs being run . . . at these facilities." <u>Id</u>. at 5, 6. Based
on the court of appeals decision, we now know that such details and
programs are among the information which would be available to the
defendant. Accordingly, the facilities category has now been shown
to include information which is directly analogous to that
contained in the programs category, a type of information which the
Independent Counsel "completely supported" protecting from
disclosure.

Under the concept embodied in CIPA § 6, the national security
concerns are to be balanced against the importance of preserving
the viability of the particular prosecution. However, in rejecting
this Department's standing to pursue an appeal in <u>Fernandez</u>, the
Court of Appeals for the Fourth Circuit concluded that,

> [w]hen independent counsel is prosecutor, the Attorney
> General need not balance the threat of public disclosure
> against the threat of ending the prosecution, because the
> Ethics in Government Act removes from his purview the
> possibility that his actions may end the prosecution.
> In this case, then, the Attorney General's only
> responsibility under CIPA is protection of classified
> information.

<u>Appeal of the United States by the Attorney General</u>, <u>supra</u>,
887 F.2d at 470.

The fact is that the application of this position to Iran-
Contra prosecutions would have prevented cases such as <u>Poindexter</u>,
<u>North</u>, <u>Secord</u>, and <u>Hakim</u> from proceeding to conclusion. The
Independent Counsel recognized, in his second interim report to
Congress, that such Iran-Contra cases could not have proceeded
without the help of the intelligence agencies, working together
with this Department, in responding conscientiously to "massive
requests for declassification."   Independent Counsel's Second
Interim Report to Congress at 60.

The Attorney General considered it important to preserve the
viability of the <u>Fernandez</u> case if at all possible. As a result,
he has sought to factor into his reconsideration decision the
relative significance of that case. The Department is, of course,
at a disadvantage in assessing the importance of a prosecution
brought by an independent counsel. However, those who are familiar
with the case assess it as a relatively weak one which would not
have been brought had Fernandez been willing to cooperate with the
investigation.   While a criminal conviction might assist the
Independent Counsel in gaining Fernandez' cooperation, other
mechanisms are available in the Federal criminal justice system to
elicit that cooperation.

6

In reaching the appropriate balance of interests under section 6(e) of CIPA, the Attorney General took into account the unanimous recommendation of the heads of the pertinent agencies that the prior section 6(e) declaration not be withdrawn. The potentially serious damage to national security which could result from the disclosure of the two categories of information is exacerbated by the prospect for additional disclosures at trial. In the words of one senior official, the damage could be "devastating." In contrast, while it is never easy to countenance the dismissal of an indicted case based on an unavailability of evidence, the damage to the Independent Counsel's overall inquiry appears to be far less significant and could even prove to be negligible. In this context the Attorney General concluded that he had no alternative but to leave the CIPA § 6(e) declaration in place.

It is, of course, not possible to assess with any degree of certainty whether the invocation of CIPA § 6(e) in _Fernandez_ could have been averted had the Independent Counsel not acquiesced in the application of CIPA by categories rather than on an item-by-item basis. What is clear, however, is that the category approach "stacked the deck" against the pretrial refinement of the case to a point where it could be tried consistent with national security constraints. In contrast, the Independent Counsel's trial team in _Poindexter_ scrupulously complied with the procedures of CIPA, thereby eliciting from the trial court fully refined pretrial rulings. As a result, in spite of the more extensive and diverse classified information problems that existed in _Poindexter_, it was tried to conclusion while the _Fernandez_ case has foundered.

Sincerely,

W. Lee Rawls
Assistant Attorney General

Enclosures

TAB - F

IN THE UNITED STATES DISTRICT COURT
EASTERN DISTRICT OF VIRGINIA
Alexandria Division

UNITED STATES OF AMERICA,	)
	)
v.	) Cr. No. 89-150-A
	)
JOSEPH F. FERNANDEZ	)
	)

NOTICE OF LODGING

The attached letter, on behalf of the Attorney General of the United States, is hereby lodged with this court for the purpose of advising it of the Attorney General's decision not to withdraw the declaration previously filed in this case on November 22, 1989, under section 6(e) of the Classified Information Procedures Act, 18 U.S.C. App. IV.

Respectfully submitted,

JAMES S. REYNOLDS
Criminal Division
U.S. Department of Justice
P.O. Box 887, Ben Franklin Station
Washington, D.C. 20044-0887
202-514-1038

U.S. Department of Justice

Washington, D.C. 20530

OCT 12 1990

Honorable Claude M. Hilton
Judge of the United States District Court
Eastern District of Virginia
200 South Washington Street
Alexandria, Virginia 22314

Dear Judge Hilton:

On November 22, 1989, the Attorney General filed a declaration under section 6(e) of the Classified Information Procedures Act (CIPA) in <u>United States v. Joseph F. Fernandez</u>, Crim. No. 89-150-A. The purpose of that declaration was to notify you formally of his objection, pursuant to his official responsibilities under CIPA, to the disclosure of two categories of classified information which you had ruled to be available to the defendant at trial. Those categories of information have been referred to generally during the course of the litigation as programs and locations.

The Attorney General's declaration urged further judicial examination of the rulings which caused him to invoke section 6(e). It was hoped that such examination would provide a basis for accommodating both the defendant's rights and the national security interests at stake, thereby allowing the <u>Fernandez</u> case to be tried to conclusion. The declaration further stated that, as expressly permitted by CIPA, the Attorney General would reconsider his invocation of section 6(e) in light of a resulting appellate court decision on the issue.

Following the dismissal of the case, the Independent Counsel did pursue an appeal. On September 6, 1990, the United States Court of Appeals affirmed your ruling. As a result, the Attorney General proceeded with a thorough reconsideration of his prior invocation of CIPA § 6(e).

That reconsideration process has been complicated in that during pretrial CIPA proceedings the Independent Counsel acquiesced in having the classified information evaluated by categories rather than on an item-by-item basis, thereby circumventing the prescription in section 6(a) of CIPA that "each item of classified information" be separately evaluated. Further, the appellate

2

ruling provides that the defendant can disclose not only the locations but also activities at those locations. As a result, the Attorney General is placed in a position of discharging his responsibilities under section 6(e) of CIPA without full knowledge of the specific items of classified information that would be disclosed at trial.

In re-evaluating the CIPA § 6(e) declaration, the Attorney General elicited detailed input from the government agencies charged with national security responsibilities. He also chaired a meeting with the heads of those agencies or their designated representatives. It was their unanimous recommendation that the section 6(e) declaration not be withdrawn. The potentially serious damage to national security which could result from the disclosure of the two categories of information is exacerbated by the prospect for additional disclosures at trial. One senior official described the potential harm which could result as "devastating."

In this context, the Attorney General concluded that he has no alternative but to continue his invocation of CIPA § 6(e). Accordingly, on behalf of the Attorney General, I hereby advise you that the section 6(e) declaration filed last November will not be withdrawn.

Sincerely,

James S. Reynolds
Principal Deputy Chief
General Litigation and
    Legal Advice Section
Criminal Division

CERTIFICATE OF SERVICE

This is to certify that on this 12th day of October 1990, I have caused copies of the attached documents to be delivered to the offices of the following persons:

Lawrence E. Walsh, Esq.
Office of Independent Counsel
Suite 701 West
555 13th Street, N.W.
Washington, D.C. 20004

Thomas E. Wilson, Esq.
Seyfarth, Shaw, Fairweather & Geraldson
815 Connecticut Avenue, N.W.
Washington, D.C. 20006-4004

JAMES S. REYNOLDS
Criminal Division
U.S. Department of Justice
P.O. Box 887, Ben Franklin Station
Washington, D.C. 20044-0887
202-514-1038

TAB-G

IN THE UNITED STATES DISTRICT COURT FOR THE
EASTERN DISTRICT OF VIRGINIA
Alexandria Division

UNITED STATES OF AMERICA   )
)

v.   )   Criminal NO. 89-150-A

)

JOSEPH F. FERNANDEZ,   )

)

    Defendant.   )

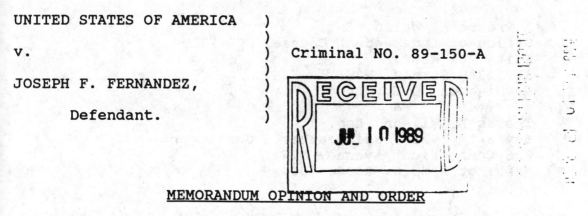

MEMORANDUM OPINION AND ORDER

This matter came before the court on defendant's motion to suppress evidence under the precedent established by _Kastigar v. United States_, 406 U.S. 441 (1972) and to order discovery and hold an evidentiary hearing on the matter.[1] While the court has written on several other aspects in this case, a brief explanation of the background of the case may be helpful in addressing this issue.

The underlying case is one of several to arise out of the Congressional investigation of the Iran-Contra Affair.[2] That investigation consisted of approximately 40 days of

---

[1] Mr. Fernandez also requested that his indictment be dismissed because he felt tainted materials were used to procure his indictment. That request has been dealt with in a previous opinion issued June 15, 1989.

[2] An incident in November 1986, when Congress undertook to investigate its suspicion that the administration was trafficking arms to Iran to bring about the release of American hostages and that the proceeds had been diverted to the Nicaraguan contras for military assistance at a time when Congress has legislated to bar such aid to these resistance forces.

public hearings conducted by Select Investigation Committees chosen from each house, followed by closed executive hearings on the matter. The public hearings commenced May 5, 1987. Prior to this, in December, 1986, the President appointed a Special Review Board, known as the Tower Commission, to conduct an investigation of the same disclosures. Also during this time period, Attorney General Meese sought appointment of an Independent Counsel to investigate possible criminal conduct in the same matter. Lawrence E. Walsh was appointed to fill this position on December 19, 1986.

As the inquiries moved forward, Congress sought the testimony of certain individuals, including in time, that of Mr. Fernandez, former CIA Chief of Station in Costa Rica. When Mr. Fernandez refused to testify, asserting his Fifth Amendment right against possible self-incrimination, he was granted use immunity pursuant to 18 U.S.C. §6001 et seq. (1982 & Supp. II 1984). His testimony was then compelled in the spring of 1987.

On June 20, 1988, a criminal indictment was returned in the District of Columbia charging defendant with violations in connection with the investigation. That case was eventually dismissed for venue reasons. Then, on April 24, 1989, Mr. Fernandez was indicted in the Eastern District of Virginia and charged with the four violations which constitute the case against him at this point: Count One charges defendant with obstructing a proceeding under 18

U.S.C. § 1505 (1982) by making false and misleading statements to the CIA's Office of Inspector General (OIG) about his role in supporting the Contras while CIA Chief of Station in Costa Rica; Count Two charges defendant with making false statements to the OIG concerning his involvement with an airstrip in Costa Rica used to support the Contras, in violation of 18 U.S.C. § 1001 (1982); Count Three charges defendant with obstructing a proceeding under 18 U.S.C. § 1505 by making false and misleading statements to the Tower Commission about his involvement with efforts to resupply the Contras; Count Four charges defendant with making false statements to the Tower Commission about his involvement with and knowledge of the Contra resupply effort, in violation of 18 U.S.C. § 1001.

Mr. Fernandez now claims that the immunized testimony he was compelled to give in the spring of 1987 is being used against him, thereby violating his Fifth Amendment rights and the use immunity he was granted when compelled to testify. The immunity statute, 18 U.S.C. §6002, provides in pertinent part:

> "no testimony or other information compelled under the order (or any information directly or indirectly derived from such testimony or other information) may be used against the witness in any criminal case, except a prosecution for perjury, giving a false statement, or otherwise failing to comply with the order." Id.

In Kastigar, the Supreme Court prescribed that the scope of the "use and derivative use" immunity was "coextensive with

3

the scope of the Fifth Amendment privilege against compulsory self-incrimination." Kastigar, supra at 448. Furthermore, Kastigar emphasized the "heavy burden" of proof borne by the United States to prove that they "had an independent, legitimate source for the disputed evidence," adding that such burden "is not limited to the negation of taint; rather it imposes on the prosecution the affirmative duty to prove that the evidence it proposes to use is derived form a legitimate source wholly independent of the compelled testimony." Id. at 460. Thus, the prosection must prove that it was not "led", directly or indirectly, to the discovery of evidence through the immunized testimony. United States v. Poindexter, 698 F.Supp. 300, 306 (D.D.C. 1988).

Accordingly, the court ordered the Office of the Independent Counsel to make pre-trial filings in camera to demonstrate the precautions taken to ensure that no use of defendant's immunized testimony was or will be made and to demonstrate the independent sources for all the evidence it will present in the Fernandez case. The court has reviewed, in camera, the submissions by the government of the body of evidence they had collected prior to Fernandez's immunized testimony, their efforts to identify the source of all subsequent additions, and their efforts to segregate such untainted material from any tainting influences; excerpts of grand jury transcripts documenting the precautions taken to avoid use of any immunized testimony; documentation of the

4

precautions taken by Independent Counsel to avoid taint from exposure to publicity and immunized testimony, including a memorandum issued the week before Fernandez was to testify warning all personnel to renew their attention to such matters; and substantial proof of Independent Counsel's legitimate independent leads to every significant witness or document.

On the basis of these filings, the court has determined that neither further discovery nor a pre-trial <u>Kastigar</u> hearing will be necessary. The defendant testified under a grant of immunity on three separate dates: April 20, May 4, and May 29, 1987. These sessions were closed to the public. The court has received written materials from the Independent Counsel demonstrating that most of the prosecutor's witnesses and documents were known to him before the first grant of immunity, and that those that were not were developed from legitimate sources independent from any immunized testimony.

In addition, from the outset, Independent Counsel undertook to enforce a prophylactic system which prevented any members of that office directly involved in the prosecution from being exposed, directly or indirectly, to the immunized testimony. Prosecuting personnel were sealed off from exposure to the immunized testimony and any publicity concerning it. They were instructed to shut off television or radio broadcasts that approached the discussion of the immunized testimony. The Independent Counsel

5

mandated use of a special form which required a description of any new evidence or lead and the identification of the source for that piece of evidence or lead.

In light of the foregoing, the court reaches its preliminary decision that the case should proceed to trial. The extensive precautions taken, coupled with the proper questioning of witnesses prior to their testimony to determine whether a given witness can testify from his or her personal knowledge and separate such testimony from any direct or indirect basis in defendant's immunized testimony, satisfies the court that defendant's Fifth Amendment rights have been and can be adequately protected as the case proceeds to trial. Specific objections to the introduction of evidence can be dealt with at the time of trial.

Accordingly, the court finds:

1. The prosecuting attorneys and Independent Counsel have not read the immunized testimony.

2. The staff at the Office of the Independent Counsel were aware of the witnesses to be called at trial and essential documents, either long before any immunized testimony was given by the defendant, or through legitimate means wholly distinct from any immunized testimony of the defendant. In fact, in many cases its investigators had already been in direct contact with the witnesses or already had possession of the proposed documents.

3. The Office of the Independent Counsel has at all times

proceeded in good faith and taken strenuous precautions to safeguard defendant's Fifth Amendment rights.

4. The government has preliminarily met its "heavy burden" under Kastigar, to demonstrate the legitimate, independent sources for all of its evidence to be presented at trial. The inquiry has uncovered no action by the government that has infringed the protection against the direct or indirect use of defendant's compelled testimony and no basis has appeared pre-trial to warrant a full blown Kastigar hearing or the preclusion of any pieces of evidence at this point in the proceedings.

5. Defendant's rights can be adequately protected by the precautions already taken, specific objections at the time of trial as necessary, and a thorough questioning of witnesses before they take the stand. Such questioning will require the witnesses to make sure that their answers to questions are based solely on their own personal knowledge and recollection of the events in question, and prohibit them from relating anything which they learned for the first time as a result of listening to or reading or hearing about immunized testimony.

For the foregoing reasons, the court concludes that a pre-trial Kastigar hearing is not warranted. The case shall proceed to trial, at which point a determination will be made on each witness through voire dire targeting possible derivation from immunized testimony and on each piece of

7

other evidence through specific objections pertaining to its derivation from immunized testimony. And it is so ordered.

_____

_____
UNITED STATES DISTRICT JUDGE

Alexandria, Virginia
July 10, 1989

TAB-H

STATEMENT OF MR. LEONARD COLE BLACK

I, Leonard Cole Black, make the following statement at the request of Mr. Daniel Marino, Esq.:

I am now, and have been for over six years, a member of the Office of Inspector General, Central Intelligence Agency (CIA). At some time in early 1988 Mr. Larry Schtasel of the Office of Independent Counsel-Iran/Contra (OIC) visited my office accompanied by one other member of the OIC and a member of CIA's Office of General Counsel. It was my understanding that Mr. Schtasel intended on that occasion to ask me questions regarding my investigation of certain activities involving Mr. Joseph F. Fernandez during his service as Chief of Station in a Central American country.

As an introductory matter, Mr. Schtasel told me that I would be responsible for ensuring that I gave him no information derived from my exposure to immunized testimony presented by certain witnesses before the U.S. House of Representatives Select Committee to Investigate Covert Arms Transactions With Iran and the U.S. Senate Select Committee on Secret Military Assistance to Iran and the Nicaraguan Opposition, hereafter referred to as the "Joint Committee." (As part of my responsibilities, I had viewed portions of the

EXHIBIT 20

testimony on television, listened to other portions on the
radio, and reviewed extensively certain printed records of the
hearings.) I told Mr. Shtasel that I could not as a practical
matter--and would not as a matter of principle--accept that
responsibility. I explained that my knowledge of
Mr. Fernandez' activities, and indeed the entire Iran-Contra
matter, was a continuum. Accordingly, there was some doubt in
my mind that I would be able to distinguish immunized testimony
from non-immunized information. I assured him that I would
answer all questions as completely and as accurately as
possible, but I would not allow him to shift the burden of
shielding him from immunized testimony to me. Mr. Shtasel
became visibly agitated, and insisted that I do so. When I
again refused, he left my office.

        Subsequently, on May 11, 1988, I was interviewed by Mr.
Shtasel in his office, preparatory to my appearance before the
Grand Jury investigating the Iran-Contra affair. Another
member of the OIC was also present. Mr. Shtasel began the
interview by reading from a prepared statement which was
designed to inform me that I would be responsible for ensuring
that none of my responses to his questions would include
information derived from the immunized testimony of witnesses
before the Joint Committee. I reminded Mr. Shtasel of our
previous confrontation on this matter, and once again refused

to accept that responsibility. During a protracted and somewhat heated exchange, Mr. Shtasel notified me that he would read the same statement before the Grand Jury on the following day. I told Mr. Shtasel that I wanted to be as cooperative as possible and I did not want to embarrass him before the Grand Jury, but that I would once again refuse to accept the responsibility. After an additional exchange, during which Mr. Shtasel frequently raised his voice and flailed his arms, I proposed the following solution to the dilemma: he would read the prepared statement before the Grand Jury and I would reply simply, "Yes, I understand." It was clearly understood at the time by Mr. Shtasel that my response would mean I understood his statement but would <u>not</u> mean that I had agreed to accept the responsibility.

Following my preparatory session with Mr. Shtasel, I discussed my concerns about the impact of immunized testimony on any statements I might make before the Grand Jury with Mr. Jeff Gibbs, the representative of CIA's Office of General Counsel who had accompanied me to Mr. Shtasel's office. I explained to him the compromise that had been worked out.

The following day I testified before the Grand Jury for approximately two hours. Prior to my testimony, and in front of the Grand Jury, Mr. Shtasel read the same prepared statement relating to immunized testimony that he had read to me the day before. When he asked if I understood the instruction, I replied, "Yes, I understand," or words to that effect. He did not ask me if I believed I could comply with that instruction. Based on our previous discussions, he most certainly knew my response would be, "No."

During my testimony before the Grand Jury, Mr. Shtasel asked me several questions relating to Mr. Fernandez' role in the construction of a clandestine airstrip in a certain Central American country. Specifically, he wanted me to repeat the varying responses Mr. Fernandez had made over a period of several weeks when I questioned him about his involvement with this airstrip. It is my recollection that at some point he asked me if I believed, based on Mr. Fernandez' responses, that he had lied to me. I responded, "He at least misled me." While I believed this to be a reasonable conclusion based on my three formal interviews with Mr. Fernandez, I cannot state unequivocally that my response was not influenced by Mr. Fernandez' statements before the Joint Committee.

Upon reflection on my Grand Jury testimony, it seems to me that to say Mr. Fernandez "lied to me" or "misled me" implies a conscious intent on his part to distort the truth. Although I have used those exact phrases--and others--to characterize at various times Mr. Fernandez' responses to my questions, there was always some doubt in my mind regarding his intent. (Mr. Fernandez was not available to me during the closing weeks of my investigation, so any confusion or contradictions in his responses remained unresolved.) It was not until Mr. Fernandez testified before the Joint Committee that the construction of the clandestine airstrip had been <u>his</u> "initiative" that I was finally certain of his intent. It is therefore a possibility that this testimony influenced my response to Mr. Shtasel's question before the Grand Jury.

Based on my discussion of the events in this case with Mr. Marino and Mr. Tom Wilson, the former prepared an initial draft of this statement for my signature. That draft required extensive changes to reflect my actual recollection of the facts. This statement is the truth to the best of my knowledge and belief.

                                          Leonard Cole Black
                                           Leonard Cole Black

WITNESSED BY: DATE:

Nancy Grundman   _6/8/8_
 Nancy Grundman

TAB – I

SUPPLEMENTAL STATEMENT OF MR. LEONARD COLE BLACK

I, Leonard Cole Black, make the following statement at the request of Thomas E. Wilson, counsel for Joseph F. Fernandez, a former CIA Chief of Station. This statement supplements my statement of June 20, 1988, which I provided at the request of Daniel Marino, an attorney with Mr. Wilson's law firm.

Subsequent to my appearance on May 12, 1988 before the District of Columbia Grand Jury investigating the Iran/Contra Affair, I was interviewed by Mr. William Hassler of the Office of Independent Counsel ("OIC"). Mr. Jeff Gibbs, a member of CIA's Office of General Counsel accompanied me to this meeting. Although Mr. Gibbs was not present at the interview I discussed it with him after it was over.

During my interview with Mr. Hassler, he informed me that the OIC planned to have me appear before the Alexandria Grand Jury investigating the activities of Mr. Fernandez. I reminded Mr. Hassler of the position that I had taken in connection with my District of Columbia Grand Jury appearance concerning my ability to distinguish what I had learned about Mr. Fernandez's activities from his immunized testimony before the U.S. House of Representatives Select Committee to Investigate Covert Arms Transactions with Iran and the U.S. Senate Select Committee on

EXHIBIT 16

- 2-

Secret Military Assistance to Iran and the Nicaraguan
Opposition (hereinafter referred to as the "Joint Committee"),
and what I had learned from non-immunized sources.

As set forth in my June 20, 1988 statement, I had informed
Laurence Shtasel of the OIC, on two separate occasions, that "I
could not as a practical matter -- and would not as a matter of
principle -- accept" the responsibility for providing only
information derived from non-immunized sources. During my
subsequent meeting with Mr. Hassler, I emphasized to him that
my views on this subject had not changed and that I was
unwilling to accept the burden of shielding the OIC and the
Alexandria Grand Jury from Mr. Fernandez's immunized testimony.

Thereupon, Mr. Hassler and I agreed that the compromise
which was worked out prior to my District of Columbia grand
jury appearance would be used again in connection with my
Alexandria Grand Jury testimony. Pursuant to that compromise,
Mr. Hassler would read before the Grand Jury a prepared
statement which was designed to inform me that I would be
responsible for ensuring that none of my responses to his
questions would include information derived from the immunized
testimony of witnesses before the Joint Committee. I would

— 3 —

then reply simply, "Yes, I understand." I made it clear to Mr. Hassler that my response would mean only that I understood his statement; it would <u>not</u> mean that I had agreed to accept the responsibility for not providing information derived from immunized testimony.

On February 7, 1989, I appeared before the Alexandria Grand Jury for approximately two hours. Prior to my testimony, and in front of the grand jury, Mr. Hassler read the same prepared statement relating to immunized testimony that Mr. Shtasel had read prior to my testimony before the District of Columbia Grand Jury and to which Mr. Hassler had referred during our preparatory meeting. When Mr. Hassler asked if I understood the instruction, I replied, "Yes, I understand," or words to that effect. I do not recall Mr. Hassler asking me if I believed that I could comply with that instruction. Based on our previous discussions, Mr. Hassler knew that, were he to have asked that question, my response would have been, "No."

During my testimony before the Alexandria Grand Jury that followed, Mr. Hassler appeared to attempt to limit his questions to what Mr. Fernandez had told me during my several interview sessions with him during January and early

- 4 -

February 1987. There is no doubt in my mind, however, that my impressions with respect to Mr. Fernandez and his activities in connection with the Iran/Contra Affair were significantly affected by my reading Mr. Fernandez's immunized testimony. In particular, my perception of Mr. Fernandez was substantially influenced by his testimony before the Joint Committee that the construction of a clandestine airstrip in Central America was his "initiative," or words to that effect.

Also, during the course of my Alexandria Grand Jury appearance, Mr. Hassler, evidently surprised by some of my answers to his questions, on at least two occasions, summoned me outside of the Grand Jury room. Once outside the Grand Jury room, Mr. Hassler and I discussed my answers to his questions with respect to issues before the Grand Jury in order to elicit the particular answers he desired. Mr. Shtasel was present on each occasion but I do not recall whether or not he participated in the discussions. Mr. Hassler and I then returned to the Grand Jury room where I continued my testimony. On each occasion, Mr. Hassler rephrased his questions in an attempt to obtain responses more to his liking.

Based on my discussion of the foregoing events with

- 5 -

Mr. Wilson and Mary Beth Sullivan of his office, they prepared
an initial draft of this statement for my review and
signature. I then made changes to that draft in order to
ensure that the information contained herein reflects
accurately my recollection of the events in question to the
greatest extent possible.

   This statement is the truth to the best of my knowledge and
belief.

                                        Leonard Cole Black
                                        Leonard Cole Black

                                        Dated:
                                        27 April 91

WITNESSED BY:

DATE:

TAB-J

IN THE UNITED STATES DISTRICT COURT

FOR THE DISTRICT OF COLUMBIA

UNITED STATES OF AMERICA,	)
	)
v.	)
	) Criminal No. 88-0236 (AER)
JOSEPH F. FERNANDEZ,	)
	)
Defendant.	)
	)

AFFIDAVIT OF NANCY D. GRUNDMAN

I, Nancy D. Grundman, being duly sworn, do hereby depose and say as follows:

1.   I am of sufficient age and competent to testify concerning the following facts as to which I have personal knowledge.

2.   I am a paralegal at the law firm of Seyfarth, Shaw, Fairweather and Geraldson ("Seyfarth, Shaw"), 1111 19th Street, N.W., Washington, D.C. 20036.

3.   On May 5, 1988, I accompanied Thomas E. Wilson, Esq., of Seyfarth, Shaw, counsel for Joseph F. Fernandez, defendant in Criminal No. 88-0236 (AER) (D.D.C.), to CIA Headquarters, Langley, Virginia. During that trip to CIA Headquarters, we interviewed Louis Dupart for approximately three-quarters of an hour. Mr. Dupart served as staff member of the CIA's Central American Task Force ("CATF") from approximately June 1985 through May 1988.

EXHIBIT 15

- 2 -

4. During the interview, Mr. Dupart stated that he had followed the joint Iran/Contra Congressional hearings that took place during the summer of 1987 very closely. He said that he had taken a personal interest in the hearings, because he was familiar with some of the events and personalities involved in those proceedings, and a professional interest because, as the Compliance Officer for the CATF, he felt obliged to keep abreast of the hearings in order to brief his superiors on pertinent developments.

5. Shortly after Mr. Fernandez testified on May 29, 1987 under a grant of immunity before the Committees sitting in executive session, Mr. Dupart secured a copy of the transcript of that testimony and read it more than once. In fact, Mr. Dupart annotated the transcript and made it available to any CIA personnel who wished to see it.

6. Mr. Dupart further stated that, between early 1987 and April 1988, he was interviewed by various representatives of the Office of Independent Counsel ("OIC") on twelve separate occasions. On Wednesday, April 27, 1988, he testified before the grand jury for approximately three hours. Mr. Dupart informed us that, during several of his many interviews with the OIC, he was <u>not</u> warned that he should avoid providing any information derived from immunized testimony.

7. Mr. Dupart explained that he believes the Congressional testimony helped him put together pieces of the Iran/Contra puzzle. He stated that he was fascinated and

- 3 -

enthralled by the Congressional hearings because they filled out a mosaic of something of which he had been a part. Mr. Dupart told us that it would have been impossible for his mental impressions of the events relating to the Iran/Contra Affair, including Mr. Fernandez's alleged involvement, not to have been influenced by the Congressional hearings, including Mr. Fernandez's compelled testimony.

Further affiant sayeth not.

Nancy B. Grundman

Subscribed to and sworn before
me this 22nd day of July, 1988

Bonnie V. Jones
Notary Public

My Commission expires

                    March 14, 1988

Norman H. Gardner, Jr.

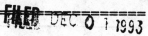

United States Court of Appeals
For the District of Columbia Circuit

FILED DEC 0 1 1993

RON GARVIN
CLERK

IN THE
UNITED STATES COURT OF APPEALS
FOR THE DISTRICT OF COLUMBIA CIRCUIT

Division No. 86-6

IN RE: Sealed Comments
(NORMAN H. GARDNER, JR.)

Division For the Purpose of
Appointing Independent Counsel
Ethics in Government Act of 1978, Amended

**COMMENTS OF NORMAN H. GARDNER, JR.
ON THE FINAL REPORT OF THE INDEPENDENT COUNSEL
INVESTIGATING THE IRAN/CONTRA AFFAIR**

John F. Conroy
GORDON & BARNETT
1133 21st Street, N.W.
Suite 450
Washington, D.C. 20036
(202) 833-3400

Counsel for Norman H.
Gardner, Jr.

December 1, 1993

UNITED STATES COURT OF APPEALS
DISTRICT OF COLUMBIA CIRCUIT

IN RE: Sealed Comments

(NORMAN H. GARDNER, JR.)

)   Division For the Purpose of
)   Appointing Independent Counsel
)   Ethics in Government Act of 1978,
)   Amended
)
)   Division No. 86-6
)
)   **(FILED UNDER SEAL)**

**COMMENTS OF NORMAN H. GARDNER, JR.
ON THE FINAL REPORT OF THE INDEPENDENT COUNSEL
INVESTIGATING THE IRAN/CONTRA AFFAIR**

The Final Report of the Independent Counsel
investigating Iran/Contra (Final Report) contains several
references to Mr. Norman Gardner, and he has, accordingly, been
afforded an opportunity to review and comment on those portions
of the Final Report in which he is mentioned. The following
remarks upon those portions of the Final Report constitute Mr.
Gardner's comments regarding it.

At all times pertinent to the Iran/Contra
investigation, Mr. Gardner served as a special assistant to the
Deputy Director for Operations of the Central Intelligence
Agency, Mr. Clair George. In that role the Independent Counsel's
report mentions Mr. Gardner approximately eight times, but only
two references to him appear to contain assertions of active
participation in obstructive conduct. These comments will deal
with those two "detailed" assertions, without making an effort to
comment on every reference to Mr. Gardner in the Final Report.
The reader will be asked, however, to evaluate any inferences of
wrongdoing he or she might read into other references to Mr.

Gardner in light of the fairness and accuracy of the two "detailed" assertions upon which he now comments.

Those "detailed" assertions against Mr. Gardner essentially suggest that he may have been involved in a "concerted effort to withhold information from, or lie to, Congress" (Final Report, p. 323). Specifically, it is claimed that by invoking his 5th Amendment privilege against self-incrimination when called before an Iran/Contra grand jury, Mr. Gardner frustrated efforts to make a case involving such charges. This claim is untrue, and it is inconceivable that the Independent Counsel, in preparing his report, did not know it to be untrue.

I. CIA Officer #7

In the first of the two "detailed" references to Mr. Gardner's activities, he is accused of helping to frustrate efforts by the Independent Counsel to determine if the CIA was aware of the pre-employment activities of one CIA Officer #7, and to determine whether the Agency's knowledge regarding CIA Officer #7, if any, was conspiratorially withheld from Congress. To demonstrate that such a conspiracy existed, and that it might be inferred that Mr. Gardner was somehow a party to it, the Independent Counsel points, at pp. 237-240 of the Final Report, to Mr. Gardner's invocation of 5th Amendment privilege when called before the Iran/Contra grand jury on August 7, 1991. At that time he was asked three questions about CIA Officer #7:

1. Whether he knew a CIA Officer #7;

2.   Whether, prior to October 14, 1986 he had been aware of CIA Officer #7's connections with the private benefactor organization that flew out of **[classified]** to assist the Contras or Nicaraguan resistance forces; and

3.   Whether, prior to Clair George's appearance before the House Permanent Select Committee on Intelligence on October 14, 1986 he had informed Clair George of what he knew about CIA Officer #7's connection with the private benefactors in terms of resupplying the Contras.

The import of the Independent Counsel's reference to Mr. Gardner's invocation of privilege, which did in fact take place, is that Mr. Gardner was withholding, and the Independent Counsel was therefore unable to determine, Gardner's state of knowledge regarding the activities of CIA Officer #7, and, more particularly, the answers to the three questions posed. The truth is quite different.

In early 1987 Mr. Gardner began a course of interviewing with the Independent Counsel, and testifying before Iran/Contra grand juries, with the status of a "witness", and without the benefit of counsel. Counting both informal interviews and appearances before Iran/Contra grand juries, Mr. Gardner cooperated in giving information and testimony to the Independent Counsel on 10 separate occasions during this investigation.

In 1990, during the trial of <u>United States v. Poindexter</u>, Mr. Gardner was subpoenaed as a defense witness. After testifying for the defense, he was cross-examined by an

Associate Independent Counsel who was prosecuting Admiral
Poindexter.   The cross-examination was based in part on an FBI
Form 302, Summary of Interview, which is a written report made by
an FBI agent, and which purported to summarize an OIC office
interview of Mr. Gardner in June, 1987. See, United States v.
Poindexter, Transcript of Trial, pp. 2671-2674. Mr. Gardner was
asked several questions by this Associate Independent Counsel
regarding the extent of, and timing of, his knowledge of the HAWK
missile shipment to Iran of November 25, 1985. He was challenged
with the suggestion that he had at an earlier time recited a
different version of events. Mr. Gardner denied that he had done
that, but believed his credibility had been damaged by the misuse
of the FBI 302 report, which Mr. Gardner knew to be inaccurate.
On redirect examination, Mr. Gardner had an opportunity to direct
the jury's attention to some of the dozens of mistakes in the FBI
302 (United States v. Poindexter, Transcript of Trial, pp. 2703-
2705), but he remained upset that the Office of Independent
Counsel had chosen to cross-examine him on the basis of a
document which the prosecutors had to have known to be seriously
flawed. He believed that the petit jury was unfairly being asked
to believe that he had somehow changed an earlier story and was
therefore an untrustworthy witness. To prevent this from
happening again, Mr. Gardner laid down conditions for future
cooperation with the Independent Counsel. He said he would speak
to the Independent Counsel only before a grand jury where his
responses would be transcribed, pursuant to a subpoena, and with

his status as a "witness" set forth in writing and read into the record of proceedings.

With that background, Mr. Gardner received a communication from the Independent Counsel's office in April, 1991 requesting him to cooperate further with their ongoing inquiry into Iran/Contra. He said he would do so, but only if his previously stated conditions were met, because he did not trust the accuracy of the FBI's 302 reports, and did not want to permit the creation of inaccurate documents which could be used against him unfairly in the future.

The Independent Counsel accepted Mr. Gardner's conditions, and on April 19, 1991 he was subpoenaed as a "witness" directly into the grand jury. His status as a "witness" was read into the record, and, still without benefit of counsel, he was then questioned for about 3 1/2 hours. One of the primary areas of questioning was his knowledge of, dealings with, and reporting on, the activities of CIA Officer #7. Mr. Gardner testified for almost forty transcript pages (Grand Jury testimony of April 19, 1991, pp. 36-64) about CIA Officer #7 and stopped only when the Associate Independent Counsel ran out of questions. His memory for details was not complete, but he responded to every question. He told the grand jury he had met and interviewed CIA Officer #7, had taken detailed notes of the interview, and had left those notes behind at the CIA when he retired. He testified about how CIA Officer #7 came to his attention, how and why he had determined to send him to the CIA General Counsel's office to tell his story, why he did not perceive CIA Officer #7's activities prior to joining the Agency to be of concern to the Agency, and that he did not recall if he had briefed Clair George on this interview, but that if it took place prior to a Congressional hearing, he probably had done so. Mr. Gardner's testimony about CIA Officer #7 ceased after questions about CIA Officer #7 were exhausted, and not before. He answered, fully and to the best of his ability, every question put to him regarding CIA Officer #7, and every other topic about which the OIC chose to question him.

On July 16, 1991 Mr. Gardner received another telephone call from an FBI agent working for the Independent Counsel. Mr. Gardner was being sought once again to be "interviewed" by the Independent Counsel. He said he would voluntarily do so, but again only on the terms he had now established. The FBI agent hung up, and within one-half hour, Mr. Gardner was called by an Associate Independent Counsel and advised his status in the investigation had been upgraded to that of a subject, and he was asked if he intended to get a lawyer. He answered that he did not know, because of the expense involved, and the telephone conversation concluded. The next day he was served with a grand jury subpoena identifying him as a subject, and the day following that he retained counsel.

Mr. Gardner's lawyer, at the time he was retained, did not possess a security clearance that would permit him to discuss anything substantive about Iran/Contra with Mr. Gardner, but promptly made applications for the necessary security clearances. While these clearances were being sought, the Independent Counsel insisted on Mr. Gardner appearing before the grand jury. His

counsel protested that Mr. Gardner's unfettered right to

assistance of counsel would be denied him if counsel was not

fully cleared to discuss all the facts involved. The Independent

Counsel took the position that an interim, SECRET security

clearance, which Mr. Gardner's counsel was given almost

immediately, would suffice. An impasse was reached and Mr.

Gardner, through counsel, filed a Motion For Protective Order

aimed at modifying his subpoena. (Attachment 1.) The

Independent Counsel was also advised that Mr. Gardner's lawyer

was sufficiently concerned about the 6th Amendment considerations

involved in the matter that if his Motion For Protective Order

were to be denied, he would have Mr. Gardner invoke his privilege

against self-incrimination until such time as proper clearances

and full counselling could be provided. (Attachment 2.) With

regard to the legitimacy of the concern Mr. Gardner's counsel

expressed regarding the level of his security clearance, it is

noteworthy that every page of transcript from the April 19, 1991

grand jury session, when Mr. Gardner discussed CIA Officer #7,

has been classified TOP SECRET and was, therefore, inaccessible

to counsel while he held no more than an interim, SECRET

clearance.

After a hearing on August 7, 1991, the Motion For

Protective Order directed to the grand jury subpoena was denied

by the District Court (Attachment 3), Mr. Gardner was taken into

the grand jury, and, over counsel's protest, was compelled to

recite over and over again before the grand jury his claim of 5th

Amendment privilege. His interrogation on this occasion was
conducted before the same grand jury that had heard his testimony
in April, and his questioner was the same prosecutor who
interrogated him then. He was asked the three questions about
CIA Officer #7 set out on p. 3, *infra*. To each question, upon
the advice of counsel, he responded by invoking his 5th Amendment
privilege. When the prosecutor was satisfied that an adequate
record had been made, Mr. Gardner was excused. Within a month
counsel had obtained TOP SECRET clearance, but Mr. Gardner was
never called again and no effort was ever made to immunize him.

Now, in his Final Report, the Independent Counsel says
he could not get information regarding CIA Officer #7 from Mr.
Gardner because of his claim of privilege before the grand jury.
A complete review of the facts makes clear that that
representation is false, and that the Independent Counsel must
know it is false. The questions asked of Mr. Gardner before the
grand jury on August 7, 1991, at a time when the Independent
Counsel knew that for technical reasons Mr. Gardner was under
counsel's instruction to invoke privilege, were designed to
create an impression that information was being denied the
prosecutors, but the questions were the same ones he had already
answered in April. That false impression has now been
memorialized in the Independent Counsel's report. The truth is
the Independent Counsel knew the answers to the questions Mr.
Gardner was asked on August 7, 1991 because Mr. Gardner had
answered them under oath on April 19, 1991. To create the
impression that information from Mr. Gardner was denied to the

Independent Counsel, and that that denial somehow impeded the
Independent Counsel's investigation, is deceitful. This slight
of hand with the known facts is particularly deplorable in view
of the fact that the Final Report is designed to stand as the
definitive statement of what actually occurred during the
Independent Counsel's efforts to resolve the Iran/Contra
controversy.

II.   The November 25, 1985 Flight

The second "detailed" reference in the Final Report to
Mr. Gardner's activities relates to a shipment of HAWK missiles
to Tehran, Iran on November 25, 1985, utilizing an airplane owned
and operated by a CIA proprietary airline. According to the
Final Report:

> ...the evidence suggests a
> concerted effort by CIA officials
> to withhold information from, or
> lie to, Congress about the 1985
> shipment of HAWK missiles to Iran.

(Final Report, p. 323.)

This alleged misconduct could not be prosecuted, says
the Independent Counsel, in part because Mr. Gardner, when asked
about his knowledge of the flight of November 25, 1985, took the
5th Amendment and later refused to make a proffer of information
to the Independent Counsel. Once again, the implication that Mr.
Gardner was withholding information from the Independent Counsel
is demonstrably false.

9

A. **The Invocation of Privilege**

Mr. Gardner's invocation of his 5th Amendment privilege
before the grand jury occurred at the same grand jury appearance
as did his refusal to testify about CIA Officer #7, and his
privilege was invoked for the same technical reason, involving
his attorney's security clearance. Again the Associate
Independent Counsel questioning him was fully aware that Mr.
Gardner had already revealed his knowledge regarding the
November 25, 1985 arms shipment to Tehran to prosecutors, not
just once, but twice, and had even testified to every detail of
it in United States v. Poindexter (see Transcript of Trial, pp.
2640-2708).

In October, 1987, Mr. Gardner gave a lengthy interview
to an Associate Independent Counsel and an FBI agent, with the
agent again acting as note-taker, in which he talked almost
exclusively about the November 25, 1985 flight, and his knowledge
of it in 1985. At his April 19, 1991 grand jury appearance he
was questioned further about that flight for 44 transcript pages.
He stopped answering only when the prosecutor ran out of
questions. This episode took place before the same grand jury
and Associate Independent Counsel that questioned Mr. Gardner on
August 7, 1991. In the trial of United States v. Poindexter, the
substance of his testimony related entirely to the November 25,
1985 flight and the consequences flowing from it.

At the 1987 interview Mr. Gardner indicated he was
aware that a CIA proprietary airline might be involved in the
November 25, 1985 shipment before the flight took place, but that

he believed the cargo was being sent by Israel to Iran. He
believed the cargo was oil drilling equipment, he understood that
Oliver North was involved in the matter, and he guessed the
flight might be connected to the release of hostages.

At his April 19, 1991 grand jury appearance he
testified that he had forgotten the agency's involvement in the
November 25, 1985 flight as the CIA went about, in November 1986,
reconstructing its involvement in the "arms for hostages"
initiative with Iran. He testified that he did not recall this
flight until sometime after November 18, 1986, and subsequent to
helping Director Casey prepare for his Congressional testimony on
November 19, 1986. (See Grand Jury transcript, April 19, 1991 at
pp. 122, 134.) At the trial of Admiral Poindexter he testified
to these same recollections, adding only anecdotal details.

Mr. Gardner testified that he was specifically reminded
of the flight, and the CIA's role in it, by November 20, 1986 as
Director Casey was finalizing his testimony. Director Casey,
voluntarily and without prompting, informed the Congress of the
CIA's involvement in the November 25, 1985 flight on the morning
of November 21, 1986 in his prepared remarks to the House
Permanent Select Committee on Intelligence.

The Independent Counsel may wish to press the notion
that a conspiracy to withhold information from Congress with
regard to the November 25, 1985 flight to Tehran existed at the
CIA between November 18, 1986, when Clair George briefed
Congressional staffers there without identifying any CIA "arms
for hostages" involvement in 1985, and November 21, 1986, when

Director Casey disclosed it to Congress, however strained such a theory might appear. It should be remembered, in that regard, that Director Casey disclosed the flight and the CIA's involvement at his first opportunity before Congress, that Deputy Director George cannot be found to have had knowledge of the flight during his November 18, 1986 briefing, and that no evidence exists to establish that Norman Gardner failed to report any information he had to anyone, or in any other way was involved in a cover-up of information.

What is abundantly clear about the November 25, 1985 flight, however, is that by invoking his 5th Amendment privilege before the grand jury on August 7, 1991, Mr. Gardner did not deny the Independent Counsel access to his version of events relating to it. The facts are that the very prosecutor who questioned Mr. Gardner had already heard sworn answers to the questions Mr. Gardner was asked on August 7th the previous April 19th, before the same grand jury. He also had a copy of Mr. Gardner's FBI 302 interview and his <u>Poindexter</u> trial testimony to use for comparative evaluation. It apparently somehow suited the prosecutor's purpose to embarrass Mr. Gardner before the grand jury by having him invoke privilege to questions he had already answered, but it certainly did not deny to the Independent Counsel Mr. Gardner's recollection of events. To permit the Final Report to state that it did, and that that denial frustrated prosecution, is more than unfair to the facts, it is a manifest injustice to Mr. Gardner.

12

Norman Gardner was made a subject of the Iran/Contra investigation one week after Alan Fiers entered a guilty plea to withholding information from Congress. Alan Fiers implicated Clair George, Mr. Gardner's boss, in similar activity. To make a case against Mr. George, the Independent Counsel used its prosecutive muscle in an effort to intimidate Mr. Gardner into providing information he had said he did not have. That is what his grand jury appearance on August 7, 1991 was all about, not a search for an untold story.

B.   The Failure to Proffer

In very late October or early November, 1991, Mr. Gardner's attorney received a telephone call from an Associate Independent Counsel advising that the Office of Independent Counsel (OIC) was considering how to "proceed" in Mr. Gardner's situation. Specifically, counsel was advised that the OIC had a list of questions that it wanted Mr. Gardner to answer, or comment on, and that in order to evaluate Mr. Gardner's responses to these questions, it would accept a "proffer" from Mr. Gardner's attorney. In this case, a proffer was to involve counsel previewing for the prosecutors what answers his client would give if, in the future, Mr. Gardner were to be asked certain questions. The prosecutors through this process would evaluate the value to their prosecution of these prospective replies and offer counsel some appropriate "benefit" for his client if those previewed answers were subsequently given as evidence.

13

On November 5, 1991 Mr. Gardner's attorney met with
three Associate Independent Counsels in furtherance of the
process of proferring. At that time Mr. Gardner had not been
approached by the Office of Independent Counsel since invoking
his 5th Amendment privilege on August 7, 1991 before the grand
jury. His lawyer, on November 5, 1991, reminded the prosecutors
that if they wanted Mr. Gardner to testify, based upon what they
already knew, they could immunize him. They advised they wanted
further information, listed numerous questions to which they
wanted further response, and allowed Mr. Gardner's attorney to
make note of them, but they never responded to the suggestion
that Mr. Gardner be immunized. Mr. Gardner's attorney left that
meeting to review matters with his client.

At their subsequent review it became clear to Mr.
Gardner and his counsel that due to the repetitious nature of the
questions asked, he could not successfully proffer information
without some possibility of coming into conflict with earlier
sworn testimony. At this point, more than four years had passed
since Mr. Gardner's first formal interview with investigators,
and he had provided information on 10 separate occasions. The
Independent Counsel's office nonetheless refused to permit him
the opportunity to review his prior testimony before giving
further testimony. Thus, if he decided to cooperate, he was
going to face the prospect of a perjury charge if he made a
mistake, or gave what satisfied the Independent Counsel as a
conflicting version of the facts, while giving further testimony,

six years after the events in question. For these reasons, Mr.
Gardner opted not to make a proffer.

III. <u>Other Matters</u>

While it is fair to say that Mr. Gardner reads the
Final Report with a jaundiced eye, he nonetheless believes that
other references made to him in the Final Report are intended to
suggest wrongdoing on his part, without ever accusing him of
anything. Such perceived insinuations are difficult to defend
against without giving them greater dignity than they deserve.
Accordingly, Mr. Gardner will respond to this group of references
by using just one example of the amount of factual error the
Independent Counsel will condone in order to "support"
insinuations of misconduct.

The Final Report describes two asserted events, both of
which the Report claims occurred on November 18, 1986, to
insinuate that Mr. Gardner was twice involved in possible
wrongdoing. In fact, however, as evidence developed by the
Independent Counsel makes abundantly clear, it was it was
physically possible for only one of the episodes to have occurred
at all. On that November 18th there was a meeting at Oliver
North's office involving Lt. Col. North, Mr. Gardner and CIA
Subject #2. That same day there was a briefing at CIA
headquarters on the "arms for hostages" initiative given by Clair
George to Congressional staffers from both the Senate and House
intelligence committees, which Mr. Gardner and CIA Subject #2
also attended. But there was only <u>one</u> meeting with Lt. Col.

North, and <u>one</u> Congressional briefing on that day, and the Final Report does not claim otherwise. Nevertheless, at p. 240 of the Final Report, the Independent Counsel states that Mr. Gardner and CIA Subject #2 went from the CIA briefing of the Congressional staffers to Lt. Col. North's office and while meeting with Lt. Col. North engaged in what may have been a criminal conspiracy. At p. 312 the Final Report says just the opposite: that Mr. Gardner and CIA Subject #2 <u>first</u> met with Lt. Col. North at his office and <u>then</u> travelled to the CIA to attend Mr. George's briefing of Congressional staffers, and at that time engaged in what may have been a criminal conspiracy. Leaving aside the soundness of the Independent Counsel's factual inferences, only one of these two scenarios could actually have occurred. To offer both to the reader within 80 pages of one another in the Final Report suggests that the Independent Counsel is not even concerned about plausibility in making assertions of wrongdoing.

What seems to intrigue the Independent Counsel in both the above settings is the prospect that Mr. Gardner and CIA Subject #2 may have acted as conduits in a cover-up conspiracy engineered by Lt. Col. North and Mr. George. An objective analysis of that proposition, as set forth in the Final Report, shows that an inference of wrongdoing cannot be supported as to either sequence of events, much less to both.

In the scenario that involves the briefing at the CIA occurring first, and then the meeting at Lt. Col. North's office, p. 240, some handwritten notes of North's were found by investigators for Attorney General Meese several days after

November 18th in a security "burn bag" in North's office. These
notes apparently resulted from the meeting with Mr. Gardner and
CIA Subject #2 on November 18th. The notes referred to some of
the subject matters raised at Clair George's briefing of
Congressional staffers, and included the reference "not reveal
Dick Secord." From this the Independent Counsel is asking the
readers of the Final Report to conclude that through Mr. Gardner
and CIA Subject #2 Clair George informed Lt. Col. North that the
CIA had not disclosed the activities of Richard Secord in
connection with the "arms for hostages" initiative. Unanswered
are such questions as when Lt. Col. North made the notation in
question, what caused him to make it, whether "not reveal Dick
Secord" was something North assumed not to have happened because
it was not mentioned by Mr. Gardner or CIA Subject #2, or whether
Mr. George was even in possession of the knowledge regarding
Richard Secord that was supposedly withheld at the briefing.

In the scenario that has events running in the opposite
direction, p. 312, Mr. Gardner and CIA Subject #2 meet with Lt.
Col. North at his office on November 18th and then travel to the
CIA to attend Clair George's briefing. In this version Lt. Col.
North, Mr. Gardner and CIA Subject #2 have discussed the
beginnings of the "arms for hostages" initiatives at North's
office. Lt. Col. North indicated to the two CIA representatives
that the agency's involvement in that activity actually began
with an arms flight in November 1985, while Mr. Gardner and CIA
Subject #2 believed the first CIA involvement came after a
presidential "finding" in January 1986. The two CIA men then

returned to their headquarters and attended Clair George's
briefing of Congressional staffers at which the start date of CIA
involvement in the "arms for hostages" deal was reported by Mr.
George to be in January of 1986. The conclusion to be drawn, the
Final Report suggests, is that armed with knowledge that the CIA
was involved in "arms for hostages" activity in 1985, Mr. Gardner
and CIA Subject #2 were silent at Clair George's briefing and
thus allowed Congressional staffers to be misled as to timing.
Unanswered here, of course, are such questions as did the two CIA
officials accept what Lt. Col. North said, did they seek to
verify Lt. Col. North's claim by checking it out before
publicizing it, and did they inform Mr. George who made his own
judgment as to what to disclose at his briefing? Unanswered as
well, and more fundamentally, is the question of why Mr. George
and his staff would conspire to withhold from Congressional
staffers information which the Director of Central Intelligence
willingly provided to the Congress three days later, at the
hearing for which the Congressional staffers were being briefed.

      No matter how lame the suggestions of wrongdoing
against Mr. Gardner may be at pp. 240 and 312 of the Final
Report, one fact is manifest. They cannot both be right. The
two CIA officials could not possibly have passed themselves going
in opposite directions on the George Washington Parkway as they
travelled to be in two places at one time. The Final Report,
however, accuses them of exactly that. That the Report recites
two mutually exclusive versions of one series of events as if
both were true, and both were evidence of unproven wrongdoing,

provides the true measure of the veracity of this Report. This attempt to damn Mr. Gardner with supposition and unprovable inference, after he on numerous occasions provided answers to every question put to him, is inexcusable, and cannot go unremarked.

Respectfully submitted,

GORDON & BARNETT

By: _____
John F. Conroy (959791)
1133 21st Street, N.W.
Suite 450
Washington, D.C. 20036
(202) 833-3400

ATTORNEY FOR NORMAN H.
GARDNER, JR.

CERTIFICATE OF SERVICE

I HEREBY CERTIFY that on this ____ day of December, 1993, a copy of the foregoing Comments of Norman H. Gardner on the Final Report of the Independent Counsel Investigating the Iran/Contra Affair was mailed first class, postage prepaid, to:

> Office of Independent Counsel
> 1726 M Street, NW
> Suite 300
> Washington, DC 20036

John F. Conroy

ATTACHMENT-1

IN THE UNITED STATES DISTRICT COURT
FOR THE DISTRICT OF COLUMBIA

```
                                    )
                                    )
IN RE:  Grand Jury Subpoena         )
                                    )     Misc. No. _____
July 16, 1991 (NORMAN GARDNER)      )     SEALED
                                    )
                                    )
_____)
```

MOTION FOR PROTECTIVE ORDER

Pursuant to the provisions of Rule 6, Federal Rules of Criminal Procedure, the movant, Mr. Norman Gardner, by and through his counsel, respectfully requests that this Court enter an order requiring that Mr. Gardner's present subpoena to appear before the grand jury be continued until such time as Mr. Gardner's counsel has obtained necessary security clearance to consult with, and give advice to, his client.

Further details in support of this Motion are contained in Movant's Memorandum of Points and Authorities In Support of Motion For Protective Order.

Respectfully submitted,

SACHS, HOROWITZ & BONARD

By: _____
John F. Conroy (959791)
1140 Connecticut Avenue, N.W.
Suite 900
Washington, D.C. 20036
(202)828-8223

ATTACHMENT 1

CERTIFICATE OF SERVICE

I hereby certify that on August __5__, 1991 I caused a copy of the foregoing Motion For Protective Order, Memorandum of Points and Authorities thereto, and proposed Order to be hand delivered to:

Craig A. Gillen, Esquire
Associate Counsel
Office of Independent Counsel
555 13th Street, N.W., Suite 701W
Washington, D.C. 20004

John F. Conroy

IN THE UNITED STATES DISTRICT COURT
FOR THE DISTRICT OF COLUMBIA

_____
)
)
)
IN RE: Grand Jury Subpoena   )
)   Misc. No. _____
July 16, 1991 (NORMAN GARDNER))   SEALED
)
)
_____)

MEMORANDUM OF POINTS AND AUTHORITIES
IN SUPPORT OF MOTION FOR PROTECTIVE ORDER

BACKGROUND

Norman Gardner is the former Assistant to the Deputy
Director of Operations of the Central Intelligence Agency. Due
to his position in the Operations directorate at CIA, he has
been called upon to testify before the grand jury investigating
the "Iran-Contra affair" on repeated occasions dating to
February of 1987. In four (4) separate appearances Mr.
Gardner, not being represented by counsel, testified as a
cooperating "witness" in the independent counsel's inquiry. As
recently as April 17, 1991 Mr. Gardner was advised in writing
by the Office of Independent Counsel that he held the status of
a "witness" in that inquiry.

On July 16, 1991 Mr. Gardner was sent yet another
subpoena to testify before the grand jury on July 19, 1991 (the
"July subpoena", Attachment 1). It is that subpoena which is
at issue in this Motion. Upon receipt of the July subpoena,

which advised Mr. Gardner that his status had now been changed
to that of a subject of the grand jury inquiry, he retained
counsel. Counsel obtained a continuance of Mr. Gardner's grand
jury appearance date to a future date to be determined.
Counsel then met with representatives of the Office of
Independent Counsel and explained that before any considered
judgment could be made regarding Mr. Gardner's continuing
cooperation in the investigation, counsel had to be able to
fully and freely discuss all aspects of this matter with his
client. The problem that counsel identified to the prosecutors
was, of course, his lack of a security clearance to discuss any
classified matters.

While an interim SECRET security clearance was
subsequently granted to counsel, it was immediately apparent
that in order to familiarize himself with the context of the
present investigation, and Mr. Gardner's relationship to it, a
clearance well beyond SECRET would be needed. The necessary
background investigation to obtain such a clearance was
initiated in late July.

On August 1, 1991 arrangements were made to have Mr.
Gardner review, on August 6, 1991, his prior testimony and FBI
reports of interview so as to be ready for a possible further
grand jury appearance. At the same time his counsel was to be
provided excerpts of testimony given to Congressional
committees by persons other than Mr. Gardner that contained
material classified no higher than SECRET, so that he could

begin to develop some background on the present inquiry. While
Mr. Gardner and his counsel were agreeable to this arrangement
a follow-up call from the OIC put the condition on this review
that Mr. Gardner must then testify before the grand jury on
Wednesday, August 7, 1991. On behalf of Mr. Gardner, counsel
stated that if such a time frame were forced upon him, he would
advise Mr. Gardner to invoke his constitutional privilege not
to testify before the grand jury. At that point the
arrangement to permit the review of documents by either Mr.
Gardner, or counsel, was withdrawn and counsel was advised that
Mr. Gardner would be compelled to sit before the grand jury in
order to invoke his privilege not to testify.

DISCUSSION

In the July subpoena, which is the document which
governs Mr. Gardner's further appearance before the grand jury,
the Office of Independent Counsel has guaranteed Mr. Gardner
two (2) things as a matter of right, the right to invoke his
constitutional privilege not to testify, and the right:

> [i]f you have retained counsel, [. . . to have
> . . .] a reasonable opportunity to step outside
> the Grand Jury room to consult with counsel if
> you so desire.

By affording that right to Mr. Gardner the OIC is
following long-standing Justice Department policy, and well
established precedent, e.g., United States v. Leighton, 265 F.
Supp. 27, 38 (S.D.N.Y., 1967) cert. den. 390 U.S. 1025 (1968).
Mr. Gardner, having retained counsel, has specifically chosen

to avail himself of his right to consult with counsel during any further grand jury appearance(s), particularly in light of the admonition in the July subpoena that the grand jury is investigating possible false statement violations made before it.

Having appeared before the grand jury on four (4) separate occasions dating to 1987, Mr. Gardner could in a further grand jury appearance misrecollect either a long-past event, or his prior testimony about it. In either case an innocent discrepancy in testimony could be viewed as a violation of 18 U.S.C. § 1623 by a prosecutor predisposed to find such violations. For that reason, if no other, the ability of Mr. Gardner to fully and candidly consult with his attorney must not be abridged. The right afforded by the grand jury to "consult" with counsel does not really exist otherwise.

It is necessary to point out that should Mr. Gardner appear before the grand jury on August 7, 1991 and invoke his privilege not to testify, his problems are unlikely to be diminished. If, as seems at least probable, the Independent Counsel is prepared to grant Mr. Gardner immunity from prosecution so that he must testify, he will remain exposed to possible perjury charges. At that point he would be in the position of having to testify, while exposed to prosecution based on that testimony, while unable to have the effective advice of counsel because attorney and client would not be able to talk to each other about any highly classified subject

- 4 -

matter pertinent to his testimony. Such a situation would
nullify the grand jury's promise to permit Mr. Gardner to
"consult" with his attorney.

    The Office of Independent Counsel need only delay Mr.
Gardner's appearance until Mr. Gardner's counsel has obtained
the necessary security clearances, and consulted with his
client, or expedite the clearance process by some other means
so that a true consultation between attorney and client can
take place.

    WHEREFORE, the applicant prays that the Court order
that his grand jury appearance now scheduled for August 7, 1991
at 9:30 a.m. be delayed until such time as his counsel has
obtained appropriate security clearances and a reasonable time
for consultation with counsel has elapsed.

                          Respectfully submitted,

                          SACHS, HOROWITZ & BONARD

                    By: _____
                          John F. Conroy (959791)
                          1140 Connecticut Avenue, N.W.
                          Suite 900
                          Washington, D.C.   20036
                          (202)828-8223

ATTACHMENT 1

AO 110 (Rev 12/89) Subpoena to Testify Before Grand Jury

United States District Court

for the   DISTRICT OF Columbia

TO:

Norman H. Gardner, Jr.
1572 Goldenrain Ct.
Reston, VA 22092

SUBPOENA TO TESTIFY
BEFORE GRAND JURY

SUBPOENA FOR:

☒ PERSON   ☐ DOCUMENT(S) OR OBJECT(S)

YOU ARE HEREBY COMMANDED to appear and testify before the Grand Jury of the United States District Court at the place, date, and time specified below.

PLACE	COURTROOM
United States District Court United States Courthouse 3rd & Constitution Avenue, N.W. Washington, D.C. 20001	Grand Jury Room 1 Third Floor
	DATE AND TIME July 19, 1991 10:00 a.m.

YOU ARE ALSO COMMANDED to bring with you the following document(s) or object(s):°

See attached Advice of Rights.

☐ *Please see additional information on reverse.*

This subpoena shall remain in effect until you are granted leave to depart by the court or by an officer acting on behalf of the court.

U.S. MAGISTRATE OR CLERK OF COURT	DATE
Nancy M. Mayer-Whittington, Clerk	July 16, 1991
(BY) DEPUTY CLERK *Margaret L. Napier*	
This subpoena is issued upon application of the United States of America	NAME, ADDRESS AND PHONE NUMBER Craig Gillen, Associate Counsel Office of Independent Counsel 555 13th Street, N.W., Suite 701W Washington, D.C. (202) 383-8967

AO 110 (Rev. 12/89) Subpoena to Testify Before Grand Jury

RETURN OF SERVICE (1.

	DATE	PLACE
RECEIVED BY SERVER		
SERVED	DATE	PLACE

SERVED ON (PRINT NAME)

SERVED BY (PRINT NAME) | **TITLE**

STATEMENT OF SERVICE FEES

TRAVEL	SERVICES	TOTAL

DECLARATION OF SERVER(2)

I declare under penalty of perjury under the laws of the United States of America that the foregoing information contained in the Return of Service and Statement of Service Fees is true and correct.

Executed on _____
Date   Signature of Server

_____
Address of Server

ADDITIONAL INFORMATION

1. Grand jury witnesses are entitled to a $40.00 fee for each day they testify before the grand jury. A witness Attendance Certificate must be completed in order to receive this fee.

2. Witnesses are entitled to be reimbursed for all travel expenses relative to their grand jury appearance. Reimbursement is based on per diem and prevailing government rates in accordance with GSA regulations.

3. In order to assure that government rates are obtained, please contact Ms. Margaret Jackson in the Office of Independent Counsel at (202) 383-8987, prior to making ticketing and hotel arrangements.

(1) As to who may serve a subpoena and the manner of its service see Rule 17(d), Federal Rules of Criminal Procedure, or Rule 45(c), Federal Rules of Civil Procedure.

(2) "Fees and mileage need not be tendered to the witness upon service of a subpoena issued on behalf of the United States or an officer or agency thereof (Rule 45(c), Federal Rules of Civil Procedure; Rule 17(d), Federal Rules of Criminal Procedure) or on behalf of certain indigent parties and criminal defendants who are unable to pay such costs (28 USC 1825, Rule 17(b) Federal Rules of Criminal Procedure)".

Advice of Rights
attached to the
Grand Jury Subpoena <u>Ad</u> <u>Testificandum</u>
to Norman H. Gardner, Jr.

As a subject of the grand jury's investigation, please be advised of the following rights:

A.   The Grand Jury is conducting an investigation of possible violations of federal criminal law involving, <u>inter alia</u>, conspiracy to commit offense against the United States, 18 U.S.C. § 371; knowing and willful false or fraudulent statements, 18 U.S.C. § 1001; obstruction of proceedings before departments, agencies, and committees, 18 U.S.C. § 1505; false declarations before grand jury or court, 18 U.S.C. § 1623; and concealment, removal or mutilation of records, 18 U.S.C. § 2071.

B.   You may refuse to answer any question if a truthful answer to the question would tend to incriminate you.

C.   Anything that you do say may be used against you by the Grand Jury and/or in a subsequent legal proceeding.

D.   If you have retained counsel, the Grand Jury will permit you a reasonable opportunity to step outside the Grand Jury room to consult with counsel if you so desire.

IN THE UNITED STATES DISTRICT COURT
FOR THE DISTRICT OF COLUMBIA

IN RE: Grand Jury Subpoena	))))))))	Misc. No. _____
July 16, 1991 (NORMAN GARDNER)		SEALED

ORDER

The Court having considered the Motion of Mr. Norman Gardner to continue the date of his appearance before the grand jury, and the opposition thereto, and having determined that good cause has been shown why such Motion should be granted, it is therefore:

ORDERED, that the grand jury appearance of Mr. Norman Gardner be, and hereby is, continued until such time as counsel for Mr. Gardner has obtained the security clearances necessary to permit him to discuss all aspects of matters being investigated by the grand jury with his client, and that a further period of one week be granted after such security clearance is obtained for Mr. Gardner and his counsel to consult.

                               _____
                               United States District Judge

Dated:_____

Copies to:

John F. Conroy, Esquire
Sachs, Horowitz & Bonard
1140 Connecticut Avenue, N.W.
Suite 900
Washington, D.C. 20036

Craig A. Gillen, Esquire
Associate Counsel
Office of Independent Counsel
555 13th Street, N.W.
Suite 701W
Washington, D.C. 20004

ATTACHMENT – 2

SACHS, HOROWITZ & BONARD

1140 CONNECTICUT AVENUE, N.W.
WASHINGTON, D.C. 20036-4002
(202) 828-8200
TELECOPIER: (202) 828-8273

WRITER'S DIRECT DIAL NUMBER

(202) 828-8223

August 2, 1991

VIA MESSENGER

Craig A. Gillen, Esquire
Associate Counsel
Office of Independent Counsel
555 13th Street, N.W.
Suite 701 W
Washington, D.C. 20004

Dear Mr. Gillen:

Rather than permit your letter of August 2, 1991 to
constitute the documentary record of the discussions my client,
Mr. Norman Gardner, and I have had with your office, I am
writing to put our discussions in proper context, and to
correct the factual assertions set forth in your correspondence.

As you are aware, your subpoena to Mr. Gardner of July
16, 1991 changed his status in your ongoing investigation from
that of "witness" to that of "subject". As a witness in your
investigation Mr. Gardner repeatedly cooperated with you and
the staff of the OIC by appearing for six (6) separate
interviews at your offices, and by making four (4) separate
grand jury appearances, all without benefit of counsel. When
you elected to change his status to that of a subject on
July 16, 1991 without explanation or apparent justification,
Mr. Gardner predictably sought the advise of counsel. The
first thing I did was obtain an extension of his scheduled July
19, 1991 grand jury appearance date, since only two (2) days'
actual notice was being given to him by your office.

The second thing I did was meet with representatives of
the OIC and explain to them that not having a proper security
clearance I was not in a position to fully and freely discuss
my client's circumstances with him. Your office has never,
until the evening of August 1, 1991, even intimated that it
intended to put Mr. Gardner back in the grand jury without my

Craig A. Gillen, Esquire
Associate Counsel
August 2, 1991
Page 2

having had an opportunity to be cleared to counsel him.
Specifically, a grand jury date of August 2, 1991 was never
mentioned, and the notion that my client and I would be asked
to read portions of documents on August 6, 1991, which we might
or might not be able to discuss, and then make an educated
decision as to whether or not to testify before the grand jury
on August 7, 1991, was simply ludicrous. It was on that basis
that I advised you that if forced into that position my client
would, on my advice, invoke his privilege not to testify. You
replied that in that case we could not read any documents and
my client would be forced, contrary to the practice in this
district, to invoke his constitutional privilege in an actual
appearance before the grand jury.

        You seem to have concluded that because I will not
accept your representations of what security clearance level
will suffice for me to represent Mr. Gardner, and because I
have determined to proceed cautiously in that regard, that
Mr. Gardner is to be abused and harassed before the grand jury
by having to perform a ritual invocation of privilege before a
group of people before whom he has repeatedly testified in the
past. Please understand that I reserve all my rights to seek
protection against this denial of my client's right to counsel,
and I personally object most strongly to your proceeding before
the grand jury in such a manner.

                            Sincerely,

                            John F. Conroy

JFC/emp

ATTACHMENT – 3

UNITED STATES DISTRICT COURT
FOR THE DISTRICT OF COLUMBIA

IN RE: GRAND JURY SUBPOENA   )
JULY 16, 1991 (NORMAN GARDNER))   **Misc. No. 91-219**
)   **(UNDER SEAL)**
_____)

FILED

O R D E R   AUG 7 1991

CLERK, U.S. DISTRICT COURT
DISTRICT OF COLUMBIA

This comes before the Court on the Motion for Protective Order filed by Norman Gardner, who has been subpoenaed to appear before the Grand Jury. The Office of Independent Counsel (OIC) opposes the motion. After giving careful consideration to the motion and the opposition thereto and the arguments of counsel, the Court concludes that the motion must be denied.

Attorney John F. Conroy, who represents Mr. Gardner, contends that he is unable to effectively advise his client with reference to the exercise of his right against self incrimination because he only has an interim "Secret" clearance and that the questions put to his client, although falling within "Secret" clearance, may require him to discuss matters with his client that are "Top Secret." OIC contends that it does not intend to delve into matters that may require "Top Secret" clearance and that the objection asserted by Mr. Gardner is premature.

At this point in time the Court agrees with the OIC. Mr. Gardner should appear before the Grand Jury and, as counsel represent, he will have on opportunity to step out and consult with his counsel. Should the concerns expressed by Mr. Gardner

ATTACHMENT 3

materialize, then they may be addressed to the Court.

It is hereby

ORDERED that the motion for a protective order is denied.

AUG 7 1991

_____

JOHN GARRETT PENN
United States District Judge

H. Lawrence Garrett, III

December 2, 1993

United States Court of Appeals
For the District of Columbia Circuit

FILED DEC 0 2 1993

RON GARVIN
CLERK

Mr. Ron Garvin, Clerk
United States Court of Appeals
For the District of Columbia
3rd and Constitution Avenue, N. W.
Washington, D. C. 20001

Dear Mr. Garvin:

This is in response to your letter apprising me of the Court's granting me an opportunity to review and, if desired, submit any comments or factual information I desire for possible inclusion as an appendix to the Final Report of the Independent Counsel ("IC") in the Iran-Contra matter. For reasons that follow, I would ask that my comments be appended to the record, and I would further urge the Court not to release the IC's report.

As a general observation, the report presents an incomplete and biased portrayal of my conduct; however, there are three conclusary references which I find to be particularly disparaging. They require clarification because they are at best, fundamentally non-factual; and at worst, purposefully misleading. These comments appear at pages 438 and 441 and in footnotes 123 and 310. The deceptiveness of the IC's conclusions can be illustrated by simply viewing the facts underlying these comments in the context in which they occurred.

The first is a paragraph found on page 438, which reads as follows:

> "Although Garrett's purported inability to recall anything about his *efforts* to obtain Weinberger's notes was sufficiently implausible to undermine Garrett's credibility, it would have been *difficult* to prove beyond a reasonable doubt that Garrett had intentionally perjured himself five years after writing his April 1987 memorandum. The evidence indicated that Garrett was not a willing accomplice in withholding Weinberger's notes from Congress."   (Emphasis added)

Mr. Ron Garvin

        The term "efforts" refers to an April 17, 1987 memorandum and an April 29, 1987 memorandum which I signed and forwarded to Secretary Weinberger and Deputy Secretary Taft, respectively. The IC refers to these memoranda in the paragraph immediately preceding the quoted paragraph.

        Both memos were prepared by my staff and signed by me in the normal course of business. I simply did not recall their existence until they were dramatically brought to my attention, with zeal and skepticism, by the IC's agent during my appearance before the Grand Jury on October 28, 1992--some five years, six months and eleven days after the fact. That the IC would assert that the <u>failure to recall, some 5 1/2 years later,</u> the existence of two memos, written by others, and signed by me in the normal course of managing the myriad legal affairs of the Department of Defense--with some 6000 attorneys--was somehow "sufficiently implausible to undermine (my) credibility"--itself begs credulity. (Emphasis added)

        The IC's assertion that "it would have been difficult to prove beyond a reasonable doubt that Garrett had intentionally perjured himself five years after writing his April 1987 memorandum", is understandable not because of the passage of time, but rather because no factual predicate for such a charge existed. The IC should know it, his agents who wrote the final report should know it, certainly any first year Assistant United States Attorney <u>would</u> know it. The IC chose instead to indict by innuendo-- contemptible conduct for one charged with upholding the public trust.

        The second issue cited by the IC is found on page 441 of the Final Report under the title: "DOD's Lack of Cooperation in the OIC's Investigation of Weinberger". At footnote 310, it states that my "chronological files ... were not produced until October 1992 in response to a Grand Jury subpoena despite a specific request for such files in May 1992."

        The IC fails to note that I relinquished my duties as the General Counsel of the Department of Defense on August 6, 1987. Upon departing the Office of the General Counsel, to assume the duties as the Under Secretary of the Navy, all of my files were packed by Navy personnel and stored somewhere in the Pentagon. To this day, I have no knowledge of what was packed, or where such items are stored. Further, while a specific request for such files may have been made in May 1992--some 4 1/2 years after my departure from that office-- no such request was ever communicated to me, to the best of my knowledge and belief.

Mr. Ron Garvin

One further issue that requires comment is found at footnote 123, wherein the IC asserts that my "April 17, 1987 memorandum contradicts (my) 1992 affidavit, which asserted that (I) did not discuss with Weinberger 'the specific details' of any Iran/Contra document request." To the best of my knowledge and belief, other than to apprise him generally of their existence, I did not personally discuss with Secretary Weinberger the numerous requests that the Department of Defense was receiving. The fact that I forwarded a written memorandum to him does not, I submit, without more, contradict my 1992 affidavit. That the IC chooses to so mischaracterize the existence of the memorandum only serves to underscore the reckless and irresponsible conduct of this IC's operations. By intentionally misrepresenting the evidence as to me, the Independent Counsel violated his oath of his office. I can only assume that he did so as to others as well.

Justice Sutherland eloquently explained the well known and familiar obligation of a federal prosecutor to uphold justice when conducting the duties of the office. In <u>Berger v. United States</u> Justice Sutherland wrote:

> The United States Attorney is the representative not of an ordinary party to a controversy, but of a sovereignty whose obligation to govern impartially is as compelling as its obligation to govern at all; and whose interest, therefore, in a criminal prosecution is not that it shall win a case, but that justice shall be done. As such, he is in a peculiar and very definite sense the servant of the law, the twofold aim of which is that guilt shall not escape or innocence suffer. He may prosecute with earnestness and vigor-indeed, he should do so. But, while he may strike hard blows, he is not at liberty to strike foul ones. It is as much his duty to refrain from improper methods calculated to produce a wrongful conviction as it is to use every legitimate means to bring about a just one. <u>Berger v. United States</u>, 295 U.S. 78, 88 (1935).

The Court may also be interested to know that in order to insure the accuracy of any final report as it might relate to me, I asked the IC to provide copies of my statements to IC investigators, as well as copies of my testimony before the Grand Jury. See <u>In re Sealed Motion</u>, 880 F. 2d 1367, 138 (D. C. Spec. Div. 1989) (per curiam). The IC promptly and summarily denied my request. Having denied me the opportunity to receive and review my own statements, as contemplated by the Court, the IC now makes selective use of Rule 6(e) and related materials to support his own self-serving purposes.

Mr. Ron Garvin

It was exactly these abuses that prompted the Senate to adopt an amendment to the Independent Counsel Reauthorization Act to safeguard the reputations of individuals caught in the vortex of an IC investigation. As passed by the Senate, the bill would restrict the nature of an IC's report to the facts without engaging in either speculation or expressions of opinions as to the culpability of individuals unless that culpability or those activities rise to a level of an indictable offense, in which case the Independent Counsel would be duty bound to seek an indictment. See 139 Cong. Rec. CR. S.15886. (daily additions ed. Nov. 17, 1993) (Statement of Sen. Cohen)

Regrettably, without this Court's intervention, only those who serve their country in high office in the future will benefit from such protections. The so-called public's right to know will not be abridged by prohibiting the release of this report. The Iran/Contra matter has been fully investigated and the public record is immense. The release of this report, though, will malign the reputations of many honest, dedicated public servants, and because it carries the official imprimatur of the IC's office, its existence in the public domain will continue to unjustly impugn them in the future.

Thank you again for affording me the opportunity to set the record straight. I am attaching copies of my affidavit, a copy of my request to the IC for copies of my statements and Grand Jury testimony, and a copy of the IC's reply. I ask that these documents be inserted in the record together with this statement, and I urge and respectively submit that the public interest will not be served by the release of this report.

Sincerely,

H. Lawrence Garrett, III

Attachments

AFFIDAVIT OF LAWRENCE H. GARRETT, III

1. I am currently the Secretary of the Department
of the Navy.

2. From early February 1986, until early August
1987, I served as the General Counsel of the Department of
Defense ("the Department") under Secretary of Defense Casper W.
Weinberger.

3. I first met Secretary Weinberger in the late
fall of 1985, when I interviewed for the position of General
Counsel. Since that time, I have had numerous opportunities to
work with and observe Secretary Weinberger. In my opinion, he is
a man of the utmost integrity and has the highest regard for the
Constitution and other laws of the United States.

4. On or about November 28, 1986, the Department
received a letter addressed to the Secretary from then Attorney
General Edwin Meese seeking documents related to or referring to
the Iran-Contra affair. The office of the General Counsel was
assigned the responsibility to comply and respond to this and all
subsequent requests for documents received by the Department. I
appointed Assistant General Counsel Edward Shapiro to carry out
the aforementioned assignment. Mr. Shapiro put a team together,
consisting of attorneys from the office of the General Counsel as
well as an attorney from each of the military services, in order

to gather relevant documents and respond to the aforementioned requests, as well as anticipated requests from various Governmental agencies.

5. Mr. Shapiro's office drafted a memorandum regarding the request, which was sent under my signature to all offices and components within the Department. Although the immediate office of the Secretary of Defense was not named as an addressee of the memorandum, his office would have been covered organizationally. In normal course, the Executive Secretariat should have received a copy of the memorandum and arranged for collection of all relevant documents from the Secretary's suite of offices. In my experience, it would be highly unusual for a Secretary of Defense, or other principal officers of the Department, personally to search his or her office in response to this or any other document request. Such activity is the responsibility of, and is normally carried out by, his or her immediate administrative staff.

6. Document requests were and are frequent and numerous within the Department, probably numbering in the thousands each year. Such requests include Congressional requests, requests under the Freedom of Information Act (FOIA), and discovery requests in the many lawsuits in which the Department or one of its components is a party.

7. I do not recall discussing with Secretary Weinberger the specific details of the November 28th request, or any subsequent request. It is not likely that I would have discussed requests for information with him other than in

very general terms. I do recall apprising the Secretary from
time to time that the Department was receiving such requests. I
recall that Secretary Weinberger treated very seriously the
requests for documents and factual information concerning the
involvement of the Department in the Iran-Contra affair. The
Secretary was adamant that the Department cooperate fully and be
completely forthcoming with respect to all such requests. We
never discussed the possibility of withholding any documents
responsive to the many requests received. I am confident that no
documents were intentionally withheld.

       8. Between November 1986 and the time I left the
General Counsel's office in August 1987, the Department received
numerous document requests relating to the Iran-Contra
investigations. While I do not recall the specific procedures
followed concerning each request, I am confident that the
Department attempted to comply fully with each such request.

       9. On at least two occasions, I assisted in
preparing Secretary Weinberger for his testimony before Congress
regarding the Iran-Contra affair. To my knowledge, the purpose
of the preparation sessions was to refresh Secretary Weinberger's
recollection of facts about which he had knowledge and to
generally apprise him of the sequence of events which occurred
within the Department. To the best of my knowledge and belief,
no effort was made to conceal knowledge from the Congress, or any
other investigative bodies.

10. I recall that when the Iran-Contra story broke in November/December 1986, Secretary Weinberger expressed his staunch opposition to the selling of arms to Iran; and he expressed his regret that his position on the matter had not been followed. From the time the Department received its first request and throughout my time of service with him, his direction was always the same whenever the subject came up: cooperate fully. Secretary Weinberger was not, in my experience, a "detail person". He dealt in broad policy matters, leaving the execution of his policy decisions to the various agencies and military departments under his authority and control. It was my perception that he knew little, if anything, about the details regarding the manner in which elements of the Department carried out their role in the transfer of arms to Iran.

11. I have been told that Secretary Weinberger maintained personal diary notes that were not produced in response to the various document requests. As I mentioned previously, I did not personally question Secretary Weinberger about the existence of personal notes or diaries. With the benefit of hindsight, he would have been better served had I done so. I do recall that early on in the process I told his secretaries that a document request had been received and asked them whether Secretary Weinberger had any notes regarding the Iran-Contra affair. They said he did not have any such notes. This did not surprise me since it comported with my own observations that Secretary Weinberger did not take notes at meetings that I attended.

12. Secretary Weinberger at all times directed full
cooperation and compliance with all of the investigating bodies.
I am confident that if I or members of my staff had asked him
specifically whether he kept diary notes, he would have provided
them so that any relevant portions could be given to the
requesting entities.

13. In all of my dealings with Secretary
Weinberger, I have never known him intentionally to misrepresent
or lie about anything. As with us all, sometimes his memory of
past events is not strong. I am absolutely confident that any
failure of the Department to produce Secretary Weinberger's
diary notes was the result of oversight and not an effort to
withhold information. Based upon my knowledge of and experience
with him, I am also sure that Secretary Weinberger did not lie to
either Congress or the Office of the Independent Counsel about
his diary notes. I am confident he did not associate his diary
notes with the requests for documents being made of the
Department.

14. There is no individual for whom I have higher personal regard as to his honesty and integrity than Secretary Weinberger.

H. LAWRENCE GARRETT, III

Subscribed and sworn before me
this 28th day of April, 1992.

Colleen A. Ercole

Notary Public

My Commission Expires:_____

MY COMMISSION
EXPIRES FEB. 28. 1995

BAKER
&
HOSTETLER
COUNSELLORS AT LAW

WASHINGTON SQUARE SUITE 1100 • 1050 CONNECTICUT AVENUE, N.W. • WASHINGTON, D.C. 20036-5304 • (202) 861-1500
FAX (202) 861-1783 • TELEX 2357276
WRITER'S DIRECT DIAL NUMBER (202) 861-1541

January 11, 1993

Lawrence Walsh, Esquire
Office of Independent Counsel
555 13th Street, N.W.
Suite 701 West
Washington, DC 20004

Re: H. Lawrence Garrett, III

Dear Mr. Walsh:

On behalf of our client, H. Lawrence Garrett, III, this is to request copies of FBI interview summaries (302s) and transcripts of interviews and grand jury testimony of our client in connection with investigations being conducted by your office. This request would encompass three interviews conducted by your staff in late Spring, 1987, April, 1992, and May, 1992, and grand jury appearances in May and October 1992. Mr. Garrett is entitled to this information prior to the issuance of a report by your office in order to assure that his interests are protected. See, In re Sealed Motion, 880 F.2d 1367 (D.C. Cir. 1989).

Your prompt attention to this request would be appreciated.

Sincerely,

Richard A. Hauser

cc: H. Lawrence Garrett, III

OFFICE OF INDEPENDENT COUNSEL
555 THIRTEENTH STREET, N.W.
SUITE 701 WEST
WASHINGTON, D.C. 20004
(202) 383-8940

January 14, 1993

Mr. Richard A. Hauser, Esq.
Baker & Hostetler
Washington Square
1050 Connecticut Avenue, N.W.
Suite 1100
Washington, D.C. 20036-5304

Re: H. Lawrence Garrett, III

Dear Mr. Hauser:

Thank you for your letter dated January 11, 1993,
to Independent Counsel Walsh, which requested copies of your
client's statements to investigators and his Grand Jury
testimony regarding Iran/Contra matters.

As you know, this Office permitted Mr. Garrett to
review copies of his prior testimony and statements before
his Grand Jury testimony in October 1992. At this time,
prior to the completion of our Final Report and its filing
with the Court, there is no legal requirement that we provide
the requested material. See In re Sealed Motion, 880 F.2d
1367, 1368 (D.C. Cir. Spec. Div. 1989) (per curiam).
Accordingly, and consistent with the practice of this Office
regarding Grand Jury witnesses, we will not comply with your
request.

Very truly yours,

LAWRENCE E. WALSH
Independent Counsel

By: *[signature]*
John Q. Barrett
Associate Counsel
(202) 383-5479

RECEIVED

JAN 15

cc: sent to HLG III 1/22/93

Robert M. Gates

United States Court of Appeals
For the District of Columbia Circuit

FILED SEP 2 8 1993

RON GARVIN
CLERK

September 22, 1993

Mr. Ron Garvin
Clerk, United States Court of Appeals
   for the District of Columbia Circuit
Washington, D.C. 20001-2866

> Re: Order Under Seal, United States Court of Appeals
> for the District of Columbia Circuit, Division for
> <u>Appointing Independent Counsels, No. 86-6</u>

Dear Mr. Garvin:

This responds to your letter of August 9, 1993, in which you advised me of an Order Under Seal issued by the United States Court of Appeals for the District of Columbia Circuit, Division for the Purpose of Appointing Independent Counsels. Pursuant to that Order, I have reviewed those portions of the Final Report of Independent Counsel Lawrence W. Walsh (the "Report") that you identified and made available as relevant to me.

The Independent Counsel has concluded, however grudgingly, that the evidence developed over a nearly six year investigation did not warrant any legal action against me. For that, I am pleased. Indeed, the Report offers no information, documents, or testimony regarding my actions during the events under review that have not been fully aired and judged on several prior occasions, including most recently by the United States Senate during the process of my confirmation as Director of Central Intelligence in 1991.

At the same time, I am disappointed that the Report does not draw upon sworn testimony of a number of individuals before the Senate Select Committee on Intelligence ("SSCI") that was both exculpatory and placed my actions in some context. Instead, the Report engages in what can only be described as a worst-case analysis, often drawn out of context, and supported by innuendo and leaps of logic that are not supported by the record as a whole. For example, the Report asserts that I made two

- 2 -

"demonstrably incorrect" statements in my six years of testifying
on this matter. This assertion as to each of these two
statements does not stand up to analysis.

        The Kerr Information. First, the Report alleges that I
made an incorrect statement when I testified that the first I
recall hearing of a possible diversion of funds was on October 1,
1986. It was on that date that Mr. Charles Allen advised me of
his suspicions of such a diversion. The Report states that Mr.
Richard Kerr testified that he had conveyed Allen's concerns to
me some time earlier and suggests that my failure to recall that
conversation is incriminating.

        While the Report accurately notes my testimony that I
did not remember the conversation, it inexplicably neglects to
mention that I never denied that the conversation with Mr. Kerr
had taken place. Indeed, I consistently stated simply that I did
not remember the conversation.

        The Report also states that I told Mr. Kerr to keep me
informed, yet it neglects to mention that Kerr himself has
testified to the SSCI that he never came back to me with further
information. Furthermore, in September 1991, Kerr testified
publicly and under oath as to the circumstances under which he
had raised the matter with me -- testimony the Independent
Counsel's Report never mentions. Specifically, Kerr told the
SSCI:

                ....[I] think it is quite easy to understand
        from my perspective, quite easy to understand why Bob
        Gates might not remember. First of all, I did not do
        this as an element of high drama as something that was
        terribly exciting and a breaking piece of intelligence.

                I did it as a piece of information that I
        considered to be very speculative and without having
        any context or anything to put it in, merely
        information to make sure that someone, my boss, knew a
        piece of information. I would have done that about a
        lot of other kinds of information outside this in terms
        of rumors, intelligence, things that were happening
        that I had no certainty about, but nevertheless would
        make sure that you give somebody a heads up. I did it
        in that context.

- 3 -

.......[I]t is quite easy for me to understand
from my own perspective, someone coming in and giving
me information like this that I couldn't put in
context, getting a lot of different inputs from people,
that it is quite possible to forget that and to not
recall that.

This exchange and its implications were fully reviewed by the
SSCI in 1991, well documented in their report, and found to lack
basis for concluding that I had misled anyone in my statements
about the exchange.

Finally, the Report's statement on page 23 that
Mr. Allen told me in the summer of 1986 of his concerns is simply
factually incorrect, even according to the Report itself.
Neither Mr. Allen nor Mr. Kerr have ever testified that Allen
came to me before October 1. Indeed, Allen has testified that I
was "surprised" when he reported his suspicions to me on October
1. The evidence assembled in the Report substantiates this
point.

In sum, the Report's conclusion that I made a
"demonstrably incorrect" statement neglects to explain how a
failure to remember a conversation, while not denying that it
might have taken place, is demonstrably incorrect. Moreover, the
Report unfairly omits sworn testimony from Kerr before the Senate
that detailed extenuating circumstances surrounding the brief
conversation that makes my inability to remember it far more
understandable than suggested in the Report.

Knowledge of Col. North's Role. The second alleged
"incorrect statement" is based on the Report's suggestion that I
knew of Lt. Col. North's operational role with the Contras. This
insinuation rests entirely on two brief exchanges with Admiral
Poindexter, in neither of which was the subject of Contra
operations even mentioned.

The first such exchange occurred when I told Poindexter
that a CIA officer scheduled to take over North's
responsibilities for Central America on the NSC staff should have
no contact with the private benefactors. It was common knowledge
in Washington at that time that North was the contact point for
putting the private donors (including Americans) in touch with
the Contra leaders.

- 4 -

In a remarkably unfair and distorted manner, the Report identifies an action I took to ensure that CIA avoid even the appearance of impropriety, turns it upside down, and asserts that it reflected my knowledge of improper actions by North. In a time of extraordinary suspicion of CIA's role with the Contras, when Congress had prohibited certain direct aid to the Contras, I did not want any CIA officer even remotely involved with the private benefactors. That was my sole reason for raising the matter with Poindexter. I did not know at the time of any impropriety by the NSC staff relating to the Contras.

The Report also points to Admiral Poindexter's asking me if CIA was interested in buying some of the private benefactors' equipment as they discontinued their activities -- and my response that I would check on it -- as evidence that I knew about North's operational control of the private benefactor effort. I testified repeatedly that it made sense to me that the White House would want to see the private benefactor effort discontinued once Congress again approved U.S. Government support for the Contras. Because the White House had encouraged the private benefactors to support the Contras, Poindexter's suggestion that CIA consider purchasing some of their equipment did not seem improper -- foolish perhaps, but not improper. It certainly did not evidence to me operational control by the NSC. When I did as I said I would, and passed the question along to the Directorate of Operations, I was told it was a bad idea and dropped it.

Indeed, the Report as well as sworn testimony and depositions before the Senate Select Committee on Intelligence made abundantly clear that not one person could be found who had talked to me about North's operational role. And why would they? By the time I became DDCI in April 1986, the Reagan Administration was well on the way to securing Congressional approval for CIA to resume military aid to the Contras -- and CIA's efforts were focused on readying the new program and sorting out the bureaucratic problems associated with it.

In order to fulfill my new responsibilities, I began meeting regularly with Alan Fiers, the Chief of the CIA's Central American Task Force, in order to follow the progress of the new program. These were the matters Fiers discussed with me. Whatever Fiers' unspoken assumptions were about my prior knowledge, this is why -- as the Report so tellingly declares -- Fiers "would not testify that he had spoken of North's operational role to Mr. Gates." Fiers "would not testify" in this manner because he could not so testify.

- 5 -

Further, the Report fails to mention that all of the other key CIA operational officers having some role in Central America and questioned by the SSCI testified under oath that they had not discussed any such NSC or North role with me.

In short, the assertion that I made an "incorrect statement" pertaining to my knowledge of North's operational role is supported by no evidence or testimony, only suspicion and innuendo so extreme as to turn actions intended to ensure compliance with the rules into supposition that they bespoke knowledge of violations of the rules. Again, the Report's conclusions are unfair and without basis.

Casey/Poindexter Meeting. A last factual correction is necessary. The Report states that Casey and I met with Poindexter on November 6, 1986, to discuss what to do about allegations that profits from the arms sales had been diverted to other projects. **This is not accurate**. There was no mention at that meeting of a possible diversion. Casey and I raised again the need to go public with the entire Iran arms sales story, and Casey again urged Poindexter to have the White House Counsel review the entire matter. Poindexter said he did not trust the Counsel and still hoped to get more hostages out. I testified to this exchange repeatedly; a memorandum of conversation I wrote promptly after the meeting confirms this. Nothing in the Report contradicts this.

*   *   *   *

I acknowledged to the Senate in 1991 that I had not been as aggressive as I should have been in pursuing Mr. Allen's concerns after October 1, 1986. But the record is clear that those actions I took throughout this period were consistently aimed at ensuring CIA's compliance with the law, full disclosure of CIA's role, and making the only part of this matter about which I was aware -- the Iran arms sales -- public. I insisted on getting a copy of the January 1986 finding; I insisted on bringing in the CIA General Counsel and then insisted on following his advice; in November 1986, I insisted that we hold nothing back and that where we lacked information we should go to retirees to get it. In connection with my confirmation hearings in 1991, the SSCI took numerous sworn statements that evidence my constant directions in November 1986 to lay out all the facts in testimony. None of these facts about my role are in the Report. The Independent Counsel has not been judicious and fair in his approach.

- 6 -

I have always cooperated fully with the multiple Iran-Contra investigations -- the SSCI, the HPSCI, the CIA's Inspector General, the Tower Board, the Congressional Iran-Contra Committee, the DCI's Special Counsel, _and_ the Independent Counsel. As Acting Director of Central Intelligence from December 1986 to May 1987, I began the flow of countless CIA documents and witnesses to investigators. When problems or obstacles arose, I cleared them away until the arrival of DCI William Webster, at which time I recused myself from any further participation in Executive Branch decision-making relating to Iran-Contra -- a situation that continued until my retirement last January.

Despite my total cooperation, and the absence of any new evidence in documents or testimony beyond that weighed by the Senate in 1991, the Independent Counsel's Report is unjustifiably disparaging, unbalanced, filled with innuendo and insinuation, and draws conclusions not supported by the evidence. The fact is that, as the Report puts it, "the evidence did not warrant indictment" because there was no wrongdoing on my part. I did not engage in obstruction or willful misleading. The Report should have so stated.

Sincerely,

Robert M. Gates

Clair E. George

UNITED STATES COURT OF APPEALS
FOR THE DISTRICT OF COLUMBIA
Division for the Purpose of
Appointing Independent Counsels

Ethics in Government Act of 1978, as Amended

```
_____
                                 )
In re:  Oliver L. North, et al.  )
        (Clair E. George)        )        Division 86-6
                                 )        FILED UNDER SEAL
                                 )
_____)
```

**COMMENT OF CLAIR E. GEORGE ON THE FINAL REPORT OF THE
INDEPENDENT COUNSEL IN THE IRAN-CONTRA MATTER**

Clair E. George, by counsel, provides the following

comments on the Final Report (the "Final Report") of the Office

of Independent Counsel ("OIC"). OIC's conclusion that Clair

George lied to Congress about his knowledge of what came to be

known as the Iran-Contra affair must be carefully analyzed. Any

judgment about the integrity of those conclusions must take into

account the following:

1.   **OIC's false assertion that Mr. George "refused to
     cooperate" with the investigation.**

OIC states categorically that Mr. George "refused to

cooperate" with the investigation, Final Report p. 223, n.1.

This is a distorted and misleading statement.

Mr. George was notified in July, 1991, one day after Alan

Fiers had plead guilty, pursuant to a cooperation agreement,

that he was a target of OIC's criminal prosecution. First
Trial[1] Transcript at 1392-1393. In August, 1991, Mr. George and
his counsel met with Independent Counsel Lawrence Walsh and his
deputy Craig Gillen. In that meeting, Mr. Walsh asked Mr.
George to cooperate with the investigation on the following
basis: Mr. George would plead guilty to a misdemeanor of false
statement to the United States Congress in violation of
18 U.S.C. Section 192, and cooperate by giving testimony about
the knowledge and participation in the Iran-Contra affair of
individuals "above" him in the Reagan Administration. OIC would
notify the sentencing judge of Mr. George's cooperation. This
would likely result in a non-jail sentence.

Mr. George insisted he had no one "to give up." This was
roundly disbelieved by the prosecutors.

Through counsel, Mr. George countered with the following
proposal: OIC would begin debriefing Mr. George immediately and
exhaustively, with no immunity to protect him from prosecution
for any offenses he might confess to during the interviews.
Thereafter, OIC would put Mr. George into the grand jury where,

---

[1]   Mr. George was tried twice. A transcript of the first
trial was purchased. Mr. George's counsel never obtained a
complete copy of the second trial transcript because there were
no funds to purchase it.

without immunity and under oath, he could be asked questions without limitation. <u>Then</u>, and <u>only</u> <u>after</u> those exercises were completed, OIC would polygraph Mr. George on any issues it wished. If his polygraph reported deceptive answers, he would be prosecuted for anything OIC wished, based not only on the events of 1986 and 1987 before the Congress but also on statements made to OIC or the grand jury.

Although Mr. Walsh at first appeared to be interested, after consultation with Mr. Gillen, the offer was rejected. Indeed, OIC was <u>not</u> interested in Mr. George's evidence and cooperation. The <u>sine</u> <u>qua</u> <u>non</u> of its dealings with him after Mr. Fiers plead guilty was a conviction of Mr. George. By this time, the prosecution of Oliver North had been decimated and OIC knew it was in trouble in the <u>Poindexter</u> appeal. The credibility of OIC's operation, as well as its cost-effectiveness, was an embarrassment to it and a growing scandal in the legal community. OIC needed someone who would give up someone "above" him for prosecution. Mr. George would not be that person. As a result, he became a twice-tried defendant.

2.   <u>**The Racial Implications of OIC's Conduct in Jury Selection**</u>.

The original indictment charged Mr. George in 10 counts with false statements, perjury, and obstruction of justice.

Within the false statement and perjury counts there were 9
testimonial statements upon which a jury would be asked to
render a verdict. Thus, the number of actual counts charged
were less than the number of verdicts the jury would be asked to
return.

In January, 1992, the U.S. Court of Appeals for the
District of Columbia Circuit ruled on the Poindexter appeal.
Poindexter v. United States, 951 F.2d 369 (D.C. Cir.), cert.
denied, 113 S.Ct. 656 (1992). As a result, the obstruction of
Congress counts were doomed. The prosecutors realized this and
consented to dismiss one of those counts outright. However,
they reindicted Mr. George in May, 1992, in an attempt to
salvage the obstruction counts from the dispositive Poindexter
precedent. Over objection, the trial court sustained this
reindictment and the case proceeded to trial on 9 counts.

A mistrial was declared, the jury having hung
overwhelmingly in favor of acquittal on all counts. On retrial,
OIC dismissed the Poindexter-tainted obstruction of justice
counts and proceeded to prosecute on seven counts of false
statements, perjury, and obstruction of justice before the grand
jury.

The first jury was comprised of 9 blacks and 3 whites.
After the mistrial, the prosecutors employed a local lawyer as a
consultant, inter alia, to assist them in selecting a jury for

the second trial. The reason for OIC's retention of the local
lawyer, who was black, became clear at the second trial.

The second jury was comprised of 12 blacks. The jury pool
from which they were selected contained 3 whites. The
prosecution had 6 peremptory challenges. The prosecutors
peremptorily struck all the whites, who were positioned "deep"
in the numerical order for possible selection. In other words,
the prosecutors calculated that, notwithstanding several jurors
who could have made up the twelve before the whites were
reached, (thus, theoretically, the whites might not have been
reached at all for selection) the whites were to be stricken.
The Court accepted the prosecution's explanation of why it
struck all the whites. The explanations, in the defense's view,
were a pretext to avoid having a white juror, especially a white
foreperson.[2] The experience of the first trial was one the

---

[2]   At the second trial, in the argument pursuant to <u>Batson v.
Kentucky</u>, 476 U.S. 79 (1986), the defense cited an article
appearing in the <u>Washington Post</u> dated August 28, 1992, and
attached hereto as Exhibit A, in which an unidentified source
familiar with the prosecution's view described the foreperson as
"very articulate, educated and forceful" and played a major role
in persuading most of his fellow jurors. While the <u>Washington
Post</u> editorial calling for no retrial saw these characteristics
as "attributes rather than negatives", it is clear OIC saw them
pejoratively, as traits that set the foreperson apart from the
other predominantly black, and, by implication, inarticulate,
uneducated and docile jurors. The prosecutor in his argument

prosecution wanted to avoid even at the expense of racial
exclusion. Clearly, if the jurors excluded were black in favor
of an white panel, the racist implication would have been more
consistent with historical experience. What occured in this
instance, however, was no less odious.

3.   **OIC's treatment of Mr. George's two trials as**
      non-events.

Clair George was tried twice. He was acquitted of all but
2 counts of a 7 count (originally 10, but 3 were dismissed
before the second trial) indictment whose verdict form called
for 13 separate verdicts of guilt or acquittal. In the Final
Report only four references to testimony from either trial were
cited in support of OIC's findings. The trials, as far as OIC
is concerned, were superfluous, as if they never occurred. The
highest authority cited to support OIC's conclusions about Mr.
George is grand jury testimony. The principal witness in the
grand jury was a person, Alan Fiers, an admitted perjurer, who
was totally discredited under cross-examination at the trials.

_____

denied it was he who made that statement reported in the Post
but did not deny that a member of the OIC staff had done so.
Second Trial Transcript p. 618.

See, e.g., First Trial Transcript at pp. 1393-1394, 1399-1400, 1405-1407, 1415-1416, 1444-1445, 1459-1462, 1473-1477.[3] Indeed, on all counts in which Mr. Fiers gave testimony, Mr. George was acquitted. Mr. Fiers should not enjoy renewed credibility in the Final Report as if the trial testimony was irrelevant.

4. **OIC's knowledge of and intentional reliance on fabricated documents as well as evidence rejected by the Court.**

OIC cites 3 documents that are at the cornerstone of their incriminating conclusions about Mr. George:

a.   Government Exhibit 119, Tab H. Two pages from a briefing book prepared for Mr. George's appearances on October 10 and 14, 1986 before congressional committees.

b.   Government Exhibit 66B, page 44 from Mr. George's deposition testimony before the Senate Select Committee on

---

[3]   On cross-examination, Mr. Fiers admitted he and CIA Director William Casey, in flat violation of their commitment to Congress, continued funding a banned secret project through the illegal diversion of funds by false invoicing - all without the knowledge of Mr. George. In fact, Mr. Fiers' gave specific instructions to CIA personnel not to disclose this activity to Mr. George. First Trial transcript at pp. 1442-1454.

Secret Military Assistance to Iran and Nicaraguan

Opposition.

c.   Government Exhibit 189, a rumpled piece of paper

purportedly retrieved from Oliver North's burnbag, offered

for the first time in the second trial.

GOVERNMENT EXHIBIT 119, TAB H

OIC claims Government Exhibit 119, Tab H represents a

single two-page document containing information on its second

page the Committee was seeking but was not disclosed by Mr.

George when asked. The significance of this is that there is no

evidence that the second page was in the briefing book at the

time the question was asked.[4]

The evidence conclusively showed at the second trial that

the material in Government Exhibit 119, Tab H was contained in 2

documents, each of a single page's length, prepared on different

typewriters, and found elsewhere in CIA files, including Mr.

---

[4]   Moreover, the briefing book materials had been purged by
OIC itself, as the exhibit contains references to pages of
material having been removed on the authority of an Associate
Independent Counsel who apparently had control over the exhibit.
In other words, Government Exhibit 119 was not properly
maintained during the years it was in the possession of OIC.

George's, separately and wholly disconnected from each other.[5]

While this might have come as a surprise to OIC at the second trial when first disclosed, the prosecutors' persistence in urging upon subsequent witnesses that Tab H contained a single document rather than two appropriately was rebuffed by the trial judge.

None of this is reported in the Final Report. Rather, without the trial court to keep the prosecutor honest, the Final Report intentionally, falsely characterizes Tab H as a single document rather than two documents.

GOVERNMENT EXHIBIT 66B, P. 44.

In the first trial the prosecutor, in his opening statement, quoted Mr. George's testimony on April 24, 1987 and

---

[5]   The Tab H evidence did not become significant until Mr. George was under cross-examination in the first trial. No particular attention was previously given to its physical composition. Certainly, none was directed toward its composition until after the first trial when the defense was on notice it would be a major evidentiary item in the second trial. It was during preparation for the second trial that the two-document discovery was made. Copies of the two documents in Tab H are attached hereto as Exhibit B. They are not a single document as evidenced by the different typefaces (or fonts) of the documents. See for example, the letter "g" and the shape of the commas on each of the pages. These pages were admitted as Defense Exhibits 313 and 314.

told the jury it crystallized the importance and the falsity of

the statements Mr. George made in October and in November, 1986.

See First Trial transcript at p. 735.

The transcript of that supposedly incriminating statement

is cited in the Final Report for its purportedly probative

impact.

Nowhere in the Final Report is it recounted that the

steno-mask reporter, who transcribed the testimony, admitted her

transcript of the April 24 testimony was not verbatim, and that

she saw herself as an interpreter of what she hears, especially

when persons talk simultaneously, or over one another, or when

interrupting one another. First Trial Transcript at 2015-2024.

It is obvious the steno-mask reporter's testimony in the

first trial proved nothing because in the second trial the tape

recording of Mr. George's testimony and not the transcript was

used by OIC as evidence. In the second trial, the tape revealed

that Mr. George began his answer to the first part of the

question before he heard the entire question and continued his

answer even as the remainder of the question was being phrased.

In a side-by-side format, these are the renditions:[6]

Original transcript excerpt (DX 295)		Revised during trial (GX 66B)
Q: When did you know that Secord and North were associated together in their efforts on behalf of the Contras?		Q: When did you know that Secord and North were associated together in--
	V	A: Well--
	O	Q: --their efforts--
	I	A: I--my--my--
A: Well, my mind is so riveted on the day when I saw them both standing there together, that I might have to say if there was ever any question, that was the day, in the White House Situation Room.	C	Q: --on behalf of the
	I	Contras?
	N	A: My mind is so riveted on
	G	the day when I saw them both standing there together that
	O	I, you know, might have to
	V	say if there was ever any
	E	question, that was the day in
	R	the White House Situation Room.

<u>See</u> First Trial Transcript at p. 2036-2038.

The transcript of an exchange between Mr. George and his questioner on April 24, 1987 does not do justice to the dynamic of the interaction of the two parties to that colloquy. Only upon hearing it will it be understood that the parties were talking over one another. In effect, Mr. George was answering

_____

[6] It should be noted that, since there was no charge in the indictment based on this testimony, the jury was not asked to deliver a verdict on it.

only that part of the question which asked "When did you know
that Secord and North were associated together?" and not the
part of the question which continued with the words "on behalf
of the Contras." The tape of that April 24 testimony exists, is
not in Mr. George's counsel's possession, but should be made a
part of the record of the Final Report. It can be found in
OIC's records as well as in the records of the United States
Senate Select Committee on Secret Military Assistance to Iran
and the Nicaraguan Opposition.

GOVERNMENT EXHIBIT 189

The government claimed Exhibit 189 was a handwritten note
of Col. North. This document, upon which so much of OIC's
conclusions are based, was never offered in the first trial.
The trial judge rejected its admission in the second trial as
not meeting any rule of evidence justifying its admission.

Assuming the exhibit to be Col. North's handwritten note of
a briefing given to him by two CIA officials after Mr. George
had met with Congressional staffers regarding the arms for
hostages operation, there were three witnesses who could have
been called to give testimony as to what transpired in the
briefing of Col. North. Any one of them could have identified
the exhibit and given his testimony about it. Each of those
witnesses had been interviewed or appeared before the grand jury
on numerous occasions: Col. North, 18 appearances before the

grand jury; Norman Gardner, Mr. George's special assistant, 6
OIC interviews and 4 appearances before the grand jury; Mr.
George's other special assistant, whose name is classified, 2
OIC interviews. As in the case of other witnesses who testified
in the prosecution's case, one or more of these persons could
have been compelled to testify under immunity (18 U.S.C. Section
6001 et seq.) Indeed, Col. North was immunized for his numerous
grand jury appearances. None was called.

Thus, the prosecutors never submitted any evidence to
support their view of the probity of this inadmissible exhibit.
Yet, it is presented in the Final Report as if it were important
evidence of Mr. George's guilt.

Far from constituting evidence to support OIC's
conclusions, the handling of these exhibits both at trial and in
the Final Report raises serious questions about the honesty and
integrity of anyone responsible for their submission in either
instance.

5. **The never-pleaded, never-proved, but now argued conspiracy theory.**

The overriding theme of the Final Report is that OIC
uncovered an administration-wide conspiracy to deceive the
Congress and the American people about the facts surrounding the
Iran-Contra Affair.

This was never pleaded or charged in Mr. George's
indictment. It was never proved in either of Mr. George's

trials. It was only in the prosecution's rebuttal argument in
summation at the second trial that for the first time, and
without fear of contradiction, the prosecutor argued such a
conspiracy existed.

When counsel moved for a mistrial on the ground that the
prosecutor's statement was wholly without any basis,
inflammatory and prejudicial, the trial judge denied the motion
telling counsel, "you'd kill me if I did [grant the motion]."

Of course, the Final Report compounded that "last word" in
its conclusion about Clair George. There, it set up the straw
man proposition the two trials of Mr. George eventually refuted:
the view that the Iran-Contra operation was run by the NSC with
the awareness and involvement of departments of the Government
and the CIA. From this OIC concludes Mr. George was in a
position to give "crucial information to Congress" but instead
"chose to evade, mislead and lie." What is missing in this
syllogism is proof of Mr. George's personal knowledge versus
what was known by CIA as an institution. Surely, the hung jury
and the later verdict of acquittal on almost all of the counts
in the case require a more precise statement of what this
prosecution has established. Putting Mr. George in jeopardy
twice, with such modest conviction results, cries out for an
analysis of his relationship to the facts that takes into
account the impact of those jury results. Rather, OIC's general
conclusion, unburdened by the juries' responses to Mr. George's

-14-

place in the facts, is cited to drive a specific conclusion about Mr. George's knowledge at certain points in time in October, November, and December, 1986. This is fallacious reasoning. It is an uncontroverted principle of the criminal law that the <u>allegata</u> and <u>probata</u> must coincide. Here, allegations and proof never met and the synapse connecting allegations against Mr. George with proof of his guilt was only in the mind of the prosecutor.

6.   **The verdicts support nothing of which OIC propounds in the Final Report**.

Attached hereto as Exhibit C is the verdict returned in the second trial.

It is remarkable that the Final Report contains no analysis of the charges that Mr. George lied to the grand jury and obstructed that body's investigation of the Iran-Contra affair when he appeared before it in 1991. It certainly cannot be because he was acquitted of these counts, as his acquittal on other counts did not prevent OIC from expressing his views of Mr. George's culpability as to those charges.

Moreover, these verdicts do not support the notion that there was a conspiracy in which Mr. George was a participant. The jury acquitted him on all counts in which Alan Fiers was the principal witness. Mr. George was convicted on two counts. They represent nothing in the larger picture of a conspiracy. Had Mr. George not been pardoned by President Bush, any judgment

of conviction, including probation and a fine, would have been
appealed.   It should be noted that, after the pardon was
announced, the OIC moved that the indictment, on which the jury
returned its verdicts of guilty, and before a judgment of
conviction was imposed, be dismissed with prejudice.   Mr. George
stands convicted of nothing.

7.   Conclusion.

The Final Report regarding Mr. George is revisionist
history, having no respect for the truth or the rule of law.   It
is the product of a vengeful, abusive prosecutor and his staff
who, in typical fashion, have chosen to write their own
vindication and then seek to have it released.   In the process,
they compound the injustice perpetrated by the ineptness of
their investigation, its astronomical costs, and its paltry,
meaningless results.

> Respectfully submitted,
>
> Richard A. Hibey (74823)
> Anderson, Hibey & Blair
> 1708 New Hampshire Ave., NW
> Washington, D.C. 20009
>
> Counsel for Clair E. George

December 3, 1993

EXHIBIT – A

AUG 28 1992 A1

The Prosecutor, The Foreman, And the Jury

George Case Deadlock Suggests U.S. Faced Unforeseen Obstacles

By George Lardner Jr. and Walter Pincus
Washington Post Staff Writers

Iran-contra prosecutors still think they have a strong case against former CIA spy chief Clair E. George, but their failure to win over even a majority of the jurors at his first trial suggests they may face bigger obstacles than they realize.

According to sources familiar with the prosecution's view, the mistrial declared Wednesday was an aberration brought about by a jury foreman who played a major role in persuading most of his fellow jurors that the government had not proved George guilty on any of the nine counts brought against him.

NEWS ANALYSIS

The foreman [Steven C. Kirk] was very articulate, educated and forceful," one source said. "You've got to consider that there was an unusual set of dynamics here. Often when you get a hung jury," you start out with someone [like Kirk] who has strong convictions."

But some defense lawyers who have been following the case said it has a fundamental flaw. They said independent counsel Lawrence E. Walsh is trying to make a convicted felon out of a basically decent, hard-working, patriotic public servant who got no payoff or personal gain from his disputed actions.

"A jury focuses on individuals," said Robert S. Bennett, lawyer for former secretary of defense Caspar W. Weinberger, who is being prosecuted by Walsh's office on charges of obstruction, perjury and lying about the Iran-contra affair to Congress and to Walsh's investigators.

"Jurors ask themselves, 'Is this a good guy or a bad guy? ... Is this someone we should make a criminal?' " Bennett said.

"The fundamental flaw in Walsh's cases is that he is pursuing 'decent,' honorable Americans 'for highly questionable crimes. Juries have to understand, and a good lawyer lets them know, they are making a decision that affects a person forever."

George, a veteran of 33 years in the CIA before his retirement in 1987 as deputy director for operations, has been accused in six counts of lying to several congressional committees and a federal grand jury about the Iran-contra affair and obstructing their investigations of the scandal.

U.S. District Judge Royce C. Lamberth declared a mistrial in the case Wednesday when the jurors said they were unable to reach a unanimous verdict on any count after four weeks of testimony and six days of deliberations. The judge scheduled a new trial to start Oct. 19.

Foreman Kirk said in an interview that from the first tally last Thursday, a majority of jurors always voted 'Not guilty' on every count. Kirk himself was

ASSOCIATED PRESS
Retrial on nine Iran-contra counts of perjury and obstruction is set Oct. 19 for ex-spy chief Clair George.

impressed with the portrayal of the CIA—by prosecution witnesses and George—as an agency that tried hard to live within the restrictions imposed by Congress in the mid-1980s on military aid to the contra rebels in Nicaragua.

"I'm surprised that professionals in the CIA did their best to get their field officers to obey" the rules laid down by Congress, said Kirk, a former law student who is a fund-raising consultant for charitable organizations and described himself as a liberal Democrat.

He said the jurors did not believe that the CIA intended to cover up what the Reagan White House was doing covertly to keep the rebels supplied with arms during this period.

CIA officials "just wanted to make it clear the CIA was not involved" in the supply network, Kirk said. And because no evidence was presented that CIA officials were conspiring to cover up what they knew, Kirk reasoned it made no sense that George was trying to do so on his own.

Sources familiar with the prosecutors' thinking said they saw the case in much simpler terms. In the prosecution's view, when George had been asked questions about what he knew of individuals involved in the contra network and the covert arms-for-hostages dealings with Iran, he lied.

Throughout the trial, George expressed genuine indignation over having been indicted for doing what he, and the agency, had always done. Agency officials were accustomed to telling Congress only as much as they wanted to tell, using semantics and cleverly crafted responses to avoid saying more.

The jury was divided over the question of whether this amounted to criminal conduct in George's case, with a majority saying it did not. As Kirk put it, "was George navigating the narrows" or was he committing a crime? Kirk said that in his view, the prosecution was "nit-picking," a phrase George used repeatedly in his courtroom testimony.

Income G

Study Says 'Ric

By Spencer Rich
Washington Post Staff Writer

The income gap between fifth of the nation's families bottom fifth grew wider in during the 1980s, accord study released yesterday.

"The rich got richer and got poorer," in most of the 4 including Virginia and M said the report by the C Budget and Policy Prioriti eral nonprofit policy analys isation.

In others, the lowest-inc went up but the top fifth faster. The figures are deri the Census Bureau's majo surveys, which are based income before payment of

The only states where between the top income and the bottom got smal Alaska, Delaware, Mont braska, North Dakota, Sc olina and Washington.

Looking at all familie wide, regardless of state, author Isaac Shapiro sai 1979 the average incom lowest fifth of families, me 1992 dollars, was $10,891 middle fifth it was $36,65 the top fifth $83,587.

In the last three year 1980s, average annual in tionally, in 1992 dollar $10,287 for the lowest fif ilies. It rose slightly to $3 the middle fifth. It went to $96,769 for the top fift

---

Silicone Trig

Associated Press

LONDON, Aug. 27—A dy has revealed antibodic silicone, a finding suppor ulation that breast implant er devices can trigger s ness, investigators said to

"This is the first dem of any specific immune silicone in humans," said rector Randall Goldblum man biological chemistry tics department at the Un Texas Medical Branch in C

The study is based on dren who had severe reac silicone-coated tubes planted to treat birth def

9/31/92 — Wash. Post

Another Trial for Clair George?

IT IS SURELY a setback to Iran-contra prosecutor Lawrence Walsh's office that a federal jury here has failed to convict former CIA official Clair George on nine counts involving perjury, obstruction and making false statements. A mistrial was declared Wednesday after four weeks of prosecution and six days of deliberation. Craig Gillen, who tried the case for the special prosecutor's office, immediately requested a retrial, and one has been set for October 19.

Mr. George was charged with misleading Congress and the independent counsel in their investigations, but the jury could not agree that the verbal exchanges, evasive and incomplete as they may have been, amounted to a crime. Interviews with jurors after the trial revealed that a substantial majority voted for acquittal each time the jury was polled. The jury itself was representative of the community, and though one observer close to the the prosecutor's office blamed the mistrial on a "very articulate, educated and forceful" foreman—attributes rather than negatives, we would say—there is no reason to doubt that each juror voted his conscience.

Will the prospects for conviction be better a second time around? We doubt it, and we think it's a high-risk choice for Mr. Walsh. While many courtroom observers believed that the government had made a good case, the majority of the jurors did not buy that version of the facts. Both sides deny that this was a case of jury nullification—where the jury tacitly accepts the fact that the defendant has committed what is technically a crime, but refuses to convict for other reasons involving their own sense of justice. But that is certainly possible. Judge Royce Lamberth likened Mr. George's résumé to that of a war hero in the intelligence community. The combination of this background and the difficulty of proving criminal intent makes conviction at any time problematic.

Mr. Walsh's investigation, now in its sixth year, has accomplished a great deal. The facts of the conspiracy and the role played by the major participants have all been brought out. Some of those principally involved have paid a penalty, and a precedent has been set that should serve as a warning to future public officials who might ignore congressional directives and go off on detours of their own. Even if Mr. George is retried and convicted, little more will be gained. We think there should be no retrial.

ATTACHMENT – B

SUBJECT: Felix RODRIGUEZ

Felix Ismael RODRIGUEZ Mendigutia was an Independent
Contractor from September 1960 until March 1970 (with an
interruption in service from February to October 1963 when he
served in the U.S. Army).   In March 1970 Rodriguez became a
Contract Employee. He remained in that status until 21 April
1976, when he was medically retired after having been disabled in
a helicopter crash in Viet Nam.

2.   Subsequent to Mr. Rodriguez' retirement, he[had]
occasional[contact with the CIA

                                                    ]The Agency
provided him with funds, in 1976 and 1977, when Mr. Rodriguez
received death threats which were determined to have been related
to his Agency service, to enhance the security of his residence
and his privately owned vehicle. In 1984, arrangements were made
for Mr. Rodriguez to broker the introduction of an Agency Officer
to a prominent[Central American]figure. [

                                           ] The available
record does not show whether the introduction was made or any
reimbursement of expenses was actually made to Rodriguez.

3.   In 1984 Mr. Rodriguez applied for re-employment as an
Independent Contractor. The 1984 application was withdrawn before
approval. An Office of Personnel index card indicates that a 1985
application for re-employment was disapproved on security
grounds. The Office of Security, Clearance Division, however, has
no record of the 1985 application. The 1984 application and the
1985 application, if one was made, appear to have been generated
by the Special Operations Group (SOG), which was interested in Mr.
Rodriguez for his military expertise, rather than by either LA
Divisions. [

        ]

DO   44831

SUBJECT: Felix RODRIGUEZ:

[CIA officer #2   ] met Rodriguez in Central
America this past spring. Rodriguez said that he was there as
an advisor on counterinsurgency matters to the Salvadoran air
force, and that he also participated in (unnamed) private
benefactors' efforts to assist the FDN. [#2   ] Rodriguez
that he would be happy to see Rodriguez socially from time to
time, but that Rodriguez would have to understand that, as a
CIA staff employee, [#2] could not become involved in any
way with any effort to aid the contras. Rodriguez indicated
that he understood, and [#2] has never talked to him again.

DO   44830

ATTACHMENT – C

UNITED STATES DISTRICT COURT
FOR THE DISTRICT OF COLUMBIA

United States of America	)
v.	)
Clair E. George,	) Crim. No. 91-0521
Defendant.	)

FILED

DEC 9 - 1992

Clerk, U.S. District Court
District of Columbia

VERDICT FORM

We, the jury in the above-captioned case, have reached a
unanimous verdict as to the following Counts of the Indictment:

Count 1

_____   _____
    Not Guilty   Guilty

If the verdict is NOT GUILTY, that is all you need to decide on
Count One.

If the verdict is GUILTY, we unanimously find beyond a
reasonable doubt that defendant is guilty as to the following
statement or statements underlined below (place a check-mark
beside each statement as to which the jury unanimously finds the
defendant to be guilty):

_____ A.   [MR. GEORGE]: . . . We learned that support
              flights had American citizens involved.

              [SENATOR KERRY]: When was this?

              [MR. GEORGE]: Oh, I would say probably
              around March of this year, Senator. However,
              we were not aware of their identities.

_____ B.   [MR. GEORGE]: . . . However, to reiterate my
              opening remarks, we did not directly or
              indirectly assist them. We provided a great
              deal of intelligence about supplies into
              Nicaragua, and I believe that those of you who
              followed the "National Intelligence Daily"
              over the last two or three months will have
              noted that we have provided several articles
              about the growing amount of supplies being
              provided overland and by air to the Contras
              inside Nicaragua. I would only conclude in
              saying that at no time did we attempt to
              investigate those Americans. That is not our
              responsibility. On those occasions in the
              past, where we have come across Americans who
              we have determined were violating law, we have
              made that information available to the
              Department of Justice. We do not know the
              individuals involved in this affair which led
              to the downing of the airplane, and we do not
              know the details of supply routes which they
              used.

2

Count 2

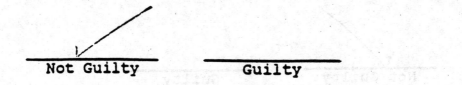

Not Guilty   Guilty

<u>Count 3</u>

_____   _____
        Not Guilty   Guilty

If the verdict is NOT GUILTY, that is all you need to decide on
Count Three.

If the verdict is GUILTY, we unanimously find beyond a
reasonable doubt that defendant is guilty as to the following
statement or statements underlined below (place a check-mark
beside each statement as to which the jury unanimously finds the
defendant to be guilty):

_____A.   [MR. CHAIRMAN]: There are a number of
             airplanes that take off there to supply the
             Contras regularly. You don't know who they
             are?

             [MR. FIERS]: We know the airplanes by type.
             We knew, for example, there were two C-123's
             and two C-7 cargoes. We knew that they were
             flying out of Ilopango and we knew they were
             flying both from Aguacate and Aguacate into
             Nicaragua. We knew in some cases less
             frequently that they were flying down the
             Pacific air corridors into southern Nicaragua
             for the purposes of resupply, but as to who
             was flying the flights and who was behind
             them, we do not know.

             [MR. CHAIRMAN]: And you still don't?

             [MR. FIERS]: No.

             [MR. GEORGE]: <u>No, sir</u>.

_____B.   [MR. FIERS]: We know from the newspapers
             that a company called Corporate Air Services
             is the company that appears to have some
             involvement with them, but --

             [MR. GEORGE]: <u>What we know at this
             point is</u> as [Alan] says, <u>is from the press</u>.

4

Count 4

| Not Guilty | Guilty |

Count 5

——————————————   ————————✓————————
        Not Guilty   Guilty

If the verdict is NOT GUILTY, that is all you need to decide on
Count Five.

If the verdict is GUILTY, we unanimously find beyond a
reasonable doubt that defendant is guilty as to the following
statement or statements underlined below (place a check-mark
beside each statement as to which the jury unanimously finds the
defendant to be guilty):

✓____ A.   [MR. HALL]: Was it your understanding
                 that Colonel North or anybody else in the
                 National Security Council or any private
                 parties would have some responsibilities and
                 roles in the financial transactions?

                 [MR. GEORGE]: I'm told that an individual
                 that had -- I'm told after the fact that an
                 individual who did have a role in the
                 financial affairs of this enterprise was
                 Richard Secord.

                 [MR. HALL]: Were you aware of any role that
                 Colonel North played?

                 [MR. GEORGE]: I have no information on
                 Colonel North and funds.

                 [MR. HALL]: Can you tell us what role Secord
                 did play?

                 [MR. GEORGE]: I cannot. Please.

_____ B.   [MR. HALL]: Are there any other details
                 associated with this project that you have
                 not discussed with us that you are aware of?

                 [MR. GEORGE]: No. Again I tell you the
                 people from our Directorate were involved,
                 the people from the other Directorates
                 involved. The critical thing to me was the
                 Finding and the fact that we were told that
                 we were going to get involved in it.
                 Surprise of how that Finding was handled.

6

The delegation of the responsibility to
support what I believe was a National
Security Council initiative. The people that
I sent out to do it. I am sure they told me
many, many things that I, sitting here before
you, can't recall off the top of my head, and
I have again, as I said, gone out of my way
not to sit down with Mr. Cave and Mr. Twetton
and everyone else and say now let's all
remind each other what happened here, because
I understand that's the way it should be.
But I at no time felt uncomfortable that the
law was broken or that we knew money was
being siphoned off or --

[MR. HALL]: Did you have --

[MR. GEORGE]: I was a little disturbed about
some of the players in the affair. I think I
was worried about -- I was worried about, you
know, who was Hakim and where is his role in
this, and the good General Secord whom I had
never laid eyes on but whose name I was
familiar with.

<u>Count 6</u>

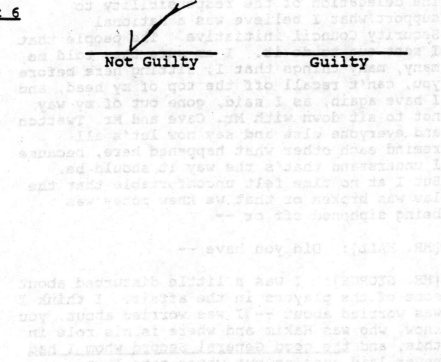

Not Guilty   Guilty

Count 7

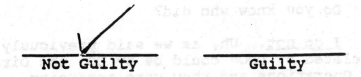

_____ Not Guilty   _____ Guilty

If the verdict is NOT GUILTY, that is all you need to decide on Count Seven.

If the verdict is GUILTY, we unanimously find beyond a reasonable doubt that defendant is guilty as to the following statement or statements underlined below (place a check-mark beside each statement as to which the jury unanimously finds the defendant to be guilty):

_____A. · Q.   During our meeting in our office, the Office of Independent Counsel, you indicated that you did not edit anything out of these drafts?

A.   I do not recall editing these drafts at all.

_____B.   Q.   Okay.

A.   I was finally handed Draft Number whatever it was, and that was it.

_____C.   Q.   On page two of Draft 3, at the bottom of that I will read the following sentence and it has three lines through it. It says, "Subsequent to the 1984 cutoff, Ilopango airfield in San Salvador was used to support democratic resistance as a transit point for congressionally authorized humanitarian assistance." And then by the third line through that sentence, it say, "Deleted by DDO."

First of all, is that your handwriting?

A.   It's not my handwriting.

Q.   Did you direct that that portion of the draft be excised?

A.   I cannot believe I did.

9

_____D. Q. Do you know who did?

A. <u>I do not</u>. Uh, as we said previously, "deleted by DDO" could be by DO, the Director of Operations and they were confusing terminologies. <u>I do not recall getting to this kind of detail in preparing this statement</u>.

Dated: ~~November~~ December 9, 1992

<u>   </u>
                          Foreperson of the Jury

CERTIFICATE OF SERVICE

I HEREBY CERTIFY that I have this 3rd day of December, 1993, caused a copy of the foregoing Comment of Clair E. George on the Final Report of the Independent Counsel in the Iran-Contra Matter to be hand-delivered to:

Independent Counsel Lawrence Walsh
Office of Independent Counsel
1 Columbus Circle, N.E.
Room G-320
Washington, D.C. 20544

Richard A. Hibey

Thomas C. Green

United States Court of Appeals
For the District of Columbia Circuit

FILED SEP 3 0 1993

RON GARVIN
CLERK

THOMAS C. GREEN
3738 HUNTINGTON ST. N.W.
WASHINGTON D.C. 20015

September 27, 1993

The Honorable David B. Sentelle
The Honorable John D. Butzner
The Honorable Joseph T. Sneed
United States Circuit Judges
United States Court of Appeals
District of Columbia Circuit
333 Constitution Avenue, NW
Washington, DC 20001-2866

Dear Judges Sentelle, Butzner and Sneed:

I am writing to avail myself of the opportunity to comment on the Report of Independent Counsel Lawrence Walsh as provided for in your Order filed on August 5, 1993, in the matter of Oliver L. North, et al.

There are a number of inaccurate statements and conclusions concerning my conduct published in Chapter 7 of the Report and in a very few other brief passages and footnotes. Two portions of the Report require specific comment.

First, Independent Counsel, in his discussion of my contact with Fawn Hall on the night of November 25, 1986, raises the possibility that I knew that Ms. Hall and Lt. Col. North were engaged in removing documents from the Old Executive Office Building when I departed with them that night. The Report appropriately concedes that its entire equivocal assessment of my conduct is based only on speculation concerning the extent of my knowledge. Nevertheless, it is disconcerting that such speculation is permitted in this type of Report which will be publicly reviewed by individuals who may ignore or not appreciate the useless value of speculation in connection with an Independent Counsel's investigation. That the speculation is absolutely false is confirmed by the affidavit of Ms. Hall attached to this letter. It should also be noted that the following morning, November 26, 1986, I ceased my representation of Lt. Col. North and introduced him to new counsel, whom he retained.

Second, at page 101 of Chapter 1 of the Report, Mr. Walsh describes a meeting between Lt. Col. North and Robert McFarlane which occurred on Sunday, November 23, 1986. I attended that meeting very briefly, which was the only time I ever met or spoke with Mr. McFarlane. In his deposition testimony on July 2, 1987, before the U.S. House of Representatives, Select Committee to Investigate Covert Arms Transactions with Iran, Mr. McFarlane recalled why I came to speak to him. Although the transcript was reviewed by the Office of Independent Counsel, Mr. Walsh's Report fails to mention that

portion of Mr. McFarlane's deposition testimony which
specifically related to my presence at the subject meeting:

> Q.   Did he (Lt. Col. North) discuss whether or
>   not he had spoken to Attorney General Meese
>   on Saturday or early Sunday?
>
> A.   No.
>
> Mr. Garment: Wasn't he going to see Meese
> that afternoon?
>
> THE WITNESS: Well he was, but I am not sure
> he told me that. The only other thing that I
> haven't already recounted here in that
> meeting was that when his attorney came in we
> all sat down. His attorney, Mr. Green, I
> think by way of introduction, just kind of
> said autobiographical things, that he had
> been [an] Assistant U.S. Attorney and he had
> been associated with I guess he said problems
> of this kind, but that he went on to say that
> he had always found it best in proceedings
> like this that you just simply told your
> story truthfully and let the chips fall where
> they may or something like that, which didn't
> make any particular impression, and about
> that time General Secord or somebody knocked
> at the door, it turned out to be General
> Secord.... McFarlane deposition at pp. 672-
> 673.

Although there are several other misstatements in the
report in connection with references to me, they are not so
significant as to require public comment.

                                   Sincerely yours,

                                   Thomas C. Green

AFFIDAVIT

City of Washington   )
)   ss:
District of Columbia   )

         Fawn Hall, being first duly sworn, avers and deposes as follows.

         1. On November 25, 1986, I telephoned Lt. Col. Oliver North and told him that he had to return to his office. He told me he would return and that Tom Green would be with him. As of this time I had never met Tom Green. It was my understanding that Mr. Green was an attorney with whom Mr. North was consulting.

         2. When Lt. Col. North and Mr. Green arrived at the office, I was introduced to Mr. Green. I did not engage in any additional conversation with Mr. Green while in the office that evening. Mr. Green did not accompany me into Lt. Col. North's inner office where Lt. Col. North and I had a private discussion. When we emerged, we left the office almost immediately, accompanied by Mr. Green. I never told Mr. Green that I was removing documents from the office that evening, and I am confident that Mr. Green had no knowledge of that fact.

         3. When we got near or in the elevator located down the hall from Lt. Col. North's office, I tried to indicate subtlety to Lt. Col. North, not Mr. Green, that I wanted to give Lt. Col. North the documents. I do not know what, if anything, Mr. Green saw or heard at that moment; nor do I know what, if

- 2 -

anything, Mr. Green perceived to be happening. I did not talk to Mr. Green, and I do not recall that Mr. Green said anything.

4. After we left the EOB, Lt. Col. North and I started to cross 17th Street, N.W. I again attempted with either a word or a gesture made to Lt. Col. North, not to Mr. Green, that I wanted to give Lt. Col. North the documents. As of that moment I had no conversation with Mr. Green; nor, to my recollection, had Lt. Col. North. As I tried to gesture or speak to Lt. Col. North, Mr. Green, whom I recall was walking a bit behind Lt. Col. North and me, told me to wait until we were inside his car. Again, I do not know what, if anything, Mr. Green saw which inspired his only remark. I clearly had not said anything to Mr. Green about any documents. I understood him to be cautioning me and Lt. Col. North not to have any conversation in public.

5. Not until I was inside Mr. Green's car did I remove any documents and hand them to Lt. Col. North, who was in the back seat. Mr. Green would only have seen me give documents to Lt. Col. North. I did not reveal the content of the

- 3 -

documents while I was in Mr. Green's car. I recall no further
contact with Mr. Green after he departed that evening and after
he stopped representing Lt. Col. North.

_____
Fawn Hall

Subscribed and sworn to before me this 5th day of March, 1990

_____
Notary Public

My Commission expires: January 14, 1995

Ambassador Donald P. Gregg

UNITED STATES COURT OF APPEALS
FOR THE DISTRICT OF COLUMBIA CIRCUIT **FILED** DEC 0 2 1993

Division for the Purpose of
Appointing Independent Counsels

RON GARVIN
CLERK

Ethics in Government Act of 1978, as Amended

In re: Oliver L. North, et al.   Division No. 86-6

MOTION OF AMBASSADOR DONALD P. GREGG
TO APPEND HIS COMMENTS TO THE
FINAL REPORT OF THE INDEPENDENT COUNSEL

Ambassador Donald P. Gregg respectfully moves pursuant to the order

of this Court dated August 5, 1993 and 28 U.S.C. § 594(h)(2) to have his comment,

and the comment of his attorney, Judah Best, included as an appendix to the final

report of the Independent Counsel.

December 2, 1993

Respectfully submitted,

Judah Best
DEBEVOISE & PLIMPTON
555 13th Street, N.W.
Washington, D.C. 20004

Attorneys for Ambassador Donald P. Gregg

COMMENT OF AMBASSADOR DONALD P. GREGG

The Office of the Independent Counsel has at last finished its investigation. Throughout the course of this seven-year process, I have fully cooperated with Judge Walsh, his staff, the FBI and all others associated with the investigation. I have always told the truth, have never made an effort to mislead or confuse anyone and did everything I possibly could to dispel doubts anyone might have had about my actions. I am proud of my actions and my testimony which has remained consistent and unchanged.

I am innocent of any wrongdoing whatsoever. Nevertheless, unable to make any sort of case against me, the Walsh staff, in the penultimate sentence of the chapter in their report dealing with my actions in 1986, accuses me of "acts of concealment." Their assertion is that I should have publicly contradicted a statement made by the White House in October 1986 that there was no official US Government connection to a Contra resupply plane shot down in Nicaragua. I was not called on to make any statement on that issue; and I was in no position to do so at the time because I did not yet know enough of the facts.

What is the basis for the Walsh staff assertion? I can only surmise that it is vindictiveness, because there is no basis for the accusation in the report.

In looking at events that they associated with me, the Walsh staffers were never able to grasp either the concept of "compartmentation," or the "need to know" principle that were fully employed by Oliver North and his associates. Felix Rodriguez, a long-time intelligence officer, understood these things, and lived by them. North recruited Felix into his Contra supply network and told Felix not to tell me. Felix respected that -- he knew I had no "need to know" and that in fact I was better off not knowing some of the ill-conceived things being done by North's associates. Only in August 1986 had things become so bad that Felix felt he had to tell me part of the story. Judge Walsh and his staff never could fathom the "need to know" principle. Their naive and stubbornly-held assumption was that since Felix and I were long time friends, we would have told each other everything. In the intelligence world, such is not the case.

The most difficult and painful part of my cooperation with the Walsh staff was my agreement in 1990 to submit to a polygraph examination. As a CIA officer, I had routinely been subjected to polygraph interrogations. I had always found the process personally difficult and degrading. I agreed to one more test since I had nothing whatsoever to hide, and hoped that the test might end the years of harassment and calculated press leaks by the Independent Counsel staff. To my utter surprise and dismay, I was told that my answers "indicated deception." I immediately called the White House legal office and the Walsh staff (Craig Gillen) to tell them that I had failed the test, and for the first time retained legal counsel. My outstanding lawyer, Judah Best, arranged for me to take an impartial polygraph test with a nationally-known polygrapher. Richard O. Arther, who conducted the second series of tests over a period of two days, is one of the most acclaimed experts in his field. Mr. Arther reviewed the questions posed to me in the Independent Counsel's test and found them inadequate to serve as the basis of forming a conclusion as to the truthfulness of my answers. (I am attaching a copy of Mr. Arther's curriculum vitae to this comment.)

The second test, taken in November 1990, I passed without difficulty. It showed clearly that I had told the truth about my knowledge of the Iran-Contra affair. Its questions, covering the same ground as the first test, were far better formulated, and more clearly focused.[1]

My reaction, at the end of this endless process is anger at Judge Walsh and his staff. I cooperated with them fully, told the truth at every turn, received strong confirmation from the Senate to become US Ambassador to Korea, and yet, at the end of a chapter that repeatedly acknowledges my consistent and truthful testimony, they say that I committed "acts of concealment."

---

1.   The questions posed by Mr. Arther are as follows:

    1.   While the 1980 hostages were still in Iran, did you then know of a plan to delay their release until after the election?

    2.   While under oath, did you deliberately tell even one lie about Felix Rodriguez?

    3.   Before August 8, '86, did George Bush and you discuss the sale of arms to Iran?

    4.   While under oath, did you deliberately tell even one lie about Ollie North?

Mr. Arther concluded that I told the truth when I answered "No" to all four of his pertinent test questions.

- 2 -

I absolutely reject this unwarranted accusation. It has no support in fact and is utterly without foundation in law, as is explained in the attached comment of my counsel, Judah Best. I am deeply angered that after all these years and all the millions of dollars spent, such a flawed, vindictive and biased report has been produced by Judge Walsh and his staff.

Donald P. Gregg

Donald P. Gregg

December 1, 1993

SCIENTIFIC LIE DETECTION, INC.

Utilizing the Sixth Generation of The Arther Polygraphs

Suite 1400   200 West 57th Street   New York, N.Y. 10019
(212)   755-5241

RICHARD O. ARTHER, M.A., A.C.P.
President

CATHERINE A. ARTHER, M.A., A.C.P.
Certified Polygraphist

RICHARD O. ARTHER, M.A., A.C.P.

Richard O. Arther graduated in 1951 with high honors from Michigan State University with a Bachelor of Science in Police Administration. In 1960, he obtained his Master's in Psychology from Columbia University.

Following graduation in 1951, he began his polygraph internship in Chicago at John E. Reid & Associates. His instructors were Mr. Reid, who was then already considered the world's most outstanding polygraphist, and Fred E. Inbau, the noted Northwestern University Professor of Criminal Law. After six months of intensive training, during which time he was their only student, Mr. Arther received his certificate as an Expert Polygraphist.

He remained with the firm as Mr. Reid's Chief Associate. While there, he was selected to conduct research work for the U.S. Office of Naval Research. This special project took one year to complete.

Mr. Arther remained in Chicago until July 1953, at which time he came to Manhattan to establish on West 57th Street the first full-time polygraph suite east of Chicago. His suite has been on West 57th Street ever since.

In 1958, Mr. Arther founded Scientific Lie Detection, Inc. His expert polygraph testimony has been accepted in six New York State Supreme Court cases, three of which were on behalf of the prosecution. He has administered polygraph examinations to over 26,000 persons.

In 1964, Mr. Arther founded the New York State Polygraphists, which is the organization of the state's 48 leading polygraphists. During its first eight years he was either President or Chairman of the Board.

Mr. Arther also founded in 1964 the New Jersey Polygraphists, which has 97 members. He was the Association's Secretary-Treasurer for its first ten years. In 1985, he was elected its first Life Member.

Mr. Arther was one of the eight founders in 1965 of the American Polygraph Association. This Association has honored him many times with various awards, such as Certificates of Merit and the Professional Service Award.

Mr. Arther was one of the seven founders in 1977 of the American Association of Police Polygraphists and served on its first Board of Directors. In 1980, he received its "Polygraphist of the Year" award and in 1990 its first award ever for "Professional Achievement".

He is the only person who is one of the founders of both the American Polygraph Association and the American Association of Police Polygraphists.

In addition, Mr. Arther is a Charter Distinguished Fellow in The Academy of Certified Polygraphists. Since its start in 1973, he has been the Executive Director of this organization which now has over 300 members.

In 1977, Mr. Arther was selected as Chief Polygraph Consultant to the prestigious U.S. House of Representatives Assassination Committee, which investigated the murders of both President John F. Kennedy and Reverend Martin Luther King.

RICHARD O. ARTHER
Expert Polygraphist Since 1951

Founder, 1964
New York State Polygraphists

Founder, 1964
New Jersey Polygraphists

President Since 1964
National Training Center of Polygraph Science

Managing Editor Since 1966
The Journal of Polygraph Science

From 1954 through 1962, Mr. Arther was on the Police Science Staff of Brooklyn College. In addition, for 3 years he was on the Police Science Staff of Seton Hall University, for 2 years on the staff of New York University's Graduate School of Public Administration, and for 2 years on the staff of the John Jay College of Criminal Justice. During the past 30 years he has presented several dozen college-level seminars, including for each of the past 11 years at Louisiana State University.

In 1958, Mr. Arther was a Co-Founder of The National Training Center of Polygraph Science, where since 1964 he has served as School Director. For the past 31 years this school has offered the greatest number of basic courses of any polygraph school in the world. He has been in charge of teaching the profession to an estimated 1,800 polygraphists, including those from the United States Army, Coast Guard, Customs Service, and Marine Corps as well as the first 22 polygraphists ever trained for the Royal Canadian Mounted Police, 62 polygraphists for the New York State Police, 14 other state police departments, numerous other state investigative organizations, and for several hundred sheriff and police departments as well as foreign governments.

In 1987, he taught in Mexico City the first polygraphists ever trained there for the Mexican Federal Government and then returned to present their first polygraph seminar. In 1987, he also taught in San Salvador polygraphists for the El Salvador Government. Since then he has returned to San Salvador 10 additional times to teach his basic course and to conduct advanced polygraph seminars.

Approximately 11,000 polygraphists/investigators have attended his 177 personally-conducted seminars, which he has presented in 31 states as well as Canada, Europe, and Latin America. He has personally conducted more seminars than all other polygraphists combined.

Starting in 1952, Mr. Arther has developed many polygraph procedures which are acknowledged to be major breakthroughs in advancing the polygraph profession.

The Arther VI Polygraph, which was designed and is manufactured according to his specifications, is the world's only polygraph which is restricted in its sale, since it is sold only to governmental agencies and those private experts of high ethical reputation.

For professional journals Mr. Arther has contributed approximately 400 articles dealing with the polygraph, interrogation, and scientific investigation. In 1953, he materially assisted Fred E. Inbau and John E. Reid in writing the third edition of *Lie Detection and Criminal Interrogation*. According to the bibliographical *Truth and Science*, Mr. Arther has written more articles than anyone else in the history of the polygraph profession, which is now 106 years old.

Mr. Arther is the senior author of *Interrogation for Investigators* and was the sole author of the noted college text, *The Scientific Investigator*, which had five printings.

In 1966, Mr. Arther founded *The Journal of Polygraph Science* and from its start has been its Managing Editor. It is the oldest of all polygraph publications.

Mr. Arther belongs to various non-polygraph professional organizations, including the Special Agents Association (1953), the National Counter Intelligence Corps Association (1962), and AFOSISA (1990). Since 1954 he has been an Associate Member of the International Association of Chiefs of Police and since 1972 a Life Member of both the National Sheriffs Association and the Military Police Association. Since 1974 he has been a member of an organization devoted to financially helping the families of policemen, firemen, and volunteer ambulance technicians killed in the line of duty.

His name has appeared in many biographical publications, including *Who's Who in the World*, *Who's Who in the East*, and *Who's Who in Finance and Industry*.

July 1991

COMMENT SUBMITTED ON BEHALF OF AMBASSADOR DONALD P. GREGG

This comment is provided to point out a serious legal infirmity in the suggestion in Chapter 29 of the Report of the Office of the Independent Counsel ("OIC") that Ambassador Gregg engaged in "acts of concealment."

The OIC admits that it has failed to find evidence sufficient to support any charge against Ambassador Gregg. But in the final few sentences of Chapter 29, the OIC gratuitously asserts that he "remained silent as administration representatives publicly stated that there was no U.S. involvement in the flight" of Eugene Hasenfus and characterizes this silence as "concealment".

Ambassador Gregg in his separate comment has eloquently expressed his indignation at this totally unjustified and unsupported charge. We wish to add that the assertion is also without any legal foundation. Having admitted that they have no case against Ambassador Gregg, the OIC has resorted to the tactic of trumping up a charge of "remaining silent" which has no basis in law.

In the introduction to Chapter 29, the OIC states that Ambassador Gregg and his deputy, Col. Samuel J. Watson III, "were investigated for possible false testimony regarding their denial of knowledge of [Felix] Rodriguez's involvement in [Oliver] North's contra resupply operation." (emphasis added). As to two aspects of the Ambassador's testimony, namely his denials that he introduced North to Rodriguez or that North had contacted him before recruiting Rodriguez, the OIC concluded that "the evidence suggests that Gregg's denials are correct." The third element of Ambassador Gregg's testimony considered by the OIC, according to its Final Report, was his denial that he was aware prior to August 1986 of Rodriguez's involvement in contra resupply. The OIC states that this question is "more problematic," but grudgingly concludes -- citing among other things the strong corroborating testimony of Felix Rodriguez -- that there was insufficient evidence to support any prosecution.

Instead of concluding the Chapter on Ambassador Gregg with the frank admission that it had failed to find evidence sufficient to support any charge concerning his testimony the OIC added these final two paragraphs:

There was strong evidence that following the shootdown of the Hasenfus plane, Gregg and Watson were aware of North's connection to the resupply operation. Rodriguez informed them of North's involvement in August 1986, and Rodriguez called Watson on October 6, 1986; to let him know that the downed plane was one of North's. They remained silent as administration representatives publicly stated that there was no U.S. involvement in the flight.

Despite these acts of concealment, the evidence did not prove that Watson or Gregg committed a chargeable offense following the Hasenfus shootdown. No chargeable offense could be proved beyond a reasonable doubt.

The implication is that if Ambassador Gregg had sufficient knowledge at the time to contradict the statements of others to the press -- which Ambassador Gregg denies -- his remaining silent would somehow constitute an offense. This suggestion is plainly contrary to law and highly irresponsible. There is no federal crime of "concealment." The closest analogue is misprision of felony[1], and under this statute it is clear that mere silence does not constitute an offense. Every court that has addressed the issue has held that misprision of felony requires that the defendant take an affirmative step to conceal the criminal activities of another. See, e.g., United States v. Waters, 885 F.2d 1266, 1275 (5th Cir. 1989); United States v. Goldberg, 862 F.2d 101 (6th Cir. 1988); United States v. Ciambrone, 750 F.2d 1416, 1417 (9th Cir. 1984).

For example, in United States v. Ciambrone, the Ninth Circuit reversed the ruling of the district court which found the defendant guilty of misprision of felony. 750 F.2d at 1416. In Ciambrone, the key issue was whether the defendant undertook any affirmative act of concealment. The Ninth Circuit states: "[t]he starting point of our analysis is the proposition that mere silence without some affirmative act, is insufficient evidence, of the crime of misprision of felony." Id. at 1418 (internal quotations omitted). In Ciambrone, the defendant made a partial truthful disclosure to the Secret Service but failed to reveal certain other information. The government contended that the partial disclosure satisfied the affirmative act requirement of the statute. The Ninth Circuit, however, disagreed and held that the misprision of felony statute cannot be rationally interpreted to criminalize partial disclosure of a crime when "remaining totally silent is not a violation." Id. at 1418.

It is clear then that "remaining silent" is not a violation of any law, and the contrary suggestion by the OIC in the final two paragraphs of Chapter 29 demonstrates how unfair its Report is with regard to Ambassador Gregg. We submit

---

1.   Whoever, having knowledge of the actual commission of a felony cognizable by a court of the United States, does not as soon as possible make known the same to some judge or other person in civil or military authority under the United States, shall be fined not more than $500 or imprisoned not more than three years or both 18 U.S.C. § 4.

that these paragraphs are totally unjustified and ask that this comment and that of Ambassador Gregg be included in the appendix to place the paragraphs in proper perspective.

December 2, 1993

Judah Best
DEBEVOISE & PLIMPTON
555 13th Street, N.W.
Washington, D.C. 20004

Attorneys for Ambassador Donald P. Gregg

David D. Gries

Central Intelligence Agency

Washington, D.C. 20505

November 1, 1993

Mr. Ron Garvin
Clerk, United States Court of Appeals
District of Columbia Circuit
Washington, DC 20001-2866

Dear Mr. Garvin:

Pursuant to your communications dated August 12, 1993 and
September 24, 1993, I am enclosing my comment concerning points
made on pages 312 and 314 of the Final Report of the independent
counsel. I hope it will be possible to include my comment as an
appendix to the Final Report.

Yours Sincerely,

David D. Gries

Enclosure

UNITED STATES COURT OF APPEALS
FOR THE DISTRICT OF COLUMBIA CIRCUIT
Division for the Purpose of Appointing Independent Counsels
Division 86-6

In re: Final Report of the Independent Counsel,
Statements concerning David Gries

FILED, NOV 0 1 1993

RON GARVIN
CLERK

The draft Final Report makes statements about me on pages 312 and 314 that require clarification.

Statement on page 312

"...CIA Director of Congressional Affairs David Gries echoed George's remarks. Again, these statements ignored the November 1985 Hawk shipment carried by a CIA proprietary."

Comment: On November 18, 1986 when I "echoed George's remarks" at a meeting with Congressional staff, I was unaware, as were many others, that a Hawk shipment had been made in November 1985 prior to the January 17, 1986 finding. I had no independent knowledge of the Hawk shipment and at that time was not involved in Agency operations. In echoing George's statement, I was relying on information sent to the Office of Congressional Affairs by other Agency offices in preparation for the November 18, 1986 meeting with Congressional staff. Three weeks after the meeting, CIA Director Casey corrected the record in December 8, 1986 testimony before the House Appropriations Subcommittee on Defense. By that time, more complete information was available. Casey repeated the correction on December 10, 1986 before the House Foreign Relations Committee. I accompanied him on both occasions and thus considered my own statement corrected as well.

Statement on page 314

"(3) David Gries's denial that there had been CIA support for the Iran arms sales prior to the January 17 finding..."

"As in most other investigations involving illegal false statements, the key question in assessing the liability of senior CIA officials for these statements were, first, whether each official knew at the time he spoke that his statement was false, and second, whether the official deliberately made that statement."

Comment: My denial quoted in (3) above on page 314 refers back to the November 18, 1986 meeting with Congressional staff when I "echoed George's remarks" that CIA had not assisted the Iran arms sales prior to the January 17, 1986 finding. As noted in my comment for page 312, I was unaware when I made the denial that a Hawk shipment had been made in November 1985. The mistake was corrected three weeks later in testimony to Congress.

Conclusion

My purpose in clarifying the statements made about me on pages 312 and 314 is to show that my incorrect statement of November 18, 1986 was based on lack of independent knowledge of the November 1985 Hawk shipment and therefore was not a deliberately false statement. My error was corrected in testimony before Congress three weeks later.

Albert Hakim

Albert Hakim
16375 Aztec Ridge Drive
Los Gatos, CA 95032
(408) 395-0500

Ron Garvin, Clerk
United States Court of Appeals
District of Columbia Circuit
333 Constitution Ave., N.W.
Room 5409
Washington, D.C. 20001

November 30, 1993

RE: Iran Contra - Oliver L. North, et al.
          (President Ronald W. Reagan)

Dear Mr. Garvin:

I am attaching herewith a set of documents concerning my Response,
Affirmative Defense and Counter Claim, as well as my Opposition to
A Stay of the case relevant to Civil Case No: 93-1202 A (E.D. Va)
in connection with the above matter.

These documents are to serve as my response to the final report of
the Independent Council.

I am also separately enclosing a "working summary of Iran Contra
activities and Legal Process" which document shows the
unconstitutional doctrine of Walsh "Everyone is guilty until proven
innocent" and which continues to be the basis of his report and the
above civil case.

Those interested should examine these documents which are the first
set of documents which reveal the factual case of Iran Contra in a
simple and non-complex language. "The funds do not belong to the
USG therefore the Boland Amendment was not violated".

Thank you.

Respectfully,

Albert Hakim

F:GARVIN.CLK

Working Summary of the Iran Contra Activities and Legal Process

1. Albert Hakim and many other individuals who put themselves at the service of USG interests experienced a series of dynamics that will be deemed shameful when in the annals of American History they are reviewed with distance and perspective.

2. When the covert operation became the focus of public awareness the Reagan administration handled the exposure as if it was a guilty party. It therefore, lost the opportunity to take responsibility for the activities and, as such, to protect their sensitive and proper mission.

3. By acting as if they were engaged in some "inappropriate" affair, the administration "invited" a level of scrutiny and concern that may have been avoidable.

4. This attention created an avalanche of inquiry that had many political agendas following the imagined scent of blood.

5. This country had been through an inquiry that smacked of cover-up, extra-Constitutional conduct and political treachery just ten years earlier and as a nation we knew how to react to the thought that a similar event was happening again.

6. The unfortunate aspect to the events relating to Reagan is that, unlike those of Nixon, these events did not revolve around an attempt to keep and maintain political power; they centered on the efforts of a powerful but politically limited nation to afford assistance to freedom fighters whose very roots were similar to those of our founding fathers, an attempt to free American hostages from a dangerous, politically charged and unpredictable environment and finally an attempt to create a dialogue of mutual interest with another nation with whom we had found ourselves in great public enmity but with whom we had many common objectives and interests. (Iran). The common thread between these two endeavors was the response to the threat of communism and specifically Russian imperialism. By fighting Russian sponsored insurgency and by helping another nation stand up to the prospective threat of Russian invasion we helped stem the tide of an expansionist country in the last throes of its expansionism.

7. The activities themselves were not manifestly illegal and were certainly defensible to the American people; had the President decided to stand up for the policy he had inititiated and supported. Instead, by acting as if something had been done that was regrettable in a moral, legal or political sense, the president showed a political vulnerability that invited the sharks into the boat. Unfortunately for the participants, the president was far away from the boat when his advisors started the finger pointing process.

8. Throughout the entire process of revelation and investigation, the pressure has been on those participants to "give up" the President.

9. As the administration distanced itself from the activities of the Iran Contra initiatives, it abandoned people in the United States and around the world who were quietly working to enable USG interests to be realized.

10. The bulk of these people had been participating solely because the President or his representatives had asked them in the name of the Executive Branch and under the guise of a legal process that insured legality and official endorsement.

11. Once the scrutiny began the participants in the "field" were not only left without the support that was due them, they became the focus of blame for the activities themselves. This abandonment served the Reagan political needs for distance and had a devastating effect on those left holding the bag.

12. From an international political perspective, the participants knew that they were part of a series of covert events that might need to be "denied" in an official sense but none of the participants expected the nation that engaged their services itself to turn so brutally against them.

13. Albert Hakim's story is representative and by no means unique. He was functioning as a private citizen who made a business arrangement with the USG to assist them in a variety of foreign policy objectives. His motivation was both capitalistic and patriotic.

14. The dynamic between the two major political parties was predictable once Reagan showed weakness rather than strength on this issue. The wild card was the dynamic adopted and created by Independent Counsel Walsh in his investigations.

15. Once the Reagan administration decided to abandon those offering assistance a variety of things happened. Many people were jailed in Middle East countries as their role on behalf of the USG became known. In Beruit, alone, over ten people were jailed and were abandoned by the USG. Interestingly, the Ayatollah eventually exerted influence to effect the release of these people even though they were associated with "our" side. Perhaps the Iranians understood that these people were working to achieve a fundamental shift in political thinking that would have left some of the historic tension in the dust by emphasizing common economic interests.

16. Tens of millions of dollars of commitments to individuals were left unpaid and unacknowledged even though official representatives of the USG had been present when most of the commitments had been made.

17. Hakim had to bear millions of dollars of legal fees, public ridicule and interference in his business that left it unable to function in the sense that it had before.

18. The USG breached its contractual arrangements and then set the Independent Counsel upon Hakim in an effort to avoid legitimate claims against it.

19. Throughout the entire affair, Albert Hakim has told a consistent, truthful and simple version of the events. In all these years, he descriptions have never wavered. He has said that he made a "for profit" business relationship with the USG, that he was pleased to be of service to the interests of the USG and that he felt he could assist in the achievement of the objectives by enacting his global approach to business which allowed historically adversarial parties to achieve a peaceful dynamic by focusing on common economic interests and through the experience of shared success to find more meaningful common ground. This "fourth option", as Hakim has often described this phenomena was the foundation of the "Hakim Accords". If allowed to be implemented, the "Accords" would have brought all the hostages home, stopped new hostage taking and changed the shape of tension in the Middle East region. In addition, it would have created an inertia of reliance upon the United States for trade facilitation that would have led to strategic alliances amongst traditionally distrustful enemies. Most surprising, the Iranians were willing to underwrite this effort in a major financial way.

20. The treatment by the USG through the Office of the Independent Counsel (OIC) has been marked by changing stories, deceptive evidence gathering, tortious business interference, misrepresentations, attempts to undermine the benefit of the presumption of innocence that Americans enjoy as the hallmark of our democracy, fabrications and a personal twist to prosecution and litigation that even the news media has observed..

21. The OIC began their existence as a tool for the political process. In the end they spent almost $40,000,000.00. For that sum, they were able to achieve no convictions for malfeasance or misfeasance relating to the substantial sums that were passed through the channels. No one was convicted of by passing Congressional mandate and no one was convicted of any form of personal enrichment. However, the OIC has continually repeated its accusations as if they are fact and then hid behind CIPA as an excuse for not achieving any legal results. In fact, it was the defense in the criminal cases that was working so hard to lift the CIPA restrictions so that they could shed the light of day upon their affairs and thus receive the exoneration to which they were entitled.

22. The OIC proffered theories of conduct that ranged from a rogue group of outlaw diplomats out for their own profit, to an agency relationship amongst the participants that was operating expressly for no profit but was willing to pay for all the costs of the operations and take all the risks if something went wrong. The OIC told the rogue story to the Swiss Government to induce them to freeze accounts under the control of Hakim and when that hold was about to be released because of the lack of proof of that criminal conduct, the OIC changed its story and requested a hold because Hakim et al **were** official USG agents who had yet to make an "accounting" of the proceeds.

23. When other defendants like Tom Clines were subject to prosecution the government did not have the evidence to bring charges so it created a false scenario that illegally got some Swiss banking documents from the Swiss government by requesting them for an unrelated case and then utilized them out of context against Clines. At the same time he could not get access to the complete records which might have exonerated him because the US held back and had destroyed probative documents.

24. Throughout this ordeal, Albert Hakim's conduct has been consistent and stalwart. When the other participants left the bargaining table with the Iranians, Hakim stayed and finished the process that resulted in the freedom of hostage David Jacobsen. Judge Gessell noted that the sole reason for the release of that hostage was that Hakim, at his own cost, stayed in Europe and continued meetings that were extraordinarily dangerous so that the hostages could be freed. Hakim stayed on for business when the others were running for cover because he so believed in the validity of the fourth option and upon seeing the response to the concept from former enemies he stayed to see it through. His last assignment in these matters was and is for the State Department and he has not abandoned that assignment for all these years. He stands ready to do the right thing and merely wants the USG to uphold its side of the bargain and meet to discuss a logical resolution of the affairs.

IN THE UNITED STATES DISTRICT COURT
FOR THE EASTERN DISTRICT OF VIRGINIA

UNITED STATES OF AMERICA,	)	
	)	
Plaintiff,	)	CIVIL NO. 93-1202-A
	)	
v.	)	
	)	
RICHARD VERNON SECORD,	)	ANSWER, AFFIRMATIVE DEFENSES,
and ALBERT HAKIM,	)	AND COUNTERCLAIM OF
	)	ALBERT HAKIM
Defendants.	)	
_____	)	(JURY TRIAL DEMANDED)

Albert Hakim, Defendant, files his Answer, Affirmative Defenses, Counterclaim and responds as follows:

ANSWER

With respect to each numbered allegation, Defendant Albert Hakim admits, denies and alleges as follows:

1. Admits that the caption identifies the United States as plaintiff.

2. The answering defendant is without knowledge or information sufficient to form a belief as to the truth of the allegation and therefore denies.

3. Admits.

4. Admits that Hakim contracted with the United States Government (hereafter 'USG") in the fall of 1984 to assist and participate in the furtherance of US foreign policy objectives but as to the rest of the paragraph, denies.

5. Admits that Albert Hakim was a shareholder in STTGI and that STTGI was a California corporation. Deny that STTGI did business in Virginia or had its principal office in Vienna, Virginia.

6. Admits that Hakim was Chairman of the Board and Secord was President of STTGI. Deny that STTGI was involved in any fashion in Albert Hakim's activities as an independent contractor to the USG. Further deny that Hakim acted in Virginia in any manner which caused the alleged harm which is alleged to give rise in the US claims.

1

7. Admits that Hakim has traveled to Virginia, deny as to allegations relating to banking on behalf of the transactions or conducting business as an independent contractor or any other actions giving rise to claims herein.

8. Deny.

9. Deny.

10.- 22. The answering defendant is without knowledge or information sufficient to form a belief as to these allegations and therefore denies them.

23. Admits that Hakim entered into an independent contractor relationship with the USG to facilitate a variety of transactions at the request of the USG through Secord. Deny Hakim was "recruited."

24. Deny.

25. The answering defendant is without sufficient information or knowledge to form a belief as to this paragraph and therefore denies.

26. The answering defendant is without sufficient information or knowledge to form a belief as to this paragraph and therefore denies.

27. Admits that this answering defendant was retained as an independent contractor to devise strategies which would further USG foreign policy. Deny that this defendant's activities were directed or controlled by the USG.

28. Deny.

29. Deny.

30. Denies that all operations of the enterprise ceased in November 1986. Admit that the funds were frozen pursuant to treaty. This answering defendant is without sufficient information or knowledge to form a belief as to the amount of money in accounts on 12-31-86.

31. Deny.

32. Admits except deny as to Zucker's credentials.

33. Deny.

34. Admits that Hakim had previously utilized the fiduciary services of CSF .

35. The answering defendant is without knowledge or information sufficient to form a belief with respect to this paragraph and therefore denies.

36. Deny as to Secord's direction to Zucker, admit that Hakim gave directions to Zucker but denies as to specific information in this paragraph.

37. Deny.

38. Deny.

39. Admits that accounts were opened, denies inaccurate description contained in balance of paragraph.

40. Deny.

41. Deny.

42. Deny.

43. Admits that some funds were raised from foreign governments.

44. Deny.

45. Deny.

46. Deny. Government authorization existed for the structure that was implemented, which was not accurately described in this paragraph.

47. The answering defendant is without sufficient knowledge or information to form a belief and therefore denies.

48. Deny.

49. Deny.

50. The answering defendant is without sufficient knowledge or information to form a belief and therefore denies.

51. The answering defendant without knowledge or information to form a belief and therefore denies.

52. Deny as to direction by North or more "active" support of "Contras".

53. Admits that account was opened and denies the characterization and description included in the paragraph.

54. The answering defendant is without sufficient knowledge or information to form a belief and therefore denies.

55. The answering defendant is without sufficient knowledge or information to form a belief and therefore denies.

56. The answering defendant is without sufficient knowledge or information to form a belief and therefore denies.

57. Deny.

58. Deny.

59. Deny.

60. Deny.

61. The answering defendant is without sufficient knowledge and information to form a belief as to this paragraph and therefore denies.

62. The answering defendant is without sufficient knowledge and information to form a belief as to this paragraph and therefore denies.

63. The answering defendant is without sufficient knowledge and information to form a belief as to this paragraph and therefore denies.

64. The answering defendant is without knowledge and information sufficient to form a belief as to this paragraph and therefore denies.

65. The answering defendant is without knowledge and information sufficient to form a belief as to this paragraph and therefore denies.

66. The answering defendant is without knowledge and information sufficient to form a belief as to this paragraph and therefore denies.

67. Deny.

68.-79. The answering defendant is without knowledge and information sufficient to form a belief and therefore denies.

80. Denies with respect to receiving direction from North, admits paying the CIA and does not remember the price.

81.- 90. The answering defendant is without knowledge and information sufficient to form a belief and therefore denies.

91. Admits that details became public and denies that the operation ceased.

92. -93. The answering defendant is without information and knowledge sufficient to form an opinion and therefore denies.

94. -95. Deny.

96. Denies as to North's instructions, admits to purchasing radios, supporting the DEA, helping with the hostages and arranging meetings around the world.

98. - 104. Denies as to North's direction of activities and disputes inaccurate description.

105. Admits but agreement which is still classified, as far as Hakim knows, included agreements on Middle East relations that were much more involved than the release of the hostages.

106. Deny. Hakim represented the interests of the US but did not hold himself out as a representative of the US.

!07. Deny.

108. Deny

109. The answering defendant is without knowledge and information sufficient to form a belief and therefore denies.

110. Deny. Hakim represented the interests of the US but never held himself out to be officially affiliated with the government.

111. The Answering defendant is without knowledge or information sufficient to form a belief and therefore denies.

112. - 141. Deny.

142. Deny. Defendant pled guilty to the misdemeanor of aiding the supplementation of a federal salary.

143. - 157. Deny.

158. Deny. All testimony and records support that the United States Government ("USG") contracted with the Defendant with the knowledge and approval of his receiving a "reasonable" profit from the contract relationship.

159. Deny. The "contract" specifically permitted the defendant to make a profit from the transactions he was asked to facilitate, in addition the "contract" specifically excluded the requirement to make an accounting, and the moneys in question were never USG funds. The defendant was never an "agent" or " subagent" of the United States and the relationship was specifically designed by the parties to avoid that structure. Because the United States has declined to fulfill its commitments under the contract the defendant has not made any profit from the transactions and in fact, has had to bear the cost of the transactions personally.

160.-162. Deny.

163. Deny. No profit was made, no agency existed, and the money in question was never the property of the USG.

164. - 166. Deny. Under the conditions of the contract, there has been no conversion.

167. - 174. Deny. The civil agreement has not been breached by the defendant. Long before the USG began to request specific acts of performance, the defendant through counsel had made demands that were material to the implementation of the agreement and which were the specific obligation of the USG. These demands were never answered and as a consequence the defendant could not perform his part of the agreement.

175. -181. Deny.

182. - 187. Deny. The described actions do not constitute a breach of the agreement and would not have been necessary had the government acted in good faith with respect to its obligations under the civil agreement.

188. - 194. Deny. In contradiction to all evidence and testimony concerning this aspect of the contract.

195. - 197. Deny. This answering defendant stands ready to perform all obligations under the civil agreement and the contract under which services for the benefit of the United States were rendered so long as the USG also tenders its performance and cures its breach .

The Defendant denies the complaint and asks the court to deny the prayer for relief as not being legally, factually or equitably justified.

6

AFFIRMATIVE DEFENSES

1. Failure to State Claims.

The Complaint fails to state a claim upon which relief can be granted.

2. Failure to Join Indispensable Parties.

The plaintiff has failed to join indispensable parties to this action per Rule 19, Federal Rules of Civil Procedure.

3. Statute of Limitations.

A. Count I is barred by the applicable Statute of Limitations, including but not limited to 28 U.S.C. s.2415.

B. Count II is barred by the applicable Statute of Limitations, including but not limited to 28 U.S.C. s. 2415.

C. Count III is barred by the applicable Statute of Limitations, including but not limited to 28 U.S.C. s. 2415.

D. Count IV and V are barred by the applicable Statute of Limitations, including but not limited to 28 U.S.C. s. 2415.

E. Count VI is barred by the applicable Statute of Limitations, including but not limited to 28U.S.C. s. 2415 and 28 U.S.C. s. 3306.

4. Laches.

Counts I, II, III, IV, V, VI, VII, VIII, are barred by laches.

5. Equitable Defenses.

To the extent the United States seeks relief based upon principles of Equity for relief in Equity, the action is barred and should be denied because:

A. The United States comes to this court with unclean hands and should receive no relief. The United States found itself with the need to create a financial structure that could be used to achieve foreign policy objectives that were very sensitive and possibly dangerous to the people that were in a position to help the U.S. achieve these results. In addition, the U.S. was prohibited by the Boland Amendment from directly expending U.S.

Treasury funds to achieve the objective of continuing support for the Nicaragua freedom fighters ("Contras"). In an effort not to abandon the Contras, sympathetic foreign governments and individuals were encouraged to donate funds to their efforts. These funds were managed through the transactions arranged through the defendant's international commercial structure. The defendant was contracted to provide these services because his business structure fit the criteria defined as critical to the USG. These criteria included the following (i) that the individual be of no danger to US national security; (ii) that the individual understand the intelligence community and be known to them; (iii) that the individual have an existing international commercial and banking infrastructure; and (iv) that the individual be resourceful and creative. The Defendant possessed these characteristics and as such, he agreed to provide the needed transactional support. In addition, the Defendant agreed to directly assist in the creation of a basis of communication between Iran and the US. The United States had spent great sums of money and had put extraordinary effort into the task of creating dialogue with the Iranians. Despite these efforts the US was not able to effect this result. At great risk (personally, professionally and financially) to the Defendant, this channel of communication was established. Representatives of the USG were present when financial commitments relating to the communications channel were made. These obligations were known by and approved by the USG. Throughout the negotiations relating to the civil agreement, the OIC was apprised of these obligations. Meetings were held with the OIC and members of the US intelligence and foreign policy community. Language relating to these obligations were included in the civil agreement. The USG has refused to meet these obligations or even to discuss them despite repeated requests by Defendant's civil counsel. In addition, other aspects of the contractual arrangement have been disregarded, misrepresented, abandoned and otherwise treated with bad faith by the government.

B. The Defendant has never been asked by his client to either stop performing under the contract or for a final report to reconcile outstanding issues. The last official contact from the client was a transfer of authority from the CIA to the State Department. Given the covert nature of the assignment, it is up to the State Department to meet with the Defendant and discuss the resolution of these matters. The Defendant is prepared to meet with his client at any time to resolve these matters. Further, the Defendant believes that, given an opportunity to meet with his client, the matter could be completely resolved in a very short time.

C. The USG had an adequate remedy at law, which it chose not to pursue and should now be barred.

E. If the Defendant was an agent _de jure_, the United States abandoned him, destroyed evidence which would be relevant to this suit, failed to agree to reasonable compensation, disavowed the agency on certain occasions when it was politically convenient, disavowed any direct involvement in the operation and represented to the Government of Switzerland that the Defendant was involved in wholly illegal, criminal conduct, unauthorized by the United States. When that tact was ineffective the USG shifted their argument to say that <u>NOW</u> the defendant was an agent and because of the authorized nature of the work the remedies should prevail.

6. <u>Statute of Frauds and Parol Evidence Rule.</u>

The action is barred by the applicable Statute of Frauds of the applicable law, including but not limited to Article 2, Section 2-201 of the applicable UCC and by the Parol Evidence Rule of applicable law since the sales were between merchants, confirmed in writing and duly performed and consummated. The United States cannot now change the price or modify the terms of the sales.

7. <u>Set Off.</u>

Any funds found to be due the United States should be set-off against reasonable compensation and indemnity due this Defendant as a result of the Counterclaim filed hereunder.

8. <u>Express Contract.</u>

Plaintiff cannot claim an implied contract, since there was an express contract, or a series of express contracts, so far fully performed by the Defendant who continues to perform in good faith.

9. <u>Equitable Estoppel.</u>

Plaintiff should be estopped to assert a constructive trust or receive other similar equitable relief since:

      A. The policy for the operations and the format thereof were approved by the Plaintiff.

      B. Plaintiff did not wish to know the financial and other details so that it could, at its discretion, disavow the activities. Plaintiff further, required as part of the contract that the financial records of the various transactions be made in such a fashion that their revelation would protect those foreign nationals who were covertly assisting the achievement of US foreign policy objectives. Plaintiff never imposed any financial restrictions on Defendant, knew that this was Defendant's profit venture and raised no objections for over two years to Defendant's activities.

      C. Defendant was reasonably led to believe that what he was doing was approved and that he was free to manage funds related to the transaction in the manner he wished so long as the goals of the operations were achieved - which they were.

      D. The Defendant relied to his great detriment on the statements, actions, representations and omissions to act of the Plaintiff.

E. The Defendant was not ever given instructions as how to perform his work. Only objectives were communicated to the Defendant, the decision about what tactics to use to implement the objectives were left totally to the discretion of the Defendant.

F. It would be unjust and inequitable for Plaintiff to achieve a windfall from Defendant's services.

10. <u>Waiver.</u>

Plaintiff, with knowledge that the Defendant was engaged with the expectation of making a profit from performing the contracted work, made no objection to the sales prices of the goods and, in fact, set the prices which the United States was to receive from the transactions. In addition, the prices to charge for the goods were set by the "commercial third party cutout", co-defendant Secord. Plaintiff waived the right to change the terms of the sale and the conditions and terms of the Defendant's engagement.

11. <u>Duress.</u>

Plaintiff used duress to coerce the Defendant's acquiescence to the Civil Agreement. The threat of continued criminal prosecution and the threat of government abrogation of the criminal plea agreement were the tools wielded by the government to eliminate the Defendant's consideration of his considerable contract and equitable rights as a party to the transactions when he signed the Civil Agreement. The OIC deliberately included language to hide their use of extreme duress to force the Defendant's agreement to the civil agreement. It would be unjust and inequitable for the Plaintiff to exert rights under this agreement.

12. <u>Collateral Estoppel and Stare Decisis.</u>

Plaintiff has adopted a legal and factual theory with Defendant's privy opposite to the one adopted here, which resulted in guilty pleas. It is collaterally estopped to change its position or is so barred by the doctrine of <u>Stare Decisis.</u>

Wherefore, Defendant moves this court to dismiss the complaint, with prejudice and with an award of attorney's fees to Defendant pursuant to 28 U.S.C. 2412, if Defendant has retained counsel pursuant to local Rule VII.

COUNTERCLAIM

Albert Hakim, Defendant/ Counter Claimant (sometimes "Hakim") files this counterclaim against the USG and alleges as follows:

THE PARTIES

1. Counterclaimant , (sometimes referred herein as "Hakim"), is a citizen and resident of the State of California, and a citizen of the United States.

2. The Counterclaim Defendant is the Government of the United States of America; including its various Executive Branch agencies and departments (i.e. the Central Intelligence Agency, the Department of State, the Department of Justice, the National Security Council, the Office of the President of the United States and the Department of Defense).

JURISDICTION

3. This is an action for two causes of Breach of Contract - Specific Performance, two causes of Breach of Contract Damages, Declaratory Judgment, Unjust Enrichment, Injunction and other Equitable Relief. This court has jurisdiction because there is an actual justicable controversy between the parties, one of which is the United States, and the amount in controversy exceeds $50,000.00.

BACKGROUND

4. Counterclaimant Hakim was requested by the United States Government through Co- Defendant Richard Secord, the commercial cutout, to assist in achievement of certain U.S. foreign policy objectives by managing the implementation of a series of transactions to further these foreign policy objectives of the United States. The transactions in question, had both a logistical and financial component.

5. In addition, Counterclaimant was also asked, on behalf of the United States Government, to develop a channel for communication and discussion with the Government of Iran. The channel was to serve two purposes, (i) to effect the release of the hostages and (ii) to create a basis of communication to explore areas of mutual interest between the two governments.

11

6. Hakim was asked to and did pass cash to officials of the United States Department of Justice Drug Enforcement Administration.

7. Hakim was asked to and did, on behalf of the United States Government Central Intelligence Agency, negotiate for and purchase a ship, the Erria, to be used by the Central Intelligence Agency for covert operations.

8. Hakim was asked to make payments to a bank account which he understood to be an account of the United States Government's Central Intelligence Agency.

9. Throughout Hakim's activities, it was repeatedly emphasized by representatives of the United States Government, who frequently invoked the name of the President, that the activities he was undertaking involved covert operations on behalf of the U.S. Government and the need for secrecy was strictly emphasized.

10. Counterclaimant Hakim, was requested by the CIA and, subsequently, the State Department to arrange contacts with Iranian Government representatives.

11. The engaging representatives of the United States understood and agreed with specificity that Hakim was undertaking these various activities to make a profit and that the profit was to come from various sources including a secondary markup, added by the commercial cut out for the benefit of Hakim, to the transactions he managed. The primary source of compensation was to financed by the Iranians in the form of a joint venture funded by the Government of Iran to finance the completion of then, and possibly, now Top Secret "Hakim Accords". These moneys included funds for the intermediaries who assisted in establishing the release of the hostages through that point in time and the release of the rest of the hostages upon completion of the Accords. In addition, the U.S. government was a party to agreements made by Hakim but with the cognizant and tacit approval of the USG to facilitate the creation of a "second channel" of communication with Iran and the achievement of other U.S. foreign policy objectives through the use of subcontractors. These agreements required the United States to fund obligations pursuant to these understandings. In fact the "second channel" was effectively created and some hostages were released solely as a result of Hakim's endeavors. Had the USG not interfered with Hakim's efforts it is highly likely that all of the hostages would have been freed in a very short time, thus reducing the imprisonment of some of the hostages for periods of years.

12. Hakim never set the prices for which items were to be bought from the United States. All these prices were set by the appropriate agencies who were party to the transactions.

13. All the funds which Hakim was asked to manage came from donations from sympathetic foreign governments and wealthy individuals worldwide. No funds were sourced through the United States Government.

14. The transactions were structured in such a fashion that Hakim was personally liable should a transaction or cargo be lost or destroyed.

15. The contractor relationship was designed by the USG so that no accounting of the transactions was requested, expected or required.

16. The transactions were designed to be self supporting from a cash standpoint and would have been had not the USG interfered with the US approved Iranian funding of these endeavors. This interference took place as the USG undermined the political and business relationship Hakim had created with the "second Channel" and moderate individuals from the Iranian government.

17. Counterclaimant was informed that this request was directed through the Executive Branch pursuant to a Presidential finding and was both legal and supported by the US Intelligence and Armed Forces Communities.

18. Counterclaimant was informed that the scope of his assignment included the need to maintain the transactions as covert, to make sure that any paper trail relating to the transactions could not be used to trace the identities of the various participants whose assistance to the United States foreign policy objectives could put them and their families in jeopardy.

19. Secord was requested to be a "third party commercial cutout". A commercial cut out is an individual who is qualified to be sensitive to covert activities. Such individuals are often retired government officials with intimate knowledge and experience in such activities. Additionally, these individuals either qualify or can qualify for government security clearances. Finally these individuals must qualify for commercial activities, have access to individuals with a knowledge of commercial dealings with governments or have both.

20. Counterclaimant was requested to function as a private independent contractor. As such, he was to manage the transactions logistically and financially. The funds were to be managed and were managed through the Counterclaimant's preexisting international commercial and banking network.

COUNTERCLAIM I
(Breach of Contract - Specific Performance)

21. Counterclaimant realleges and incorporates by reference paragraphs 1 through 20 as though fully set forth herein.

22. By virtue of the conduct in this count and at all times during the conduct of the transactions described herein, the USG was a party to a contract with the Counterclaimant.

23. This contract included a description of the objective results desired by the USG, a description of the terms and conditions under which the results were to be achieved, a description of the compensation to be earned, a description of how and by whom the costs of the transactions were to be born.

24. These components provided for a compensation package for Hakim, the requirement that no complete or traceable financial records be maintained, that certain aspects of the transaction be classified as confidential and, therefore, pending a determination from the client that these details can and should be disclosed, they will be kept confidential, the understanding that the USG would provide the proscribed compensation and remuneration for subcontractors including the coverage of their expenses incurred as a result of the assistance proffered.

25. The Counterclaimant performed his obligations as requested and specified. Now the plaintiff argues that, after the fact, the contract should be recast and that there should be an accounting, funds explicitly part of the compensation package should be turned over to the USG even though the USG had nothing to do with their source and that the subcontractors who risked their very lives in the furtherance of the US objectives should be completely abandoned.

26. Defendant USG has materially breached its contract with Counterclaimant Hakim by reneging on the terms and conditions of the agreement, interfering with one negotiated aspect of the compensation package, by failing to fulfill obligations to subcontractors and by sabotaging the other component of the compensation agreement.

27. Despite repeated requests to do so, the USG has wrongfully failed and refused to perform any of its obligations under the contract.

28. The Counterclaimant has been harmed by the Defendant's material breaches of this contract.

29. The Counterclaimant's legal remedies are inadequate because of the Counterclaimant's inability to achieve the results required under the contract without the USG's assistance in ascertaining and fulfilling its obligations under the contract.

30. Because the Legal remedies are inadequate, Hakim seeks specific performance of defendant USG's contractual obligations to allow the surplus funds to remain under the control of the Counterclaimant, to ascertain and fulfill all obligations to subcontractors and intermediaries, and to refrain from asking for an accounting when the original

arrangements specifically requested that the records not be maintained in the fashion necessary to facilitate an accounting.

COUNTERCLAIM II
(Breach of Contract Damages)

31. Plaintiff realleges and incorporates by reference paragraphs 1 through 29 as though fully set forth herein.

32. This is a claim against Counter Defendant United States of America.

33. The agreement for services between the USG and Albert Hakim constitutes a legally enforceable contract between the United States and Hakim .

34. Defendant USG materially breached its contract with Hakim by impeding the Iranian funding of the venture which would have funded the implementation of the Hakim Accords. This funding would have substantively paid for the costs of the intermediaries and subcontractors and provided Hakim with his stipulated profit. In addition, the USG impedance meant that an agreement to free the remaining hostages and not to take others was not implemented and the hostages had to wait several more years to actually gain their freedom.

35. Despite repeated requests to do so, the USG wrongfully failed and refused to perform their obligations to facilitate and support the Iranian funded venture supporting the Hakim Accords under the service contract between the USG and Albert Hakim_ or any of the other components of the contract.

36. Counterclaimant has been harmed by defendant's material breaches of this contract and suffered material damages as a consequence of defendant's breach of contract.

37. Albert Hakim is entitled to actual damages sustained as a consequence of defendant's breach of contract. When clearance is given by the client to provide supporting detail, the actual uninflated damages will approximate $50,000,000.00 with an additional amount of required indemnification of approximately $15,000,000.00.

COUNTERCLAIM III
(Breach of Contract- Specific Performance)

38. This count is based upon the Civil Agreement signed between the USG and the Counterclaimant Hakim on November 8, 1989.

39. The Counterclaimant believes that the Civil Agreement is void based upon the affirmative defense of duress as claimed in the affirmative defense designated #11. In the

15

event that the court rules that the civil agreement has efficacy, it still serves the interests of the Counterclaimant, as the agreement was breached by the USG long before a demand for specific actions was requested by the government. The initial communication about the lack of performance came from Hakim's counsel in a letter dated July 16, 1990 to the Government concerning their lack of performance relating to Section 5.

40. Section 3(c) and 5 were included to accommodate the unpaid intermediaries and subcontractors. The section was included after Hakim and his counsel had meetings with the OIC (including Walsh) and representatives for the CIA. The obligations of the USG with respect to these remaining parties was openly discussed and reference to these potential claims was, accordingly, included in the document.

41. On August 3, 1990, after a two day negotiation session with the OIC relating to the uncompleted civil agreement in the San Francisco office of Hakim's attorneys, the OIC wrote to Hakim through his counsel to officially give notice of the breach of the civil agreement. That letter became the foundation for the Government's claims in the current law suit.

42. The government's characterization of the civil agreement is both a distortion of the facts and a presentation of unwarranted conclusions. The civil agreement is exactly what its title states: a civil contract between the two parties both, presumably, with equal bargaining power vis a vis its poorly drafted terms. The allegations in this complaint misspeak the terms of the agreement and the respective obligations of the parties, in a manner clearly designed to suggest that Hakim is the only uncooperative party.

43. In the Agreement the USG is obligated "to use its best efforts to obtain the withdrawal of any impediments to the release of all monies maintained... in a manner..." that insures that $1.7million is placed in a corporate (or any other) account to be designated by Hakim. In addition, by the unequivocal language of the agreement itself, the entire United States Government is obligated to provide information to the Swiss "regarding the merit of any remaining claims to the funds maintained..." in Switzerland.

44. Hakim was obligated by the agreement to comply "with all reasonable requests by...the USG for assistance on obtaining the funds in the manner set forth in paragraph 2a..." of the Agreement. He is not obligated to commit economic, if not actual suicide in the process. The applicable language relating to outstanding claims was included because the USG has a duty to fulfill its obligations to those who offered assistance and because some of those who were unpaid have actually threatened the life of the Counterclaimant. The inclusion of language to protect the interests of the "Second Channel" intermediaries has alleviated the threats. It is particularly distressing to have the government disavow that obligation when members of the USG and the Iranian Government were present and participants during the commitment process.

45. The complaint's characterization of Hakim's condition precedent to cooperation is indicative of the bad faith with which the USG has approached this agreement. The civil agreement was clearly drawn to clarify the respective rights of the parties and their respective rights to certain funds in Switzerland. Hakim is only in a position to contract on his own behalf. The USG had contracted for the entire United States. Neither contracting party is in a position to deter other independent claims to the accounts. For the US to suggest that Hakim assume sole responsibility for such other independent claims, without being willing to attempt to assist, is in itself a breach of the United States obligations under the Agreement.

46. The language of paragraph 5 is unequivocal. The Characterizations included in the complaint are irrelevant, misleading and false. It is particularly egregious to suggest, that the Unites States only obligation under Paragraph 5 is to provide information regarding claims to the $1.7million allotted to the Counterclaimant.

47. The USG has refused to provide any information concerning outstanding claims, including claims that it was party to creating.

48. Defendant USG has materially breached its contract by refusing to fulfill its obligations thereunder, by failing to assist in the clearance of outside claimants and by failing to use the best efforts of the entire Governmental structure to ascertain and assist in the clearance of those claims when the vast majority of them are known intimately to the USG.

49. Despite repeated requests to do so, the USG has wrongfully failed and refused to perform any of its obligations required under its contract with Hakim.

50. The Counterclaimant has been harmed by the defendant's material breaches of the contract.

51. The Counterclaimant's legal remedies are inadequate because the Counterclaimant's ability to assist in the clearance of outstanding claims is totally dependent upon the USG willingness to fulfill its obligations under the Civil Agreement.

52. Because legal remedies are inadequate, The Counterclaimant seeks specific performance of defendant USG's obligation under the Civil Agreement.

COUNTERCLAIM IV
(Breach of Contract-Damages)

53. Plaintiff realleges and incorporates by reference paragraph 1through 52 as though fully set forth herein.

54. This is a civil claim against the United States Government.

55. The civil agreement executed between the United States and Hakim, referenced in paragraphs 38 through 52 of this Counterclaim and incorporated as though fully set forth herein, constitutes a legally, enforceable contract between the parties; unless the court has ruled that it is not valid due to the nature of the threatened criminal prosecution and other duress utilized by the government to secure its affirmation by counterclaimant.

56. Defendant USG has materially breached its contract as indicated above.

57. Despite repeated requests to do so, USG has wrongfully failed and refused to perform any of its obligations under the civil agreement.

58. The Counterclaimant has been harmed by defendant's material breaches of this contract and suffered damages as a consequence of defendant's breach of contract.

59. The Counterclaimant is entitled to actual damages as a consequence of defendant's breach of contract.

COUNTERCLAIM V
(Unjust Enrichment)

60. Counterclaimant realleges and incorporates by reference paragraphs 1 through 52 as though fully set forth herein.

61. By virtue of the facts alleged in this count, Plaintiff voided its obligations under the contract and blocked monies that were never owned by the USG and but were always designed by the parties to belong to the Counterclaimant.

62. As a result of the conduct described in this count, Plaintiff wrested control of the funds from the rightful party entitled to control and have continued to assert control over certain monies to which it is not entitled.

63. In consequence of the acts set forth in this count, Plaintiff is on the verge of becoming unjustly enriched at the expense of the Defendant Hakim, under circumstances dictating that, in equity and good conscience, the money should be returned to the Counterclaimant's control.

COUNTERCLAIM VI

(Conversion)

64. Counterclaimant realleges and incorporates by reference paragraphs 1 through 52 as though fully set forth herein.

65. In November of 1986, the Office of Independent Counsel, utilizing the international division of the Department of Justice and pursuant to a Treaty of Mutual Assistance between the Unites States and Switzerland sought to and received a blocking or freezing of what has been referred to as "Enterprise Funds".

66. At the time of the blocking of the funds held in various Swiss and other foreign accounts controlled from Switzerland certain third parties, employees and related persons working for the Counterclaimant were left unpaid and unreimbursed.

67. The USG in November of 1986 and continually until April 1992, misrepresented the facts and circumstances surrounding the events in question to the Swiss government and continually indicated that the Counterclaimant was involved in an unauthorized criminal rogue adventure of his own, that he was about to be indicted with co- conspirators relating to the diversion of US funds for personal use. The entire time that the USG was pursuing this tact with the Swiss government they knew the contrary was, in fact, the truth.

68. In fact, no individual or entity was ever indicted for any crime relating to the diversion of funds and the Counterclaimant pled guilty to the misdemeanor of aiding and abetting the supplementation of a federal salary.

69. The Swiss Government (after investigation of the facts and a determination that no criminal conduct had even been alleged let alone proven), declined to continue the treaty freeze. The United States then filed an untimely appeal of the decision of the Swiss Government (Federal Police Office) resulting in a decision by the Swiss Supreme Court that the United States failed to file a timely appeal.

70. The United States then proceeded in the Spring of 1993 as an ordinary civil party to file an action equivalent to asking for a temporary injunction blocking the funds against the Counterclaimant and others. No evidentiary hearing was granted and it was procured by misrepresenting the facts to the Swiss Court without sworn testimony or even sworn affadavits. A "temporary injunction" was granted and the United States proceeded to validate its claim against the Counterclaimant for the funds. On September, 21 1993, the United States filed an action in Switzerland virtually identical to this one alleging the

19

same facts and seeking the identical relief. **After seven years and over thirty million dollars in legal fees, the USG now changed its story from that which characterized the Counterclaimant as a rogue criminal who stole the funds to that of an duly authorized agent who breached his fiduciary agent duty and therefore had an obligation to return funds in his possession.**

71. In this case, as in the previous circumstances, the USG knows that what is being promulgated is patently false. The USG should not be permitted to shop theories until it finds one that "works" regardless of any consideration for the truth.

72. In consequence of the acts set forth in this count, Plaintiff wrongfully exerted control over moneys obtained from the transactions set forth in this count. Such moneys rightfully belong to and are the property of the Counterclaimant and Plaintiff's exertion of dominion and control through knowingly false declarations to the Swiss authorities is in denial of the Counterclaimant's right over its property.

73. The Counterclaimant has suffered actual damages of at least $11,000,000.00 by virtue of Plaintiff's wrongful conversion to their control and Plaintiff's should be ordered to facilitate a release of all funds to the Counterclaimant.

COUNTERCLAIM VII
(Declaratory Judgment)

74. Counterclaimant realleges and incorporates by reference paragraphs 1through 52 and 64 through 73 as though fully set forth herein.

75. By virtue of the conduct described in this count, and at all times during the operation of the transactions in question, the USG had contracted with the Counterclaimant to provide certain services as an independent contractor.

76. Counterclaimant believes that the United States has no interest of any kind whatsoever in funds generated through the transactions. None of the originating funds came from the United States, none of the transactions involving agencies of the United States involved less than full payment as defined by that agency, no member of the United States Government controlled any of the funds at any time and none of the transactions except for payments for material involved the United States.

77. The USG claims here and in Switzerland that it believes that it is entitled to the funds superior to any right title and interest of Counterclaimant.

78. Hakim was not designated either officially or unofficially in writing or otherwise as an agent. The USG has contended consistently in cases and policies on which agency is sought to be imposed against it that it has to adhere to specific statutory

protocol in order to legally act to appoint agents. "Apparent Agency" is a concept available to third party creditors, not to a principal attempting to create an Agency de jure.

79. Counterclaimant believes that he was not an agent of the USG because of the following:

A. The United States claimed no accounting, nor portion of the proceeds at any time until November of 1986. The agreement for services excluded the requirement for an accounting and did require that the contractor not keep records for his own use that could be utilized in a fashion to undermine the covert nature of the arrangements or put those assisting the USG in danger.

B. The Counterclaimant was not subject to the control of any agency or instrumentality of the USG. He worked independently making all of his own strategic and operational decisions.

C. The contacts utilized to achieve the results indicated were those of the Counterclaimant.

D. The Counterclaimant assumed the risk of loss, not the United States. The Counterclaimant was required to pay for all goods in advance, bear all costs for fees, expenses, attorneys, freight, etc.

E. None of the entities utilized to facilitate the transactions were covered or protected by the Federal Tort Claims Act or similar Acts. The USG specifically disavowed any recognition of nor responsibility to persons working for, through or under Hakim or his companies on the grounds that neither Hakim nor his companies were US instrumentalities.

F. If injured or killed (which was likely given the unpredictable nature of the work which was requested) neither he nor his family would have been covered by any federal compensation.

G. The United States disavowed, at times, any form of express or constructive agency in denying responsibility for claims of others but began to articulate this theory only as a means for making claims to recover the funds.

H. The United States, in US v. Claire George; and US v. Clines; represented to the Court and Jury that Secord was a third party commercial cutout.

I. The President of the United States affirmed the "third party" relationship in his finding when the arrangement was confirmed.

80. If, however, the Counterclaimant is adjudicated to have been an agent (which he in good faith believes he was not) then the USG, as principal violated the following

duties to Counterclaimant, for which it is liable and for which Counterclaimant claims a lien on the funds:

A. The USG had a duty which it breached to provide Hakim with adequate information and competent advice concerning the nature of the Counterclaimant's acts.

B. The United States had a duty, which it breached, to deal in good faith with the Counterclaimant. Instead Counterclaimant was subject to government harassment and ridicule by various agencies of the United States including the IRS, the FBI, the OIC, etc. for diligently performing the services requested by the government. He has been required to retain counsel and fight USG litigation continuously.

C. The US had a duty, which it breached, to indemnify the Counterclaimant.

D. The US had a duty, which it breached, to pay reasonable compensation for the services rendered and to pay his reasonable costs and expenses. Instead, the US has utilized every conceivable agency of the government to insure that the Counterclaimant had no access to funds in order to make him incapable of defending himself.

81. In the event that an agency relationship is adjudicated, counterclaimant had and has a legal right to retain titular possession of the funds, until the USG agrees upon a reasonable fee for services and costs and expenses that have been incurred as a result of the foregoing and other breaches of duties by the USG.

82. Counterclaimant requests an adjudication, if necessary, of the amount of and his entitlement to reasonable compensation, costs, indemnification and a Declaration and mandatory and prohibitory injunction that said compensation be first deducted from the funds before repatriation of the balance, if any.

PRAYER FOR RELIEF

WHEREFORE, counterclaimant, Albert Hakim, demands judgment:

Under Counterclaim I:

(1) That Plaintiff /Defendant ("USG") be ordered to cause all orders freezing funds to be lifted in all countries where such actions are in force;

(2) That all funds associated with the transactions be declared to be under the permanent control of the Defendant/ Counterclaimant ("Hakim");

(3) That the USG be forced to utilize its best efforts to ascertain and satisfy the claims of subcontractors and other intermediaries to whom legitimate obligations were made;

(4) That the USG ascertain and satisfy the claims of Hakim relating to expenses and a "reasonable" profit;

(5) That the USG refrain from demanding an accounting for funds as under the original agreement.

Under Counterclaim II:

(1) That the USG be ordered to pay actual and exemplary damages;

Under Counterclaim III:

(1) That, in the unlikely event that the court does not void the Civil Agreement due to the duress that was used to secure Hakim's acquiescence, the USG be ordered to comply with all provisions of the agreement;

(2) That the USG be ordered to utilize its best efforts to ascertain and satisfy the outstanding claims by other claimants of which the USG has specific knowledge;

(3) That the USG be ordered to cooperate with Hakim to complete their obligations under the agreement.

Under Counterclaim IV:

(1) That the USG be ordered to pay actual and exemplary damages.

Under Counterclaim V:

(1) That the USG be ordered to effect the release of all orders freezing or otherwise denying Hakim control of the funds and not to attempt to limit such control in the future.

Under Counterclaim VI:

(1) That the USG be ordered to release all claims to the transaction funds and to effect a release of all orders restricting Hakim's control over the funds.

Under Counterclaim VII:

(1) Declaratory Judgment adjudicating that Hakim is entitled to all interests and control of all transaction funds and also reasonable compensation and indemnification for Hakim and his subcontractors;

(2) An injunction, temporary and permanent in nature, restraining and preventing the Unites States from interfering with the quiet enjoyment of Hakim in and to the transaction funds as may finally be adjudicated to be under his control and ordering the United States to represent the Final Declaration of this Court to the Swiss Courts and to take such action a n perform such acts as may be required to enforce this court's declaration;

(3) A Preliminary injunction requiring the United States to "unfreeze" funds now on deposit so that Hakim may pay counsel in this proceeding;

(4) A judgment for costs and attorneys fees pursuant to the Equal Access to Justice Act under 28 U.S.C. 2412 if Defendant can ultimately retain counsel pursuant to Local Rule VIII.

Respectfully submitted,

Date: Nov. 29-93

Albert Hakim
in propria persona
16375 Aztec Ridge Drive
Los Gatos, California 95032
phone 408- 395-0500
fax 408- 354- 4245

Supplemental Background and Supplemental Prayer For Relief
On behalf of Defendant - Counterclaimant Albert Hakim
CIVIL NO.93-1202-A

1. Albert Hakim and many other individuals who put themselves at the service of USG interests experienced a series of dynamics that will be deemed shameful when in the annals of American History they are reviewed with distance and perspective.

2. When the covert operation became the focus of public awareness the Reagan administration handled the exposure as if it was a guilty party. It therefore, lost the opportunity to take responsibility for the activities and, as such, to protect their sensitive and proper mission.

3. By acting as if they were engaged in some "inappropriate" affair, the administration "invited" a level of scrutiny and concern that may have been avoidable.

4. This attention created an avalanche of inquiry that had many political agendas following the imagined scent of blood.

5. This country had been through an inquiry that smacked of cover-up, extra-Constitutional conduct and political treachery just ten years earlier and as a nation we knew how to react to the thought that a similar event was happening again.

6. The unfortunate aspect to the events relating to Reagan is that, unlike those of Nixon, these events did not revolve around an attempt to keep and maintain political power; they centered on the efforts of a powerful but politically limited nation to afford assistance to freedom fighters whose very roots were similar to those of our founding fathers, an attempt to free American hostages from a dangerous, politically charged and unpredictable environment and finally an attempt to create a dialogue of mutual interest with another nation with whom we had found ourselves in great public enmity but with whom we had many common objectives and interests. (Iran). The common thread between these two endeavors was the response to the threat of communism and specifically Russian imperialism. By fighting Russian sponsored insurgency and by helping another nation stand up to the prospective threat of Russian invasion we helped stem the tide of an expansionist country in the last throes of its expansionism.

7. The activities themselves were not manifestly illegal and were certainly defensible to the American people; had the President decided to stand up for the policy he

Supplemental Background and Prayer1

had inititiated and supported. Instead, by acting as if something had been done that was regrettable in a moral, legal or political sense, the president showed a political vulnerability that invited the sharks into the boat. Unfortunately for the participants, the president was far away from the boat when his advisors started the finger pointing process.

8. Throughout the entire process of revelation and investigation, the pressure has been on those participants to "give up" the President.

9. As the administration distanced itself from the activities of the Iran Contra initiatives, it abandoned people in the United States and around the world who were quietly working to enable USG interests to be realized.

10. The bulk of these people had been participating solely because the President or his representatives had asked them in the name of the Executive Branch and under the guise of a legal process that insured legality and official endorsement.

11. Once the scrutiny began the participants in the "field" were not only left without the support that was due them, they became the focus of blame for the activities themselves. This abandonment served the Reagan political needs for distance and had a devastating effect on those left holding the bag.

12. From an international political perspective, the participants knew that they were part of a series of covert events that might need to be "denied" in an official sense but none of the participants expected the nation that engaged their services itself to turn so brutally against them.

13. Albert Hakim's story is representative and by no means unique. He was functioning as a private citizen who made a business arrangement with the USG to assist them in a variety of foreign policy objectives. His motivation was both capitalistic and patriotic.

14. The dynamic between the two major political parties was predictable once Reagan showed weakness rather than strength on this issue. The wild card was the dynamic adopted and created by Independent Counsel Walsh in his investigations.

15. Once the Reagan administration decided to abandon those offering assistance a variety of things happened. Many people were jailed in Middle East countries as their role on behalf of the USG became known. In Beruit, alone, over ten people were jailed and were abandoned by the USG. Interestingly, the Ayatollah eventually exerted influence to effect the release of these people even though they were associated with"our" side. Perhaps the Iranians understood that these people were working to achieve a fundamental shift in political thinking that would have left some of the historic tension in the dust by emphasizing common economic interests.

Supplemental Background and Prayer2

16. Tens of millions of dollars of commitments to individuals were left unpaid and unacknowledged even though official representatives of the USG had been present when most of the commitments had been made.

17. Hakim had to bear millions of dollars of legal fees, public ridicule and interference in his business that left it unable to function in the sense that it had before.

18. The USG breached its contractual arrangements and then set the Independent Counsel upon Hakim in an effort to avoid legitimate claims against it.

19. Throughout the entire affair, Albert Hakim has told a consistent, truthful and simple version of the events. In all these years, he descriptions have never wavered. He has said that he made a "for profit" business relationship with the USG, that he was pleased to be of service to the interests of the USG and that he felt he could assist in the achievement of the objectives by enacting his global approach to business which allowed historically adversarial parties to achieve a peaceful dynamic by focusing on common economic interests and through the experience of shared success to find more meaningful common ground. This "fourth option", as Hakim has often described this phenomena was the foundation of the "Hakim Accords". If allowed to be implemented, the "Accords" would have brought all the hostages home, stopped new hostage taking and changed the shape of tension in the Middle East region. In addition, it would have created an inertia of reliance upon the United States for trade facilitation that would have led to strategic alliances amongst traditionally distrustful enemies. Most surprising, the Iranians were willing to underwrite this effort in a major financial way.

20. The treatment by the USG through the Office of the Independent Counsel (OIC) has been marked by changing stories, deceptive evidence gathering, tortious business interference, misrepresentations, attempts to undermine the benefit of the presumption of innocence that Americans enjoy as the hallmark of our democracy, fabrications and a personal twist to prosecution and litigation that even the news media has observed..

21. The OIC began their existence as a tool for the political process. In the end they spent almost $40,000,000.00. For that sum, they were able to achieve no convictions for malfeasance or misfeasance relating to the substantial sums that were passed through the channels. No one was convicted of by passing Congressional mandate and no one was convicted of any form of personal enrichment. However, the OIC has continually repeated its accusations as if they are fact and then hid behind CIPA as an excuse for not achieving any legal results. In fact, it was the defense in the criminal cases that was working so hard to lift the CIPA restrictions so that they could shed the light of day upon their affairs and thus receive the exoneration to which they were entitled.

22. The OIC proffered theories of conduct that ranged from a rogue group of outlaw diplomats out for their own profit, to an agency relationship amongst the participants that was operating expressly for no profit but was willing to pay for all the

costs of the operations and take all the risks if something went wrong. The OIC told the rogue story to the Swiss Government to induce them to freeze accounts under the control of Hakim and when that hold was about to be released because of the lack of proof of that criminal conduct, the OIC changed its story and requested a hold because Hakim et al **were** official USG agents who had yet to make an "accounting" of the proceeds.

23. When other defendants like Tom Clines were subject to prosecution the government did not have the evidence to bring charges so it created a false scenario that illegally got some Swiss banking documents from the Swiss government by requesting them for an unrelated case and then utilized them out of context against Clines. At the same time he could not get access to the complete records which might have exonerated him because the US held back and had destroyed probative documents.

24. Throughout this ordeal, Albert Hakim's conduct has been consistent and stalwart. When the other participants left the bargaining table with the Iranians, Hakim stayed and finished the process that resulted in the freedom of hostage David Jacobsen. Judge Gessell noted that the sole reason for the release of that hostage was that Hakim, at his own cost, stayed in Europe and continued meetings that were extraordinarily dangerous so that the hostages could be freed. Hakim stayed on for business when the others were running for cover because he so believed in the validity of the fourth option and upon seeing the response to the concept from former enemies he stayed to see it through. His last assignment in these matters was and is for the State Department and he has not abandoned that assignment for all these years. He stands ready to do the right thing and merely wants the USG to uphold its side of the bargain and meet to discuss a logical resolution of the affairs.

For the reasons of justice and equity, Albert Hakim respectfully requests that the history and context of these matters be considered by the court in evaluating these issues.

Respectfully submitted,

Albert Hakim
16375 Aztec Ridge Drive
Los Gatos,, CA 95032
408-395-0500
fax 408-354-4245

Supplemental Background and Prayer4

IN THE UNITED STATES DISTRICT COURT
FOR THE EASTERN DISTRICT OF VIRGINIA

UNITED STATES OF AMERICA,	)	
	)	CIVIL NO. 93-1202-A
Plaintiff	)	
	)	
v.	)	
	)	
ALBERT HAKIM,	)	
	)	
_____	)	

MEMORANDUM OF DEFENDANT, ALBERT HAKIM,
IN OPPOSITION TO MOTION OF U.S. FOR A STAY OF PROCEEDINGS

The United States filed this action on September 21, 1993, at the same time that it filed a virtually identical action in Geneva, Switzerland.

Defendant Hakim filed, on November 30 1993, his Answer, Affirmative Defenses, and Counterclaim. The case is set for Pretrial Conference in January, 1994 and Trial in February or March.

Now the United States has apparently decided that it is more convenient for its strategy to proceed in Switzerland first, and concluded that it is more probable that it will prevail there,1

---

1 For the purposes of this motion, Hakim will not respond to each item of the "statement of the Swiss proceedings" recited by the Plaintiff. Hakim contends that it is wildly inaccurate. For example, the U.S. conveniently omitted the Federal decision tossing the United States out of court for failure to "timely file" (a decision it regards as "procedural"). It was then required to resort to proceedings as a private party. No evidentiary hearing has ever taken place, the courts simply relying upon "the papers" the U.S. has submitted. Needless to say, the U.S. has yet to proffer the true facts to the Swiss Courts. Hakim has yet to have his day in Swiss Court.

hence guaranteeing for the United States a <u>res judicata</u> effect of the decision of the Swiss Courts. The Court should deny the motion.

In general, when there is a pending proceeding, regarding the same parties and same claims in a foreign country, comity between the two sovereign states is implicated. The first jurisdiction to reach a judgment may be pled as <u>res judicata</u> in the other.

Parallel proceedings in two countries involving the same claim should ordinarily be allowed to proceed simultaneously, at least until a judgment is reached in one which can be pled as <u>res judicata</u> in the other. See <u>Lake Airways Ltd. v. Sabena, Belgian World Airlines</u>, 731 F.2d 909 (D.C. Cir. 1984), <u>Sea Containers Ltd. v. Sten AB</u>, 890 F.2d 1205 (D.C. Cir 1989), <u>Gau Shan Company, Ltd. v. Bankers Trust Company</u>, 956 F. 2d 1349 (6th Cir. 1992).

The United States claims that its Motion is based upon a desire to "avoid needless duplication of civil litigation, conserve judicial resources..." etc. This lately held ideal is hardly credible from the party who initiated this litigation. It is much more likely that the motivation for this motion is the real likelihood (having lately examined the issues and defenses and the probability of an early trial on the "rocket docket") that its claim will be reviewed first here and defeated in a U.S. Court actually receiving evidence and reviewing U.S. Law.

In deciding on an appropriate disposition of the motion, this court will likely engage in a weighing of many factors. See, <u>Black & Decker Corp. v. Sanyei America Corp.</u>, 650 F.Supp. 406 (N.D. Ill.

1986). What the United States offers as rationale for a stay <u>here</u> are problems it has encountered with its strategy and tactics <u>in Switzerland</u> in connection with its multifarious barrage of litigation against these defendants. What should be determinative, however, are the rights of <u>both parties</u>. Here, the United States will have its day in Court on the relevant and ultimate issue: "Agency".

Here, important substantive rights of the Defendant would be severely prejudiced by a tilt towards the litigation tactics of the Unties States. The following are just some of the factors the Court may wish to consider.

1. The transactions challenged by the United States occurred here. The United States relies on these facts and the background of U.S. investigations, suits and proceedings to explain and justify its position to the Swiss Courts.

2. All of the parties to the facts in issue are here.

3. The witnesses, including relevant government agencies are here. Indeed, a review of the attachments to the motion show that the U.S. is in substance litigating a domestic, U.S.-based case in Switzerland against U.S. citizens.

4. The applicable law is that of the Unites States (federal common law or Virginia State Law). This Court, rather than a Swiss Court, is better equipped to deal with these issues and others, such as Classified Information Protection Act ("CIPA") issues.

5. The relevant documents to the issues originate in Washington and Virginia. Switzerland will not be able to enforce

subpoenas nor document production from the U.S. territory to Switzerland.

6. It will be substantially easier and less expensive for the parties to subpoena documents and persons here. It will be financially impossible for the defendant to transport them to Geneva, a fact well known to the immensely rich Government whose resources spent on this case have apparently no known limit.

7. The Defendant has defenses available to him under United States Law not available in Switzerland.

8. The Defendant has filed a Counterclaim here under U.S. Law which could be determinative of his position. No such procedure is available in Swiss Law. As such, the rights of both parties are not protected equally in the Swiss Courts and the stay would serve to limit the presentation of facts and issues accordingly. While the United States claims that it can merely "dismiss" this case at any time before trial, Hakim doubts it.

9. The key issue raised by the Plaintiff is whether Defendant was its Agent. That issue is best decided by a U.S. Court under U.S. law, not a Swiss Court applying U.S. Law and attempting to construe it. In this regard, it more than appears that the U.S. is attempting to "engineer" the trier of fact. This "engineering" is especially important because the <u>key issue that will be raised by the defendant is breach of contract</u> and in Switzerland the process would not permit this issue to be raised. The issue of forum shopping has been faced before in similar circumstances with fair results, antithetical to the U.S. position. See, <u>Ronar, Inc. v.</u>

<u>Wallace</u>, 649 F. Supp 319 (D.Me. 1986).

Comity generally requires that the domestic court exercise jurisdiction concurrently with the foreign court. <u>Laker Airways Ltd. v. Sabena, Belgian World Airlines</u>, 731 F.2d 909 926-27 (D.C. Cir. 1984). As between American and Foreign courts, the mere filing of a suit in one forum does not cut off the preexisting right of an independent forum to regulate matters subject to its prescriptive jurisdiction. <u>Id</u>. at 927. Comity also requires that the parties and the issues in both litigations be the same or sufficiently similar, such that the doctrine of <u>res judicata</u> can be asserted. <u>Herbstein v. Bruetman</u>, 743 F.Supp. 184, 187-88 (S.D.N.Y. 1990). If the foreign court reaches a judgment first, that judgment can then be pled as <u>res judicata</u> in the domestic court. <u>Id.</u> at 188. See <u>Hilton v. Guyot</u>, 16 S.Ct. 139, 143 (1985). In <u>Hilton</u>, the court held that comity should allow a foreign country judgment conclusive effect so as to precluded a retrial of the merits of the case as long as the trial abroad was fair and impartial and before a court of competent jurisdiction, and there was no fraud in procuring the judgment. While there appears to be a genal respect and enforcement of foreign judgments, comity does not always require recognition of the judgment.2 The principle of

---

2 Thus far, the Swiss procedure is somewhat Draconian. The funds were frozen without a hearing from 1986 to 1992. The case for Temporary Injunction was on unsworn "papers" with no evedentiary hearing nor right of cross-examination.

international comity, which is in itself discretionary, permits
permissive rather than mandatory recognition of a foreign judgment
by the court. <u>Cunard Steamship Co. v. Salen Reefer Services AB</u>,
773 F. 2d 452 (1985).

Thus, in the present case, the fact that the United States has
filed the exact same case, against the same parties and alleging
the same issues, in Switzerland, has little effect on the proceeding in the Untied States.
Both actions can proceed concurrently at least until a judgment is
reached in one which can then be asserted as <u>res judicata</u> in the
other.

Moreover, it would appear wiser and more economical for the
<u>Swiss</u> proceeding to be stated until the U.S. proceeding is
concluded, rather than the reverse.

The motion should be denied.
Respectfully submitted,

Albert Hakim
in propria persona
16375 Aztec Ridge Drive
Los Gatos, CA 95032
(408) - 395 - 0500
Fax (408) - 354 - 4245
Date: Nov. 29 93

Charles Hill

November 22, 1993

United States Court of Appeals
District of Columbia Circuit
333 Constitution Avenue N.W.
Washington D.C. 20001-2866

To the Court:

I appreciate the opportunity offered to me by the Court to
comment and submit factual information on relevant portions of
the final report of the Office of Independent Counsel. On
September 3, 1993 in Room 5809 of the United States Court House
in Washington, D.C. I was permitted to read Chapter 24, Part VII
and an additional selection of individual pages provided to me by
the Clerk of Court. My comments, submissions, and requests
follow.

1. Chapter 24 of Part VII is in large part a prosecutor's brief
against me which sets out the prosecutor's case in detail,
declares that the prosecution's case could be established "beyond
a reasonable doubt," and asserts various subjective judgments,
legal conclusions, and gratuitous characterizations about me.
The Report then states that the OIC decided not to prosecute
because, inter alia, "an issue of fact" central to the case
"might create reasonable doubt in the minds of the jurors."

Publication of Chapter 24 of Part VII would amount to
prosecution of me by means other than due process of law; i.e.,
by officially authorized public defamation. I therefore request
that Chapter 24 of Part VII remain under seal.

2. The "issue of fact" is not accurately or adequately set forth
in Chapter 24, Part VII. In brief summary, the facts are as
follows:

* My notebooks presented an unusual problem, as an estimated
98 per cent of their content dealt with classified or sensitive
material on topics other than those of the Iran/Contra
investigations; entries which dealt with Iran/Contra matters were
widely scattered throughout the inextricable pages and often
represented by only a word or phrase within the context of non-
relevant material.

* A detailed, consecutive, page-by-page review by me of the
full set of notebooks was not possible because of the exigencies
of the situation in November and December of 1986 and the
requirements of my assigned official duties.

* It was my understanding at that time that neither
investigators nor the Department of State wanted non-pertinent
classified material on then-current foreign policy and national

security matters to be deposited with those conducting the investigation. Accordingly, following my initial, relatively brief (only a few days) review of the notebooks in search of reference to arms for Iran, I was instructed by the Legal Advisor of the State Department to continue to hold the notebooks in my office safe and to stand ready to return to review them with regard to topics and time periods as requested by investigators. My understanding from the Legal Advisor was that this arrangement was entirely known and acceptable to investigators. During this period Congressional Members and Staff made public reference to my notebooks and the detailed accounts they contained.

        * Under this arrangement I was requested and did return to the notebooks in late 1986 and early 1987 to review, extract, and produce entries on the Brunei solicitation, the November-December 1986 period itself, and on support for the Contras. With regard to this last search, in early 1987 the Legal Advisor, informing me that he was acting on investigators' request, instructed me to go through my notebooks to search for material on aid to the Contras. For several hours a day over the course of about two weeks I did so. The task was so time-consuming that I could not perform my official duties adequately. I found a considerable amount of material on the topic of U.S. Contra aid and turned it over to the Legal Advisor in early 1987. Because the two week effort had only covered a few months of the record when years were required, I asked the Legal Advisor to be relieved of this duty. He informed me that the material I had located appeared not to be directly relevant to the investigation and told me that I could cease my search until further notified. Therefore, the statement in the OIC final report that I "had produced to criminal and congressional investigators in 1987 only those portions of his notebooks that related to the Iran arm sales -- not to contra-related activities" is false. This is only one example of factual inaccuracies, omissions, or unwarranted conclusions contained in pages of the final report shown to me on September 3, 1993. Among them, particularly defamatory and unsubstantiated is the OIC's accusation that Mr. Platt and I colluded. My actions were in no way coordinated with Mr. Platt's at any time during the investigation.

3. In order to correct the record across the entire range of misrepresentations by the OIC, I request that the following documents be included as an appendix to the OIC's final report.

        a.) This letter, dated November 22, 1993.

        b.) My affidavit, taken by the firm of Wilmer, Cutler and Pickering, in which I describe in detail the record of availability of my notebooks to investigators. This affidavit was, I believe, filed with the Court on December 1, 1992 on behalf of that firm's client. A copy of that affidavit is attached to this letter.

3

     c.) The full transcripts of the OIC's (Mr. Gillen) interviews with me in the office of the OIC on February 21 and February 22, 1992.

     d.) The full transcript of my appearance before the Grand Jury on July 10, 1992 or, alternatively, the first part of that transcript in which the OIC (Mr. Barrett) makes clear to the Grand Jury my full cooperation with the OIC's investigation, including making myself and my notebooks available from the outset.

     The transcripts mentioned in c.) and d.) above are not within my possession or control.

4. On June 25, 1990 the OIC stated in writing that I was not a subject or a target of any investigation. At no time thereafter did the OIC ever inform me of any change in this status, including at the time they requested that I testify before the Grand Jury. At no time during the course of nearly seven years of contact with the OIC have I been represented by counsel, and at no time have I done other than fully respond and cooperate with the OIC and its requests. In view of the discrepancy between this pattern of conduct by the OIC and the hostile, prosecutorial stance taken by the OIC toward me in Chapter 24, Part VII, I ask that the Court take into consideration whether a breach in professional legal ethics has occurred.

                                     Respectfully submitted,

                                     Charles Hill

                                     Charles Hill
                                     P.O. Box 908 Yale Station
                                     New Haven, CT 06520

P.S. I also attach, for the Court's information, a letter provided to me by the National Archives pertaining to the classification of my notebooks.

UNITED STATES COURT OF APPEALS
FOR THE DISTRICT OF COLUMBIA CIRCUIT

Division for the Purpose of
Appointing Independent Counsels

United States Court of Appeals
For the District of Columbia Circuit

FILED DEC 1 1992

RON GARVIN
CLERK

In re Oliver L. North et al.   )
)   Division No. 86-6
)

DECLARATION OF CHARLES HILL

I, CHARLES HILL, declare:

1.   I am currently a "diplomat-in-residence" at Yale University in New Haven, Connecticut.

2.   From 1984 to 1989, I served as Executive Assistant to Secretary of State George P. Shultz.

3.   It was my practice, in my position as Executive Assistant, to take notes on meetings and conversations in and around the offices of the Secretary of State. I would also take notes of debriefs given to me of meetings attended by the Secretary and of information passed to me by various State Department or other Administration officials. To the extent of my ability, my notes faithfully and accurately reflected the events and information described therein.

4.   During the period June 1985 to November 1986, I recorded from time to time in my notes information concerning an initiative on the part of the members of the National Security Council staff to attempt to transfer, either directly or indirectly, military arms to Iran with the goal, among others, of the release of American citizens held hostage in Beirut. A substantial portion of this information was either hearsay or

lacking in credibility. When I thought the information was credible, I would generally pass it along to the Secretary.

5.   Soon after the revelation in a Middle Eastern publication on November 3, 1986, that such an initiative had existed and that a former United States official had traveled to Iran in May of that year to facilitate the transfer of arms to Iran and to negotiate the release of the American hostages, the Secretary directed me to review my notes to help him to reconstruct what he personally knew about the events surrounding the arms initiative from the summer of 1985 forward.

6.   The Secretary related to me those events in the internal Administration debate over the arms sales that he could recall and asked that I check his recollections against my notes.

7.   In response to that request, I immediately spent approximately one day applying myself exclusively to the task of reviewing my notes.

8.   During this and all subsequent reviews of my notes, I made no effort selectively to review or present notes that would put the Secretary or the Department in a favorable light or to avoid reviewing or presenting those that might put the Secretary or the Department in a less favorable light. My intent each time I reviewed my notes was to provide the most accurate information responsive to the particular task or request available in the time allowed.

9.   Almost immediately after I began the review of my notes, the Secretary learned that the arms sales initiative was

ongoing and asked me to redirect my efforts towards assisting him
in bringing it to an end.

10.   During the last few weeks of November 1986, the
full attention of the Secretary and his staff was focused on
marshalling for the President convincing evidence that the Iran
arms sales policy was misguided and that it should be stopped.
The effort to bring the arms sales to a halt took precedence over
my review of my notes, which was temporarily suspended.

11.   However, I did use my notes extensively in the
Secretary's effort to stop the arms for hostages initiative and
to ensure that factual details of the initiative were not kept
from the public. For example, on November 20, 1986, the
Secretary asked me to brief the State Department Legal Advisor,
Judge Abraham Sofaer, in preparation for his review of testimony
that CIA Director William Casey was scheduled to give to
Congress. I briefed Judge Sofaer based largely on my notes,
including a November 18, 1985, note that recorded a conversation
between the Secretary and then National Security Advisor Robert
McFarlane, in which Mr. McFarlane informed the Secretary of an
impending United States sponsored arms shipment to Iran. I
understand that Judge Sofaer called this note to Mr. Casey's
attention, causing Mr. Casey to change his planned testimony
denying U.S. Government participation in this transfer.

12.   On November 22, 1986, Attorney General Edwin Meese
interviewed the Secretary as part of the former's investigation
into the arms sales to Iran. I was present at that interview as

was Assistant Attorney General Charles Cooper. The Secretary
relied on my notes in responding to the Attorney General's
questions. His answers were consistent with everything I had
been able to find in my notes to that point. He also referred to
a comment to him by President Reagan two days earlier that
indicated that the President knew or had contemporaneously known
of the November 1985 arms shipment to Iran.

13. Mr. Cooper interviewed me on November 24, 1986.
The focus of Mr. Cooper's questions was on the November 1985 arms
shipment. I showed him a copy of the November 18, 1985 note
recording the conversation between Mr. McFarlane and the
Secretary and, at his request, provided him a copy of the note at
the end of the interview.

14. In late November of 1986, the Secretary instructed
Judge Sofaer to coordinate the Department's full and open
response to investigators. As part of this effort, on
November 29, he issued a directive instructing all relevant
sections of the State Department to produce all pertinent
documents to the Office of the Legal Advisor for review by FBI
agents or other investigators. The directive, which was reviewed
and approved by the Department of Justice, instructed that, in
cases of doubt as to whether particular documents were to be
produced, Department personnel were to err on the side of
disclosure.

15. As the Attorney General's investigation got
underway, it became clear to me and to Judge Sofaer that the

investigators would be interested in the notes I had taken. We
were concerned, however, that at least ninety percent of my notes
were completely unrelated to Iran-Contra issues and that many of
them were highly sensitive. In view of these concerns, I did not
turn over all of my notes, but responded to requests for notes on
particular subjects, and made the notes available in their
entirety for supervised review by FBI agents at the Department of
State. I also preserved the notes for possible future review,
pursuant to Judge Sofaer's instruction.

16. This practice with respect to my notes remained in
force for the duration of the Attorney General's investigation
and remained in effect during the subsequent investigations by
the Independent Counsel and Congress. None of my notes or other
Department documents were withheld from any Iran-Contra
investigators.

17. I spent December 1 and 3, 1986, reviewing my notes
in preparation for the Secretary's upcoming Congressional
testimony and for my own FBI interview scheduled for December 4.
In order to prepare the Secretary for his testimony, I worked
with Judge Sofaer and then State Department Executive Secretary
Nicholas Platt to put together a three-ring binder of notes and
departmental documents that indicated what the Secretary had
known about the arms for hostages initiative at key points
between May 1985 and November 1986. This notebook was not
intended to be an exhaustive review of all of my notes relevant
to the Iran-Contra Affair, which the pressure of time precluded,

but was rather a quickly assembled document intended to assist
the Secretary in his public testimony. I understand from Judge
Sofaer that he later provided this notebook to White House
counsel, Congressional investigators, and FBI agents who worked
first on the Attorney General's investigation and subsequently
reported to the Independent Counsel.

18. On December 4, 1986, I was interviewed by an FBI
agent. In answering many of the agent's questions, which focused
largely on the Iran arms initiative, I referred explicitly to my
notes. Although I indicated to the agent that my notes were
available for investigators, the agent did not request to take
any of my notes with him.

19. In late 1986, I began to receive specific requests
for collections of my notes on various specific subject matters.
For example, I was asked to compile my notes relating to Brunei
and those relating to the Contras. At no time prior to a request
to see all of the notes in the Summer of 1990 was I ever asked by
investigators to assemble for them notes specifically relating to
the arms sales to Iran.

20. In late 1986, on my own initiative, I assembled a
book of the notes I had taken on developments during the period
following the revelation of the arms sales to Iran (November
through December 1986). These notes document the Secretary's
efforts during this period to bring the arms sales to a close and
to cooperate with investigators and with Congress in making them

public. (I will refer to them herein as the "post-revelation
notes.")

21. In February of 1987, I was interviewed by
Independent Counsel staff attorney Jeffrey Toobin and an FBI
agent. Although Mr. Toobin asked me about my notes and looked
them over, he displayed little interest in any of the notes
having to do with arms shipments to Iran with the exception of
the November 1985 arms shipment.

22. In April of 1987, I was interviewed by another
Independent Counsel lawyer, Geoffrey Stewart. The questions
during this interview were focused on the Contras and on the
November 1985 arms shipment. During the interview, I observed
that Mr. Stewart was referring to some of my notes, but I was not
shown any of those notes or any other documents.

23. In May or June 1987, I understand that Judge
Sofaer's office turned over the notebooks of post-revelation
notes and notes relevant to the Contras to both the Joint
Congressional Committee and the Independent Counsel's office.

24. On June 25 and 26, 1987, I was present for the
Secretary's Independent Counsel interview in preparation for the
Secretary's possible appearance as a witness in the trial of Lt.
Col. Oliver North. The interview lasted for parts of two days;
the first day was conducted by Mr. Toobin and Mr. Stewart and the
second day by the Independent Counsel, Judge Lawrence Walsh,
himself. The focus of the interview was the Secretary's views of
the proper role of the National Security Council in the

implementation of foreign policy. During the interview, Judge
Walsh told the Secretary that he had read his testimony and
statements, but made no suggestion to the Secretary that either
his testimony or his statements were in any way inconsistent with
one another or with what the Independent Counsel knew. Judge
Walsh made no suggestion at this interview that the Secretary
might have been involved in the arms sales to Iran or the
diversion of profits to the Contras.

25. On July 27, 1987, the Secretary was interviewed by
Mr. Toobin, Mr. Stewart, and an FBI agent. During the interview,
the Secretary was questioned concerning the National Security
Council, the Contras, the Boland Amendment, and the history of
State Department knowledge concerning arms sales to Iran. The
questions posed by the Independent Counsel attorneys concerning
the shipment of arms to Iran appeared to be based upon notes that
I and others in the State Department had previously provided to
the Independent Counsel, including the post-revelation notes.

26. During the July 27, 1987, interview there was no
suggestion that the Secretary was suspected of any involvement in
the arms sales to Iran or the diversion of profits to the
Contras.

27. In March of 1988, Mr. Toobin called me to make an
appointment to review my notes. He later cancelled the
appointment.

28. On June 23, 1988, Mr. Toobin returned to the State
Department to go over with me for the first time the post-

revelation notes that I had assembled in early 1987. These notes
had been in the possession of the Independent Counsel's office
for over a year at that point. The meeting lasted approximately
half an hour. Between that time and June 1990, I was not asked
to provide further information or documents and had no other
contact with the Independent Counsel's office.

29. On June 15, 1990, I received a letter from the
Independent Counsel requesting the opportunity to examine all of
my notes from 1983 to the end of my tenure at the Department of
State. This was the first time that any investigator had made a
formal request for all of my notes. After I received the letter,
the Secretary asked Judge Sofaer to make arrangements with the
Independent Counsel's Office for the transportation, storage, and
supervision of access to my notes at a neutral repository in
Washington, D.C.

30. Shortly after receiving that letter, I received a
call from Mr. John Barrett of the Independent Counsel's office
stating that he wanted the Secretary and me to come to Washington
for further interviews concerning my notes. When Mr. Barrett
indicated that he would need to refer to my notes, I suggested
that he and his colleagues come to the Hoover Institution at
Stanford University where the Secretary and I had offices and
where the notes were then stored in a classified vault for
safekeeping. Mr. Barrett readily agreed to do so.

31. On June 21, 1990, I was interviewed in Stanford by
Mr. Barrett, another Independent Counsel staff attorney by the

name of Louise Radin, and an FBI agent. These investigators
interviewed me for one day, then conducted a one day interview
with the Secretary and returned for another half day of
questioning with me. The focus of the questions to me were the
November 1985 arms shipment, Central America, and the role of the
Vice President. There was no discussion during my interviews
with these Independent Counsel investigators of other notes or
any suggestion that the Secretary or I had, at any time, been
remiss in producing any of my notes. As had been the case with
previous Independent Counsel interviews, our interaction was
cooperative and friendly.

     32. On June 22, 1990, my employer, the Hoover
Institution, and I were subpoenaed by the grand jury
investigating the Iran-Contra matter, and I was ordered to appear
in Washington, D.C. with all of my notes.

     33. It is my understanding that Judge Sofaer then
worked out an agreement with Mr. Gillen providing for full access
to my notes under the auspices of the National Archives. In this
context, Mr. Gillen wrote to Judge Sofaer on June 25, 1990,
assuring him that I was not a subject or a target of any
investigation and that I was excused from my grand jury
appearance.

     34. On June 28, 1990, I personally brought all of my
notes to Washington, D.C., and lodged them at the National
Archives, where the Independent Counsel and his staff had full
access to the notes.

35.   In early November 1990, I was contacted by the National Archives, informing me that I could retrieve my notes. I decided instead to deed the originals to the Reagan Library, and so deeded the documents on November 21, 1990.

36.   On December 10, 1990, I was interviewed at the Hoover Institution by attorneys from the Independent Counsel's office. The questions were directed to my post-revelation notes. There was no discussion at this interview of the circumstances surrounding the production of my notes.

37.   On January 7, 1992, I received a letter from Mr. Gillen asking me to respond to 19 questions that had arisen since my December 1990 interview. The questions were all focused on what notes I had or may still have had in my possession, custody, or control which I had used to prepare the Secretary for various meetings, interviews, and testimony in the post-revelation period. I responded to this request by letter dated January 22, 1992, indicating that I had no documents in my possession, custody, or control other than copies of my notes.

38.   A few days later, Mr. Gillen contacted me by phone and informed me that his office would have to interview me again. I was not informed what the topics of the interview would be. Mr. Gillen did not indicate to me what my status was with respect to the Independent Counsel's investigation.

39.   I was interviewed by Mr. Gillen, Independent Counsel staff attorneys John Barrett and Thomas Baker, and an FBI agent on February 21 and 24, 1992, at the Office of the

Independent Counsel. The clear focus of the interview was on
1) notes the Independent Counsel had found in its review of my
notes at the National Archives and Mr. Gillen's assertion that I
had not "produced" these notes to investigators in late 1986 and
early 1987, and 2) my participation in the preparation of the
Secretary for public testimony in that same time frame with the
strong implication that I had assisted the Secretary in preparing
false testimony. I strongly refuted both suggestions, reminding
the interviewers of their full access to my notes from the outset
of the Department of Justice's investigation and describing in
detail the efforts made by the Secretary and the entire State
Department to get out the facts to the public as quickly as
possible.

          40. I understand that, in early March 1992, Mr.
Barrett sought, through the White House Counsel's Office and the
National Archives, to conduct another review of my original
notes, which I had previously donated to the Reagan Library. At
the request of the Reagan Library, by letter dated March 9, 1992,
I gave my permission to have the notes transferred again to the
National Archives for the Independent Counsel's review. It was
not revealed to me why the Independent Counsel again needed to
review the originals of my notes.

          41. On or about July 1, 1992, I was again contacted by
the Office of Independent Counsel and was informed that I would
have to return yet again to Washington for another interview and
a possible grand jury appearance. It was not disclosed to me

what the purpose of this interview would be, nor was it disclosed
whether my status with respect to the investigation had changed.

42.   I was interviewed at the Office of the Independent
Counsel on July 9, 1992, and appeared before the grand jury on
July 10, 1992.   The questioning in both sessions suggested to me
that the focus of the investigation had clearly shifted away from
the Secretary and me toward former Secretary of Defense Caspar
Weinberger and former National Security Advisor Frank Carlucci.

43.   I have since had no further contact with the
Office of the Independent Counsel.

I declare under penalty of perjury that the foregoing
is true and correct and that this declaration was executed on the
11th day of December 1992 in New Haven, Connecticut.

_____
CHARLES HILL

SENT BY:Xerox Telecopier 7020 ; 3-20-92 ; 4:20PM ;   2026474802→   95015709 82415709;# 2

United States Department of State

Washington, D.C. 20520

March 20, 1992

UNCLASSIFIED

Mr. John Fawcett
National Archives and Records
    Administration
Office of Presidential Libraries
Washington, D.C. 20408

Dear Mr. Fawcett:

The Office of Presidential Libraries requested that the Department of State review for classification 33 notebooks containing the handwritten notes of M. Charles Hill. The notes cover the period May 24, 1985, to August 4, 1987, during which time Mr. Hill served as Secretary Shultz's Executive Assistant. As a result of the National Archives and Records Administration's (NARA) request for an expeditious review and, to assist the Office of Independent Counsel with its investigation, two reviewers from the Department's Office of Freedom of Information, Privacy and Classification Review surveyed portions of the notebooks on March 13.

You requested that the Department review selected material which NARA identified, but not all of the material in question. Based on this survey, it is the Department's view, until a line-by-line review can be made, that the notebooks as a group should be considered to contain TOP SECRET/CODEWORD material in accordance with the standards of Executive Order 12356. This determination is based on the specific identification of State Department derived material which is currently and properly classified SECRET. It is also based on the identification of material similar to, or representative of, text derived from documents or information originated at third agencies of which the Department is familiar and which is classified TOP SECRET/CODEWORD subject to special handling restrictions. Furthermore, the Department's Director, Office of Freedom of Information, Privacy and Classification Review, has personally reviewed copies of some of Mr. Hill's notes in addition to being briefed on the findings of the March 13 review and determined that the notes continue to warrant the protection identified above.

If NARA requires further certification of this classification, the Department recommends that NARA afford appropriate third agencies an opportunity to review the Hill

SENT BY:Xerox Telecopier 7020 ; 3-20-92 ; 4:20PM ;   2026474802→   95015709 82415709;# 3

<u>UNCLASSIFIED</u>
-2-

notes.   In addition, a page specific classification
determination would require an additional Department review.
We understand that copies of the 33 notebooks will be retained
by NARA in Washington should further review be required.

    The Department appreciates the opportunity to review these
notebooks and would request that NARA keep this Department
advised of further developments regarding Mr. Hill's notes.
Thank you.

                                        Sincerely,

                                        James E. Baker

                                        James E. Baker
                                        Attorney Adviser

cc: Mr. John Barrett, Esq.
    Office of Independent Counsel

W. George Jameson

CENTRAL INTELLIGENCE AGENCY

WASHINGTON, D.C. 20505

Office of General Counsel

12 November 1993

Ron Garvin, Clerk
United States Court of Appeals
District of Columbia Circuit
Washington, DC 20001-2866

Dear Mr. Garvin:

On 21 September 1993 I reviewed the Final Report of the
Independent Counsel in the Iran-Contra matter. My comments
follow:

a) Page 218, fn 114. The Final Report states incorrectly
that, on 21 November 1986, I attended two hearings on Iran-
Contra held by the House and Senate intelligence committees
to hear testimony from then-DCI Casey and others. In fact,
I attended three sessions: the morning hearing of the HPSCI,
the SSCI hearing, and the second HPSCI session later that
afternoon.

b) Page 312, fn 14. Same; the Final Report is in error. I
attended the SSCI hearing and <u>both</u> HPSCI sessions.

c) Pages 317-320, including footnote 60. The Report states
that I <u>purport</u> not to recall precisely when during the week
of 19 November I learned, and informed others in CIA, of the
flight to Iran that occurred in November 1985. In fact,
when the OIC asked me several years after-the-fact, I said I
could not recall exactly on which day of that week, and at
what time of the day (which is what OIC asked me to try to
remember) I learned and reported the information about the
flight.

Thank you for the opportunity to comment. Please call (703-874-
3118) if you have any questions.

Yours truly,

W. George Jameson

Alton G. Keel, Jr.

December 3, 1993

Mr. Ron Garvin
Clerk
U. S. Court of Appeals
District of Columbia Circuit
Washington, D.C. 20001

Dear Mr. Garvin:

Please allow me to make the following corrections for the record in regard to the Final Report of the Independent Counsel:

Chapters 1 thru 4

(1)   McFarlane comment of November 18th or 19th meeting

McFarlane is reported to have indicated that at a "November 18th or 19th" meeting at which he "believed" North, Teicher, Keel and Poindexter attended at least part of, there was reference to "use of Iranian money".

As Keel has testified, he was at no meeting in which there was a discussion or mention of the use of Iranian money. Col. North testified before the Senate in open testimony to the effect that Dr. Keel, having just joined the NSC as Deputy National Security Adviser in September 1986, was unaware of the details of the Iranian hostage rescue efforts and, specifically, was not aware of the diversion of the funds from Iran to the Contras.

(2)   McFarlane's comment on November 21, 1986 discussion with Ledeen

McFarlane is reported to have stated that Ledeen mentioned to him on November 21, 1986, that Ledeen asserted that he had wanted to start speaking-out but Keel had "muzzled" him.

Ledeen in November 1986 did contact Keel, while Keel was Deputy National Security Advisor, and indicated that in his view that the administration had "a good story to tell". Keel indicated to Ledeen that the

administration was in the process of collecting all the facts about the Iran
related activities; that it was unlikely he, Ledeen, was aware of all the
relevant facts; that he thus risked putting out misinformation; and, finally,
that the activities were still classified as part of a covert operation and
could not be commented on publicly without proper authorization.

<u>Chapter 4, page 141</u>

Thompson is reported to have indicated that at a November 21, 1993,
meeting "probably attended by North, Keel and McDaniel", Adm.
Poindexter tore-up documents, which Thompson believed included a
previous Intelligence finding.

Keel had no knowledge of any previous Intelligence Finding and attended
no meeting in which he witnessed Adm. Poindexter destroying an
Intelligence Finding, nor does he have any knowledge of Adm. Poindexter
doing so.

<u>Chapter 30, page 508</u>

Regan is reported as indicating at the rehearsal preparing for the
President's press conference that "I think it was Al Keel , who was then his
[Poindexter's] assistant - it may have been still Rod McDaniel, I'm not
sure...were telling the President that he shouldn't speak up about Israel;
that Israel's role in this should be down played; we should not feature it
and he should be cautious about acknowledging the Israeli role."

Keel did <u>not</u> advise the President on how to handle the Israeli issue at the
rehearsal for the November 19, 1993 press conference. It <u>was</u> the
administration position, as reflected in issue papers prepared for the press
conference and provided to the Independent Counsel, not to comment on
<u>any</u> third country involvement, including specifically Israel, in the Iran
initiative. This position was consisted with long standing U.S.
government position not to comment on third country involvement in any
classified or covert operation.

<u>Chapter 30, page 510</u>

Pete Wallison is reported as having indicated that Keel objected "when
<u>Wallison tried to omit</u> [emphasis added] a line stating that all laws had
been complied with ", from President Reagan's planned televised speech.

<u>Chapter 31, page 528</u>

Wallison is reported as having stated that Keel "<u>proposed inserting a sentence</u> [emphasis added] that all laws had been complied with," in the draft of the Presidents planned address.

The above reports on Mr. Wallison's recollection are inconsistent. The draft speech for the President <u>contained</u> a reference to the fact that "all laws had been complied with." This <u>was</u> the position of the U.S. attorney General and the President and there was no evidence to the contrary at that date, November 13, 1986, that Mr. Wallison or anyone else was aware of or made known. On that basis, Keel did insist that the reference <u>not</u> be omitted. There was never an issue of "inserting a sentence" to this effect.

Thank you for your kind consideration in including these corrections to the Final Report.

Sincerely,

Alton G. Keel, Jr.

Michael A. Ledeen

29 September, 1993

Mr. Ron Garvin, Clerk
United States Court of Appeals
District of Columbia Circuit
Washington, D.C. 20001-2866

Dear Mr. Garvin,

In response to your kind note of 9 August, I am sending you some comments and factual information for possible inclusion as an appendix of the Final Report of the Independent Counsel.

I would also like to take the opportunity to thank you personally for your help and attention.

Yours Faithfully,

United States Court of Appeals
For the District of Columbia Circuit

FILED SEP 3 0 1993

RON GARVIN
CLERK

From Michael A. Ledeen:

Most of the material that regards my activities confirm my testimony, and my published writings, to whit: all my contacts with the Israeli Government and Manucher Ghorbanifar in 1985 were fully authorized by the United States Government, including President Reagan. Moreover, my discussions with Prime Minister Peres in the Spring of that year did not concern either hostages or weapons, but rather had to do with Iran, in an effort to improve our knowledge and understanding. It is encouraging to learn (pg. 369), for the first time, that this was precisely the information given to Secretary of State Shultz by the U.S. Ambassador to Israel Samuel Lewis.

There are some errors of fact. On pg. 14 we are told that North and I were present at the November 8, 1985 meeting between McFarlane and Kimche; neither of us attended. On pg. 17 it is alleged that North "pushed" me to encourage an intelligence relationship between CIA and Ghorbanifar. He did not; I thought it worthwhile, suggested it to North, and he approved it.

Then there are more serious matters.

On pg. 88, note 74, we find: "Ledeen was an early suspect of IC's investigation because of allegations that he personally profited from the Iran arms sales. No evidence was found supporting these allegations, although Ledeen <u>admitted</u> (my italics) that he asked Israeli arms brokers Adolf (Al) Schwimmer and Yaakov Nimrodi to open a bank account in October 1985 to cover Iran arms sales expenses. Ledeen said an account was opened in Switzerland, that Schwimmer and Nimrodi gave him the number, and that he subsequently gave it to North. After the Iran arms sales became public, he received a letter from Credit Suisse stating that the account was never used and no money was ever deposited in it."

The use of the word "admitted" is tendentious; it suggests that the IC, although faced with a total lack of evidence that I profited in any way from the Iran Initiative, still wishes to smear me.   A fair-minded author would simply have stated the facts: there is no evidence that I profited. Period. I had nothing to hide, and indeed I volunteered the information about the Credit Suisse account to investigators for the Iran-Contra Committee long before I learned that the account was never used.

Kay D. Leisz

LAW OFFICES
JANIS, SCHUELKE & WECHSLER
1728 MASSACHUSETTS AVENUE, N.W.
WASHINGTON, D.C. 20036

S. ROBERT SUTTON

RECEIVED

DEC 02 1993

CLERK OF THE UNITED
STATES COURT OF APPEALS
TELEPHONE
(202) 861-0600

December 2, 1993

BY HAND

Mr. Ron Garvin, Clerk
United States Court of Appeals
District of Columbia Circuit
Room 5409
United States Courthouse
Third Street & Constitution Ave., N.W.
Washington, D.C. 20001-2866

In Re: Oliver L. North, et al.
           (Ms. Kay D. Leisz)
           Division No. 86-6

Dear Mr. Garvin:

Enclosed for filing **under seal** in the above-referenced matter, pending before the Division for the Purpose of Appointing Independent Counsels, please find the original and three copies of our Comments of Kay D. Leisz in Response to Relevant Portion of O.I.C. Final Report. Also enclosed please find two additional copies to be file stamped and returned to us in the enclosed postage pre-paid envelope.

Your assistance and cooperation is very much appreciated.

Yours truly,

S. Robert Sutton

S. Robert Sutton

Enclosures
SRS:jm
cc: Ms. Kay D. Leisz

IN THE UNITED STATES COURT OF APPEALS
FOR THE DISTRICT OF COLUMBIA CIRCUIT

Division for the Purpose of
Appointing Independent Counsels

Ethics in Government Act of 1978, As Amended

In re:	Oliver North, et al. (Ms. Kay D. Leisz)	Division No. 86-6 **(Under Seal)**

Before: Sentelle, Presiding, Butzner and Sneed, Senior Circuit
Judges

COMMENTS OF KAY D. LEISZ IN RESPONSE
TO RELEVANT PORTION OF O.I.C. FINAL REPORT

As an "individual named" in the Final Report issued by the
Office of Independent Counsel Lawrence E. Walsh, pursuant to 28
U.S.C. § 594(h)(2), Ms. Kay D. Leisz, by and through undersigned
counsel, hereby submits these comments to the relevant portion of
said report (pages 439-441).

Ms. Leisz is a long term public servant.   She served her
government for more than twenty-four years through her employment
both on Capitol Hill and in the Pentagon.   Over the period of those
many years she worked diligently, faithfully, and with great
dedication.   In the process she developed an impeccable reputation
for honest and faithful service, and earned her country's
considerable confidence, as evidenced by her high level security

clearances. Ms. Leisz values that reputation and confidence highly, and takes great pride in the belief that she has never given anyone any grounds to question her honesty, integrity, or loyalty.

The Final Report issued by the Office of Independent Counsel Lawrence E. Walsh (the "O.I.C.") inappropriately and unfairly maligns Ms. Leisz by characterizing her June 15, 1992 deposition testimony as "flagrantly incredible" and "false." Nothing could be farther from the truth. Ms. Leisz testified honestly and candidly to the best of her ability. Indeed, it appears that the only rationale that the O.I.C. might have for being disappointed with Ms. Leisz' testimony is that she may not have said what they wanted to hear. In this regard, Ms. Leisz' testimony may serve as grounds for disappointment, but not as grounds for complaint. While Ms. Leisz may not have said what the O.I.C. wanted to hear, she did testify honestly.

In its Final Report, the O.I.C. specifically challenges Ms. Leisz' testimony as it pertains to (1) Secretary Weinberger's handwritten meeting notes, and (2) Secretary Weinberger's "diary notes" or "telephone logs." Initially, in analyzing Ms. Leisz' testimony and the allegations of "incredibility" it must be noted that Ms. Leisz has been placed at a considerable disadvantage. At the O.I.C.'s urging, Ms. Leisz has been denied access both to her own deposition testimony -- the very testimony which is challenged by the O.I.C. -- and to much of the testimony and other materials which allegedly contradict that testimony. Such a process is

2

wholly unfair and entirely lacking in normal due process protections. The O.I.C. has been permitted to challenge Ms. Leisz' credibility based upon mere citations to other witnesses' testimony without affording her so much as an opportunity to review that testimony, much less an opportunity to cross examine the witnesses. Fortunately, however, some relevant materials are available for our review. Those materials strongly support Ms. Leisz' testimony and raise questions about the O.I.C's contentions.

1. Secretary Weinberger's Handwritten Meeting Notes

On the subject of Secretary Weinberger's handwritten meeting notes, Ms. Leisz testified that after she and Secretary Weinberger had been at the Department of Defense for one year it became evident that he was not going to have time to dictate memoranda based upon those meeting notes. Accordingly, with Secretary Weinberger's blessing, she stopped maintaining a file of those notes and instead left them in the briefing books (where they had been placed by Secretary Weinberger) which were forwarded to the Correspondence and Directives Section to be broken down and filed. In this regard, two specific items are available for our review -- both of which are wholly supportive of Ms. Leisz' testimony. The first such item is the FBI 302 Report of Secretary Weinberger's October 10, 1990 interview, which the O.I.C. concedes is consistent with Ms. Leisz' testimony. Indeed, Secretary Weinberger's statement is, in relevant part, 100% consistent with Ms. Leisz' testimony:

> Weinberger advised that his secretary, Kay Leisz, used to save his notes from these briefing book pages because Weinberger had told her that he wanted to dictate memoranda of the meetings based on them. After about a year, Leisz came up to Weinberger and said, "You're never really gonna dictate from these notes are you?" Weinberger agreed that he was too busy to dictate memoranda from these notes and he gave Leisz permission to discard them. From this point on, Weinberger rarely took notes, and when he did, Leisz never saved them for him, except for rare occasions.

FBI 302 Report at p.2. Also available is the April 29, 1992 Affidavit of Thelma Stubbs Smith. Although the O.I.C. contends, in its Final Report, that Ms. Smith's Affidavit contradicts Ms. Leisz on this subject, review of paragraph 6 of that Affidavit demonstrates that Ms. Smith's testimony is entirely consistent with Ms. Leisz' testimony:

> 6. Secretary Weinberger occasionally made margin notes in briefing books. At the conclusion of a meeting, he placed the briefing book in his Out Box in the Outer office by my desk. The Correspondence & Directives Division ("C&D") was responsible for taking the documents from the Out Box and distributing them as appropriate. Accordingly, any notes regarding the Iran-Contra matter that Secretary Weinberger made in briefing books would have been turned over to C&D or the office that prepared the briefing book.

2. Secretary Weinberger's "Diary Notes"

Interestingly, all of the available materials similarly support Ms. Leisz' testimony on the subject of Secretary Weinberger's "diary notes" or "telephone logs." Ms. Leisz testified that she had no personal knowledge with respect to those notes as her job responsibilities did not require that she review or process them. Ms. Smith's April 29, 1992 Affidavit is also wholly supportive of Ms. Leisz' testimony on this subject. Like

Ms. Leisz, Ms. Smith was generally aware that Secretary Weinberger
"scribbled notes" on a pad on his desk, but had no personal
knowledge with regard to the contents of those notes, which she
viewed as personal:

> 5.   I was aware that Secretary Weinberger kept a pad on
> his desk on which he scribbled notes reflecting the date, time
> and other references to telephone calls and meetings.   I
> considered these to be personal notes. It was my belief that
> he made these notes to assist him in writing a book.

Also available is the April 21, 1992 Affidavit of General
Colin L. Powell. General Powell therein states, at paragraph 3,
that he considered those notes to be Secretary Weinberger's
"personal diary" and that he never read those notes out of respect
for their personal nature.   One cannot expect that Secretary
Weinberger's secretary would have been permitted access to
materials which Secretary Weinberger chose not to share with
General Powell, who served first as Secretary Weinberger's Senior
Military Assistant and later as Chairman of the Joint Chiefs of
Staff. Moreover, General Powell states that Secretary Weinberger's
personal notes pad "would sit on his desk with the completed pages
turned over. When he completed a pad, it would go into his desk
drawer and he would begin to write on a new pad." Powell Affidavit
at paragraph 4.   Thus, General Powell's Affidavit supports a
conclusion that Ms. Leisz' testimony concerning Secretary
Weinberger's diary notes -- that she neither reviewed nor processed
those notes -- is wholly credible and entirely truthful.

Thus, all of the available evidence is supportive of a
conclusion that Ms. Leisz testified truthfully and candidly to the

best of her ability. Indeed, review of her grand jury testimony (which was made available to us) demonstrates that she made every effort to be as honest and helpful as reasonably possible. Under these circumstances, the O.I.C.'s allegations of incredibility and falsity appear to be as unfounded as they are unfair. Accordingly, the Court should take whatever steps are available -- including redaction of the relevant section of the Final Report (pages 439-441), continued maintenance of the relevant portion of the Final Report "Under Seal," or, at an absolute minimum, inclusion of these comments as an appendix to the Final Report[1] -- to erase the blemish which the O.I.C. would attach to the good name which Ms. Leisz has worked so hard to earn.

Respectfully submitted,

Dated: December 2, 1993

S. Robert Sutton

Lawrence H. Wechsler
 D.C. Bar No. 102418
S. Robert Sutton
 D.C. Bar No. 367304
Janis, Schuelke & Wechsler
1728 Massachusetts Avenue, N.W.
Washington, D.C. 20036
(202) 861-0600

Counsel for Ms. Kay D. Leisz

---

[1] Pursuant to 28 U.S.C. § 594(h)(2) this "division of the court may release to the Congress, the public, or any appropriate person, such portions of [an O.I.C. final report] as the division of the court considers appropriate." Conversely, the Court is clearly authorized to withhold from such release such portions of an O.I.C. final report as the Court considers appropriate. 28 U.S.C. § 594(h)(2) also provides for the submission of comments by any individual named in an O.I.C. final report, and for the inclusion of such comments as an appendix to the final report.

CERTIFICATE OF SERVICE

I hereby certify that on the 2nd day of December, 1993, copies of the foregoing Comments of Kay D. Leisz in Response to Relevant Portion of O.I.C. Final Report were served by first class mail, postage pre-paid upon the Office of Independent Counsel Lawrence E. Walsh, with one copy directed to the office located at One Columbus Circle, N.E., Suite G320, Washington, D.C. 20544, and a second copy directed to the office located at 50 Penn Place, Suite 1475, Oklahoma City, Oklahoma 73118.

S. Robert Sutton

Robert C. McFarlane

Robert C. McFarlane
2101 L Street, NW
Suite 403
Washington, DC 20037

RECEIVED

OCT 25 1993

CLERK OF THE UNITED
STATES COURT OF APPEALS

October 22, 1993

Dear Mr. Garvin,

In reply to your letters of August 5 and September 24, enclosed please find my proposed corrections to the draft report by the Independent Counsel, Judge Lawrence Walsh, regarding the Iran Contra investigation. This constitutes my formal request. It supersedes my earlier letter with enclosures of September 2nd.

With best regards,

Sincerely,

Robert C. McFarlane

Mr. Ronald Garvin
Clerk
US Court of Appeals
District of Columbia Circuit
Washington, DC 20001-2866

Enclosures

Proposed Corrections
Submitted by Robert C. McFarlane

1. Chapter 1, Page 79, para 2, first sentence change to read "...Clark; Counselor of the Department of State;...and Military Assistant to Henry Kissinger when..."

Reason: The position of "Counselor of the Department," formally established in law and requiring confirmation by the Senate, is not oriented toward an advisory role to the Secretary but rather to all bureaus of the Department of State.

2. Page 79, paragraph 6, first sentence. Recommend change to read, "In 1985, McFarlane and Casey for different reasons -- were the chief advocates of ..."

Reason: My original motivation in recommending to the President that he authorize a dialogue with Iran was to determine whether five years of violent loss and economic decline brought on by the war with Iraq might have engendered formation of a viable alternative to Khomenei. When in December 1985 it became clear to me that such was not the case, I recommended to the President that the operation be ended. This is a matter of record unchallenged by any witness.

3. Page 80, right column, second full paragraph, last sentence. Recommend delete sentence.

Reason: Accuracy. Shultz inquiry to me was whether I had sent Mr. Ledeen to Israel to develop a channel to Iran. It was in this context that I replied that Mr. Ledeen not Mr. Teicher, had gone "on his own hook." This is confirmed by cables sent by Shultz to me in June or July, 1985. It is correctly recorded on page 89. Shultz apparently confused the two matters when he testified.

4. Page 103, right column, first full paragraph, last sentence. The last sentence states in effect that June 1985 was "...well after North's last surviving operations memorandum to McFarlane." This appears to represent either a typographical error or an error in fact. In that I did not leave the NSC staff until December 1985, and that North was writing memos to me until almost December 4, there is a 6-month gap in your reference.

5. Part I, Iran/Contra - The Underlying Facts, page 5, right column, last line. Recommend change to read, "...decided to withhold information about North's activities...."

Reason: Accuracy and fairness. I did not lie and was never charged with lying by the Independent Counsel. Had there been any question of my being so charged I would not have accepted the plea offer. The inaccurate characterization is not in keeping with the spirit of the plea arrangement, nor does it serve the national interest in encouraging future career professionals in government to come forward and be fully accountable in matters such as this. (Note: This false characterization is repeated in several places in the report. I would be pleased to identify each of these if allowed renewed access to the report).

Page 2

6. Page 6, left column, second full paragraph, second sentence. Recommend change to read, "Poindexter replied on behalf of...and knowingly repeated McFarlane's earlier <u>statement</u>,..."

<u>Reason</u>: See "Reason" for five above.

7. Chapter 4, Paul Thompson, page 144, left column, second full paragraph. Recommend deletion of fourth sentence, "McFarlane believed that...(through)...the letters were false."

<u>Reason</u>: Accuracy. I don't believe that I ever stated to the FBI or to anyone else, that I believed Thompson knew that the letters were "false." You may wish to check your footnote #60 which refers to an FBI interview with me on 9/13/90.

John N. McMahon

✈★ Lockheed Missiles & Space Company, Inc.

Sunnyvale, California 94088-3504 (408) 742-6211

John N. McMahon
President & CEO

October 5, 1993

Mr. Ron Garvin, Clerk
United States Court of Appeals
District of Columbia Circuit
Washington, DC 20001-2866

Dear Mr. Garvin:

Thank you for the advisory regarding the extension of time to December 3, 1993 for the review of the Final Report of the Independent Counsel in the Iran-Contra matter.

As you are aware. I had the opportunity to review the Final Report on Wednesday, September 8, 1993, in your office; and I have no motions or comments to make regarding it.

Thank you for the opportunity for the review.

Sincerely,

John N. McMahon

Edwin Meese, III

United States Court of Appeals
For the District of Columbia Circuit

FILED DEC 0 3 1993

RON GARVIN
CLERK

UNDER SEAL

IN THE UNITED STATES COURT OF APPEALS
FOR THE DISTRICT OF COLUMBIA CIRCUIT

Division for the Purpose of
Appointing Independent Counsels

Ethics in Government Act of 1978, as Amended

In re: Oliver L. North, <u>et al</u>.)))))	Division No. 86-6

Before: Sentelle, Presiding, Butzner and Snead, Senior Circuit
       Judges

EDWIN MEESE III's COMMENTS IN RESPONSE TO THE
FINAL REPORT OF INDEPENDENT COUNSEL LAWRENCE E. WALSH

Respectfully submitted,

Dated: December 3, 1993

LANDMARK LEGAL FOUNDATION
   Mark R. Levin
   Mark J. Bredemeier
   Jerald L. Hill
   Richard P. Hutchison
   Landmark Legal Foundation
   One Farragut Square South
   Washington, D.C. 20006
   (202) 393-3360

ATTORNEYS FOR EDWIN MEESE III

TABLE OF CONTENTS

I.   INTRODUCTION.. 1

II.   THE WALSH REPORT: A GRAND DELUSION..................... 2

III. THE BIG LIE: WALSH AND HIS CONSPIRACY................. 4

      A.   Significant Steps Initiated By
           Attorney General Meese <u>After</u> The
           November 24, 1986 NSPG Meeting.................... 5

           1.   November 25, 1986: Attorney General Meese
                 tells the world President Reagan knew of
                 the November 1985 HAWK shipment............. 5

           2.   Evening Of November 25, 1986/
                 Morning of November 26, 1986:
                 Attorney General initiates
                 criminal investigation...................... 7

           3.   The Attorney General's November 28, 1986
                 discovery letter to Shultz and others....... 8

           4.   Appointment and protection of
                 Independent Counsel......................... 10

      B.   Attorney General Meese:
           No Coverup, Tell The Truth........................ 11

           1.   Robert McFarlane............................ 11

           2.   George Shultz............................... 11

           3.   Oliver North................................ 12

           4.   November 24, 1986: National Security
                 Policy Group (NSPG) meeting................. 12

      C.   Walsh's Concoction Of A
           Motive For His Coverup Theory..................... 12

           1.   There was no coverup, and
                 there was no motive to coverup.............. 12

           2.   Was the November 1985 HAWK
                 shipment illegal?........................... 14

           3.   Whether the Attorney General thought
                 the November 1985 HAWK shipment
                 was "possibly" illegal is irrelevant........ 15

I.   INTRODUCTION

The Final Report of Independent Counsel Lawrence E. Walsh (hereinafter "Walsh Report") falsely accuses the President of the United States, the Vice President of the United States, the Attorney General, the Secretary of State, the Secretary of Defense, the Chief of Staff to the President, and others, of participating in a coverup of facts relating to a strategic initiative involving arms transfers to Iran. These comments will specifically rebut the preposterous claims against the Attorney General. It is assumed others will address allegations directed at them.[1] [1]

At **no** time did the Attorney General initiate or participate in any coverup of any aspect of what has become known as the "Iran-contra" matter.[2] Indeed, the Attorney General and his staff **discovered the diversion of funds** from the Iranian initiative to support the Nicaraguan Freedom Fighters. Immediately thereafter, Attorney General Meese, with the direction and support of the President, informed the American people and Congress of these facts. He also took aggressive and immediate actions to ensure that a full investigation of the entire matter would be conducted by the Department of Justice and, ultimately, an independent counsel.

The most important question that arises from the Walsh Report is **why** would a person, selected by a special judicial panel to serve as an independent counsel, so abuse his public trust and dishonor his appointment by issuing a document filled with distortions of fact, misuse of evidence, and false accusations against honorable public officials who are totally innocent of any wrongdoing?

The answer is that instead of performing a timely, competent, and thorough investigation to determine whether any real crimes were committed and, if so, to promptly prosecute them, Walsh has carried on a six-and-a-half year fruitless search for nonexistent criminal offenses and substituted politically-oriented hostility for objective fact-finding. In the process Walsh has violated numerous laws, professional standards, and ethical requirements. The true total cost of this malfeasance approximates $100,000,000.

To avoid the public criticism, official condemnation, and punitive action his conduct deserves, Walsh is using his final Report (as he did his Fourth Interim Report to Congress) to divert attention from his own failures and misconduct by falsely

---

1 Endnotes appear at the conclusion of these comments, beginning at p. a-1.

1

accusing President Reagan and his top officials of fictional offenses wholly manufactured by Walsh.

This matter has been examined intensively by Congress and investigated by the Tower Commission and Walsh. An objective and accurate review of the thousands of pages of testimony and documentary evidence produced and scrutinized during this seven year period can lead to only one conclusion: <u>There was no coverup, and any allegations of wrongdoing by President Reagan or Attorney General Meese are totally false</u>.

II.   THE WALSH REPORT: A GRAND DELUSION

Walsh's Report is patterned after the old Soviet model of justice: You're guilty because I say you're guilty, and damn the truth.

Walsh's Report is not only a grand delusion riddled with false statements, but an unconscionable act of deception intended to coverup Walsh's own unethical and illegal conduct, divert attention from Walsh's years of prosecutorial incompetence and abuse, and smear the Reagan Administration -- including President Ronald Reagan and Attorney General Edwin Meese, among others.

The Walsh Report is largely a refuge for Walsh's false statements and infirm musings about some Oliver Stone-type conspiracy to coverup the President's knowledge of what was actually a legal arms transfer that occurred in 1985. Walsh's bald assertion -- and his despicable manipulation and omission of information -- would be laughable if it were not so deplorable.

This Report conceals obvious and important facts that give the lie to Walsh's bizarre conspiracy fiction. In truth, Attorney General Meese, in a period of a few days, not only discovered the diversion of funds to the Nicaraguan Freedom Fighters, but he directed, in writing, that all information regarding the diversion **and** arms sales and shipments involving Iran be identified, produced and secured for the Federal Bureau of Investigation (FBI). Soon thereafter, the Attorney General requested the appointment of an independent counsel. Upon Walsh's appointment, Walsh had unfettered control over this body of information. And when a serious constitutional challenge was made against the very existence of an independent counsel -- thereby threatening Walsh's investigation of the so-called Iran-contra matter -- Attorney General Meese immediately exercised his own discretionary authority and appointed Walsh as a Department of Justice official to ensure that Walsh's investigation would not be hindered.

In short, Walsh accuses an innocent person, Attorney General
Edwin Meese, of a crime he knows did not happen. Walsh
calculatedly bypassed the Constitution and the judicial process
-- having never charged **any** official for the nonexistent
conspiracy he now adamantly and repeatedly urges in his Report --
to justify his 78-month-long, $100,000,000 fiasco and avoid legal
scrutiny and judicial sanctions.

Moreover, Walsh's Report violates the standards proclaimed
by the Watergate Special Prosecution Force ("WSPF"), which
condemned such a reckless abuse of power. In reporting on its
28-month-long investigation of the Watergate matter, the WSPF
wrote:

> ... A full accounting, within the confines and strictures
> that the law properly places upon prosecutors, is required
> ....

This report contains no facts about alleged criminal
activity not previously disclosed in a public forum. Many
public officials saw the Special Prosecutor as one with
special privileges to lay bare what witnesses had said and
to offer his own, personal conclusions as to what really
happened. Other persons also asserted that President
Nixon's pardon, and Congress' passage in the middle of
WSPF's work of a retroactive, 3-year statute of limitations
for campaign law violations (replacing the normal 5-year
period for initiating prosecutions) reinforced the propriety
of releasing grand jury testimony, informants' allegations,
and the confidential assertions of cooperative witnesses.

**However, for WSPF to make public the evidence it gathered
concerning the former President and others who were not
charged with criminal offenses would be to add another abuse
of power to those that led to the creation of a Special
Prosecutor's office. The Federal Rules of Criminal
Procedure prohibit the disclosure of information presented
to a grand jury except as necessary in the course of
criminal proceedings.** The American Bar Association
reinforces this stricture in its 'Code of Professional
Responsibility' and limits the circumstances under which
attorneys involved in criminal investigations are free to
make out-of-court statements about the details of their
work.

Most important, in terms of the American constitutional
system of government, is the notion of fundamental fairness
for those who, after investigation, have not been charged
with any criminal misconduct. **This consideration is
particularly important for a Special Prosecutor whose
independence considerably reduces his accountability and who
must be unusually sensitive to possible abuses of his power.**

It is a basic axiom of our system of justice that every man is innocent unless proven guilty after judicial proceedings designed to protect his rights to ensure a fair adjudication of the charges against him. Where no such charges are brought, it would be irresponsible and unethical for a prosecutor to issue a report suggesting criminal conduct on the part of an individual who has no effective means of challenging the allegations against him or of requiring the prosecutor to establish such charges beyond a reasonable doubt. (emphasis added)[3]

III. THE BIG LIE: WALSH AND HIS CONSPIRACY[4]

Conspiracy theorists are an odd lot. They take the commonplace and turn it on its head. Such is the case with Walsh.

The truth is that Walsh is not clear on what he thinks the Attorney General and the others are supposed to have conspired to coverup. At various points in his Report, he seems to be asserting that there was a coverup of the President's alleged <u>contemporaneous</u> knowledge of the November 1985 HAWK shipment. At other times, Walsh appears to argue that there was a more general coverup intended supposedly to conceal the President's knowledge of the November 1985 HAWK shipment <u>no matter when the President learned of it</u>. Walsh also claims, without any basis in fact or law, that the November 1985 shipment was illegal, but Walsh further argues that <u>whether or not</u> it was illegal, the Attorney General thought it "<u>possibly</u>" illegal and, hence, the alleged motive for the alleged coverup.

Walsh's own confusion and incoherence about his coverup theory helps explain his strenuous efforts to block virtually every request by Attorney General Meese for access to the information Walsh claims as the basis for his allegations, his avoidance of the courtroom, and his preference for wild and false public pronouncements.[5]

In advancing his convoluted coverup theory, Walsh is untruthful. He misrepresents events, ignores critical information, and implies wrongful motives where none exist. Given the severe limitation to information and time constraints placed on the Attorney General, we are able to respond to only the most egregious false statements published in Walsh's Report.

This section of the Attorney General's Comments is organized as follows:

<u>First</u>, we will present information that is already in the public record -- but that Walsh <u>omits</u> from his massive Report. This information demonstrates that actions directed and

4

undertaken by the Attorney General <u>after</u> the November 24, 1986
NSPG meeting clearly prove the infirm and irrational thinking
behind Walsh's coverup scheme.

   <u>Second</u>, we will present information that shows <u>prior</u> to the
November 24, 1986 National Security Policy Group ("NSPG")
meeting, and during his fact-finding inquiry, the Attorney
General urged those he interviewed to be truthful and not to
engage in any kind of coverup.

   <u>Third</u>, Walsh claims that the Attorney General's motive in
covering up the President's knowledge of the November 1985 HAWK
shipment was because Attorney General Meese allegedly thought
that shipment might "possibly" be illegal. Again, Walsh ignores
overwhelming, conclusive evidence to the contrary, and we will
demonstrate that Walsh's assertion is false, illogical and
irrelevant.

   <u>Fourth</u>, the Regan and Weinberger notes of the November 24,
1986 NSPG do <u>not</u> and <u>cannot</u> be interpreted as evidence of a
conspiracy to coverup the President's knowledge of the November
1985 HAWK shipment unless <u>all</u> evidence to the contrary is
ignored.

   <u>Fifth</u>, we will question why Walsh's conspiracy and coverup
story is limited to the November 1985 HAWK shipment, but excludes
the diversion of funds to the Nicaraguan Freedom Fighters.

   A.   **Significant Steps Initiated By
        Attorney General Meese <u>After</u> The
        November 24, 1986 NSPG Meeting.**

        1.   **November 25, 1986: Attorney General Meese
             tells the world President Reagan knew of
             the November 1985 HAWK shipment.[6]**

   The day following the November 24, 1986 NSPG meeting --
when Walsh claims a conspiracy to coverup the President's
knowledge of the November 1985 HAWK shipment was hatched --
Attorney General Meese held a news conference. The purpose of
the news conference was to enable reporters to ask any questions
about the Iran-contra matter, and to reveal to the American
people -- at an early date -- information the Attorney General
and his staff had gathered during the course of their short fact-
finding inquiry.

   Throughout the news conference, Attorney General Meese
cautioned that "<u>we don't have all the facts</u>," "<u>we have not
completed our inquiry</u>," and "<u>this is something we are still
looking into at the present time</u>." (emphasis added)[7] And as
described later, the Attorney General, on the evening of this
news conference, initiated a full criminal investigation.

Nonetheless, Walsh focuses on only one of more than <u>135 rapid-fire questions</u> asked of Attorney General Meese during this news conference to falsely claim that the Attorney General misled the public about the President's contemporaneous knowledge of the November 1985 HAWK shipment.

Specifically, Attorney General Meese was asked:

What details did he [the President] have about those transactions [the 1985 shipments], and when did he have them?[8]

The Attorney General answered as follows:

The president -- this is one of the things that we're recollecting now. The president was informed generally that there had been an Israeli shipment of weapons to Iran sometime during the late summer, early fall of 1985, and then he later learned in February of 1986 details about another shipment that had taken place in November '85, which had actually been returned to Israel in February of '86.[9]

Attorney General Meese's answer <u>reveals to the world</u> that the President <u>was</u> aware of the November 1985 shipment, the <u>details</u> of which -- including the February 1986 return of the missiles to Israel -- he learned in February 1986.

Furthermore, the Attorney General had <u>no</u> information indicating precisely <u>when</u> the President learned of the shipment or whether the President, in fact, had contemporaneous knowledge of it.

In addition, in his November 21, 1986 interview of Robert McFarlane, Attorney General Meese told McFarlane:

[I]f the President knew <u>earlier</u> [about the November 1985 HAWK shipment], it might even be helpful as a legal matter. (emphasis added)[10]

This is indisputable evidence that if Attorney General Meese had been told the President did, in fact, have contemporaneous knowledge of the November 1985 HAWK shipment, he would have every reason to <u>disclose</u> it to the world, <u>not</u> conceal it.

Finally, in his November 22, 1986 interview of George Shultz, the Attorney General asks Shultz if, in November 1985, McFarlane told the President about the November 1985 HAWK shipment. Shultz answered as follows:

<u>Not to my knowledge. This I don't know.</u>[11]

6

The Attorney General had <u>no</u> information indicating <u>when</u> the President learned of the shipment or whether, in fact, the President had contemporaneous knowledge of it. Walsh falsely asserts Attorney General Meese had such knowledge, but provides <u>no</u> supporting evidence. Indeed, it was Attorney General Meese's stated opinion that as a matter of law, it would be <u>helpful</u> if the President knew about the November 1985 HAWK shipment <u>earlier</u>. Walsh's claim of a scheme to coverup the President's alleged contemporaneous knowledge of this shipment is wrong as a matter of fact and wrong as a matter of logic.

>   2.   Evening of November 25, 1986/
>   Morning of November 26, 1986:
>   Attorney General initiates
>   criminal investigation.

Importantly, yet consistent with Walsh's dishonest tactics, Walsh utterly ignores all of the significant events that occurred <u>after</u> the November 24, 1986 NSPG meeting. These events unequivocally and conclusively expose the folly of Walsh's conspiratorial thinking, and demonstrate the honorable and competent actions of Attorney General Meese.

By the evening of November 25, 1986 -- just <u>one day</u> after the November 24, 1986 NSPG meeting where Walsh claims high officials conspired to coverup the President's knowledge of the November 1985 HAWK shipment -- the Attorney General determined that a criminal investigation was in order. He met with William Weld, Assistant Attorney General in charge of the Justice Department's Criminal Division, among others, and directed Weld to begin an investigation.[12] Early the next morning, November 26, 1986, the Attorney General again met with Weld and others in furtherance of the criminal investigation he had initiated the prior evening.[13]

Also on the morning of November 26, 1986, Attorney General Meese spoke with FBI Director William Webster. The Attorney General asked that the FBI assist the Criminal Division in the investigation.[14]

During the afternoon of that same day, November 26, 1986, the Attorney General held a meeting with the appropriate individuals from the Criminal Division and the FBI where they reviewed the facts that had been gathered during the Attorney General's weekend inquiry.[15]

If, as Walsh imagines, there was an effort to coverup, the Attorney General's aggressive and immediate actions in elevating -- literally overnight -- a fact-finding inquiry into a full-fledged criminal investigation, involving many career Justice Department prosecutors and FBI agents, are inexplicable. Attorney General Meese's actions triggered the involvement of the

law enforcement apparatus of the Department of Justice to
investigate what would become the Iran-contra matter, and
determine whether any laws had been violated. This is a strange
way to conduct a coverup.

Walsh ignores these important facts because they
conclusively show that <u>there was no coverup, there was nothing to
coverup, and there was no reason for a coverup</u>.

        3.   **The Attorney General's November 28, 1986
                   discovery letter to Shultz and others.**

On November 28, 1986 -- only four days after the November
24, 1986 meeting where Walsh alleges the Attorney General
"signaled" the participants to coverup the President's knowledge
of the November 1985 HAWK shipment -- Attorney General Meese
dispatched a discovery letter to Secretary Shultz and other key
administration officials and offices. With respect to the letter
to Shultz, Walsh reports on this event as follows:[16]

> On November 28, 1986, Attorney General Edwin Meese III wrote
> a letter to Shultz requesting that department information
> 'be segregated and held for review by and transmission to
> the Federal Bureau of Investigation (FBI) upon its request.'
> Meese's request applied to
>
> > '[a]ny and all material of any kind, type, or
> > description, including but not limited to, all
> > memoranda, briefing materials, minutes, handwritten
> > notes, diaries, telephone logs, ... files and other
> > documents of the ... State Department, ... from <u>1
> > January 1985 to present, concerning the following</u>
> > (emphasis added):
> >
> > '1.   <u>All arms activities involving Iran</u> (emphasis
> >   added);
> >
> > '2.   All hostage negotiations or similar communications
> >   involving arms as an inducement;
> >
> > '3.   All financial aid activities involving the
> >   Nicaraguan resistance movement which are related
> >   to Iran or Israel; [and]
> >
> > '4.   All activities of Robert C. McFarlane, ... Lt.
> >   Col. Oliver North, Vice Admiral John M. Poindexter
> >   ... relating to 1 - 3 above.'

Walsh's Report continues as follows:[17]

> In response to the Meese request, the Department of State's
> Legal Adviser Abraham D. Sofaer, and the Assistant Secretary

of State for Administration Donald J. Bouchard sent a
memorandum the next day to the senior official in each
department component that potentially would possess relevant
information ... The Sofaer/Bouchard memorandum, <u>which the
Department of Justice had reviewed and approved before it
was issued at State</u> (emphasis added), distributed a copy of
Meese's letter to each of these persons, reported that the
President had ordered the Department of Justice
investigation and stated that '[t]he Secretary has pledged
full Department cooperation. ...' The memorandum stated
that, with regard to the phrase 'All arms activities
involving Iran' in the Meese letter, the department was
interpreting this request,

> '<u>[b]ased upon consultation with the FBI, ... to
> encompass any materials concerning allegations or
> evidence of U.S. or U.S.-authorized arms shipments to
> Iran, requests by Iran for arms or alleged offers by
> the U.S., Israel, or other parties allegedly acting on
> behalf of the U.S. to supply arms</u>.' (emphasis added)

Walsh's Report further states that the Attorney General's
memorandum "<u>stated twice that the ... request covered handwritten notes ...</u>" (emphasis added)[18]

This evidence further reveals the illogic of Walsh's
conspiracy and coverup theory. We learn:

o   A few days after Walsh claims Attorney General Meese
headed a conspiracy to coverup the President's knowledge of
the November 1985 HAWK shipment, the Attorney General acted
to secure all information about any arms shipments that may
have occurred between <u>January 1, 1985 and November 28, 1986</u>.
Of course, that would <u>include the November 1985 HAWK
shipment</u>.

No one intending to coverup this matter would make such an
effort to secure this information for the FBI and later the
independent counsel. Clearly the Attorney General was
spearheading a massive search for information, which was to be
turned over to the FBI. Attorney General Meese's conduct belies
any notion of a coverup, which is why Walsh ignores this
evidence.

o   On November 29, 1986, <u>Attorney General Meese's Justice
Department "reviewed and approved"</u> a memorandum prepared by
Sofaer and Bouchard which further described the requested
information as including arms shipments to Iran or requests
by Iran for arms, or offers by the U.S. or Israel to ship
arms to Iran.

Again, rather than supporting any concept of a coverup, these contemporaneous documents prove an aggressive effort was initiated to gather information.

Walsh realizes that these documents make it impossible for him to square his coverup theory -- and his allegation of the Attorney General's prominence in it -- with the facts. <u>Walsh intentionally omits this evidence from that portion of his Report that discusses Attorney General Meese</u>. (Yet, he uses these letters in the State Department portion of his Report to condemn the alleged failure of certain parties to respond fully to the Attorney General's request.)

    4.   **Appointment and protection of Independent Counsel.**

On December 4, 1986 -- <u>only 2-weeks after he had begun his initial fact-finding inquiry</u> -- Attorney General Meese used his discretionary authority to request the appointment of an independent counsel.

On March 5, 1987 -- as a result of litigation challenging the constitutionality of the independent counsel statute -- the Attorney General again used his discretionary authority to issue a parallel appointment to Walsh. In short, that meant if the independent counsel law was found unconstitutional by the U.S. Supreme Court, Walsh could <u>continue his investigation</u> because Attorney General Meese, in essence, directed that the Department of Justice hire him.

Once again, the Attorney General's conduct in requesting the appointment of an independent counsel and protecting Walsh and his investigation from a legal challenge is further evidence that Walsh's coverup story is nonsense. Walsh knows he is being dishonest for he, again, omits this important information from the portion of his Report that discusses Attorney General Meese's conduct.

In summary, following the November 24, 1986 NSPG meeting, Attorney General Meese took steps to <u>ensure the full discovery of all information relating to the Iran-contra matter</u>, which is in complete contradiction to the baseless coverup allegation claimed by Walsh.

    o   On <u>November 25, 1986</u> Attorney General Meese publicly announced the President's knowledge of the November 1985 HAWK shipment.[19]

    o   On <u>November 25 and 26, 1986</u> Attorney General Meese initiated a formal criminal investigation.[20]

o   On <u>November 28, 1986</u> Attorney General Meese issued
     discovery letters to several key administration
     officials, including Shultz, requesting, in part, all
     information relating to arms activities involving Iran
     from January 1, 1985 through November 28, 1986 (which
     includes the November 1985 HAWK shipment).[21]

o   On <u>November 29, 1986</u> Attorney General Meese's Justice
     Department reviewed and approved a letter from Sofaer
     and Bouchard to relevant State Department personnel
     seeking all information related to arms shipments to
     Iran (which includes the November 1985 HAWK
     shipment).[22]

o   On <u>December 4, 1986</u> Attorney General Meese used his
     discretionary authority to request the appointment of
     an independent counsel to investigate the Iran-contra
     matter.

o   On <u>March 5, 1987</u> Attorney General Meese issued a
     parallel appointment to Walsh to ensure that Walsh's
     investigation would not be disrupted or ended.

Walsh concealed all of this information because he cannot
construct a conspiracy and coverup story in the face of this
compelling and incontrovertible evidence to the contrary.

B.   Attorney General Meese:
      No Coverup, Tell The Truth.

During the Attorney General's fact-finding inquiry (November
21, 1986 to November 24, 1986) he participated in several
discussions. Despite Walsh's coverup allegation, the following
statements demonstrate that the Attorney General's motives
throughout the course of the Iran-contra matter were to uncover
the facts and insist on the truth.

      1.   Robert McFarlane.

On November 21, 1986, Attorney General Meese interviewed
former National Security Council adviser Robert McFarlane. The
Attorney General told McFarlane to "not try to think how to
protect the President, just tell **exactly what happened.**"[23]

      2.   George Shultz.

On November 22, 1986, Attorney General Meese interviewed
Secretary of State George Shultz. The Attorney General told
Shultz that "[w]e have to get facts so he [President] knows
facts. And <u>no</u> coverup." (emphasis in original)[24]

3.   **Oliver North.**

On November 23, 1986, the Attorney General interviewed Lt.
Col. Oliver North.   Contemporaneous notes reveal that he told
North:

> **Want to get all facts from everyone involved. Flesh out
> different recollections. ... Worst thing [that] can happen
> is if someone tried to conceal something to protect self, RR
> [Reagan], put good spin on it. Want nothing anyone can
> call a coverup."[25]**

4.   **November 24, 1986: National Security
      Policy Group (NSPG) meeting.**

Near the close of this meeting of high administration
officials, where Walsh imagines a conspiracy to coverup the
President's knowledge of the November 1985 HAWK shipment was
secretly hatched (**even though Weinberger and Regan were taking
notes**) contemporaneous notes record that the Attorney General
stated:

> [A]nyone know anything else that hasn't been revealed - 'No'
> - any further Israeli arms sales?[26]

These open-ended questions by Attorney General Meese are
posed for the purpose of <u>eliciting</u> additional information, not
concealing it.

C.   **Walsh's Concoction Of A
      Motive For His Coverup Theory.**

1.   **There was no coverup, and
      there was no motive to coverup.**

Walsh's theory -- we think -- is that the Attorney General's
motive in leading an alleged coverup of the President's
(contemporaneous?) knowledge of the November 1985 HAWK shipment
was that he supposedly thought the shipment was "possibly"
illegal.

The short answer to Walsh is that <u>there was no coverup, so
there was no motive to coverup</u>.

As described earlier, Walsh intentionally conceals all of
the significant actions undertaken by the Attorney General
<u>subsequent</u> to the November 24, 1986 NSPG meeting -- including
Attorney General Meese's initiation of a full-fledged criminal
investigation by the Criminal Division and the FBI on November
25, 1986, the November 28, 1986 gathering for the FBI of all
information related to, among other matters, any arms shipments,

and the appointment and later protection of the independent
counsel.

It is clear that the Attorney General's motives -- to
uncover the facts and enforce the law -- were consistent and
adhered to from the beginning. His motives are known from the
interviews he conducted <u>before</u> the November 24, 1986 NSPG meeting
when he asked for the facts and the truth, to his actions <u>after</u>
the November 24, 1986 NSPG meeting when he initiated a criminal
investigation aimed at further uncovering all of the facts and
determining whether any laws had been violated. <u>These are not
the actions of someone attempting to coverup anything</u>.

But what are <u>Walsh's motives</u> in concocting a conspiracy and
coverup story that ignores critical and obvious facts and
distorts the historical record? Walsh's motives, as described
later,[27] are as follows:

o   Walsh seeks to justify his enormous and unprecedented
     expenditure of resources ($100,000,000) and the
     extraordinary length of his investigation (six-and-one-
     half-years, nearly three times as long as the Watergate
     investigation).[28]

o   Walsh seeks to divert attention from his own unethical
     and illegal conduct.[29]

o   Walsh seeks to divert attention from his record of
     incompetence and abuse.[30]

o   Walsh seeks to use his out-of-court, false statements
     to maliciously injure the reputations of innocent
     individuals.[31]

Moreover, even at this late hour, conspiracy theorist Walsh
<u>opposed</u> every request by the Attorney General for access to
Walsh's full Report and access to the vast majority of
information Walsh claims to have relied on in producing it.[32]
In other words, those Walsh accuses, in his Report, of wrongdoing
are <u>denied</u> information relating to his out-of-court allegations,
and are <u>denied</u> an opportunity to respond fully to these false
public statements. Attorney General Meese must rely on Walsh's
representations and characterizations of testimony, documents and
other information -- even though Walsh is <u>not</u> reliable, <u>not</u>
credible and <u>not</u> truthful, as demonstrated earlier in this
response.

In truth, if Walsh believes his Report and his tale of
conspiracy and coverup are accurate, he would not <u>fear</u> careful
scrutiny of his false allegations by the Attorney General.

13

2.   Was the November 1985 HAWK shipment illegal?[33]

<u>Walsh did not prosecute a single official for violating any of the laws relating to the November 1985 HAWK shipment</u>. Yet, Walsh's Report repeatedly refers to that shipment as being "illegal." If the shipment was illegal, as Walsh boldly and stridently asserts to the public, why did he refuse to bring his case into the courtroom? He could not do so because there was no criminal conduct regarding the Iran arms transaction.

In point of fact, Walsh knows that none of the relevant statutes that might relate to the November 1985 arms shipment are criminal laws. They neither specify crimes nor prescribe penalties for the actions taken by public officials in this case. A November 22, 1986 memorandum prepared by a career attorney in the Criminal Division of the Justice Department for her supervisor, which was included in the evidence available to Walsh, makes this clear.[34]

Walsh does not explain how someone "violates" laws that lack penalties and enforcement mechanisms. What constitutes "violations" of such laws, and how is it determined that "violations" have occurred? Moreover, there is no authority or precedent, and none cited by Walsh, to enable Walsh to claim that the November 1985 HAWK shipment was illegal. Nonetheless, Walsh simply announces that these laws were violated in order to advance his ludicrous theory.

In addition, the Assistant Attorney General for the Office of Legal Counsel, Charles Cooper, writing for the Department of Justice, issued three legal memoranda to the Attorney General on the legality of the arms shipments, including the November 1985 HAWK shipment. Cooper's conclusion: <u>No violations of applicable law</u>. Cooper's legal conclusion remained consistent from the time he authored his first memorandum on November 13, 1986, to his issuance of two additional memoranda on December 17, 1986. Unlike Walsh -- who provides no authority for his frequent claims that the November 1985 HAWK shipment was illegal, and who did not prosecute a single official for these alleged violations of law -- Cooper's scholarship is serious and unassailable. Indeed, rather than rehashing the arguments that disprove Walsh's claim, it is sufficient to include with this response the full text of the three Cooper memoranda for all to read.[35]

Moreover, the November 1987 Minority Report of the Congressional Committees Investigating the Iran-contra affair concluded that none of the relevant statutes were violated. Walsh ignores the significant and thorough research and analysis used by these members of Congress to reach their conclusion. Among those who signed that report was Rep. Dick Cheney, who would later become Secretary of Defense.[36]

3.   **Whether** the Attorney General thought
      the **November 1985 HAWK** shipment
      was **"possibly"** illegal is irrelevant.

Unable to provide any credible evidence or precedent for his
fraudulent assertion that the November 1985 arms shipment was
illegal, conspiracy theorist Walsh dissembles and shifts his
argument. Walsh urges that whether or not any laws were
violated, the Attorney General thought that laws were "possibly"
violated, and that was his motive for allegedly "signaling" other
high administration officials at the November 24, 1986 NSPG
meeting to coverup the President's knowledge of the November 1985
HAWK shipment.[37]

This is the second time Walsh dissembles on an important
detail of his conspiracy theory. The first occasion is when
Walsh falsely asserts that the Attorney General attempted to
coverup the President's contemporaneous knowledge of the November
1985 HAWK shipment, yet also falsely asserts that the Attorney
General attempted to coverup the fact of the President's
knowledge of the shipment (whether or not it was
contemporaneous).[38]

In fact, the Attorney General at no time believed the
President or any other Cabinet official violated any laws
relating to Iran arms shipments. As described earlier, his
belief was correct.

Nonetheless, the question is why does it matter whether the
Attorney General thought laws may have been violated? The
Attorney General was not the person who would determine if any
laws were violated. The Attorney General initiated a process --
a full-fledged criminal investigation and shortly thereafter the
appointment of an independent counsel -- which he knew would
ultimately exclude his involvement in any investigative and
prosecutorial decisions and, of course, in any determinations
regarding possible violations of law. When all of Attorney
General Meese's actions are considered in context, particularly
his efforts after Walsh's alleged conspiracy began on November
24, 1986, it is obvious that whether or not the Attorney General
thought at the time that laws may have been violated is
irrelevant and does not support any motive to coverup. It proves
the opposite.

As described earlier, Walsh's coverup story utterly ignores
several important steps taken by the Attorney General after the
November 24, 1986 NSPG meeting -- which conclusively disprove any
conspiracy concoction and conclusively disprove any relevance
Walsh attributes to Attorney General Meese's opinion as to
whether any laws may have been violated. It needs repeating:
Walsh omits the following critical evidence:

o   On <u>November 25, 1986</u> Attorney General Meese publicly
     announced the President's knowledge of the November
     1985 HAWK shipment.[39]

o   On <u>November 25 and 26, 1986</u> Attorney General Meese
     initiated a formal criminal investigation.[40]

o   On <u>November 28, 1986</u> Attorney General Meese issued
     discovery letters to several key administration
     officials, including Shultz, requesting, in part, all
     information relating to arms activities involving Iran
     from January 1, 1985 through November 28, 1986 (which
     includes the November 1985 HAWK shipment).[41]

o   On <u>November 29, 1986</u> Attorney General Meese's Justice
     Department reviewed and approved a letter from Sofaer
     and Bouchard to relevant State Department personnel
     seeking all information related to arms shipments to
     Iran (which includes the November 1985 HAWK
     shipment).[42]

o   On <u>December 4, 1986</u> Attorney General Meese used his
     discretionary authority to request the appointment of
     an independent counsel to investigate the Iran-contra
     matter.

o   On <u>March 5, 1987</u> Attorney General Meese issued a
     parallel appointment to Walsh to ensure that Walsh's
     investigation would not be disrupted or ended.

Again, it is revealing that Walsh does <u>not</u> even mention the
November 28, 1986 letter (and the November 29, 1986 letter) in
the portion of his Report that allegedly describes Attorney
General Meese's conduct in this matter. But Walsh <u>does</u> discuss
the letter in a different portion of his Report, and he says the
following:

> The memorandum [the November 28, 1986 discovery letter to
> Shultz] ... stated twice that the Meese request covered
> handwritten notes ('Please note that the request defines
> documents which are subject to production most broadly to
> include handwritten notes, diaries, telephone logs of
> Department officials ...').[43]

Walsh <u>highlights</u> the Attorney General's letter -- and his
request for notes -- when he falsely seeks to assemble
information in a dishonest effort to show wrongdoing by other
administration officials. Walsh <u>ignores</u> the letter when he
addresses the Attorney General's conduct in his Report to invent
a dishonest and false portrayal of Attorney General Meese's
motives and actions.[44]

16

The existence of the November 28, 1986 letter and the substantial weight Walsh gives to it (as a broad and far-reaching discovery request) further proves the irrelevance of the Attorney General's pre-November 28, 1986 opinion as to whether or not laws had been violated -- as Attorney General Meese launched a criminal investigation that would make such a determination -- and further proves the honesty and objectivity that motivate all of his actions.

D.   **November 24, 1986 NSPG Meeting:**
       Regan's And Weinberger's Notes.

In attempting to further his conspiracy theory, Walsh grossly misrepresents and distorts the notes of Donald Regan and Caspar Weinberger relating to the November 24, 1986 NSPG meeting. It is therefore important that the record is corrected.

Walsh contends his conspiracy and coverup theory are established by the November 24, 1986 NSPG meeting notes of Regan and Weinberger. In truth, only in Walsh's Twilight Zone could these notes mean what he claims.

1.   **Regan's November 24, 1986 NSPG notes.**

The relevant portion of Regan's notes are as follows:[45]

DTR [Regan] asked about shipment of HAWK missiles to Iran in Nov. Ed Meese answered. Shultz told in Geneva by Bud [McFarlane] - delivery of weapons & may be hostages out. Didn't approve.

Pres [President] only told may be hostages out in short order.

Plane unable to land in Iran. Another plan arranged[.] [O]nly 18 missile[s] aboard - wrong ones. No specific OK for [?]

Returned in Feb. From Israeli stocks.

Bud told Geo. [Shultz]. Hostages out first, then arms in. [D]id not take place.

May be a violation of law if arms shipped w/o [without] a finding. But Pres [President] did not know. Cap [Weinberger] denies knowing Israelis may have done this on their own. But it was a low level contact that did this, probably using Pres' [President's] name.

Walsh reads Regan's notes -- whether or not they accurately represent what transpired in that meeting -- as the Attorney General "signaling" to the others present to coverup the

17

President's (contemporaneous) knowledge of the November 1985 HAWK shipment. For all of the reasons described earlier in this response, that is <u>impossible</u>. <u>Walsh's interpretation of Regan's notes is the most illogical and far-fetched interpretation imaginable</u>.

The excerpts from Regan's notes have <u>nothing to do with the President's knowledge (contemporaneous or otherwise) of the occurrence of the November 1985 HAWK shipment</u>.

Regan's notes make clear the Attorney General is responding to a question from Regan about details of the November 1985 shipment. Attorney General Meese provided a general, but brief, rundown of the information he had gathered during the weekend fact-finding inquiry.

The most obvious reading of Regan's notes (and that Attorney General Meese considers accurate after having refreshed his memory by reviewing the full text of Regan's notes) is that the Attorney General is addressing the issue of whether the President knew of the <u>CIA's involvement in the November 1985 HAWK arms transfer at the time the shipment occurred</u>. The Attorney General is saying that the President was told that hostages may be released, that he did <u>not</u> know about the CIA's involvement, and that some lower level individual may have used the President's name to secure the CIA's involvement. This is what Regan's notes record.

Attorney General Meese specifically stated, according to Regan's notes, that [the] "<u>Pres [President] only told may be hostages out in short order</u>." (emphasis added)[46] In other words, the President was not aware of the <u>details</u> involved in the shipment when it occurred, such as the <u>CIA's role in securing a proprietary aircraft to transport the missiles</u>.

Regan's notes reinforce this by stating the Attorney General said the "<u>Plane unable to land in Iran. Another plan arranged ... No specific OK for [?]</u>." (emphasis added)[47] Again, this addresses the issue of transporting the missiles, which is where the CIA was asked to provide assistance.

Regan's notes add that Attorney General Meese said the missiles were "[r]eturned in Feb. ... " The notes then state that the Attorney General stated "Bud [McFarlane] told Geo. [Shultz]. Hostages out first, then arms in. [D]id not take place."[48]

It is at this point, <u>after</u> the Attorney General has indicated that the President did not know details about the shipment ("... only told may be hostages out in short order"[49]) and <u>after</u> the Attorney General just finished describing the transportation of the missiles and their return by Iran to Israel, that Regan's notes record the following:

May be a violation of law if arms shipped w/o [without] a
finding. But Pres [President] did not know. Cap
[Weinberger] denies knowing Israelis may have done this on
their own. But it was a low level contact that did this,
probably using Pres' [President's] name.[50]

Whether or not the November 1985 HAWK shipment "may" have
violated any law -- which it did not, and Walsh did not prosecute
any official for violating any of the statutes relating to the
shipment -- is irrelevant for the reasons described earlier.

Moreover, the core issue is what is the Attorney General
saying the President "did not know." Walsh is hopelessly lost --
as he has been during the entire six-and-a-half-years of his
investigation -- in asserting these notes reveal an attempt to
coverup the President's knowledge of the November 1985 HAWK
shipment.

The Attorney General was aware that the President had
knowledge of the November 1985 HAWK shipment (although he did not
know when the President learned about it). Contemporaneous notes
show that Shultz told Attorney General Meese on November 22,
1986:

> Shultz: You [Attorney General] should know I went to
>   President's Thursday night [November 20, 1986] ... I
>   described Bud [McFarlane's] talk with me in Geneva [in
>   November 1985, in which McFarlane mentioned the
>   shipment to Shultz]. President said oh I [knew or
>   know?] that ...[51]

Shortly thereafter, the Attorney General asks Shultz if
McFarlane advised the President about the shipment in Geneva.

> Attorney General: ... As to November [1985] talk with Bud
>   [McFarlane], no contact you know of that Bud had with
>   President then?[52]

> Shultz: Not to my knowledge. This I don't know.[53]

The information Attorney General Meese had gathered from his
November 22, 1986 interview of Shultz -- that the President had
knowledge of the November 1985 HAWK shipment (although he did not
know when the President became aware of it) -- was a positive
development. It was Attorney General Meese's stated belief that
the earlier the President knew about the shipment, the better as
a legal matter.

Indeed, in his November 21, 1986 interview of McFarlane, the
Attorney General told McFarlane:

19

If the President knew earlier [about the November 1985 HAWK shipment], it might even be helpful as a legal matter ...[54]

This is also consistent with Attorney General Meese's answer at the November 25, 1986 news conference where he said:

... The President was informed generally that there had been an Israeli shipment of weapons to Iran sometime during the late summer, early fall of 1985, and then he later learned in February of 1986 **details** about another shipment that had taken place in November of '85, which had actually been returned to Israel in February '86. (emphasis added)[55]

Clearly the Attorney General had **no motive to coverup** the President's knowledge of the shipment, but **every reason to reveal it** at the earliest opportunity. Conspiracy theorist Walsh has mangled the facts in an attempt to conform them with **his** story. He is dead wrong.

Presumably, most of those attending the November 24, 1986 NSPG meeting -- and many not at the meeting, such as former U.S. Federal District Judge Abraham Sofaer -- were aware that the President had at least a general knowledge of the shipment. Were all these individuals part of Walsh's coverup? Were they all accomplices in the commission of a felony for which they were prepared to face possible prosecution, imprisonment, and financial and personal disaster?

Furthermore, there can't be a coverup without a motive. And what motive would be so compelling to cause so many senior government officials -- with long and honorable records of public service -- to risk everything by allegedly participating in such a conspiracy? It can't be concern over the legality of the November 1985 HAWK shipment for all of the reasons described earlier. There was **no** motive to conspire to coverup the President's knowledge.

2. **Weinberger's November 24, 1986 notes.**

The portion of Weinberger's notes repeatedly referenced in Walsh's Report reads as follows:

Not legal because no finding. President not informed. (emphasis in original)[56]

Walsh concludes that these eight words prove his conspiracy and coverup theory as they demonstrate the Attorney General "signaled" those present at the meeting that the President had no knowledge of the November 1985 HAWK shipment.

That's not what this language says. When taken out-of-context, which is how Walsh considers these words, they are

20

meaningless. There is simply <u>no</u> indication of what the President was not informed about. There is not a clue. <u>And there certainly is not even a hint that this language says or means the President was not informed about the November 1985 HAWK shipment</u>. These eight words (out of several pages of notes) are so brief and sketchy as to be inconsequential when considered out-of-context.

However, if Weinberger's notes are read in context with Regan's more detailed notes, Weinberger's notes are consistent with Regan's notes. As such, Walsh's interpretation of Weinberger's notes -- like his view of Regan's notes -- is inaccurate and untruthful.[57]

E.   What About The Diversion?

Walsh's coverup story does not address this simple question: <u>Why would the Attorney General seek to coverup information about the November 1985 HAWK shipment, but not coverup the diversion of funds to the Nicaraguan Freedom Fighters</u>? The diversion raised far more serious legal issues and political dangers than the arms shipment. Indeed, it was this discovery that caused Attorney General Meese to initiate a criminal investigation.

Moreover, if the Attorney General's purpose was to coverup information that might be harmful to the President (an absurd and mindless claim), why wouldn't he have concealed or destroyed the diversion memorandum? Attorney General Meese and his staff had ample opportunity to do so. In fact, not only had they discovered the diversion memorandum during their fact-finding inquiry, but they went to great lengths to secure and protect it. Soon thereafter, the diversion was made public.

The Attorney General could not know in advance if the arms shipment would cause more damage to the President than the diversion. Indeed, he would have every reason to believe that the diversion was potentially more damaging than the arms shipment. In any event, he would have no reason to coverup one explosive event but not the other.

<u>Walsh's inconsistent story about a conspiracy to coverup the President's knowledge of the November 1985 HAWK shipment is illogical on its face</u>.

IV. WALSH'S OTHER FALSE STATEMENTS

Shortness of time and severe limits placed on the Attorney General's access to information make it impossible to address all of Walsh's false statements. Nonetheless, certain false statements by Walsh must be answered.

A. Attorney General Meese's Fact-Finding Inquiry.

During November 21, 1986 to November 24, 1986, Attorney General Meese conducted a brief yet important fact-finding inquiry. As the Attorney General said at the November 25, 1986 news conference, in response to a question, the fact-finding inquiry was initiated for the following reasons:[58]

> ... I had been in meetings -- in looking at the various aspects of the testimony -- and there appeared to be things that we didn't know because one person had done this and one person had done that -- and because of the very necessary secrecy involved in this, and the highly compartmentalized nature of the operation, a lot of people did not know certain things that were going on, that were being done by others. **My suggestion to the president was that we get all of the facts together to be sure that anyone testifying before Congress was being absolutely accurate, not only as to what they knew, but as to other facts, since they were representing the administration.** The president suggested that be done -- that the facts all be pulled together. It was in the course of that, that this information came to light.

Throughout his Report, Walsh refers to the Attorney General's fact-finding inquiry as an "investigation,"[59] despite the Attorney General's frequent public explanations that it was <u>not</u> an investigation, but an effort to ensure that those scheduled to testify before Congress did so accurately.

Attorney General Meese, prior to entering the federal government, had a long career in law enforcement in which he headed many major criminal investigations during his service as deputy district attorney in a large metropolitan area and as Vice Chairman of the California Organized Crime Control Commission. The Attorney General knew the difference between a criminal investigation and the mission he undertook on November 21, 1986.

Consistent with Attorney General Meese's statement at the November 25, 1986 news conference was his testimony before Congress on July 28, 1987, during the so-called Iran-contra hearings. There the Attorney General said: "<u>The essential point to keep in mind is that our purpose was not to conduct a criminal investigation. Indeed, on November 21, 1986, there was no hint that criminal activity was in any way implicated in the Iranian transactions. ...</u>"[60] The full text of the Attorney General's statement is attached.

Why, then, does Walsh use his Report repeatedly and falsely to refer to the November 21, 1986 to November 24, 1986 fact-finding inquiry as an "investigation"? The answer is that by distorting the truth about the inquiry, and simply referring to it as an investigation, conspiracy theorist Walsh attempts to invent sinister motives about the purpose and conduct of the inquiry.

For instance, in hit-and-run fashion, Walsh questions why more notes were not taken, why there were one-on-one meetings, why documents weren't secured earlier (a question that Walsh should answer about his six-and-a-half-year investigation). Walsh wants to create doubt, questions and cynicism about the remarkably thorough and successful four-day fact-finding inquiry voluntarily undertaken by Attorney General Meese and his small staff. In truth, as Shultz commented at the time, the Attorney General's weekend fact-finding inquiry uncovered **the essential facts that are still the essential facts today**.[61]

Among the important evidence Attorney General Meese discovered was the diversion of funds to the Nicaraguan Freedom Fighters. Essential to any coverup would be concealing any diversion evidence. Yet Attorney General Meese promptly secured and disclosed the diversion memorandum.

In contrast, Walsh's $100,000,000 operation uncovered **nothing** new about the arms shipments or the diversion. Walsh is left justifying his record of incompetence and unethical and illegal conduct by fabricating a conspiracy and coverup scheme and using out-of-court statements to smear innocent people.

B.   Walsh's Tricks And Attorney General Meese's Recollection.

Walsh alleges that Attorney General Meese's "early testimony was marked by a conspicuous lack of recollection ... OIC [Office of Independent Counsel] concerns were highlighted when Meese in the North trial was able to assist the defendant by clearly recalling in 1989 information that he had failed to recall much earlier, at a time nearer events in question. ...."[62]

Walsh's claim is nonsense. Walsh conceals the fact that he and North's counsel fully prepared the Attorney General for North's trial. **Both** sides used extensive documentation to refresh Attorney General Meese's recollection in advance of the trial.

In contrast, during much of the time Walsh's staff questioned the Attorney General (except for the North trial preparation), information that would have been helpful in refreshing Attorney General Meese's recollection was concealed.

The problem throughout Walsh's investigation is that rather than pursuing the truth, Walsh creates a story or reaches a conclusion which he then sets out to prove. This helps explain why Walsh's staff was frequently unethical and not forthcoming in their questioning of the Attorney General.[63]

C.   Posey-Corvo Investigation.[64]

The Posey-Corvo investigation involved "allegations of . . . gun-running, drug-trafficking and Neutrality Act allegations."[65] The matter was under investigation by the U.S. Attorney's office in Miami. Walsh implies that there was something sinister about a visit Mr. Meese made to Miami during this investigation.[66]

The only reason Attorney General Meese was in Miami was to visit hospitalized FBI agents who had been seriously wounded in a shootout with criminals, in which two of their fellow agents had been killed. His brief visit to Miami had nothing to do with the Posey-Corvo investigation. Perhaps Walsh can explain why he wasted government resources investigating the Attorney General's visit to Miami on April 12, 1986.

V.   WALSH'S UNETHICAL AND ILLEGAL CONDUCT: QUESTIONS OF INTEGRITY AND MOTIVE

A brief discussion of Walsh's conduct, particularly his violations of law and ethics rules, is critical to understanding Walsh's investigation and his Report.

A.   Walsh And Watergate.

In contrast to Walsh's reprehensible conduct in concocting his conspiracy theory -- which is directly contrary to the evidence in this matter -- and publishing it in his Report, the Watergate Special Prosecution Force ("WSPF") condemned such a reckless abuse of the extraordinary power granted by Congress.

The statement of the WSPF was fully set forth earlier, but particular attention should be given to the following paragraph that bears directly on Walsh's misconduct in making the false allegations in his Report:

> Most important, in terms of the American constitutional system of government, is the notion of fundamental fairness for those who, after investigation, have not been charged with any criminal misconduct. This consideration is particularly important for a Special Prosecutor whose independence considerably reduces his accountability and who must be unusually sensitive to possible abuses of his power. It is a basic axiom of our system of justice that every man is innocent unless proven guilty after judicial proceedings designed to protect his rights to ensure a fair adjudication of the charges against him. Where no such charges are

brought, it would be irresponsible and unethical for a
prosecutor to issue a report suggesting criminal conduct on
the part of an individual who has no effective means of
challenging the allegations against him or of requiring the
prosecutor to establish such charges beyond a reasonable
doubt.[67]

Unlike the sober and principled thinking exhibited in the
WSPF report, Walsh's Report is "irresponsible and unethical."
Walsh takes a sledgehammer to over 200 years of American
jurisprudence and his misconduct evidences an out-of-control
prosecutor unable and unwilling to abide by the rule of law.

B.   Walsh And His Violations Of
      The Rules Of Professional Conduct.

Every state and the District of Columbia (D.C.) have adopted
Rules of Professional Conduct or Codes of Professional
Responsibility providing ethical standards and rules guiding
attorney conduct. A violation of these standards can result in
severe disciplinary action against the transgressing attorney --
including disbarment.

Walsh, who has either practiced law in or lived in New York,
D.C. and Oklahoma, is legally bound by the ethical standards of
all three jurisdictions. As a direct result of his unscrupulous
and fraudulent public accusations of criminality on matters that
he never litigated, and against individuals he never formally
charged and whose reputations he seeks to destroy, Walsh has
violated the ethical standards of all three jurisdictions.

New York's Code of Professional Responsibility, like those
of other jurisdictions, demands the highest standard of behavior
from its attorneys. It's Preamble states, in part:

The continued existence of a free and democratic society
depends upon recognition of the concept that justice is
based upon the rule of law grounded in respect for the
dignity of the individual and the capacity of the individual
through reason for enlightened self-government. Law so
grounded makes justice possible, for only through such law
does the dignity of the individual attain respect and
protection. Without it, individual rights become subject to
unrestrained power, respect for law is destroyed, and
rational self-government is impossible.

Lawyers, as guardians of the law, play a vital role in the
preservation of society. The fulfillment of this role
requires an understanding by lawyers of their relationship
with and function in our legal system. A consequent
obligation of lawyers is to maintain the highest standards
of ethical conduct.[68]

In addition to violating New York's overarching statement of
principles, Walsh uses his Report in a manner that violates
specific rules of conduct. Disciplinary Rule (DR) 7-102, Section
A, Subpart 1 of New York's Code provides:

> ... [A] lawyer shall not ... assert a position ... or
> take other action ... when the lawyer knows or when it is
> obvious that such action would serve merely to ...
> <u>maliciously injure</u> another. (emphasis added)[69]

Subpart 5 of that same section states:

> ... [A] lawyer shall not ... [k]nowingly make a false
> statement of law or fact.[70]

There is not a particle of truth or evidence to support
Walsh's conspiracy story. That is why Walsh uses his Report to
fabricate a ridiculous accusation that cannot and would not stand
up to minimal judicial scrutiny. Indeed, as described earlier,
Walsh's Report ignores and even conceals facts that demonstrate
the irrationality of his thinking.[71] He is guilty of
"maliciously injur[ing]" Attorney General Meese and "knowingly
mak[ing] false statement[s] of law and fact" about him.

Moreover, DR 1-102, Section A, Subpart 5 of New York's Code
prohibits a lawyer from:

> Engag[ing] in conduct that is prejudicial to the
> administration of justice.[72]

The Rules of Professional Conduct for D.C. and Oklahoma
contain even more compelling language. Rule 8.4, Part (d) of the
D.C. and Oklahoma Rules states:

> <u>It is professional misconduct</u> for a lawyer to ... engage in
> conduct that is prejudicial to the administration of
> justice. (emphasis added)[73]

Walsh knows that by flagrantly and deliberately subverting
the rule of law with false and dramatic statements in his Report
-- which he intends to be repeated frequently and uncritically in
the media throughout the United States and beyond -- he may
deny Attorney General Meese any real ability to protect his
reputation. Walsh's ethical and legal violations, at a minimum,
<u>are</u> "prejudicial to the administration of justice."

C.   Questions About Walsh's Integrity:
     Violations Of Federal Law.

Walsh's out-of-court allegations about a conspiracy to coverup what was actually a legal arms transfer raises a question central to the public's understanding, evaluation and acceptance or rejection of his Report: Is the accuser, Walsh -- who bypasses the legal process while presenting himself to the public as a reliable judge of the integrity and veracity of others -- someone who brings fidelity and honesty to the discharge of his trusts? The answer is no.

Astonishingly, during the time he was independent counsel, in addition to ignoring the prophetic warnings of the Watergate prosecutors, and violating the ethical rules of his profession, Walsh repeatedly violated federal laws and regulations from which he benefited financially at taxpayer expense. This pattern of misconduct evinces a lack of judgment, competence and integrity by the chief lawyer investigating the Iran-contra matter.

Specifically, a Government Accounting Office (GAO) audit[74] of Walsh's conduct as independent counsel uncovered, among other things, the following:

> Based on records provided by Mr. Walsh, we [GAO] calculated that the total amount of unallowable reimbursements for lodging and meals for Mr. Walsh was approximately $78,000 more than the per diem rate... (emphasis added)[75]

Walsh also "used a government-leased vehicle for transportation between his office and living quarters [at the Watergate Hotel] while in Washington, D.C."[76] The GAO stated that this expense was "generally unallowable."[77]

The GAO also discovered that Walsh used government funds to travel by first class air between his home in Oklahoma and his Washington, D.C. office. The GAO stated:

> For at least his first 2 years as independent counsel, ... Walsh was reimbursed for first class air travel. Reimbursement for first class air travel is allowed, but only when its use is certified and specifically authorized. Examples of the conditions permitting first class air travel are when no other class is available and travel is so urgent it cannot be postponed or when, for security purposes or exceptional circumstances, use of travel is essential to the performance of an agency's mission. We did not find any such certifications and authorizations by Mr. Walsh.[78]

Moreover, according to the GAO, 30 members of Walsh's staff "accrued excess leave without written justifications and approvals. ... As of March 31, 1992, the 30 employees had been allowed to carry forward an estimated 5,300 hours without written justifications and approvals." (emphasis added)[79]

On October 5, 1992, Walsh asked the GAO to waive the requirement that he and his staff reimburse the taxpayers for all of these unallowable costs. On February 3, 1993, the GAO, an arm of Congress, allowed Walsh's request.[80] Remarkably, rather than being penalized or punished for clear violations of federal laws and regulations, and returning ill-gotten gains to the public treasury, the taxpayers footed Walsh's bill.

It is ironic indeed that while Walsh was an independent counsel, prosecuting others for conspiracies to defraud the United States and false statements, he sought and received numerous unallowable payments resulting from his own improper conduct. And even while he was drafting his Report -- in which he challenges the integrity and character of many innocent individuals and lectures the American people and Congress about the importance of the rule of law -- Walsh was using his position of public trust to avoid the law and enrich himself and several of his staff members.

D. Walsh's Unauthorized Disclosure Of Classified And National Security Information.

Walsh attempts to divert attention from his sorry six-and-one-half-year record by, in part, concluding that an attorney general should not have the discretion to declassify information under the Classified Information Procedures Act. Walsh complains that Attorney General Richard Thornburgh prevented him from using certain classified materials in open court. The problem, according to Walsh, is that an attorney general has "the power to block almost any potentially embarrassing prosecution that requires the declassification of information."[81]

Typical of Walsh's tactics, his Report raises the specter of sinister motives by, for instance, Attorney General Thornburgh (and virtually everyone else he dealt with during his long tenure). Walsh does not cite any facts to support his opinion or provide any explanation about the legitimate exercise of authority by Attorney General Thornburgh in protecting the national security interests of the American people.

Furthermore, Walsh conceals the fact that he had access to and use of an unprecedented amount of highly classified material (thousands of pages). He fails to mention that extraordinary efforts were made to assist him in his investigation by numerous career civil servants, employed at all the intelligence and security agencies.

But once again, while Walsh recklessly points an accusatory finger at some nonexistent event -- such as the ridiculous suggestion that an attorney general might use the security laws of this nation to coverup an embarrassing prosecution -- Walsh's own misconduct in handling highly classified information raises serious questions about his own judgment and credibility.

Amazingly, there are two known occasions when Walsh violated the national security rules of the United States. These are situations when the government <u>granted</u> Walsh access to and use of highly classified material.

The first known violation occurred near the beginning of Walsh's tenure as an independent counsel, and after he had been briefed about security procedures. <u>Walsh was seen reading highly classified material on a commercial airplane by a government contractor</u>. The government contractor, knowing that Walsh's conduct was a violation of national security rules, reported Walsh to the FBI. As a result of this transgression, Walsh received additional security training, but he was not reprimanded or otherwise punished.

Walsh violated our nation's security rules a second time. As was reported in a newspaper last fall:[82]

> A suitcase containing highly classified government documents, including secret codes, disappeared ... after an aide to Iran-contra independent prosecutor ... [who was traveling with Walsh] ... <u>checked it in at curbside</u> at Los Angeles International Airport. (emphasis added)[83]
>
> The FBI has launched an intensive effort to recover the documents, which one source said had been carried to California for an interview with ex-President Ronald Reagan.
>
> ... <u>The Justice Department complained that Walsh waited more than two weeks before notifying it of the loss, reducing chances of finding the material.</u> (emphasis added)[84] ... The Justice Department accused Walsh's office of a <u>flagrant violation</u> of security that could affect pending Iran-contra cases. (emphasis added)

The news article further says that the Deputy Attorney General of the United States, in a letter to Walsh (himself a former deputy attorney general), stated that the "<u>flagrant violation of [the security] rules ... is of particular concern in view of the prior security breaches of your office, including the transport of codeword material</u>." (emphasis added)[85]

Walsh's treatment of highly classified material -- entrusted to him by the government -- and his violations of security rules known to him, shows extraordinary arrogance, contempt for the

law, and bad judgment. Moreover, he <u>concealed</u> the fact of the
missing classified material from the Department of Justice and
the FBI for more than two weeks, thereby harming their ability to
locate the material.

Unlike most citizens, who would be punished for such
misconduct, Walsh escaped even a mild reprimand. It is yet
another irony of Walsh's Report that he seeks to judge the wisdom
of the government's procedures for declassifying national
security information -- and speculate about the integrity of
others who face imaginary conflicts -- when <u>his</u> track record on
the subject is deplorable and irresponsible, and raises serious
doubt about his judgment, credibility and reliability.

E.   Walsh's Obstructions.[86]

As has been discussed previously, Walsh makes an end-run
around our system of justice by using his Report repeatedly to
make false allegations about Attorney General Meese and others.
But Walsh's unethical resort to out-of-court smear tactics
represents only part of his effort to deny the Attorney General
any fair and true opportunity to refute Walsh's fabrications.

In particular, when Attorney General Meese was recently
informed by the Clerk of the U.S. Court of Appeals for the
District of Columbia that Walsh's Report had been filed with the
Court and the Attorney General (and other interested parties)
would be given a short period of time to submit a response, <u>Walsh
strenuously opposed every request by Attorney General Meese for
access to Walsh's full Report and the vast majority of underlying
information Walsh used to write his Report (and which Walsh cites
in his Report)</u>.

It is an essential principle of a civilized society and a
democratic government that an innocent individual who stands
accused of wrongdoing be permitted to defend himself. Walsh's
successful strategy to <u>obstruct</u> Attorney General Meese's access
to information that <u>Walsh</u> represents as the basis for his
allegations should jolt the conscience of every citizen.

There is simply <u>no</u> legitimate justification for Walsh's
obstructionist conduct in preventing the availability of this
information to the Attorney General, yet there is every
indication that Walsh fears the collapse of his absurd claims
under the weight of Attorney General Meese's scrutiny.

Incredibly, <u>Attorney General Meese will not be permitted to
read the full Walsh Report until it is released to the public. He
was only permitted to read those pages of the Walsh Report that
Walsh determined he should read</u>. This not only limits severely
the ability of Attorney General Meese to provide a written
response to Walsh's Report, but it limits his ability to comment

30

on the Report upon its release. Walsh maliciously intends to
injure the reputation of the Attorney General by releasing his
Report <u>in advance</u> of the Attorney General reading it.

In addition to Walsh's strenuous objection to providing
Attorney General Meese with access to his full Report, Walsh
opposed virtually every request by the Attorney General for
information needed to prepare his response.

For instance, throughout the pre-selected pages of Walsh's
Report to which Attorney General Meese was given access, Walsh
frequently discusses and references the secret grand jury
testimony of several parties, including the Attorney General.

Walsh's use of secret grand jury testimony is without
precedent and wholly improper. The Federal Rules of Criminal
Procedure provide, in part:

> [A]n attorney for the government ... shall not disclose
> matters occurring before the grand jury, except as otherwise
> provided for in these rules ...[87]

There is no evidence that Walsh's disclosure of secret grand
jury testimony met any of the exceptions provided under the
rules.[88] He is simply disclosing the testimony in a public
report.

In any event, given Walsh's use of and reference to such
testimony, Attorney General Meese requested a copy of these
materials. <u>Walsh opposed this request</u>.

Attorney General Meese then requested a copy of his own
grand jury testimony. <u>Walsh opposed this request</u>, but allowed
the Attorney General to read his testimony only at the
courthouse. It was soon learned that Attorney General Meese's
grand jury testimony was six inches thick and classified as "Top
Secret - Veil" and "Secret." Attorney General Meese was
prohibited from taking any notes of his testimony or discussing
the substance of his testimony in his response to Walsh's Report.
<u>While Walsh was able to discuss the Attorney General's secret,
classified grand jury testimony in concocting his Report, the
Attorney General was not provided a copy of his testimony, could
not take notes of the material, and could not discuss his
testimony in this response -- even though Walsh's claims are
said, in part, to be based on that testimony</u>.

Walsh's Report frequently uses and references confidential
FBI 302 reports, which are interview notes taken by FBI agents in
the course of an investigation.

The Attorney General requested copies of all FBI 302 reports discussed and referenced in Walsh's Report. <u>Walsh opposed this request</u>.

The Attorney General requested copies of his own FBI 302 report. <u>Walsh opposed this request</u>.

Again, <u>Walsh was able to discuss confidential FBI 302 reports in concocting his Iran-contra Report, but the Attorney General was denied access to his FBI 302 report in preparing his response</u>.

Furthermore, Attorney General Meese requested permission to contact other parties mentioned in Walsh's Report to discuss notes, testimony and comments alleged by Walsh. This is of particular importance where an individual is being accused of conspiring with these other parties. <u>Walsh opposed this request</u>.

With the degree of fairness accorded by prosecutors during the Salem witch trials, Walsh obstructed virtually every effort by the Attorney General to review the information allegedly gathered by Walsh to manufacture his inane conspiracy and coverup theory. Walsh demands that those he accuses (as well as the public) be satisfied with <u>his</u> self-serving and tortured representations and characterizations of information, and willingly accept the guilty verdict he imposes on them.

VI. CONCLUSION

<u>**There was no coverup. There was no conspiracy. And there was no misconduct of any kind by Attorney General Meese.**</u> Indeed, it was the Attorney General who discovered the diversion of funds and immediately thereafter disclosed his finding to the American people and Congress. Moreover, it was the Attorney General who took aggressive actions to ensure that a full investigation of the entire matter would be conducted by the Department of Justice and, later, an independent counsel.

Walsh's Report is thoroughly defective, and his conduct is dishonest and cowardly. Walsh's malfeasance and abuse of power are unequaled in recent American history and pose a real and serious danger to our system of justice.

Furthermore, the severe damage Walsh attempts to inflict on innocent people -- under the guise of justice -- is intended to have a devastating and lasting impact on their lives. For this he must be viewed with contempt.

History will judge Walsh harshly, and well it should.

Respectfully submitted,

LANDMARK LEGAL FOUNDATION

Dated: December 3, 1993   By ___Mark R. Levin___
                                           Mark R. Levin
                                           Mark J. Bredemeier
                                           Jerald L. Hill
                                           Richard P. Hutchison
                                           Landmark Legal Foundation
                                           One Farragut Square South
                                           Suite 906
                                           Washington, D.C.   20006
                                           (202) 393-3360

                                           ATTORNEYS FOR EDWIN MEESE III

ENDNOTES

(NOTE: The Attorney General's counsel is unable to cite to
specific pages of the Final Report of Independent Counsel
Lawrence Walsh because Mr. Meese was denied a copy of the Report.
Citations to the full Report are accordingly used in these
endnotes.)

1.   Attorney General Meese was **not** permitted access to the full
Walsh Report.   Therefore, his response is limited to that portion
of the Walsh Report to which he was given access.

2.   There are three distinct parts of the so-called "Iran-
contra" matter.
        First, the Iranian initiative intended to enhance the
national security of the United States by opening channels of
communication with moderates in Iran.   This strategy was
legitimate and legal.
        Second, the Administration's support for the Nicaraguan
Freedom Fighters and the democratization of Nicaragua.   This
strategy proved successful.
        Third, funds obtained through arms transactions from the
Iranian initiative were diverted to the Nicaraguan Freedom
Fighters.   This activity was unauthorized.   The diversion was
discovered in the four-day fact-finding inquiry conducted by
Attorney General Meese and his staff.   The Attorney General
disclosed the diversion to the public and Congress immediately.
        Questions about the legality of the diversion of funds led
the Attorney General to, among other things, request the
appointment of an independent counsel.   No limitation was placed
on the scope of the independent counsel's mandate.

3.   Watergate Special Prosecution Force Report, p. 1-2 (1975).

4.   Final Report of Independent Counsel Lawrence Walsh ("Walsh
Report").

5.   See Comments, Section V, infra.

6.   Transcript of Attorney General Meese's News Conference, The
Washington Post, November 26, 1986, at A-8-9. ("News Conference
Transcript").

7.   Ibid.

8.   Ibid.

9.   Ibid.

10.   Walsh Report.

11.   Notes of Charles Hill, aide to George Shultz, (Regarding Attorney General Meese's November 22, 1986 interview with Shultz).

12.   Based on his discovery of the diversion, Attorney General Meese determined a criminal investigation should be launched. See Notes of Edwin Meese III, Attorney General of the United States, (November 25, 1986 meeting schedule).

13.   Nov. 1987. H. R. 433, S. 216 100th Cong., 1st Sess., Report of the Congressional Committees Investigating the Iran-contra Affair With Supplemental, Minority, and Additional Views 319 (1987).   ("Congressional Report").

14.   Ibid.

15.   Ibid.

16.   Walsh Report.

17.   Ibid.

18.   Ibid.

19.   News Conference Transcript, supra.

20.   Notes of Edwin Meese III, Attorney General of the United States, (November 25, 1986 meeting schedule); Congressional Report at 319.

21.   Walsh Report

22.   Ibid.

23.   Ibid.

24.   Notes of Charles Hill, aide to George Shultz, (Regarding Attorney General Meese's November 22, 1986 interview with Shultz).

25.   Notes of John Richardson, Chief of Staff to Attorney General Edwin Meese III, (Regarding Attorney General Meese's November 23, 1986 Interview with Oliver North).

26.   Notes of Donald Regan, Secretary of the Treasury, (November 24, 1986 NSPG Meeting); Walsh Report.

27.   See Edwin Meese III's Comments in Response to the Final Report of Independent Counsel Lawrence E. Walsh ("Comments"), Section V, infra.

28.   Ibid.

29.   Ibid.

30.   Ibid.

31.   Ibid.

32.   See Response To Motion Of Edwin Meese III To Obtain A Copy
Of Independent Counsel's Final Report And For Permission To
Contact Interested Parties And To Obtain Copies Of Referenced
Documents And Testimony; Response Of Independent Counsel To
Motion Of Edwin Meese III For A Copy Of The Portion Of
Independent Counsel's Final Report Now Available To Him And A
Copy Of The May/June 1992 Deposition Transcript; Opposition To
Edwin Meese III's Motion For Reconsideration Of The Order Denying
Him The Complete Final Report Of Independent Counsel and
Permission To Contact Interested Parties In Connection With His
Response Thereto.

33.   The laws at issue are the National Security Act, 50 U.S.C.
413, et seq., the Hughes-Ryan Amendment to the Foreign Assistance
Act, 22 USC Section 2422, and the Arms Export Control Act, 22
U.S.C. Section 2753.

34.   November 22, 1986 Memorandum from Jo Ann Farrington, Special
Assistant to the Chief of the Public Integrity Section (Criminal
Division) to Gerald E. McDowell, Chief of the Public Integrity
Section (Criminal Division).

35.   See Exhibit 1, November 13, 1986 Memorandum from Charles J.
Cooper, Assistant Attorney General, Office of Legal Counsel, to
the Attorney General; Exhibit 2, December 17, 1986 Memorandum
from Charles J. Cooper, Assistant Attorney General, Office of
Legal Counsel, to the Attorney General; and Exhibit 3, December
17, 1986 Memorandum from Charles J. Cooper, Assistant Attorney
General, Office of Legal Counsel, to the Attorney General.

36.   Congressional Report (Minority Report).

37.   Walsh Report

38.   Ibid.

39.   News Conference Transcript, supra.

40.   Notes of Edwin Meese III, Attorney General of the United
States, (November 25, 1986 meeting schedule); Congressional
Report at 319.

41.   Walsh Report

42. Ibid.

43. Ibid.

44. The November 28, 1986 letter was issued by Attorney General Meese over seven years ago. Walsh opposed every effort by the Attorney General to gain access to Walsh's full Report and any information Walsh claims to have used in preparing it. This would include access to the names of all administration officials who received the November 28, 1986 letter. Such information would further demonstrate the full extent of Attorney General Meese's effort and desire to discover the truth, in direct contrast to Walsh's reprehensible accusation.

45. Notes of Donald Regan, Secretary of the Treasury, (November 24, 1986 NSPG Meeting).

46. Ibid.

47. Ibid.

48. Ibid.

49. Ibid.

50. Ibid.

51. Notes of Charles Hill, aide to George Shultz, (Regarding Attorney General Meese's November 22, 1986 interview with Shultz); Walsh Report.
     Charles Hill was an aide to Shultz. Hill was a prolific note-taker. His notes often describe meetings he never attended and conversations he never heard (many times Shultz would merely debrief Hill about a meeting or conversation). Unfortunately, Hill's notes frequently are one-part fact and two-parts incogitant ruminations. Not surprisingly, Walsh quotes Hill's notes repeatedly, even though Hill's irresponsible speculation is of no value and would not be admissible in a court of law. Indeed, Walsh questions Hill's veracity in his report. Nonetheless, Walsh uses Hill's notes in an attempt to embarrass Hill and those he writes about, and to muddle the facts.

52. Ibid.

53. Ibid.

54. Walsh Report.

55. News Conference Transcript, supra.

56. Notes of Caspar Weinberger, Secretary of Defense, (November 24, 1986 NSPG Meeting); Walsh Report.

57.   In questioning Attorney General Meese about the Weinberger notes in May 1992 -- six-and-a-half-years **after** the fact -- Walsh's deputy, Gillen, intentionally misrepresented the meaning of Weinberger's eight words by stating that they demonstrate the Attorney General was telling the others at the meeting that the President was not aware of the November 1985 HAWK shipment. (Recently Attorney General Meese was prevented from making notes of the transcript of his testimony; otherwise Gillen's unethical technique would be quoted in these Comments for all to see.) Also, Gillen did not provide the Attorney General with the full text of the notes when he questioned him.

It is anticipated that Walsh's office employed the same misleading tactics in questioning other parties about Weinberger's and Regan's notes. Walsh's purpose was to secure potentially inaccurate and contradictory testimony in support of his contrived conspiracy and coverup theory.

58.   News Conference Transcript, supra.

59.   Walsh Report.

60.   See Exhibit 4, Statement of Edwin Meese III Attorney General of the United States Before the United States Senate Select Committee on Secret Military Assistance to Iran and the Nicaraguan Opposition and the United States House of Representatives Select Committee to Investigate Covert Arms Transactions With Iran on July 28, 1987, at 13.

61.   Ibid.; Congressional Report (Minority Report).

62.   Walsh Report.

63.   Ibid.

64.   Ibid.

65.   Ibid.

66.   Ibid.

67.   See Comments, Section II, supra.

68.   Preamble, New York Lawyers Code of Professional Responsibility, (1987).

69.   Ibid.

70.   Ibid. at 91.

71.   See Comments, Section III, supra.

72.   DR 1-102, New York Lawyers Code of Professional Responsibility (1987).

73.   Rule 8.4(d), District of Columbia Rules of Professional Conduct (1991); Rule 8.4(d), Oklahoma Rules of Professional Conduct (1988).

74.   Financial Audit: Expenditures By Nine Independent Counsels, (GAO/AFMD-93-1, October 1, 1992).

75.   Ibid. at 17.

76.   Ibid. at 15.

77.   Ibid.

78.   Ibid. at 18.

79.   Ibid. at 13.

80.   Financial Audit: Expenditures By Nine Independent Counsels, (GAO/AFMD - 93-60, April 21, 1993) at 9-10.

81.   Walsh Report

82.   Classified Documents on Iran-contra Lost by Prosecutor's Aide, The Philadelphia Inquirer, Oct. 10, 1992, at 6. ("Philadelphia Inquirer Article").

83.   Walsh and his aide checked four suitcases, one contained the classified material; three of the four suit cases arrived at the baggage claim area when the airplane landed at Dulles International Airport.

84.   It took Walsh over two weeks to report his breach of national security to the FBI. It took Attorney General Meese only four days to uncover the basic facts about the Iran-contra matter.

85.   Philadelphia Inquirer Article, supra.

86.   See endnote 31, supra, and accompanying text.

87.   Fed. R. Crim. P. 6(e)(2) (1993).

88.   See Fed. R. Crim. P. 6(e)(3) (1993).

1278

U.S. Department of Justice
Office of Legal Counsel

Office of the
Assistant Attorney General

Washington, D.C. 20530

MEMORANDUM FOR THE ATTORNEY GENERAL

Re: Statutes Relevant to Recent Actions
with respect to Iran

The statutes most directly bearing on the legality of the recent missions to and transactions with Iran are the following: the Hughes-Ryan Amendment, the congressional reporting provisions of the National Security Act, and the Arms Export Control Act. Based on our understanding of the facts, we believe that the recent actions with respect to Iran, including the transfer of arms to Iran by the CIA, do not violate the Hughes-Ryan Amendment or the National Security Act. Moreover, under the the executive branch's prior interpretation of the Arms Export Control Act, this Act is inapplicable to the arms transfers to Iran.

Hughes-Ryan Amendment: The Hughes-Ryan Amendment to the legislation authorizing the operations of the Central Intelligence Agency was passed in 1974 in response to revelations of covert CIA operations. The Amendment, as amended in 1980, provides (22 U.S.C. 2422):

No funds appropriated under the authority of this chapter or any other Act may be expended on behalf of the Central Intelligence Agency for operations in foreign countries other than activities intended solely for obtaining necessary intelligence, unless and until the President finds that each such operation is important to the national security of the United States. Each such operation shall be considered a significant intelligence activity for the purpose of section 413 of title 50.

Because the President made the appropriate finding, the Hughes-Ryan Amendment does not prohibit the use of CIA funds for the transfer of arms to Iran. (S)

Congressional Oversight Provisions of the National Security Act. In 1980 the National Security Act was amended to provide for congressional oversight of significant anticipated intelligence activities. This section now provides (section 501 of the National Security Act, 50 U.S.C. 413(a)) (emphasis added):

EXHIBIT 1
Page b-1

1279

To the extent consistent with all applicable authorities and duties, including those conferred by the Constitution upon the executive and legislative branches of the Government and to the extent consistent with due regard for the protection from unauthorized disclosure of classified information and information relating to intelligence sources and methods, the Director of Central Intelligence and the heads of all departments, agencies, and other entities of the United States involved in intelligence activities shall --

(1) keep the Select Committee on Intelligence of the Senate and the Permanent Select Committee on Intelligence of the House of Representatives . . . fully and currently informed of all intelligence activities which are the responsibility of, are engaged in by, or are carried out for or on behalf of, any department, agency, or entity of the United States, including any significant anticipated intelligence activity, except that (A) the foregoing provision shall not require approval of the intelligence committees as a condition precedent to the initiation of any such anticipated intelligence activity; and (B) if the President determines it is essential to limit prior notice to meet extraordinary circumstances affecting vital interests of the United States, such notice shall be limited to the chairmen and ranking minority members of the intelligence committees, and the majority and minority leaders of the Senate. . . .

Section 501(b) of the National Security Act applies to those situations in which the President falls to give prior notice under section 501(a):

The President shall fully inform the intelligence committees in a timely fashion of intelligence operations in foreign countries, other than activities intended solely for obtaining necessary intelligence, for which prior notice was not given under subsection (a) of this section and shall provide a statement of the reason for not giving prior notice.

Section 501 of the National Security Act does not contemplate that prior notice of "intelligence activities" will be given in all instances. Subsection (b) of section (1) makes specific provision for situations in which "prior notice was not given under subsection (a)." Because subsection (a) includes situations in which the President provides notice to the full intelligence committees under subsection (a)(1)(A) and situations in which he provides prior notice restricted to designated in

1280

UNCLASSIFIED

members of the House and Senate intelligence committees under subsection (b)(1)(B); it seems clear that subsection (b) contemplates situations in which no prior notice has been given under either of these provisions. This interpretation is confirmed by a colloquy between Senators Javits and Huddleston, who were on the committee that drafted this provision. Senator Javits asked: "If information has been withheld from both the select committee and the leadership group [as section 501(b) authorizes], can it be withheld on any grounds other than Independent constitutional authority" and, if so, on what grounds?" Senator Huddleston answered: "Section 501(b) recognizes that the President may assert constitutional authority to withhold prior notice under section 501(b). A claim of constitutional authority is the sole grounds that may be asserted for withholding prior notice of a covert operation." 126 Cong. Rec. 17693 (June 20, 1980) (emphasis added).

Moreover, the preamble to the provision makes clear that disclosure is required only when such disclosure is consistent with the President's constitutional duties. Accordingly, the President is not required to make disclosure when he is acting in a situation in which he is employing his inherent foreign affairs powers. As the President made clear in his televised address to the Nation this evening, the primary purpose of the recent action with respect to Iran was diplomatic. The "intelligence activities" involved in the Iran matter consisted of the arms transfers were an integral part, and attempts to gain information relating to Americans captured abroad. These intelligence matters were inextricably intertwined with and essential to the President's foreign policy goals. We therefore believe that the President was acting at the height of his inherent power in foreign affairs. In United States v. Curtiss-Wright, 299 U.S. 304 (1936), the Court made clear that the President has plenary power over negotiations with foreign powers:

In this vast external realm [of foreign affairs] with its important, complicated, delicate and manifold problems, the President alone has the power to speak or listen as a representative of the nation. He makes treaties with the advice and consent of the Senate; but he alone negotiates. Into the field of negotiation the Senate cannot intrude; and Congress itself is powerless to invade it. As Marshall said in his great argument of March 7, 1800, in the House of Representatives, "The President is the sole organ of the nation in its external relations, and its sole representative with foreign nations."

The Court in Curtiss-Wright also quoted approvingly George Washington's message to Congress in which he refused to give the...

UNCLASSIFIED

1281

UNCLASSIFIED

House of Representatives documents relating to negotiations over the Jay Treaty, characterizing the refusal as one "the wisdom of which was recognized by the House itself and has never since been doubted." 299 U.S. at 320. Accordingly, given the strength of the argument that Congress cannot require the President to make disclosures concerning negotiations with foreign governments even after they are completed, the argument that he cannot be forced to make disclosures during the pendency of sensitive negotiations is particularly compelling. (a)

Second, we believe that a good argument can be made that section 501 of the National Security Act does not require disclosure of information in particularly sensitive circumstances, even if the President is not acting in a manner that implicates his inherent constitutional powers in foreign affairs. The preamble to Section 501 qualifies the requirements of the provision not only by reference to constitutional authorities, but also by reference to the need to keep certain national security information secret. President Carter, in his signing statement for the Intelligence Authorization Act of 1981, stated the understanding on the basis of which the bill received executive approval (emphasis added):

It is noteworthy that in capturing the current practice and relationship, the legislation pre- serves an important measure of flexibility for the President and the executive branch. It does so not only by recognizing that there are circum- stances in which a limited number of security officials, even though the congressional over- sight committees are authorized recipients of classified information, circumstances of this nature have been rare in the past I would expect them to be rare in the future.

1 As quoted in Curtiss-Wright, 299 U.S. 320-321, President Washington said:

The nature of foreign negotiations requires caution; and their success must often depend on secrecy; and even when brought to a conclusion a full disclosure of all the measures, demands, or eventual concessions which may have been proposed or contemplated would be extremely impolitic; for this might have a pernicious influence on future negotiations, or produce immediate inconveniences, perhaps danger and mischief, in relation to other powers.

UNCLASSIFIED

EXHIBIT 1
Page b-2

1282

UNCLASSIFIED SECRET

President Carter seems to have contemplated that there would be instances in which the President would restrict information even when there was no constitutional basis for doing so. Cutting against this interpretation of section 501, however, is Muddleston in which Senator Huddleston suggests that "[a] claim of constitutional authority is the sole grounds of a covert operation... asserted for withholding prior notice of a covert operation." 126 Cong. Rec. 17693 (1980). Because we believe that the President was acting in a manner that implicates his inherent powers, we need not now decide the question of whether the National Security Act permits the President to withhold prior notice on other than a constitutional basis.

Arms Export Control Act. The Arms Export Control Act places a number of restrictions on the export of arms executed under its authority, including:

1) Sales must be made only to countries with respect to which the President has found that such sales will strengthen the security of the United States and promote world peace (22 U.S.C. 2751(b)[1]);

2) The articles must be sold only for use for legitimate purposes and the recipient country must agree to use the arms only for legitimate (e.g. self-defense) purposes (22 U.S.C. 2753(a)(2));

3) A report of the proposed sale of major defense equipment valued at $14 million or more must be submitted to Congress (22 U.S.C. 2776(b)).

4) As of August 26, 1986, no arms may be exported to countries that the Secretary of State has certified as supporting terrorism. See Section 509 of the Omnibus Diplomatic Security and Antiterrorism Act of 1986. (The Secretary of State has certified that Iran supports terrorism).

The Department of Justice, however, has previously concurred in the conclusion of the Department of State that the Arms Export Control Act is not the exclusive authority for transferring arms to foreign countries and that the arms may be transferred outside the context of that statute. See Letter from William French Smith to William J. Casey (Oct. 5, 1981). In the case considered by Attorney General Smith the government relied on the CIA's authority under Section 102(d) of the National Security Act in transferring arms to a foreign country for the primary purpose of achieving certain intelligence objectives. Section 102(d) provides that it shall be the duty of CIA, under NSC direction, to perform services of common concern for the benefit of existing intelligence agencies and to perform "such other functions and duties relating to intelligence affecting the national security

UNCLASSIFIED

1283

UNCLASSIFIED SECRET

as the National Security Council may from time to time direct."[2] We understand that the arms transfer to Iran had an intelligence objective among its objectives. Accordingly, under prior precedent, section 102(d) of the National Security Act furnishes authority for the President's action, and the restrictions of the Arms Export Control Act do not apply.

We therefore believe that the Department of Justice can successfully rebut arguments that the actions with respect to Iran violated either the congressional reporting provisions of the National Security Act or the requirements of the Arms Export Control Act.

Charles J. Cooper
Assistant Attorney General
Office of Legal Counsel

---

2 We understand that the President informed members of Congress of this transaction pursuant to the section 501 of the National Security Act.

UNCLASSIFIED

EXHIBIT 1
Page b-3

1528

U.S. Department of Justice

Office of Legal Counsel

Washington, D.C. 20530

December 17, 1986

Office of the
Assistant Attorney General

MEMORANDUM FOR THE ATTORNEY GENERAL

Re: Legal Authority for Recent Covert Arms Transfers to Iran

This memorandum responds to your request for a summary of the legal authorities affecting the recently disclosed arms transfers to Iran. Because the exact details of the transfers by the government are not completely transparent, this memorandum will provide a general framework for analysis, with reference only to the basic facts that have already emerged. Although this memorandum does not deal with questions arising from the handling of the monies that Iran paid for the arms in question, the operation in which weapons were sold to Iran appears in other respects to have been lawful.

I. General Authority for Arms Transfers to Iran

As you know, there are numerous statutes that regulate the export of weapons. The principal statutes directly affecting transfers by the government are the Foreign Assistance Act of 1961[1] and the Arms Export Control Act.[2] Although both statutes establish substantially comprehensive regulatory schemes in the areas of military assistance and military sales, they do not purport to constitute the sole and exclusive authority under which the executive branch may transfer weapons to foreign nations. Thus, the limitations that the Foreign Assistance Act and Arms Export Control Act impose on arms transfers apply only to transfers undertaken pursuant to those statutes. If the sales to Iran were accomplished under other authorities, as we believe

---

[1] Codified, as amended, in relevant part at 22 U.S.C. 2311 et seq.

[2] Codified, as amended, in relevant part at 22 U.S.C. 2751 et seq.

-1-

1529

they were, these restrictions would not apply.[3]

Consistent with the President's constitutional responsibilities for conducting the foreign policy of the nation, Congress has recognized that the executive has considerable discretion to use government resources for a variety of activities not specifically authorized by statute. Most conspicuously for present purposes, section 101 of the National Security Act of 1947 assigns certain functions to the National Security Council, but expressly acknowledges that that entity may "perform[] such other functions as the President may direct," while authorizing certain functions to the Central Intelligence Agency, while authorizing that Agency to perform such other functions and duties related to intelligence affecting the national security as the National Security Council may from time to time direct." We believe that these two provisions may be relied on to support a wide range of foreign covert activities not otherwise forbidden by law.

The authorities exercised by the NSC and the CIA include the discretion to transfer arms to foreign recipients in the course of intelligence or intelligence-related activities. Congress recently confirmed the assistance of such authority in section 401 of the Intelligence Authorization Act for Fiscal Year 1986, Pub. L. No. 99-169, 99 Stat. 1002, 1006 (1985). That provision provides in relevant part:

> Sec. 401. (a)(1) During fiscal year 1986, the transfer of a defense article or defense service exceeding $1,000,000 in value by an intelligence agency to a recipient outside that agency shall be considered a significant

---

[3] It should be noted that the Department of State and the Department of Justice have both taken the position, long before the operation at issue in this memorandum, that arms may be transferred to foreign countries outside the context of the Arms Export Control Act. See Memorandum of Law on Legal Authority for the Transfer of Arms Incidental to Intelligence Collection, by David R. Robinson, Legal Adviser, Department of State; Letter from William French Smith to William J. Casey (Oct. 5, 1981).

---

[4] For a detailed discussion of the President's constitutional powers and responsibilities, as they relate to the Iran operation, see our memorandum on section 501(b) of the National Security Act.

[5] Codified as amended at 50 U.S.C. 402.

[6] Codified as amended at 50 U.S.C. 403.

-2-

EXHIBIT 2
Page b-4

1530

anticipated intelligence activity for the purpose of section 501 of the National Security Act of 1947.

(2) Paragraph (1) does not apply if--

(A) the transfer is being made to a department, agency, or other entity of the United States (so long as there will not be a subsequent retransfer of the defense articles or defense services outside the United States Government in conjunction with an intelligence or intelligence-related activity); or

(B) the transfer--

(i) is being made pursuant to authorities contained in part II of the Foreign Assistance Act of 1961, the Arms Export Control Act, title 10 of the United States Code (including a law enacted pursuant to section 7307(b)(1) of that title), or the Federal Property and Administrative Services Act of 1949, and

(ii) is not being made in conjunction with an intelligence or intelligence-related activity.

(3) An intelligence agency may not transfer any defense article or defense services outside the agency in conjunction with any intelligence or intelligence-related activity for which funds were denied by the Congress.

(b) As used in this section--

(1) the term "intelligence agency" means any department, agency or other entity of the United States involved in intelligence or intelligence-related activities;

This provision, which was made a permanent part of the National Security Act (new section 503) by the Intelligence Authorization Act for Fiscal Year 1987, was primarily intended to limit the executive's discretion to transfer arms in the course of intelligence-related activities. Its present significance, however, lies in its unambiguous recognition that the executive possesses such discretion apart from the Foreign Assistance Ac:

-3-

1531

and the Arms Export Control Act.[7] Assuming that the arms transferred to Iran were sold to that country at a legally justified price, the language of sections 101 and 102 of the National Security Act is broad enough to encompass the kind of discretion whose existence is manifestly implied in section 403 of the Intelligence Authorization Act. It follows that the NSC and/or the CIA had authority to arrange for the sale of arms to Iran as part of an intelligence or intelligence-related operation, subject to such other restrictions as Congress may have imposed by law. The remainder of this memorandum discusses the applicability of such restrictions.

7 Because subsection (a)(2) states that subsection (a)(1) does not apply to transfers made pursuant to authorities contained in the Foreign Assistance Act or the Arms Export Control Act, the clear implication is that the restriction in subsection (a)(1) applies to transfers made pursuant to some other authority.

The same implication can be drawn from other congressional actions that have imposed restrictions on covert arms transfers without suggesting that such transfers were subject to existing restrictions under the Foreign Assistance Act or the Arms Expor Control Act. For example, a provision was enacted in 1976 precluding funding for military assistance to Laos outside the confines of the Foreign Assistance Act and the Arms Export Control Act. See Pub. L. No. 93-559, sec. 12, 88 Stat. 1798 (1974) (repealed by Pub. L. No. 97-113, title VII, sec. 734(a)(1), 95 Stat. 1560 (1981)).

8 Our point here is that the charters of the CIA and NSC appear to recognize that those entities may use their facilities to arrange an arms sale to Iran. Whether these or other governmental agencies would be authorized to spend the sums of money necessary to procure and give arms to Iran is a distinct question, which need not be addressed at this time.

Because we have not seen the classified Schedule of Authorizations referred to in section 102 of the Intelligence Authorization Act for Fiscal Year 1986 or the similar schedule referred to in the FY 1985 authorization legislation, we do not know whether anything in those schedules would affect the issues addressed in this memorandum.

This memorandum does not address the legal questions that may arise from arms having been sold to Iran at prices higher than the prices at which they were made available to the CIA or NSC.

9 Whether the ultimate source of this discretion is the President's inherent constitutional authority in foreign affairs, or the cited statutes, or some other statute, is a question that need not be resolved. The crucial point is that section 403 of the Intelligence Authorization Act clearly recognizes the existence of the authority, whatever its source.

-4-

EXHIBIT 2
Page b-5

1532

1533

II. Section 501 of the National Security Act

III. The Hughes-Ryan Amendment

EXHIBIT 2
Page b-6

1534

1535

EXHIBIT 2
Page b-7

1536

(b) Action prohibition prior to execution of report

Such finding or determination [prior to the] pub finding or determination shall be taken pursuant to any date on which that finding or determination has been reduced to writing and signed by the President.

(c) Publication in Federal Register

Each such finding or determination shall be published in the Federal Register as soon as practicable after it has been reduced to writing and signed by the President. In any case in which the President concludes that such publication would be harmful to the national security of the United States, only a statement that a determination or finding has been made by the President, including the name and section of the Act under which it was made, shall be published.

(d) Information accessible to Congress prior to transmission of report

No committee or officer of either House of Congress shall be denied any requested information relating to any finding or determination which the President is required to report to the Congress, or to any committee or officer of either House of Congress, under any provision of this chapter, the Foreign Military Sales Act (22 U.S.C. 3151 et seq.), or the Foreign Assistance and Related Programs Appropriation Act for each fiscal year, even though such report has not yet been transmitted to the appropriate committee or officer of either House of Congress.

Because Hughes-Ryan and this provision are both in chapter 32 of title 22, the President would be required to reduce the required finding to writing before each covert operation if he were required to make a report concerning that finding to Congress or to any congressional committee or officer. Hughes-Ryan, however, has never required the President to make any such report concerning his findings; (1) in its present version it requires compliance with section 501 of the National Security Act, which demands certain reports about "intelligence

1537

activities."30 and "intelligence operations."31 but requires no reports about presidential findings;32 (2) as originally enacted, Hughes-Ryan required the President to report a description and scope of the operation,33 and (3) as originally introduced by Senator Hughes, the Hughes-Ryan Amendment would have required that the President provide Congress with both a report of his finding and a description of the nature and scope of each operation.34 The first of these requirements would have made the requirements of section 654 applicable, but this requirement was deleted from the final version of the bill; thus, Congress deliberately rejected the language that might have brought section 654 into play and substituted language that made section 654

_____

20 50 U.S.C. 413(a)(1) (requiring that the President "fully and currently keep certain congressional committees informed of all intelligence activities" within their jurisdiction).

21 50 U.S.C. 413(b) (requiring that the executive branch officials "fully inform the [congressional] intelligence committee of intelligence operations in foreign countries . . . for which prior notice was not given under subsection (a) of this section . . . .").

22 Section 501(a)(1)(B) 50 U.S.C. 413(a)(1)(B), might require certain executive branch officials to provide information about presidential findings, if the information is in their possession custody, or control; to a congressional intelligence committee upon that committee's request, but it does not require that the President himself make any such report. Section 501 applies only to findings as to which the President himself is required to report to Congress.

23 As originally enacted, Hughes-Ryan forbade the CIA to spend appropriated funds for covert foreign operations unless and until the President had made the requisite national security finding and had "reported[ed], in a timely fashion, a description and scope of such operation to the appropriate committees of the Congress . . . ."

24 See 120 Cong. Rec. 33,090 (1974), reproducing Senator Hughes' proposed amendment, which would have permitted the President to authorize covert operations if, but not before, he (1) finds that such operation is vital to the defense of the United States, and (2) transmits an appropriate report of his finding, together with an appropriate description of the nature and scope, of such operation to certain congressional committees.

-9-

-10-

EXHIBIT 2
Page b-8

1538

1539

25 We therefore conclude that section 501 by its own terms does not apply to the Hughes-Ryan Amendment.

This conclusion is reinforced by the structure of the Foreign Assistance Act and long-standing practice. This Act deals primarily with grant foreign aid, including military assistance. To subject covert operations, including covert arms transfers, to the requirement of section 501(c), which requires publication in the Federal Register, would not make much sense, especially now that the National Security Act contains an elaborate mechanism by which Congress is kept informed of covert operations.[26] We are informed by the General Counsel of the CIA that presidential findings made pursuant to Hughes-Ryan have never been published in the Federal Register, and that Congress has never expected to this practice. This confirms our conclusion that the language and legislative history of the statutory provisions at issue, that section 501 does not apply to presidential findings under Hughes-Ryan.

Our conclusion, that the Hughes-Ryan findings may take the form of an oral authorization for a particular operation, agrees with and by the Legal Advisor at the Department of State.

25 The language ultimately adopted by Congress was taken from the House of Representatives' version of the proposed amendment. See 120 Cong. Rec. 39,199 (1974); H.R. Conf. Rep. No. 1610, 93d Cong. 2d Sess. (1974); reprinted in 1974 U.S. Code Cong. & Admin. News 6745, 6761-65.

26 This analysis does not leave section 501 without any applications. Chapter 32 of this title 22 contains numerous provisions requiring both a presidential finding or determination and a report to Congress concerning such finding or determination. See, e.g., 22 U.S.C. 2364(a); 2370(c); 2371(b); 2414(b); 2420(b); 2754; 2753(b)(3); 2769(b)(6)(A), furthermore, chapter 32 also contains numerous provisions requiring presidential findings or determinations without also requiring congressional reports. See, e.g., 22 U.S.C. 2119(a); 2135; 2191(b); 2321(e); 2360(a); 2375. Thus, there is a meaningful distinction, reflected in the language of section 501, between findings and findings concerning which the President must report to Congress and findings concerning which no such report is required.

27 The anomalous nature of publishing notice of covert operations in the Federal Register is reduced, but not completely eliminated, by the following provision in section 501(c). "In any case in which the President concludes that such publication would be harmful to the national security of the United States, only a statement that a determination or finding has been made by the President, including the name and section of the Act under which it was made, shall be published. 22 U.S.C. 2414(c). Some covert operations could well be so sensitive that the mere publication of the section of the Act under which a presidential finding was made could in some circumstance serve to alert a foreign intelligence agency to the possible existence of the operation.

28 This conclusion is further strengthened by the nature of section 501(d), which requires the executive branch to respond to inquiries about presidential findings before the report concerning them has been transmitted to Congress. Such a provision would make no sense as applied to the covert operation findings required by Hughes-Ryan.

It should be noted that the legislative history of section 656 suggests that it was enacted in response to incidents in which (1) the Nixon Administration provided military aid to Cambodia and obtained the presidential determination required by the Foreign Assistance Act after the facts and (2) President Nixon orally determined to authorize military aid to Ceylon, but did not put the determination in writing or inform Congress until some weeks later. S. Rep. No. 631, 92d Cong. 1st Sess. (1971), reprinted in 1971 U.S. Code Cong. & Admin. News 1893, 1895-1896. The legislative history of section 656 cannot properly be used to draw inferences about the subsequently enacted Hughes-Ryan Amendment, especially if these inferences would be contrary to the language and legislative history of Hughes-Ryan itself.

29 In a classified memorandum of Oct. 29, 1977, for the Assistant to the President for National Security Affairs, which dealt with a particular proposed covert operation, Attorney General Bell opined that the President's decision that the operation was important to the national security constituted the finding required by Hughes-Ryan, "notwithstanding the fact that his finding has not been reduced to writing."

30 OLC Memorandum for the Attorney General, Oct. 25, 1977, on Requirements of the Hughes-Ryan Amendment, 22 U.S.C. 2422, at 6 & n.7.

31 Memorandum of Dec. 11, 1986, to the White House Counsel et al., on Validity of Oral Instruction to Initiate Covert Action;

-11-

EXHIBIT 2
Page b-9

IV. Other Legal Objections to the Arms Shipments

A number of other legal provisions have been mentioned as possibly raising problems about the arms transfers to Iran. None of them raises serious questions, and they warrant only a brief discussion.

A. Omnibus Diplomatic Security and Antiterrorism Act of 1986.

Section 509 of the Omnibus Diplomatic Security and Antiterrorism Act of 1986, Pub. L. No. 99-399, 100 Stat. 853, 874 (1986), which became effective August 27, 1986, amended the Arms Export Control Act by adding a new section providing:

(a) Prohibition.--Items on the United States Munitions List may not be exported to any country which the Secretary of State has determined, for purposes of section 6(j)(1)(A) of the Export Administration Act of 1979 (50 U.S.C. App. 2405(j)(1)(A)), has repeatedly provided support for acts of international terrorism.

(b) Waiver.--The President may waive the prohibition contained in subsection (a) in the case of a particular export if the President determines that the export is important to the national interests of the United States and submits to the Congress a report justifying that determination and describing the proposed export. Any such waiver shall expire at the end of 90 days after it is granted unless the Congress enacts a law extending the waiver.

The Secretary of State has identified Iran as a country that has repeatedly provided support for acts of international terrorism.

The same reasons that require treating the covert arms shipments to Iran as outside the ambit of the Arms Export Control Act also require that this new amendment to the same Act be treated as inapplicable to covert arms shipments. The President

32 49 Fed. Reg. 2836 (1984).

-13-

has independent authority, recognized in the National Security Act, for transferring arms in the course of covert intelligence related operations; the congressional notification requirement in the above-quoted provision is at odds with the congressional oversight process established in section 501 of the National Security Act; and the sparse legislative history of this new provision gives no indication of an intent to override this section. We therefore conclude that this new provision was not violated by the covert shipment of arms to Iran.

B. Export Administration Act of 1979.

Section 6(j) of the Export Administration Act of 1979, 50 U.S.C. App. 2405(j), limits the issuing of licenses for the export of goods or technology to countries that the Secretary of State has identified as having repeatedly provided support for acts of international terrorism. This statute does not apply to items on the United States Munitions List, which are covered instead by the Arms Export Control Act. Nor does the statute apply to shipments by the United States government, for which no "license" is required. The Export Administration Act is therefore inapplicable to the Iran project.

C. Executive Order 12333

It has been suggested that the Iran project in some way violated the provisions of E.O. 12333, which is the executive order dealing with the structure and conduct of the nation's intelligence effort. The Iran transfers that took place before January 17, 1986 were accomplished by inducing Israel to ship weapons, which she had obtained from the United States, to Iran on the understanding that our government would replenish Israeli stocks; we also gather that the commitment to resupply Israel was kept. As a legal matter, we believe that such a transaction is equivalent to one in which the United States sells the weapons directly to Iran.

-14-

V. Three-way Transactions Involving Israel

Robert McFarlane, formerly Assistant to the President for National Security Affairs, in the public testimony previously mentioned, has said that the arms transfers that took place before January 17, 1986 were accomplished by inducing Israel to ship weapons, which she had obtained from the United States, to Iran on the understanding that our government would replenish Israeli stocks; we also gather that the commitment to resupply Israel was kept. As a legal matter, we believe that such a transaction is equivalent to one in which the United States sells the weapons directly to Iran.

1540

1541

EXHIBIT 2
Page b-10

1542

1543

-15-

-16-

EXHIBIT 2
Page b-11

in the same way.[39]

1544

Several features of the statutes restricting retransfers support this analysis. First, the statutes clearly contemplate situations in which multiple-supplied weapons are concerned, not the United States itself. In the transferring country to make the transfer, the Arms Export source of the request, not the recipient, the recipient of American arms Control Act, for example, requires the recipient of American arms (in this case, Israel) to agree not to transfer the arms to (o third country (safe, Iran) without the President's approval, and then goes on to specify certain factors that the President must look to in considering a request for approval of any transfer.

Clearly, the statute is not aimed at situations in which the President is considering a request for approval of his own approval. The Foreign Assistance Act contains similar provisions, to which the same analysis applies.

The Arms Export Control Act also makes an express distinction between arms exports by private parties in the United States (which ordinarily require an export license) and exports by such private parties "by or for an agency of the United State Government . . . (B) for carrying out any foreign assistance or sales program authorized by law and subject to the control of the President by other means." To do so requires an export license). Analogously, a distinction should be made between Israel's transferring American-supplied arms for her own benefit (which would be subject to the retransfer requirements of the foreign Assistance Act or the Arms Export Control Act) and such transfers by or for an agency of the United States Government (which were not contemplated by the retransfer provisions of those statutes). That the United States transfers of arms to Iran were "by or for an agency of the United States Government" is clear from the fact that the Israeli shipments were made at the request of American authorities, and (i) the fact that Israel was promised and given identical replacements for the arms that she shipped to Iran.

---

[39] So far as we know, there is no legal bar to the use of Israeli help in American intelligence operations.

[40] 22 U.S.C. 2753(a).

[41] See 22 U.S.C. 2314(a)(1)(B); 2314(a).

[42] 22 U.S.C. 2770 (b)(2). Note that this provision appears to assume that there may be arms sales programs carried out pursuant to legal authorities other than the Arms Export Control Act.

1545

for the foregoing reasons, we conclude that a covert intelligence operation, authorized by the President and conducted by members of the NSC staff and/or the CIA, could lawfully have included the sale of arms to Iran. Such an operation would have been carried out pursuant to presidential powers recognized in sections 101 and 102 of the National Security Act. An oral authorization by the President would have sufficed to allow CIA participation under the Hughes Ryan amendment. The use of Israel's American-supplied weapons, under an arrangement by which Israeli stocks were later replenished, appears not to have violated the conditions under which American weapons are supplied to Israel.

Conclusion

[signature]
Charles J. Cooper
Assistant Attorney General
Office of Legal Counsel

EXHIBIT 2
Page b-12

U.S. Department of Justice
Office of Legal Counsel

December 17, 1986

Office of the
Assistant Attorney General

Washington, D.C. 20530

1546

MEMORANDUM FOR THE ATTORNEY GENERAL

Re: The President's Compliance with the "Timely Notification"
Requirement of Section 501(b) of the
National Security Act

This memorandum responds to your request that this Office review the legality of the President's decision to postpone notifying Congress of a recent series of actions that he took with respect to Iran. As we understand the facts, the President has, for the past several months, been pursuing a multifaceted secret diplomatic effort aimed at bringing about better relations between the United States and Iran (partly because of the general strategic importance of that country and partly to help end the Iran-Iraq war on terms favorable to our interests in the region); at obtaining intelligence about political conditions within Iran; and at encouraging Iranian steps that might facilitate the release of American hostages being held in Lebanon. It is our understanding that the President, in an effort to achieve these goals, instructed his staff to make secret contacts with elements of the Iranian government who favored closer relations with the United States; that limited quantities of defensive arms were provided to Iran; that these arms shipments were intended to increase the political influence of the Iranian elements who shared our interest in closer relations between the two countries and to demonstrate our good faith; and that there was hope that the limited arms shipments would encourage the Iranians to provide our government with useful intelligence about Iran and to assist our efforts to free the Americans being held captive in Lebanon.

On these facts, we conclude that the President was within his authority in maintaining the secrecy of this sensitive diplomatic initiative from Congress until such time as he believed that disclosure to Congress would not interfere with the success of the operation.

As we indicated in our memorandum of November 10, 1986, section 501 of the National Security Act permits the President to

-1-

1547

withhold prior notification of covert operations from Congress, subject to the requirement that he inform congressional committees of the operations "in a timely fashion," and that he give a statement of reasons for not having provided prior notice. We [therefore] conclude that the vague phrase "in a timely fashion" should be construed to [grant] the President wide discretion to [determine when to notify] Congress. This discretion, which is rooted at least as firmly in the President's constitutional authority and duties as in the terms of any statute, must be especially broad in the case of a delicate and ongoing operation whose chances for success could be diminished as much by disclosure while it was being conducted as by disclosure prior to its being undertaken. Thus, the statutory allowance for withholding prior notification, consistent with the President's constitutional independence and authority in the field of foreign relations, to withhold information about a secret diplomatic undertaking until such a project has progressed to a point where its disclosure will not threaten its success.

I. The President's Inherent Constitutional Powers Authorize a Wide Range of Unilateral Covert Actions in the Field of Foreign Affairs

A. The President Possesses Inherent and Plenary Constitutional Authority in the Field of International Relations

"The executive Power shall be vested in a President of the United States of America." U.S. Const. Art. II, sec. 1. This is the principal textual source for the President's wide and

---

1 The vagueness of the phrase "in a timely fashion," together with the relatively amorphous nature of the President's inherent authority in the field of foreign relations, necessarily leaves room for some dispute about the strength of the President's legal position in withholding information about the Iranian project from Congress over a period of several months. The remainder of this memorandum outlines the legal support for the President's position, and does not attempt to provide a comprehensive analysis of all the arguments and authorities on both sides of the question. This caveat, which does not alter the conclusion stated in the accompanying text, reflects the urgent time pressures under which this memorandum was prepared.

-2-

EXHIBIT 3
Page b-13

1548

inherent discretion to act for the nation in foreign affairs.[2] The clause has long been held to center on the President's plenary authority to represent the United States and to pursue its interests outside the borders of the country, subject only to limits specifically set forth in the Constitution itself and to such statutory limitations as the Constitution permits Congress to impose by exercising one of its enumerated powers. The President's executive power includes, at a minimum, all the discretion traditionally available to any sovereign in its external relations, except insofar as the Constitution places that discretion in another branch of the government.

Before the Constitution was ratified, Alexander Hamilton explained in *The Federalist* why the President's executive power would include the conduct of foreign policy. "The essence of the legislative authority is to enact laws, or, in other words to prescribe rules for the regulation of the society; while the execution of the laws and the employment of the common strength, either for this purpose or for the common defense, seem to comprise all the functions of the executive magistrate." This fundamental distinction between "prescribing rules for the regulation of the society" and "employing the common strength for the common defense" explains why the Constitution gave to Congress only those powers in the area of foreign affairs that directly involve the exercise of legal authority over American

[footnote] 2 The Constitution also makes the President Commander in Chief of the armed forces (art. II, sec. 3); given his power to make treaties and appoint ambassadors, subject to the advice and consent of the Senate (art. II, sec. 3); and to receive ambassadors and other public ministers (art. II, sec. 3); the Constitution also requires that the President "take Care that the Laws be faithfully executed (art. II, sec. 3). These specific grants of authority supplement, and to some extent clarify, the discretion given to the President by the Executive Power Clause.

[footnote] 3 *The Federalist* No. 75, at 450 (A. Hamilton) (C. Rossiter ed. 1961). This number of *The Federalist* was devoted primarily to explaining why the power of making treaties is partly legislative and partly executive in nature, so that it made sense to require the cooperation of the President and the Senate in that special case.

-2-

1549

citizens.[4] As to other matters in which the nation acts as a sovereign entity in relation to outsiders, the Constitution delegates the necessary authority to the President in the form of

[footnote] 4 Congress's power "[t]o declare War, grant Letters of Marque and Reprisal, and make Rules concerning Captures on Land and Water," art. I, sec. 8, cl. 11, like the power "[t]o define and punish Piracies and Felonies committed on the high Seas, and Offences against the Law of Nations," art. I, sec. 8, cl 10, and the power "[t]o regulate Commerce with foreign Nations," art. I, sec. 8, cl 3, reflects the fact that the United States is, because of its geographical position, necessarily a nation in which a significant number of citizens will engage in international commerce. A declaration of war immediately alters the legal climate for Americans engaged in foreign trade and is therefore properly treated as a legislative act necessarily binding on an important section of the private citizenry. Similarly, Congress's broad power over the establishment and maintenance of the armed forces, art. I, sec. 8, cls. 12-16, reflects their obviously important domestic effects. In accord with Hamilton's distinction, however, the actual command of the armed forces is given to the President in his role as Commander in Chief. Treaties (in those making the Senate participates under art. II, sec. 3) have binding legal effect within our borders, and are most notable for the significantly small role that Congress plays.

EXHIBIT 3
Page b-14

1550

the "executive Power.".[5]

The peremptorily exclusive authority of the President in foreign affairs was asserted at the outset by George Washington and acknowledged by the first Congress. Without consulting Congress, President Washington determined that the United States would remain impartial in the war between France and Great

1551

Britain.[6] Similarly, the First Congress itself acknowledged the breadth of the executive power in foreign affairs when it established what is now the Department of State. In creating this executive department, Congress directed the Secretary of State[7] head [i.e. the person now called the Secretary of State] to carry out certain specific tasks when entrusted to him by the President, as well as "such other matters respecting foreign affairs as the President of the United States shall assign to the said department." Just as the first President and the first Congress recognized that the executive function contained all the residual power to conduct foreign policy that was not otherwise delegated by the Constitution, subsequent historical practice has generally confirmed the President's primacy in formulating and

-9-

[5] As one would expect in a situation dealing with implied constitutional powers, argument and authority can be mustered for the proposition that Congress was intended to have a significant share of the foreign policy powers not specifically delegated by the Constitution. Perhaps the most oft-cited authority for this position is James Madison's "Helvidius Letters" (reprinted in part in E. Corwin, The President's Control of Foreign Relations 16-27 (1917)), where he cautioned against construing the President's executive power so broadly as to reduce Congress's power to declare war to a mere formality. Madison's argument was directed principally at countering some overstatements made by Alexander Hamilton in his "Pacificus Letters" (reprinted in part in E. Corwin, supra, at 8-13). Madison's argument is not properly interpreted to imply that Congress has as great a role to play in setting policy in foreign affairs as in domestic matters. Even Jefferson, who was generally disinclined to acknowledge implied powers in the federal government or in the President, wrote: "The transaction of business with foreign nations is executive altogether; it belongs, then, to the head of that department, except as to such portions of it as are specially submitted to the Senate. Exceptions are to be construed strictly." 5 Writings of Thomas Jefferson 161 (Ford ed. 1895). While we agree that Congress has some power to curb a President who persistently pursued a foreign policy that Congress felt was seriously undermining the national interest, especially in cases where Congress's constitutional authority to declare war was implicated, well-settled historical practice and legal precedents have confirmed the President's dominant role in formulating, as well as in carrying out, the nation's foreign policy.

[6] Proclamation of the President, April 22, 1793, reprinted in 1 Messages and Papers of the Presidents 156-157 (J. Richardson ed.). President Washington also warned that his Administration would pursue criminal prosecutions for violations of his neutrality proclamation. Although such prosecutions were upheld at the time, a rule that would prohibit such prosecutions was recognized by the Supreme Court relatively soon thereafter. Compare Henfield's Case, 11 F. Cas. 1099, 1102 (C.C.D. Pa. 1793) (No. 6,360) (Jay, C.J.), with United States v. Hudson & Goodwin, 11 U.S. (7 Cranch) 32 (1812). It is worth emphasizing that Presidents have sometimes encountered constitutional obstacles when attempting to pursue foreign policy goals through actions in the domestic arena, but have rarely been interfered with in taking diplomatic steps, or even military actions short of war, outside our borders. The present significance of President Washington's proclamation has less to do with the particular actions he might have taken in the domestic sphere than with his claim that foreign affairs are generally within the constitutional domain assigned to the Executive. This claim is consistent with the Constitution and has now been reinforced by long historical practice.

[7] Act of July 27, 1789, 1 Stat. 28-29. See also Act of Jan. 10, 1799, 1 Stat. 613 [similar provision currently codified at 18 U.S.C. 951], which made it a crime for any person to attempt to influence the conduct of foreign nations with respect to a controversy with the United States.

carrying out American foreign policy.[8]

1552

The Supreme Court, too, has recognized the President's broad discretion to act on his own initiative in the field of foreign affairs. In the leading case, United States v. Curtiss-Wright Export Corp., 299 U.S. 304 (1936), the Court drew a sharp distinction between the President's relatively limited inherent powers to act in the domestic sphere and his far-reaching discretion to act on his own authority in managing the external relations of the country. The Supreme Court emphatically declared that this discretion derives from the Constitution itself and that congressional efforts to act in this area must be evaluated in the light of the President's constitutional ascendancy:

It is important to bear in mind that we are here dealing not alone with an authority vested in the President by an exertion of legislative power, but with such an authority plus the very delicate, plenary and exclusive power of the President as the sole organ of the federal government in the field of international relations--a power which does not require as a basis for its exercise an act of Congress, but which, of course, like every other governmental power, must be

1553

exercised in subordination to the applicable provisions of the Constitution. It is quite apparent that if, in the maintenance of our international relations, embarrassment--perhaps serious embarrassment--is to be avoided and success for our aims achieved, congressional legislation which is to be made effective through negotiation and inquiry within the international field must often accord to the President a degree of discretion and freedom from statutory restriction which would not be admissible were domestic affairs alone involved. Moreover, he, not Congress, has the better opportunity of knowing the conditions which prevail in foreign countries, and especially is this true in time of war. He has his confidential sources of information. He has his agents in the form of diplomatic, consular and other officials. Secrecy in respect of information gathered by them may be highly necessary, and the premature disclosure of it productive of harmful

-7-

____
[8] The fact that Presidents have often asked Congress to give them specific statutory authority to take action in foreign affairs may reflect a practical split of courtesy and compromise rather than any concession of an absence of inherent constitutional authority to proceed. For example, President Franklin Roosevelt requested that Congress repeal a provision of the Emergency Price Control Act that he felt was interfering with the war effort; he warned, however, that if Congress failed to act, he would proceed on the authority of his own office to take whatever measures were necessary to ensure the winning of the war. 88 Cong. Rec. 7044 (1942).

As one would expect, of course, Congress has not always accepted the most far-reaching assertions of presidential authority. See also Youngstown Sheet & Tube Co. v. Sawyer, 343 U.S. 579 (1952) (Constitution did not authorize President to take possession of and operate privately owned steel mills that had ceased producing strategically important materiel during labor dispute); id. at 635 (Jackson, J., concurring) (the Constitution enjoins upon [the government's] branches separateness but interdependence, autonomy but reciprocity. Presidential powers are not fixed but fluctuate, depending upon their disjunction or conjunction with those of Congress.).

-8-

EXHIBIT 3
Page b-16

1554

Results.[9]

sioned on this principle, the Supreme Court rejected the argument that Congress had improperly delegated a legislative function to the President when it authorized him to impose an embargo on an area going to an area of South America in which a war was taking place. The Court's holding hinged on the essential insight that the embargo statute's principal effect was merely to remove any question about the President's power to pursue his foreign policy objectives by enforcing the embargo _within_ the borders of

[9] 299 U.S. at 319-320 (emphasis added). See also _Chicago & Southern Air Lines v. Waterman S.S. Corp._, 333 U.S. 103, 109 (1948) (President possesses in his own right certain powers conferred by the Constitution on him as Commander-in-Chief and as the Nation's organ in foreign affairs"); _Id._ at 109-111 (refusing to read literally a statute that seemed to require judicial review of a presidential decision taken pursuant to his discretion to make foreign policy); _Id._ at 111 ("it would be intolerable that courts, without the relevant information, should review and perhaps nullify actions of the Executive taken on information properly held secret."); _quoted with approval in United States v. Nixon_, 418 U.S. 683, 710.

In _Perez v. Brownell_, 356 U.S. 44, 57 (1958) (citations omitted), the Court stated, "Although there is in the Constitution no specific grant to Congress of power to enact legislation for the effective regulation of foreign affairs, there can be no doubt of the existence of this power in the law-making organ of the Nation. The _Perez_ Court, however, was reviewing the constitutionality of a statute in whose drafting the Executive branch had played a role equivalent to one of Congress's own committees. _Id._ U.S. at 57. Furthermore, the statute at issue in _Perez_ provided that an American national who voted in a political election of a foreign state would thereby lose his American nationality. If the President lacks the inherent constitutional authority to deprive an American of his nationality, then the _Perez_ Court's language about "regulation of foreign affairs" may refer only to "regulation of domestic affairs that affect foreign affairs." In any case, _Perez_ should not be read to imply that Congress has broad legislative powers that can be used to diminish the President's inherent Article II discretion.

1555

this country.[10] As the Court emphatically stated, the President's authority to act in the field of international relations is plenary, exclusive, and subject to no legal limitations save those derived from applicable provisions of the Constitution itself. As the Court noted with obvious approval, the Senate Committee on Foreign Relations acknowledged this principle at an early date in our history:

"_The President is the constitutional representative of the United States with regard to foreign nations._ We manage our concerns with foreign nations and must necessarily be most competent to determine when, how, and upon what subjects negotiation may be urged with the greatest prospect of success. _For his conduct he is responsible to the Constitution._ The committee consider this responsibility the surest pledge for the faithful discharge of his duty. They think the interference of the Senate in the direction of foreign negotiations calculated to diminish that responsibility and thereby to impair the best security for the national safety. The nature of transactions with foreign nations, moreover, requires caution

[10] See 299 U.S. at 327 (effect of various embargo acts was to confide to the President "an authority which was cognate to the conduct by him of the foreign relations of the government") (quoting _Panama Refining Co. v. Ryan_, 293 U.S. 388, [] (1935) (emphasis added). This implies that while the President may in some cases need enabling legislation in order to advance his foreign policy by controlling the acquisition of American citizens on American soil, he needs no such legislation for operations and negotiations outside our borders.

[11] Because the presidential action at issue in _Curtiss-Wright_ was authorized by statute, the Court's statements as to the President's inherent powers could be, and have been, characterized as dicta. See, e.g., _Youngstown Sheet & Tube Co. v. Sawyer_, 343 U.S. 579, 635 n.1 (1952) (Jackson, J., concurring). We believe, however, that the _Curtiss-Wright_ Court's broad view of the President's inherent powers was essential to its conclusion that Congress had not unconstitutionally delegated legislative authority to the President. Furthermore, the Supreme Court has since reaffirmed its strong commitment to the principle requiring the "utmost deference to presidential responsibilities" in the military and diplomatic areas. _United States v. Nixon_, 418 U.S. 683, 710 (1974).

EXHIBIT 3
Page b-17

399 U.S. at 319 (emphasis added) (quoting U.S. Senate, Reports, Committee on Foreign Relations, vol. 8, p. 24 (Feb. 15, 1816)); it follows inexorably from the *Curtiss-Wright* analysis that congressional legislation authorizing extraterritorial diplomatic and intelligence activities is superfluous, and that statutes infringing the President's inherent Article II authority would be unconstitutional.

D. Secret Diplomatic and Intelligence Missions Are at the Core of the President's Inherent Foreign Affairs Authority

The President's authority over foreign policy, precisely because its nature requires that it be vide and relatively unconfined by preexisting constraints, is inevitably somewhat ill-defined at the margins. Whatever questions may arise at the outer reaches of his power, however, the conduct of secret negotiations and intelligence operations lies at the very heart of the President's executive power. The Supreme Court has repeatedly so held in modern times. For example:

Not only, as we have shown, is the federal power over external affairs in origin and essential character different from that over

12 See **United States ex rel. Knauff v. Shaughnessy**, 338 U.S. 537, 542 [citations omitted]:

The exclusion of aliens is a fundamental act of sovereignty. The right to do so stems not alone from legislative power but is inherent in the executive power to control the foreign affairs of the nation. When Congress prescribes a procedure concerning the admissibility of aliens, it is not dealing alone with a legislative power. It is implementing an inherent executive power.

See also **Worthy v. Regan**, 270 F.2d 905, 910-912 (D.C. Cir. 1959) (statute giving President authority to refuse to allow Americans to travel to foreign "trouble spots" simply reinforces the President's inherent constitutional authority to impose the same travel restrictions).

internal affairs, but participation in the exercise of the power is significantly limited. In this vast external realm, with its important, complicated, delicate and manifold problems, the President alone has the power to speak or listen as a representative of the nation. He makes treaties with the advice and consent of the Senate; but he alone negotiates. Into the field of negotiation the Senate cannot intrude; and Congress itself is powerless to invade it.

United States v. Curtiss-Wright Export Corp., 299 U.S. 304, 319 (emphasis in original). The Court has also, and more recently, emphasized that this core presidential function is by no means limited to matters directly involving treaties. In **United States v. Nixon**, 418 U.S. 683 (1974), the Court invoked the basic *Curtiss-Wright* distinction between the domestic and international contexts to explain its rejection of President Nixon's claim of an absolute privilege of confidentiality for all communications between him and his advisors. While rejecting this sweeping and undifferentiated claim of executive privilege as applied to communications involving domestic affairs, the Court repeatedly and emphatically stressed that military or diplomatic secrets are in a different category: "... such secrets are intimately linked to the President's Article II duties, where the Courts have traditionally shown the utmost deference to presidential responsibilities." 418 U.S. at 710 (emphasis added).

Such statements by the Supreme Court reflect an understanding of the President's function that is firmly rooted in the nature of his office as it was understood at the time the Constitution was adopted. John Jay, for example, offered a concise statement in *The Federalist*:

13 See also *Id.* at 706 ("a claim of need to protect military, diplomatic, or sensitive national security secrets" would present a stronger case for denying judicial power to make in-camera inspections of confidential material); *Id.* at 712 n.19 (recognizing "the President's interest in preserving state secrets").

Note also that the *Curtiss-Wright* Court expressly endorsed President Washington's refusal to provide the House of Representatives with information about treaty negotiations after the negotiation had been concluded. 299 U.S. at 320-322. A fortiori, such information could be withheld during the negotiations.

EXHIBIT 3
Page b-18

1558

It seldom happens in the negotiation of treaties, of whatever nature, but that perfect secrecy and immediate dispatch are sometimes requisite. There are cases where the most useful intelligence may be obtained, if the persons possessing it can be relieved from apprehensions of discovery. Those apprehensions will operate on those persons whether they are actuated by mercenary or friendly motives; and there doubtless are many of both descriptions, who would rely on the secrecy of the President, but who would not confide in that of the Senate, and still less in that of a large popular assembly. The convention have done well, therefore, in so disposing of the power of making treaties, that although the President must in forming them act by the advice and consent of the Senate, yet he will be able to manage the business of intelligence in such manner as prudence may suggest.

So often and so essentially have we heretofore suffered from the want of secrecy and dispatch that the Constitution would have been inexcusably defective if no attention had been paid to those objects. Those matters which in negotiations usually require the most secrecy and the most dispatch are those preparatory and auxiliary measures which are not otherwise important in a national view, than as they tend to facilitate the attainment of the objects of the negotiation.

Jay's reference to treaties "of whatever nature" and his clear explicit discussion of intelligence operations make it clear that he was speaking, not of treaty negotiation in the narrow sense, but of the whole process of diplomacy and intelligence-gathering. The President's recent Iran project file comfortably within the terms of Jay's discussion.

14 The Federalist No. 64, at 392-393 (J. Jay) (C. Rossiter ed. 1961) (emphasis in original). Jay went on to note that "should any circumstance occur which requires the advice and consent of the Senate, he may at any time convene them." Id. at 393. Jay did not, however, suggest that the President would be obliged to seek such advice and consent for actions other than those specifically enumerated in the Constitution.

13

1559

c. The President Has Inherent Authority to Take Steps to Protect the Lives of Americans Abroad

Perhaps the most important reason for giving the federal government the attributes of sovereignty in the international arena was to protect the interests and welfare of American citizens from the various threats that may be posed by foreign powers. This obvious and common sense proposition was confirmed and relied on by the Supreme Court when it held that every citizen of the United States has a constitutional right, based on the privileges or immunities clause of the Fourteenth Amendment, to demand the care and protection of the Federal government over his life, liberty, and property when on the high seas or within the jurisdiction of a foreign government. Accordingly, the Supreme Court has repeatedly intimated that the President has inherent authority to protect Americans and their property abroad by whatever means, short of war, he may find necessary.

An early judicial recognition of the President's authority to take decisive action to protect Americans abroad came during a mid-nineteenth century revolution in Nicaragua. On the orders of the President, the commander of a naval gunship bombarded a town where a revolutionary government had engaged in violence against American citizens and their property. In a later civil action against the naval commander for damages resulting from the bombardment, Justice Nelson of the Supreme Court held that the action could not be maintained.

As the executive head of the nation, the President is made the only legitimate organ of the general government, to open and carry on correspondence or negotiations with foreign nations in matters concerning the interests of the country or of its citizens. It is to him, also, the citizens abroad must look for protection of person and of property, and for the faithful execution of the laws existing and intended for their protection. For this purpose, the whole executive power of the country is placed in his hands, under the Constitution, and the laws passed in pursuance thereof. . . .

Now, as it respects the interposition of the executive abroad, for the protection of the lives or property of the citizen, the

15 Slaughter-House Cases, 83 U.S. (16 Wall.) 36, 79 (1873).

EXHIBIT 3
Page b-19

1560

suit out of necessity rest in the Discretion of the President. Acts of lawless violence, or of threatened violence to the citizen or his property, cannot be anticipated and provided for; and the protection to be effectual or of any avail, may, not infrequently, require the most prompt and decided action. Under our system of government, the citizen abroad is as much entitled to protection as the citizen at home.

The great object and duty of the government is the protection of the lives, liberty, and property of the people composing it, whether abroad or at home; and any government failing in the accomplishment of the object, or the performance of the duty, is not worth preserving.

Durand v. Hollins, 8 F. Cas. 111, 112 (C.C.S.D.N.Y. 1860) (No. 4,186) (emphasis added).

Later, the full Court confirmed this analysis in an opinion holding that the President has inherent authority to provide bodyguards, clothed with federal immunity from state law, to protect judicial officers, even when they are travelling within the United States in the performance of their duties. In re Neagle, 135 U.S. 1 (1890). Rather than base its decision on a narrow analysis of the statute of federal judges, the Court held that the President's duty to "take Care that the Laws be faithfully executed" includes any obligation [sic] that is properly inferrible [sic] from the Constitution itself. Our Court specifically stated that these were not limited to the express terms of statutes and treaties, but included the rights, duties and obligations growing out of the Constitution itself, our international relations, and all the protection implied by the nature of the government under the Constitution. As the Court pointed out, Congress itself had approved this position when it ratified the conduct of the government in using military force to secure the release of an American who had been taken prisoner in Europe. Noting that Congress had voted a medal for the naval officer who had threatened to use force to obtain the American's release, the Court asked, "Upon what act of Congress then existing can any one lay his finger in

16 U.S. Const., art. II, sec. 1.

17 In re Neagle, 135 U.S. at 59.

18 Id. at 64 (emphasis added).

15

1561

support of the action of our government in this matter?"[19] If military force may be used on the President's own discretion to protect American lives and property abroad, surely the less drastic means employed by President Reagan during the Iran project were within his constitutional authority.

II. Any Statute Interfering with the President's Inherent Authority to Conduct Foreign Policy Would Be Unconstitutional and Void.

Congress has traditionally exercised broad implied powers in overseeing the activities of Executive Branch agencies, including probes into departments of the Federal Government to expose corruption, inefficiency or waste. McGrain v. Daugherty, 273 U.S. 135, 177 (1927); see also McGrain v. Daugherty, 273 U.S. 135, 161-164 (1922). This power of oversight is grounded in Congress's need for information to carry out its legislative function. Because the executive departments are subject to statutory regulation, Congress can usually demonstrate through appropriations levels, that it has a legitimate need for the information necessary to make future regulatory and appropriations decisions in an informed manner. McGrain, 273 U.S. at 175.

As the Supreme Court has observed, however, the congressional power of oversight "is not unlimited: McGrain, 250 U.S. at 161." It can be exercised only in aid of a legitimate legislative function traceable to one of Congress's enumerated powers. See McGrain, 273 U.S. at 173-174. The power of oversight cannot constitutionally be exercised in a manner that would usurp the functions of either the judicial or Executive branches. Thus, the Supreme Court has held that by investigating the affairs of a business arrangement in which one of the government's debtors was interested, "the House of Representatives not only exceeded the limit of its own authority, but assumed a power which could only be properly exercised by another branch of the government, because it was in its nature

19 Id. The fact that such a statute may have existed, see Espionage Act of July 27, 1868, ch. 249, sec. 1, 15 Stat. 223, 224 (current version at 22 U.S.C. 1732) (authorizing the President to use such means, short of war, as may be necessary to obtain the release of Americans unjustly held prisoner by foreign governments), does not diminish the force of the Supreme Court's statement that no such statute would be needed to support such an exercise of executive power.

20 It is worth observing that Congress's oversight powers are no more explicit in the Constitution than are the President's powers in foreign affairs. See McGrain, 273 U.S. at 161.

16

EXHIBIT 3
Page b-20

clearly judicial." Kilbourn v. Thompson, 103 U.S. 168, 192 (1881). The same principle applies to congressional inquiries that would trench on the President's exclusive functions. "Lacking the judicial power given to the Judiciary, [Congress] cannot inquire into matters that are exclusively the concern of the Judiciary. Neither can it supplant the Executive in what exclusively belongs to the Executive." Barenblatt v. United States, 360 U.S. 109, 112 (1959) (emphasis added).[21]

It is undoubtedly true that the Constitution does not contemplate "a complete division of authority between the three branches." Nixon v. Administrator of General Services, 433 U.S. 425, 443 (1977). Nevertheless, there are certain quintessential executive functions that Congress may not exercise in the guise of its "oversight power." Congress, for example, may not give its own agents the power to make binding rules "necessary to or advisable for the administration and enforcement of a major statute." Buckley v. Valeo, 424 U.S. 1, 281 (1976) (White, J., concurring in part). Nor may Congress unilaterally alter the rights and duties created by a prior statutory authorization. INS v. Chadha, 462 U.S. 919, 951 (1983). In general, the management and control of affairs committed to the Executive Branch, even those given to the Executive by Congress itself, must remain firmly in the control of the President. Myers v. United States, 272 U.S. 52, 135 (1926). A fortiori, the conduct of affairs committed exclusively to the President by the Constitution must be carefully insulated from improper congressional interference in the guise of "oversight" activities.

This principle has three immediately relevant corrolaries. First, decisions and actions by the President and his immediate staff in the conduct of foreign policy are not subject to direct review by Congress. "By the constitution of the United States, the President is invested with certain important political powers, in the exercise of which he is to use his own discretion, and is accountable only to his country in his political character, and to his own conscience." Marbury v. Madison, 5 U.S. (1 Cranch) 137, 164 (1803).[22]

---

[21] On its facts, Barenblatt did not involve an inter-branch dispute. The Court upheld a contempt citation issued by a House Committee against a witness who refused to answer questions about his ties with the Communist Party.

[22] Obviously, Congress may investigate and consider the President's past actions when performing one of its own assigned functions (for example, while giving advice and consent to treaties or appointments, deciding whether to issue a declaration of war, or during the impeachment process).

Second, while Congress unquestionably possesses the power to make decisions as to the appropriation of public funds, it may not attach conditions to Executive Branch appropriations that require the President to relinquish any of his constitutional discretion in foreign affairs. Just as an individual cannot be required to waive his constitutional rights as a condition of accepting public employment or benefits, so the President cannot be compelled to give up the authority of his office as a condition of receiving the funds necessary to carry out the duties of his office.[23] To leave the President thus at the mercy of the Congress would violate the principle of the separation of powers in the most fundamental manner. The Federalist indicates that one great "inconveniency" of republican government is the tendency of the legislature to invade the prerogatives of the other branches, and that one of the main concerns of the Framers was to give the other branches the "necessary constitutional means and personal motives to resist [such] encroachments."[24] In an effort to address this problem the Constitution provides that the President's personal compensation cannot be altered during his term of office,[25] and it must be acknowledged that the President's constitutional independence is even more precious and

---

[23] The doctrine of unconstitutional conditions has pervasive application throughout the law. For a good general statement of the doctrine, see Frost & Frost Trucking Co. v. Railroad Commission, 271 U.S. 583, 594 (1926):

> If the state may compel the surrender of one constitutional right as a condition of its favor, it may, in like manner, compel a surrender of all. It is inconceivable that guaranties embedded in the Constitution of the United States may thus be manipulated out of existence.

[24] The Federalist No. 51, at 321-322 (J. Madison) (C. Rossiter ed. 1961).

[25] U.S. Const., art. II, sec. 1, cl. 7; The Federalist No. 51, at (J. Madison) (C. Rossiter ed. 1961); Id. No. 73, at 441-442 Hamilton).

vulnerable than his personal independence."[26]

Third, any statute that touches on the President's inherent authority in foreign policy must be interpreted to leave the President as much discretion as the language of the statute will allow. This accords with the well-established judicial presumption in favor of construing statutes so as to avoid constitutional questions whenever possible. Because the President's constitutional authority in international relations is by its very nature virtually as broad as the national interest and as indefinable as the exigencies of unpredictable events, almost any congressional attempt to curtail his discretion raises questions of constitutional dimension. Those questions can, and must be, kept to a minimum in the only way possible, by resolving all statutory ambiguities in accord with the presumption that recognizes the President's constitutional independence in international affairs.

iii. **Statutory Requirements That the President Must Report to Congress About His Activities Must Be Construed Consistently With the President's Constitutional Authority to Conduct Foreign Policy.**

In 1980, the National Security Act of 1947 was amended to provide for congressional oversight of "significant anticipated intelligence activities." This section now provides (section

---
[26] See 41 Op. A.G. 230, 233 (1955):

It is recognized that the Congress may grant or withhold appropriations as it chooses, and when making an appropriation may direct the purposes to which the appropriation shall be devoted. It may also impose conditions with respect to the use of the appropriation, provided always that the conditions do not require operation of the Government in a way forbidden by the Constitution. If the practice of attaching invalid conditions to legislative enactments were permissible, it is evident that the constitutional system of the separability of the branches of Government would be placed in the gravest jeopardy.

[27] "[I]t 'a serious . . . tion of the statute is fairly possible by which [a serious . . . te of constitutionality] may be avoided . . . a court should adopt that construction." Califano v. Yamasaki, 442 U.S. 682, 693 (1979) (quoting Crowell v. Benson, 285 U.S. 22, 62 (1932)).

501(a)) of the National Security Act, 50 U.S.C. 413(a)) (emphasis added):

To the extent consistent with all applicable authorities and duties, including those conferred by the Constitution upon the executive and legislative branches of the Government, and to the extent consistent with due regard for the protection from unauthorized disclosure of classified information and information relating to intelligence sources and methods, the Director of Central Intelligence and the heads of all departments, agencies, and other entities of the United States Government involved in intelligence activities shall —

(1) keep the Select Committee on Intelligence of the Senate and the Permanent Select Committee on Intelligence of the House of Representatives fully and currently informed of all intelligence activities which are the responsibility of, are engaged in by, or are carried out for or on behalf of, any department, agency, or entity of the United States, including any significant anticipated intelligence activity, except that (A) the foregoing provision shall not require approval of the Intelligence committees as a condition precedent to the initiation of any such anticipated intelligence activity, and (B) if the President determines it is essential to limit prior notice to meet extraordinary circumstances affecting vital interests of the United States, such prior notice shall be limited to the Chairman and ranking minority members of the Intelligence committees, the Speaker and minority leader of the House of Representatives, and the majority and minority leaders of the Senate.

For situations in which the President fails to give prior notice under section 501(a), section 501(b), 50 U.S.C. 413(b), (emphasis added) provides:

The President shall fully inform the intelligence committees in a timely fashion of intelligence operations in foreign countries, other than activities intended solely for obtaining necessary intelligence, for which prior notice was not given under subsection (a) of this section and shall provide a statement of the

EXHIBIT 3
Page b-22

1566

reasons for not giving prior notice.[28]

The delicate connection between the "timely notice" requirement of section 501(b) and the President's "inherent constitutional authority" is acknowledged in section 501(a), is dramatically confirmed by a colloquy between Senators Javits and Huddleston, both of whom were on the committee that drafted this provision. Senator Javits asked, "If information has been withheld from both the select committee and the leadership group (as section 501(b) envisages) can it be withheld on any grounds other than 'independent constitutional authority' section 501(b), on what grounds?" Senator Huddleston answered, "Section 501(b), as I recognize that the President may assert constitutional authority to withhold prior notice of covert operation [sic]; but would not be able to claim the identical authority to withhold timely notice under section 501(b). A claim of constitutional authority is the sole grounds that may be asserted for withholding prior notice of a covert operation." 126 Cong. Rec. 17693 (1980)

1567

(emphasis added).[29] If, as Senator Huddleston contended, section

[29] A similar colloquy took place on the floor of the House between Rep. Boland, Chairman of the House Select Committee on Intelligence, and Rep. Hamilton:

Rep. Hamilton: As I understand that subsection, it allows the President to withhold prior notice entirely; that is, he does not inform anyone of that circumstance. He only has to report in a timely fashion.

Is that a correct view of subsection (b)?

Rep. Boland: In response to the gentleman, let me say that the President must always give at least timely notice.

126 Cong. Rec. 28,392 (1980). Thus, Rep. Boland clearly, if reluctantly, confirmed Rep. Hamilton's interpretation. During the floor debates, several senators also acknowledged that the proposed legislation did not require that Congress be notified of all intelligence activities prior to their inception. According to Senator Nunn, the bill contemplated that "in certain instances the requirements of secrecy preclude [a] prior consultation with Congress." 126 Cong. Rec. 11,117 (1980)(statement of Sen. Nunn). See also Id. at 11,119 (statement of Sen. Huddleston)("Section 501(b) recognizes that the President may assert constitutional authority to withhold prior notice of covert operations . . . ."). Id. at 11,103 (statement of Sen. Bayh).

[28] Section 501 of the National Security Act does not contemplate that prior notice of "intelligence activities" will be given in all instances. Subsection (b) of section 501 makes specific provision for situations in which "prior notice was not given under subsection (a). Because subsection (a) includes situations in which the President provides notice to the full intelligence committees under subsection (a)(1)(A) and situations in which he provides prior notice restricted to designated members of Congress, including the chairmen and ranking members of the House and Senate intelligence committees under subsection (a)(1)(B). It seems clear that subsection (b) contemplates situations in which no prior notice has been given under either of these provisions.

In the course of the floor debates, some senators stated that the situations in which prior notice was not required would be very rare. See, e.g., 126 Cong. Rec. 26,276 (1980) (remarks of Sen. Inouye). Such statements are of direct relevance to determining the scope of the prior notice requirement. First, the executive branch has always agreed that instances of deferred reporting will be rare and had consistently given prior notice. Second, Section 501 at the very least permits the President to defer notice when he is acting pursuant to his independent constitutional authority; the scope of this authority is determined, not by legislators' view of the Constitution, but by the Constitution itself. Third, the draftsmen of section 501 decided that because the scope of the President's constitutional authorities and duties was in serious dispute, the legislation would not attempt to resolve the issues separating the parties to the dispute. See 126 Cong. Rec. 11,123 (1980) (statement of Sen. Javits). The ambiguities of subsection (b) reflect Congress' inability to override the executive branch's view of the President's constitutional authority. That dispute cannot now be settled, contrary to the Executive's position, by reference to the statements of individual Congressmen who had a narrow view of the President's constitutional role.

22

EXHIBIT 3
Page b-23

151-793 O - 94 - 18 : Vol.3

1568

1569

33

34

EXHIBIT 3
Page b-24

1570

1571

after the undertaking as a whole was completed or terminated.[38]

Conclusion

Section 501(b) of the National Security Act of 1947 must be interpreted in the light of section 501 as a whole and in light of the President's broad and independent constitutional authority

EXHIBIT 3
Page b-25

1572

Charles J. Cooper
Assistant Attorney General
Office of Legal Counsel

EXHIBIT 3
Page b-26

1660

U.S. Department of Justice

STATEMENT

OF

EDWIN MEESE III
ATTORNEY GENERAL OF THE UNITED STATES

BEFORE THE

UNITED STATES SENATE SELECT COMMITTEE ON SECRET
MILITARY ASSISTANCE TO IRAN AND THE NICARAGUAN OPPOSITION

AND THE

UNITED STATES HOUSE OF REPRESENTATIVES SELECT COMMITTEE TO
INVESTIGATE COVERT ARMS TRANSACTIONS WITH IRAN

ON

JULY 28, 1987

1661

Chairman Inouye, Chairman Hamilton, Members and Counsel of
these Committees:

I welcome this opportunity to come before these Committees
and assist in your review of this Administration's Iranian policy
initiatives, as well as other activities aimed at providing
funding for the Freedom Fighters in Nicaragua. A number of
witnesses have preceded me and provided an accounting of the
policy decisions that were and were not made, and have described
efforts undertaken for the ostensible purpose of furthering those
policies. As I join the witnesses before you, it might be useful
to address what I see as the larger perspective of these hearings
before turning to the specifics of my limited involvement in
certain events.

As a threshold matter, it is important to understand that
the Constitution commits to the President the conduct of United
States' foreign affairs, just as it gives to the Congress certain
responsibilities for the formulation of our country's foreign
policy. The strategic initiative regarding Iran was the
President's policy. Providing assistance to the Freedom
Fighters, within the constraints of the law, was and is also the
President's policy. The President has taken full responsibility
for these policies. He has already said that mistakes were made
in their implementation, and it is clear as well that he neither
approved nor knew about the diversion of funds from the Iranian
arms transfers to the democratic forces in Central America.

EXHIBIT 4
Page b-28

1662

-2-

To the extent one may disagree with the President's policies, there are appropriate ways of making that disagreement known. In regard to the mistakes that were made in implementing the President's policies, the President has already taken steps to correct those problems and he continues to work to ensure that they will never happen again. In regard to any possible illegal conduct by anyone involved in various aspects of this matter, an Independent counsel has been appointed and is investigating. Let us not forget that Congress, in enacting the Independent Counsel statute, gave to him the responsibility as much to exonerate as to prosecute, depending upon the state of the evidence and the legal conclusions that it compels.

The Administration has thoroughly cooperated with the Independent Counsel and will continue to do so. Whatever legal questions there may be concerning the constitutionality of the Independent Counsel statute, there should be no doubt about the wisdom of seeking an Independent counsel in this instance. Indeed, to preclude possible adverse court rulings, I gave Judge Walsh a parallel appointment within the Department of Justice to ensure that his investigation would continue uninterrupted to its completion. It is imperative, both in fairness to the Independent counsel and to those individuals who have been involved in the Iran-Contra matter, that his efforts not be prejudged or impeded.

1663

-3-

With those preliminary observations, let me turn to my participation in the events you are reviewing. As the Attorney General of the United States, it is, of course, one of my responsibilities to serve as the nation's chief law enforcement officer. In that capacity, I am privileged to assist the President in making sure that the laws of the United States are faithfully executed. In addition, as prescribed in the Judiciary Act of 1789 which created the office of attorney general, I am assigned the responsibility of providing legal advice and opinions to the President on such matters and at such times as he directs. Further, the Attorney General is, and has since 1791 been, a member of the President's Cabinet, and thus has the distinctly separate role as one of the general advisors to the President and the Executive Branch. My exposure to the Iran-Contra matter was not confined to any one of those areas of responsibilities, but from time-to-time touched them all. I believe one can better appreciate my limited role in the events of the period by understanding in which of the several capacities I was approached for advice and assistance.

Some eight months ago, the President asked me, as his principal legal advisor, to develop a factual overview of the events related to the Iranian initiative. During that hectic weekend in November, 1986, we were able to piece together a basic outline of what is now known as the Iran-Contra story, which has been essentially validated during the extensive investigations which have occurred since.

EXHIBIT 4
Page b-29

I mention this because after many months of televised hearings and intensive press coverage, some might understandably have difficulty recalling that, as we embarked on our fact finding inquiry on November 21, few inside or outside the government understood the true nature and scope of the Iran matter, let alone knew of the many details of all related activities and events. I certainly had no such knowledge.

My first exposure to the Iran initiative was in reality ather brief. I recall on January 7, 1986, being asked to attend a meeting with the President in the Oval Office along with the Secretaries of State and Defense, the Vice President, the White ouse Chief of Staff, the Director of Central Intelligence, the National Security Assistant, and perhaps one other member of the NSC staff. Parenthetically, let me state that my calendar shows -- and I have been told by others -- that on the previous day the Deputy Attorney General, Lowell Jensen, and I met with Lieutenant Colonel Oliver North who gave us a short briefing on an Iranian initiative. I do not specifically remember that meeting.

At the meeting on January 7th in the President's office, Admiral Poindexter and Director Casey raised the proposed Iran initiative. As described, the initiative involved overtures to "more moderate" elements in Iran and the cultivation of a relationship that could, in the future, be to the geopolitical advantage of the United States. The proposal was also described as possibly helping to end the long Iran-Iraq war. The

-4-

1664

initiative was also seen as a means for decreasing Iranian sponsorship of terrorism, forestalling Soviet designs on the area, and gaining Iranian assistance for the release of the Americans being held hostage in the Middle East. We discussed Israeli suggestions concerning the initiative, especially concerning a transfer of arms from the United States and assistance in the release of hostages from Iran as a means of establishing with each side the good faith of the other. One legal issue that was raised concerned the appropriate statutory authority for an arms transfer as part of the strategic initiative. I was present at the meeting both as the President's legal advisor and as a member of the Cabinet. Based on my familiarity with a 1981 opinion by Attorney General William French Smith, I concurred with the view of Director Casey that it would be legal for the President to authorize arms transfers pursuant to the National Security Act.

Admiral Poindexter and Director Casey favored the initiative; Secretary Shultz and Secretary Weinberger opposed it. My own counsel was that, while very close, the benefits seemed to outweigh the risks, especially since I had the impression that a time frame of 30 to 60 days was contemplated and that the risks were, therefore, short-term.

-5-

1665

EXHIBIT 4
Page b-30

1666

-6-

It is my recollection that the meeting included a brief discussion that a presidential finding would be necessary because of the proposed involvement of the Central Intelligence Agency. I believe there was also a discussion of the necessity of notifying Congress and the legality of delaying that notification because of the extreme hazard to the hostages and others. I do not recall anyone at the meeting arguing in favor of immediate notification. With regard to the legality of the delay, I do recall stating that I believed a short delay was appropriate but wanted to examine the statute before I agreed that such a postponement would be permissible. At the conclusion of the meeting, the President decided that the project was worth pursuing and directed Admiral Poindexter and Director Casey to proceed.

I should add parenthetically that it was not my understanding at that meeting that anyone was discussing an arms-for-hostages transaction, or that the President understood the proposal in those terms. Quite the contrary, no deals were to be made with any of the groups who had taken or were holding American hostages. The President was firm on this point. A limited number of defensive weapons were to be sold to certain Iranians to demonstrate the United States' good faith. They, in turn, as a display of their good faith, were to negotiate separately with forces in Lebanon for the return of the American hostages. No direct dealings with the hostage-takers nor the payment of any type of ransom were ever contemplated.

1667

-7-

Following the January 7 meeting and over the next ten days, I attended one or possibly two follow-up meetings which included Director Casey, Admiral Poindexter, CIA General Counsel Sporkin and me. The one meeting I most clearly recall occurred on January 16, 1986. I believe Secretary Weinberger also attended at least part of that meeting. We discussed section 501 of the National Security Act, the law involving notification to Congress of certain covert activities. General Counsel Sporkin explained his analysis of the statute. After reviewing the statute, I concurred with the Central Intelligence Agency's advice that notification to Congress could, in the circumstances, be postponed due to the imminent danger facing the hostages.

In this regard, I should emphasize that the expectation at the meetings that I attended in January was that the Administration would notify Congress as soon as possible after the hostages were on board an airplane, out of the Middle East, and under the control of the United States. There was no desire or plan to keep this matter from the Congress. There was simply a recognition that this was a highly sensitive activity and that human lives were at stake -- the lives of the American hostages and the lives of the more pragmatic Iranian elements who were willing to attempt a relationship with the United States. We were all acutely aware that if word of the initiative got out, however innocently or inadvertently, it would likely be fatal to the hostages and others helping in their release. It is precisely because of this concern that knowledge of this operation within the Administration was so closely held and shared on only a strict "need-to-know" basis.

EXHIBIT 4
Page b-31

1668

-8-

Indeed, I was not even kept advised of the Iranian Initiative after rendering advice in January of 1986. Apparently there was no continuing need for me to know of efforts undertaken to implement this program. In that regard, I had not been included as a necessary participant in 1985 when the concept of an Iranian strategic Initiative had first been suggested and developed. And I, along with some other members of the National Security Council, had not been informed at any time in 1985 about any arms shipments that occurred during that year or about any related presidential findings prepared or signed prior to January, 1986. I had no awareness of such matters until I learned of them for the first time in November, 1986, and thereafter.

As the testimony of others before these Committees has indicated, there were only two occasions that I can recall in the summer of 1986 when Department of Justice matters prompted a conversation between me and Admiral Poindexter that related to the Iranian Initiative. On both occasions, I acted in my capacity as the country's chief law enforcement officer. The first arose as a result of an inquiry from within the Department of Justice concerning a criminal investigation originating in New York relating to arms smuggling to Iran. The suspects in the investigation alleged that the U.S. government had authorized their arms sales. Criminal Division attorneys had asked that I check to be sure that no such authorization existed. I

1669

-9-

therefore called Admiral Poindexter and received his assurance that the arms sales in question had not been authorized and were not connected with the Iranian Initiative. A declaration was subsequently filed in court stating this fact.

The second incident occurred around the end of October, 1986. Admiral Poindexter telephoned me to inquire about a federal investigation which included an air carrier known as Southern Air Transport. He advised that the airline was involved in efforts concerning the Iranian Initiative that were at a critical stage. He therefore asked whether it might be possible to delay a scheduled visit of investigators to Southern Air for around ten days so as not to disrupt this activity. I informed Admiral Poindexter that we could not impede, weaken or interfere with the investigation, but that I would check with FBI Director Webster to ascertain if it might be possible to delay certain non-urgent aspects of the inquiry.

Through Associate Attorney General Trott, I was informed by Director Webster on October 30, 1986, that the delay could properly take place without in any respect adversely affecting the investigation. I have since been advised by Director Webster that this is precisely what occurred, that the investigation of Southern Air Transport resumed on November 26, and that it was in no way prejudiced by the delay.

EXHIBIT 4
Page b-32

-10-

1670

In early November of 1986, events occurred which were of great consequence to the Iranian Initiative. On or about November 4, following publication of a story in a Middle Eastern journal, American newspapers began to print widely varying accounts of the matter. On November 7, I advised Charles Cooper, Assistant Attorney General for the Office of Legal Counsel -- the office that assists me in my responsibility as legal advisor to the President and the Executive Branch, including national security matters -- that his efforts would probably be needed on the legal issues that might arise in regard to the Iranian initiative. The following Monday (November 10) I attended a meeting with the President and other advisors at which the Iranian initiative was generally discussed.

On November 13, the President addressed the nation on the Iranian activities. Six days later, on November 19, he held a press conference on the subject. At Admiral Poindexter's invitation, I attended a meeting in his office the next afternoon, with Director Casey, Assistant Attorney General Cooper, and for most of the time, NSC Counsel Paul Thompson and Lieutenant Colonel North. I was invited, as the President's legal advisor, to review legal aspects of the Iranian Initiative prior to Administration witnesses giving scheduled testimony and briefings before Congress.

-11-

1671

I recall seeing for the first time at that meeting a draft chronology of events that, from all appearances, had been prepared earlier in the day by the National Security Council staff. In addition, drafts of proposed testimony were distributed -- again, which I was seeing for the first time. Those documents were reviewed and discussed, and corrections and revisions were made at the suggestion of those who had knowledge of specific events.

Questions have been raised during prior hearings of these Committees about my participation in this meeting and whether I "acquiesced" in the statements included in the proposed testimony being prepared. The truth is, I did not at the time have knowledge sufficient to allow me to make any sort of judgment regarding the accuracy of the proposed testimony, or the prepared chronology, or the revisions or corrections that were being suggested. You will recall that the Iranian operation had been rigorously compartmentalized, and only those with a "need to know" were brought into the planning and implementation. Thus, while I was generally aware on November 20, 1986, that there may have been arms transfers to Iran by Israel in 1985, I had no personal knowledge about such shipments, about our role (if any) in assisting with the transfers, or about the contemporaneous knowledge of other Administration officials concerning the details of these shipments.

EXHIBIT 4
Page b-33

1672

-12-

It was after that meeting, late that evening, when I first learned, in a secure telephone conversation with Mr. Cooper, that there were apparent differences in the recollections of the Secretary of State, former National Security Assistant Robert McFarlane, and perhaps others. I was concerned that great care be taken to resolve these differences so that accurate testimony would be given at the Congressional hearings and briefings the next day. I believed that, because the Iranian initiative had been such a highly sensitive matter and because it had been so rigidly "compartmentalized," no one seemed to have all the facts and all seemed to me to be trying to piece together various parts of the story without full knowledge of the events. As a consequence, there appeared to be considerable confusion as to what occurred when; and the many conflicting and inconsistent news stories only seemed to exacerbate the situation.

It was for this reason that I went to see the President the next day. I advised him of my concerns, and recommended that he have someone undertake a fact-gathering review into the Iranian initiative to ascertain a fuller and more accurate picture of the events and activities that had occurred. The President agreed totally with my assessment and directed me to commence an immediate review. He asked that I complete this task before the National Security Planning Group meeting on this subject that was scheduled for 2:00 p.m. on Monday, November 24.

1673

-13-

It might be helpful if I spend a just few minutes on the activity that took place during that weekend. The essential point to keep in mind is that our purpose was not to conduct a criminal investigation. Indeed, on November 21, 1986, there was no hint that criminal activity was in any way implicated in the Iranian arms transactions. Indeed I later learned that the Criminal Division had separately conducted its own independent review of criminal statutes that might possibly be involved, and as reflected in a memorandum dated November 22, 1986, found no basis to suspect that crimes had been committed.

Early Friday afternoon, after my meeting with the President, I discussed the matter of the fact-gathering inquiry with FBI Director William Webster, who concurred that it would be inappropriate to utilize FBI investigators. Our purpose, plain and simple, was to find out what the facts really were and report to the President. I therefore put together a small team of lawyers who were knowledgeable about national security matters and proceeded to systematically talk with each of the persons having information about the Iranian initiative and to review the applicable documents. As Secretary Shultz said in his testimony last week, our efforts in the space of just over three days turned up the essential facts that are still the essential facts today. Obviously, much more information and many additional details have been uncovered by the various investigations and months of effort that have been taken place since that weekend. But the basic outline of facts that the President and I related to Congress and the public on November 25, 1986, remains intact today.

EXHIBIT 4
Page b-34

-14-

1674

From the afternoon of Friday, November 21, 1986, through the evening of Monday, November 24th, a number of people were interviewed, documents were examined and information was obtained from the relevant agencies that had participated in the strategic Iran initiative. Much of the information we obtained has previously been provided to these Committees by the witnesses that have appeared before you and in the depositions and documents which are part of your record. Therefore, I will not chronicle in detail the events of that weekend, but will, of course, be happy to respond to any questions you may have about it.

During our review, we discovered facts indicating that funds obtained from the arms transfers in Iran had been diverted to the Democratic Resistance Forces in Nicaragua. I brought this information to the President, who determined that it should be reported promptly to the Congress and to the American people, and that immediate corrective action should be taken.

Therefore, on Tuesday, November 25, 1986, a briefing for Congressional leaders was held at 11:00 a.m. and a news conference was conducted at noon. Although our information was by no means complete, and we recognized that much investigative activity would follow, the President requested that I disclose all that we had learned to date so that there would be no claim of withholding of information or charge of "cover-up."

-15-

1675

Several actions were immediately commenced to pursue necessary followup investigations and remedial actions.

The President announced that he was convening a Special Review Board to investigate and make recommendations to ensure that the mistakes made in implementing national security policy in this case would not occur again.

We also took immediate action concerning the possible criminal law implications of the information which had been uncovered. I, therefore, met with Assistant Attorney General William Weld, who heads the Department's Criminal Division, to discuss the initiation of an investigation by his attorneys and the FBI into the possible violation of criminal statutes. That process was well underway by the same evening. I also directed Deputy Attorney General Arnold Burns to contact the White House Counsel to secure all files in the NSC offices.

As these steps were being taken, it was clear to me that the initiation of an Independent Counsel investigation was probable. The activities of the Criminal Division included the initial inquiry to determine whether the legal and factual predicates required by the statute were present. By December 2, I had concluded that seeking an Independent Counsel was appropriate and advised the President of this fact.

EXHIBIT 4
Page b-35

1676

-16-

On December 4, the formal request for assignment of an Independent Counsel was presented to the Special Division of the Court of Appeals for the District of Columbia Circuit. That request was ultimately granted and Lawrence Walsh was appointed as Independent Counsel. Since then, I have continued, in accordance with the President's wishes and my own best judgment, to be fully supportive of and cooperative with all the official inquiries into this matter. Today is my sixth session of testimony on this matter. Others in the Department and elsewhere in the Administration have also appeared multiple times; and there has been an unprecedented willing disclosure of perhaps millions of pages of sensitive government documents.

That, in brief, is my knowledge of events surrounding the matters under consideration by these Committees. But I would be remiss if I did not comment on one of the often-stated goals of these hearings -- the need for a constructive relationship between the Executive and Legislative Branches in the conduct of foreign policy.

We have heard some harsh criticism of the Executive Branch over the past several months -- some of which is deserved; some of which is not. Obviously, the destruction of documents and any breakdown of communications within and outside the Administration deserves serious review and reflection. But no branch of government has a monopoly on good intentions, and no branch is without its faults and problems.

EXHIBIT 4
Page b-36

Richard R. Miller

December 3, 1993

Ms. Marilyn R. Sargent
Chief Deputy Clerk of the Court
United States Court of Appeals
 for the District of Columbia Circuit
333 Constitution Avenue, N.W.
Room 5409
Washington, D.C. 20001

Dear Ms. Sargent:

As we discussed I have enclosed the original and three copies of the
petition and supporting documents for consideration by Judges Sentelle, Butzner and
Sneed. As I indicated there maybe some sensitive or classified material in the petition
letter and the supporting documents. I would be happy to discuss these in person.

Sincerely,

Richard R. Miller

10117A Tamarack Drive
Vienna, Virginia 22182
Office 703/715-8888
Home 703/255-9793

December 2, 1993 **United States Court of Appeals**
For the District of Columbia Circuit

FILED DEC 0 3 1993

RON GARVIN
CLERK

Clerk of the Court
United States Court of Appeals
 for the District of Columbia Circuit
333 Constitution Avenue, N.W.
Room 5409
Washington, D.C. 20001

In re: Oliver L. North, et al.   Division No. 86-6

Clerk of the Court:

According to the Order entered August 5, 1993 by Judges Sentelle, Butzner and Sneed, I am submitting the following for consideration by the Court, and petition that certain sections of the Report by Independent Counsel Lawrence Walsh be suppressed or, in the alternative, amended. In the event that the court decides not to grant this petition then I request that this letter and its accompanying documents be made a part of the record.

In reviewing the final report by Independent Counsel Lawrence E. Walsh it became clear that information contained in certain passages pertaining to me is incorrect. What is particularly disturbing is that the information in question is not relevant in the least to the guilty plea which I entered or to my subsequent testimony used by Judge Walsh in his failed attempt to convict Lt. Col. North on a similar charge. Judge Walsh's only reason for misrepresenting the facts seems to be an effort to paint a picture of me and Frank Gomez as profiteers. I have admitted to participating in improper solicitations for contributions for military materials using a non-profit tax deductible foundation but have steadfastly denied any personal gain from my activities. The report's characterization of me and Mr. Gomez was not part of the information filed by the Independent Counsel at the time of my guilty plea and was not introduced in any way in the subsequent court proceedings. This leads to the question of whether these are actual errors or politically motivated character assassinations. In either case they have no place in this report.

The repeated assertion in the report that there were $6,323,020 raised for the "contras" and that "only $3,306,882 went to contra support," is absolutely false and disproved by the documents and testimony in Judge Walsh's possession. It is highly uncomfortable for me to defend a man whose guilty plea sealed my fate, but Carl Channell successfully raised and forwarded to me $3,275,000 for direct humanitarian and military assistance to keep the freedom fighters alive until the resumption of U.S. aid. I in turn sent those funds where Col. North told me to. The continuing assertion from others, an assertion supported by innuendo in Judge Walsh's report, is that these funds did not make it to their intended beneficiaries. That is an utter lie.

Specifically, in one of two such passages, Judge Walsh charges that "NEPL (National Endowment for the Preservation of Liberty) in 1985 and 1986 received $6,323,020 for the contras. Because of overhead costs, commissions and salaries taken by the fund-raisers, it disbursed to the contras at North's direction only $3,306,882." This is untrue. The Independent Counsel started its 1987 inquiries of Carl Russell Channell and the National Endowment for the Preservation of Liberty (NEPL) after a disgruntled former employee accused him of raising $10 million for the freedom fighters, and only sending on to them $1 million. This charge later proved to be false and Judge Walsh never brought this witness to trial. In fact, the Independent Counsel knows that NEPL conducted and raised money for several public education campaigns including programs focused on the freedom fighters of Nicaragua, the Reagan Administration's Strategic Defense Initiative, an effort to erect a "freedom torch" in Berlin and others.

The attached report, "1985/1986 Summary of National Endowment for the Preservation of Liberty Program Expenditures" provides a careful detailing of expenditures made by IBC on NEPL's behalf in executing its part of these programs. The report's validity has never been challenged by Judge Walsh. That report clearly states that in 1985 and 1986 NEPL funded and executed The Central American Freedom Program. It was a difficult and

2

hard fought public awareness campaign designed to support the Reagan Administration's

efforts to convince Congress and the public to support the Nicaraguan Freedom Fighters. This

effort was credited by the administration with helping to change political opinion in favor of the

freedom fighters. In fact NEPL and its donors were lavishly praised by President Reagan for

their efforts. This program was originally budgeted for $2,000,000 but ultimately spent closer

to $1,200,000 in professional fees and program expenditures. The balance of approximately

$500,000 in 1985 and 1986 program payments to IBC were for direction and execution of

NEPL's SDI program and several other minor projects. All of these payments and their

resulting expenditures are contained in the "1985/86..." report to NEPL and were readily

available to the Independent Counsel's office.

This report was issued to NEPL at a time of great controversy and was the only

reliable road map the Independent Counsel's office had at the time it began its inquiry.

However, Judge Walsh chose to ignore its contents when writing his final report.

What is equally disturbing is that through my early cooperation Assistant

Independent Counsels Michael R. Bromwich and David M. Zornow received nearly 80,000

pages of document production from the offices of International Business Communications.

These documents include, but are by no means limited to, the television and print

advertisements and schedules for all of NEPL's public education efforts, including reams of

reports on such things as public tours by resistance figures designed to bolster public opinion.

They also included hours of videotapes from film crews inside Nicaragua used in

documentaries as part of the program. The fact that the subpoena produced 80,000 pages is

clear and irrefutable evidence of the extensive professional work done by IBC for NEPL.

Judge Walsh chose to ignore this evidence in writing his report.

In fact, it is the Central American Freedom Program and a subsequent effort by

NEPL to develop similar public support for President Reagan's Strategic Defense Initiative that

make up the majority of the $1.7 million in professional and program expenses paid to IBC by

NEPL for the years 1985 to 1986. Unfortunately, the Independent Counsel has chosen to

obscure these facts and infer that this money came to IBC's principals personally.

In several references including one on Page 191, Judge Walsh seeks to infer that I and Frank Gomez personally received the $1.7 million mentioned above. This is an absolute falsehood and readily disproved by the documents subpoenaed by his office. In those documents are the personal tax returns of Richard Miller and Francis Gomez, IBC's principals. As the attached final IRS audit report on my 1984, 1985, 1986 and 1987 returns clearly shows, my 1985 income was $27,066 and 1986 was $138,844 (the 1986 number actually included deferred 1985 income in the amount of $45,000). Rather than the $1.7 million that the Independent Counsel alleges, I actually earned $165,910 for those two years, or $82,955 average per year. Francis Gomez earned less than that amount and I see no purpose in embarrassing him by reporting it here. However, his returns were also available to the Independent Counsel's office. Furthermore, IBC had several other substantial clients during this period and the personal income derived from IBC by me and Mr. Gomez was for work on their accounts as well. Consequently, for the Independent Counsel to infer that we got rich off of our work for NEPL or Col. North's activities is proven false by the evidence.

What the Independent Counsel's office also has in its subpoenaed documents, and seems unwilling to rely on, are the records of the bank transfers and acknowledgment letters from all the receiving organizations. Instead of characterizing all the expenditures directed by Col. North as "Contra support" the report should show the diversity of the recipients including all the humanitarian organizations that benefited from this aid. Excluding them is only intended to paint an inaccurate picture. These records detail a disbursement history to all three factions of the Nicaraguan Resistance, not just the FDN. These records also detail the dispersal of funds to Miguel Cardinal Obando, Archbishop of Managua; The Gulf and Caribbean Foundation for prosthetic surgery for wounded fighters; Friends of the Americas for refugee and orphan releif programs in Honduras; and the Unified Nicaraguan Opposition (UNO) for the entire operating budget for Washington office.

This record of disbursements includes several payments to a subsidiary that I set up to help recover the costs of participating in this difficult venture. Through agreement with Col. North that organization, World Affairs Counselors Inc., received approximately

$450,000 in payments to off-set the costs associated with our participation in this effort. As the earlier mention of my tax returns indicates, these funds never came to me or Frank Gomez personally and obviously only barely covered the associated costs of the efforts we put forward. At no time did I, Col. North, or anyone involved in this inquiry, through document or testimony, characterize these funds as "commissions" as Judge Walsh does three times in his report (page 191, para. 3, 4 & 5). Col. North agreed to these reimbursements because, as our tax returns confirm, we could no longer afford to provide these services without these reimbursements. Characterizing them as "commissions" is a cheap shot that should not have made it's way into the Independent Counsel's final report.

From the beginning of this inquiry I cooperated fully. Perhaps this response is weighted by some greater disappointment that the Independent Counsel's report does not judge people on the basis of the facts presented through testimony and evidence. Independent Counsel Walsh has instead allowed political commentary to take the place of a clear and honest recital of the truth. For this reason I petition the court to instruct the Independent Counsel to remove these references to me or correct them. I have included a listing of the changes I seek the court to instruct Judge Walsh to make. Since the Independent Counsel's original passages are so defamatory, if the court grants this petition, in whole or in part, I ask that the attached list of requested changes not be made part of the record if in any way possible. Additionally, given the inaccurate nature of the present language in the final report, I ask to have the right to respond and seek suppression of any language amended by the Independent Counsel and submitted to the court.

Thank you.

Sincerely,

Richard R. Miller
10117A Tamarack Drive
Vienna, Virginia 22182
703/255-979

5

Requested Changes to Final Report
by Independent Counsel Lawrence Walsh
Proposed by Richard R. Miller

The proposed changes are annotated to reflect requested removals, using strikeouts (ex.; ~~commissions~~) and insertions, using underlining (ex.; **reimbursements**). All proposed changes are in bold. In each instance the full text or passage in question is provided and where possible page numbers are included.

1. **Pg., unknown**

   "NEPL (National Endowment for the Preservation of Liberty) in 1985 and 1986 received $6,323,020 for the contras. Because of overhead costs, commissions and salaries taken by the fund-raisers, it disbursed to the contras at North's direction only $3,306,882."

   requested change -

   "NEPL (National Endowment for the Preservation of Liberty) in 1985 and 1986 received $6,323,020 for **its contra-related political and public education campaigns as well as direct financial support to** the contras. ~~Because of overhead costs, commissions and salaries taken by the fund-raisers, i~~ **It** disbursed to the contras at North's direction ~~only~~ $3,306,882."

2. **Pg. 187, para. 1**

   "...Spring 1984,..." This is an obvious error in dates.

   requested change -

   "Spring 198**5**"

3. **Pg. 190, para. 8**

   "In 1985 and 1986 NEPL received $10,385,929 in total contributions for a variety of causes. The major contra-related contributions from June 1985 to November 1986 totaled $6,323,020. Of this, only $3,306,882 went to contra support, disbursed at North's direction as follows: $1,238,000 to the Swiss Enterprise account Lake Resources; $1,080,000 transfers to Calero; and $488,882 to other Contra-related activities."

   requested change -

   "In 1985 and 1986 NEPL received $10,385,929 in total contributions for a variety of causes. The major contra-related contributions from June 1985 to November 1986 totaled $6,323,020. Of this, ~~only~~ $3,306,882 went to **direct financial support for the** contra**s and other Nicaraguan political and humanitarian organizations** ~~support~~, disbursed at North's direction as follows: $1,238,000 to the Swiss

1985/86 Summary of
National Endowment for the
Preservation of Liberty
Program Expenditures

INTERNATIONAL BUSINESS COMMUNICATIONS
1912 Sunderland Place N.W. ● Washington D.C. 20036

INTERNATIONAL BUSINESS COMMUNICATIONS
1912 SUNDERLAND PLACE N.W.
WASHINGTON D.C. 20036-1608
TELEPHONE 202 659.8551
TELEX 3719713 SCUSA

M E M O R A N D U M

TO: Carl Russell Channell
               President
               National Endowment for the
               Preservation of Liberty

FROM: Richard R. Miller
               Senior Partner

DATE: February 16, 1987

SUBJECT: 1985/86 summary of NEPL program expenditures

This memorandum and the materials attached to it constitute the report you requested on the application of the funds provided to IBC by NEPL in 1985 and 1986 in connection with the Central American Freedom Plan (CAFP), other NEPL programs and for the purpose of providing humanitarian aid in Central America. We have prepared or collected the following materials based on a thorough review of our records:

1. An executive summary of 1985 and 1986 expenditures which includes both the program costs of CAFP, other NEPL programs and the amount of humanitarian aid given by NEPL through IBC.

2. A comprehensive, chronological list of all NEPL deposits to our accounts and IBC expenditures in the execution of your programs for each year.

3. Documentation provided by the managing directors of Intel-Cooperation Inc. (originally I.C. Inc.), including a copy of the Memorandum of Association (corporate charter) filed with the government of the Cayman Islands and a schedule of the receipts and disbursements of that company for 1985 and 1986.

4. Copies of the retainer letter between NEPL and IBC and our program spending document that includes planning for the January 1986 Winter Meeting.

5. Copies of the wire transfers and bank orders used by IBC to distribute the humanitarian aid funds listed in section 2 and summarized in section 1.

You are familiar with our efforts in connection with the CAFP.
In addition, the funds NEPL provided for humanitarian assistance
have been applied to particularly worthy purposes. For example,
your generosity has saved the arm of a little girl who was shot
by the Sandinistas and paid for the reconstructive surgery in the
United States that repaired the faces and limbs of young freedom
fighters. You have also supported some of the best scholarly
work by Nicaraguans and helped to support education efforts by
exiles who wanted to bring their story to America.

Adolfo Calero has personally thanked you and me and has written
to you thanking you for the help we provided to the Nicaraguan
Development Council. Another major recipient is the Unified
Nicaraguan Opposition (UNO), the political umbrella organization
of the Nicaraguan Democratic Resistance. As your representative we
have heard from other officials of the movement, and they have
gratefully acknowledged the direct assistance we sent on to them.

IBC also distributed funds through Intel Co-operation Inc. to
several organizations exempt from American taxation under section 501(c)(3) of the Internal Revenue Code. They are:

    Gulf and Caribbean Foundation

    Friends for the Americas

    Nicaraguan Development Council

    Latin American Strategic Studies Institute

    Institute on Terrorism and Subnational Conflict

All of these recipients have pledged that their donations were
used solely for humanitarian purposes and, given the nature of
their organizations, we are confident that such is the case,
since it is consistent with their programs in the region.

Some of the funds, as shown in the attached materials, were
deposited to the account of Lake Resources, Inc., at Credit Swiss
Bank in Geneva at the request of Lt. Col. Oliver L. North. At
the present time we are unable to obtain from him any information
concerning the application of those funds after deposit to the
Lake Resources account. However, we were assured by him at the
time that the funds were to be applied solely for humanitarian
assistance.

If you have any questions about this report, we would be happy to
discuss them with you.

EXECUTIVE SUMMARY OF

IBC RECEIPTS AND EXPENDITURES FOR

NEPL FUNDS IN 1985 AND 1986

<u>1985</u>   <u>Total Deposits</u> $1,497,222.00

PROGRAM COSTS

Professional Fees	$351,397.15	
(1986 Payments on CAFP made in Dec)	+140,000.00	
1985 Pro. Fee payments		491,397.15
Program Expenses		104,119.85
HUMANITARIAN AID		901,705.00

<u>1986</u>   <u>Deposits</u>   3,433,098.79

PROGRAM COSTS

Professional fees	786,204.00	
(Prepaid in 1985)	<140,000.00>	
1986 Pro. Fees payment		652,311.36
Program Expenses		388,743.33
HUMANITARIAN AID		2,392,044.10

<u>1985/1986 Humanitarian aid breakdown</u>

85 Direct assistance payments	81,705.00	
85 Payments via Intel Cooperation	390,000.00	
85 Payments via Lake Resources	430,000.00	
TOTAL 1985		901,705.00
86 Direct assistance payments	42,044.10	
86 Payments via Intel Cooperation	2,350,000.00	
TOTAL 1986		2,392,044.10
<u>GRAND TOTAL</u>		$3,293,749.10

ACCOUNT REVIEW 1985

National Endowment for the Preservation of Liberty
American Conservative Trust

The following account review uses two designations for transactions; Debit, for any expenditure undertaken for NEPL or ACT; Deposit, for all checks and wire transfers written to IBC.

DATE	ITEM	DESCRIPTION	DEBIT AMOUNT	DEPOSIT AMOUNT
5/13	Deposit	NEPL		5,000.00
5/22	Debit	Stamps	44.00	
5/23	Debit	Office Supplies	571.89	
5/24	Debit	Color Photos	263.94	
5/29	Debit	FARA Books	11.00	
6/5	Debit	Office Supplies	226.52	
6/5	Debit	Couriers	745.95	
6/3	Deposit	NEPL		5,000.00
6/6	Debit	Copying Press Release	95.40	
6/6	Debit	Hill Deliveries	235.40	
6/7	Debit	Photocopying	458.60	
6/7	Debit	Copying Press Release	26.50	
6/11	Deposit	NEPL		5,000.00
6/19	Debit	Travel Expenses	2,200.00	
6/20	Debit	Cash for Travelers Checks	3,500.00	
6/20	Debit	Postage	40.00	
6/25	Debit	Hill Delivery	26.75	
6/25	Deposit	NEPL		5,000.00
7/3	Deposit	NEPL		5,000.00
7/15	Deposit	NEPL/CAFP		130,000.00
7/15	Debit	Friends of Freedom Commercial TULIN	30,000.00	
7/15	Debit	Messengers	549.80	
7/15	Debit	Photocopying	227.40	
7/15	Debit	Travel	820.28	
7/17	Deposit	NEPL		5,000.00
7/17	Deposit	NEPL-CAFP		25,000.00
7/18	Debit	Subcontractor -Schwatrz	2,000.00	
7/19	Deposit	NEPL-CAFP		80,000.00
7/22	Debit	Avcom	81.94	
7/22	Debit	Directories	308.00	
7/22	Debit	Radio/TV Monitoring	45.98	
7/22	Debit	VCR	350.00	
7/22	Debit	Photos	210.94	
7/22	Debit	News conference Translations	500.00	
7/22	Debit	Maps	100.00	

DATE	ITEM	DESCRIPTION	DEBIT AMOUNT	DEPOSIT AMOUNT
7/22	Debit	Daily Newspapers Mailing	135.00	
7/22	Debit	Radio/TV Monitoring	116.38	
7/22	Debit	Reprints-U.S. Strategic Review	197.34	
7/22	Debit	Photocopying	368.30	
7/22	Debit	Federal Express	930.55	
7/22	Debit	Office Supplies	531.36	
7/23	Debit	NPR Tape	20.00	
7/23	Debit	Telephones	1,100.00	
7/23	Debit	Pyramid Videos	497.52	
7/24	Debit	IDU Conference Ticket	1,000.00	
7/25	Debit	Miami Car	82.58	
7/26	Debit	May to June Travel	6,235.66	
8/12	Debit	Travel-Wesley Smith	1,500.00	
8/12	Debit	Postage	100.00	
8/15	Debit	National Journal	5.00	
8/15	Debit	FPA Books	8.50	
8/15	Debit	Cinema East	3,295.00	
8/23	Deposit	NEPL-CAFP		80,000.00
8/23	Debit	Wesley Smith-travel	3,121.00	
9/3	Deposit	NEPL		10,000.00
9/3	Debit	Newspapers	159.00	
9/4	Debit	Newsweek	26.87	
9/4	Debit	Telephones	226.78	
9/5	Deposit	NEPL-CAFP		21,000.00
9/5	Debit	Freinds of Freedom -TULIN	30,000.00	
9/11	Debit	Camera Crew	7,550.00	
9/11	Debit	Wesley Smith	500.00	
9/12	Debit	Couriers	689.00	
9/12	Debit	Writers Subcontract	10,005.00	
9/12	Deposit	NEPL-CAFP		26,300.00
9/12	Debit	Film Producer	3,000.00	
9/13	Debit	Film Crew Expenses	1,000.00	
9/13	Debit	Film Crew Fees	850.00	
9/16	Debit	Adcom	8.99	
9/16	Debit	Dubbing	30.00	
9/17	Debit	Telephone	100.00	
9/16	Debit	U.S. News Reprints	60.00	
9/17	Debit	Video Rental	232.00	
9/17	Debit	Film Crew Travel	410.00	
9/17	Debit	Casual Labor	70.00	
9/18	Deposit	NEPL-CAFP		10,000.00
9/18	Debit	Translations	398.00	
9/20	Deposit	NEPL		132,000.00
9/20	Debit	Friends of Freedom	130,000.00	
9/20	Deposit	NEPL		100,000.00
9/24	Debit	Postage	70.07	
9/24	Debit	Travel	1,256.00	
9/26	Debit	Friends of Freedom -I.C. Inc.	100,000.00	
9/26	Debit	Film Crew Fees	231.00	
9/26	Deposit	NEPL		5,000.00

DATE	ITEM	DESCRIPTION	DEBIT AMOUNT	DEPOSIT AMOUNT
9/26	Debit	Journal of Amer. Pol.	392.20	
9/30	Debit	U.S. News Reprints	60.00	
10/3	Debit	Sprint on tapes	47.50	
10/3	Debit	Travel	1,452.00	
10/4	Debit	Travel-Refugee	218.00	
10/7	Deposit	NEPL-CAFP		10,000.00
10/7	Debit	Postage	26.40	
10/8	Debit	TV Tape Dubbing	248.00	
10/8	Debit	TV Tape Dubbing	68.00	
10/8	Debit	Heritage Publications	8.95	
10/11	Deposit	NEPL-CAFP		10,000.00
10/11	Debit	Postage	98.34	
10/15	Debit	Presentation Boxes	84.59	
10/15	Debit	S. Christian Books	211.47	
10/16	Debit	Telephones	3,081.28	
10/16	Debit	Video Equipment	196.50	
10/16	Deposit	NEPL		10,000.00
10/16	Debit	Presentation Boxes	83.79	
10/17	Debit	Trevor Books	380.65	
10/18	Debit	Film Crew	10,000.00	
10/18	Deposit	NEPL		270,000.00
10/21	Debit	Postage	200.00	
10/22	Debit	Travel	3,616.00	
10/23	Debit	Film Crew Expenses	4.90	
10/23	Deposit	NEPL-CAFP		10,522.00
10/25	Debit	Film Crew Fees	1,101.36	
10/25	Debit	Gomez Expenses	4,181.00	
10/25	Debit	Friends of Freedom -I.C. Inc.	250,000.00	
10/28	Debit	Couriers	987.00	
10/28	Debit	Press Club Room	154.90	
10/28	Debit	Videotaping	49.82	
10/30	Deposit	NEPL		63,000.00
10/30	Deposit	ACT		9,500.00
10/30	Debit	Forbes	4.00	
11/6	Debit	Video Editing	330.00	
11/4	Debit	Flores Expenses	37.78	
11/4	Debit	Flores Labor	204.25	
11/7	Debit	Video Transmission	400.00	
11/8	Debit	Friends of Freedom -I.C. Inc.	40,000.00	
11/8	Debit	Mailgrams	1405.00	
11/8	Debit	Photographs	165.63	
11/8	Debit	Postage	82.80	
11/14	Debit	Hotel for Producer	102.66	
11/15	Debit	Travel for Flores	1010.00	
11/15	Debit	Postage	112.00	
11/17	Debit	Travel-CAFP	2,973.00	
11/19	Deposit	NEPL-CAFP		10,000.00
11/19	Debit	Expenses-CAFP Producer	1,357.32	
11/19	Debit	CAFP Travel	2,088.50	
11/19	Debit	CDS-Photocopying	20.36	
11/20	Debit	Miami Trip Clemons	550.00	

DATE	ITEM	DESCRIPTION	DEBIT AMOUNT	DEPOSIT AMOUNT
11/20	Debit	CDS-ACT Copying	108.44	
11/20	Debit	Postage	100.00	
11/27	Debit	Photocopying	27.35	
11/27	Debit	Keffer Expenses	35.86	
12/3	Debit	Speech UNO travel to D.C.	6,000.00	
12/4	Debit	Expenses, Freedom House	7.50	
12/6	Deposit	NEPL		400,000.00
12/6	Deposit	NEPL		7,500.00
12/10	Debit	Photocopying	7.28	
12/11	Deposit	NEPL		7,400.00
12/11	Debit	Telephone	3,700.00	
12/11	Debit	Newspaper	1.30	
12/11	Debit	Travel-CAFP	4,161.00	
12/12	Debit	Producer Fees-CAFP	10,000.00	
12/12	Debit	Radio Tape	50.00	
12/13	Debit	Flores Travel	60.00	
12/16	Debit	Tape of TV	16.96	
12/16	Debit	Friends of Freedom	300,000.00	
12/16	Deposit	NEPL		20,000.00
12/18	Debit	Postage	124.00	
12/20	Debit	USSR-FARA Reg.	13.50	
12/20	Debit	Travel	334.08	
12/20	Deposit	NEPL		20,000.00
12/24	Debit	Gomez Expenses	51.00	
12/29	Debit	Books	40.54	
12/30	Debit	Couriers	777.45	
12/30	Debit	Travel	2,655.45	

Total Debits   1,005,824.85

Total Deposits   1,497,222.00

ACCOUNT REVIEW 1986

National Endowment for the Preservation of Liberty
American Conservative Trust

The following account review uses two designations for transactions; Debit, for any expenditure undertaken for NEPL, ACT
or Sentinel; Deposit, for all checks and wire transfers
written to IBC.

DATE	ITEM	DESCRIPTION	DEBIT AMOUNT	DEPOSIT AMOUNT
1/2	Debit	Photocopying	200.00	
1/2	Deposit	NEPL		20,000.00
1/2	Deposit	NEPL		10,000.00
1/2	Debit	VCR-TV	753.00	
1/3	Debit	ZGS-Dubbing	114.00	
1/3	Debit	ZGS-Dubbing	138.00	
1/3	Debit	Air Courier	66.00	
1/3	Debit	FEDEX	861.00	
1/3	Debit	Newsletter	91.20	
1/3	Debit	Saxitone-Tape Recorder	427.09	
1/3	Debit	FEDEX	24.00	
1/7	Debit	Travel-CAFP	5,128.77	
1/7	Debit	PBS Terrorism Film	356.50	
1/7	Debit	U.S. News and W.R.	58.24	
1/7	Debit	Couriers	143.15	
1/7	Debit	Supplies	1,362.42	
1/7	Debit	Film Crew	10,000.00	
1/8	Deposit	NEPL		400,000.00
1/9	Debit	Cable-TV Guide	79.50	
1/9	Debit	Travel-CAFP Film Crew	1,010.00	
1/10	Debit	Travel-CAFP Film Crew	1,515.00	
1/10	Debit	Tape Dubs	45.58	
1/10	Debit	Courier	51.45	
1/13	Debit	FEDEX	27.50	
1/13	Debit	Postage	22.00	
1/13	Debit	Friends of Freedom -I.C. Inc.	360,000.00	
1/14	Debit	TV Guidebook	246.50	
1/17	Debit	Copying	54.55	
1/17	Debit	Copying	414.34	
1/17	Debit	Copying	22.05	
1/17	Debit	FEDEX	1,006.00	
1/17	Debit	FEDEX	16.50	
1/17	Debit	FEDEX	25.50	
1/17	Debit	FEDEX	16.50	
1/17	Debit	Copying	89.04	

DATE	ITEM	DESCRIPTION	DEBIT AMOUNT	DEPOSIT AMOUNT
1/17	Debit	Videotape	$100.00	
1/20	Debit	Letter Copying	118.04	
1/20	Deposit	NEPL		$5,000.00
1/20	Deposit	NEPL		20,000.00
1/24	Debit	Traveler's Checks-CAFP	404.00	
1/28	Debit	Cameron Analysis	10,000.00	
1/28	Debit	Copying	85.33	
1/28	Debit	Traveler's Checks for Wesley Smith	3,605.70	
1/29	Debit	DHL Couriers	993.00	
1/29	Debit	Postage	132.00	
1/30	Debit	Radio Shack	62.68	
1/30	Debit	Western Union	402.60	
1/30	Debit	Telephone	2,007.90	
1/31	Deposit	NEPL		50,000.00
2/3	Debit	Dubbing	45.58	
2/7	Debit	Travel CAFP	2,885.68	
2/5	Debit	Traveler's Checks-CAFP	505.00	
2/5	Deposit	NEPL		20,000.00
2/5	Deposit	NEPL		756.84
2/5	Debit	Tape Dubbing	34.05	
2/6	Debit	Tape Stock	235.00	
2/7	Debit	VHS Dubbing	20.00	
2/7	Debit	Copying	31.87	
2/7	Debit	CAFP-Schwartz Subcontractor	900.00	
2/10	Debit	Traveler's Checks-CAFP	202.00	
2/10	Deposit	NEPL		100,000.00
2/10	Debit	Smith Report Grant	3,307.00	
2/10	Debit	Book	17.97	
2/12	Debit	Traveler's Checks-CAFP	1,212.00	
2/13	Debit	Tape Recorder	107.05	
2/13	Debit	Films	2,338.00	
2/13	Debit	News Tapes	105.00	
2/13	Debit	Translators	236.25	
2/13	Debit	Tapes-Goodman	408.16	
2/13	Debit	Tape-Dubs	298.00	
2/13	Debit	Tape-Dubs	112.00	
2/13	Debit	Taping-News	200.00	
2/13	Debit	Photography	756.84	
2/13	Debit	Javelin Press	112.50	
2/13	Debit	Public Brod. Dubs	26.52	
2/13	Debit	Flores-Auto CAFP	47.90	
2/13	Debit	Presentation Materials	1,778.11	
2/14	Debit	VCR-Rental	91.40	
2/13	Debit	TELEX	65.43	

DATE	ITEM	DESCRIPTION	DEBIT AMOUNT	DEPOSIT AMOUNT
2/13	Debit	Photo Publishers	79.50	
2/13	Debit	Supplies for Presentations	138.71	
2/13	Debit	Terrorism Film Dub	495.00	
2/13	Debit	Telephone	380.60	
2/13	Debit	Wire to Speaker-CAFP	900.00	
2/13	Debit	Tape Dubbing	190.00	
2/14	Debit	Computer for Smith Report	1,000.00	
2/14	Debit	CAFP Subcontract-Schwartz	750.00	
2/14	Debit	Travel Expenses-Schwartz	60.50	
2/14	Debit	Traveler's Checks-CAFP	1,010.00	
2/14	Debit	CAFP Travel-Flores	2,031.59	
2/17	Debit	Sandwiches-CAFP meeting	60.80	
2/18	Debit	Tape Dubs-Smith	249.00	
2/18	Debit	FEDEX	84.00	
2/18	Debit	Supplies for Speaker Program	1,139.67	
2/18	Debit	TELEX	95.18	
2/18	Debit	Couriers	362.40	
2/18	Debit	Copying	1,265.29	
2/18	Debit	Travel-CAFP	2,701.11	
2/18	Debit	TV/Market Guide	60.00	
2/18	Debit	Reimb. CAFP Expenses	126.88	
2/18	Debit	Postage	176.00	
2/18	Debit	PR Aids-Press Release	1,100.00	
2/19	Debit	Radio/TV Monitoring	127.20	
2/19	Debit	Traveler's Checks-CAFP	1,010.00	
2/19	Debit	Travel Expenses	72.00	
2/19	Debit	Tape Recorders	347.15	
3/4	Debit	Wesley Smith Expenses	1,254.34	
3/4	Deposit	NEPL		28,750.00
3/3	Deposit	NEPL		7,000.00
3/6	Debit	NDC-Donation	25,000.00	
3/7	Debit	LASSI-Briefing Book	25,000.00	
3/7	Deposit	NEPL		65,000.00
3/7	Deposit	CAFP-Traveler's Checks		1,100.00
3/8	Debit	CAFP Exps-Schwartz	505.00	
3/10	Debit	Traveler checks-CAFP	505.00	
3/11	Debit	Traveler checks-CAFP	141.35	
3/11	Debit	Travel Reimb.-CAFP	6,740.69	
3/11	Debit	Photo's-Wesley Smith	23.10	
3/12	Debit	Traveler checks-CAFP	808.00	
3/12	Debit	Translations-Smith Report	2,028.00	

DATE	ITEM	DESCRIPTION	DEBIT AMOUNT	DEPOSIT AMOUNT
3/12	Debit	Smith Report Printing	1,580.78	
3/14	Debit	Postage	110.00	
3/14	Debit	Traveler checks-CAFP	808.00	
3/14	Debit	Traveler checks-CAFP	505.00	
3/10	Debit	Furniture for Office	2,544.10	
3/14	Debit	CAFP Subcontractor-Schwartz	2,100.00	
3/17	Debit	KMOL-TV Tape	52.81	
3/17	Deposit	NEPL		263,000.00
3/17	Debit	WCJB Tape	50.00	
3/19	Debit	Printing	1,625.47	
3/20	Debit	Traveler checks-CAFP	1,010.00	
3/21	Debit	Expenses-CAFP Speaker	200.00	
3/21	Debit	Travel-CAFP	4,590.00	
3/21	Debit	CAFP Subcontract-Semilla	1,714.34	
3/21	Debit	Expense Reimb.-Smith	1,437.72	
3/21	Debit	Videotape Production Crew	6,206.85	
3/24	Debit	Office Rent	4,500.00	
3/24	Debit	Computer Rental-Smith	270.06	
3/24	Debit	Traveler checks-CAFP	404.00	
3/25	Debit	UPS	7.49	
3/25	Debit	Subcontractor-Smith	2,520.00	
3/26	Debit	Smith News Conference Room Rental	399.74	
3/26	Debit	Audio Dubbing	25.00	
3/28	Debit	CAFP Subcontractor-Castellanos	1,500.00	
3/28	Debit	CAFP Subcontractor-Schwartz	1,650.00	
3/26	Deposit	NEPL		724,990.00
3/26	Debit	CAFP Bills-AMEX	8,838.96	
3/31	Debit	Press Conference Releases	43.64	
4/1	Debit	CAFP-Videotape Dubs	132.50	
4/1	Debit	WCLF-TV Videotape	56.25	
4/1	Debit	Maps-SDI	21.09	
4/2	Debit	Smith Expenses	1,312.84	
4/2	Debit	Smith UPS	10.81	
4/2	Debit	Smith Report Supplies	2,385.15	
4/7	Debit	Couriers	1,772.15	
4/7	Debit	FEDEX	40.00	
4/7	Debit	FEDEX	13,678.50	
4/7	Debit	Telephone	535.00	

DATE	ITEM	DESCRIPTION	DEBIT AMOUNT	DEPOSIT AMOUNT
4/7	Debit	IRD-Speaker CAFP	800.00	
4/8	Debit	Bumper Stickers	1,953.00	
4/9	Debit	Telephone	4,885.30	
4/9	Debit	Freinds of Freedom -I.C. Inc.	740,000.00	
4/8	Debit	Translator CAFP	1,799.00	
4/14	Deposit	NEPL		100,650.00
4/14	Debit	Cong. Quarterly Maps	42.18	
4/15	Debit	CAFP Subcontractor-Castellanos	196.00	
4/16	Debit	Congressional Direct.	26.00	
4/18	Debit	Printing-CAFP	216.00	
4/18	Debit	Telephone	1,934.31	
4/18	Deposit	NEPL		29,977.00
4/21	Deposit	NEPL		170,000.00
4/21	Debit	Flores Expenses-CAFP	83.09	
4/21	Debit	Telephone	800.00	
4/21	Debit	AMEX	42,960.00	
4/18	Debit	Telephone	966.09	
4/21	Debit	Photographer	305.00	
4/21	Debit	CAFP Expen.-Castellanos	301.19	
4/28	Debit	Postage	110.00	
5/5	Debit	Tape Stock	280.37	
5/2	Debit	National Review Reprint	1.00	
5/5	Debit	Congressional Record	218.00	
5/5	Debit	Photo Reproduction	222.87	
5/7	Debit	NEPL Printing	447.56	
5/5	Debit	U.S. Documents	5.00	
5/8	Deposit	NEPL		1,250,000.00
5/8	Debit	ACYPL Dinner	1,000.00	
5/9	Debit	Postage	16.41	
5/14	Debit	Nightline Transcript	2.00	
5/14	Debit	Friends of Freedom -I.C. Inc.	1,250,000.00	
5/15	Debit	Supplies	805.66	
5/15	Debit	Copying	398.60	
5/15	Debit	NPC Room Rental	355.86	
5/15	Debit	Interpass	1,100.00	
5/15	Debit	WETA Tapes	25.00	
5/15	Debit	WETA Transcripts	130.00	
5/15	Debit	Translations	2,300.00	
5/15	Debit	Couriers	1,487.57	
5/15	Debit	SDI Brochure Design	2,019.57	
5/15	Debit	Videotape Dub	25.00	
5/15	Debit	WTLV Tape	100.00	
5/16	Debit	Expenses-CAFP	5.10	
5/21	Debit	Postage	110.00	
5/23	Debit	AMEX	11,585.66	
5/29	Debit	Couriers	235.25	
5/29	Debit	Telephone	1,312.53	
6/1	Debit	Audio tape Dub	40.00	
6/3	Debit	Maps-CAFP	5.30	

DATE	ITEM	DESCRIPTION	DEBIT AMOUNT	DEPOSIT AMOUNT
6/3	Debit	Video Production	761.00	
6/9	Debit	Portfolios-CAFP	74.40	
6/11	Debit	SDI Briefing Books	669.04	
6/13	Debit	Copying	2,022.29	
6/13	Debit	NEPL Maps	39.08	
6/16	Debit	NEPL Maps	150.00	
6/16	Deposit	NEPL		72,929.00
6/19	Debit	AMEX	4,799.12	
6/19	Debit	Telephone	1,137.26	
6/19	Debit	Couriers	248.00	
6/19	Debit	Photography	414.00	
6/19	Debit	Radio/TV Monitoring	442.66	
6/19	Debit	Supplies	965.53	
6/19	Debit	Nova Tapes	4.00	
6/19	Debit	FEDEX	1,580.50	
6/19	Debit	FEDEX	574.85	
6/19	Debit	FARA Registrations	2.40	
6/19	Debit	NEPL Maps	150.00	
6/23	Debit	National Journal	93.28	
6/23	Debit	Eason Associates-SDI Brochure	12,000.00	
6/27	Debit	NEPL Tape Dubs	40.00	
6/27	Debit	NEPL Tape Dubs	175.00	
7/1	Debit	Postage	110.00	
7/10	Debit	Translations	697.00	
7/10	Debit	Couriers	272.25	
7/10	Debit	Telephone	306.47	
7/10	Debit	FEDEX	333.25	
7/10	Debit	Supplies	813.67	
7/10	Debit	Photography	58.30	
7/10	Debit	Lion Recording	11.13	
7/10	Debit	Smith final Expenses	600.00	
7/16	Debit	Forbes Reprint	6.50	
7/17	Deposit	NEPL		46,193.00
7/21	Debit	Travel-CAFP	3,000.00	
7/21	Debit	Traveler Checks-CAFP	606.00	
7/24	Debit	Traveler Checks-CAFP	1,111.00	
7/24	Debit	Flores Expenses	51.13	
7/24	Debit	FEDEX	255.75	
7/24	Debit	Graphics-SDI	212.00	
7/24	Debit	Printing	126.66	
7/24	Debit	Radio/TV Monitoring	152.64	
7/24	Debit	TV Production	566.04	
7/24	Debit	AMEX	5,036.85	
7/24	Debit	Telephone	200.00	
7/24	Debit	FEDEX	21.50	
7/29	Debit	Catterton Printing	315.50	
7/31	Debit	NEPL Expenses	42.10	
7/31	Deposit	NEPL		6,100.00
8/4	Debit	SDI Graphics	2,500.00	

DATE	ITEM	DESCRIPTION	DEBIT AMOUNT	DEPOSIT AMOUNT
8/12	Debit	Recording Services	126.60	
8/12	Debit	Expenses-CAFP	40.44	
8/18	Deposit	NEPL-SDI		14,000.00
8/18	Debit	SDI Subcontractors	5,000.00	
8/21	Debit	Couriers	234.50	
8/21	Debit	Telephones	200.00	
8/21	Debit	Nexis Searches	2,847.10	
9/15	Debit	Wesley Smith Final Expenses	296.70	
9/15	Debit	AMEX	15,062.01	
9/18	Debit	Cagle and Associates-NEPL-SDI	2,403.33	
9/18	Debit	Couriers	533.75	
10/9	Debit	Couriers	272.25	
10/14	Deposit	NEPL		20,000.00
10/22	Debit	AMEX	41,768.13	
10/22	Deposit	NEPL		7,652.95
10/30	Debit	SDI-Writer Subcontract	7,600.00	
10/30	Debit	NEPL-SDI Supplies	119.85	
10/30	Debit	NEPL-SDI News Conference	597.57	
10/30	Debit	NEPL-SDI Defense News	65.00	
10/30	Debit	Radio/TV Monitoring	322.74	
10/30	Debit	Photos-NEPL	159.00	
10/30	Debit	NEPL-Tape Dubs	164.30	
10/30	Debit	NEPL Books	50.00	
10/30	Debit	FEDEX	1,263.00	
10/30	Debit	FEDEX	266.00	
10/30	Debit	FEDEX	171.75	
10/30	Debit	Copying	652.41	
10/30	Debit	Guillen Expenses	17.60	
10/30	Debit	TELEX	229.24	
10/30	Debit	Lawyer Fees	12,658.62	
10/30	Debit	Nexis	1,293.67	
11/3	Debit	Bank Luemi	10,000.00	

Total Debits   2,780,787.43

Total Deposits   3,433,098.79

THE COMPANIES LAW

Company Limited by Shares

MEMORANDUM OF ASSOCIATION

OF

I.C. INC.

1. The name of the Company is "I.C. INC."

2. The Registered Office of the Company will be situate at the offices of Cayhaven Corporate Services Limited, Swiss Bank Building, Fort Street, George Town, P.O. Box 1043, Grand Cayman, Cayman Islands, British West Indies.

3. The objects for which the Company is established are:

    (i) To distribute any benevolent contributions made by foundations, private organisations and individuals to other worthy benevolent organisations and political entities representing such organisations.

    (ii) To acquire any shares, stocks, debentures, debenture stock, bonds, mortgages, notes, bankers' acceptances, obligations and other securities issued by any company, corporation or undertaking of whatever nature and wheresoever constituted or issued or guaranteed by any government, sovereign ruler, commissionners, trust authority or other body of whatever nature, by original subscription, syndicate participation, tender purchase, exchange or otherwise and to subscribe for the same either conditionally or otherwise and to guarantee the subscription thereof.

    (iii) To buy, sell and deal in all commodities and commodity futures, including silver and to buy sell and deal in bullion and specie, to receive money and valuables for safe custody or otherwise other than on deposit repayable by cheque or order, to collect and transmit money and securities, to grant and issue letters of credit, circular notes and to manage and advise on the management of securities and investments.

    (iv) To carry on business as capitalists, financiers, concessionaires, brokers and merchants and to undertake and carry on and execute all kinds of financial, commercial and trading operations, except banking and trust operations, and to

- 2 -

carry on any other business which may seem to be capable of
being conveniently carried on in connection with any of these
objects or calculated directly or indirectly to enhance the
value of, facilitate the realisation of, or render profitable
any of the Company's property or rights.

(v)   To provide or procure management, including the management of
investments and other property, administrative, sales and
technical assistance, service and advice on a contract, loan,
secondment, employment or other basis and to provide consultants
staff and employees who will give management, administrative,
sales, marketing and technical assistance, service and advice to
any person or company anywhere in the world on any matter or any
type of business whatsoever and to act as managers, registrars,
administrators, secretaries, auditors, accountants of bodies
corporate or unincorporate in any part of the world, for the
Company's account or for third parties.

(vi)   To buy, sell, deal in, trade, transact, lease, hold, improve,
sub-divide, or develop real estate, and the fixtures and
personal property incidental thereto or connected therewith and
to acquire by purchase, lease, hire or otherwise, lands and all
forms of buildings or constructions or any interest therein and
to improve the same generally to hold, manage, deal with and
improve the property of the Company, and to sell, lease,
mortgage, pledge or otherwise dispose of the lands, buildings
and constructions or other property of the Company.

(vii)   To carry on the business of farming in all its branches,
including without prejudice to the foregoing generality arable
and fruit farmers, dairy and poultry farmers, live stock
breeders of every variety of animal whether bred of pedigree
stock or otherwise, and also fishermen.

(viii)   To contract for public or private loans and to negotiate,
underwrite and issue the same; without prejudice to the
foregoing generality with reference to commodity, commodity
futures, or foreign exchange contracts to enter into conditional
or forward contracts for the acquisition or disposal of any such
assets.

Original submission did not include pages 3 through 7.

- 8 -

(xxx) To do all such things as may be considered to be incidental or

conducive to the above objects or any of them.

AND IT IS HEREBY DECLARED that the objects of the Company as

specified in each of the foregoing paragraphs of this clause (except

only in so far as otherwise expressed in any such paragraph) shall be

separate, distinct and independent objects of the Company and shall

not be in anywise limited by reference to or inference from any other

paragraph or the order in which the same shall occur or the name of

the Company.

AND IT IS FURTHER HEREBY DECLARED that the Company will not trade in

the Cayman Islands with any person, firm or corporation except in

furtherance of the business of the Company carried on outside the

Islands; Provided that nothing in this section shall be construed as

to prevent the Company effecting and concluding contracts in the

Islands, and exercising in the Islands all of its powers necessary

for the carrying on of its business outside the Islands.

4. The liability of the members is limited.

5. The capital of the Company is US$900,000.00 divided into 900,000

shares of a nominal or par value of US$1.00 each provided always that

subject to the provisions of the Companies Law, Cap. 22 as amended

and the Articles of Association the Company shall have power to

redeem any or all of such shares and to sub-divide or consolidate the

said shares or any of them and to issue all or any part of its

capital whether original, redeemed, increased or reduced with or

without any preference, priority or special privilege or subject to

any postponement of rights or to any conditions or restrictions

whatsoever and so that unless the conditions of issue shall otherwise

expressly provide every issue of shares whether stated to be

Ordinary, Preference or otherwise shall be subject to the powers on

the part of the Company hereinbefore provided.

Certified to be a true and correct copy

SIG......................................
       WOODWARD L. TERRY
DATE... 16.5.86 ....

- 9 -

We, the several persons whose names, addresses and descriptions are

subscribed are desirous of being formed into a Company in pursuance of

this Memorandum of Association, and we respectively agree to take the

number of shares in the capital of the Company set opposite our respective

names.

NAMES, ADDRESSES AND DESCRIPTIONS OF SUBSCRIBERS	NUMBER OF SHARES TAKEN BY EACH SUBSCRIBER
CAYHAVEN CORPORATE SERVICES LIMITED P.O.Box 1043, George Town, Grand Cayman Per: (Sgd.) David G. Bird David G. Bird - Director	One Share
DAVID G. BIRD P.O.Box 265, George Town, Grand Cayman (Sgd.) David G. Bird Attorney-at-Law	One Share
ALASTAIR J.N. LOUDON P.O.Box 265, George Town, Grand Cayman (Sgd.) Alastair J.N. Loudon Attorney-at-Law	One Share

Dated April 25, 1985

(Sgd.) C. KIPLING
Witness to the above signatures:Christiane Kipling

Address: P.O.Box 265, Grand Cayman

Occupation: Secretary

I,   DELANO O. SOLOMON
Registrar of Companies in and for the Cayman Islands DO HEREBY CERTIFY
that this is a true copy of the Memorandum of Association of "I.C. INC.".

Dated this   26th day of APRIL 1985

CERTIFIED SPECIAL RESOLUTIONS OF THE SHAREHOLDERS

OF

I.C. INC.

"RESOLVED that the amended Memorandum of Association be and is hereby adopted in place of and to the entire exclusion of the existing Memorandum of Association."

"RESOLVED that the name of the Company be changed to INTEL CO-OPERATION INC."

WE HEREBY CERTIFY THAT THE ABOVE ARE TRUE COPIES OF RESOLUTIONS OF THE SHARE-HOLDERS OF THE COMPANY WHICH WERE ADOPTED ON 9TH MAY, 1986.

CAYHAVEN CORPORATE SERVICES LIMITED

Per:...............................
Secretary

13th May, 1986

and transmit money and securities, to grant and issue ——————

INTEL CO-OPERATION INC.

Schedule of Receipts

**April 25, 1985 (date of incorporation)
to December 31, 1985:**

Sept. 27, 1985	I.B.C.	100,000.00
Oct. 29. 1985	I.B.C.	250,000.00
Nov. 13, 1985	I.B.C.	80,000.00
Nov. 13, 1985	I.B.C.	40,000.00
Nov. 27, 1985	Bank.draft - Continental Bank	5,000.00
		475,000.00

**January 1, 1986
to December 31, 1986:**

Jan. 1, 1986	I.B.C.	360,000.00
Apr. 4, 1986	I.B.C.	740,000.00
May 15, 1986	I.B.C.	1,250,000.00
Aug. 7, 1986	Nat. Endowment for Preservation Liberty	100,000.00
Oct. 2, 1986	Nat. Endowment for Preservation Liberty	200,000.00
Oct. 8, 1986	Nat. Endowment for Preservation Liberty	100,000.00
Oct. 21, 1986	Nat. Endowment for Preservation Liberty	50,000.00
		2,800,000.00

INTEL CO-OPERATION INC.

Schedule of Distributions

April 25, 1985 (date of incorporation)
to December 31, 1985:

Oct. 8, 1985	Lake Resources Inc.	100,000.00
Nov. 1, 1985	Lake Resources Inc.	150,000.00
Nov. 1, 1985	Alpha Services S.A.	100,000.00
Nov. 14, 1985	Lake Resources Inc.	48,000.00
		398,000.00

January 1, 1986
to December 31, 1986:

Jan. 2, 1986	Barclays Bank, Miami	40,000.00
Jan. 21, 1986	Barclays Bank, Miami	20,000.00
Jan. 21, 1986	Lake Resources Inc.	360,000.00
March 17, 1986	Riggs Nat. Bank - Katyal	15,000.00
Apr. 11, 1986	Lake Resources Inc.	650,000.00
Apr. 21, 1986	Gulf & Caribbean Foundation	14,254.00
May 5, 1986	1st American Bank - Carlos Ulet	10,000.00
May 9, 1987	Barclays Bank, Miami, Denise Ponce	11,000.00
May 14, 1986	World Affairs Counselors Inc. (WACI)	10,000.00
May 16, 1986	WACI ...	125,000.00
June 4, 1986	Alpha Services	15,000.00
June 13, 1986	Barclays Bank, Miami	500,000.00
June 13, 1986	Bank Leumi - F. Arguello	7,000.00
June 13, 1986	Latin American Strategic Studios Institute	5,000.00
June 13, 1986	Institute on Terrorism & Subnational Conflict	75,000.00
June 13, 1986	Intercontinental Bank, Miami	10,000.00
July 3, 1986	Friends of the Americas	125,000.00
July 14, 1986	WACI ...	38,000.00
July 28, 1986	Bank Leumi	7,000.00
July 28, 1986	Latin American Financial Services	55,700.00
July 28, 1986	Latin American Strategic Studies Institute	5,000.00
July 28, 1986	Barclays Bank, Miami	10,000.00
July 28, 1986	Gulf & Caribbean Foundation	6,928.00
July 29, 1986	WACI ...	10,000.00
	Carried forward	2,124,882.00

		Brought forward . 2,124,882.00
August 29, 1986	WACI	10,000.00
Sept. 19, 1986	Latin American Strategic Studies Institute	20,000.00
Sept. 19, 1986	Bank Leumi – Fredrick Arguello	7,000.00
Sept. 19, 1986	Latin American Strategic Studies Institute	5,000.00
Sept. 26, 1986	Alpha Services S.A.	100,000.00
Oct. 2, 1986	Alpha Services S.A.	150,000.00
Oct. 2, 1986	WACI	20,000.00
Oct. 7, 1986	WACI	49,000.00
Oct. 8, 1986	WACI	10,000.00
Oct. 21, 1986	WACI	5,000.00
Oct. 21, 1986	Bank Leumi – Frederick Arguello	10,000.00
Oct. 21, 1986	Agro Bank – Polca S.A.	25,000.00
Nov. 12, 1986	WACI	10,000.00
Nov. 12, 1986	Latin American Strategic Studies Institute	5,000.00
Nov. 26, 1986	WACI	65,000.00
Nov. 26, 1986	Alpha Services S.A.	75,000.00
Dec. 18, 1986	WACI	100,000.00
Dec. 18, 1986	Latin American Strategic Studies Institute	10,000.00
		2,800,882.00

NATIONAL ENDOWMENT
FOR THE
PRESERVATION OF LIBERTY

August 1, 1985

305 FOURTH ST., N.E.
SUITE 1000
WASHINGTON, D.C. 20002

Mr. Richard R. Miller
President
International Business Communications
1523 New Hampshire Ave., NW
Washington, D.C. 20009

Dear Mr. Miller:

This letter is a formal retainer agreement between International
Business Communications and the National Endowment for the
Preservation of Liberty. While we have engaged I.B.C. for work on
programs of the Endowment and the political action committee, The
American Conservative Trust, at a fluctuating monthly fee we would
like to undertake a more formal arrangment.

The present agreement made verbally by you, me and Daniel L. Conrad,
NEPL Executive Director, called for a monthly retainer of fifteen
thousand dollars plus expenses. This agreement was made before the
proliferation of our public education and political programs. With
this in mind we agree to begin paying I.B.C. a monthly retainer of
forty thousand dollars and we understand that I.B.C. reserves the
right to increase the charges to the Endowment to meet increases in
costs such as personnel and operating expenses. At the time of
billing and throughout the month I.B.C. will try to apprise us of
potential extraodinary costs.

As you spend money collected from us to pay for programs you manage
for us we will meet occassionally to discuss immediate and near-future
expense needs. Since our programs are fast developing and can take on
urgency not normally encountered in the public relations field, we
understand that you may make occassional demands for cash deposits to
cover major expenditures.

For the next few months you should be reviewing the cost of this
arrangment to International Business Communications. Should we
determine that these agreed upon operating standards do not work, we
reserve the right to renegotiate the retainer arrangement. You will
provide Mr. Conrad with written or oral cost analysis at the time of
submission of your expenses and time and billing records.

If this agreement is acceptable please countersign this letter and
return it to us.

Sincerely,

Carl Russell Channell
President

Richard R. Miller
President

January 20, 1986

Mr. Carl Russell Channell
President
National Endowment for the
   Preservation of Liberty
305 fourth Street, N.E.
Washington, D.C. 20002

Dear Mr. Channell;

Thank you for including me in your winter meeting in Palm Beach,
Florida this month. The chance to help plan the execution of
programs by the National Endowment for the Preservation of
Liberty, the American Conservative Trust were very useful in
planning the I.B.C. level of effort needed to carry out our
responsibilities to you.

The agenda of the Endowment and its related organizations is very
ambitious and will take an extraordinary amount of talent,
manpower and creative effort. I.B.C. is prepared to undertake
this effort. We will however need to revamp our financial
arrangments with you.

Here-to-date we have concentrated on the Nicaraguan public
education effort and special programs designed to support the
President in obtaining his goals in Central America. Now we are
to undetake a manmouth program to educate the American Public,
senior government officials and influencial Americans. This
program will require major outlays of personnel and will require
in and of itself the use of several senior level consultants.
The monthly fees for this program alone will be forty thousand
dollars plus expenses.

In your outline of the the 1986 programs, you have also directed
that I.B.C. design and implement a program to promote the
public's support of President Reagan's Strategic Defense
Initiative. This program will require the development of a major
briefing book for policymakers and SDI champions, the direction
of a speakers tour and consultation with your advertising
agencies on advertising campaigns. This effort will be
undertaken for a monthly fee of twenty thousand dollars and
expenses. I.B.C. will be responsible for all additional
consultant fees necessary to run this program.

The third program that you have asked us to consider working on
are the Future of Freedom Seminar Series. These programs would
undertaken by The American Conservative Trust and funded funded

1

by contributors under an arrangment to be designated by you at a later time. However, we will incur expenses in the development of these programs and may need additional consultants and consulting organizations to be involved in the effort. Such additional consultants will be your financial responsibility through reimbursement to us. We will not undertake such efforts without your verbal approval.

Your terrorism film and conference ideas are not yet assigned to I.B.C. but we understand that may change at a later date.

Also, we understand that your Constitutional Minutes Project may also be assigned to us as a 1986 program but that formal agreement on this will wait until a later date.

Finally, one aspect of our financial arrangments needs to be clarified going into this year. We are not in a position to know the final purpose and use of all the services you request of us. As the "TO-DO" list reaches thirty and forty items at a given time, we simply execute the tasks you assign us as we can. In this operational mode it is impossible for us to independently bill your various organizations for specific work hours. Therefore it will be your responsibility to internally identify the end user of our billed services. We trust that this is an area that you and your lawyers are quite capable of handling yourselves.

The impact of your efforts on behalf of the President have been major and unique. We look forward to serving you in your efforts in 1986.

If this letter represents your understanding of our relationship, please countersign to letter and return it to me.

Sincerely,

Richard R. Miller
President
I.B.C.

Carl Russell Channell
President
NEPL

CENTRAL AMERICAN

FREEDOM PROGRAM

CENTRAL AMERICAN FREEDOM PROGRAM

Introduction

1986 is destined to be a landmark year in the advancement of freedom throughout the world. After a generation of increasing tyranny and authoritarianism, the winds of change are rising. These winds are carrying freedom movements on four continents toward a victory over communist domination.

And Ronald Reagan, leading a rejuvenated America, has caught these winds of change. He is dramatically aligning American policy, resources, and moral support with the force of that gathering storm.

President Reagan's policy, when fully developed, is destined to trigger the overthrow of communist tyranny. This will happen around the world, in Afghanistan, Angola, Mozambique, Kampuchea and, most important, Nicaragua.

America's relationship with communist Nicaragua experienced an absolute moral and political reversal when Ronald Reagan became President of the United States.

The Carter Administration, like millions of Nicaraguans, had been fooled by the communists who captured the leadership of the anti-Somoza revolution in 1979. Once in power, the communist junta began systematically lying to the world about the true policies and purposes of their revolutionary government.

But Ronald Reagan was not fooled. So, moved by new leadership, American policy toward Nicaragua's communist government changed sharply in 1981. Then the U.S. declared support for the Nicaraguan Freedom Fighters.

Since 1981, opposition to the communist-controlled Nicaraguan regime has gradually become a very powerful internal democratic movement. It claims the support of over 25,000 well armed Nicaraguans and literally hundreds of thousands of ordinary Nicaraguans. Nearly 400,000 (one out of every six Nicaraguans) lives under Freedom Fighter protection.

The democratic forces have endured years of conflict with a communist army easily six times their number. More remarkably, they have steadily increased their ranks in the midst of the struggle. These democratic forces continued to gain strength even during the year and a half that United States aid was suspended.

1986 finds the democratic forces stronger than ever. But so is their communist enemy. Ronald Reagan has offered decisive assistance to the democratic forces. And, if this assistance is fully endorsed by the Congress, it could, in fact, carry them to victory over communism in Nicaragua this year.

When victory occurs, it will have historic and political significance throughout the Western Hemisphere. Its impact will be felt by every Freedom Fighter in the world. Its possibility will haunt every communist dictator.

Finally, Ronald Reagan's actions will herald a new dynamic American policy. It is a policy of materially supporting freedom movements struggling to overthrow communist regimes. Freedom is on the offensive.

Description of the Problem

If Ronald Reagan is to succeed in meeting the needs of Freedom Fighter movements for years to come, it will be necessary to create a deep reservoir of public support for Freedom Fighters and the President's policy.

Such public support will come only if the American people truly understand the stakes and the opportunities the Reagan policies embody.

The memories of Vietnam, however inapplicable, remain fresh, as does the urge to have America fight for clearly recognizable just causes. So President Reagan, if he is to be successful, must carry into this foreign policy arena the unified support of the American people.

In spite of the headlines and the debates during the last five years, the American public remains woefully ignorant about Nicaragua. They don't understand the clear threat it poses to vital American security interests.

A 1985 public opinion poll showed more than one-third of those surveyed did not know which side the United States supports. Twenty percent thought we support the (communist) government!

A later poll found that among those aware of U.S. policy, 58% said we should not be giving aid to the Democratic Opposition.

It is tragic, but not surprising that so many people are ill-informed, and that so many oppose our policies. It's not surprising because the American public is the victim of an intense, sophisticated multi-million dollar disinformation campaign. It is being conducted by opponents of the President.

The Sandinistas abuse the freedoms in the U.S. that they deny to their own people. They do this by hiring a Washington law firm and two public relations firms under contract to spread disinformation.

They are aided by the Soviet Union and Cuba. The Soviets and Cubans already spend tens of millions of dollars to shape public policy in America. Their actions are supported by a vast network of communist and leftist activist sympathizers. Soviet spokesmen regularly seek tv time. Phil Donahue gave Nicaraguan dictator Ortega an hour in October.

These people operate at the grass-roots level and in Washington. They use the media and all the tools at their disposal to undermine the policies of our elected government.

This is why President Reagan needs the support and cooperation of clear-thinking, patriotic Americans. We must counter the disinformation program of the Sandinistas. We must educate the public on the policies, the players, the dangers and the realities.

The National Endowment for the Preservation of Liberty is helping the President do just that.

Solution

The National Endowment for the Preservation of Liberty has undertaken a nationwide program of indefinite duration known as the CENTRAL AMERICAN FREEDOM PROGRAM.

The overriding goal of this program is to educate the American people. It will show the realities of communism in Nicaragua. It will show the threat to U.S. national security.

We have chosen television as the major vehicle. We believe it is the most successful to carry our educational and informative messages to the public.

The CENTRAL AMERICAN FREEDOM PROGRAM will require the National Endowment for the Preservation of Liberty to spend $2,000,000 in the next 90 days.

This is over $160,000 every week for public education and information on the issue of Nicaragua. A longer, $3 million program is under consideration and will be implemented if required to fully educate the American public.

When our program achieves its public awareness goals, it will become a useful model for similar activities by other in the future. Our program is truly unique. It has become the pioneering effort in this area.

Central American Freedom Program
==

The National Endowment for the Preservation of
Liberty is focusing its education program on seven
issues. They are:

1) Nicaraguan communist persecution of
   its citizens;

2) Denial of religious and political
   rights;

3) The creation of an aggressive armed
   Soviet satellite on the North American
   continent;

4) The creation of Cuban bases inside
   Nicaragua;

5) The threat Nicaragua now poses to its
   neighbors both through state terrorism
   and outright aggression;

6) Support for revolution in El Salvador;

7) Betrayal of the true anti-Somoza democratic
   revolution by the Nicaraguan communists.

The issues listed above represent the principal
points our programs will make in the minds of Americans.
We are also emphasizing other issues such as the origin,
nature, organization and objectives of the Freedom
Fighters.

We are developing the images of the UNO leadership.
We are graphically showing the situation facing over
400,000 Nicaraguan refugees. And we are presenting the
political and human rights goals of the Freedom Fighters
themselves.

Public Affairs Components

Central American Freedom Program

The Sandinistas have two public relations firms and two law firms either registered as foreign agents or working sub rosa in the United States.

They have a combined budget of $2 million. They are using this war chest to concentrate on the districts of Congressmen who have opposed aid to the Freedom Fighters.

They have also stepped up the use of Op-Eds and articles in national newspapers written by sympathetic Americans. They have planted disinformation, too, like the recent articles accusing the FDN of drug trafficking.

An ignorant and misinformed public is one of the principal objectives of the communists. They recognize that ignorance and apathy in local communities across America leaves the doors wide open to the opponents of Administration policy.

And given the activism of those opponents, they are the ones who are often visible to members of Congress. A legislator who only hears from the critics can ignore logic and danger. He can vote to deny U.S. assistance to those on the front lines in the battle against communism in our hemisphere. So, the public must be better informed.

The public is quite unaware of the true nature of the Sandinistas as well as the existence of a viable democratic alternative. They do not support efforts to overthrow any government and fear U.S. involvement in another Vietnam.

This ignorance and the isolation it produces have been the Sandinista's principal advantages in the debate. We intend to evaporate those advantages through the use of truth.

Objectives

As Congressional debate heats up on this issue, we should expect the Sandinistas, their foreign agents and liberal sympathizers to give it all they have.

We are in the last weeks of a national campaign to be decided by the American public. If the public remains apathetic, the President's democratic initiative will be defeated.

If we are successful, America will have a policy that
sounds the death knell of America's post-Vietnam feeling
of impotency.   It will end America's retreat from her
responsibilities as the leader of the free world.

To accomplish this, the National Endowment for the
Preservation of Liberty is addressing four audiences using
specifically targeted communications strategies:

The public - Through the use of strong negative
images of the Sandinistas recently reported in
the media.

Policymakers - Democratic leadership issues
provide the groundwork for more challenging arguments that
can influence liberals and moderates.

Congress - Through issues now associated with
America's leadership role in supporting democracy in the
region against the developing communist threat. NEPL, as
an educational organization, is not permitted to engage in
lobbying activities. Our co-sponsor, Sentinel, is
permitted to engage in lobbying activities and will
undertake the responsibility of bringing this important
issue to the attention of members of Congress.

Freedom Fighter Leadership - Without a sound
belief in the capabilities of the resistance's
leadership, no policy can succeed in Congress.

Program Elements

Time is short and we are fighting for public support
over a wide geographic area. So, we are treating this
like a national educational campaign, with March 15 as our
target.

We are using the methodology of national political
campaigns. We are seeking to emphasize the disturbing
truth about the communist control over Nicaragua. We
are debating the unclaimed issues to our advantage.
And we are reinforcing our positive public perceptions
to educate and inform.

We are using advertising and public affairs programs
for each of the four program objectives listed above.
They are being handled as follows:

The Public - The public has been exposed
recently to several negative images of the Sandinistas.
We use these images to reinforce the public perception
that the Sandinistas are communists and tyrannical
dictators. We employ the following techniques:

Television advertising - We have analyzed
Congressional action on the last aid package. Based
on this research, we are producing materials for

television spots which focus on:

1) Daniel Ortega's trip to Moscow and the
   $220 million commitment he received from
   the Soviets for offensive military weaponry.

2) The recent crackdown on human rights
   directed against the entire Nicaraguan
   population.

3) Ortega's purchase of $3,500 in designer
   eyeglasses while his people starve.

4) The communists militarization of Nicaragua
   through Soviet, Libyan, East German, Cuban
   and other advisors, and the use of Nicaragua
   as a command center for subversion of her
   democratic neighbors.

5) That Cubans are now proved to be actively
   involved in combat.

6) That Nicaragua has become a lair and a
   refuge.

7) The humiliation of Pope John II when he was
   spat upon and heckled when he tried to
   conduct Mass in Managua.

<u>Spokesman program</u> - using the prototype program
already underway, we are placing speakers in 50
markets between now and March 15, 1986.

These speakers are booked into a civic club or
professional organization in a market. Then
they are scheduled for television, radio and
newspaper interviews.

The speakers come from the ranks of the United
Nicaraguan Opposition (UNO) leadership. They can
defend all UNO participants.

They focus on Sandinista excesses and UNO as the
democratic alternative. The principal concentration
for these speakers are the southern and western
states.

Battlefield Videotape - Sandinista state security
agents rigidly control the movements of foreign
correspondents, especially television journalists in
or visiting Nicaragua. That control is exercised
through:

1) Escort "guides" and interpreters;

2) Denial of access to selected parts of the
   country;

3) Imposition of "taboo" themes;

4) Screening and censorship of footage for export;

5) Monitoring of telephones and telex;

6) Expulsion or denial of entry to any offenders.

At the same time, coverage from the northern border is extremely arduous and far from the areas where the Resistance is operating.

The result is timid, selective, highly censored and heavily biased television coverage. Battle zones are only presented from the Sandinista perspective.

We are providing major media outlets and local television stations with videotape from the field. It shows scenes never seen before in the U.S.

It includes combat footage and evidence of Sandinista atrocities. We are also providing footage and commentary on events inside Managua and other major population centers.

This footage will be used in three ways:

1) An experienced advertising agency is producing advertising for distribution in as many as 50 selected markets across the United States.

2) A satellite feed will be edited and fed each time new footage is obtained. These feeds will reach approximately 200 television stations in the U.S. Usage reports will be received daily.

3) A new documentary on the face of communism in Nicaragua and the use of internal repression will be produced. This theme will be countered with a segment showing the Freedom Fighters as the logical outgrowth of Sandinista tyranny.

Policymakers

Given the compressed time frame, policymakers can be best reached through an effort that is visible in Washington and the national media. The issues used to reach Congress should be centered on America's leadership responsibilities in this hemisphere.

The primary effort is focused in specially selected areas of the country, but we are reinforcing this effort with a public affairs and education program including:

A. Articles and Op-Eds written by prominent American leaders on Nicaragua as a center of terrorism. We will use recent revelations of Nicaraguan arms being used in the Colombian Supreme Court assaults.

We will cite evidence of Libyan, PLO and Iranian

terrorists working in Nicaragua. From these facts, we will produce articles for paid distribution, single placement in national newspapers and general media distribution.

B. Religious persecution of all faiths can be used to touch and educate the public, producing a positive effect on the policymakers.

Jewish, Catholic and Protestant organization publications are being approached to interview defectors and religious figures who know the persecution firsthand.

The National Endowment for the Preservation of Liberty is arranging a series of meetings with religious leaders and journalists. We will also help to produce an article by a prominent American religious figure for paid distribution.

C. Another Cuba on the North American Continent is unacceptable to almost all Americans. If the issue is picked up by constituents it would be a strong message for policymakers.

The National Endowment for the Preservation of Liberty is utilizing these arguments in the speakers program already underway. An American exiled Cuban has been commissioned to write an article for paid distribution throughout the U.S.

A Cuban exile leader has been added to the spokesman program.

D. Drugs and politics are a bad mix. Nicaragua's support for and role in narcotics trafficking are issues with which no one can publicly disagree.

We will ask Don Johnson of MIAMI VICE, or a strong anti-drug figure such as Rosie Greer, to give a briefing on the drug trafficking evidence the Administration has on the Sandinistas.

He will be asked to write an Op-Ed piece for national distribution through paid and direct placements.

The National Endowment for the Preservation of Liberty would seek to get this super-spokesman on major television shows such as TODAY and GOOD MORNING AMERICA.

We would also produce a news spot for satellite distribution.

E. The Sandinistas are violating human rights at an unprecedented level in this hemisphere.

The National Endowment for the Preservation of
Liberty is providing radio, television and
newspaper interviews with two researchers who
have compiled a report on Sandinista human rights
violations.

They are being commissioned to do an update on
their report with a trip to Honduras and Costa
Rica. On their return they will hold a
Washington news conference and issue a report to
Congress through a respected Senator or
Congressman.

F.   The Revolution of 1979 has been betrayed by the
     Sandinistas. The National Endowment for the
     Preservation of Liberty will produce a news spot
     for satellite distribution on the lives of three
     former Sandinistas who now fight with the
     FDN/UNO.

Congress

We expect to reach Congress primarily through the
media we will be using for the policymakers. However, special
briefings will also be used to educate specific target
audiences within this group.

These briefings will be arranged by our co-sponsor,
Sentinel. Briefings may feature drug enforcement experts or
political scientists who have studied Cuban expansionism.

Freedom Fighter Leadership

The National Endowment for the Preservation of
Liberty has begun to provide spokesmen training for the
leadership and provide information feedback to reinforce
that training. We will provide UNO leaders with public
opinion analyses.

When possible, we are incorporating the UNO
leadership in events and briefings that further their
image of unity.

Conclusion

Without an opportunity to see the truth about the
Sandinistas, the American public will defeat democracy in
Nicaragua.

Through its public education program, the National
Endowment for the Preservation of Liberty will give the
President a chance to free this continent of communism.
We will strike a decisive blow for democracy.

CENTRAL AMERICAN FREEDOM PROGRAM BUDGET

1. Television field projects

   Personnel

   - field producer
   - camera man
   - sound man
   - correspondent

   Equipment

   - six cameras
   - sound package
   - editing machine
   - character generators

   Transportation

   - airfares
   - ground transportation
   - local travel

   Travel expenses

   - in-country expenses
   - U.S. travel for editing

   Studio time

   - in-country studio for editing
   - U.S. production facilities

   Tapes supplies

   - tape stock
   - battery packs
   - lights and reflectors

   ($60,000 per month for 5 months) $ 300,000

2. Marketing of field TV programs

   (5 projects at $24,000 per)   120,000

3. Speaking tour program

    Tour to include:
    - speaking engagements
    - editorial board meetings
    - television interviews
    - radio interviews
    - newspaper interviews
    - briefings for church, business,
      labor, political, and college
      organization leaders

    Costs for tours
      (January to March 15, 1986)

    Travel
        (7 weeks, 2 speakers,
         each week $8,700) $121,800

    Per diem for speakers
        ($220 per day, 5 days per
         trip, 7 weeks for 2
         speakers per week)   15,400

    Expenses
        (ground transportation, phones,
         tips, $800 per trip, for 14
         one week schedules)   11,200

                             SUBTOTAL   148,400

4. Supplementary services, including:
    - postage
    - telephones
    - telex
    - couriers
    - translations

        ($4,700 per month for 5 months)   27,750

5. Administration/Coordination, including:

    Professional staff:
    - 2 senior partners
    - 1 local coordinator
    - 1 Program Coordinator
    - 1 Senior Writer
    - 2 Account Executives
    - 1 Media Coordinator

    Verification of Placement
    - clipping retrieval
    - polling data assembling
    - monitoring network feedback

        ($53,500 for 2 months, January
         to March 15)   107,000

6.   Advertising and paid media

Television advertising:

Production of 4 TV messages	$ 80,000
D.C. media buys	225,000
Nationwide market buys	750,000
SUBTOTAL	1,055,000

7.   National Media Placement

- Network and syndicated TV and Radio
- National newspapers
- National periodicals

158,850

8.   Polling and research

- national
- local

83,000

GRAND TOTAL $2,000,000

"Big Bill"

Frank Hyman

Jensen

1986

(Jim Baker Show)
Edelman?
75 Ft Rich here advance team Bush

ACTION PLAN FOR 1986 PROGRAMS OF THE
AMERICAN CONSERVATIVE TRUST
AND
THE NATIONAL ENDOWMENT FOR THE PRESERVATION OF LIBERTY

Introduction - This action plan is divided into five specifically focused programs as directed by Mr. Channell. In each case the contractor and subcontractor designations are indicated. The programs are as follows:

FRIENDS OF FREEDOM PROGRAM - This program is an effort to directly support the President's initiatives in Central America and Nicaragua through political and educational institutions in the region. This program is based on direct grants to religious, political, academic and professional organizations in Latin and Central America.

CENTRAL AMERICAN FREEDOM PROGRAM - This program is an effort to educate the American public, policy makers and the media on the issues surrounding Nicaragua and the President's policy toward it. It incorporates a wide variety of public education tools including television productions, spokesmen tours, Op-Ed articles, commissioned journalistic documentaries and television advertising. The program goal is to establish a national consensus that will allow official American support for democracy as a policy.

SDI SUPPORT PROGRAM - This program is designed to support the President's Strategic Defense Initiative through a public education program. This program is based on the political assessment that the Soviets will seek to undermine the President and the national consensus he now enjoys on SDI. This issue will be focused in the Congress and media for the next 21 months, through two Congressional funding cycles, as the Soviets set up their misinformation program to combat SDI. The NEPL program is designed to provide strong public information programs in the national media, through televised messages, feature productions, and print advertising in the nationally read newspapers. The program will also provide media, academic and political organizations with speakers or guest journalist works to develop support for the President.

FUTURE OF FREEDOM SEMINAR SERIES - This program is a series of briefings for high level conservative activists on critical foreign policy, monetary and national issues. The ACT will seek to host a series of formal meetings with a senior government official to brief senior ACT and NEPL contributors on current critical issues dealing with the national security, international terrorism, regional conflict resolution, as well as international monetary policy, domestic spending and tax policy. For the most part these events will be quiet, private gatherings hosted by ACT and featuring a briefing by a senior member of the Administration.

TERRORISM: A US RESPONSE - This program is an educational effort directed towards increasing public awareness of the connection between terrorism against Western governments and Soviet political brinksmanship. This program will use television, print and periodical distributions to communicate the need for a national program to combat terrorism. It will focus public attention on the role of the Congress, the President and our allies in combatting terrorism.

For each program discussed, this action plan outlines the key issues addressed by the program, an evaluation of present circumstances, the program objectives and the program elements to reach those objectives. In each case the contractor and subcontractor relationships are indicated, as are the specific communications vehicles selected for use in achieving the program's objectives.

Central American Freedom Program

Introduction

1986 is destined to be a landmark year in the advancement of freedom throughout the world. After a generation of increasing tyranny and authoritarianism, the winds of change are rising. These winds are carrying freedom movements on four continents toward a victory over communist domination. And Ronald Reagan, leading a rejuvenating America, has caught these winds of change and is dramatically aligning American policy, resources, and moral support with the force of that gathering storm which is destined to overthrow communist tyranny in Afghanistan, Angola, Mozambique, Kampuchea and, most important, Nicaragua.

America's relationship with communist Nicaragua experienced an absolute moral and political reversal when Ronald Reagan became President of the United States.

The Carter Administration, like millions of Nicaraguans, had been fooled by the communists who captured the leadership of the anti-Somoza revolution in 1979. Once in power, the communist junta began systematically lying to the world about the true policies and purposes of their revolutionary government.

But Ronald Reagan was not fooled. So, moved by new leadership, American policy toward Nicaragua's communist government radically changed in 1981 and declared support for the Nicaraguan Freedom Fighters began.

Since 1981, opposition to the communist-controlled Nicaraguan government has gradually become a very powerful internal democratic movement. It claims the support of over 25,000 well armed Nicaraguans and literally hundreds of thousands of ordinary Nicaraguans. The democratic forces have not only endured years of conflict with a communist army easily six times their number, but have steadily increased their ranks in the midst of the struggle. These democratic forces continued to gain strength even during the year that United States aid was cut off.

1986 finds the democratic forces stronger than ever. But so is their communist enemy. Ronald Reagan, however, is preparing to offer decisive assistance to the democratic forces which, if fully endorsed by the Congress, could in fact carry to them to victory over communism in Nicaragua this year. When victory does in fact occur, it will have historic and political significance throughout the western Hemisphere. Its impact will be felt by every Freedom Fighter in the world. Its possibility will haunt every communist dictator. Finally, Ronald Reagan's actions will herald a new dynamic American policy of materially supporting freedom movements struggling to overthrow communist regimes.

Description of the Problem

If Ronald Reagan is to succeed in meeting the needs of the
Freedom Fighter movements for years to come, it will be necessary
to create a deep reservoir of support for the Freedom Fighters
and the President's policy.   Such public support will come only
if the American people truly understand the stakes and the
opportunities the Reagan policies embody.   The memories of
Vietnam, however inapplicable, remain fresh, as does the urge to
have America fight for clearly recognizable just causes.   So
President Reagan, if he is to be successful, must carry into this
foreign policy arena the unified support of the American people.

The National Endowment for the Preservation of Liberty is
helping the President do just that.

Solution

The National Endowment for the Preservation of Liberty has
undertaken a nationwide program of indefinite duration known as
The Central American Freedom Program.   The overriding goal of
this program is to educate the American people and political
elites about the nature of communism in Nicaragua and the threat
to U.S. national security.

We have chosen television as the major vehicle we believe
will be most successful in carrying our educational and
informative messages to the public.

The Central American Freedom Program will require the
National Endowment for the Preservation of Liberty to spend over
one million, four hundred thousand dollars in the next ninety
days.   This means allocation of over one hundred thousand dollars
every week for public education and information on the issue of
Nicaragua.

If our program achieves its public awareness goals, it will
become a useful model for similar activities by others in the
future.   Our program is truly unique.   It has become the
pioneering effort in this area.

Central American Freedom Program

The National Endowment for the Preservation of Liberty has
decided to focus its education program on seven issues.   They
are:

1) Nicaraguan communist persecution of its citizens;

2) Denial of religious and political rights;

3)   The creation of an aggressive armed Soviet satellite
     on the North American continent;

4)   The creation of Cuban bases inside Nicaragua;

5)   The threat Nicaragua now poses to its neighbors both
     through state terrorism and outright aggression;

6)   Support for revolution in El Salvador;

7)   Betrayal of the true anti-Somoza democratic
     revolution by the Nicaraguan communists.

     The issues listed above represent the points our programs
want to make in the minds of Americans. We will also discuss
other issues such as who the Freedom Fighters are.   We will
develop the images of the UNO leadership. We will graphically
show the situation facing over three hundred thousand Nicaraguan
refugees.   And we will discuss the political and human rights
goals of the freedom fighters themselves.

Public Affairs Components of Central American Freedom Program

The Sandinistas have two public relations firms and two law firms either registered as foreign agents or working subrosa in the United States. They have a combined budget of two million dollars and are concentrating on the districts of Congressmen who have opposed aid to the Freedom Fighters. They have also stepped up the use of Op-Eds and articles in national newspapers written by sympathetic Americans, as well as the planting of disinformation such as recent articles accusing the FDN of drug trafficking.

The public is quite unaware of the true nature of the Sandinistas as well as the existence of a viable democratic alternative. They do not support efforts to overthrow any government and fear U.S. involvement in another Vietnam. This ignorance and the isolationism it produces have been the Sandinista's principal advantages in the debate. We intend to evaporate those advantages through the use of truth.

Objectives

With the Congressional debate heating up on this issue, we should expect the Sandinistas, their foreign agents and liberal sympathizers to give it all they have. We are in the last weeks of a national campaign to be decided by the American public. If the public stays apathetic Congress will defeat the President's democratic initiative. If we are successful, America will have had, debated and changed, and then debated and changed back, a policy that sounds the death knell of America's post-Vietnam feeling of impotency *and retreat from world responsibilities.*

To accomplish this we must address four audiences using specifically targeted communications strategies:

The public - Through the use of strong negative images of the Sandinistas recently reported in the media.

The Congress - Through issues now associated with America's leadership role in supporting democracy in the region.

Policymakers - Democratic leadership issues provide the groundwork for more challenging arguments that can influence liberals and moderates.

Freedom Fighter Leadership - Without a sound belief in the capabilities of the resistance's leadership, no policy can succeed in Congress.

Program Elements

We propose to approach this program with the understanding that we are under considerable time constraints and are fighting for public support in areas widely dispersed across the United States. Therefore, we propose to treat this as a national political campaign, with March 15 as our target. Using the methodology of national political campaigns, we will seek to utilize our opponents negatives, debate the unclaimed issues to our advantage and reinforce our positive public perceptions.

We will use advertising and public affairs programs for each of the four program objectives listed above. They will be handled as follows:

<u>The Public</u> - The public has been exposed recently to several negative images or impressions of the Sandinistas. We will use these images to reinforce the public perception that the Sandinistas are communists and tyrannical dictators. We should employ the following techniques;

Television advertising - following research into the Congressional votes cast on the last aid package, we will produce materials that ~~will be used by Robert Goodman and Associates to~~ focus on -

1) Daniel Ortega's trip to Moscow and the $220 million commitment he received from the Soviets *in hard lethal military support.*

2) The recent crackdown on human rights in Nicaragua *against the entire population of the nation.*

3) Ortega's purchase of $3,500 in designer eyeglasses while his people starve.

4) The *communist* militarization of Nicaragua through *Libyan, East German* Soviet and Cuban advisors and the use of Nicaragua as a command center for subversion of her democratic neighbors.

5) The incident when Pope John II was spat upon and heckled when he tried to say Mass in Nicaragua *signalling an era of religious persecution*

6) That Cubans are now proved to be actively involved in combat.

Spokesman program - using the prototype speakers program begun by I.B.C., NEPL will place speakers in 50 markets between now and March 15, 1986. These speakers will be

Department of the Treasury — Internal Revenue Service
Income Tax Examination Changes

Name and Address of Taxpayer	SSN or EI Number	Filing Status	Return Form No.
RICHARD R. & JOYCE E. MILLER 4500 ORANGEWOOD LANE BOWIE, MD 20715	147-44-2912	JOINT	1040
	Person with whom examination changes were discussed	Name and Title TAXPAYER	

1. Adjustments to Income	Year: 1984	Year: 1985	Year:
A. CLIENT REIMBURSED INCOME	$	$ -1,083,330	$
B. CONSULTING INCOME		-243,300	
C. CLIENT REIMBURSED EXPENSE		977,540	
D. LEGAL & PROFESSIONAL FEES		20,000	
E. CONSULTING FEES		266,900	
F. MARRIED COUPLE DEDUCTION		224	
G.			
H.			
I.			
J.			
K.			
2. Total Adjustments	0	-61,958	
3. Taxable income shown on return or as previously adjusted	7,552	88,624	
4. Corrected taxable income	7,552	27,060	
5. Tax 64-Table 65-Table	480	3,874	
6.			
7. Corrected tax liability	480	3,874	
8. Less A. POLITICAL CONTRIBUTION		100	
Credits B. GENERAL BUSINESS CREDIT	272		
C.			
D.			
9. Balance (line 7 less total of lines 8A thru 8D)	208	3,874	
10. Plus A. SELF-EMPLOYMENT TAX		2,913	
Additional B.			
Taxes C.			
D.			
11. Total corrected income tax liability (line 9 + 10A,B,C,D)	208	6,787	
12. Total tax shown on return or as previously adjusted	208	30,341	
13. Deficiency or Overassessment (line 11 adjusted by line 12)	0	-23,554	
14. Adjustments to prepayment credits	0	0	
15. Balance due or Overpayment (line 13 adjusted by line 14) not including interest	0	-23,554	
16. Penalties, if any (See Summary of Assorted Penalties)	$ 0	$ 2,000	$

Other Information

Examiner's Signature	District	Date
JAMES E. DOWNS	BALTIMORE, MD	07/21/89

Consent to Assessment and Collection – I do not wish to exercise my appeal rights with the Internal Revenue Service or to contest in the United States Tax Court the findings in this report. Therefore, I give my consent to the immediate assessment and collection of any increase in tax and penalties, and accept any decrease in tax and penalties shown above, plus any interest as provided by law. It is understood that this report is subject to acceptance by the District Director.

Note: If a joint return Signature of Taxpayer	Date	Signature of Taxpayer	Date
was filed, both tax- payers must sign. *(signature)*	8-4-89	*(signature)*	8-4-89
By		Title	Date

Department of the Treasury - Internal Revenue Service
Income Tax Examination Changes

Name and address of taxpayer	S S or E I Number	Filing Status	Return Form No
MILLER, RICHARD R. & JOYCE B. 4502 ORANGEWOOD LANE	147-44-2912	JOINT	1040
	Person with whom examination changes were discussed	Name and title RICHARD R. MILLER TAXPAYER	
BOWIE, MD 20715			

1. Adjustments to Income	Year: 1986	Year: 1987	Year:
A. SCHEDULE C LOSS - WINE SELLER	$ 1,841	$ 22,081	$
B. LEGAL FEES - SCHEDULE C		44,127	
C. MARRIED COUPLE DEDUCTION	-184		
D. ITEMIZED DEDUCTIONS	-317	-34,842	
E.			
F.			
G.			
H.			
I.			
J.			
K.			
2. Total adjustments	1,340	31,366	
3. Taxable income shown on return or as previously adjusted	137,504	16,949	
4. Corrected taxable income	138,844	48,315	
5. Tax 86-SchG 87-SchD	42,722	9,775	
6.			
7. Corrected tax liability	42,722	9,775	
8. Less A. POLITICAL CONTRIBUTION	100		
credits B.			
C.			
D.			
9. Balance (line 7 less total of lines 8A thru 8D)	42,622	9,775	
10. plus A. SELF-EMPLOYMENT TAX		479	
Additional B. ALTERNATIVE MINIMUM TAX		2,892	
taxes C. TAX ON IRA		359	
D.			
11. Total corrected income tax liability (line 9 + 10A,B,C,D)	42,622	13,505	
12. Total tax shown on return or as previously adjusted	46,827	2,778	
13. Deficiency or Overassessment (line 11 adjusted by line 12)	-4,205	10,727	
14. Adjustments to prepayment credits	0	0	
15. Balance due or Overpayment (line 13 adjusted by line 14) not including interest	-4,205	10,727	
16. Penalties, if any (See Summary of Asserted Penalties)	$ 0	$ 2,304	$

Other Information

Examiner's Signature _James E. Downs_ *James E. Downs*   District   Baltimore, MD   Date 10/16/89

Consent to Assessment and Collection   I do not wish to exercise my appeal rights with the Internal Revenue Service or to contest in the United States Tax Court the findings in this report. Therefore, I give my consent to the immediate assessment and collection of any increase in tax and penalties, and accept any decrease in tax and penalties shown above, plus any interest as provided by law. It is understood that this report is subject to acceptance by the District Director.

Note: If a joint return Signature of Taxpayer   Date   Signature of Taxpayer   Date
was filed, both tax-   _[signature]_ 11/9/89   _Joyce Miller_ 11/9/89
payers must sign   Title
By

GOBIERNO ECLESIASTICO

ARZOBISPADO DE MANAGUA

A Quien Concierna:

El infrascrito Arzobispo de Managua, Miguel
Card. Obando Bravo, hace constar que Mons. Federico
Argüello, es Protonotario Apostólico "Supra Numerum",
Capellán Conventual "Ad Honorem" de la Soberana y Mi-
litar Orden de Malta. Es un Sacerdote de confianza,
Párroco de San Sebastián de Diriamba, de la Arquidió-
cesis de Managua .

Agradeceré la ayuda que le puedan prestar.

Atentamente.

+Miguel Card. Obando

+Miguel Card. Obando Bravo.
Arzobispo de Managua.

Managua, 14 de Agosto de 1988.

English Translation:

To whom it may concern:

The undersigned Archbishop of Managua, Miguel Cardinal Obando Bravo, states that Monsignor Federico Arguello, is Protonotary Apostolic "Supra Numerum," Conventual Chaplain "Ad Honorem" of the Sovereign and Military Order of Malta. He is a preist who has my trust, Pastor of Saint Sebastian of Diriamba, Archdiocese of Managua.

I will be grateful for any assistance you can give him.

Sincerely,

Miguel Cardinal Obando
Archbishop of Managua

Managua, August 14, 1986

March 31, 1987

International Business Communications
Att. Mr. Richard Miller
Washington.

Dear Mr. Miller: I have received from you $41,000.

I accepted your contributions for the church and the poor
people of Nicaragua.

Thank you for your help.

Msgr. Federico Arguello P.A. K.M.

INSTITUTE ON TERRORISM AND SUBNATIONAL CONFLICT

SUITE 330

1133 20TH STREET. N.W.

WASHINGTON. DC 20036

———

TELEPHONE (202) 429-4913

April 8, 1987

Mr. Richard R. Miller
IBC
1912 Sunderland Place, N.W.
Washington, D.C. 20036-1608

Dear Mr. Miller:

This is to confirm that the Institute on Terrorism and
Subnational Conflict received an anonymous contribution of
$ 75,000.00 by wire transfer to the Institute's account on
June 25, 1987. We noted on the receipt from the bank that the
wire transfer had a reference to Intel-Cooperation.

For your records, the Institute is a 501 (C) (3) non-profit
tax-deductible institution as ruled by the IRS.

Sincerely,

Neil C. Livingstone

LASSi

March 11, 1987

Richard Miller
International Business Communications
1912 Sunderland Place

Washington D.C 20036

Dear Mr. Miller,

This letter is to certify that the Latin American Strategic Studies Institute has received $75,000 in 1986 through the good offices of International Business Communications. Thank you for assisting LASSI in its educational work.

Sincerely yours,

Father Thomas F. Dowling
Executive Director

Directorio Nacional

November 12th. 1985

Mr. Carl Russell Channel
National Endowment for the Preservation of Liberty
2032 Belmont Road, Apt. 608
Washington, D.C.

Dear Spitz:

    This is to ackonwledge reciept of the $ 25,000 you sent to
us; you sure work fast! We are very greatful for your support.

    Needless to say, we are looking forward to your continued
asistance in our struggle for freedom and democracy in Nicaragua.

    Best wishes and may God bless you.

                                    Sincerely,

                                    Adolfo Calero Portocarrero.
                                    Presidente. UNO-FDN

WASHINGTON, D.C.

December 5, 1985

Mr. Carl Russell Channell
President
American Conservative Trust
Suite 210
305 4th St. N.E.
Washington, D.C. 20002

My Dear Friend Spitz,

    I wish to thank you for all the support you have provided us
this year. Now we need your support to help several hundred
families who remained in Nicaragua. These women and children
have been expropriated by the Sandinistas and are constantly
harrassed and intimidated. All because a member of their family
has joined our struggle for freedom. These people have been
deprived of even the basic means to survive in Communist Nicaragua.

    The brave decision these families make to stand and silently
help our struggle is their commitment. They intend to provide us
information and assistance in our country. This will cost them a
great deal. Their Christmas will be hard and lean.

    We ask your help, as you have done so well in the past, to
keep these families alive. We need $50,000.00 dollars through
the holiday season. Please help us to sustain those who have
stayed behind so that those of us on the front lines can survive.

    God bless you for your past efforts and constant faith in
us.

                              Sincerely,

                              [signature]

                              Adolfo Calero

Directorio Nacional

January 5th, 1987

Mr. Carl Russell Channell
National Endowment for the
        Preservation of Liberty
1331 Pennsylvania Ave. N.W.
Washington, D.C.

Dear Spitz:

     Now that we are in a new year it is a good time to reflect
on and thank all those who have stood by us in our time of
struggle.

     Throughout our worst period of public condemnation because
of misinformation efforts by our critics, and despite Congress's
unwillingness to support us, you and your contributors were
constant.   The public education effort you mounted was critical
to re-emergence of a national foreign policy consensus to support
freedom in Nicaragua.   The UNO supporters who participated in
your program were impressed with the thoroughness and scope of
the interviews and public speaking opportunities you arranged.
Your television messages hit home for many of us who have seen
the sandinistas at close range.   While mounting an effort to
change public opinion and educate policy makers was a formidable
task, you were up to it.

     Had you only aided our struggle for political freedom with
your education programs that would have been enough. But you and
the members of the National Endowment for the Preservation of
Liberty did not stop there.   Your generous contributions made it
possible for us to support our work by maintaining decent living
conditions for our people.   As I know I have told you in the
past, the freedom forces have become provider and protector for
thousands of families. We find ourselves providing for those the
sandinistas have abused and turned into refugees.   This peasent
stock is our foundation and our future.

                                                       cont...

In 1986 your gifts, by our count well over one million dollars, to us and supporting organizations are what made the difference. The greatest aid you provided us was your efforts in the public education arena to avaken America to the need to aid freedom in Nicaragua. The millions it cost to see this effort through were well worth it. The simplest of things still cost money, and when these things must be purchased for tens of thousands, the cost is enormous. We have used your generous gifts to buy the needs for thousands including dry milk for the smallest mouths we feed; vital surgical supplies to treat wounded soldiers and medicines to fight off diseases that could ravage our camps. Finally we have used your generosity to help train our people in democratic ideals and in the need to educate all Nicaraguans in the ways of liberty and respect for human rights, and also to make our plight known throughout the world.

Yet even with the New Year and aid from Congress we are in difficulty. The U.S. officials we must work with have informed us that none of the money Congress is sending can be used to clear old bills. This is most unfortunate because our food, clothing and medical suppliers in Central America have demanded payment of two million dollars for supplies purchased on credit before President Reagan signed the Bill Congress passed. Without the ability to apply the new aid to this final bill we are in danger of losing our chief supply lines. With congress divided on the issue of aiding us, these supply lines must stay open. Otherwise we could again find ourselves without aid and no where to turn.

Please help us. This two million dollar need is urgent! Everyday brings new threats of supply cutoffs. As I always do I want to say thank you on behalf of all of us, and to urge you to do more. We welcome your help and bless you for your dedication. Please continue to tell our story to the American public, and to educate policy makers and influential Americans also.

With our best wishes for the continued success of your efforts for freedom, and our profound gratitude, we wish you and your Organization a Happy New Year.

            Sincerely,

            Adolfo Calero

Directorio Nacional

January 10, 1986

Mr. Carl Russell Channell
National Endowment for the
  Preservation of Liberty
305 Fourth Street, N.E.
Washington, D.C. 20002

Dear Spitz:

As we enter the new year it is important that we say thank you to our friends. The struggle we have undertaken is monumental. But, we will be victorious.

The resources you expended on our behalf have helped to keep our people from starvation and sickness. When the United Sates Congress cut off the aid to us, our fighting forces were greatly impaired, but what Congress did not see was the pain and suffering this brought to our troops.

The lack of medical care, decent clothing, food and hygiene materials was critical. Your kind donations at this critical time went to fill that void. Lots of the boots you see on American television and the medicines we have used to treat wounded and sick alike are due to the generosity of your contributors. The food that sustained us in our long wait for congress to come to our aid again is from your good will.

Pleases accept the sincerest thanks from us for these patriotic gifts. And, as always I end my thank you with a request to please do more. With the help of friends of freedom such as you, we can continue.

Sincerely,

Adolfo Calero

Directorio Nacional

January 15, 1986.

Richard R. Miller
1523 New Hampshire Avenue, N.W.
Suite 200
Washington, D.C. 20036

Dear Mr. Miller:

Enclosed you will find copy of the thank-you letters sent by
Mr. Adolfo Calero.

Needless to say, Mr. Calero is very grateful for your support in
our struggle for freedom and democracy in Nicaragua.

May God Bless you!

Sincerely,

Manuel Porro

Directorio Nacional

April 27, 1987

Mr. Carl Russell Channell
President
National Endowment for the
 Preservation of Liberty
1331 Pennsylvania Ave. NW
Washington, D.C. 20004

Dear Spitz:

    The crush of events of the last two months has prevented
me from writing you to properly thank you for your support.
The funds that you have raised have helped us greatly to meet
the many challenges we face.   The $1,030,000 plus the $200,000
from Lake Resources in direct remittances to our Organization
through Alpha Services helped us to clothe, feed and medically
treat thousands.

    As you know, the humanitarian challenge is not the only
one we've faced. Even with the staunch and unswerving support
of President Reagan, misinformation about what we are doing
continues to be circulated.   The $41,000 that were received
from you in support of our public education efforts in the
United States was very much needed ($31,000 for the Nicaraguan
Development Council and $10,000 for the Nicaraguan Business
Council), as was the $170,244.10 you gave to support affiliated
political education efforts outside the United States.

    The speed with which you have responded to our needs has
been greatly appreciated. The $25,000 you sent after my 1985
Christmas appeal is typical and shows that the National Endowment
for the Preservation of Liberty is strongly behind us.

    Once again, my deepest thanks for the contributions to
our cause that your fundraising efforts have made possible.

                         Sincerely,

                         Adolfo Calero
                         President
                         UNO-FDN

CONFIDENCIAL

PROYECTO DOCUMENTAL

PRESUPUESTO

<u>PASAJES</u> (3 personas)	Mia-Tegu-Mia	$ 350.- c/u	$ 1,050.00
	Tegu-Mga-Tegu	$ 180.- c/u	540.00
		Total pasajes	$ 1,590.00
<u>EXCESO EQUIPAJE</u>	Mia-Tegu-Mia		800.00
	Tegu-Mga-Mia		400.00
		Total exceso	$ 1,200.00

<u>VISAS-IMPUESTOS</u>   Honduras-Nicaragua .... $ 100.00

<u>HOTELES</u> (2 personas)	$65.- c/u por día - 14 días Nic.		$ 1,820.00
	$60.- c/u por día - 2 días Hon.		240.00
	Total hoteles		$ 2,060.00

<u>TRANSPORTE</u> - carro y chofer - $100.- al día - 14 días........ $ 1,400.00

<u>COMIDA</u> (2 personas) $ 36.-c/u por día - 14 días .... $ 1,008.00

<u>MISCELANIA</u> - fondos extras de emergencia .... $ 2,642.00

TOTAL PRESUPUESTO PROYECTO .... $ 10,000.00
                                                          ===========

NOTA: Es de suma importancia que esto proyecto sea mantenido en absoluto
        secreto.

CAYHAVEN CORPORATE
SERVICES LIMITED
SWISS BANK BUILDING
GEORGE TOWN, GRAND CAYMAN
CAYMAN ISLANDS

CORPORATE MANAGEMENT
& ADMINISTRATION

MAILING ADDRESS:
P. O. BOX 1043

TELEPHONE: 809-949-5444
CABLES CAYHAVEN
TELEX: (0293) 4287 CAYHAVN C
TELEFAX: GROUPS II & III
809-949-6252

OUR REF DMP/erd/c-2561

YOUR REF

Gulf and Caribbean Foundation
517 3rd Street
S.E. Washington D.C. 20003
USA

1st August 1986

Dear Sirs,

Please find enclosed a draft made payable to yourselves in the amount of
US$6928.00 at the request of Intel Co-Operation Inc.

Yours faithfully,

David M. Piesing
Senior Administrator

Encl.

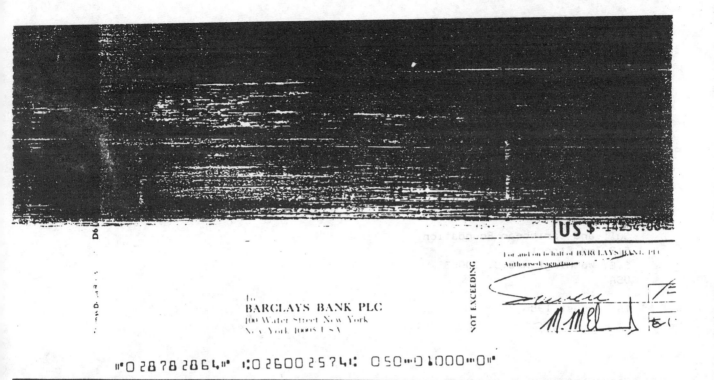

BARCLAYS BANK PLC

GRAND CAYMAN

02878286   APRIL 21,1986

THE GULF & CARIBBEAN FOUNDATION * * * * *

1-257
260

CAYMAN ISLANDS
5¢
STAMP DUTY PAID

US $ 14254.00

PROSTHETICS LABORATORIES, INC.

2753 S.W. CORAL WAY
MIAMI, FLORIDA 33145

(305) 443-1339

PEDRO L. LLANES, R.T.
Prosthetist — Orthotist

INVOIC
No   2

ARTIFICIAL LIMB:
SPINAL & LEG B
ARCH SUPPORTS
CORSETS

SOLD   Fuerzas Aereas Salvadorenas
TO   BAse Aerea Ilopango
       San Salvador, El Salvador

DELIVERED
TO   SAME

PO #		TERMS	DATE DELIVERED April & June 86		TECH Pedro L. LLanes	
DATE	QUANTITY	DESCRIPTION			PRICE	AMO
7-3-86	1	Below Knee Prosthesis			$ 1,150.00	$ 1,1
"	3	Above Knee Prosthesis(finishing)			550.00	1,6
"	1	Below Knee Prosthesis(finishing)			350.00	3
"	6	Rubber Sleves			32.00	1
			Total amount			$ 3,3
"	*	F.D.Y.				1,8.
"	*	T.D.Y.				1,6.
		GRAND TOTAL				$ 6,7

PROSTHETICS LABORATORIES, INC.
2753 S.W. CORAL WAY
MIAMI, FLORIDA 33145

PEDRO L. LLANES, R.T.
Prosthetist — Orthotist

(305) 443-13:

July 3, 1986

Gulf Caribean Foundation
517 3rd St S.E.
Washington, D.C. 20003

ATTN: Dan Kuykendall

Dear Mr. Kuykendall:

Enclosed you will find a brief explanation of services
rendered April and June 1986.

1 Below Knee Prosthesis	$ 1,150.00
3 Above Knee Prosthesis (finishing)	1,650.00
1 Below Knee Prosthesis (finishing)	350.00
6 Rubber Sleves	192.00
Total	$ 3,342.00

T.D.Y. April 16-20 1986 @ 100.00 a day 5 days

Mr. LLanes	500.00
Dr. Gonzalez	500.00
Air fare round trip	825.00
Total	1,825.00

T.D.Y. June 20-23 1986 4 days

Mr. LLanes	400.00
Dr. Gonzalez	400.00
Air fare round trip	825.00
Total	1,625.00

Total amount of this bill is $ 6,792.00

I will certainly appreciate your prompt response to this
matter.

Thank you

Pedro L. LLanes R.T.

PLL/gc

Robert Gonzalez Jr., M.D.

1900 UNIVERSITY DRIVE
PEMBROKE PINES, FLA 33024

DADE - 62
BROWARD - 9(

April 7, 1986

Gulf Caribbean Foundation
517 3rd St., S.E.
Washington, D.C. 20003

Gentlemen:

Please find enclosed invoices and total charges for
prosthesis, food, and accomodations for Mr. Pedro Llanes, R.
and Robert Gonzalez Jr., M.D.

Mr. Pedro Llanes stay was for 5 days, and Dr. Robert Gonzale
stay was for 7 days, each was allowed $100.00 per day for
expenses, making the total for Mr. Llanes $500.00,
and for Dr. Gonzalez, $700.00

Invoice # 2537 from Prosthetics Laboratories, Inc. is
self explanatory, and total charges for these services.
are $11,950.00.

Plane fare round trip , plus tax, for both Mr. Llanes and
Dr. Gonzalez totaled $825.00.

All expenses were as follow:
Mr. Llanes's expenses	$500.00
Dr. Gonzalez's expenses	700.00
Prosthesis	11,950.00
Plane fares	825.00
	$13,975.00

Please remit check as soon as possible in the amount of
$13,975.00 made out to Dr. Robert Gonzalez Jr., P.O. Box
64407, Uleta, Fla. 33164. We will greatly appreciate
your expediting funds, as material is needed to finish
prosthesis, which work is in progess.

Very truly yours,

ROBERT GONZALEZ JR, M.D.

RG:ec

PROSTHETICS LABORATORIES, INC.

2753 S.W. CORAL WAY
MIAMI, FLORIDA 33145

(305) 443-1339

INVOICE

№ 253

ARTIFICIAL LIMBS
SPINAL & LEG BRAC:
ARCH SUPPORTS
CORSETS

PEDRO L. LLANES, R.T.
Prosthetist — Orthotist

SOLD TO	F.A.S. Base Aerea Ilopamgo San Salvador, El Salvador
DELIVERED TO	Same

PO #		TERMS	DATE DELIVERED	TECH Pedro L. LLanes R

DATE	QUANTITY	DESCRIPTION	PRICE	AMOUNT
4-4-86	3	A.K.Temporaries	$ 1,550.00	4,650.
"	2	Safety Knees	350.00	700.
"	3	B.K.Temporaries	950.00	2,850.
"	3	B.K.Definitive	1,250.00	3,750.
		Total amount		11,950.

5/26/86

Jose Arnulfo Escobar
M

Taquicardista (FAS) = 3ᵈ Squadron

Dr. V. Gonzalez Jr   Max Gomez.

HISTORY

SKIN
- dry, burning, itch
- pimple, or rash
- bleeding problem
- bruises easily

HEAD/NECK
- face pain
- headaches
- pain or jerks in neck
- lumps/swelling in neck

EYES
- wears eyeglasses
- decline in vision
- eyes black/water, itch
- blurry vision
- sees halos
- double vision

EARS
- earache
- running ear
- trouble hearing
- noises in the ears

MOUTH

NOSE/THROAT

RESPIRATORY

CARDIOVASCULAR
- dizziness
- racing heart
- pains/tightness in chest
- heart murmur
- hot flashes
- leg cramps
- ankles/feet swell
- high blood pressure

DIGESTIVE

MUSCULOSKELETAL
- handicapped
- aches in shoulder/back
- aching feet
- pain/stiffness in joints
- swelling in joints
- swelling in armpits/groin
- back pain with coughing

NEUROLOGICAL
- numbness in body
- frequently trembles
- fainting problem
- nervous fits/convulsions
- handwriting has changed
- knee gives way walking

ALLERGIES

GENERAL

PSYCHIATRIC
- depressed
- attention/memory lapses
- nervous with strangers
- shy/sensitive
- easily angered/irritated
- bad dreams/thoughts
- worrier
- bites nails
- work/family problems
- sexual problem
- considered suicide
- wanted psychiatric help
- presently under treatment

PREGNANCIES

MEDICATIONS
- penicillin, sulfa
- other antibiotics
- aspirin
- other pain drugs
- codeine
- sedatives
- sleeping drugs
- laxatives
- hormones
- diet pills
- other

IMMUNIZATIONS
- flu 19__
- measles 19__
- mumps 19__
- polio 19__
- smallpox 19__
- tetanus 19__
- typhoid 19__
- other 19__

TESTS
- chest x-ray 19__
- colon x-ray 19__
- gallbladder x-ray 19__
- kidney x-ray 19__
- stomach x-ray 19__
- G.I. series 19__
- electrocardiogram 19__
- T.B. skin test 19__
- blood tests 19__
- sigmoidoscopy 19__
- other tests 19__

Date of last exam

Dr. _____

HOSPITALIZATIONS

REASON HOSPITALIZED	YEAR

Rt. leg below Lt Knee . (Rt. Lateral
ANTERIOR TIBIAL NERVE

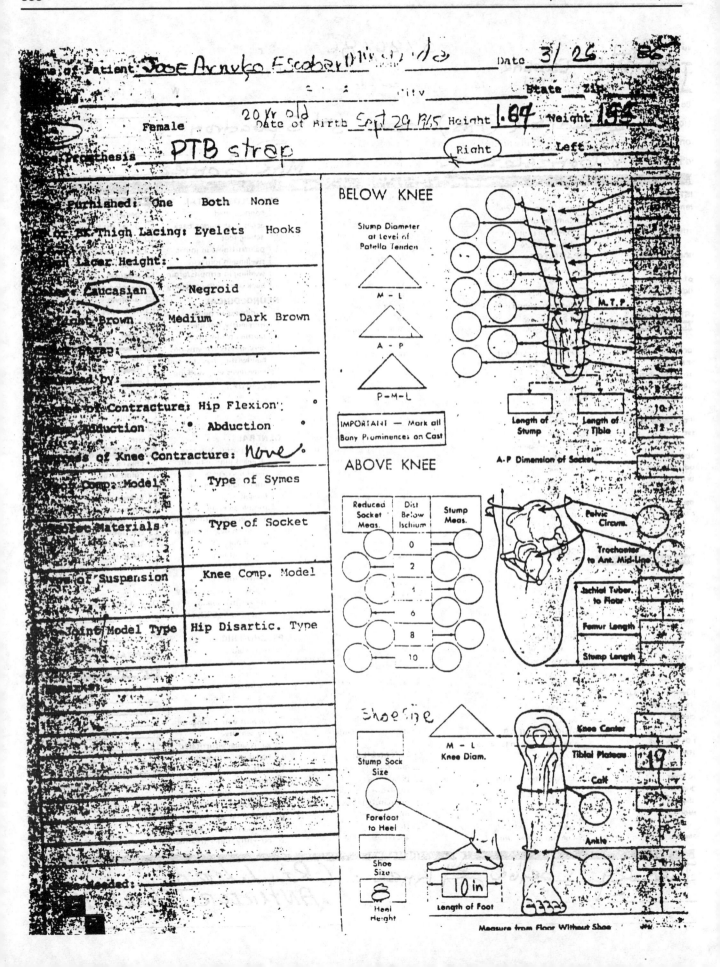

Name of Patient: Jose Arnulfo Escobar Miranda   Date 3/26 86

City   State   Zip

Female   20 yr old Date of Birth Sept 29 1965 Height 1.64 Weight 195

Prosthesis PTB strap   (Right)   Left

BELOW KNEE

Furnished: One   Both   None

for AK Thigh Lacing: Eyelets   Hooks

Liner Height:

(Caucasian)   Negroid

Light Brown   Medium   Dark Brown

Straps:

Used by:

Degree of Contracture: Hip Flexion

Adduction   Abduction

Degree of Knee Contracture: None

Comp. Model	Type of Symes
Materials	Type of Socket
Type of Suspension	Knee Comp. Model
Joint Model Type	Hip Disartic. Type

Stump Diameter at Level of Patella Tendon

M - L

A - P

P - M - L

IMPORTANT — Mark all Bony Prominences on Cast

Length of Stump   Length of Tibia

A-P Dimension of Socket

M.T.P.

ABOVE KNEE

Reduced Socket Meas.	Dist Below Ischium	Stump Meas.
	0	
	2	
	4	
	6	
	8	
	10	

Pelvic Circum.

Trochanter to Ant. Mid-Line

Ischial Tuber. to Floor

Femur Length

Stump Length

Shoe Size

Stump Sock Size

Forefoot to Heel

Shoe Size

Heel Height

M - L
Knee Diam.

Knee Center

Tibial Plateau

Calf

Ankle

10 in
Length of Foot

Measure from Floor Without Shoe

3/26/86 Jun 12-62

Rene Armando Lopez
Age - 24   Date of Birth   Air Force

Occupation **Paracaidista (FAS)**   3rd Squadron

Phone

Referred by **Dr. R. Gonzalez Jr.**   Max Gomez

HISTORY	SKIN	DIGESTIVE	MUSCULOSKELETAL	MEDICATIONS
parents	☐ dry, burning, itch	☐	☐ handicapped	☐ penicillin, sulfa
brothers or sisters	☐ pimples or rashes	☐ pains in stomach	☐ aches in shoulder/back	☐ other antibiotics
brothers or sisters	☐ bleeding problem	☐ bloated after eating	☐ aching feet	☐ aspirin
of children	☐ bruises easily	☐	☐ pain/stiffness in joints	☐ other pain drugs
children	**HEAD/NECK**	☐ heartburn	☐ swelling in joints	☐ codeine
	☐ face pain	☐ hard to swallow	☐ swelling in armpits/groin	☐ sedatives
ARY ILLNESSES	☐ headaches weekly	☐	☐ back pain with coughing	☐ sleeping drugs
	☐ pain or jerking neck	☐ diarrhea	**NEUROLOGICAL**	☐ laxatives
	☐ lumps/swelling in neck	☐ constipation	☐ numbness in body	☐ hormones
s or rheumatism	**EYES**	☐ pain with stools	☐ frequently trembles	☐ diet pills
or allergies	☐ wears eyeglasses	☐	☐ fainting problem	☐ other
or kidney problem	☐ decline in vision	☐	☐ nervous fits/convulsions	**IMMUNIZATIONS**
g tendency	☐ eyes blank/watery itch	☐	☐ handwriting has changed	☐ flu 19__
sions or epilepsy	☐ blurry vision	**URINARY**	☐ knee gives way walking	☐ measles 19__
	☐ sees halos	☐ pass with pain	**ALLERGIES**	☐ mumps 19__
al or stomach ulcer	☐ double vision	☐ hard to control urine	List:	☐ polio 19__
ease	**EARS**	☐ urgency		☐ smallpox 19__
	☐ earaches	☐		☐ tetanus 19__
roblem	☐ running ears	☐	**GENERAL**	☐ typhoid 19__
ood pressure	☐ trouble hearing		☐ failed past health test	☐ other 19__
s breakdown	☐ noises inside ears		☐ changed jobs re health	**TESTS**
	MOUTH		☐ motion sickness	☐ chest x-ray 19__
losis	☐	**MALE GENITAL**	☐ not enough exercise	☐ colon x-ray 19__
or cancer	☐ sore tongue		☐ fatigue	☐ gallbladder x-ray 19__
	☐ sores/swollen gum		☐ trouble sleeping	☐ kidney x-ray 19__
LNESSES	☐ trouble with teeth		☐ generally too hot or cold	☐ stomach x-ray 19__
	☐ partial denture		☐ recent change in weight	☐ G.I. series 19__
tis	☐ full dentures		☐ loss of appetite	☐ electrocardiogram 19__
pox	**NOSE/THROAT**		☐ always hungry	☐ T.B. skin test 19__
ulitis	☐ frequent colds	**FEMALE GENITAL**	☐ 5 cups coffee/tea daily	☐ blood tests 19__
	☐ running nose		☐ smokes tobacco	☐ sigmoidoscopy 19__
ema	☐ ear		☐ 2 alcoholic drinks daily	☐ other tests 19__
hoids	☐ sneezing		☐ smokes marijuana	
	☐		☐ used heroin, LSD, etc.	Date of last exam
rashes	☐		☐ lived outside U.S	
easu	**RESPIRATORY**		**PSYCHIATRIC**	Dr.
	☐ frequent chest colds		☐ depressed	
(German or 3 day)	☐ wears medication		☐ can't relax	**HOSPITALIZATIONS**
(red or 5 day)	☐ coughs up mucus		☐ cries a lot	
cleosis	☐ has cough due to cold		☐ attention/memory lapses	
	☐ coughing spells		☐ hopeless outlook	REASON HOSPITALIZED
s or neuritis	☐ often short of breath		☐ indecisive	
itis	☐ wheezes		☐ nervous with strangers	
	CARDIOVASCULAR		☐ shy/sensitive	
ic fever	☐ tires quickly climbing stairs		☐ easily angered/irritated	
disease	☐ dizziness	**PREGNANCIES**	☐ bad dreams/thoughts	
disease	☐ racing heart	☐ gravida	☐ worrier	
undice	☐ pains/tightness in chest	☐ para	☐ bites nails	
	☐ heart murmur	☐ cesareans	☐ work/family problems	
nesses	☐ hot flashes	☐ premature births	☐ sexual problem	
	☐ leg cramps	☐ miscarriages	☐ considered suicide	
	☐ ankles/feet swell	☐ stillbirths	☐ wanted psychiatric help	
	☐ high blood pressure	☐ abortion	☐ presently under treatment	

REMARKS

move left knee

Name of Patient: Kene Armando Lopez   Phone _____   Date 3/26/86

Air Force (FAS)   City _____   State ____ Zip ____

____ Female   Date of Birth _____   Height 1.64   Weight 122 lb

Prosthesis _____   Right ____   Left ____

Furnished: One   Both   None

BK Thigh Lacing: Eyelets   Hooks

Lacer Height: _____

Color: Caucasian   Negroid

Light Brown   Medium   Dark Brown

Strap: _____

Fitted by: _____

Degree of Contracture: Hip Flexion ___°

Adduction ___°   Abduction ___°

Degrees of Knee Contracture: ___°

Foot Comp. Model	Type of Symes
Socket Materials	Type of Socket
Type of Suspension	Knee Comp. Model
Hip Joint Model Type	Hip Disartic. Type

Remarks: _____

Data Needed: _____

BELOW KNEE

Stump Diameter at Level of Patella Tendon

M – L

A – P

P–M–L

IMPORTANT — Mark all Bony Prominences on Cast

Length of Stump   Length of Tibia

M.T.P.

A-P Dimension of Socket

ABOVE KNEE

Reduced Socket Meas.	Cast Below Ischium	Stump Meas.
	0	19
	2	17½
	4	15⅜
	6	13½
	8	
	10	

Pelvic Circum.

Trochanter to Ant. Mid-Line

Ischial Tuber. to Floor   30"

Femur Length   B"

Stump Length   B

M – L Knee Diam.

Stump Sock Size

Forefoot to Heel

Shoe Size

Heel Height

Length of Foot   9"

Knee Center   17"

Tibial Plateau

Calf   13½

Ankle   9"

Measure from Floor Without Shoe

ORELLANA Lemos ARTURO   6/26/82   JUN-29-65

21

Occupation PARACAIDISTA - (FAS)   3rd squadron.

referred by DR. R. GONZALEZ Jr   Responsible Party MAX GOMEZ

HISTORY	SKIN	DIGESTIVE	MUSCULOSKELETAL	MEDICATIONS
parents	☐ dry, burning, itch		☐ handicapped	☐ penicillin, sulfa ☐
	☐ pimples or rashes		☐ aches in shoulder/back	☐ other antibiotics ☐
brothers or sisters	☐ bleeding problem		☐ aching feet	☐ aspirin ☐
	☐ bruise easily		☐ pain/stiffness in joints	☐ other pain drugs ☐
brothers or sisters	HEAD/NECK	heartburn	☐ swelling in joints	☐ codeine ☐
	☐ face pain	hard to swallow	☐ swelling in armpits/groin	☐ sedatives ☐
number of children	☐ headaches weekly	vomited blood	☐ back pain with coughing	☐ sleeping drugs ☐
children	☐ pain or jerking neck		NEUROLOGICAL	☐ laxatives ☐
	☐ lumps/swelling in neck		☐ numbness in body	☐ hormones ☐
HEREDITARY ILLNESSES	EYES		☐ frequently trembles	☐ diet pills ☐
	☐ wears eyeglasses		☐ fainting problem	☐ other ☐
	☐ eyes blurs/waters/itch		☐ nervous fits/convulsions	IMMUNIZATIONS
	☐ blurry vision	URINARY	☐ handwriting has changed	☐ flu 19__
	☐ sees spots		☐ knee gives way walking	☐ measles 19__
	☐ double vision		ALLERGIES	☐ mumps 19__
	EARS			☐ polio 19__
	☐ earache			☐ smallpox 19__
	☐ trouble hearing		GENERAL	☐ tetanus 19__
	MOUTH		☐ failed past health test	☐ typhoid 19__
high blood pressure			☐ changed jobs re health	☐ other 19__
			☐ motion sickness	TESTS
			☐ not enough exercise	☐ chest x-ray 19__
				☐ colon x-ray 19__
				☐ gallbladder x-ray 19__
ILLNESSES	NOSE/THROAT			☐ T.B. skin test 19__
				☐ blood tests 19__
	RESPIRATORY		PSYCHIATRIC	☐ sigmoidoscopy 19__
				☐ other tests 19__
	CARDIOVASCULAR	PREGNANCIES		HOSPITALIZATIONS
	☐ heart murmur			REASON HOSPITALIZED
	☐ hot flashes			
	☐ leg cramps			
	☐ ankles/feet swell			
	☐ high blood pressure			

IMPORTANT MARKS

Rt. Keg - below Rt knee.   (Possible permanent PROSTESIS →

Name of Patient ARTURO Orellanas lemos   Date 3/26/86

Address   City   State Zip

☐ Male ☐ Female   Date of Birth   Height 1.70 Weight 119

Prosthesis   Right R   Left

BELOW KNEE

Furnished: One   Both   None

Lock Thigh Lacing: Eyelets   Hooks

Lacer Height:

☐ Caucasian   ☐ Negroid

☐ Light Brown ☐ Medium   ☐ Dark Brown

Strap:

Lined by:

Type of Contracture: Hip Flexion

Hip Adduction   Abduction

Degree of Knee Contracture:

Hip Comp. Model	Type of Symes
Socket Materials	Type of Socket
Type of Suspension	Knee Comp. Model
Joint Model Type	Hip Disartic. Type

*Date of ambulation
may 10-1985.*

*may be perform →
permanent prostesis →*

Date Needed:

BELOW KNEE

Stump Diameter
at Level of
Patella Tendon

3 3/4
M - L

A - P

P - M - L

IMPORTANT — Mark all
Bony Prominences on Cast

Length of Stump   Length of Tibia

ABOVE KNEE

A-P Dimension of Socket

Reduced Socket Meas.	Dist Below Ischium	Stump Meas.
	0	
	2	
	4	
	6	
	8	
	10	

Pelvic Circum.

Trochanter to Ant. Mid-Line

Ischial Tuber. to Floor

Femur Length

Stump Length

M - L
Knee Diam.

Stump Sock Size

6½
Forefoot to Heel

Shoe Size

10

Heel Height

Knee Center

Tibial Plateau

Calf   13

Ankle   7½

Length of Foot

Measure from Floor Without Shoe

JUAN JOSE ORTIZ GOMEZ 3/26/86 **AIR FORCE** MARZO 16/6

19 S M W D Sep

upation **PARACHIDISTA (FAS** 3rd SQUADRON

Phone Previous

erred by **DR. R. GONZALEZ Jr.** Responsible Party **MAX GOMEZ**

Y HISTORY
g parents
g brothers or sisters
brothers or sisters
ber of children
g children

ITARY ILLNESSES

HEDITARY ILLNESSES	FAMILY
ma	☐
tis or rheumatism	☐
ma or allergies	☐
der or kidney problem	☐
ding tendency	☐
ulsions or epilepsy	☐
etes	☐
enal or stomach ulcer	
disease	☐
problem	☐
blood pressure	☐
us breakdown	☐
e	
culosis	
r or cancer	☐

ILLNESSES
OTHER ILLNESSES
hitis
en pox
iculitis
e
ysema
rrhoids
or rashes
disease
d
es (German or 3 day)
es (red or 5 day)
nucleosis
s
gia or neuritis
atitis
atic fever
d disease
al disease
y jaundice
illnesses

SKIN
☐ dry, burning, itch
☐ pimples or rashes
☐ bleeding problem
☐ bruises easily

HEAD/NECK
☐ face pain
☐ headaches weekly
☐ pain or jerking neck
☐ lumps/swelling in neck

EYES
☐ wears eyeglasses
☐ decline in vision
☐ eyes blink/water itch
☐ blurry vision
☐ sees halos
☐ double vision

EARS
☐ earache
☐ running ears
☐ trouble hearing
☐ noises in ears

MOUTH
☐ change in taste sense
☐ sore tongue
☐ parts of gums
☐ bad breath
Last Visit to dentist

NOSE/THROAT
☐ frequent head cold
☐ catarrhal
☐ often sore throat
☐ wheeze

RESPIRATORY
☐ cough up mucus
☐ has coughed up blood
☐ cough repeats
☐ often short of breath
☐ wheeze

CARDIOVASCULAR
☐ tires quickly climbing stairs
☐ dizziness
☐ racing heart
☐ pains/tightness in chest
☐ heart murmur
☐ hot flashes
☐ leg cramps
☐ ankles/feet swell
☐ high blood pressure

DIGESTIVE

URINARY

MALE GENITAL

FEMALE GENITAL

PREGNANCIES

MUSCULOSKELETAL
☐ handicapped
☐ aches in shoulder/back
☐ aching feet
☐ pain/stiffness in joints
☐ swelling in joints
☐ swelling in armpits/groin
☐ back pain with coughing

NEUROLOGICAL
☐ numbness in body
☐ frequently trembles
☐ fainting problem
☐ nervous fits/convulsions
☐ handwriting has changed
☐ knee gives way walking

ALLERGIES
List:

GENERAL
☐ failed past health test
☐ changed jobs re health
☐ motion sickness
☐ not enough exercise
☐ fatigue
☐ trouble sleeping
☐ generally too hot or cold
☐ recent change in weight
☐ loss of appetite
☐ always hungry
☐ 5 cups coffee/tea daily
☐ smokes tobacco
☐ alcohol drinks daily
☐ smokes marijuana
☐ used heroin, LSD, etc
☐ lived outside U.S.

PSYCHIATRIC
☐ depressed
☐ can't relax
☐ cries a lot
☐ attention/memory lapses
☐ hopeless outlook
☐ indecisive
☐ nervous with strangers
☐ shy/sensitive
☐ easily angered/irritated
☐ bad dreams/thoughts
☐ worrier
☐ bites nails
☐ work/family problems
☐ sexual problem
☐ considered suicide
☐ wanted psychiatric help
☐ presently under treatment

USE	MEDICATIONS	
☐	penicillin, sulfa	☐
☐	other antibiotics	☐
☐	aspirin	☐
☐	other pain drugs	☐
☐	codeine	☐
☐	sedatives	☐
☐	sleeping drugs	☐
☐	laxatives	☐
☐	hormones	☐
☐	diet pills	☐
☐	other	☐

USE	IMMUNIZATIONS	YEAR
☐	flu	19
☐	measles	19
☐	mumps	19
☐	polio	19
☐	smallpox	19
☐	tetanus	19
☐	typhoid	19
☐	other	19

USE	TESTS	YEAR
☐	chest x-ray	19
☐	colon x ray	19
☐	gallbladder x ray	19
☐	kidney x-ray	19
☐	stomach x ray	19
☐	G.I. series	19
☐	electrocardiogram	19
☐	T.B. skin test	19
☐	blood tests	19
☐	sigmoidoscopy	19
☐	other tests	19

Date of last exam

Dr.

HOSPITALIZATIONS

REASON HOSPITALIZED	YEAR

REMARKS

eft Leg - below Knee.

Patient: **Juan Jose Ortiz Gomez**   Date **3/26/86**

City _____ State ___ Zip ____

Female   Date of Birth _____   Height _____ Weight **119**

Prosthesis **Possible Permanent**   Right _____ Left **6 1/2**

Furnished: One   Both   None

BK Thigh Lacing: Eyelets   Hooks

Lacer Height: _____

Caucasian   Negroid

Light Brown   Medium   Dark Brown

Contracture: Hip Flexion

Adduction   Abduction

Knee Contracture: **Full Range**

	Type of Symes
Foot Comp. Model	Type of Socket
Socket Materials	
Type of Suspension	Knee Comp. Model
Knee Joint Model Type	Hip Disartic. Type

Remarks: **Limited distal pressure**

Date of injury: **May 10 - 1985**

Possible Permanent Prosthesis

BELOW KNEE

Stump Diameter at Level of Patella Tendon

3 1/2 M - L

2 3/4 A / P

P - Y - L

IMPORTANT — Mark all Bony Prominences on Cast

Length of Stump   Length of Tibia

A-P Dimension of Socket

M.T.P.

ABOVE KNEE

Reduced Socket Meas	Dist. Below Ischium	Stump Meas.
	0	
	2	
	4	
	6	
	8	
	10	

Pelvic Circum.

Trochanter to Ant. Mid-line

Ischial Tuber. to Floor

Femur Length

Stump Length

M - L Knee Diam.

Stump Sock Size

Forefoot to Heel

Shoe Size

Heel Height

Length of Foot

Rt. Leg

Knee Center

Tibial Plateau **19 1/2**

Calf **13 1/2**

Ankle **8 1/2**

Measure from Floor Without Shoe

OO5   Date **3/26/86**   Birth Date **MARZO 13 - 65**

SALVADOR AMADO   M   **AIR FORCE.**

fernandez Guido Birth   S   M   W   D   Sep

on **PARACAIDISTA (FAG)**   Comp. **1ª Squadron Mando de Servicio**

by **DR. K. GONZALEZ. ~r.**   Previous Phys.   Responsible Party **MAX Gomez.**

...TORY
...nts
hers or sisters
...ers or sisters
...children
...dren

...Y ILLNESSES

...ARY ILLNESSES		FAMILY
...r rheumatism	☐	
...allergies	☐	
kidney problem	☐	
...ndency	☐	
...s or epilepsy	☐	
...	☐	
or stomach ulcer	☐	
...	☐	
...lem	☐	
...d pressure	☐	
...reakdown	☐	
...sis	☐	
cancer	☐	

...NESSES

...THER ILLNESSES	
...ox	
...ns	
...e	
...ds	
...shes	
...se	
...temar. or 3 (yr)	
...ed or 5 day)	
...eosis	
or neuritis	
...ts	
...fever	
...sease	
...sease	
...undice	
...sses	

SKIN
☐ dry, burning, itch
☐ pimples or rashes
☐ bleeding problem
☐ bruises easily

HEAD/NECK
☐ face pain
☐ headaches weekly
☐ pain or jerking neck
☐ lumps/swelling in neck

EYES
☐ wears eyeglasses
☐ decline in vision
☐ eyes blink/water/itch
☐ blurry vision
☐ sees halos
☐ double vision

EARS
☐ earaches
☐ running ears
☐ trouble hearing
☐ noises inside ears

MOUTH
☐ change in taste sense
☐ sore tongue
☐ sore/swollen gums
☐ trouble with teeth
☐ partial dentures
☐ full dentures
Last Visit to dentist date

NOSE/THROAT
☐ frequent head colds
☐ running nose
☐ nasal congestion
☐ sneezing spells
☐ spontaneous nosebleed
☐ sore, hoarse throat

RESPIRATORY
☐ frequent chest cold
☐ ...
☐ coughs up mucus
☐ has cough or sore throat
☐ coughing spells
☐ often short of breath
☐ wheeze

CARDIOVASCULAR
☐ tires quickly, climbing stairs
☐ dizziness
☐ racing heart
☐ pains/tightness in chest
☐ heart murmur
☐ hot flashes
☐ leg cramps
☐ ankles/feet swell
☐ high blood pressure

DIGESTIVE
☐ nausea
☐ pain in stomach
☐ bloated after eating
☐ burps a lot
☐ heartburn
☐ hard to swallow
☐ vomited blood
☐ diarrhea
☐ constipation
☐ pain with stools
☐ rectal bleeding
☐ grey stools
☐ black bloody stools
☐ recent change in bowel habits

URINARY
☐ pass urine
☐ hard to start urine
☐ urine ...
☐ urinate many while awake
☐ frequency while asleep
☐ loss of bladder control
☐ ...

MALE GENITAL
☐ prostate problem
☐ weak urine flow
☐ sores or on testicles
☐ ...
☐ ...discharge
☐ loss of sex function

FEMALE GENITAL
☐ ... last PAP
☐ last period
☐ ...problem
☐ ...
☐ ...bleed
☐ ...
☐ ...
☐ ...
☐ ...
☐ pain with intercourse
☐ do not reach climax

PREGNANCIES
___ gravida
___ para
___ cesareans
___ premature births
___ miscarriages
___ stillbirths
___ abortion

MUSCULOSKELETAL
☐ handicapped
☐ aches in shoulder/back
☐ aching feet
☐ pain/stiffness in joints
☐ swelling in joints
☐ swelling in armpits/groin
☐ back pain with coughing

NEUROLOGICAL
☐ numbness in body
☐ frequently trembles
☐ fainting problem
☐ nervous fits/convulsions
☐ handwriting has changed
☐ knee gives way walking

ALLERGIES
List: _____
_____

GENERAL
☐ failed past health test
☐ changed jobs or health
☐ motion sickness
☐ not enough exercise
☐ fatigue
☐ trouble sleeping
☐ generally too hot or cold
☐ recent change in weight
☐ loss of appetite
☐ always hungry
☐ 5 cups coffee/tea daily
☐ smokes tobacco
☐ 2 alcoholic drinks daily
☐ smokes marijuana
☐ used heroin, LSD, etc
☐ lived outside U.S.

PSYCHIATRIC
☐ depressed
☐ can't relax
☐ cries a lot
☐ attention/memory lapses
☐ hears voices, sees things
☐ indecisive
☐ nervous with strangers
☐ shy/sensitive
☐ easily angered/irritated
☐ bad dreams/thoughts
☐ vulgar
☐ bites nails
☐ work/family problems
☐ sexual problem
☐ considered suicide
☐ wanted psychiatric help
☐ presently under treatment

USE	MEDICATIONS	
☐ penicillin, sulfa		☐
☐ other antibiotics		☐
☐ aspirin		☐
☐ other pain drugs		☐
☐ codeine		☐
☐ sedatives		☐
☐ sleeping drugs		☐
☐ laxatives		☐
☐ hormones		☐
☐ diet pills		☐
☐ other		☐

USE	IMMUNIZATIONS	
☐ flu		19__
☐ measles		19__
☐ mumps		19__
☐ polio		19__
☐ smallpox		19__
☐ tetanus		19__
☐ typhoid		19__
☐ other		19__

USE	TESTS	YEAR
☐ chest x-ray		19__
☐ colon x-ray		19__
☐ gallbladder x-ray		19__
☐ kidney x-ray		19__
☐ stomach x-ray		19__
☐ G.I. series		19__
☐ electrocardiogram		19__
☐ T.B. skin test		19__
☐ blood tests		19__
☐ sigmoidoscopy		19__
☐ other tests		19__

Date of last exam

Dr. _____

HOSPITALIZATIONS

REASON HOSPITALIZED	YEAR

REMARKS

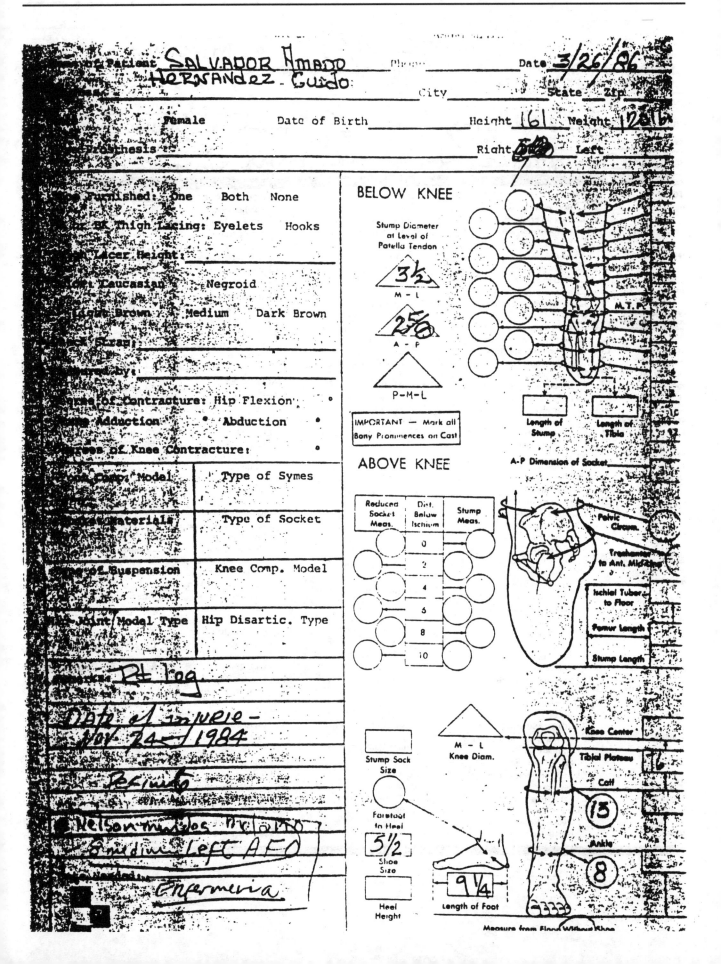

rt No. __OU6__

ne __José Luis Pineda Gomez__ 3/26/86 __NOV-25-1965__ AIR FORCE.

Date of Birth

age __20__ S M W D Sep

tance

upation __PARACAIDISTA (FAS)__ Squadron de Mando y Servicio

. Phone Previous

ned by __Dr. R. Gonzalez Jr__ Max Gomez.

Y HISTORY

g parents

g brothers or sisters

d brothers or sisters

ter of children

g children

XTARY ILLNESSES

HEREDITARY ILLNESSES

nra
ritis or rheumatism
me or allergies
der or kidney problem
ding tendency
ulsions or epilepsy
etes
denal or stomach ulcer
disease
t
t problem
blood pressure
rous breakdown
re
rculosis
or or cancer

ILLNESSES

OTHER ILLNESSES

chitis
ken pox
rticulitis
ma
hysema
oorrhoids
ia
s or rashes
r disease
aria
sles (German or 3 day)
sles (red or 5 day)
nonucleosis
mps
algia or neuritis
creatitis
o
umatic fever
roid disease
ereal disease
low jaundice

er illnesses

SKIN
- dry, burning, itch
- pimples or rashes
- bleeding problem
- bruises easily

HEAD/NECK
- face pain
- headaches weekly
- pain or jerking neck
- lumps/swelling in neck

EYES
- wears eyeglasses
- decline in vision
- eyes blink/water itch
- blurry vision
- sees halos
- double vision

EARS
- earaches
- running ears
- trouble hearing
- noises inside ears

MOUTH
- change in
- sore tongue
- partial dentures
- full dentures

Last Visit to dentist

NOSE/THROAT
- frequent head cold
- runny nose
- sinus trouble

RESPIRATORY
- frequent chest colds
- sweat more than usual
- cough up mucus
- has coughed up blood
- coughing spells
- often short of breath
- wheezes

CARDIOVASCULAR
- tires quickly climbing stairs
- dizziness
- racing heart
- pains/tightness in chest
- heart murmur
- hot flashes
- leg cramps
- ankle feet swell
- high blood pressure

DIGESTIVE

URINARY

MENSTRUATION

PREGNANCIES
- miscarria
- prema
- still births
- live births

MUSCULOSKELETAL
- handicapped
- aches in shoulder/back
- aching feet
- pain/stiffness in joints
- swelling in joints
- swelling in armpits/groin
- back pain with coughing

NEUROLOGICAL
- numbness in body
- frequently trembles
- fainting problem
- nervous fits/convulsions
- handwriting has changed
- knee gives way walking

ALLERGIES
List.

GENERAL
- failed past health test
- changed jobs re health
- problem sleeping
- not enough exercise
- fatigue
- trouble sleeping
- apparently too hot or cold
- recent change in weight
- loss of appetite
- always hungry
- cups coffee/tea daily
- smokes tobacco
- drinks daily

PSYCHIATRIC
- depressed
- can't relax
- cries a lot
- suffer from memory lapses
- hopeless outlook
- indecisive
- nervous with strangers
- shy/sensitive
- easily angered/irritated
- bad dreams/thoughts
- worrier
- bites nails
- work/family problems
- sexual problem
- considered suicide
- wanted psychiatric help
- presently under treatment

MEDICATIONS
- penicillin, sulfa
- other antibiotics
- aspirin
- other pain drugs
- codeine
- sedatives
- sleeping drugs
- laxatives
- hormones
- diet pills
- other

IMMUNIZATIONS
- flu 19__
- measles 19__
- mumps 19__
- polio 19__
- smallpox 19__
- tetanus 19__
- typhoid 19__
- other 19__

TESTS
- chest x-ray 19__
- colon x-ray 19__
- gallbladder x-ray 19
- kidney x-ray 19
- stomach x-ray 19
- G I series 19
- electrocardiogram 19
- T.B. skin test 19__
- blood tests 19__
- sigmoidoscopy 19__
- other tests 19__

Date of last exam

Dr

HOSPITALIZATIONS

REASON HOSPITALIZED	YEAR

REMARKS

t. leg below Rt. Knee.

Pt. want to Runs agains — Pt athletic

Patient Jose Luis Pineda Gomez   Date 3/26/86

City _____ State ___ Zip ___

___ Female   Date of Birth _____ Height ___ Weight ___

Prosthesis PTS liner _____   (Right)   Left

Furnished: One   Both   None

Thigh Lacing: Eyelets   Hooks

Lacer Height: _____

Caucasian   Negroid

Light Brown   Medium   Dark Brown

Strap: _____

Lined by: _____

Type of Contracture: Hip Flexion _____ °

Adduction _____ °   Abduction _____ °

Degrees of Knee Contracture: _____ °

Comp. Model	Type of Symes
Materials	Type of Socket
Type of Suspension	Knee Comp. Model
Model Type	Hip Disartic. Type

Date of Injurie
24 /85

Candidate meet
area of injurie of
tinul to have a
perminent PROSTSIS

BELOW KNEE

Stump Diameter
at Level of
Patella Tendon

△ 4/8 M - L

△ 3 1/2 A - P

△ P-M-L

IMPORTANT — mark all
Bony Prominences on Cast

Length of Stump

Length of Tibia

A-P Dimension of Socket

M. Tir

ABOVE KNEE

Reduced Socket Meas.	Dist Below Ischium	Stump Meas.
	0	
	2	
	4	
	6	
	8	
	10	

Pelvic Circum.

Trochanter to Ant. Mid-line

Ischial Tuber. to Floor

Femur Length

Stump Length

Stump Sock Size

Forefoot to Heel

9

Shoe Size

Heel Height

△ M - L Knee Diam.

Knee Center

Tibial Plateau   20"

Calf

Ankle

Length of Foot

Measure from Floor Without Shoe

No. ‥ UU 1   3/26/86   Oct 20/ 1954

Jose Ricardo Guardo Hernandez / AIR FORCE (FAS)

Age 32   Date of Birth   S M W D   Sep

nce ✓

ation PARACAIDISTA   2ND Squadron

hone   Previou

ed by DR. Robert Gonzalez   Max Gomez

HISTORY
arents

erothers or sisters

rothers or sisters

r of children

children

ARY ILLNESSES

DITARY ILLNESSES	FAMILY
s or rheumatism	
or allergies	
r or kidney problem	
g tendency	
sions or epilepsy	
es	
hal or stomach ulcer	
ease	
problem	
lood pressure	
s breakdown	
uluus	
or cancer	

LLNESSES

OTHER ILLNESSES	
itis	
n pox	
cuitis	
a	
serus	
rhoids	
r rashes	
isease	
a	
es (German or 3 day)	
es (red or 5 day)	
nucleosis	
s	
gia or neuritis	
eatitis	
atic fever	
d disease	
al disease	
n jaundice	
ilinesses	

SKIN
- [ ] dry, burning, itch
- [ ] pimples or rashes
- [ ] bleeding problem
- [ ] bruises easily

HEAD/NECK
- [ ] face pain
- [ ] headaches weekly
- [ ] pain or jerking neck
- [ ] lumps/swelling in neck

EYES
- [ ] wears eyeglasses
- [ ] decline in vision
- [ ] eyes blink/water/itch
- [ ] blurry vision
- [ ] sees halos
- [ ] double vision

EARS
- [ ] earaches
- [ ] running ear
- [ ] trouble hearing
- [ ] noise in the ears

MOUTH

NOSE/THROAT
- [ ] frequent head cold
- [ ] running nose

RESPIRATORY
- [ ] coughs up phlegm
- [ ] has coughed up blood
- [ ] coughing spells
- [ ] often short of breath
- [ ] wheezes

CARDIOVASCULAR
- [ ] tires quickly climbing stairs
- [ ] dizziness
- [ ] racing heart
- [ ] pains/tightness in chest
- [ ] heart murmur
- [ ] hot flashes
- [ ] leg cramps
- [ ] ankles/feet swell
- [ ] high blood pressure

DIGESTIVE

URINARY

MALE GENITAL

FEMALE GENITAL

PREGNANCIES

MUSCULOSKELETAL
- [ ] handicapped
- [ ] aches in shoulder/back
- [ ] aching feet
- [ ] pain/stiffness in joints
- [ ] swelling in joints
- [ ] swelling in armpits/groin
- [ ] back pain with coughing

NEUROLOGICAL
- [ ] numbness in body
- [ ] frequently trembles
- [ ] fainting problem
- [ ] nervous fits/convulsions
- [ ] handwriting has changed
- [ ] knee gives way walking

ALLERGIES
List.

GENERAL
- [ ] failed past health test
- [ ] changed jobs for health
- [ ] section of back
- [ ] not enough exercise
- [ ] fatigue
- [ ] trouble sleeping
- [ ] unusually hot or cold
- [ ] recent change in weight
- [ ] loss of appetite
- [ ] always hungry
- [ ] 5 cups coffee/tea daily
- [ ] smokes tobacco
- [ ] 2 alcoholic drinks daily
- [ ] smokes marijuana
- [ ] used heroin, LSD, etc.
- [ ] lived outside U.S.

PSYCHIATRIC
- [ ] depressed
- [ ] restless
- [ ] cries a lot
- [ ] memory lapses
- [ ] bleak outlook
- [ ] indecisive
- [ ] nervous with strangers
- [ ] shy/sensitive
- [ ] easily angered/irritated
- [ ] bad dreams/thoughts
- [ ] worrier
- [ ] bites nails
- [ ] work/family problems
- [ ] sexual problem
- [ ] considered suicide
- [ ] wanted psychiatric help
- [ ] recently under treatment

USE	MEDICATIONS	WHEN TAKEN
[ ]	penicillin, sulfa	[ ]
[ ]	other antibiotics	[ ]
[ ]	aspirin	[ ]
[ ]	other pain drugs	[ ]
[ ]	codeine	[ ]
[ ]	sedatives	[ ]
[ ]	sleeping drugs	[ ]
[ ]	laxatives	[ ]
[ ]	hormones	[ ]
[ ]	diet pills	[ ]
[ ]	other	[ ]

USE	IMMUNIZATIONS	YEAR
[ ]	flu	19__
[ ]	measles	19__
[ ]	mumps	19__
[ ]	polio	19__
[ ]	smallpox	19__
[ ]	tetanus	19__
[ ]	typhoid	19__
[ ]	other	19__

USE	TESTS	YEAR
[ ]	chest x-ray	19__
[ ]	colon x-ray	19__
[ ]	gallbladder x-ray	19__
[ ]	kidney x-ray	19__
[ ]	stomach x-ray	19__
[ ]	G.I. series	19__
[ ]	electrocardiogram	19__
[ ]	T.B. skin test	19__
[ ]	blood tests	19__
[ ]	sigmoidoscopy	19__
[ ]	other tests	19__

Date of last exam

Dr

HOSPITALIZATIONS

REASON HOSPITALIZED	YEAR

REMARKS

Name of Patient _Jose Ricardo Guardado Almendez_   Date _3/27/86_

City _____ State ___ Zip ___

Female   Date of Birth _____   Height _169_ Weight _138 lb_

Type of Prosthesis _Bilateral AK_   Right _____ (Left)

Furnished: One   Both   None

BK Thigh Lacing: Eyelets   Hooks

Lacer Height: _____

Caucasian   Negroid

Light Brown   Medium   Dark Brown

Strap: _____

Secured by: _____

Type of Contracture: Hip Flexion   °
Hip Adduction   • Abduction   °

Degrees of Knee Contracture: °

Foot Comp. Model	Type of Symes
Socket Materials	Type of Socket
Type of Suspension	Knee Comp. Model
Joint Model Type	Hip Disartic. Type

Remarks:
Injury Date NOV. 24/85

Par de Mocasines -

Recommended: _____

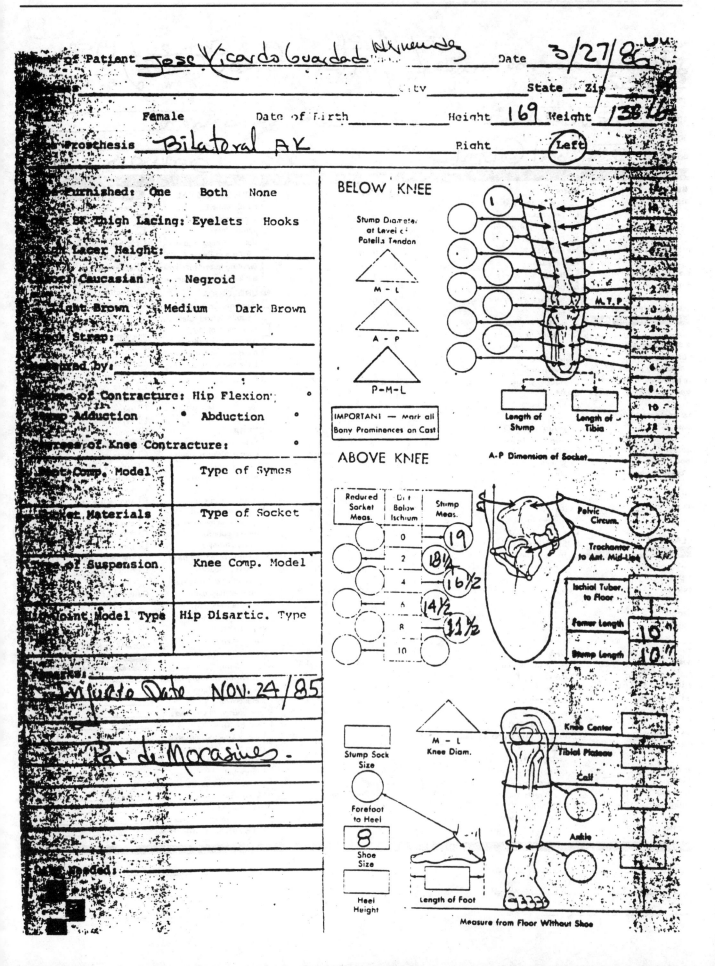

BELOW KNEE

Stump Diameter at Level of Patella Tendon

M - L

A - P

P - M - L

IMPORTANT — Mark all Bony Prominences on Cast

Length of Stump   Length of Tibia

A-P Dimension of Socket _____

ABOVE KNEE

Reduced Socket Meas.	Dist. Below Ischium	Stump Meas.
	0	19
	2	18½
	4	16½
	6	14½
	8	11½
	10	

Pelvic Circum.

Trochanter to Ant. Mid-Line

Ischial Tuber. to Floor

Femur Length _10"_

Stump Length _10"_

M - L Knee Diam.

Stump Sock Size

Forefoot to Heel

Shoe Size _8_

Heel Height

Length of Foot

Knee Center

Tibial Plateau

Calf

Ankle

Measure from Floor Without Shoe

Name of Patient _Jose Ricardo Guardado Hernandez_ Date _3 / 26 / 86_

Address _____ City _____ State __ Zip ____

__ Female __ Date of Birth _____ Height _1·69_ Weight _13?_

Type of Prosthesis _Bilateral AK_ (Right) ~~____~~ Left Ⅰ

| Furnished: | One | Both | None |

BK Thigh Lacing: Eyelets Hooks

Lacer Height: _____

Color: Caucasian Negroid

Light Brown Medium Dark Brown.

Back Strap: _____

Measured by: _____

Degree of Contracture: Hip Flexion: °

Hip Adduction ° Abduction °

Degree of Knee Contracture: °

Foot Comp. Model	Type of Symes
Socket Materials	Type of Socket
Type of Suspension	Knee Comp. Model
Hip Joint Model Type	Hip Disartic. Type

Remarks:

NOV. 24/85

Ron de Moorsines (signature)

__ Needed: _____

BELOW KNEE

Stump Diameter
at Level of
Patella Tendon

M – L

A – P

P–M–L

IMPORTANT — Mark all
Bony Prominences on Cast

Length of Stump

Length of Tibia

A–P Dimension of Socket

ABOVE KNEE

Reduced Socket Meas.	Dist. Below Ischium	Stump Meas.
	0	18¾
	2	18¼
	4	17
	6	15¼
	8	13⅜
	10	12¼

Pelvic Circum.

Trochanter to Ant. Mid-Line

Ischial Tuber. to Floor

Femur Length 12"

Stump Length 2"

M – L
Knee Diam.

Knee Center

Tibial Plateau

Calf

Stump Sock
Size

Forefoot
to Heel

8

Shoe Size

Ankle

Heel Height

Length of Foot

Measure from Floor Without Shoe

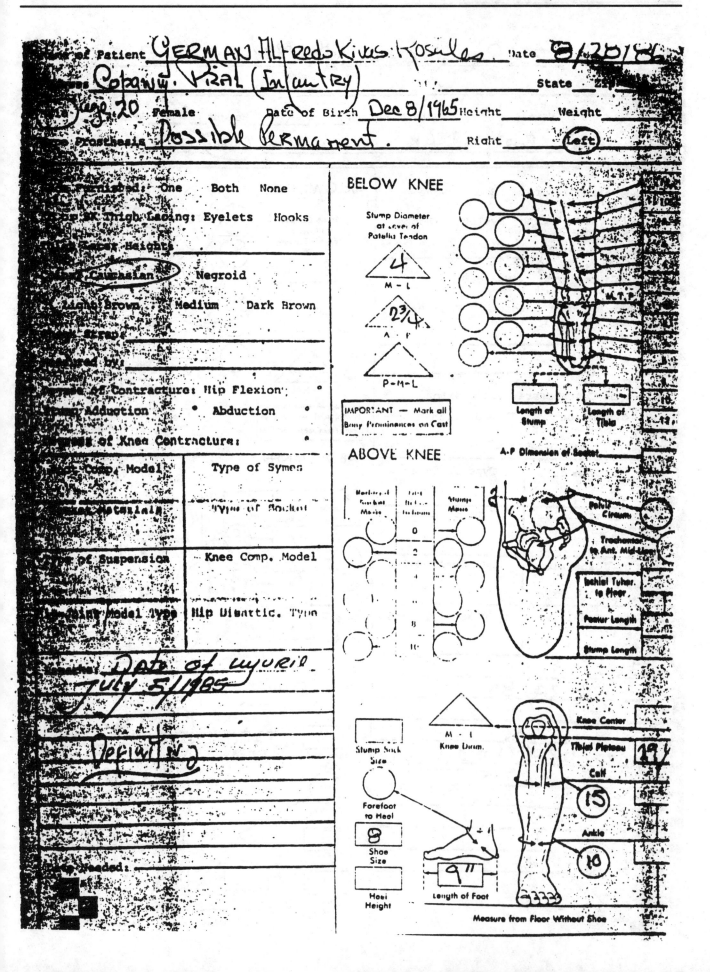

FRIENDS OF THE AMERICAS
912 NORTH FOSTER DRIVE
BATON ROUGE, LOUISIANA 70806
(504) 926-5707

March 12, 1987

PERSONAL AND CONFIDENTIAL

Mr. Richard Miller
International Business Communications
1912 Sunderland Place, N. W.
Washington, D. C. 20036

Dear Mr. Miller:

This is to confirm that we received your contribution on
July 15, 1986 in the amount of $125,000.00.

As you know, Friends of the Americas is a non-profit
public charity with an active program of service thru 46
projects in 18 countries of Latin America.

Your contribution was used for the general purposes of
the organization which include the operation of medical clinics
for women and small children, elementary schools, agricultural
projects, the Christmas box project and general administration.

None of these funds were used for any other purpose or
diverted to any other organization. Specifically, none of these
funds were used for military or paramilitary purposes, such
as participants in the Civil War in Nicaragua.

With appreciation for your generous support, and with
kindest regards, I remain

Sincerely,

Diane A. Jenkins
Executive Director

NICARAGUAN
DEVELOPMENT
COUNCIL.

27 April, 1987.

Mr. Richard Miller, President,
International Business Communications,
1912 Sunderland St.,
Washington, D.C.

Dear Sir:

On behalf of the Nicaraguan Development Council,
I wish to acknowledge receipt of the following funds
from the Internatioal Business Communications:

1- $6,000.00, in December, 1985.

2- $25,000.00, on 6 March, 1986.

3- $10,000.00, on 13 June, 1986.
4-   And $10,000.00, through Barclay's Bank, Miami,
for the Nicaraguan Business Council.

                    Sincerely yours,

                    Bosco Matamoros,
                    Executive Director, N.D.C.

REFINADORA COSTARRICENSE
DE PETROLEO, S. A. We paid
TELEFONO: 23-96-11 — APARTADO: 4351 — TELEX 2215
SAN JOSE, COSTA RICA a u to Frank

handwritten: Mr Robelo who p...

ORDEN DE ENTREGA Y FACTURA

Nº 49237

PLANT PLANTEL	CODE CODIGO 6670	DATE FECHA 4/4/1985		PRODUCTS PRODUCTOS	QUANTITY GLS. CANTIDAD	PRICE PRECIO	AMOUNT VALOR
CUSTOMER NAME NOMBRE DEL CLIENTE	JET FLEET CORP.			AV – GAS 100			
CUSTOMER ADDRESS DIRECCION DEL CLIENTE	SAN JOSE			JET A – 1 litros	2000	¢18:00	¢36000 c
TRUCK OR PIT No. (CAMION No.) GMC-391	HOMESTATION (BASE) A·S·M						
UNIT (UNIDAD)	SERIE No.)	RANK (GRADO)		$\frac{¢36.000^{00}}{¢50^{00}}$ = U.S.$ 720^{00}			
☐ DEFUELER	☐ RESERVISED	TERM (CONDICIONES) R/,					
PLACE OF DELIVERY (LUGAR DE LA ENTREGA) Aeropuerto Santamaria							
PLANE (AVION)							
MODEL (MODELO)	SERIE (SERIE)	SERIAL NUMBER (SERIE No.)					
FLIGTH NUMBER (VUELO No.) privado	CREDIT CARD No. (CARNET No.)	CONTRAC No. (CONTRATO No.) NIIAK					

RECEIVED He recibido ... productos descritos
HE RECIBIDO LOS PRODUCTOS DESCRITOS
LIBRES DE AGUA

	TOTAL COST COSTO TOTAL	¢36000 c

Verificado Recope | Aceptado cliente

CUSTOMER'S SIGNATURE - FIRMA DEL CLIENTE

METER - MEDIDOR	PRODUCT PRODUCTO A - 1	PRODUCT PRODUCTO
FINAL READING LECTURA FINAL	3437153	
INITIAL READING LECTURA INICIAL	3436953	
PRODUCT DELIVERED PRODUCTO ENTREGADO	200	

REFINADORA COSTARRICENSE
DE PETROLEO, S. A.
CEDULA 3 - 101 - 007749
Inscripción: Tomo 49, Folio 515, Asiento 369

SERVICE BY HECHO POR Amedeo Bolan	TIME START - COMENZO TIME FINISH - TERMINO
PAYMENT RECEIVED BY PAGO RECIBIDO POR	CHECK CHEQUE	CASH EFECTIVO

ORIGINAL

INTERNATIONAL BUSINESS COMMUNICATIONS
1912 SUNDERLAND PLACE, N W
WASHINGTON, D C 20036-1608
TELEPHONE (202) 659-6550
TELEX 3718712 IBCUSA

October 1, 1987

Mr. Leonardo Sommariba
6501 N.W. 36th Street
Miami, Florida 33166

Dear Nayo:

Adolfo suggested that I send you a copy of the letter I sent to Ernesto
Palazio requesting acknowledgement of the grants we made to the Unified
Nicaraguan Opposition in 1986. It has been over two months and we have
not yet heard from Ernesto.

Adolfo thought you might be able to help me get the document I need.
I would appreciate any help you can give me. If I don't get a response
soon it will cost me a lot of money which I would prefer not to spend.

Thank you for your assistance in this matter.

Sincerely,

Richard R. Miller
Managing Partner

Enclosure

July 21, 1987

INTERNATIONAL BUSINESS COMMUNICATION
1912 SUNDERLAND PLACE, N.W.
WASHINGTON, D.C. 20036-1608
TELEPHONE (202) 659-6550
TELEX 3718712 IBCUSA

Mr. Ernesto Palazio
Washington Representative
Unified Nicaraguan Opposition
C/O Nicaraguan Resistance - USA Office
2623 Connecticut Avenue, NW
Washington, D.C. 2008

Dear Mr. Palazio:

As you know I helped to secure a grant for the creation and operation of the
UNO Washington Office in 1986. Through your predecessor we transferred a total
of $100,244.10 in grant money for the operation of your office. What you did
not know then, and what we are in a position to confirm to you now, is that
these funds were raised by The National Endowment for the Preservation of Liberty and expended by me in your behalf. Listed below is a breakdown of the expenditures that includes their form and date:

Payee	Form	Date	Amount
CORT office furniture	IBC check	3/10/86	$ 2,544.10
Jadgdish Katyal - rent	IC Inc. wire	3/17/86	15,000.00
Real Estate agent - rent	IBC check	3/24/86	1,500.00
Jadgdish Katyal - rent	IBC check	3/24/86	4,500.00
1ST American Bank - Carlos Ulvert - admin.	IC Inc. wire	5/5/86	10,000.00
Barclay's Bank - Carlos Ulvert - admin.	IC Inc. wire	5/9/86	11,000.00
Latin America Services Denise Ponce per Ulvert final admin. grant	IC Inc. wire	7/28/86	55,700.00
TOTAL			$100,244.10

We ask that you acknowledge these grants to your organization and that you confirm the use of those funds for the purposes stated to us, namely the operation
of a Washington Office for the Unified Nicaraguan Opposition. In addition, if
the funds were used for any purpose other than political action, public education or lobbying, we would appreciate knowing this.

Thank you for your assistance in this matter.

Sincerely,

Richard R. Miller
Managing Partner

Ross Perot

H. R. PEROT
1700 LAKESIDE SQUARE
12377 MERIT DRIVE
DALLAS, TEXAS 75251

August 27, 1993

Mr. Ron Garvin
Clerk
United States Court of Appeals
District of Columbia Circuit
Washington, DC 20001-2866

Dear Mr. Garvin:

It is my understanding that my name is mentioned in Judge Walsh's Final Report in connection with my supplying funds for use by certain government agencies in connection with efforts to obtain the return of hostages held by extremist groups in Lebanon. The inclusion of this information in the report which deals largely with a number of unrelated activities does not specifically mention Lebanon.

The Independent Counsel's report does not make it clear that I was asked to help on a matter in Beirut, Lebanon -- not Iran Contra or Nicaragua.

The supplying of funds for the use of obtaining the return of American hostages held in Lebanon was done at the request of the White House. This effort had no connection to Nicaragua or the Iran Contra issue.

Thank you for allowing me to clarify the record.

Please include this as an appendix to Judge Walsh's final report.

Sincerely,

Ross Perot

RP/sb

Ambassador Nicholas Platt

SHAW, PITTMAN, POTTS & TROWBRIDGE
A PARTNERSHIP INCLUDING PROFESSIONAL CORPORATIONS

2300 N STREET, N.W.
WASHINGTON, D.C. 20037-1128
(202) 663-8000
FACSIMILE
(202) 663-8007

R. KENLY WEBSTER, P.C.
(202) 663-8200

December 3, 1993

United States Court of Appeals
For the District of Columbia Circuit

FILED DEC 0 3 1993

RON GARVIN
CLERK

Hand Delivered

United States Court of Appeals
for the District of Columbia Circuit
Division for the Purpose of Appointing
Independent Counsels
Sentelle, Presiding, Butzner and Sneed,
Senior Circuit Judges
United States Courthouse
333 Constitution Avenue, N.W.
Washington, D.C.

Re: Independent Counsel Lawrence Walsh -
       Ambassador Nicholas Platt

Gentlemen:

I represent former Ambassador Nicholas Platt in connection with his cooperation with Independent Counsel Lawrence Walsh's investigation arising out of matters relating to Oliver L. North. I have previously corresponded with Ron Garvin, Esq., the Clerk of this Court, and was afforded the courtesy of reviewing all references to Ambassador Platt in the proposed report of the Independent Counsel.

The purpose of this letter is to request this Court to delete from the report all references to Ambassador Platt or, in the alternative, to seal all portions of the report which make reference to him. In addition, Ambassador Platt requests that his personal letter to the Court, which is forwarded herewith, be made a part of the appendix to the report and that the letter also be placed under seal. The reasons for these requests are set forth below.

As a matter of background, Ambassador Platt cooperated fully with the Independent Counsel to the limited extent that his assistance was needed. This cooperation included a voluntary interview by Independent Counsel, voluntarily producing all documents requested, and voluntarily providing testimony to the grand jury during one session. At all times Ambassador Platt answered all questions directed to him. Preceding his assistance to the Independent Counsel, Ambassador Platt cooperated fully with investigators who also requested documents and information from him.

SHAW, PITTMAN, POTTS & TROWBRIDGE
A PARTNERSHIP INCLUDING PROFESSIONAL CORPORATIONS

United States Court of Appeals
for the District of Columbia Circuit
Division for the Purpose of Appointing
Independent Counsels
December 3, 1993
Page Two

At no time during the investigation did the independent counsel take action to bring any charges against Ambassador Platt, nor did it threaten to do so.

Ambassador Platt's testimony related to his activities in support of former Secretary of State George Shultz who was also supported at the time by Executive Assistant Charles Hill. Neither former Secretary Shultz nor Mr. Hill was charged as a result of the investigation. I understand that both have provided submissions to the panel.

As the panel well knows, the history of grand jury activity in this country reflects a sacred principle of secrecy, especially with respect to individuals who are not charged after a thorough investigation. Independent Counsel Walsh's report, as it pertains to Ambassador Platt, makes various accusations, contains unflattering innuendo, and in general adversely impacts on the reputation of Ambassador Platt, whose lifetime of service with the State Department was highly distinguished, culminating with ambassadorships to The Philippines and to Pakistan. The history of our tradition of grand jury secrecy and basic principles of fundamental fairness dictate that all adverse references to Ambassador Platt be either stricken from the report or placed under seal.

Examples of unnecessary and unflattering slurs contained in the report are:

º "Both Platt and Hill were evasive about the origin and meaning of the term 'Polecat'." p. 328, fn 22.

º There is a heading entitled "Possible Collusion by Platt and Hill." p. 348.

º "But Hill and Platt each professed not to remember this conversation when they were shown Platt's contemporaneous note." p. 349.

º "Despite this disclaimer, Platt did recall a few relevant points." p. 368. The disclaimer was that he had "virtually no independent memory of the events of 1985 and 1986." p. 368.

º "Asserting a joint defense with Shultz, Platt asserted this privilege with respect to conversations with persons other than his own attorney, including Shultz's counsel." p. 409, fn 410.

º "Platt's testimony showed signs of rehearsal." p. 372, fn 411.

º "The evidence that Platt deliberately withheld relevant notes is inconclusive." p. 373.

SHAW, PITTMAN, POTTS & TROWBRIDGE
A PARTNERSHIP INCLUDING PROFESSIONAL CORPORATIONS

United States Court of Appeals
for the District of Columbia Circuit
Division for the Purpose of Appointing
Independent Counsels
December 3, 1993
Page Three

As may be seen from the foregoing, the unflattering comments are a collection of innuendo and lack substance or fact. Such slurs have no place in our system of jurisprudence, particularly given the reverence with which grand jury secrecy is held and the time-honored reasons therefor.

In addition to the request that the references to Ambassador Platt be stricken from the report, or, in the alternative, that they be placed under seal together with Ambassador Platt's letter enclosed herewith, it is further requested that this letter be placed in the appendix of the report and also held under seal.

Thank you for your consideration of this request.

Sincerely,

R. Kenly Webster

RKW:ewc

enclosure

131 East 69th St.
New York, N.Y. 10021

United States Court of Appeals
For the District of Columbia Circuit

FILED DEC 0 3 1993

RON GARVIN
CLERK

November 25, 1993

United States Court of Appeals
District of Columbia Circuit
333 Constitution Avenue N.W.

Washington, DC

To the Court,

I am grateful to the Court for letting me read the passages relating to me in the final report of the Office of the Independent Counsel(OIC). As a citizen I was taught from childhood to respect the US system of justice, and devoted more than thirty years in government service promoting and defending American values overseas. As a result, when the OIC asked for my cooperation, I complied to the best of my ability throughout the years of its work.

At the outset, I provided through the office of the Counsel to the State Department the portions of my notes it deemed relevant to the OIC's request. I appeared readily every time FBI or OIC staff requested an interview (travelling from ambassadorial posts in the Philippines and Pakistan on two occasions to do so). I acknowledged from the beginning the existence of 4500 pages of handwritten notes that I had taken during the period January 2, 1985-February 12, when I was Executive Secretary of the Department of State. When the OIC asked later for the entire body of my notes, I supplied them immediately. This was done in a spirit of cooperation. I acted in good faith.

It was not until I had read Chapter 24 of Part VII of the Independent Counsel's Report that I realized the exent to which my cooperation with the OIC had resulted in a formal investigation of my conduct. The report acknowledged that my notes had been among the most important evidence made available to the OIC, and concluded that there was no case against me. In the course of reaching that conclusion, the report discussed in detail a variety of damaging allegations--that I had deliberately withheld information; that I had colluded with Charles Hill to do so-- while acknowledging correctly that these charges could not be substantiated. The report, in effect, is a prosecutorial brief which attempts an indictment without providing the protection normally associated with due process. I

ask the court to consider whether public release of Chapter 24 of P
art VII is appropriate or proper.

Sincerely,

Nicholas Platt

Adm. John M. Poindexter, Ret.

FULBRIGHT & JAWORSKI
L.L.P.

A REGISTERED LIMITED LIABILITY PARTNERSHIP
801 PENNSYLVANIA AVENUE, N.W.
WASHINGTON, D.C. 20004-2604

TELEPHONE: 202/662-0200
TELEX: 197471
FACSIMILE: 202/662-4643

WRITER'S DIRECT DIAL NUMBER:
202/662-4505
RICHARD W. BECKLER, PARTNER

HOUSTON
WASHINGTON, D.C.
AUSTIN
SAN ANTONIO
DALLAS
NEW YORK
LOS ANGELES
LONDON
ZURICH
HONG KONG

December 3, 1993

United States Court of Appeals
For the District of Columbia Circuit

FILED DEC 03 1993

RON GARVIN
CLERK

VIA HAND DELIVERY

Honorable David B. Sentelle
Presiding Judge, Special Division for the
    Purpose of Appointing Independent
    Counsels
United States Court of Appeals for the
    District of Columbia Circuit
Constitution Avenue & John Marshall Place, N.W.
Washington, D.C. 20001

Re: Independent Counsel's Final Report

Dear Judge Sentelle:

Pursuant to the Special Division's Order of August 5, 1993, counsel for Admiral John M. Poindexter have reviewed those portions of the Independent Counsel's Final Report (the "Report") that have been designated as "relevant" to Admiral Poindexter. I am writing on behalf of Admiral Poindexter to request that the Special Division, pursuant to its authority and responsibility under 28 U.S.C. § 594(h)(2) "to protect the rights of any individual named in such report," enter an order precluding the public release of the Report.

The Report is offensive and prejudicial to Admiral Poindexter's rights in at least two respects. First, in a chapter of the Report titled *United States v. John M. Poindexter*, the Independent Counsel purports to summarize the history of his investigation and prosecution of Admiral Poindexter, while employing a selective memory and a pro-prosecution spin at every turn. The most audacious aspect of this revisionist history is the Independent Counsel's attempt to discredit the Court of Appeals' decision reversing Admiral Poindexter's convictions. While essentially ignoring the majority view of the Court that Admiral Poindexter was tried in violation of his fifth amendment rights and that one of the statutes under which he was convicted could not constitutionally be employed to criminalize his conduct, the Independent Counsel cites selectively to the dissenting opinion of one judge, suggesting that it be considered a compelling refutation of the majority opinion. The Independent Counsel's version of these events conveniently neglects to mention that even the

December 3, 1993
Page 2

dissenting judge acknowledged that Admiral Poindexter's fifth amendment rights had not been adequately protected during his trial and that at least one, and perhaps all, of Admiral Poindexter's convictions could not survive scrutiny under the Constitution. In sum, the Independent Counsel's revisionist history of the trial and appellate proceedings of the *Poindexter* case seeks only to cloud the accurate history of those proceedings that is already a matter of public record. *See United States v. Poindexter*, 951 F.2d 369 (D.C. Cir. 1991) (publicly reported decision of Court of Appeals overturning all of Admiral Poindexter's convictions), *cert. denied*, 113 S. Ct. 656 (1992).

The Report is even more offensive and prejudicial in its gratuitous discussion of a conspiracy charge against Admiral Poindexter that was narrowed prior to trial. When Admiral Poindexter initially was indicted with Oliver North, Richard Secord, and Albert Hakim, all four were charged with a broad-ranging conspiracy to defraud the United States government. Admiral Poindexter's case later was severed from the others and, prior to his trial, Judge Greene, *at the request of the Independent Counsel*, narrowed the Indictment by eliminating the "conspiracy to defraud" allegations. Having determined that it could not proceed with the allegations in court, the Independent Counsel now attempts to try the case in his Report. He devotes an entire chapter of his Report to

> an attempt to present in an abbreviated fashion what *would have been* Independent Counsel's case at a conspiracy trial of North, Secord, Poindexter and Hakim, and an explanation of the criminal nature of their actions.

Final Report, Part III - The Operational Conspiracy: A Legal Analysis, p. 55 (emphasis added).

It is difficult to imagine a more unfair and illegitimate assault on the integrity and character of an individual than this purported "explanation of [Admiral Poindexter's] criminal . . . actions." It is patently offensive to even the most basic notions of due process for an agent of the United States government, in the person of the Independent Counsel, to elect not to proceed in a court of law with an accusation

December 3, 1993
Page 3

of criminal wrongdoing against a citizen and subsequently attempt to prosecute that individual on the same accusation in the "court" of public opinion.

For these reasons, I respectfully request on behalf of Admiral Poindexter that the Special Division exercise its authority to preclude public disclosure of the Report. The Independent Counsel's actions to date have failed to convict Admiral Poindexter of any crime, but they have caused great anguish and suffering for him and his family. Public disclosure of the Report will serve only to advance further the Independent Counsel's illegitimate and meritless crusade to tarnish the character of a man who devoted his life to serving his country with humility, honor, and dignity.

Alternatively, if the Court permits public disclosure of the Report, I ask that this letter be included in the appendix to the Report, *see* 28 U.S.C. § 594(h)(2), so that the public may be informed of the characteristic unfairness of this Independent Counsel's final act.

Respectfully submitted,

Richard W. Beckler

RWB/clg
cc: Independent Counsel Lawrence E. Walsh
       Keith A. Jones, Esq. (Firm)
       Joseph T. Small, Jr., Esq. (Firm)
       Frederick Robinson, Esq. (Firm)
       Stephen M. McNabb, Esq. (Firm)
       Michael G. McGovern, Esq. (Firm)

Gen. Colin L. Powell, USA, Ret.

General Colin L. Powell, USA (Ret)
1317 Ballantrae Farms Drive
McLean, Virginia 22101

29 November 1993

United States Court of Appeals
For the District of Columbia Circuit

Mr. Ronald Garvin
Clerk, United States Court of Appeals
District of Columbia Circuit
Washington, D.C. 20001

FILED NOV 3 0 1993

RON GARVIN
CLERK

Dear Mr. Garvin,

Thank you for the opportunity to address the matters raised
by the Iran-Contra Independent Counsel in his Final Report. In
concluding his investigation, the Independent Counsel has found
that my role does not warrant any further action. Since I was
never a subject of his investigation but only a witness, this is
no surprise.

The Independent Counsel has nevertheless seen fit to impugn
my character in an extensive document to which I have been
accorded only a limited opportunity to respond. This statement
is provided to set the record straight.

In the three specific sections in which my name appears,
the Report alleges that: (1) I had "detailed information" of the
transfer of arms to the Iranians in 1985 (contrary to my sworn
testimony that, to the best of my knowledge, I first learned of
the transfers in 1986); (2) my 1987 testimony regarding what and
when I knew of the 1985 transfers was less than truthful; and
(3) my 1987 deposition regarding Secretary Weinberger's diary
and notes "was at least misleading" and "hardly constituted full
disclosure." Through innuendo and unfounded accusations, the
Independent Counsel attacks my reputation, impugns my character,
and calls me a liar -- all while conceding I committed no
offense.

I intend to establish two truths about Iran-Contra and my
participation in this investigation. First, I testified
repeatedly and truthfully that I had no awareness of the 1985
transfer of arms to Iran until 1986. Second, there are no
discrepancies between my 1987 testimony in my deposition before
the Select Committee to Investigate Covert Arms Transactions
with Iran and my 1992 statement to the Independent Counsel. The
Independent Counsel's contrary suggestions are simply
misstatements of facts and improper characterizations of my
actions. Throughout this entire ordeal, I was truthful and
fully cooperative.

Personal Knowledge of 1985 Arms Sales to Iran

The Executive Summary concludes that "General Colin Powell, Weinberger's senior military aide, and Richard L. Armitage, ...also had detailed knowledge of the 1985 shipments from Israeli stocks. Armitage and Powell had testified that they did not learn of the November 1985 HAWK missile shipment until 1986." Despite the Independent Counsel's suggestion, above, that I lied to investigators, I did not learn of the shipments until well after they were made. The statement that I had "detailed knowledge" is totally unsubstantiated and totally untrue.

I knew of <u>the proposal</u> to ship missiles from Israel to Iran when it was made in late 1985. The Independent Counsel <u>confuses knowledge of the proposal with knowledge of the shipments</u> themselves. The first I heard about a proposal to ship HAWKs to Iran was in November 1985, when Secretary Weinberger asked me to examine and report the legal implications of such a transaction. I referred the question to Mr. Henry Gaffney, Acting Director of the Defense Security Assistance Agency. Mr. Gaffney concluded that the missiles could not be given to Israel or Iran without first notifying Congress. I passed that information to Mr. Weinberger, both orally and in a point paper provided by Mr. Gaffney. That ended my involvement with and knowledge of the affair until 1986, when I learned the transfer had been made.

Knowledge of Mr. Weinberger's "Diary"

The Independent Counsel makes most of his accusations against me in the context of the alleged "withholding" of Secretary Weinberger's notes. Following are some of the statements he makes about my testimony to investigators regarding those notes:

"Although Powell generally was a cooperative witness, his 1992 statements describing Weinberger's notes in detail and characterizing them as a "personal diary" (footnote 287) necessarily raise questions about Powell's 1987 statements to congressional investigators."

(Footnote 287: "Powell's detailed 1992 account of Weinberger's notetaking, while quite helpful to the OIC, was also consistent with a defense strategy to demonstrate that Weinberger was not secretive about his notes. Indeed,

Powell, who cooperated extensively with Weinberger's
counsel, provided increasingly vivid descriptions of
Weinberger's notes as the investigation progressed.")

. . .

"The Independent Counsel determined that most of Powell's
early statements regarding the Iran initiative were
forthright and consistent. But some were questionable and
seem generally designed to protect Weinberger. Because the
Independent Counsel had no direct evidence that Powell
intentonally made false statements, however, these matters
were not pursued."

. . .

"In light of his statements in 1992 (denying Weinberger had a
diary or memos, but admitting he took notes) Powell's 1987
deposition was at least misleading ... His oblique reference
to Weinberger's notes hardly constituted full disclosure."

. . .

"While Powell's prior inconsistent statements could have been
used to impeach his credibility, they did not warrant his
prosecution."

The above sequence progresses from discussing facts, to
suggesting that my testimony was suspect at some points and
probably false at others, to concluding that my involvement,
knowledge, and testimony to investigators provided the bases for
impeachment of credibility but not prosecution.

At the time of my 1987 testimony, I had never read or been
privy to the notes that Secretary Weinbverger had taken and that
I had alluded to. Nor did I have any idea what their content
was, their importance, or what use he made of them. Five years
later in 1992, after his notes were retrieved from the Archives
and thoroughly examined by Independent Counsel, I was shown many
of these personal notes dealing with the period represented by
the events that formed the subject of the investigation. The
Independent Counsel's staff, in fact, asked me to look at
specific notes and their contents. In 1992, these notes and
their contents <u>were the subject of the inquiry</u>.

In 1992, I provided an affidavit to Mr. Weinberger's
attorneys describing in more detail what I knew of his
notetaking practices, as it had assumed a whole new relevance.
I stated that Mr. Weinberger would jot down various calls and
events during the day on 5" x 7" sheets of paper from a pad he

kept on his desk. These notes were personal; I was never privy to their contents nor did I know, other than that he put them in his desk drawer, what he did with them afterward. This report juxtaposes my testimony in such a way as to suggest that I lied at one point or another. In truth, the "inconsistencies" Independent Counsel alleges are due to the different focus of the questions asked in 1987 and 1992. On one hand, I was asked by congressional staff in 1987 whether Mr. Weinberger kept any records at all of his daily activities. I replied truthfully that he took notes, but did not have a diary -- a permanent record summarizing important events. My 1992 affidavit, on the other hand, focused in depth on the notes I said he took and my understanding that the notes were personal. Since I, his senior military assistant, was not privy to them, they could have been nothing but personal.

Independent Counsel now alleges that my earlier testimony to Congress about Mr. Weinberger's notes was "misleading," supporting this conclusion with his observation that I "provided increasingly vivid descriptions of Weinberger's notes as the investigation progressed." In my 1987 testimony to congressional staff, which focused on whether Mr. Weinberger kept a permanent record of events and thoughts, I said he had no diary but that he made notes. The distinction, again, was based on the nature of Mr. Liman's question, which focused on the permanence of the record. In my later affidavit, which focused on my recollection of his note-taking practices per se, I described his notes as a diary to convey the idea that they were private and personal, as opposed to an official record. As used in the context of the question <u>on both occasions</u>, my meaning was clear, consistent, and understood throughout this investigation <u>by those asking the questions</u>.

What was not consistent throughout the investigation was the level of detail to which I was asked to testify about Mr. Weinberger's notes. I progressed from general questions from congressal staff in 1987 to entire questioning sessions in 1992 after the notes had been subpoenaed and after I had been shown the notes and given an opportunity to read them. Certainly, as the later questions referred to specific jottings on the notes vice questions such as whether the Secretary had maintained a diary, my answers became "increasingly vivid." Until investigators showed me the notes, I had no idea what detail or information they contained. Independent Counsel now uses this sequence of events against me. Rather than fairly and logically attributing the increasing detail of my testimony to the increasing detail of the questions and the information investigators gave me, he concludes I misled them. This is simply not true.

4

Any characterization of my testimony as less than truthful is purely reflective of Independent Counsel's lack of evenhandedness in portraying the context in which it was presented. At best, the distinction drawn by Independent Counsel is of such triviality that it is a shocking assertion by an officer of the court. The Independent Counsel himself, after sullying my reputation without cause, finally concludes the matter is non-prosecutable.

The Review and Comment Process

In addition to the substantive issues listed above, the review and comment procedures imposed hardly allow for a fair and fully informed response. While I appreciate the court's need to insure confidentiality, I am concerned by several of the restrictions imposed:

- I was provided only part of the full report. The final report is well over a thousand pages long. I was permitted to review less than one hundred pages. I was advised that these were the pages "relevant" to my involvement in the investigation. The predecision on relevance by the Independent Counsel and the resultant filtering of information precluded me from fully appreciating the context in which my testimony appears. (This is in contrast to at least one other addressed in the investigation who was provided full access - President Reagan).

- While permitted to read the "relevant" portions of the report, neither I nor my attorney was allowed to make copies. These constraints thus limited our ability to study the report in depth, reflect on the meanings and implications of difficult passages, and draft a coherent legal and factual analysis. A far better and fairer approach would have been to allow me and the other principals to make copies of at least the relevant portions or preferably the entire report. We could then have written a more specific, focused, and meaningful response. As it is, this response addresses generally only the small portion of the report we could read.

If this were a criminal prosecution, the limitations imposed upon my ability to fashion a meaningful response would constitute denial of due process. While I appreciate the opportunity to rebut the Independent Counsel's overt and implied attacks on my character, the unreasonable procedural constraints narrow that opportunity considerably. This is especially unfair considering the unfettered power the Independent Counsel had to prepare and publish his report. I note that this limitation on access to the full investigation is also inconsistent with the practice of other Independent Counsel.

5

Conclusion

There is nothing more I can say. My reputation stands on
its own. I am concerned, however, that in a country that prizes
justice for all, above all, the government established to
preserve justice should not be allowed to trample the very
rights it is sworn to uphold. These are principles the
Independent Counsel seems to have forgotten or ignored. If I
were simply to allow the Independent Counsel's Report to stand
without comment or protest, I would be surrendering the very
rights that I and so many others have fought so long and hard to
defend.

Colin L. Powell

Rafael Quintero

LAW OFFICES
OF
ROBERT WINTHROP JOHNSON II

1050 POTOMAC STREET, N.W.
WASHINGTON, D.C. 20007
(202) 337-6817
TELEFAX (202) 337-3462

United States Court of Appeals
For the District of Columbia Circuit

FILED DEC 0 3 1993

RON GARVIN
CLERK

December 3, 1993

Ron Garvin, Clerk
United States Court of Appeals
District of Columbia Circuit
United States Courthouse
Fifth Floor
333 Constitution Avenue, N.W.
Washington, D.C. 20001-2866

    Re: <u>Report of Lawrence E. Walsh, Esq., the Independent
            Counsel in re: Oliver L. North, et al.</u>

Dear Mr. Garvin:

    I am writing to respond to certain comments in the
Independent Counsel's Report (the Final Report), relating to my
client, Rafael Quintero. Mr. Quintero was actively involved in
the efforts to equip and supply the Nicaraguan freedom fighters
(the Contras) seeking to overthrow the Sandinista regime and
restore democracy in Nicaragua.

    Mr. Quintero is concerned about the accuracy of certain
remarks about him in the Final Report attributed to Felix
Rodriguez. The remarks were made in the following context: Mr.
Rodriguez, while assisting the Contras under the cover identity
"Max Gomez", was told that a "Mr. Green" would be one of his
contacts in the Contra resupply program. "Mr. Green" was, to
Felix Rodriguez's surprise, the <u>nom de guerre</u> of Rafael Quintero
whom he had known for over thirty-three years. Mr. Rodriguez is
reported to have said that, when "Mr. Green's" identity became
known to him, he did not want to work with Mr. Quintero because
of Mr. Quintero's association with General Secord, Tom Clines,
and Ed Wilson, and their alleged connections with Libya.

    My client wants to set the record straight to show that Mr.
Rodriguez's hesitation about working with him was caused by an
animus of long duration, dating from their joint work with other
Cuban freedom-fighters and the U.S. intelligence services during

2

the Bay of Pigs operation and before. Mr. Quintero and Mr.
Rodriguez were closely associated in these efforts and
disagreements arose between them over strategy, tactics, and
organizational and operational matters.

These resentments on the part of Mr. Rodriguez, rather than
doubts about Mr. Quintero's integrity and loyalty, led to the
reported uncomplimentary remarks about Mr. Quintero. Mr.
Rodriguez was simply surprised when he learned that "Mr. Green"
was actually Rafael Quintero. Obviously Mr. Rodriguez did not
want to work on the Contra program with a person who was familiar
with him from anti-Castro operations in Cuba and who had served
as his superior in certain cases.

Mr. Rodriguez's own statements in his book, Shadow Warrior,
(Simon & Schuster, 1989) detail these long-standing disagreements
with Mr. Quintero. A close reading of that book, and familiarity
with still-classified materials, will reveal Mr. Rodriguez's need
to take credit for operational successes, and to assign blame to
others for less-than-successful operations.

This propensity led to the unfortunate remarks about Mr.
Quintero. History will prove that Mr. Quintero has dedicated
many years to advancing the cause of freedom in Cuba, Nicaragua,
and many other places in Latin America, and has put his life at
risk many times.

I trust that these comments will be included in the
Independent Counsel's Final Report.

                                        Sincerely,

                                        Robert W. Johnson II
                                        for Rafael Quintero

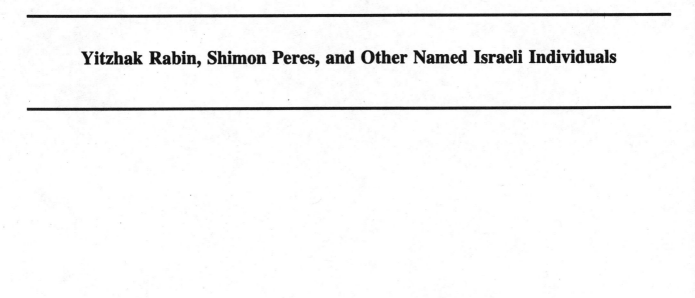

Yitzhak Rabin, Shimon Peres, and Other Named Israeli Individuals

SIDLEY & AUSTIN
A PARTNERSHIP INCLUDING PROFESSIONAL CORPORATIONS

1722 EYE STREET, N.W.
WASHINGTON, D.C. 20006
TELEPHONE 202: 736-8000
TELEX 89-463
FACSIMILE 202: 736-8711

CHICAGO
———
LOS ANGELES
———
NEW YORK

125th
Anniversary
1866-1991

LONDON
———
SINGAPORE
———
TOKYO

United States Court of Appeals
For the District of Columbia Circuit

FILED DEC 0 3 1993

RON GARVIN
CLERK

WRITER'S DIRECT NUMBER

(202) 736-8559

To: The Hon. Judges of the United States Court of Appeals for the District of Columbia
Circuit, Division for the Purpose of Appointing Independent Counsels, Ethics in
Government Act of 1978, As Amended

Re: In Re Oliver L. North, et al.   Division No. 86-6
Comments of Individual Officials of the Government of Israel
on the Final Report of the Independent Counsel for Iran-Contra Matters

Date: December 3, 1993

Pursuant to the Orders of this Court advising Yitzhak Rabin, Shimon Peres and other
named Israeli individuals of their right under the above-referenced Act to submit any comment or
factual information for possible inclusion as an appendix of the Final Report of Lawrence E. Walsh,
Esquire, the Independent Counsel in the above-referenced matter, we are herewith transmitting the
Comments of the Hon. Shimon Peres, Foreign Minister of Israel. Foreign Minister Peres' comments
also include comments by Prime Minister Rabin and other named Israeli individuals.

Due to the very limited portions of the Final Report that have been made available to
Israeli officials, these comments are necessarily limited in scope to the impressions gained from the
review that was permitted. The Government of Israel and Israeli individuals have requested more
complete access to information contained within the Final Report; however, to date, that access has
been denied. The Government of Israel and these individuals reserve their right to supplement these
comments when and if additional portions of the Final Report are made available.

Foreign Minister Peres has asked us to forward to this Court his and his
Government's expression of their deep respect for and gratitude to this Court for the opportunity
granted by this Court for the submission of the attached Comments.

Sincerely,

SIDLEY & AUSTIN

By _____
Melvin Rishe

Counsel to Shimon Peres,
Yitzhak Rabin and other
named Israeli individuals

Enclosure

**COMMENTS OF INDIVIDUAL OFFICIALS OF THE GOVERNMENT OF ISRAEL
ON THE FINAL REPORT OF THE INDEPENDENT COUNSEL
FOR IRAN-CONTRA MATTERS**

United States Court of Appeals
For the District of Columbia Circuit

December 3, 1993

FILED DEC 0 3 1993

<u>**Comments of Shimon Peres, Foreign Minister Of Israel**</u>

RON GARVIN
CLERK

I.   <u>General Comments</u>

These Comments are submitted by Shimon Peres, Foreign Minister of Israel, who was Prime Minister of Israel when the Iran-Contra events occurred. Officials of the Government of Israel ("GOI") acting in this matter reported ultimately to Mr. Peres, and these comments reflect information provided by these individuals. Due to the limited portions of the Final Report of the Independent Counsel ("IC") that were made available to Israeli officials, these comments are limited in scope to the impressions gained from the review that was permitted, and these individuals and the GOI reserve their right to supplement these comments when and if additional portions of the Final Report are made available. Following the general comments provided in the initial sections of comments, specific comments on particular statements in the Final Report are set forth on behalf of a number of Israeli individuals mentioned in the Final Report.

The Final Report contains numerous references to individuals who, as officials of the GOI, were acting in their official capacities when they participated in events that are described in the Final Report and when they later provided information to United States Government ("USG") investigating authorities. Among others, these individuals included the then-Prime Minister, Shimon Peres, the then-Defense Minister, Yitzhak Rabin, and the then-Director-General of the Ministry of Foreign Affairs, David Kimche.

These comments are submitted on behalf of these individuals and they also reflect the Government they represented. They are intended to clarify certain aspects of their involvement as well as the Israeli involvement in the Iran Affair and the ensuing investigations. These comments are made necessary by the impression gained from a review of limited excerpts of the Final Report that, in some instances, do not reflect accurately or completely the events that occurred and the unprecedented role of Israeli individuals and the GOI in extending cooperation to the USG.

It is well-known now that the supply of certain arms to Iran, in connection with the Iran Affair, was part of a joint operation undertaken on a Government-to-Government basis between the USG and the GOI. In conducting this operation, numerous individuals were selected to serve their governments in pursuing a mission which, at the time, offered significant potential benefits to the two governments, to individuals then held hostage, and to the cause of regional and world peace.

Israeli individuals, acting on behalf of their government, acted in good faith in pursuing their mission. When the Iranian operation was transformed into a USG Iran-Contra investigation, these individuals extended themselves considerably to cooperate with the investigation and to help develop a complete understanding of the true facts and motivations underlying these events. However, this cooperation and the facts and motivations that surrounded their participation in the Iran Affair events unfortunately do not appear to be reflected accurately in the Final Report. These comments are intended to help facilitate a more accurate historical perspective on these matters.

II.   Government of Israel Cooperation

When the "Iran-Contra affair" became known to the public, USG officials in both the Executive and Congressional branches indicated that they were launching extensive investigations into it. Immediately, the GOI made it very clear to both branches of the USG that the GOI intended to cooperate fully with them. This cooperation was aimed at assisting the USG's investigatory bodies in uncovering the facts about what had happened on the Iran side of this controversy, which was the only part of these events in which the GOI had any involvement. In fact, the cooperation that was thereafter extended was unprecedented in international law and relations.

By the beginning of 1987, several weeks after the outlines of what happened initially became known, the GOI had already communicated to the USG, through government-to-government channels, that the GOI would cooperate with USG officials in investigating what had occurred. In accordance with the international norm in such matters, the GOI communicated its view that the most appropriate and efficacious means of providing cooperation would be through direct, government-to-government channels, in which the two sovereign states could transmit and exchange all relevant information.

From the outset, the GOI committed itself to cooperate with official United States governmental bodies investigating those developments, such as the Select Congressional Committees appointed to conduct this investigation on behalf of the Congress and the IC. From that point on, the GOI continually and repeatedly expressed to the USG its willingness to share very detailed and sensitive information, including substantial materials which the GOI was developing through its own special investigation of the Iran aspect of this matter.

In order to facilitate communication of GOI-developed information to the Select Congressional Committees investigating the Iran-Contra affair, the GOI and the Committees entered into an agreement under which the GOI provided information and materials to advance the Congressional investigation. On February 18, 1987, Senate Select Committee Chairman Daniel K. Inouye and House Select Committee Chairman Lee Hamilton thus announced their agreement with the GOI on cooperation, noting that the Prime Minister of Israel had been "extremely cooperative" and that Israel wanted to provide the Committees with all the information which Israel had. Rep. Hamilton stated that he was "very pleased" with the understanding between Israel and Congress.

Once there was an agreement in principle, even before the terms of that agreement were worked out, the GOI began to extend its cooperation wholeheartedly. Thus, although the formal agreement for GOI cooperation with the Congressional Select Committees was not signed until June 25, 1987, as an act of goodwill and to demonstrate the GOI's readiness to assist the Select Committees' investigation, a Financial Chronology was submitted to the Committees by April 25, 1987, two months before the Agreement was signed.

This spirit of bilateral cooperation, moreover, continued throughout the investigation and was noted in the Appendix to the Final Report of the Select Committees, on page 690, as follows:

> The Committees received unprecedented cooperation from the State of Israel. Israel entered into an agreement with the Committees to prepare and provide extensive financial and historical chronologies entailing the role of Israel and individual Israelis in the Iran initiative from 1985 through 1986 . . . Israel agreed to obtain and review relevant documents from Israeli participants and to interview Israeli nationals. With the specific agreement of the Government of Israel, information from the Israeli chronologies is used in this Report. The Committees used

this material sparingly and only where it was the best or only evidence of relevant facts.

As the Select Committees' Report indicated, the GOI cooperated extensively with and facilitated the Committees' investigations. The GOI provided critical information which identified key investigative directions, led the Committees to other major evidence, and provided evidence which could not have been obtained by the Committees from any source. The bilateral cooperation which marked the GOI's interactions with the Committees reflected the continuing close relations between Israel and the United States and the desires of the leaders of Israel to report on the truth of what had occurred.

The same extensive cooperation provided to the Congressional Select Committees was also offered, from the outset, to the IC and his investigative team. Unfortunately, the IC refused for more than a year to enter into an agreement with the GOI and to respect the sovereign status of the GOI. Instead, while negotiations to reach an agreement were in process, the IC chose to engage in confrontations with the GOI and its officials. Thus, for example, the IC placed former senior officials of the GOI on an immigration watch list and prepared subpoenas to serve upon them should they arrive in the United States. In a move which was unprecedented in international relations among nations, and which disturbed the United States Department of State, the IC then caused a subpoena to be served upon David Kimche, the former Director-General of the Israel Ministry of Foreign Affairs, the most senior career position in the Foreign Ministry.

Mr. Kimche was confronted with a USG subpoena when he was visiting the United States. As a result of a late evening knock at his hotel door, he was confronted by two federal agents and a subpoena demanding his appearance before a Grand Jury within two days. If United States officials were treated similarly when visiting foreign countries, USG outrage would be expressed in no uncertain terms, and rightfully so. The GOI was no less

disturbed by this serious breach of international law and etiquette. As a result, the GOI was

forced to enter a United States courtroom in order to protest the IC's conduct and contest the

validity of the subpoena.

The IC's confrontational approach was considered in court proceedings in which

the U.S. State Department also intervened to express its serious concerns about the IC's tactics

and legal positions. After many months of court proceedings and related delays, when it was

apparent that the court would not condone the IC's disregard for international norms between

sovereigns, the IC in March 1988 finally entered into an agreement with the GOI on

investigative cooperation that respected the sovereignty of the State of Israel.

While the process of entering into the cooperation agreement was much more

laborious and time-consuming than had been the case in connection with the Iran-Contra

investigation conducted by Congress, after agreement was reached the GOI began immediately

to provide the IC with a great deal of information, including chronologies, bank account data,

written answers to numerous questions, and other documents, which contributed significantly

to the IC's investigation and findings, providing important leads and corroborative evidence and

insights for use by the IC. In fact, this extensive level of GOI cooperation was unique in the

history of international relations and reflected the close connection between the USG and the

GOI. The cooperation entailed the GOI undertaking an extensive investigation, interviewing

every Israeli who had been involved in the Iran Affair, tracing a complicated network of

financial transactions and making all that information available to the IC. In addition, there

was a constant flow of information from the GOI to the IC as questions were raised, and Israeli

investigators were asked to clarify numerous aspects and track down numerous leads.

Having extended such cooperation, the GOI and the individuals who worked on its behalf and cooperated with the IC should have anticipated receiving some praise in the IC's Final Report. Congress recognized and praised such efforts and similar recognition would have been appropriate from the IC. Instead, however, the Report reflects an air of unjustified criticism, unfounded allegations of noncooperation and a complete failure to recognize and acknowledge the enormous extent of cooperation that was extended.

When the Iranian operation was underway, Israeli officials understood that this action had been approved at the highest levels of the USG and that it represented an extremely sensitive and important operation from the USG perspective. Full cooperation was extended and United States confidences were respected and protected. When this operation was transformed into a matter of internal USG strife and investigation, the GOI and its officials were naturally torn by the need to produce evidence which would be used to evaluate the conduct of USG officials with whom Israeli officials had worked closely and whose character and motivation they highly respected. Nevertheless, as an accommodation to the USG requests, and in a spirit of cooperation between close allies, the GOI extended its cooperation thoroughly and professionally. Having extended such cooperation voluntarily, on a sovereign-to-sovereign basis, the GOI did not expect such cooperation to be the subject of criticism in the Report, rather than praise.

The manner by which the GOI's cooperation is treated in the Final Report is unwarranted. Readers of the Final Report should appreciate the extent of cooperation that was provided by the GOI to the USG because of the extremely close ties that bind the two Governments. Because of these ties, the GOI initiated a substantial effort by a dedicated team of high-level GOI officials to ensure that the information was provided to the USG in an open, accurate and forthcoming manner. Throughout the course of the USG investigation, moreover, the GOI did not diminish, in any way, its commitment to provide assistance in the investigation.

III. Principal Concerns With IC Report

1. The Report Appears To Obscure The Fact That The Iran Affair Was A U.S., Not An Israeli Initiative

While counsel to the GOI and Israeli individuals was permitted to read only a small number of pages in the Final Report, containing specific references to a number of GOI officials, those pages were unfortunately replete with inaccuracies. The Final Report's treatment of important facts appears to have created a significant distortion, shifting the responsibility for the Iran initiative from the USG and, in particular, certain USG officials, to the GOI and its officials. For example, going back to the beginning of Israel's involvement in this initiative, the Final Report asserts that many aspects of this initiative, including the effort to obtain the release of hostages and provide arms to Iran, were Israeli initiatives, while the facts are quite to the contrary. Thus, contrary to the Final Report's assertion, the very idea of an Iran-related initiative was raised initially by Michael Ledeen at a May 3, 1985 meeting with Mr. Peres, which Mr. Ledeen requested. At that meeting, on behalf of the National Security Council, Mr. Ledeen suggested an Iranian initiative. Mr. Peres responded that, if the U.S. asked for Israeli cooperation, the GOI would do whatever was possible. In fact, arms shipments were not discussed at that meeting.

It is important to note that all of the initial contacts with the GOI regarding the Iran initiative involved Ledeen, who was acting explicitly on behalf of National Security Advisor Robert McFarlane. It was understood from the outset that his actions represented actions on behalf of the USG. As a result, in every respect, the GOI believed that it was responding to a joint venture initiated and approved by senior American officials, including President Ronald Reagan. In fact, Israeli officials, including the Prime Minister and Minister of Defense, made it clear on virtually every occasion when they had contact with cognizant USG officials that Israel was not interested in proceeding with any of these activities regarding Iran unless such activities were a joint U.S.-Israel venture with the express approval of the highest levels of the USG.

From the very outset of U.S. involvement, the GOI sought the express approval of President Reagan for the shipment of any TOW missiles from Israel to Iran; in fact, even the very first shipment from Israel of such missiles was made only after the GOI received President Reagan's personal approval. Furthermore, senior Israeli officials repeatedly asked their National Security Council contacts to make sure that Secretary of State George Shultz was aware of these developments. It was express GOI policy throughout its involvement to make certain that the most senior USG officials knew about the Iran initiative, approved of it, and viewed it as a joint venture between these two allied governments.

The Final Report continues erroneously with this theme of Israeli, rather than U.S. initiatives, when it addresses the involvement of Prime Minister Peres and Defense Minister Rabin in specific events. These officials are portrayed as being involved in minute details relating to the planning and implementation of the Iranian initiative, when that was not the case. For example, the Final Report states that, in a trip to the United States in November 1985, then-Defense Minister Rabin discussed in detail and sought U.S. approval for a prospective HAWK missile transaction with Iran. In fact, Defense Minister Rabin became aware of the HAWK transaction when he was briefed about it after meeting with McFarlane in November 1985. As a result, every reference to Defense Minister Rabin's discussions with

U.S. officials in November 1985 about the HAWK transaction is erroneous.

It is important to recognize the fundamental point that at no time in 1985 or

1986 did the GOI provide any weapons to Iran without express prior approval from the USG.

At each point in this process, the GOI was responding to USG requests that a joint effort be

undertaken to improve the American strategic position (and, of course, that of Israel, as well)

with Iran. In the course of that process, the USG sought other beneficial results in addition to

freeing the hostages in Lebanon. The Final Report appears to disregard these basic facts and,

to some extent, shifts responsibility for the Iran initiative and many of its specific

manifestations from the USG to the GOI.

2.   **Israel Did Not Suggest And Had No**
        Involvement In The Diversion Of Funds To The Contras

In what is a very serious distortion of the facts, the Final Report refers to Lt.

Col. North's testimony at the Poindexter trial, attributing to Amiram Nir, the then-Prime

Minister's Special Advisor for Anti-terrorism (in December 1985 or January or February 1986)

the idea for the diversion of funds to the Contras, and links that allegation with a November

14, 1985 meeting between North and Nir, at which they discussed hostage matters. This

linkage connects two unrelated sets of discussions and improperly suggests Israeli responsibility

for the diversion idea.

In fact, any assertion or inference in the Final Report that Nir or the GOI

initiated the notion of a diversion of funds is wholly unfounded and incorrect. To begin with,

the North-Nir meeting on November 14, 1985 had nothing to do with and did not include any

reference to the Iran initiative, since Nir was then completely uninformed about that subject.

It was not until later in December 1985 that Nir became involved in the Iran matter. His discussion with North on November 14 was completely divorced from any Iran-related developments. For the Final Report to suggest anything different about the November 14 meeting, or the notes cited by the Final Report relating to that meeting, is completely unwarranted and in total disregard of the detailed, documented submission provided by the GOI to the IC.

Moreover, as the Final Report itself states, North mentioned in passing to Israeli Ministry of Defense officials at a meeting in New York on December 6, 1985 that he intended to divert funds from the Iran arms sales to the Contras. Notes taken by an Israeli official present at that meeting include reference to such a statement by North. Since the GOI had no knowledge about or involvement or interest in such a diversion, North's statement was viewed by the note-taking GOI official as of no particular significance.

It is most significant that, on that date, December 6, 1985, Nir was not yet informed in any respect about the Iranian developments. In fact, at a meeting in London on December 7, 1985 attended by North, Kimche and other officials, North asked whether Nir was informed about the Iranian operation and was told that he was not. Since this question was posed by North after North had already told other Israeli officials that he intended to divert profits to the Contras, it follows that Nir could not possibly have been the source of the diversion idea. It would have been impossible for Nir to have suggested an idea which pre-dated Nir's having acquired any knowledge about the Iranian developments.

3.   The Final Report Misrepresents Israel's Role

Besides improperly attributing the Iranian initiative to the GOI, as noted in subsection 1 above, the Final Report also appears to fundamentally misrepresent Israel's role in 1985 and 1986 regarding the Iran initiative, downplaying the U.S. role and placing greater responsibility on Israel. Thus, the Final Report frequently errs in its references to events, making it appear as if the GOI was pressing for USG approvals when, in fact, official USG approvals had already been provided. For example, President Reagan's approval for the Israeli sale and replenishment by the USG had already been communicated to the GOI by Ledeen on July 23, 1985. Notwithstanding this communication, the GOI assigned Mr. Kimche to meet with Mr. McFarlane on August 2, 1985, in order to reconfirm the President's explicit approval of the USG initiative and the supply of TOW missiles to Iran. Furthermore, it was at this August 2 meeting, very early in the process, that the GOI impressed upon American officials the GOI's strong view that Secretary Shultz should be brought into the picture. That was the GOI's position at that stage, and throughout the evolution of these events, because the GOI at all times was willing to participate in such a joint activity only if it was absolutely clear that the Administration wanted Israel to do so.

The Final Report also contained references which suggest that Israeli officials were dealing with NSC officials in order to avoid dealing with the State or Defense Departments. As noted above, nothing could be further from the truth. As routine matters, GOI officials sometimes interacted with NSC officials and at other times with State or Defense Department officials. For instance, even the Final Report mentions the meeting between Mr. Meron, of the GOI Ministry of Defense, and Mr. Armacost, of the U.S. State Department, to discuss the replenishment issue. Such conduct was in no way pernicious or even significant; in fact, it is common practice for foreign governments to deal with either the NSC or the State or Defense Departments, depending upon the specific issues involved.

Israel's role is also erroneously reflected in the Final Report's assertion that, in late August 1985, McFarlane communicated President Reagan's approval of the initial Israeli arms shipment to Kimche. In fact, as noted above, Presidential approval had been communicated to Israel one month earlier. It is therefore not accurate to portray the GOI as having been out in front of the USG regarding these activities, when such was not the case.

The Final Report also states that after October 7, 1985, the U.S. was extremely reluctant to proceed any further with the matter, but that Ghorbanifar and the Israelis continued to push it. This assertion ignores the fact that Ledeen continued to be actively involved during this period, participating in meetings on behalf of the USG and urging the process forward. Such urgings were understood as reflecting the will and desire of the Administration.

The Final Report also contains significant errors regarding the HAWK missile transaction. First, the Final Report asserts a Rabin initiative with McFarlane in November 1985, at a time when the then-Defense Minister had not yet been briefed on the HAWK sale. Second, the Final Report asserts that technical difficulties with the initial HAWK deliveries were associated with Israel's inability to obtain landing clearances in a European country. In fact, it was never Israel's task or responsibility to get such clearances; rather, North had told GOI officials that Secord would be handling these clearances on behalf of the U.S. Once again, the Final Report appears to be placing a leadership role on Israel that was not in fact the case.

A serious error regarding the Israeli role is also made by the Final Report in its treatment of a January 2, 1986 meeting in Washington, attended by Poindexter, North and Nir. The Final Report states that Nir told the others that Israel would be willing to go ahead with a new transaction without a replenishment commitment from the U.S., thus again conveying the notion that the GOI was out in front on this issue. In fact, Nir's major position at that meeting was that Israel's only pre-condition to performing its part of the joint venture with the U.S. was that agreement had to be reached between Israel and the U.S. in advance on a timetable, method and price for replenishment of any IDF stocks that would be used for sales to Iran. In this regard, Nir emphasized military tensions with Syria then being manifested.

The specific instances of erroneous assertions in the Final Report represent examples of an approach which, unfortunately, does not illuminate the facts. Rather, these examples tend to generate incorrect inferences which are detrimental to the GOI. While these inferences are drawn from only a limited glimpse of the report, at this writing, Mr. Peres and other GOI officials are not in a position to draw conclusions regarding the impressions one would draw from a reading of the Final Report as a whole.

As the comments in Section IV below indicate in detail, many of the excerpts of the Final Report reviewed by counsel to the GOI and reported to the GOI officials who investigated these events or were involved in them are neither accurate nor credible. They lead to conclusions which do not support the factual reality that ——

    a.   the Iran initiative was a USG initiative for which Israeli support was solicited;

    b.   the GOI was immediately responsive and fully supportive of the U.S. initiative because of (i) a shared belief in the importance of its objectives and out of a sincere desire to help a friend (i.e., the United States) in need and (ii) respect for the USG officials involved in the process;

    c.   the GOI took painstaking steps to ensure that the highest officials of the USG, including President Reagan and Secretary of State Shultz, approved the initiative;

-14-

d.   the GOI was not involved in any fashion in the origination or

implementation of a plan to divert funds for Contra purposes, and only

belatedly learned of these activities; and

e.   the GOI has extended full cooperation to the USG authorities investigating

the Iran-Contra Affair on the sole condition that the cooperation be on a

sovereign-to-sovereign basis.

IV.   Factual Inaccuracies In The Final Report

1.   Introduction

The pages that were provided by the Court to counsel for certain present and

former officials of the GOI came in loose form from various Sections of the Final Report.

All in all, those pages appeared to represent only a very small portion of the Final Report.

While they were sufficient to alert GOI officials to the concerns discussed in the previous

sections of these Comments, the denial of greater access to the Final Report, as had been

requested, necessarily limits the comments that can or should be made.

In reviewing the pages that were provided, it became clear that, although the

Final Report appears to contain very specific details about the events surrounding the Iran

Affair, neither those details nor many of the conclusions reached or reported in the Final

Report are always consistent with facts. For the sake of historical accuracy and fairness, this

section of the Comments reviews specific facts and opinions in the Final Report that do not

appear to be completely accurate.

Page references in this section relate to the specific page numbers that were set

forth on the pages that were provided by the Court for review. Unfortunately, exactly where these pages are found in the Final Report was often not clear, since the pages were not provided in any precise textual context and copies of the Report's index and Table of Contents were also not provided.

2.   **Comments Of Individuals**

● **Errors Perceived By Messrs. Rabin And Peres**

(1)   **Part I, pages 9-12:**

The Final Report notes in these pages that Michael Ledeen, a part time consultant to the National Security Council, obtained National Security Advisor Robert McFarlane's approval to meet in Israel with Prime Minister Shimon Peres "to explore whether Israel would share information on Iran with the United States." It then quotes Ledeen as indicating that "Peres expressed displeasure with Israel's intelligence on Iran and suggested that the United States and Israel should work together to improve their information about and policies toward Iran. He also mentioned a recent Iranian request to buy artillery shells from Israel. Israel would grant the request, Peres said, only if the United States had no objection. Ledeen agreed to relay the question of the proposed weapon sale to McFarlane."

Comment:

The initiative to begin Israeli-U.S. cooperation vis a vis Iran was suggested by Mr. Ledeen on behalf of the National Security Council at the meeting on May 3, 1985. It was not an Israeli initiative or suggestion. Mr. Peres' response was that, if the U.S. requests Israeli cooperation, Israel would, of course, do whatever is possible. The issue of supplying arms to Iran was raised only later.

* * *

(2)   **Part I, pages 13-14**

The text notes that Mr. Rabin asked McFarlane if the United States still approved

of the Israelis selling arms to Iran and McFarlane said that President Reagan approved. It

notes that Mr. Rabin described the contemplated Hawk sale.

Comment:

At this November 15, 1985 meeting referenced in the Final Report, the HAWK

sale was not discussed, since Mr. Rabin was informed about Prime Minister Peres' decision

on the HAWK transaction only the day after the meeting. Mr. Rabin approved the transaction,

provided there would be proper replacements for the delivered missiles.

                              *   *   *

(3)   The text also notes that, on Sunday, November 17, 1985, just two days

after McFarlane's meeting with Rabin, Rabin telephoned North to say that Israel was ready to

go forward with a shipment of 80 HAWKS, once replenishment issues were worked out.

Comment:

Mr. Rabin did not telephone Col. North in this regard. Mr. Schwimmer was

in touch with Col. North on this matter.

                              *   *   *

(4)   **Chapter 1, page 89**

The Final Report notes that in May 1985, Ledeen traveled to Israel where he

met with Shimon Peres. Peres asked him to convey a request back to McFarlane. Peres said

Iran wanted to purchase U.S. made artillery shells from Israel and Israel could not make the

sale without United States approval. Subsequent to the meeting, Ledeen got back to Peres indicating that he had checked it out with the U.S. authorities and it was okay, but only one shipment was approved.

Comment:

This description is not accurate. Arms shipment were not discussed at this meeting.

* * *

(5) It is further noted that, in November, "Israeli Defense Minister Rabin called McFarlane in Geneva and told him there was a problem getting an arms shipment through a European country."

Comment:

This is not accurate. Mr. Rabin asked only for an answer regarding replacement of TOW missiles.

* * *

(6) Mr. McFarlane's testimony is quoted as follows: "I believe that his [Rabin's] purpose in coming was simply to reconfirm that the President's authority for the original concept was still valid. We hadn't changed our minds. And I reconfirmed that was the case."

Comment:

The main purpose of Mr. Rabin's meeting with Mr. McFarlane was to ascertain replacement for the TOW missiles.

* * *

(7)   It is further noted that, later in November, "Israeli Defense Minister Rabin called McFarlane in Geneva and told him there was a problem getting an arms shipment through a European country."

Comment:

This is not accurate. Mr. Rabin asked only for an answer regarding replacement of TOW missiles.

*   *   *

(8)   **Chapter 1, page 99**

In footnote 177, it is noted that "Israel never gave OIC access to financial accounts or records."

Comment:

This is not true. Israel furnished the OIC with all accounts and records as detailed in the Agreement with the IC.

*   *   *

(9)   **Chapter 8, page 171**

The text notes the following:

North, in his testimony, attributed to Nir and Ghorbanifar the idea for a diversion of arms sales funds to the Contras. In the Poindexter trial, although uncertain, he fixed the date in December 1985 or January or February of 1986. As early as November 14, 1985, North's notebooks show that he discussed with Nir a plan to obtain release of the hostages by payments to certain Middle East factions. The questions they discussed included: How to pay for; how to raise and a possible solution was to set up a 'joint' Israeli-U.S. 'cover op'.

Comment:

The assertions here are incorrect. Nir could not have suggested the diversion, since North expressed his intention to divert funds from the arms sales to the Contras on December 6, 1989, before Nir was involved in the Iranian transactions.

*   *   *

(10)   The text notes that, according to the Israelis, North apparently told Israeli defense officials at a meeting in New York on December 6, 1985 that he intended to divert funds from the arms sales to the Contras.

Comment:

An Israeli official present at the meeting noted North's above-mentioned statement in minutes he wrote during the meeting.

*   *   *

(11)   The text further notes that the diversion of the funds for the Contras was only one "dimension" of a much larger theft of Government funds generated by the Iran and Israeli replenishment transactions."

Comment:

The GOI had nothing to do with, and was entirely unaware of any "theft".

*   *   *

(12)   Chapter 15, pages 205-6

It is noted that Casey was an early advocate of finding an opening to Iran and was one of the individuals in the Administration who was wholeheartedly in favor of pursuing the Israeli initiative, because he was looking for a new broader policy.

Comment:

As mentioned above, this activity did not result from an Israeli initiative: it was a U.S. initiative to start U.S.-Israeli cooperation on Iran.

*   *   *

(13)   It is further noted that Michael Ledeen's talks with Mr. Peres led to a direct approach by Israeli officials to McFarlane to obtain President Reagan's approval to ship U.S.-supplied TOW missiles to Iran in exchange for the release of the American hostages in Beirut.

Comment:

From the outset, Israeli officials were concerned that before the GOI joined the U.S. initiative, it should be approved as a U.S. initiative at the highest levels of the USG. That concern led to the discussions with McFarlane.

*   *   *

(14)   **Chapter 24, page 333**

In a quotation from notes by Charles Hill, the Final Report states: "We are being had. Isr [Israel] desperate for a big arm trade..."

Comment:

The U.S. was never "being had" by Israel and Israel was never desperate for an Iran arms deal. Israel only responded to the USG's request for assistance in dealing with Iran and especially regarding the release of hostages.

*   *   *

(15)　Chapter 24, 337-8

The text notes that although Secretary Shultz stated as recently as February 1992 that he still believed that Rev. Weir was released to bring pressure on Kuwait to release the Dawa prisoners, and not because of the Israeli arms shipments, he could not maintain that he was never informed that Israel made the arms shipments at or before the time of the Weir release.

Comment:

The fact is that Rev. Weir was released on September 15, 1985, on the same day and immediately after the shipment from Israel of 408 TOW missiles arrived in Iran. None of the people involved denied that his release was a result of the shipment.

*　　　*　　　*

(16)　The text further notes that a proposal was under consideration involving 3300 TOWS and it states:

> Shultz reported that he told Poindexter that the new proposal raised "all (the) same probls (problems) as before. A payment Blows our policy. Shultz complained to Armacost "so it's not dead (Israeli Prime Minister Shimon) Peres came to me on some things and to the NSC (staff) on others.

Comment:

It is common practice that certain matters are discussed with the NSC and others with the State Department and vice versa.

*　　　*　　　*

(17)　Part II, pages 29-30

The text notes that the IC was effectively blocked from interviewing Israeli nationals by the GOI, although the IC attempted to subpoena them on visits to the U.S. In a footnote to this comment, the text also notes that, in February 1987, the GOI entered into an agreement with the Select Congressional Committees, unbeknownst to the IC until after-the-fact, and that, to obtain information, the IC in May 1987 was forced to issue subpoenas to Kimche and others. Thereafter, at the request of the State Department and in accordance with lengthy negotiations with the Israelis, the IC eventually agreed to withdraw the subpoena and accept a commitment by the Israelis to supply the IC with historical and financial chronologies and with additional information. The footnote ends by stating that "the chronologies, although highly useful in certain respects, were not a true substitute for live witness testimony."

Comment:

This is not an accurate or fair depiction of the events or of the unprecedented cooperation that was extended by the GOI. That cooperation is discussed in Section II above, containing Mr. Peres' comments on GOI cooperation.

*   *   *

(18)   **Part III, pages 69-70**

The text notes that Israel encountered difficulties in the shipment of the HAWKS and that Defense Minister Rabin called McFarlane and McFarlane directed North to help with the shipment.

Comment:

Mr. Rabin did not call Mr. McFarlane as described. On November 21, the last day of Mr. Rabin's stay in the U.S., Mr. McFarlane, who was in Geneva, returned a call placed by Mr. Rabin to the White House. Mr. Rabin was anxious to receive an answer about the replacement of the 504 TOW missiles Israel had delivered to Iran. In the discussion that followed, Mr. Rabin made it clear that, if the U.S. did not consider the Iranian issue as a joint U.S.-Israel project, Israel would not pursue the matter any longer.

* * *

(19) The text further notes that the Israelis paid Secord $1 million for his assistance. When the HAWK shipments were cancelled, Secord was left with a surplus of $800,000.

Comment:

The payment was made in response to a request from Col. North, who claimed that the above sum was required to cover the cost of flying the HAWK missiles to Iran.

* * *

(20) Thereafter, the text notes that the November 1985 transaction was the subject of an indictment in three respects: (1) North's direction that Israeli funds intended to cover the transportation cost for delivery of materials to Iran be deposited into an Enterprise bank account; (2) the Enterprise's retention and use of excess Israeli funds; and (3) Poindexter and North's attempted concealment in November 1986 of NSC participation in the 1985 transaction. In the course of the initial Israeli arms sales, McFarlane, Poindexter and North became involved in the initiative and a pattern of using arms sales to Iran to generate funds was established.

Comment:

It should be stressed that the existence of "excess Israeli funds" resulted from North's exaggerated pricing of the replacement TOW's. Furthermore, as mentioned above, this was an NSC initiative and Israel had absolutely no role in the activities relating to the subsequent use of funds.

(21)   Chapter 4, page 138

In a section dealing with "Thompson's Role in the November 1985 HAWK

shipment and the Destruction of the Findings," it notes that in November 1985, Israel Defense

Minister Rabin called McFarlane for assistance in making a shipment of U.S.-made HAWK

missiles from Israel to Iran. It thereafter describes the assistance that was provided and

Thompson's role.

Comment:

As has been noted, Defense Minister Rabin did not call McFarlane for assistance

in connection with the shipment of the HAWK missiles. It was Col. North who informed Mr.

Schwimmer that there were difficulties in obtaining landing approval and that he asked Gen.

Secord to obtain such approval.

*   *   *

(22)   Chapter 18, page 249

The Final Report again discusses an attempt by Mr. Rabin to obtain assistance

from the U.S. for the shipments that were being made from Israel to Iran, and deals with the

role Secord played after he was enlisted to be the problem-solver for the Israelis.

Comment:

As mentioned above, Mr. Rabin did not ask for U.S. assistance for those

shipments.

*   *   *

(23)   Part I, pages 11-19

The text notes that McFarlane met at the White House on July 3, 1985 with

David Kimche, the Director-General of the Israeli Foreign Ministry. At that meeting, Kimche raised the possibility of renewed political dialogue between the U.S. and Iran. Kimche said that the Iranians would use their influence over radical groups in Lebanon to obtain release of American hostages. The Iranians, however, would expect a reciprocal show of good faith from the U.S. "most likely in the form of military equipment." McFarlane thereafter discussed Kimche's proposals with President Reagan.

Comment:

Mr. Kimche met Mr. McFarlane following the NSC initiative which had been communicated by Mr. Ledeen to Prime Minister Peres at their meeting on May 3, 1987. Mr. Kimche sought to ascertain if President Reagan approved of the initiative, which included delivery of U.S.-made TOW missiles from Israel to Iran. Israel and Kimche were not the driving forces in pursuing the cooperation with Iran. Israel only responded favorably to U.S. requests.

*   *   *

(24)   The text further notes that, in mid-July 1985, McFarlane informed Shultz, Weinberger and Casey of the Israeli proposal and that the "Kimche and Schwimmer proposal" was briefed to the President.

Comment:

As mentioned above, the proposal was in accordance with an NSC initiative. It was not a "Kimche and Schwimmer proposal."

*   *   *

(25)   The text notes that Kimche met with McFarlane at the White House on August 2, 1985. The main issue they discussed was whether the U.S. would sell weapons to Iran or permit Israel to sell U.S.-manufactured equipment to Iran and then give Israel

replacements for that equipment. McFarlane promised that he would respond after consultation

with the President.

Comment:

In the August 2 meeting, McFarlane and Kimche discussed various aspects of

the joint U.S.-Israel operation. McFarlane reconfirmed the President's interest in the operation

and his personal approval of the delivery of 100 U.S.-made TOW missiles from Israel to Iran.

*   *   *

(26)   The text further notes that, not later than August 23, 1985, the President

wrote in his diary that he received a "secret" phone call from McFarlane that a man high up

in the Iranian Government believed he could deliver all or some of the kidnap victims. As a

result, the President decided to go forward. McFarlane then communicated the President's

approval to Kimche.

Comment:

As discussed above, the President's approval was reconfirmed to Mr. Kimche

at the August 2 meeting with McFarlane.

*   *   *

(27)   The text notes that Ghorbanifar claimed that the TOWs fell into the wrong

hands but he hoped that further shipments would result in the release of hostages. It then notes

that, after this great disappointment, the Israelis tried to move things forward by convening a

meeting in Paris on September 4 and 6. After that meeting, there was apparent resolution to

proceed.

Comments:

As a result of the second TOW shipment, Rev. Weir was released. Furthermore, at the meeting in Paris on September 4-5, Mr. Ledeen represented the U.S. and the decision to proceed was a joint U.S.-Israeli decision.

* * *

(28)   The text notes that, during this time, McFarlane told the Israelis that the Americans wanted William Buckley to be the first hostage released. After the September 14 delivery of the TOWs, there was a hostage release on September 15; however, instead of Buckley, Rev. Benjamin Weir was released. When this was raised, Ghorbanifar said that Buckley was too sick to be released, so they took Weir instead.

Comment:

This is not accurate. Although North specifically demanded the release of Buckley after the first shipment, at the September 5 Paris meeting, Ledeen said that, based on their sources, the Americans believed that Buckley was already dead.

* * *

(29)   The text notes that North did not participate in certain important meetings, but did participate in follow-up meetings. At these meetings, it was absolutely clear that the U.S. was extremely reluctant to proceed with this matter any further. However, Ghorbanifar and the Israelis continued to push it. It is then noted that, to keep it moving, Ledeen maneuvered a meeting between Kimche and McFarlane in Washington on November 8, 1985, with North and Ledeen also present. The Final Report states that "Kimche pressed McFarlane not to abandon the efforts to contact moderate Iranians through Ghorbanifar and Israel."

Comment:

This is not accurate. Ledeen, as long as he represented the NSC, participated in all meetings, as did North during the same period (except for one meeting). Recommendations for further action (e.g. HAWK missiles delivery) were taken jointly. At the November 8 meeting, although McFarlane expressed his doubts about the hostage transactions, he demanded continuation of the ties with Karrubi.

* * *

(30)   It is also noted that the project began to deteriorate because of technical difficulties associated, among other things, with Israel's inability to getting landing clearances.

Comment

The U.S., and not Israel, undertook through McFarlane and North to receive landing approval for the aircraft carrying the HAWK missiles, and failed.

* * *

(31)   The text describes a meeting that took place on December 8, 1985, at which there were heated exchanges with Kimche and Ghorbanifar "both whom favored more arms for hostages shipments." Thereafter, North wrote to Poindexter, taking issue with McFarlane and favoring going forward with the Kimche/Ghorbanifar proposals.

Comments:

The meeting on December 8 with McFarlane's participation was mainly a dialogue between McFarlane and Ghorbanifar, which resulted in disagreement. Notwithstanding that disagreement, in a meeting with Kimche immediately after that meeting, McFarlane asked Kimche whether Israel would be willing to supply a shipment of several hundred TOW missiles.

Moreover, McFarlane stressed the importance of convening a meeting with Karrubi, which he would personally attend.

*   *   *

(32)   The text notes that McFarlane briefed the President on December 10, in the presence of Weinberger, Casey and Reagan. McFarlane recommended strongly that the U.S. step out of this transaction. Again there was no decision by the President. After the meeting, however, it is noted that Poindexter sensed the President's willingness to continue with the transaction, since he was obsessed with doing whatever possible to free the hostages. As such, U.S. involvement continued.

Comment:

On November 26, North sent a telephone message to Kimche stating that the U.S. wanted to carry on, even if the supply of additional arms was necessary, and that everything, including replacements and money, would be covered by the U.S.

*   *   *

(33)   The text notes that on January 2, 1986, Nir came to Washington to meet with Poindexter and North. At that time, Nir proposed a broad new initiative involving 500 TOW missiles to Iran and the release of Hezbolla prisoners in Southern Lebanon. The Final Report states that Nir also noted that Israel was willing to go forward with this transaction without a commitment from the U.S. to replenish any equipment that Israel gave up. The Report states that Nir's proposal was well received.

Comment:

This is not accurate. On the contrary, at the meeting with Poindexter on January 4, Nir stressed that Israel's only condition for performing its part was an agreement with the U.S., in advance, on the time table, method and price for the replenishment of IDF

stocks reduced by the supply of 4000 TOW missiles to Iran.

*   *   *

(34)   <u>Chapter 8, page 168</u>

The Final Report notes that some time during May 15 and 16, Israel deposited

a total of $1.685 million in the Lake Resources account and that, although the Israelis expected

the replenishment to be paid from mark-ups on the Iran weapons sales, they finally agreed to

pay this amount after Nir was informed that sufficient funds were not being generated.

Further complicating the matter, the Final Report states, Israel had expected to

pay for the replacement of TOWs it sent to Iran in 1985 from Enterprise mark-ups on the

1,000 TOWs sold to Iran in February 1986. According to the Israelis, North claimed that the

proceeds were less than anticipated and would not cover the cost of the replenishment.

<u>Comment</u>:

North's claim proved to be incorrect. According to U.S. Army Ordnance

records, as reported by the Select Committees, the price of the replaced TOW missiles was

much lower than that quoted by North.

*   *   *

(35)   It is noted that Kimche pressed McFarlane not to abandon the efforts to

contact moderate Iranians through Ghorbanifar and Israel.

<u>Comment</u>:

It was the U.S. that decided to continue and work through Ghorbanifar after a

thorough investigation conducted in January 1986, when Ghorbanifar was invited to the U.S.

for this purpose, and not because of Israeli pressure.

-31-

- **Error Perceived By Mr. David Kimche, Former
  <u>Director-General Of The Ministry Of Foreign Affairs</u>**

<u>Chapter 24</u>

In the very limited materials that were made available to me from the Final Report, there is a reference in Chapter 24 indicating that I leaked information to Newsweek regarding a meeting I had with Mr. McFarlane.

<u>Comment</u>:

There is absolutely no truth to the suggestion that I leaked any information regarding my meeting with Mr. McFarlane to Newsweek. The instructions given to all Israeli officials involved in this matter required that all information be treated in strictest confidence and as classified information. I followed that instruction at all times and, to my knowledge, it was also followed strictly by the other Israeli individuals involved in the matter.

●   **Error Perceived By Mr. Adolph Schwimmer,**
    <u>**Former Special Advisor To Prime Minister Peres**</u>

<u>**Chapter 1**</u>

In the very limited materials that were made available to me from the Final
Report, there is a suggestion in Chapter 1 that I had an agreement with Michael Ledeen to share
gains from the sales to Iran.

<u>**Comment**</u>:

There is no truth or basis whatsoever for a suggestion that I received any gain
from the Iranian transaction or that I had any agreement with Michael Ledeen to share in any
of the proceeds from the sales to Iran.   It is also my understanding that Michael Ledeen
received no financial benefits from these transactions.

Former President Ronald W. Reagan

UNITED STATES COURT OF APPEALS
FOR THE DISTRICT OF COLUMBIA CIRCUIT

Division for the Purpose of
Appointing Independent Counsel
Division No. 86-6

United States Court of Appeals
For the District of Columbia Circuit

FILED DEC 0 3 1993

RON GARVIN
CLERK

RESPONSE OF FORMER PRESIDENT RONALD W. REAGAN TO FINAL REPORT OF THE INDEPENDENT COUNSEL FOR IRAN/CONTRA MATTERS

Theodore B. Olson
John A. Mintz
Theodore J. Boutrous, Jr.
John K. Bush
GIBSON, DUNN & CRUTCHER

Attorneys for Former President Ronald W. Reagan

December 3, 1993
Washington, D.C.

IN THE UNITED STATES COURT OF APPEALS
FOR THE DISTRICT OF COLUMBIA CIRCUIT

Division for the Purpose of
Appointing Independent Counsels

Ethics in Government Act of 1978, As Amended

In re: Oliver North, et al.

Division No. 86-6

(Under Seal)

SUBMISSION OF RESPONSE OF FORMER PRESIDENT
RONALD W. REAGAN TO FINAL REPORT OF THE
INDEPENDENT COUNSEL FOR IRAN/CONTRA MATTERS

Former President Ronald W. Reagan lodges herewith his Response to the
Final Report of the Independent Counsel for Iran/Contra Matters.

December 3, 1993

Respectfully submitted,

THEODORE B. OLSON
JOHN A. MINTZ
THEODORE J. BOUTROUS, JR.
JOHN K. BUSH
GIBSON, DUNN & CRUTCHER
1050 Connecticut Avenue, N.W.
Washington, D.C. 20036-5303
(202) 955-8500

*Attorneys for Former President Ronald W.
Reagan*

UNITED STATES COURT OF APPEALS
FOR THE DISTRICT OF COLUMBIA CIRCUIT

Division for the Purpose of

Appointing Independent Counsel

Division No. 86-6

United States Court of Appeals
For the District of Columbia Circuit

FILED DEC 0 3 1993

RON GARVIN
CLERK

RESPONSE OF FORMER PRESIDENT
RONALD W. REAGAN TO
FINAL REPORT OF THE
INDEPENDENT COUNSEL FOR
IRAN/CONTRA MATTERS

Theodore B. Olson
John A. Mintz
Theodore J. Boutrous, Jr.
John K. Bush
GIBSON, DUNN & CRUTCHER

Attorneys for Former President Ronald W. Reagan

December 3, 1993
Washington, D.C.

TABLE OF CONTENTS

PRELIMINARY STATEMENT

President Reagan first learned in November of 1986 that proceeds from United States Government arms sales to Iran may have been diverted to assist the Nicaraguan resistance movement. He responded immediately by opening the records of his Administration to congressional investigators and to an independent investigating commission headed by former Senator John Tower. He waived claims of executive privilege and instructed his subordinates to cooperate fully with all investigations. He asked his Attorney General to seek the appointment of an independent counsel to investigate and, where appropriate, to prosecute any violations of criminal law arising from the events that became known as Iran-Contra.

Lawrence E. Walsh was appointed on December 19, 1986, to serve as Iran-Contra Independent Counsel. President Reagan cooperated fully with that investigation from its inception. He provided the Independent Counsel with unlimited access to the records of his Administration. He answered the Independent Counsel's questions under oath in writing and in person. He allowed the Independent Counsel access to all relevant portions of his diaries. He denied no information to the Independent Counsel. His cooperation has been both unlimited and unstinting.

President Reagan has never publicly criticized any aspect of the investigation or conduct of Independent Counsel Walsh. He has refrained from any statement or conduct that might in any way be perceived as an impediment to the investigation. He declined requests to pardon individuals being investigated by the

1

Independent Counsel. He did everything within his power to ensure that the Independent Counsel had the fullest authority and unfettered discretion to conduct his investigation.

The Independent Counsel has now completed his almost seven-year investigation, and it is now both appropriate and necessary for former President Reagan to respond. As many others have commented, and as his Final Report reveals, the Independent Counsel has permitted his investigation to become both excessive and vindictive. He has abused his authority. He has used his office to intimidate and harass individuals and otherwise to damage the lives of the persons he was given license to investigate. He and his Final Report have violated the policies of the Department of Justice that he was required by law to uphold, and he has disregarded the standards and ethics imposed uniformly on public prosecutors. His Final Report exceeds the authority given to him by law. He has used it to disseminate false and unfounded speculation, opinion and innuendo. His Final Report is not a chronicle of facts, but a prolonged justification of his own excessive investigation and a defamation of the individuals he was empowered to investigate.

Independent Counsel Walsh found no credible evidence of personal wrongdoing by President Reagan or violation by the former President of any criminal laws. *See, e.g., Final Report of the Independent Counsel for Iran/Contra Matters*, Vol. I, at xiii (Aug. 4, 1993) ("[T]he investigation found *no* credible evidence that President Reagan violated *any* criminal statute.") (emphasis added) [hereinafter *Final Report*]; *id.* at 445 (the former President's "conduct *fell well short of criminality*") (emphasis added). Yet in his Final Report the Independent Counsel attempts to indict President Reagan for alleged misconduct by others and to hint, without the benefit of any evidence, at wrongdoing by the former President himself.

The Independent Counsel's Final Report is the product of almost seven-years work involving sixty-eight lawyers and hundreds of investigators. It is

several hundred pages and several hundred-thousand words long. It is based upon
years of secret grand jury interrogations to which only the Independent Counsel has had
access. It is therefore impossible for anyone injured by the Report adequately to
respond to it without comparable resources and access to the same materials.
However, the following pages respond to the principal assertions and conclusions of the
Independent Counsel. They demonstrate that, except for matters already considered by
Congress and the courts, the Independent Counsel's speculation and conclusions
regarding alleged misconduct by many individuals, including former President Reagan,
are without foundation, and reflect, at best, a misunderstanding of the events he has
investigated and a slanted and completely misleading rendition of them.

EXECUTIVE SUMMARY

The Facts Of Iran-Contra

The essential facts of Iran-Contra are as follows:

1.   In the summer of 1985, the Reagan Administration, at the urging and with the assistance of the Israeli government, determined to explore forming a relationship with moderates in the government of Iran who were preparing to seek power upon the death of Ayatollah Khomeini. The Iranians offered to demonstrate their "bona fides" by attempting to assist the United States in achieving the release of American hostages being held in Lebanon. To demonstrate the good faith of the United States in engaging in these discussions, the United States agreed to sell a limited amount of arms to these moderate Iranian government officials. President Reagan was informed of and approved the Iranian initiative, which at first involved Israel's shipment of U.S.-made TOW and HAWK missiles to Iran, and subsequently involved direct shipments of a limited amount of arms to Iran by the United States. Three hostages were released during the eighteen-month Iranian initiative, which was first publicly reported on November 3, 1986, and terminated shortly thereafter.

2.   Beginning in 1983, Congress sought to impose a series of legal restrictions on the use of certain appropriated funds by the Reagan Administration to support the Nicaraguan Democratic Resistance, or "Contras," in their efforts to resist the excesses and expansionism of the communist "Sandinistas," who had seized control

of the Nicaraguan government in 1979. Congress enacted and subsequently repeatedly amended appropriations riders, the so-called Boland Amendments, to restrict certain Executive Branch agencies from providing certain types of aid to the Contras. President Reagan acted in compliance with the Boland Amendments and directed his subordinates to do so as well.

      3.   In connection with a preliminary investigation of the Iranian arms sales directed by Attorney General Edwin Meese III over the weekend of November 21-23, 1986, the Attorney General's staff discovered a memorandum in the files of Lt. Col. Oliver L. North indicating that funds from the Iranian arms transactions may have been diverted to support the Contras. President Reagan was first informed on November 24, 1986, that a diversion may have occurred, and on November 25, 1986, the President and the Attorney General held a press conference to disclose the discovery of the possible diversion of funds. President Reagan moved immediately thereafter to assist congressional investigations of these events, authorized the creation of an independent Executive Branch investigation and urged the appointment of an independent counsel by the Judiciary to conduct a third investigation. He opened the records of his Administration to these three separate independent investigations.

Response Of Former President Reagan
To The Independent Counsel's Final Report

      The Response of former President Reagan to the Final Report demonstrates the following:

      1.   The Iran-Contra Independent Counsel has misused and abused the reporting process that is mandated by the independent counsel statute. The Final Report unfairly and unnecessarily injures the rights and reputations of individuals, relies on innuendo, speculation and conjecture instead of proof, violates established

standards governing the conduct of prosecutors, and improperly relies on secret grand jury materials to support the Independent Counsel's many accusations.

        2.   The Independent Counsel's principal accusation in his Final Report is that officials at the highest levels of the Reagan Administration engaged in a "cover-up" designed to conceal the fact that President Reagan had contemporaneous knowledge of the 1985 Iranian arms shipments. There was, however, no "cover-up." To the contrary, President Reagan repeatedly insisted, both publicly and privately, that the complete facts of Iran-Contra be publicly aired and that his Administration cooperate fully with investigators. Moreover, the evidence is overwhelming that the essential facts of the Iranian initiative were readily and repeatedly disclosed by President Reagan and his top advisers. The contemporaneous notes of participants in the meetings referred to by the Independent Counsel independently refute the notion of a cover-up and demonstrate that the Independent Counsel has falsely depicted the events that he purports to describe. In fact, President Reagan's knowledge of the 1985 arms transactions supports, not undermines, the legality of those transactions.

        3.   The Independent Counsel's contention that President Reagan and his senior advisers and Cabinet officials participated in a strategy to make National Security Council ("NSC") staff member Lt. Col. North, and National Security Advisers Robert C. McFarlane and John M. Poindexter "scapegoats" with respect to Iran-Contra is demonstrably false. President Reagan took full responsibility for the Iranian initiative from the outset. He also accepted responsibility for all actions within the scope of his instructions taken by his subordinates in support of the Contras. But he was not aware of and could not responsibly be blamed for the diversion of funds to the Contras, the destruction of records by individuals acting contrary to his instructions or other conduct that was not authorized or sanctioned. The "scapegoat" theory of the Independent Counsel has been advanced and repeatedly rejected since the first public revelation of Iran-Contra, and was rejected by the Independent Counsel himself in the

cases that he prosecuted. His Final Report adds nothing to the record except his own, internally inconsistent, personal theory.

     4.   The Independent Counsel repeatedly seeks to convey the impression that high-ranking Reagan Administration officials, including the President, violated civil laws and Executive Orders in carrying out the Iranian initiative, particularly with regard to the 1985 arms shipments. But there is, in fact, strong authority supporting the legality of the Iranian arms shipments. The President had the power and responsibility to take certain measures to advance U.S. policies and interests and the constitutional discretion to protect the lives and liberty of Americans in foreign countries. The President properly relied on legal experts to ensure that his actions were lawful, as the Independent Counsel grudgingly acknowledges. The Iranian initiative was consistent with other applicable laws, and the Independent Counsel has provided no reasoned legal analysis to the contrary.

     5.   Although the Independent Counsel concedes that there is "*no credible evidence that the President authorized or was aware of the diversion of profits from the Iran arms sales to assist the contras,*" *Final Report*, Vol. I, at 443 (emphasis added), his Final Report indulges in the irresponsible speculation that the President must have known about the diversion. However, that speculation has no evidentiary support whatsoever, and is directly contradicted by the findings of the Tower Commission and the Congressional Committees that investigated Iran-Contra. President Reagan has consistently, unequivocally and categorically stated that he had no knowledge of the diversion, and every bit of credible evidence in the record -- including the voluminous record compiled by Independent Counsel Walsh -- is consistent with the President's clear and unwavering position on this point. The Independent Counsel's Report adds nothing new beyond his capricious speculation.

     6.   The Independent Counsel asserts that President Reagan is responsible for "set[ting] the stage" for alleged violations of the law by his subordinates

by expressing his continuing public support for the Contras. *See id.* at xiii. However, President Reagan gave repeated instructions to members of his Administration to follow the law and abide by the Boland restrictions. The activities authorized by President Reagan complied with the Boland Amendments and all other laws of the United States. The Independent Counsel has been unable to establish that any conduct by the President violated the various vague appropriations riders referred to as the Boland Amendments.

RESPONSE OF FORMER PRESIDENT REAGAN CONCERNING THE INDEPENDENT COUNSEL REPORTING PROCESS

I

THE FINAL REPORT ACKNOWLEDGES THAT PRESIDENT REAGAN VIOLATED NO CRIMINAL LAWS BUT NONETHELESS CONTAINS FALSE, INACCURATE AND IRRESPONSIBLE SPECULATION, INNUENDO, AND HYPERBOLE, AND IMPROPER POLICY AND CONSTITUTIONAL PRONOUNCEMENTS

The Independent Counsel's Final Report acknowledges that President Reagan did not violate any criminal laws or engage in any personal wrongdoing in connection with any aspect of the Iran-Contra controversy. While his language betrays his attitude and bias, the Independent Counsel concedes, as he must, that the former President's "conduct *fell well short of criminality*." *Final Report*, Vol. I, at 445 (emphasis added). The Independent Counsel found "*no* credible evidence that President Reagan violated *any* criminal statute." *Id*. at xiii (emphasis added). Thus, if nothing else, the Independent Counsel's Report serves to confirm what the Tower Commission and Congressional Committees concluded over six years ago:

(a)   President Reagan did not authorize and was not aware of any diversion of funds from the Iranian arms sales to the Contras. *See, e.g., id*. at xiii ("The OIC could not prove that Reagan authorized or was aware of the diversion

9

or that he had knowledge of the extent of North's control of
the contra-resupply network."); *id.* at 447 (same); *id.* at 443
("Independent Counsel found no credible evidence that the
President authorized or was aware of the diversion of profits
from the Iran arms sales to assist the contras . . . ."); *id.* at
457 ("Independent Counsel could not prove that President
Reagan knew there was Government involvement in the
Hasenfus operation."); *id.* at 446 ("Independent Counsel
found no prosecutable evidence that the President expressly
authorized or was informed of the illegal features of North's
operational participation in the covert contra-resupply
operation and his financing of the operation.").

       (b)   "[C]riminal proceedings against [President
Reagan] were always unlikely." *Id.* at xvi. President
Reagan had no knowledge of the underlying facts of Iran-
Contra that the Independent Counsel alleges "were
criminal." *Id.* at 445. Nor did President Reagan make any
"criminal misrepresentations regarding them." *Id.*; *see also*
id. at 465 (no proof that the President "knew that the
statements being made to Congress were false, or that acts
of obstruction were being committed"); *id.* at 469-70 ("it
would be impossible to prove beyond a reasonable doubt
that any misstatement was intentional or willful").

However, the Independent Counsel has not confined his Report to "the work of the independent counsel," 28 U.S.C. § 595(b)(2),[1] or limited his analysis to matters within his prosecutorial jurisdiction, which was explicitly limited to the investigation and prosecution of crimes.[2] Instead, he has quite brazenly used his Report to argue for or hint at conclusions that, as he admitted to *The New York Times*, "'we were not able to prove'."[3] The result is an excessive, hyperbolic, emotional screed that relies on speculation, conjecture, innuendo, and opinion instead of proof. The Independent Counsel has improperly used the shield of an official report to disseminate grand jury material protected by statutory law and the Constitution from disclosure, to launch defamatory personal attacks, and to make imperial pronouncements as to how the government should be structured and how he would have dealt with hostages in Lebanon, a changing political dynamic in Iran, and a civil war in Nicaragua.

As Attorney General and later Supreme Court Justice Robert Jackson once observed:

> The prosecutor has more control over life, liberty and
> reputation than any other person in America. His discretion
> is tremendous. He can have citizens investigated and, if he
> is that kind of person, he can have this done to the tune of
> public statements and veiled or unveiled intimations . . . .
> While the prosecutor at his best is one of the most beneficent
> forces in our society, when he acts from malice or other
> base motives, he is one of the worst.

---

[1]   All citations to the independent counsel statute in this Response are to the 1983 version of the statute, which generally governs Independent Counsel Walsh's investigation. *See* 28 U.S.C. § 591 (1988) (note explaining effective dates).

[2]   *See* December 19, 1986 Order of Appointment, *reprinted in Final Report*, Vol. II, at 777-79.

[3]   Spencer, *Lawrence Walsh's Last Battle*, N.Y. Times, July 4, 1993, § 6 (Magazine), at 11, 33 (quoting Mr. Walsh).

R. Jackson, *The Federal Prosecutor*, Address Delivered at the Second Annual
Conference of United States Attorneys, Apr. 1, 1940. For these reasons, prosecutors
do not issue reports,[4] they do not pronounce persons guilty of crimes who have not
even been indicted, much less tried and convicted, and they do not engage in innuendo,
speculation, supposition and assertions of guilt by implication.[5] The independent
counsel law, however, requires an independent counsel to file a final report. But that
provision does not license its abuse in the gross and reckless manner of this
Independent Counsel. The Iran-Contra Independent Counsel's extraordinary and
inappropriate Final Report ignores all established prosecutorial standards or concerns
for the rights of the individuals whom he has investigated. His irresponsible abuse of
authority makes this comprehensive response by former President Reagan to his many
improper charges both appropriate and necessary.

II

THE FINAL REPORT IS REPLETE WITH HIGHLY IMPROPER STATEMENTS AND MATERIAL

Independent Counsel Walsh's Final Report is permeated with improper
statements and material. The following is a small sample of the Report's multitude of
abuses.

---

[4]   The filing of reports by independent counsels is "a complete departure from the
authority of an United States Attorney," and "contrary to the practice of federal grand jury
investigations." *In re Sealed Motion*, 880 F.2d 1367, 1369-70 (Spec. Div. D.C. Cir.
1989).

[5]   The Department of Justice regulations and policies, which the Independent Counsel
must follow unless it is impossible, *see* 28 U.S.C. § 594(f), ban precisely such statements
and conduct. *See infra* pages 21-22.

A. Expressions Of Opinion Concerning Alleged Criminal Law Violations

Independent Counsel Walsh's Report quite freely brands certain individuals as criminals even though they were never indicted or convicted or their convictions were overturned:

(a)   The Report makes the blanket assertions that "senior Reagan Administration officials engaged in a concerted effort to deceive Congress and the public about their knowledge [of arms sales to Iran]," and participated in a "cover-up," *Final Report*, Vol. I, at xi, although no convictions were obtained to support such an extraordinary charge, and although every percipient witness to the events denies that any "cover-up" was ever intended, discussed or implemented.

(b)   Although the Independent Counsel acknowledges that the convictions of Admiral Poindexter and Lt. Col. North "were reversed on appeal on constitutional grounds," he denies the legal effect of those judicial decisions and disregards the presumption of innocence to which those not convicted of a crime are entitled by declaring that the decisions overturning those convictions "in no way cast doubt on the *factual guilt* of the men convicted." *Id.* at x (emphasis added); *see also id.* at 122 ("the congressional hearings did nothing to hold North or others responsible for the *crimes they committed*") (emphasis added); *id.* ("Despite the dismissal of North's convictions, the prosecution of the case showed that even individuals entrenched in national security matters can be held accountable for *crimes committed* in the course of their official duties.") (emphasis added); *id.* at 136 (even though set aside, Admiral Poindexter's "conviction showed . . .

that . . . *obstructing and lying to Congress is a serious act worthy of felony conviction*") (emphasis added).

(c)   Despite the fact that President George Bush pardoned Secretary of Defense Caspar W. Weinberger prior to trial, the Independent Counsel again re-argues the **"Government's Case Against Weinberger**," *id.* at 415 (bold in original), and states, among other things, that Mr. Weinberger "*lied to investigators* to conceal his knowledge of the Iran arms sales," *id.* at 405 (emphasis added), "*deliberately withheld his own notes* from Congress and *falsely denied* to congressional investigators that he had contemporaneous notes," *id.* at 417 (emphasis added), and made "*false statements* to the Select Committees" regarding his knowledge of Saudi Arabian contributions to the Contras, *id.* at 422 (emphasis added).

(d)   Ignoring President Bush's pardon of former CIA official Claire E. George after trial but prior to appeal, the Independent Counsel states without equivocation or qualification that Mr. George "chose to *evade, mislead and lie*" to Congress and the grand jury. *Id.* at 245 (emphasis added).

B.   Innuendo As To Alleged Criminal Law Violations

The Report contains page after page of innuendo that former President Reagan and others might have transgressed criminal laws even though the Independent Counsel neither found nor offers any evidence to support such outrageous suggestions. For example:

(a)   The Report makes the false and wholly unwarranted slander that "President Reagan *created the conditions which made possible the crimes* committed by others by his secret deviations from

14

announced national policy . . . and by his open determination to keep the contras together 'body and soul' despite a statutory ban on contra aid." *Final Report,* Vol. I, at 445 (emphasis added).

    (b)   The Report inexplicably and without even a scintilla of evidence -- indeed, all the evidence is to the contrary -- asserts that President Reagan "*permitted the creation of a false account* of the Iran arms sales to be disseminated to Congress and the American people." *Id*. at 445-46 (emphasis added).

    (c)   While the Report grudgingly concedes that President Reagan committed no crimes, it does so in a way that is clearly intended to suggest that it is the Independent Counsel's personal view that the former President's innocence is nothing more than a legal technicality. For example, the Report is forced to acknowledge that "President Reagan's conduct fell well short of criminality," but then immediately adds the phrase, "*which could be successfully prosecuted.*" *Id*. at 445 (emphasis added); *see also id*. ("it *could not be proved beyond a reasonable doubt* that President Reagan . . . made criminal misrepresentations . . . .") (emphasis added); *id*. at 446 ("No *direct* evidence was developed . . . .") (emphasis added); *id*. ("Independent Counsel found no *prosecutable* evidence . . . .") (emphasis added).

    (d)   The Report repeatedly implies that there is less to the President's innocence of criminal misconduct than meets the eye, making suggestive statements such as "[t]he President's own activities on behalf of the contras were not *on the face of it* activities forbidden by criminal law," *id*. at 452 (emphasis added), and observing that

15

prosecution of the former President "would have required more [evidence] than [certain individuals] were willing to give," *id*.

(e)   The Report makes calculated and sweeping generalizations assessing blame on President Reagan that are obviously intended directly to nullify its specific statements exonerating the President from criminal misconduct: "The *tone* in Iran/contra was set by President Reagan," and "[w]hen a President . . . chooses to *skirt the laws or to circumvent them*, it is incumbent upon his subordinates to resist, not join in." *Id*. at 566 (emphasis added). And, "the ignorance of the 'diversion' asserted by President Reagan . . . in no way absolves [him] of responsibility for the underlying Iran and contra operations." *Id*. at xi.

(f)   The Independent Counsel admits that Chief of Staff Donald T. Regan committed no crimes, but cannot resist implying just the opposite by adding that there was "no *usable* evidence that [Regan] was attempting to orchestrate a story [to conceal the President's knowledge of the 1985 arms shipments], or that he was helping Meese do it." *Id*. at 523 (emphasis added).

C.   Speculation As To Events, Motives And Knowledge Of Individuals

Lack of proof has not constrained Independent Counsel Walsh from offering his personal speculation concerning events that "might" have occurred and what individuals, including former President Reagan, "might" have known. For example:

(a)   Although he concedes that there is no "direct evidence" that the former President knew of the possible diversion of funds to the Contras -- and points to no "indirect" or remotely credible evidence supporting any such theory -- the Independent Counsel hypothesizes that "it was doubtful that President Reagan would tolerate the successive Iranian affronts during 1986 unless he knew that the arms sales continued to supply funds to the contras." *Final Report,* Vol. I, at 446. A few pages later he adds: "In spite of his insulation from North and his activities by McFarlane and Poindexter, President Reagan *had to know* the contras were being held together." *Id.* at 452 (emphasis added). Thus, the Independent Counsel draws the bewildering and utterly fanciful conclusion that President Reagan would not have continued dealing with the Iranians had he not known that it was somehow beneficial to the Contras. This bizarre logic typifies the Independent Counsel's tactic of allowing his imagination to substitute for fact.

(b)   The Independent Counsel speculates, without any evidence and, indeed, contrary to a wealth of evidence available to him, including evidence from the President's own diaries, that "the President's most senior advisers and the Cabinet members on the National Security Council participated in a strategy to make . . . McFarlane, Poindexter and North the scapegoats whose sacrifice would protect the Reagan Administration in its final two years." *Id.* at xi. Not a shred of evidence exists, even from the alleged objects of the "scapegoat" operation, that such a plan even existed or was implemented. It may serve the Independent Counsel's objective to tarnish President Reagan to make the charge, but it is utterly fraudulent.

(c)   The Independent Counsel engages in conjecture that high-level officials agreed on an elaborate six-year cover-up strategy based on what was *not* said at a November 24, 1986 senior

advisers meeting about the state of the President's knowledge of the

1985 HAWK shipment to Iran, *see, e.g., id.* at 542-45, even

though the Independent Counsel recognizes that Chief of Staff

Regan disclosed in testimony to Congress only three weeks later

that President Reagan knew about the HAWK shipment.[6]

      (d)   Instead of proof, Independent Counsel Walsh offers

only his own subjective observation that the "most plausible

explanation for Meese's conduct [in November 1986] is that he *was*

trying to get Shultz to change his recollection" about the

President's knowledge of the 1985 HAWK shipment. *Id.* at 545

(emphasis in original). He also engages in after-the-fact guesswork

that "[i]n the November 24 senior advisers' meeting, it *appears*

Meese was trying to signal the other senior advisers that the official

position should be that the President didn't know," and that

Attorney General "Meese's motives . . . are implicit." *Id.*

(emphasis added).

D.   Assertions That President Reagan Deliberately Violated Civil Laws Restricting Arms Sales And Covert Action

      The Independent Counsel has not limited his Report to matters within his

prosecutorial jurisdiction, which extends only to investigations of criminal law

violations. For example:

      (a)   Although the Department of Justice issued a legal

opinion that the 1985 Iranian arms shipments were consistent with

---

[6]   *See, e.g., id.* at 519 n.90 ("Since his earliest testimony before [Congress] on December 16, 1986, Regan repeatedly stated that McFarlane briefed the President during the November 1985 Geneva summit on a shipment of arms from Israel to Iran.").

laws relating to arms sales, Independent Counsel Walsh draws from the ether a pronouncement that such actions violated the law. While the Independent Counsel nowhere presents a reasoned legal opinion refuting the views of the Attorney General, the Assistant Attorney General and the CIA General Counsel, who expressed strong convictions on the subject, the Independent Counsel argues, without authority, to the contrary. Independent Counsel Walsh refers to the Justice Department's opinion finding the sales legally authorized to be nothing more than a "post hoc position," *Final Report,* Vol. I, at ix n.1, and then argues without any legal research or analysis of his own that "[t]here was no way in which President Reagan's action could be squared with the Arms Export Control Act," *id.* at 453. The difference between the Justice Department's *post hoc* analysis and the Independent Counsel's *post hoc* contradiction is that the former explains its conclusions and cites authorities for it, while the Independent Counsel's assertion is simply a naked assertion without any research, reasoning or authority.

(b)   Similarly, Independent Counsel Walsh flatly declares, with only the barest legal analysis and no supporting authority, that **"The Boland Amendment was Violated."** *Id.* at 67 (bold in original).

(c)   The Report broadly pronounces, again without legal reasoning, explanation or authority, that "regardless of criminality, President Reagan, the secretary of state, the secretary of defense, and the director of central intelligence and their necessary assistants . . . skirted the law, some of them broke the law, and almost all of them tried to cover up the President's willful activities." *Id.* at 561; *see also id.* at 562 (the "Iran/contra affair . . . was the product of two foreign policy directives by President Reagan which skirted the law"); *id.* at xiii (referring to the "President's disregard for civil laws enacted to limit presidential actions abroad -- specifically the Boland Amendment, the Arms Export Control Act and congressional-notification requirements in covert-action laws").

Thus, although the Independent Counsel could not prove criminal law violations, and could not document or otherwise establish violations of non-criminal enactments, he has chosen to imply that completely lawful conduct "skirted" the law or set a "tone" that encouraged others to violate the law. Such irresponsible rhetoric is unwarranted and violates the rules, standards and ethics governing prosecutors.

Indeed, the Independent Counsel's assertions regarding individuals who were not even indicted, much less tried and convicted of any crime, are completely at odds with traditional prosecutorial practice. As the Special Division of the United States Court of Appeals responsible for overseeing the work of the Independent Counsel has stated, "[f]iling a report that may be made public where no indictment is returned is a complete departure from the authority of an United States Attorney following the return of a no bill by a grand jury." *In re Sealed Motion*, 880 F.2d 1367, 1370 (Spec. Div. D.C. Cir. 1989). The decision not to prosecute "an individual for a crime is . . . rarely subject to . . . public scrutiny." *In re Donovan*, 877 F.2d 982, 990 (Spec. Div. D.C. Cir. 1989) (quoting *Fund for Constitutional Gov.* v. *National Archives*, 656 F.2d 856, 863 (D.C. Cir. 1981)). Thus, "[i]f normal Department of Justice procedures had been followed," a conclusion that the parties investigated committed no crimes and should not be indicted "could have been made by the

Department following a grand jury investigation and no public report of the grand jury investigation would have been authorized." *Id.*[7]

While the final report requirement is, in and of itself, at odds with Department of Justice policy, Independent Counsel Walsh was required to comply with Department of Justice rules, regulations, and ethical provisions when determining the *content* of his Final Report.[8] And Department of Justice regulations expressly provide that public disclosures by prosecutors should be limited to "incontrovertible, factual matters, and should not include subjective observations." 28 C.F.R. § 50.2(b)(3). "[W]here background information or information relating to the circumstances of an arrest or investigation would be highly prejudicial or where the release thereof would serve no law enforcement function, such information *should not be made public.*" *Id.* (emphasis added). The Department of Justice also flatly prohibits release of "*[a]ny*

---

[7] The American Bar Association ("ABA") Criminal Justice Section recently summarized Department of Justice policy as follows:

> Details of non-independent counsel investigations within the Department that do not result in an indictment or plea are confidential. There are no reports filed with the court or any other outside body. In most instances, the subject of the investigation is not even notified of the results of the matter. In some cases, where there has been a substantial amount of media attention, the Department will send a letter or call the subject's counsel stating that the investigation has ended without any charges being filed. The Department will then either make no public statement or limit its public statement to the fact that the investigation is over without charges being filed.

ABA Section of Criminal Justice, Report with Recommendations to the House of Delegates, *The Independent Counsel Act: Its History, Problems and Solutions* 12 (Aug. 1993); *see also Reauthorization of the Independent Counsel Law: Hearing Before the Subcomm. on Oversight of Government Management of the Sen. Comm. on Governmental Affairs*, 102d Cong., 2d Sess. 62 (1992) (statement of George J. Terwilliger III, Deputy Attorney General, U.S. Department of Justice) ("The Department's career prosecutors may not speculate on the evidence or make public statements about a case that does not result in prosecution.").

[8] The independent counsel statute demands that "except where not possible, [an independent counsel shall] comply with written or other established policies of the Department of Justice respecting enforcement of the criminal laws." 28 U.S.C. § 594(f).

opinion as to the accused's guilt . . . ." *Id.* § 50.2(b)(6)(vi) (emphasis added); *see also*

United States Attorneys' Manual § 1-7.001 (1988) ("Generally, even the existence of

particular criminal investigations should not be acknowledged or commented on.").

   The Department of Justice regulations effectuate the ethical standards

imposed on prosecutors generally. These ethical responsibilities preclude a prosecutor

from expressing any opinion "as to the accused's guilt or innocence or as to the merits

of a case," the credibility of witnesses, and any evidence that the prosecutor knows

would be inadmissible at trial. *See ABA Standards for Criminal Justice*, Fair Trial

Standard 8-1.1(b); *see also ABA Model Rules of Professional Conduct,* Rule 3.6.

While these ethics provisions generally focus on the need to ensure a fair trial, their

rationale -- that persons who have not been convicted in a court of law should not

receive punishment in the form of reputational damage that flows from being

wrongfully branded a criminal by a government official -- is equally applicable to the

independent counsel "final report" process.[9]

---

[9] On November 18, 1993, the Senate voted to reauthorize the independent counsel law
and to amend the final report provision to ensure that independent counsels are "preclude[d]
. . . from expressing an *opinion* or *conclusion* as to the *culpability* of any of the individuals
involved," where no indictment is brought against them. 139 Cong. Rec. S15,886 (Nov.
17, 1993 daily ed.) (statement of Sen. Cohen) (emphasis added); *see* 139 Cong. Rec.
S15,973 (Nov. 18, 1993 daily ed.). The Senate confirmed that the "final report should be a
simple declaration of the work of an independent counsel," and concluded that such reports
should only "pertain[ ] to those cases in which [the independent counsel] has sought
indictments . . . ." 139 Cong. Rec. S15,886 (Nov. 17, 1993 daily ed.) (statement of Sen.
Cohen). Indeed, "the purpose of the amendment is quite clear, to restrict the nature of the
report to the *facts without engaging in either speculation or expressions of opinion as to the
culpability of individuals* [against whom no indictment is brought]." *Id.* (emphasis added);
see also id. (statement of Sen. Levin) ("the purpose of the amendment . . . is . . . to avoid
having independent counsel[s] state conclusory opinions that the subject of an investigation
engaged in criminal wrongdoing in the absence of bringing an indictment against that
person"); *id.* at S15,887 (statement of Sen. Dole) ("we have modified this final report
language, because [if] Lawrence Walsh could not indict you or could not convict you, he
would try to do it in the court of public opinion by filing some report, in effect venting his
spleen on somebody he was not able to convict along the way").

Independent Counsel Walsh, however, has chosen to ignore completely Department of Justice regulations and ethical standards, and engage in speculation as to the guilt or innocence of persons who were never the subject of prosecution.

E. Critiques Of Executive Branch Policies And Practices, And Accusations That President Reagan Violated His Own Policies

The Independent Counsel was appointed to investigate whether crimes were committed. He was given no mandate by the public, Congress or the Court that appointed him to pronounce his own views on Executive Branch policies or constitutional doctrine. Yet, without any training, experience or electoral mandate, he has gone well beyond his narrow judicial assignment to report on his prosecutorial activities by offering criticisms of Executive Branch policies and operation, and also by advancing his personal views that President Reagan may have "violated" President Reagan's policies:

(a)   Independent Counsel Walsh contends that President Reagan "disregard[ed] Executive Order 12333," by which President Reagan established a mechanism for the President to decide whether the CIA, as opposed to some other intelligence agency, should be used in a covert action outside the United States. *See Final Report,* Vol. I, at 455-56.

(b)   The Report accuses President Reagan of "secretly deviat[ing] from [President Reagan's] announced national policy," and "disregarding the Administration's public policy prohibiting arms sales to nations supporting terrorism," implying that a President in conducting covert intelligence policy must invariably adhere rigidly to past public policy pronouncements irrespective of exigent circumstances. *Id.* at 445; *see also id.* at 561 (President Reagan and

his top advisers "committed themselves . . . to two programs contrary
to . . . national policy.").

      (c)   The Report levels gratuitous critiques concerning the
manner in which the Reagan Administration operated. *See, e.g., id.* at
445 ("Having bypassed accountability to Congress, the President failed
either to establish an effective system of accountability within the
Administration or to monitor the series of activities he authorized.").

      (d)   The Report surmises that Iran-Contra was a product of
the "desire of persons in high office to pursue controversial policies
and goals." *Id.* at 565. But Independent Counsel Walsh has neither
the mandate nor the expertise to determine whether government
officials with both the expertise and the legal responsibility to exercise
it should pursue "controversial" policies.

F.   The Independent Counsel's "Overall Observations And Conclusions On Iran-Contra Matters"

      This aspect of the Report, which is not even remotely contemplated by the
independent counsel statute, articulates the Independent Counsel's policy views,
opinions, theories of government, criticisms of those whose decisions impeded in some
fashion the single-minded pursuit of his own goals, and offers philosophy regarding the
structure of government. Thus, the Independent Counsel:

      (a)   complains that "[t]ime and again this Independent
Counsel found himself at the mercy of political decisions of the
Congress and the Executive branch," *Final Report,* Vol. I, at 564;

      (b)   offers his thoughts on "important lessons for the future,"
id. at 555;

      (c)   expresses his views, criticisms and advice concerning
Congress' performance of its oversight function with respect to the

Executive Branch, *see id.* at 555-59; *id.* at 561 ("Congress destroyed the most effective lines of inquiry by giving immunity to" Lt. Col. North and Admiral Poindexter "so that they could exculpate and eliminate the need for the testimony of President Reagan and Vice President Bush.");

(d)   attacks the decisions of the United States Court of Appeals for the District of Columbia Circuit reversing the convictions in the *North* and *Poindexter* cases, *id.* at 556-57;

(e)   challenges as illegitimate the Attorney General's application of the Classified Information Procedures Act ("CIPA") process and standards for protecting classified information, *id.* at 565; and

(f)   exalts the importance of the role of independent counsels in our system of government, *see id.* at 561, 563-64.

In short, the Independent Counsel found fault and deficiencies in the structure, decisions and motives of all three branches of government: the Legislative, the Executive, and the Judicial. Only Independent Counsel Walsh knows how to conduct foreign policy, adjudicate criminal cases and investigate charges of misconduct in the Executive Branch.

G.   Constitutional Pronouncements

The Report digresses into *ex cathedra* pronouncements concerning the constitutional separation of powers:

(a)   Independent Counsel Walsh contends that our system of government was defectively designed by the Framers of the Constitution and could not survive without independent counsel investigations: "Given the enormous autonomous power of both the Legislative and Executive

branches in the modern state, *the rightly celebrated*

constitutional checks and balances are inadequate, alone, to

preserve the rule of law upon which our democracy

depends." *Final Report,* Vol. I, at 563 (emphasis added).

      (b)   The Independent Counsel offers his

constitutional theory about how to make "our system of

government . . . function properly." *Id.* at 566.

      (c)   The Independent Counsel contends that the

Reagan Administration took actions that conflicted with "the

constitutional system of checks and balances." *Id.* at 565.

H.   Improper Reliance On Grand Jury Materials

      Finally, the principal conclusions, assertions and conjecture contained in

the Final Report are hopelessly intertwined with and predicated on information put

before, developed by or arising from the grand jury. For example, the Independent

Counsel relies on:

      (a)   The double hearsay grand jury testimony of Lt. Col.

North's assistant, Robert Earl, concerning a telephone call between

President Reagan and Lt. Col. North: "North told him that the

President said it was important that the President not know" about the

diversion of funds to the Contras. *Final Report*, Vol. I, at 465. Lt.

Col. North's alleged statement to his assistant was not true. Even Lt.

Col. North acknowledges that no such statement was made in his

conversation with President Reagan. *Id.* Yet the Independent Counsel

offers this snippet of grand jury testimony, knowing that it is false.

(b)   A paraphrase of purported grand jury testimony of Charles Hill, an assistant to Secretary of State Shultz. Mr. Hill allegedly speculated that in November 1986 Attorney General Meese "was trying to get Shultz to back off his claim that the President had admitted knowing about the [1985] HAWK shipment." *Id.* at 544. This also is untrue, but the Independent Counsel offers it as fact.

(c)   The Independent Counsel's characterization and summation (not the text) of 1992 grand jury testimony of Chief of Staff Regan regarding the November 24, 1986 "senior advisers" meeting. *See id.* at 511, 545. Independent Counsel Walsh imagines, without any credible evidence, and against the uniform testimony of all persons present, that at this meeting a "cover-up" was commenced to conceal the fact that President Reagan had contemporaneous knowledge of the 1985 HAWK missile shipment from Israel to Iran. As will be demonstrated in the following pages of this Response, this accusation is at once the Independent Counsel's most extravagant and most demonstrably false theory.

There are hundreds more such references.[10] They have no place in a public report if grand jury secrecy is to mean anything at all. Indeed, the filing of final reports by independent counsels based upon grand jury material "is contrary to the

---

[10]   There are at least 648 specific references of one kind or another to grand jury testimony or exhibits from 62 different witnesses scattered throughout the 566-page text of Volume I of the Final Report, or an average of more than one such reference per page. In the 27-page chapter concerning former President Reagan (*see Final Report*, Vol. I, at 445-72), there are at least 26 such references, averaging approximately one grand jury citation a page, including testimony from seven different witnesses.

practice of federal grand jury investigations," *see In re Sealed Motion*, 880 F.2d at 1369, and seriously undermines the constitutional guarantee of grand jury secrecy.[11]

III

THE INDEPENDENT COUNSEL HAS CONSISTENTLY ABUSED THE REPORTING PROCESS AND MADE DISCLOSURES TO THE PRESS TO INJURE THE RIGHTS OF THE INDIVIDUALS WHOM HE HAS INVESTIGATED

A.   The Interim Reports

The Independent Counsel has repeatedly used the "interim" reporting process established by the independent counsel statute to publish improper comments concerning his investigation and to disseminate damaging information concerning individuals. The independent counsel statute provides that an independent counsel "may make public from time to time, and shall send to the Congress statements or reports on the activities of such independent counsel." 28 U.S.C. § 595(a). But the Iran-Contra interim reports did not constitute status reports to Congress or the public. Instead, the reporting mechanism was used as a vehicle to disseminate slanted, intemperate, and even angry outbursts by the Independent Counsel to condemn his adversaries and the parties he was investigating.

For example, following the dismissal of the prosecution of former CIA official Joseph Fernandez on national security grounds, the Independent Counsel

---

11   The constitutional guarantee of grand jury secrecy has its strongest application where, as here, investigations and deliberations pertain to individuals who were completely exonerated of any criminal wrongdoing, such as former President Reagan. *See, e.g., United States* v. *Sells Engineering, Inc.*, 463 U.S. 418, 424 (1983) ("Grand jury secrecy . . . is 'as important for the protection of the innocent as for the pursuit of the guilty'.") (quoting *United States* v. *Johnson*, 319 U.S. 503, 513 (1943)). Yet the independent counsel reporting process is completely at odds with the guarantee of grand jury secrecy especially where a final report relies extensively on grand jury testimony to discuss the conduct of persons who may have been subjects of a grand jury inquiry but were never indicted.

submitted and published a 61-page harangue against Attorney General Richard Thornburgh, suggesting that "the Attorney General undervalued the principle that all persons are accountable to the law." Second Interim Report, Executive Summary at 1, *reprinted in Final Report,* Vol. II, at 511. The report attacked the motives, good faith, and integrity of the Attorney General and U.S. intelligence agencies, calling their actions "comic," "wasteful," "ritualistic and patronizing," and generally ridiculing their decisions with regard to the disclosure of classified information. *See id.* at 40, 53, *reprinted in Final Report*, Vol. II, at 552, 565.[12] This was not a periodic report on the Independent Counsel's activities, but a sullen tantrum disguised as a report.

The Third Interim Report, filed a week after the indictment of former Secretary of Defense Caspar Weinberger, contained inappropriate statements about the direction and goals of the "final phase" of the investigation. It implied that "officials at the highest level of government" had engaged in a conspiracy to obstruct justice. *See* Third Interim Report at 1, 7, *reprinted in Final Report*, Vol. II, at 575, 581. The report hinted in tabloid style at "new and disturbing evidence" that "provided a significant shift in our understanding of which Administration officials had knowledge of Iran/Contra, [and] who participated in its cover-up." *Id.* at 7, *reprinted in Final Report*, Vol. II, at 581. The report concluded in a melodramatic and self-righteous flourish: "It is not a crime to deceive the American public, as high officials in the Reagan Administration did for two years," but "it is a crime to mislead, deceive and lie

---

12   The Independent Counsel omits from his Report any mention of his own conduct with respect to sensitive national security documents. *See, e.g.,* Johnston, *Federal Agents are Investigating Loss of Iran-Contra Papers,* N.Y. Times, Oct. 10, 1992, at A6. ("Federal agents are investigating a missing suitcase of classified documents that Lawrence E. Walsh, the Iran-Contra prosecutor, lost after he met secretly last summer with President Ronald Reagan in Los Angeles . . . . The loss of the suitcase prompted an angry letter from Deputy Attorney General George J. Terwilliger 3d, who accused Mr. Walsh of a 'flagrant violation' of security procedures for safeguarding classified materials."); Ledeen, *Lawrence Walsh, Grand Inquisitor,* The American Spectator, Mar. 1993, at 18, 20 (observing that "impatience with annoying security regulations has been one of the leitmotifs of Walsh's activities" and cataloguing allegations of the Independent Counsel's security breaches).

to Congress." *Id.* Mr. Walsh accompanied this interim report with numerous national

television interviews[13] that ignited a frenzy of speculation in the media that he was

about to indict former President Reagan.[14]

The Fourth Interim Report followed President Bush's pardon of Secretary

of Defense Weinberger and others. In it, the Independent Counsel presented a

prolonged argument containing, as he put it, **"THE GOVERNMENT'S CASE**

AGAINST WEINBERGER." Fourth Interim Report at 20 (bold in original),

reprinted in Final Report, Vol. II, at 604. It declared that "there was *overwhelming*

evidence that Weinberger *committed serious crimes* in making *false statements* and

concealing evidence from congressional investigators and federal prosecutors." *Id.* at

88 (emphasis added), *reprinted in Final Report,* Vol. II, at 672. And the report

suggested that the Weinberger trial might have served what the Independent Counsel

perceived to be the valuable purpose of incriminating other "high-ranking officials in

the Reagan Administration" who were never formally charged with violating the law.

Id.

---

[13]   For example, Independent Counsel Walsh appeared on ABC's *Nightline,* and confirmed
that his investigation was "moving toward the center of power" and that President Reagan
was at the "center of power." *Nightline: A Conversation With Lawrence Walsh* 4 (ABC
television broadcast, June 23, 1992). Later in the interview, the Independent Counsel
unmistakably implied that the former President was the principal remaining subject of the
investigation, acknowledging that his probe was continuing to seek to assess criminal
responsibility for Secretary Weinberger's alleged actions against a higher-level official and
"there's only actually one [official] who was senior to Caspar Weinberger." *Id.* at 7. He
added that, had President Reagan been more forthcoming about Iran-Contra, Congress
would have then had an opportunity to "decide whether it wanted to deal with impeachment
or not." *Id.* at 8.

[14]   *See, e.g.,* Pincus, *Walsh May Seek Indictment of Reagan in Iran-Contra -- Meese,
Shultz, Regan Also Seen Targeted,* Wash. Post, July 26, 1992, at A1; Pincus, *More High
Officials May Be Indicted In Iran-Contra Case, Walsh Says,* Wash. Post, June 26, 1992, at
A6 ("The concluding inquiry, Walsh said, will focus on whether there was a conspiracy
among top Reagan Administration officials, including former President Ronald Reagan.").

Thus, Mr. Walsh has repeatedly used the reporting process to smear in advance those he would seek to prosecute or those whom he was unable to prosecute. His Final Report continues the pattern.

B. Improper Statements To The Media

There also has been a pattern of inappropriate and damaging public statements to the media throughout Independent Counsel Walsh's investigation reaching far beyond the reporting process. As former Independent Counsel Alexia Morrison stated, Mr. Walsh's office

> "took the . . . approach . . . that it's okay to comment
> beyond the parameters of your public acts. While
> indictments were brought, there were also comments about
> potential criminal liability, the direction the investigation
> was going to take, and descriptions of particular acts that
> were part of a purported conspiracy that was never
> charged."

Greenya, *Feeding Frenzy Fallout*, The Washington Lawyer, Sept.-Oct. 1993, at 28, 37 (quoting Ms. Morrison); *see also* 139 Cong. Rec. S15,857 (Nov. 17, 1993 daily ed.) (statement of Sen. Cochran in connection with independent counsel law reauthorization) ("'Lawrence Walsh and other special prosecutors have not only sought indictments and pushed trials, but they have eagerly sought the airwaves and the news pages to make wild or bitter allegations against their targets that have little to do with their legal cases and everything to do with either frontier justice or naked ambition'.") (quoting Norman Ornstein article in Sept. 20, 1993 edition of *Roll Call*).[15]

---

[15] The Independent Counsel has had innumerable meetings with journalists, both on and off the record. *See, e.g.,* Ledeen, *supra* note 12, at 21 (observing that the Independent Counsel "had so much direct contact with the press . . . several months of his media calendar [reveal] that he would often process journalists like so many widgets on an assembly line, bringing in a new one every forty-five minutes for hours on end").

It is not possible to chronicle the innumerable occasions on which the Independent Counsel has made damaging public comments on the targets of his investigation. However, the following example typifies the Independent Counsel's pattern of extra-judicial public commentary concerning the alleged guilt or misconduct of his targets.

Immediately following President Bush's December 24, 1992 pardon of Secretary of Defense Weinberger and others, Independent Counsel Walsh issued an official statement accusing individuals of crimes and promising that his final report would do so as well:

> President Bush's pardon of Caspar Weinberger and other Iran-contra defendants undermines the principle that no man is above the law. It demonstrates that powerful people with powerful allies can commit serious crimes in high office -- deliberately abusing the public trust -- without consequence.
>
>   *   *   *
>
> The Iran-contra cover-up, which has continued for more than six years, has now been completed with the pardon of Caspar Weinberger. We will make a full report on our findings to Congress and the public describing the details and extent of this cover-up.
>
> Weinberger's early and deliberate decision to conceal and withhold extensive contemporaneous notes of the Iran-contra matter radically altered the official investigations and possibly forestalled timely impeachment proceedings against President Reagan and other officials. Weinberger's notes contain evidence of a conspiracy among the highest-ranking Reagan Administration officials to lie to Congress and the American public . . . .
>
> Weinberger's concealment of notes is part of a disturbing pattern of deception and obstruction that permeated the highest levels of the Reagan and Bush Administrations.

*   *   *

> In light of President Bush's own misconduct, we are
> gravely concerned about his decision to pardon others who
> lied to Congress and obstructed official investigations.

Text of Walsh Response to Bush Pardon, L.A. Times, Dec. 25, 1992, at A21.

In an interview that evening on the *MacNeil/Lehrer Newshour*, Mr. Walsh asserted that "Mr. Weinberger lies as well in press interviews . . . as he does when he testified before Congress." *MacNeil/Lehrer Newshour: Focus -- Pardons* 4 (television broadcast, Dec. 24, 1992). Mr. Walsh charged that President Bush had "pardoned a person who committed the same type of misconduct that he did." *Id*. at 5-6. He also directly accused President Reagan of having had a "deliberate intent to violate the Arms Export Control Act," and of "deliberately defying a statute which Congress had enacted to prevent the sale of U.S. arms to terrorists or to those who supported terrorism." *Id*. at 4. He stated unequivocally then what he repeats in his Final Report, still without evidence, that there was a "November 1986 cover-up by high-ranking Reagan appointees to prevent Congress [from] learning that the President had deliberately defied the Arms Export Control Act," and repeated his charge that this "cover-up" was designed to forestall impeachment of President Reagan. *Id*. at 4-5.[16]

Only one month before he filed his Final Report, the Independent Counsel expressed his speculation to *The New York Times* that, contrary to all of the evidence, including all the evidence in his Report, President Reagan *did* have knowledge that

---

[16]   These and other similar inflammatory and improper statements were repeated without restraint by Independent Counsel Walsh, who went on *Nightline* and pronounced Secretary Weinberger guilty of lying to both Congress and the Independent Counsel. *See, e.g.*, *Nightline: Bush Pardons Weinberger, Iran-Contra Group* 2 (ABC television broadcast, Dec. 24, 1992) (Caspar Weinberger "lied just as readily to the media as he lied to Congress. He's making it quite clear that his first line of defense when he has a troublesome problem is to lie."); *id.* ("Caspar Weinberger lied to Congress and lied to my office . . . . He deliberately lied to Congress.").

funds from the Iranian arms sales were being diverted to the Contras. The Independent

Counsel stated:

> "In order to assume Reagan had no idea that money
> from this arms deal was being funneled secretly into
> Nicaragua, you'd have to assume the President authorized
> the second flight to go forward in total ignorance that he was
> feeding the contras, that he once again stuck his neck out,
> after having his head knocked off three times by three
> disappointments with these arms shipments and no hostages
> coming out. Is it believable that the President went through
> this embarrassing charade for a year if he didn't know he
> was getting money for the contras?"

Spencer, *supra* note 3, at 30 (quoting Mr. Walsh).[17] The *Times* also quoted Mr. Walsh

as promising that his final report would discuss "things we were not able to prove," and

the article said that Mr. Walsh was willing "to include conjecture and speculation" in

the report. *Id*. at 33. Thus, Mr. Walsh made clear to the public in advance that his

report would include unprovable conjecture and speculation on certain specified

subjects. He did not wait for publication of his Final Report before leaking its contents

to the media.

IV

THE INDEPENDENT COUNSEL'S ABUSE OF THE REPORTING PROCESS REQUIRES A COMPREHENSIVE RESPONSE

The Independent Counsel and his staff have ignored, broken or run

roughshod over every rule restricting prosecutors from making damaging public

statements about the subjects of criminal investigations. As former Judge Robert Bork

observed, "'Walsh's prosecutorial team has behaved in ways more morally questionable

---

17   This precise speculative and undocumented theory is set forth in slightly different
      language in the *Final Report,* Vol. I, at 446; *see infra* page 114.

than did their victims.'" 139 Cong. Rec. S2520 (Mar. 9, 1993 daily ed.) (remarks of Sen. Dole quoting Judge Bork). Former Watergate Special Prosecutor Henry Ruth has expressed the view that it would be "irresponsible and unethical for a prosecutor to issue a report suggesting criminal conduct on the part of someone" who was never indicted. Freiwald, *Unindicted, Unvindicated; McKay Remarks on Meese Guilt Draw Fire*, Legal Times, July 25, 1988, at 1 (quoting Associate Special Prosecutor Henry Ruth). Yet the Independent Counsel has engaged in precisely the kind of "highly prejudicial" and "subjective" speculation, innuendo and obloquy that Justice Department and other prosecutors are prohibited from making public, including this Independent Counsel's personal views regarding the guilt or innocence of individuals whom he did not formally charge or against whom he failed to sustain convictions.

The Independent Counsel has no right to go beyond a statement of incontrovertible fact concerning his investigation, personnel, expenditures, prosecutions and convictions. He has no right and no moral license to damage unconvicted and innocent persons. His Report should not be a political platform or bully pulpit. He has a duty to exercise his awesome power responsibly and with restraint.

The individuals who are the targets of the Independent Counsel's untempered and intemperate wrath have no way fully to respond to the Independent Counsel's indiscriminate and wrongful charges of criminal, civil, moral and constitutional wrongdoing. The Report is largely predicated on secret grand jury material, Independent Counsel interviews, handwritten notes and other similar material to which the individuals named in the Report have little or no access. Very often, the Independent Counsel paraphrases, summarizes or characterizes brief portions of these materials to which only he has access in advancing some of his most damaging theories and accusations. President Reagan's motion to have access to these materials was opposed by the Independent Counsel and was denied.

35

Moreover, the individuals named in the Report have neither the resources nor the time to respond completely to the myriad allegations and accusations of Independent Counsel Walsh. The Independent Counsel utilized 68 lawyers and a staff of 112 persons over the course of six and one half years (*Final Report*, Vol. II, at 753-67) at a cost of over $37,000,000 (*id*. at 723) to prepare his Report. This latter figure does not include the fees of a Harvard Law School professor and two senior partners of major law firms who assisted the Independent Counsel on a *pro bono* basis. *Id*. at 754-56. And these tabulations do not include Executive Branch personnel performing services for the Independent Counsel, such as the FBI agents who conducted over 3,400 separate interviews. *Id*. at 734. The Report, as Independent Counsel Walsh puts it, "is a product of all who have served" in his office, "the lawyers, the investigators, and the support staff." *Final Report*, Vol. I, at v. More than forty people, including seventeen attorneys, worked directly on the Report. *Id*.

The text of Volume I of the Report is 566 pages long and contains approximately 400,000 words. It refers to and cites literally thousands of documents, interviews and transcripts. It discusses, by name, the conduct of over 450 persons. Entire chapters of the Report are written on dozens of individuals. It chronicles numerous indictments, pleas, trials and appeals. According to the Independent Counsel, who held office longer than all except one of the nation's Attorneys General, the preparation of the Final Report of his single-mission odyssey was "[o]ne of the most difficult and important tasks" of his office. *Id*.

The Report describes the actions of scores of former subordinates, aides and associates of President Reagan. Many of those persons testified many times in several different forums (congressional oversight committees, the Tower Commission, the Iran-Contra Congressional Committees), before grand juries and in trials over a period of years. The Independent Counsel has constructed his lengthy narrative from this testimony, books and articles, handwritten notes, and from tens of thousands of other pieces of information from thousands of sources. It would require months and vast resources to respond in equal measure to the full Report. However, despite these limitations and disadvantages, former President Reagan offers the following specific responses to the contents of the Final Report.

151-793 O - 94 - 25 :Vol.3

THE FACTS:
IRAN-CONTRA AND PRESIDENT REAGAN'S
INVOLVEMENT IN IRAN-CONTRA MATTERS

The facts of Iran-Contra matters have been the subject of a multitude of hearings, depositions, reports and books. After the Tower Commission issued its 175-page report of its investigation of Iran-Contra in February 1987, *see Report of the President's Special Review Board* (Feb. 26, 1987) [hereinafter *Tower Commission Report*], Congress conducted a lengthy and thorough investigation during the Spring and Summer of 1987, including weeks of public hearings, culminating in the publication of a 700-page report. *See* House Select Comm. to Investigate Covert Arms Transactions with Iran & Senate Select Comm. on Secret Military Assistance to Iran and the Nicaraguan Opposition, *Report of the Congressional Committees Investigating the Iran-Contra Affair With Supplemental, Minority, and Additional Views*, H.R. Rep. No. 433, S. Rep. No. 216, 100th Cong., 1st Sess. (1987) [hereinafter *Iran-Contra Congressional Report*].

The congressional hearings are transcribed in thirteen publicly available volumes containing thousands of pages of testimony and documentary exhibits. *See The Iran-Contra Investigation: Joint Hearings Before the House Select Comm. to Investigate Covert Arms Transactions with Iran and the Senate Select Comm. on Secret Military Assistance to Iran and the Nicaraguan Opposition*, 100th Cong., 1st Sess. (1987) [hereinafter *Iran-Contra Congressional Hearings*]. Also available to the public

38

are twenty-seven volumes of deposition testimony taken in conjunction with the congressional hearings, comprising approximately over twenty-five thousand pages. *See Iran-Contra Congressional Report*, Appendix B [hereinafter App. B].

In addition to the foregoing Iran-Contra material, there are (1) the hundreds of thousands of pages of other documents reviewed by the Tower Commission, Congressional Committees and the Office of Independent Counsel; (2) the hundreds of thousands of pages of interviews, depositions, interrogatories and testimony taken by the Tower Commission, Congressional Committees and the Office of Independent Counsel; and (3) the dozens of published memoirs and accounts of Iran-Contra events. The Independent Counsel has now added a three-volume Final Report, based upon thousands of pages of interviews, notes, documents and other materials assembled by the Independent Counsel. The Iran-Contra events are therefore among the most meticulously investigated incidents in United States history. These multiple and lengthy investigations have inevitably generated some confusion and reflect some inconsistencies in recollection or recording of events.

However, it is neither possible nor necessary to reiterate all of the facts of Iran-Contra. The discussion that follows is a general overview of President Reagan's involvement in the pertinent Iran-Contra events. This summary is generally based upon the public record, including prior testimony and statements of the former President and his advisers and contemporaneous documents. Although neither President Reagan nor any other official involved in Iran-Contra has a complete and clear recollection of the specific details of certain events,[18] the basic facts of the President's activities are not

---

[18] While the complicated events relating to Iran-Contra have been the subject of intense scrutiny over the past seven years, at the time the events in which the President was directly involved occurred, they were only a small segment on the spectrum of the President's activities. As President Reagan explained in his interrogatory answers:

                                        [Footnote continued on next page]

disputed, and have long been on the public record. The Independent Counsel's seven-year investigation and Report reveal no additional evidence that changes in any material respect the factual findings of the Tower Commission and the Congressional Committees regarding President Reagan's involvement in Iran-Contra. However, because the Independent Counsel's Report confuses that record and, as a result, reaches distorted and inaccurate conclusions, it is important to set forth briefly the undisputed central facts of Iran-Contra.

I
THE IRANIAN INITIATIVE

A.   Background

With the fall of the government of Shah Mohammed Reza Pahlavi in early 1979 and its replacement by a Shiite Muslim government led by Ayatollah Ruhollah Khomeini, Iran was transformed from a close ally of the United States into an implacable, unstable and dangerous enemy. Remaining diplomatic ties between the

---

[Footnote continued from previous page]

> During the period January 1, 1983 to November 25,
> 1986, I made official visits to various foreign countries,
> participated in major summits with our allies and with the
> leadership of the Soviet Union, and met in Washington and had
> other communications with leaders from numerous foreign
> countries. Moreover, I had national defense and domestic
> responsibilities involving extensive communications with
> Congress, my Cabinet and other parties. All of these activities
> were preceded, accompanied, or followed by a substantial
> volume of briefing material, decision memoranda and other
> documentation.

Answers of the President of the United States to Interrogatories, Introduction at 1-2, *In re Grand Jury Investigation* (D.D.C. Nov. 24, 1987) [hereinafter President's Answers to Interrogatories].

United States and Iran were completely severed on November 4, 1979, when Iranian militants took over the U.S. Embassy in Tehran and held American diplomats hostage for 444 days. One of the actions taken in response by the United States was to place an embargo on all trade with Iran, including the shipment of arms to that country.

In January of 1981, President Reagan took office. In July of 1981, a Reagan Administration Senior Interdepartmental Group ("SIG") recommended that, while the United States should maintain its embargo on arms sales to Iran, the U.S. policy of discouraging third-country transfers of arms to Iran should be relaxed. *See Iran-Contra Congressional Report* at 159. Otherwise, the SIG concluded, there was a danger either that Iraq would succeed in its aggression against Iran or Iran would turn to the Soviet Union for weaponry to defeat Iraq, thereby increasing Soviet influence in Iran to the detriment of American interests. *Id.* Three years later, the NSC staff also recommended that the United States reevaluate its position towards Iran. *See Tower Commission Report* at III-3, B-2. Nevertheless, the Reagan Administration's policy continued to be one of discouraging third-country arms transfers to Iran. *See id.* at III-3; *Iran-Contra Congressional Report* at 159.

Because of Iran's vital and strategic location and capabilities, the Reagan Administration continued to believe that it was in the interest of the United States to be alert for opportunities to explore ties with moderates in the Iranian government who were preparing to seek power upon the death of Ayatollah Khomeini. *See* R. Reagan, *An American Life* 504-05 (1990) [hereinafter Reagan, *An American Life*]. There was "talk worldwide [that] Ayatollah Khomeini . . . might not. . . live [long]" and "we were aware that there were groups placing themselves in position to perhaps become the government of Iran." Deposition of Ronald W. Reagan 14 (Feb. 16, 1990), *United States* v. *Poindexter*, No. CR 88-0080-HHG (D.D.C.) [hereinafter Reagan Depo.]. Thus, "[f]rom our point of view, reestablishing a friendly relationship with this strategically located country -- while preventing the Soviets from doing the same

41

thing -- was very attractive," and "[w]e wanted to ensure that the next government in
Tehran was moderate and friendly." Reagan, *An American Life* at 504.

In June 1985 National Security Adviser Robert C. McFarlane circulated a
draft National Security Decision Directive to Administration officials proposing that the
United States change certain aspects of its Iranian policy in order to establish a closer
relationship with Iran in the post-Khomeini era and to counter the Soviet Union's
attempts to increase its influence in that country. *See Tower Commission Report* at III-
3 to -4. Among the proposals in this draft was the "provision of selected military
equipment as determined on a case-by-case basis." Draft of National Security Decision
Directive, *U.S. Policy Toward Iran* at 5 (June 17, 1985).

In July 1985 Mr. McFarlane met at the White House with David Kimche,
the Director General of the Israeli Foreign Ministry, who informed Mr. McFarlane that
certain Iranian officials had expressed an "interest . . . in establishing contact with the
United States," and asked whether the United States was "interested in talking to
them." Testimony of Robert C. McFarlane [hereinafter McFarlane Testimony], *in
Iran-Contra Congressional Hearings,* 100-2, at 43. Mr. Kimche argued that "Israel
had concluded that these people were legitimate and sought over time to be able to
influence change in Iran away from the rather extreme policies of the time to a . . . less
violent coexistence with their neighbors." *Id.* According to Mr. Kimche, the Iranians
had proposed to demonstrate their "bona fides" by attempting to "influence the captors
of the United States and other countries' hostages in Lebanon to release them." *Id.*; *see
also Tower Commission Report* at III-5.

B.   The August And September 1985 TOW Shipments

On July 18, 1985, a few days after President Reagan's abdominal surgery
in Bethesda Naval Hospital, Mr. McFarlane met with the President and Chief of Staff
Donald T. Regan. While President Reagan has been unable to recall the details of this

meeting, which took place in his hospital room while he was still recovering from surgery, *see* Reagan Depo. at 16-17; *see also Tower Commission Report* at III-6,[19] Mr. McFarlane testified that he informed the President of an Israeli proposal to respond to an Iranian request for TOW missiles. McFarlane Testimony, *in Iran-Contra Congressional Hearings*, 100-2, at 45. According to Mr. McFarlane, "the President said that . . . the idea of strengthening" the moderate Iranians through arms sales as "the means to rally the army or revolutionary guards to them was not an outrageous notion." *Id.* at 46.[20]

Mr. McFarlane understood that his meetings with the President in the hospital and a few days later resulted in presidential approval of limited shipment of U.S.-made weapons by Israel to groups in Iran opposed to terrorism. *See Iran-Contra Congressional Report* at 166-67.

The pros and cons of the Israeli proposal were considered at an August 6, 1985 meeting at the White House attended by the President, Vice President George Bush, Mr. Regan, Secretary of State George P. Shultz, Secretary of Defense Weinberger, Mr. McFarlane and Central Intelligence Agency ("CIA") Director William J. Casey. Secretary Shultz and Secretary Weinberger gave their reasons for opposing the sale, as they did at other times during the Iran initiative. *See* G. Shultz, *Turmoil and Triumph* 796 (1993) [hereinafter Shultz, *Turmoil and Triumph*];

---

[19]   On the day before this meeting, President Reagan wrote in his diary: "Some strange soundings are coming from some Iranians. Bud M. will be here tomorrow to talk about it. It could be a breakthrough on getting our seven kidnap victims back. Evidently the Iranian economy is disintegrating under the strain of war."

[20]   Chief of Staff Donald T. Regan has said that he does not recall any specific discussion of arms during the July 18 hospital meeting. *See, e.g.,* D. Regan, *For the Record* 20 (1988) [hereinafter Regan, *For the Record*]; Tower Commission Interview of Donald T. Regan at 5 (Jan. 7, 1987). However, it is not disputed that President Reagan was first made aware of the Iranian proposal at the time of the July 18 hospital meeting or soon thereafter. *See, e.g.,* Deposition of Donald T. Regan at 51 (Mar. 3, 1987) [hereinafter Regan 3/3/87 Depo.], *reprinted in Iran-Contra Congressional Report*, App. B, Vol. 22, at 576.

C. Weinberger, *Fighting For Peace: Seven Critical Years in the Pentagon* 368-69 (1990) [hereinafter Weinberger, *Fighting For Peace*]. However, President Reagan determined that approval of the arms shipment -- a "single order of TOW missiles" that "would not have changed the balance [of the Iran-Iraq conflict] in any way" -- might be justified in light of assurances from Israeli officials that the Iranians receiving the arms "did not support terrorism" and that the Iranians might be able to facilitate release of the American hostages in Lebanon. Reagan Depo. at 18-19.

Mr. McFarlane testified that a few days after the August 6 meeting, President Reagan gave his approval for Israel "to sell modest levels of TOW missiles or other military spares and items to Iran and to come to the United States and be allowed to purchase replacements." McFarlane Testimony, *in Iran-Contra Congressional Hearings*, 100-2, at 49. According to Mr. McFarlane, the President based his approval on his understanding that the arms sales would "not affect the balance of the war, . . . [would] not be used for terrorist purposes, and . . . [would] not include major end items." *Id.* at 49-50.

On August 20, 1985, the Israelis shipped 96 TOW missiles to Iran. This shipment was followed by another Israeli shipment of 408 TOW missiles to Iran on September 14, 1985.

Mr. McFarlane explained that while the President did not separately approve the September 1985 TOW shipment, he had interpreted the President's decision in August as authorizing "Israel to negotiate sales without any need to come back to him for approval of each specific one." *Id.* at 67.

While his memory of the specific circumstances of his approval of the TOW shipments by Israel is not detailed, President Reagan has never disputed Mr. McFarlane's recollection and the conclusion subsequently reached by both the Tower Commission and the Congressional Committees that he gave general approval to Israel's plan to ship TOW missiles before any shipment occurred. *See Tower*

Commission Report at III-6 to -8, B-19, B-20; *Iran-Contra Congressional Report* at 6, 163, 166-68. He has acknowledged and explained his decision and his reasons for it on numerous occasions including in his book, *An American Life*, at 506-07, in 1990.

C.   The November 1985 HAWK Shipment

In early November 1985, during briefing for the upcoming American-Soviet summit in Geneva, Mr. McFarlane informed President Reagan of a new Israeli plan involving the shipment of arms to Iran. *See Tower Commission Report* at III-9. According to Mr. Regan, who was present at this meeting, President Reagan was told "that there [was] something up between Israel and Iran" and that "[i]t might possibly lead to our getting some of our hostages out." Testimony of Donald T. Regan [hereinafter Regan Testimony], *in Iran-Contra Congressional Hearings*, 100-10, at 12. Mr. Regan testified to the Tower Commission that McFarlane told the President "to expect that a shipment of missiles would come from Israel through a third country to Iran, and that the hostages would come out." *Tower Commission Report* at III-9; *see also* Regan 3/3/87 Depo. at 56, *reprinted in Iran-Contra Congressional Report*, App. B, Vol. 22, at 580-81.[21]

McFarlane testified that on November 15 he told Israeli Defense Minister Yitzhak Rabin that the United States approved the Israeli plan "based upon recent questions and reaffirmations by the President that I had received." McFarlane Testimony, *in Iran-Contra Congressional Hearings*, 100-2, at 51.

On November 19, the first day of the Geneva Summit, while President Reagan was preparing for his first meeting with Soviet General Secretary Mikhail Gorbachev, Mr. McFarlane briefed the President and Mr. Regan regarding the Israeli

---

[21]   According to Mr. Regan, President Reagan was informed "on the margins of his briefings for the Gorbachev meeting to expect that there is going to be a shipment of arms coming . . . missiles, transshipped through Israel into Iran, and the hostages will come out." Tower Commission Interview of Donald T. Regan at 14 (Jan. 7, 1987).

plan to ship additional arms to Iran.[22] According to Mr. Regan, Mr. McFarlane "told the President the details of" a "complicated operation" "to sell eighty HAWK antiaircraft missiles to Iran through the Israelis." Regan, *For the Record* at 319:

> [T]he Israelis would deliver the missiles from their own stockpile to a secret destination in Portugal. There they would be loaded aboard three transport planes and flown to Tabriz. As soon as the first plane was airborne, word would be flashed to the Iranians by clandestine means and the Iranians would tell the terrorists who were holding the five U.S. citizens hostage in Lebanon to release them. The plane would not land and no missiles would be delivered until all five Americans had been handed over to the American Embassy in Beirut.

Id.[23]

According to Mr. Regan, the President was told that the HAWK shipment and hostage release were scheduled for November 21. After that date, the Israeli plan called for the United States to

> give the Israelis eighty new Hawk missiles to replace the ones they had delivered to the Iranians; forty additional Hawks would be given to the Iranians in a separate transaction. In return the Iranians would guarantee that no more American hostages would be taken by terrorists.

Id.

---

22   Mr. Regan initially believed that Secretary Shultz was also present when the President was briefed in Geneva. *See* Regan, *For the Record* at 319-20. However, Mr. Shultz apparently was not at the briefing on November 19, but rather learned of the proposed HAWK shipment when Mr. McFarlane telephoned him later. *See* Shultz, *Turmoil and Triumph* at 798 n.8.

23   Mr. Regan testified before Congress that Mr. McFarlane informed President Reagan at the Geneva meeting that around eighty HAWK missiles would be delivered to Iran via a warehouse in a third country. Regan Testimony, *in Iran-Contra Congressional Hearings*, 100-10, at 13; *see also* Testimony of Donald T. Regan Before the Senate Select Committee on Intelligence at 16 (Dec. 16, 1986).

Mr. McFarlane's recollection of the Geneva meeting generally parallels that of Mr. Regan. According to Mr. McFarlane, he told the President that a shipment of arms from Israel was on the way to Iran and that he hoped hostages would be released as a result of this shipment. McFarlane Testimony, *in Iran-Contra Congressional Hearings*, 100-2, at 53. Mr. McFarlane testified that when he informed President Reagan of the HAWK shipment, he did not ask for the President's specific approval of this shipment. *See id.* at 261. According to Mr. McFarlane, "the President provided the authority in early August for Israel to undertake, to sell arms to Iran, and to then come to the United States for replenishment, to buy new ones." *Id.* "That didn't require then the Israelis to come back to us on each occasion and get new approval." *Id.*

Although President Reagan recalls that he was told at the time of the Geneva summit "that there was a possibility that the hostages might be released," President's Answers to Interrogatories, Answer No. 24, he does not have a clear recollection of the details of the briefings he received from Mr. McFarlane during this period regarding the shipment of HAWK missiles, *see id*; Reagan Depo. at 33-38. As Mr. Regan has explained, the HAWK shipment was "[q]uite obviously . . . not the number one topic on our minds" during briefings preparing President Reagan for his meetings with General Secretary Gorbachev. Regan Testimony, *in Iran-Contra Congressional Hearings*, 100-10, at 13.[24] This was an historic and vitally important

---

[24] The Tower Commission recounted some of President Reagan's foreign policy activities during this period:

> The Soviet foreign minister visited Washington. Preparations for the Geneva Summit with General Secretary Gorbachev were under way; this included four Presidential speeches on arms control, human rights, regional issues, and U.S./Soviet bilateral [sic] relations. The President delivered an address to the United Nations on the occasion of its 40th Anniversary. The President met with twelve to fifteen heads of State in New York and

[Footnote continued on next page]

meeting between the two superpowers. As the world now knows, it led to the most
important changes in U.S.-Soviet relations in 40 years and, in many respects, was
instrumental in ending the cold war. President Reagan was intensely involved in
making this summit a success. President Reagan, however, did not dispute the
recollections of Mr. Regan,[25] Secretary Schultz[26] and Mr. McFarlane[27] and the
conclusions of the Tower Commission[28] and Congressional Committees[29] that the
President was informed in advance of the 1985 HAWK shipment.[30]

On December 5, 1985, Admiral John M. Poindexter, who succeeded Mr.
McFarlane as National Security Adviser, presented President Reagan a Finding

---

[Footnote continued from previous page]

> Washington. In the middle of this hectic schedule, on October 7,
> 1985, the Achille Lauro was seized by four Palestinian hijackers.

Tower Commission Report at III-8.

[25]   *See, e.g.,* L. Cannon, *President Reagan: The Role of a Lifetime* 622 (1991)
[hereinafter Cannon, *President Reagan*] ("'Did Ronald Reagan approve shipment of HAWK
missiles to Iran in 1985? Definitely yes.'") (quoting interview with Donald Regan, Feb. 2,
1990).

[26]   Secretary Shultz testified that President Reagan had indicated that he had been
contemporaneously informed of the 1985 HAWK shipment. Testimony of George P.
Shultz [hereinafter Shultz Testimony], *in Iran-Contra Congressional Hearings,* 100-9, at
44-45. Also, according to Mr. Schultz's testimony before the Tower Commission, he told
an associate on November 22, 1985, that "'Bud [McFarlane] says he's cleared with the
President' on the plan." *Tower Commission Report* at III-9.

[27]   *Tower Commission Report* at B-38.

[28]   *Id.* at III-9.

[29]   *Iran-Contra Congressional Report* at 175, 176, 178.

[30]   President Reagan's diary entries contemporaneous with the HAWK shipment also
indicate that he had knowledge of the shipment. Access to the President's relevant diary
entries was provided by the President to the Tower Commission, the Congressional
Committees and to the Independent Counsel, who reviewed them in 1987. *See Final Report*
Vol. I, at 466 & n.126 (quoting diary entries and noting review was conducted in 1987);
see also Tower Commission Report at III-2 (noting access provided to review relevant diary
entries); *see Iran-Contra Congressional Report* at xvi (same).

prepared by the CIA General Counsel (now a Federal District Court Judge)[31] that affirmed in writing the President's approval for the CIA's assistance in transporting the November HAWK shipment from Israel to Iran. *See* Reagan Depo. at 231-34. The Finding retroactively approved the actions of the CIA in providing "assistance . . . to private parties" through "the provision of transportation, communications, and other necessary support" as part of an "attempt to obtain the release of Americans held hostage in the Middle East." Exhibit SS-4 (unsigned version of Finding) *in Iran-Contra Congressional Hearings,* 100-6, at 427; *see* Testimony of John M. Poindexter [hereinafter Poindexter Testimony], *in Iran-Contra Congressional Hearings,* 100-8, at 17-18, 123-35.

Admiral Poindexter testified that he destroyed this Finding in November 1986. *Id.* at 18. However, the Congressional Committees determined that the President did, indeed, sign the Finding. *See Iran-Contra Congressional Report* at 195. Although President Reagan does not have a specific recollection of the time of and circumstances surrounding his signing of that particular Finding, he has never denied having done so. Reagan Depo. at 232; *see also* President's Answers to Interrogatories, Answer No. 27.

D. The December 7, 1985 Meeting

On December 7, 1985, President Reagan met with Mr. Regan, Secretary Shultz, Secretary Weinberger, Mr. McFarlane, Admiral Poindexter and Deputy CIA Director John N. McMahon in the White House residence. *See Tower Commission Report* at III-10, B-42; *Iran-Contra Congressional Report* at 197-98. The purpose of the meeting was to review the initiative with Iran, its results and its future.

---

[31]   *See* Testimony of Stanley Sporkin [hereinafter Sporkin Testimony], *in Iran-Contra Congressional Hearings,* 100-6, at 119-27.

Secretary Weinberger and Secretary Shultz opposed any further arms shipments to Iran "in the strongest possible terms." Weinberger, *Fighting For Peace* at 372; *see also* Shultz, *Turmoil and Triumph* at 799. And, although he later did not recall having opposed the arms shipments, Mr. Regan also apparently questioned the wisdom of the proposed transaction. *See* Reagan, *An American Life* at 510 ("'George Shultz, Cap and Don are opposed.'") (quoting diary); *Iran-Contra Congressional Report* at 198 (noting that Regan also objected to further arms shipments). President Reagan, however, resisted arguments against continuing the Iran initiative. *See id.* As Mr. Weinberger recalled, "the President was . . . very concerned about the fate of our hostages, and extremely unhappy that apparently nothing could be done to release them." Weinberger, *Fighting For Peace* at 373.

In his autobiography, President Reagan gave the following description of his exchange with Secretaries Weinberger and Shultz during the December 7 meeting:

> At that meeting on Pearl Harbor Day, 1985, when we considered continuing and possibly even expanding the covert operation begun the previous summer, they [Secretaries Weinberger and Shultz] made their opposition clear to me forcefully. They didn't argue that the plan involved a swap of arms for hostages, but they contended that if information about it ever leaked out (and George insisted that it would), it would be made to *look* as if we were.
>
> My response to them was that we were *not* trading arms for hostages, nor were we negotiating with terrorists.
>
> "Look," I said, "we all agree we can't pay ransom to the Hizballah to get the hostages. But we are not dealing with the Hizballah, we are not doing a thing for them. We are trying to help some people who are looking forward to becoming the next government of Iran, and they are getting the weapons in return for saying that they are going to try to use their influence to free our hostages."

50

Reagan, *An American Life* at 512.[32] According to Secretary Shultz, the President said
at the December 7 meeting that he didn't "feel we can leave any stone unturned in
trying to get the hostages back."[33]

As a result of the arguments made by Secretary Weinberger and Secretary
Shultz, the President "decided to wait" before making a final decision, *see* Reagan, *An
American Life* at 512:

> The Pearl Harbor Day meeting ended without me making a
> decision, although I said I wanted to keep the channels open
> and asked Bud McFarlane to take the next step and meet
> again with the principals involved in the negotiations. I told
> him to say we wanted a dialogue directly with responsible
> Iranians, and that the Iranians could prove they were
> responsible by freeing the hostages, but that we would not
> trade arms for hostages.

Id. at 512-13; *see also Tower Commission Report* at III-10; *Iran-Contra Congressional
Report* at 199.

---

[32] President Reagan told a biographer that Secretaries Weinberger and Shultz "'turned out
to be right'" in warning that if the arms shipments ever became public "it would look like
we were trading arms for hostages.'" Cannon, *President Reagan* at 631 (quoting interview
with President Reagan, Feb. 10, 1989). The President added:

> "I didn't at the time see how it possibly could, when we were
> dealing with some people who had to literally hide from their
> own government to save their lives. . . . But I never convinced
> them [Weinberger and Shultz]. And now, as I say, they turned
> out to be right."

Id. (quoting President Reagan).

[33] This meeting and the President's comments during the meeting have been exhaustively
reported and investigated. The fundamental fact is that it constituted a discussion of
alternatives and no decisions resulted. Mr. Shultz testified that the President's remarks did
not have the tone of "the President advocating violating the law," but rather was "the kind

[Footnote continued on next page]

51

E.   January 1986

On January 6, 1986, Admiral Poindexter presented to President Reagan an Israeli plan to ship 3,000 TOW missiles to Iran. The President indicated general agreement with the plan. Poindexter Testimony, *in Iran-Contra Congressional Hearings*, 100-8, at 30. Admiral Poindexter presented the President a draft of a Finding to authorize the plan to proceed as a covert operation. President Reagan indicated his approval on the draft. *See id.*

On January 7, the Israeli plan was discussed at the full NSC meeting attended by President Reagan, the Vice President, Mr. Regan, Secretary Schultz, Secretary Weinberger, Attorney General Edwin Meese III, Admiral Poindexter and Mr. Casey. Secretary Schultz and Secretary Weinberger again voiced their opposition to any arms shipment, while others either favored the plan or were neutral. Schultz Testimony, *in Iran-Contra Congressional Hearings*, 100-9, at 33; Schultz, *Turmoil and Triumph* at 803. In response to Secretary Weinberger's concerns regarding compliance with the Arms Export Control Act, the Attorney General gave his opinion that the arms sales would be legal if made pursuant to the National Security Act and the Economy Act. *See* Testimony of Edwin Meese III [hereinafter Meese Testimony], *in Iran-Contra Congressional Hearings*, 100-9, at 197-98; Weinberger Testimony, *in Iran-Contra Congressional Hearings*, 100-10, at 142-43. The Attorney General referred to a written legal opinion rendered in 1981 by then-Attorney General William French Smith that concluded "that the CIA could legally sell to third countries weapons obtained from the Defense Department under the Economy Act." *Iran-Contra Congressional Report* at 203; *see* Meese Testimony, *in Iran-Contra Congressional Hearings*, 100-9, at 197,

---

[Footnote continued from previous page]

of statement that I'm sure we all make sometimes when we are frustrated." Schultz Testimony, *in Iran-Contra Congressional Hearings*, 100-9, at 32.

208-09; Weinberger Testimony, *in Iran-Contra Congressional Hearings,* 100-10, at 142-43.

Another legal issue discussed was whether Congress had to be notified in advance of the sale. There were "grave concerns about leaks and whether these would endanger the lives of the hostages and/or the people with whom we were dealing in Iran." E. Meese, *With Reagan* 255 (1992) [hereinafter Meese, *With Reagan*]:

> The tenor of the discussion was that once arrangements were concluded and the hostages had been freed -- or were on their way to freedom -- Congress would be notified.

Id.; see also Tower Commission Report at B-62 (quoting Mr. Meese).

At the conclusion of the meeting, President Reagan had decided to go forward with the Israeli plan. *See* Meese Testimony, *in Iran-Contra Congressional Hearings,* 100-9, at 197. According to the Attorney General, the President was "very firm" in making the point that "no deals were to be made with any of the groups who had taken or were holding American hostages." *Id.*

> A limited number of defensive weapons were to be sold to certain Iranians to demonstrate the United States' good faith. They, in turn, as a display of their good faith, were to negotiate separately with forces in Lebanon for the return of the American hostages. No direct dealings with the hostage-takers nor the payment of any type of ransom was ever contemplated.

Id.

On January 17, 1986, Admiral Poindexter presented President Reagan a Finding that was identical to the January 6 draft Finding except that the words "third parties" was added to the list of entities to be assisted by the CIA. *Iran-Contra Congressional Report* at 208. Also, the cover memorandum recommended that the United States ship the TOWs directly to Iran rather than use Israel as an intermediary in order to ensure compliance with provisions of U.S. law. *Id.* President Reagan agreed to the proposed modification and signed the Finding. *See* President's Answers to Interrogatories, Answer No. 32.

F.   February-November 1986

In February 1986 two shipments totalling 1,000 TOW missiles were made to Iran with the President's approval. In May President Reagan approved a shipment of 508 TOW missiles to Israel to replace those that had been sold to the Iranians. Also that same month, the President authorized Mr. McFarlane to lead a delegation to Tehran to meet with Iranian officials. *See Tower Commission Report* at III-16. In July President Reagan approved the shipment to Iran of HAWK spare parts requested by the Iranians. *See id.* at III-17.

In late October President Reagan authorized the shipment of 500 TOWs. *See id.* at III-19. Israel delivered these TOWs from its stock on the same day. *See id.*[34]

The Iranian initiative became public on November 3 when the Lebanese newpaper *Al-Shiraa* published an article regarding Mr. McFarlane's trip to Iran in May of 1986.

II

THE NICARAGUAN INITIATIVE

A.   Background

On July 17, 1979, President Anastasio Somoza Debayle and his family fled Nicaragua. Opponents of Somoza, known as the National Liberation Front, or Sandinistas, seized control of the Nicaraguan government. After they achieved power,

---

[34]   Five hundred U.S. TOWs were shipped to Israel as replacements on November 7. *Id.* at B-184.

the Sandinistas restricted the liberties of the Nicaraguan people and began to intervene

in the affairs of their neighbors. As Congress found in 1983:

> (1)   the Government of National Reconstruction
> of Nicaragua [Sandinistas] has failed to keep solemn
> promises, made to the Organization of American States in
> July 1979, to establish full respect for human rights and
> political liberties, hold early elections, preserve a private
> sector, permit political pluralism, and pursue a foreign
> policy of nonaggression and nonintervention;
>
> (2)   by providing military support (including arms,
> training, and logistical, command and control, and
> communications facilities) to groups seeking to overthrow
> the Government of El Salvador and other Central American
> governments, the [Sandinista] Government. . . has violated
> article 18 of the Charter of the Organization of American
> States which declares no state has the right to intervene,
> directly or indirectly, for any reason whatsoever, in the
> internal or external affairs of another state; . . .

Intelligence Authorization Act for Fiscal Year 1984, Pub. L. No. 98-215, § 109(a), 97

Stat. 1473, 1475 (1983).

The House Intelligence Committee, whose chairman was Representative

Edward P. Boland, found that Nicaragua was directly responsible for providing

weaponry and other support to communist insurgents in El Salvador:

> [T]his (Salvadoran) insurgency depends for its life-blood --
> arms, ammunition, financing, logistics and command-and-
> control facilities -- upon outside assistance from Nicaragua
> and Cuba. This Nicaraguan-Cuban contribution to the
> Salvadoran insurgency is longstanding. It began shortly
> after the overthrow of Somoza in July, 1979. It has
> provided -- by land, sea and air -- the great bulk of the
> military equipment and support received by the insurgents.

H.R. Rep. No. 122, 98th Cong., 1st Sess., at 2 (1983); *see also* International Security

and Development Cooperation Act of 1985, Pub. L. No. 99-83, § 722(c)(2)(C)(vi), 99

Stat. 190, 252 (1985) ("[Nicaragua] has committed and refuses to cease aggression in the form of armed subversion against its neighbors in violation of the Charter of the United Nations, the Charter of the Organization of American States, the Inter-American Treaty of Reciprocal Assistance, and the 1965 United Nations General Assembly Declaration on Intervention.").

B.   The Boland Amendments

Notwithstanding its findings regarding the human rights violations and expansionist activities of the Sandinista regime, Congress sought to impose a series of somewhat vague legal restrictions on the use of certain appropriated funds by the Reagan Administration to support the Nicaraguan Democratic Resistance, or Contras, in their efforts to resist the Sandinistas. President Reagan had first authorized covert aid to the Nicaraguan resistance in November 1981, as part of an arms interdiction program designed to stem the flow of arms from Nicaragua to communist insurgents in El Salvador and other countries. A little over a year later, on December 21, 1982, the first Boland Amendment was enacted into law. *See* Further Continuing Appropriations of 1983, Pub. L. No. 97-377, § 793, 96 Stat. 1830, 1865 (1982). This legislation prohibited two agencies, the CIA and Department of Defense ("DOD"), from giving assistance to any "group or individual, not part of a country's armed forces . . . for the purpose of overthrowing the Government of Nicaragua or provoking a military exchange between Nicaragua and Honduras." *Id.* The first Boland Amendment did not forbid the CIA or DOD from aiding arms interdiction efforts. Nor did it purport to prohibit a variety of other activities.

In 1983 Congress enacted legislation that provided $24 million for the Nicaraguan resistance. *See* Department of Defense Appropriations Act for Fiscal Year 1984, Pub. L. No. 98-212, § 775, 97 Stat. 1421, 1452 (1983). In addition, Congress enacted a second version of the Boland Amendment providing that once the $24 million had been expended, the Nicaraguan Democratic Resistance was to receive no more funding from the CIA, DOD, "or any other Agency or entity of the United States *involved in intelligence activities*." Intelligence Authorization Act for Fiscal Year 1934, Pub. L. No. 98-215, § 108, 97 Stat. 1473, 1475 (1983) (emphasis added).

When the $24 million was exhausted, Congress refused President Reagan's request in 1984 for additional funding, and the Boland Amendment was reenacted, without changes. *See* Temporary Continuing Appropriations Act, Pub. L. No. 98-441, § 106(c), 98 Stat. 1699, 1700-01 (1984); Continuing Appropriations Act for Fiscal Year 1985, Pub. L. No. 98-473, § 8066, 98 Stat. 1837, 1935-36 (1984).

In the summer of 1985, immediately after a congressional vote denying funds to the Contras, Nicaraguan President Daniel Ortega made a trip to Moscow. Soon thereafter, Congress changed its position and reinstated financial assistance to the Contras, this time in the form of humanitarian aid. *See* International Security and Development Cooperation Act of 1985, Pub. L. No. 99-83, § 722(g)(1), 99 Stat. 190, 254 (1985). The legislation, however, prohibited the CIA and DOD from distributing the aid. *Id.*

Yet another version of the Boland Amendment was enacted as part of the Further Continuing Appropriations Act of 1985. *See* Pub. L. No. 99-190, § 8050, 99 Stat. 1185, 1211 (1985). This version prohibited the CIA, DOD, "or any other agency or entity of the United States *involved in intelligence activites*" from providing assistance to the Nicaraguan Democratic Resistance except as provided in a classified funding scheme enacted as part of the Act. *Id.* (emphasis added).

Finally, in October 1986, Congress approved $100 million in additional assistance to the Nicaraguan resistance, *see* Continuing Appropriations for Fiscal Year 1987, Pub. L. No. 99-591, §§ 206(a)(1)-(2), 100 Stat. 3341-299-300 (1986), but placed a cap on aid above that amount, *see id.* § 209(c), 100 Stat. at 3341-301.

C.   The Reagan Administration's Response To The Boland Amendments

As President Reagan has written, "[f]rom the outset of our program of covert operations in Central America, my instructions were that everything we did must be done legally." Reagan, *An American Life* at 476-77. Yet, the President did not believe the Boland Amendments restricted his constitutional power to support the Nicaraguan Democratic Resistance, except with respect to the expenditure of funds appropriated by the Congress from the Treasury of the United States. Each version of the Boland Amendment was a rider to and limitation upon an appropriations bill.

> While I battled with Congress to get support for the Contras
> reinstated, I felt we had to do everything we legally could do
> to keep the force in existence. I told the staff: We can't
> break the law, but, within the law, we have to do whatever
> we can to help the Contras survive.

Id. at 484. President Reagan "wanted the Contras maintained as a force, to the fullest extent that was legal, until I could convince Congress to appropriate new funds for the freedom fighters." *Id.* at 485.

President Reagan thus authorized and participated in efforts to persuade third countries to provide financial support for the Contras. As the President has explained:

> I knew that there must be among our allies other
> countries that shared our concern about the threat to
> democracy in Latin America, and I believed we should
> communicate to them our strong convictions regarding the
> importance of tangible international support for the Contras.
> Several countries responded and extended help -- a case of
> friendly nations believing we all had a stake in fighting for
> democracy.

Id. at 484. President Reagan "believed, then and now, that the president has the absolute constitutional right and obligation to share such thoughts and goals with leaders of other nations." *Id.*

In meeting with leaders of foreign countries to discuss support for the Contras, President Reagan acted in reliance upon the legal advice of Attorney General William French Smith. In June 1984 the Attorney General concluded that "he saw no legal concern if the United States Government discussed this matter with other nations so long as it was made clear that they would be using their own funds to support the Contras and no U.S. appropriated funds would be used for this purpose." Sporkin Memorandum for Record, 6/26/84, Subj: "Nicaragua," ER 21615.

President Reagan also met with private American citizens to thank them for providing financial assistance to the Contras. As President Reagan has explained:

> I said, "there has to be a way to help these private citizens who otherwise wouldn't know how to get help to the Contras or buy the supplies they need; there must be ways we can help or counsel them if somebody says we've raised some money and want to help the Contras; somebody ought to be able to tell them what channel to use." The staff . . . asked me to thank citizens who had contributed humanitarian assistance to the Contras, and I was happy to do so.

Reagan, *An American Life* at 485. But President Reagan "repeatedly insisted that whatever we did had to be within the law, and I always assumed that my instructions were followed." *Id.*

At the time of the events in question, President Reagan was assured by his aides that all of the activities of his subordinates in supporting the Contras were in compliance with the law. *See id.* And, he has accepted responsibility for all actions taken by his subordinates that were within the scope of his instructions. "As president, I was at the helm, so I am the one who is ultimately responsible" for the Administration's policy of supporting the Nicaraguan Democratic Resistance. *Id.* at 487.

III

EVENTS OF NOVEMBER-DECEMBER 1986

When a Lebanese publication first published information concerning the shipment of American arms to Iran, the Reagan Administration was compelled to respond cautiously because public disclosure of certain facts might have jeopardized the lives of hostages and the lives of persons in Iran with whom the Administration had been in communication.[35] At the same time, the President took steps to ensure that there would be a full public accounting of the actions of his Administration.

The President directed the Attorney General immediately to assemble all relevant information. From November 21 to November 23, the Attorney General and other members of his staff conducted personal interviews and reviewed documents related to the Iranian initiative. During this investigation, a member of the Attorney General's staff discovered a memorandum in Lt. Col. Oliver L. North's files "describing a plan to direct profits from the arms transactions with Iran to support the Nicaraguan freedom fighters." Meese, *With Reagan* at 244.[36] When questioned, Admiral Poindexter and Lt. Col. North stated that a so-called "diversion" of funds from Iran to the Contras had occurred. *Id.* According to Attorney General Meese, "[w]e were . . . told that only three people in the U.S. government had known about it -- North, Poindexter, and McFarlane." *Id.* With respect to the arms shipments to

---

[35] The Lebanese publication appeared on November 3, 1986, the day after American hostage David Jacobsen was released. Mr. Jacobsen's release was preceded by the release of the Reverend Lawrence Martin Jenco on July 26, 1986, and the Reverend Benjamin Weir on September 15, 1985. President Reagan has written that the report of the Iranian initiative resulted in "our expectations of bringing home [additional hostages] go[ing] up in smoke." Reagan, *An American Life* at 527. "It was one of the most unpleasant experiences of my presidency to watch this happen -- hoping it would not happen, then accepting the reality that the other hostages weren't going to be coming home." *Id.*

[36] The so-called "diversion memorandum" is reprinted as Exhibit DTR-22 in *Iran-Contra Congressional Hearings,* 100-10, at 330-38.

Iran, but not any diversion of funds from those shipments, the Attorney General was told by Mr. McFarlane that President Reagan had given general advance approval. Meese Testimony, *in Iran-Contra Congressional Hearings,* 100-9, at 231.

Attorney General Meese informed the President of the alleged diversion on the morning of November 24, 1986. President Reagan had had no prior knowledge of the subject. Later that day, President Reagan met with his top advisers to discuss the Administration's relationship with the individuals in Iran with whom they had been dealing, and relationships with Iran and other middle eastern nations in light of the public disclosures of the arms sales. That meeting is discussed in more detail *infra* at pages 74-84.

At a press conference on November 25, President Reagan and the Attorney General disclosed what they had learned about the planned diversion. On November 26 the President appointed former U.S. Senator John Tower, former National Security Adviser Brent Scowcroft and former U.S. Senator and Secretary of State Edmund Muskie to a Special Review Board, which became known as the Tower Commission. *See* Statement by the President, Special Review Board for the National Security Council, 22 Weekly Comp. Pres. Doc. 1605 (Dec. 1, 1986). President Reagan charged the Tower Commission with learning and disclosing all facts related to the Iran-Contra matter and evaluating the implications to the National Security Council system. *See Tower Commission Report* at III-1 (the President "wanted 'all the facts to come out'"). On December 16-17 the Senate and House of Representatives appointed special committees to investigate the Iran-Contra matter. The President waived claims of executive privilege and directed that his Administration cooperate fully with the investigations of the Tower Commission and Congressional Committees.

On December 4 the Attorney General, on instructions from President Reagan, requested the appointment of an independent counsel. *See Final Report*, Vol. II, at 771-74. On December 19 the Special Division of the United States Court of

Appeals for the District of Columbia Circuit appointed Independent Counsel Walsh to investigate and, where appropriate to undertake prosecutions related to Iran-Contra. *See In re: Oliver L. North*, No. 86-6 (D.C. Cir. Spec. Div. Dec. 19, 1986), *reprinted in Final Report*, Vol. II, at 777-79.

RESPONSE TO STATEMENTS IN FINAL
REPORT CONCERNING PRESIDENT REAGAN

Time and resources do not permit former President Reagan to respond to every statement concerning him in the Final Report. The following responds to the Independent Counsel's principal assertions regarding the former President's involvement in Iran-Contra matters.

I

THE INDEPENDENT COUNSEL'S SPECULATION CONCERNING A "COVER-UP" IS UNWARRANTED, UNSUPPORTED BY ANY EVIDENCE, DENIED BY EACH ALLEGED PARTICIPANT, INHERENTLY IMPLAUSIBLE, CONTRADICTED BY OVERWHELMING EVIDENCE, IRRATIONAL AND IRRESPONSIBLE

Independent Counsel Walsh asserts that "senior Reagan Administration officials" engaged in a "concerted effort" "to deceive Congress and the public about their knowledge of and support for [the Iran-Contra transactions.]" *Final Report*, Vol. I, at xi. He charges that officials at the highest level of the Reagan Administration engaged in a "cover-up," *id.*, to "protect the President and themselves from the consequences of the possibly illegal 1985 shipments from Israeli stocks," *id.* at xvi, and that the President and his top national security advisers "permitted the creation of a false account of the Iran arms sales to be disseminated to Congress and the American people," *id.* at 445-46.

In particular, the Independent Counsel's "cover-up/conspiracy" theory focuses on the November 1985 HAWK missile shipment, *see, e.g., id.* at 39, and a November 24, 1986 meeting of senior Administration officials during which Attorney General Meese responded to a question by indicating that President Reagan may not have been informed in advance concerning some aspect of the HAWK shipment, *see, e.g., id.* at 542-43. According to Independent Counsel Walsh, the Vice President, the Attorney General, the Secretary of Defense, the Secretary of State, the Chief of Staff for the President, and others took Mr. Meese's ambiguous response to an unclear question as a signal of some sort that from that date forward they were to act in unison to lie to Congress and the Independent Counsel and conceal the President's knowledge of the 1985 arms transactions, to withhold relevant notes for years in order to conceal the fact that President Reagan had contemporaneous knowledge of the HAWK shipment, and otherwise to shield the public and investigating authorities from information concerning the President's awareness in 1985 of the arms shipments that year. But this theory of a concentrated and prolonged conspiracy to conceal President Reagan's knowledge of the 1985 arms shipments is nothing more than the Independent Counsel's fantasy. It is factually without any foundation, irresponsible and squarely inconsistent with mountains of contrary evidence.

The Independent Counsel's "cover-up" theory is difficult to describe because it makes so little sense and defies not only logic and common sense, but so many inconvenient facts. It apparently assumes that in November of 1986, eight or more top-level Reagan Administration officials released the story of the diversion of Iranian weapons sale profits to the Contras as a smokescreen to distract attention from the far more threatening story that the President had approved illegal arms sales to Iran. The alleged "cover-up" of the "real story" was theoretically so successful that it was discovered only in the last days of the Lawrence Walsh Independent Counsel investigation when he reviewed theretofore concealed notes of the November 24, 1986 White House meeting in which the "cover story" was developed.

The Independent Counsel's theory springs from his interpretation of a remark made by Attorney General Meese at a meeting convened for and devoted to future Middle East relationships. At this meeting, the Attorney General supposedly denied that the President had known of arms shipments to Iran in 1985. The Independent Counsel believes that certain of the attendees at the meeting knew that the statement was not true, but said nothing. By this silence, a conspiracy among those present was supposedly created to conceal the President's knowledge of the 1985 arms shipments because the transactions were allegedly illegal and the President would have faced impeachment proceedings had his knowledge of the shipments been revealed.

This conspiracy theory has no evidence to support it, builds upon a probably erroneous reconstruction of a brief digression within a two-hour meeting, is denied by every single person present at the meeting, and is so permeated with inconsistencies and contradictions that no objective person familiar with the facts has taken the charge seriously. Nevertheless, it is a theory that Independent Counsel Walsh has chosen to embrace and disseminate in court documents, through inappropriate communications directly, or through subordinates, to the press, and now to memorialize in his Final Report. But the Independent Counsel cannot begin to prove the theory because it is not true.

The "cover-up" theory is completely contradicted by (1) President Reagan's repeated public and private insistence that the complete facts of the Iran-Contra matter be publicly aired and that his Administration cooperate fully with investigators; (2) the evidence demonstrating that the facts of the matter were fully and often disclosed on the public record by participants in the alleged conspiracy; (3) the contemporaneous notes of the November 24, 1986 meeting; (4) the contemporaneous notes from the other November meetings that the Independent Counsel contends paved the way for the November 24 conspiracy; and (5) the fact that the President's knowledge in 1985 of the arms shipments actually sustained rather than undermined the legality of those shipments.

A. President Reagan Acted Promptly To Insist Upon Full And Complete Disclosure Of The Facts

President Reagan's immediate and unconditional response to the November 1986 revelations that mushroomed into the Iran-Contra controversy was to insist on full and complete disclosure of all pertinent facts to the public, congressional committees and investigating bodies. From the beginning, he followed a consistent course of openness and cooperation. In this regard, he took the following steps:

- On November 21, 1986, he ordered the Attorney General to conduct an immediate investigation and to make his findings available to the public.

- On November 26, 1986, he appointed the Tower Commission to investigate the matter fully and to report to the American people.

- He asked his Attorney General to seek the appointment of an independent counsel, and pursuant to that request, Lawrence Walsh was appointed independent counsel on December 19, 1986.

- He ordered his subordinates to cooperate fully with investigations conducted by the Tower Commission, Congress and the Office of Independent Counsel.

- He waived claims of executive privilege as to all investigations of Iran-Contra.

- He cooperated fully with the Tower Commission, Congress and the Independent Counsel, giving them access to all relevant Administration records, including access to relevant portions of his personal diary. He answered grand jury questions under oath, and he voluntarily consented to an interview under oath by the Independent Counsel.

President Reagan's cooperation with investigatory bodies and his insistence that his subordinates do the same were recognized by both the Tower Commission and the Congressional Committees investigating the Iran-Contra matter. The Tower Commission concluded:

> By at least November 20, the President took steps to ensure that all the facts would come out. From the President's request to Mr. Meese to look into the history of the initiative, to his appointment of this Board, to his request for an Independent Counsel, to his willingness to discuss this matter fully and to review his personal notes with us, the Board is convinced that the President does indeed want the full story to be told.

Tower Commission Report at IV-12 to -13.

The November 1987 report of Congress states:

> The President cooperated with the investigation. He did not assert executive privilege; he instructed all relevant agencies to produce their documents and witnesses; and he made extracts available from his personal diaries . . . .

Iran-Contra Congressional Report at xvi.

The two federal judges who presided over the two most important Iran-Contra trials commended President Reagan for his extraordinary and unprecedented cooperation with the Independent Counsel:

> During his presidency, President Reagan cooperated with Independent Counsel's investigation to an unusual extent and over a considerable period. Voluminous materials, classified and nonclassified, running into hundreds of thousands of pages of White House documents were made available.

United States v. *North*, 713 F. Supp. 1448, 1449 (D.D.C. 1989) (Judge Gerhard Gesell).

> President Reagan has repeatedly stated his willingness to cooperate with all official bodies investigating the so-

called Iran-contra affair, and . . . he has, in fact, faithfully
carried out that pledge. Thus, he has cooperated with the
Tower Commission and the Independent Counsel, in
addition to the grand jury, and he has dispatched his senior
aides to testify before congressional committees.

United States v. *Poindexter*, 732 F. Supp. 142, 153 (D.D.C. 1990) (Judge Harold

Greene).

In short, any theory of a "cover-up" is flatly contradicted by President

Reagan's complete cooperation with investigators and his insistence that his

Administration make full public disclosure of the facts of Iran-Contra. The Tower

Commission, the Congressional Committees and two federal judges all agreed that

President Reagan had been cooperative and open.

**B.   President Reagan's Knowledge Of The 1985 Arms Shipments
        Was Disclosed By The Administration Immediately And
        Repeatedly On The Public Record**

The Independent Counsel's speculation of a "cover-up" is not only

inconsistent with President Reagan's actions, but fails utterly to take into account the

prompt and full disclosure on the public record of the President's knowledge of the

1985 arms shipments. Many officials, including Secretary of State Shultz, National

Security Adviser McFarlane and Chief of Staff Regan testified freely from the very

beginning of the Iran-Contra investigations about the precise extent and scope of the

President's involvement in the 1985 transactions. No one has sought to conceal the

President's knowledge and approval of these shipments. This is not an issue that the

Independent Counsel discovered in 1992. The Congressional Committees and their

staff, the Tower Commission and its investigators, the Independent Counsel and his

scores of investigators and lawyers, dozens of independent journalists, witnesses, and

many others have been discussing the subject for seven years. Discussion of it may be

found in the Tower Commission Report, the congressional committee testimony and report, documents received by the Independent Counsel, and even books by the

participants that have discussed when and how the President was informed of and

approved the 1985 transactions. A few of many such instances are set forth below.

1. **Official Public Disclosures Of The President's Knowledge Of The 1985 HAWK Missile Shipment**

- On December 16, 1986, Mr. Regan testified before the Senate Select Committee on Intelligence that Mr. McFarlane had briefed President Reagan on the HAWK shipment at the Geneva Summit in November 1985. Mr. Regan testified that Mr. McFarlane told "us that there was movement in the Iranian situation and some type of arms shipment being contemplated . . . . [S]ince that time I have found out . . . [i]t was the shipment of HAWK missiles to Iran." Testimony of Donald T. Regan Before the Senate Select Committee on Intelligence at 16-17 (Dec. 16, 1986). Mr. Regan also testified that during the December 7, 1985 meeting between the President and his senior advisers "there was much discussion about the shipment of those HAWK missiles." *Id.* at 20. Mr. Regan recalled that the "HAWK missiles had already been sold at that point," but there was nonetheless "a discussion of the sale," "a discussion of the shipment of HAWKS," and "discussion about the need for a Finding." *Id.* at 140; *see also id.* at 25-26. Thus, as the Independent Counsel is forced to recognize, "Regan's testimony on the November 1985 HAWK missile shipment to Iran has been *consistent, acknowledging that McFarlane briefed the President in Geneva on the HAWKs shipment as it was about to take place.*" *Final Report*, Vol. I, at 519 (emphasis added).

- In 1987, the Independent Counsel was permitted to and did review President Reagan's diary, including entries contemporaneous with the HAWK shipment in November 1985 that indicate that the President was aware of the Iranian initiative. The Independent Counsel's Final Report acknowledges that the President's diary entries show "clearly [that] he was following the course of the initiative." *Id.* at 466 & n.126. Whatever difficulties the Independent Counsel had in reviewing diaries or notes made by other witnesses, he had no such problems with President Reagan, who made all pertinent diary entries available to the Tower Commission, congressional investigators and the Independent Counsel.

- In his January 7, 1987 interview with the Tower Commission, Mr. Regan declared that in briefings leading up to the November 1985 Geneva Summit, "[w]e [he and President Reagan] were told in quite some detail . . . about a shipment that would originate . . . and would come out and would be transshipped through Israel and all of our hostages would come out." Tower Commission Interview of Donald T. Regan at 11 (Jan. 7, 1987). Later in that same interview, he reiterated that "[t]he President . . . was told . . . on the margins of his briefings for the Gorbachev meeting to expect that there is going to be a shipment of . . . missiles, transshipped through Israel into Iran, and the hostages will come out." *Id.* at 14.

- In his 1988 book, Mr. Regan declared: "During the Geneva Summit, Bud McFarlane had told the President the details of a plan to sell eighty HAWK antiaircraft missiles to Iran through the Israelis." Regan, *For the Record* at 319.

- The February 2, 1987 Report of the Senate Select Committee on Intelligence regarding its preliminary inquiry into the Iran-Contra affair states "Regan testified that McFarlane informed the President in Geneva that some type of arms shipment was being considered, and that if the operation were successful, hostages might be freed," and Secretary of State Shultz testified that he "was told by McFarlane that [McFarlane] had cleared it with the President." *See* Report of the Senate Select Committee on Intelligence, *Preliminary Inquiry into the Sale of Arms to Iran and Possible Diversion of Funds to Nicaraguan Resistance* 11 (Feb. 2, 1987).

- The February 26, 1987 Tower Commission Report explicitly concluded that "Chief of Staff Regan told the Board that the President *was informed in advance* of the Israeli HAWK shipment but was not asked to approve it. He said that McFarlane told the President early . . . on the margins of his briefings for the Geneva Summit to expect that a shipment of missiles would come from Israel through a third country to Iran, and the hostages would come out." *Tower Commission Report* at III-9.

- Secretary of State Shultz told the Tower Commission that it was his understanding that "Bud [McFarlane] . . . cleared with the President" the plan to ship HAWKs through Israel to Iran. *Id.*; *see also id.* at B-37.

- Mr. McFarlane told the Tower Commission that, in his view, the President gave general approval of "the Israeli sale of modest levels of arms of a certain character" and that "with that approval Israel could

70

transfer or sell modest levels without further concrete approval." *Id.* at B-38. And he specifically testified to the Tower Commission that he informed the President of the HAWK shipment in Geneva. *Id.*

- The Congressional Committees explicitly found that "[t]he President did know of the Iran arms sales, and he made a deliberate decision not to notify Congress." *Iran-Contra Congressional Report* at 415. Mr. McFarlane "brought aspects of the plan" to ship HAWK missiles to Iran "to the attention of the President." *Id.* at 175. Specifically, in a section entitled **"McFarlane Briefs the President,"** Congress said that "McFarlane told the President about the developing plans for the HAWK transaction shortly before they left on November 17 for a summit meeting with Soviet leaders in Geneva." *Id.* at 176. Mr. Regan explicitly verified this in his congressional testimony. *See* Regan Testimony, *in Iran-Contra Congressional Hearings*, 100-10, at 13.

- The Congressional Committees also concluded that "[w]hile they were still in Geneva, McFarlane updated the President and Chief of Staff . . . on the status of the HAWK shipment and the anticipated hostage release. McFarlane informed them that the Israelis were about to ship the weapons, and expressed hope that the hostages would come out by the end of the week. McFarlane specifically told the President that Israel was about to deliver 80 HAWK missiles . . . , and that Israel wanted the United States to replace those missiles." *Iran-Contra Congressional Report* at 178 (footnotes omitted); *see, e.g.,* Regan Testimony, *in Iran-Contra Congressional Hearings*, 100-10, at 13 (confirming that Mr. McFarlane briefed the President in Geneva on the November 1985 Israeli shipment to Iran and "made it clear that the item that was being delivered was HAWK missiles . . . . Certainly he said HAWK missiles in Geneva."); *id.* at 24; *id.* at 91.

- Secretary of State Shultz told Congress in his July 23, 1987 testimony that President Reagan *himself* had indicated that he had been contemporaneously informed of the November 1985 HAWK shipment. *Iran-Contra Congressional Report* at 298, 309; *see also* Shultz Testimony, *in Iran-Contra Congressional Hearings,* 100-9, at 44-45.

- The Congressional Committees noted that when only one hostage was released following the August-September TOW shipments from Israel to Iran, "[t]he President persisted. In November [1985], he authorized Israel to ship 80 HAWK anti-aircraft missiles in return for all the hostages." *Iran-Contra Congressional Report* at 7.

- The Congressional Report also concluded that the December 5, 1985 "retroactive" "Finding was evidence of the Administration's contemporaneous knowledge of the HAWK shipment." *Id.* at 197.

- In his memoirs former Attorney General Meese wrote: "As for the HAWK shipments -- though discussions on the matter were conducted in the hurried atmosphere surrounding the November 1985 summit -- we have good evidence that the President approved the initiative in question, a point on which Bud McFarlane and Don Regan, for once, emphatically agreed." Meese, *With Reagan* at 267.

2. Official Public Disclosures Of The President's Knowledge Of The 1985 TOW Missile Shipments

- On November 13 and 14, 1986, Administration press conferences that were convened to amplify on the President's November 13, 1986 Address to the Nation disclosed that the United States had condoned and the President had authorized the 1985 TOW shipments from Israel to Iran. *See Final Report,* Vol. I, at 460-61; *see also infra* pages 84-86.

- Diary entries by former President Reagan made available to the Tower Commission, the Congressional Committees and the Independent Counsel in 1987 indicate his general awareness of the Iranian initiative in July and August of 1985 and "suggest[ ] [the President's] approval for the [August] Israeli TOW shipment." *Final Report*, Vol. I, at 466.

- In a March 19, 1987 press conference, the President himself confirmed that he verbally approved the TOW missile shipments in 1985. *See* The President's News Conference, 23 Weekly Comp. Pres. Doc. 274 (Mar. 19, 1987).

- The Congressional Report states categorically that, prior to the TOW shipments, "in the summer of 1985 the President authorized Israel to proceed with the sales." *Iran-Contra Congressional Report* at 6.

- The Tower Commission Report declared that "[w]e believe that an Israeli request for approval of such a transfer [of TOWs] was discussed before the President in early August. . . . The President agreed to replenish Israeli stocks. We are persuaded that he most likely provided this approval prior to the first shipment by Israel." *Tower Commission Report* at III-8. It also added that, "[i]n coming to this conclusion, it is of paramount importance that the President never opposed the idea of Israel transferring arms to Iran. Indeed, four months after the August shipment, the President authorized the United States government to undertake directly the very same operation that Israel had proposed. Even if Mr. McFarlane did not have the President's explicit prior approval, he clearly had his full support." *Id.*

- In a section of its report entitled "*The President Is Informed*," Congress stated that Mr. McFarlane had briefed President Reagan generally on the Israeli plan to ship TOW missiles to Iran in July 1985 while the President was in the hospital recuperating from surgery. *Iran-Contra Congressional Report* at 166-67 (bold in original).

- In another section of the report, entitled "*The Israeli Arms Sales Are Authorized*," Congress stated: "The Tower Board concluded that the President most likely approved the Israeli [TOW missile] sales before they occurred. *The evidence supports that conclusion*. The Israelis expressly sought the President's approval of the Israeli sales and confirmation that the Secretary of State had been consulted. By McFarlane's own admission, he told the Israelis that they were authorized to sell the TOWs. McFarlane had no motive to approve a sale of missiles to Iran if the President had not authorized it. Moreover, Ledeen testified that McFarlane told him of the President's decision. McFarlane also contemporaneously reported the President's approval to Kimche." *Id.* at 167-68 (emphasis added; bold in original; footnote omitted).

There are dozens of additional examples of testimony or commentary beginning in 1986 and continuing throughout 1987 concerning the President's knowledge of the 1985 arms sales, the Administration meetings at which these issues were discussed, discussions regarding compliance with the Arms Export Control Act and various other related subjects. The plain, simple and indisputable fact is that although there are minor and understandable differences in recollection and variations in the amount each person remembered about each event, all pertinent facts concerning the President's knowledge and approval of the 1985 transactions were disclosed and were the subject of concentrated investigative attention by all investigating bodies from the very beginnings of the controversy. It is devastating to the Iran-Contra Independent Counsel's twisted conspiracy theory that after years of investigation, his Report does not contain a single fact concerning President Reagan's knowledge in 1985 of the 1985 arms transactions that was not disclosed to and reported by the Tower Commission and the Congressional Committees over six years ago.

C.   The Independent Counsel Has Misunderstood And Completely Mischaracterized The November 24, 1986 Senior Advisers Meeting

The Independent Counsel's "cover-up" theory is premised on the view that, at the November 24, 1986 senior advisers meeting, the Attorney General orchestrated a plan, adopted by silence on the part of senior Administration officials, to hide from the public the President's knowledge of the 1985 HAWK shipment. The Independent Counsel asserts that the November 24, 1986 meeting was convened to discuss the 1985 arms transactions, their legality, and the President's involvement in them. *See, e.g., Final Report*, Vol. I, at 464, 542-44. According to the Independent Counsel, "Meese reported his findings, . . . reviewed the 1985 activities and asserted that the 1985 arms shipments could have been illegal. Meese reported further that, contrary to what Shultz had told him, the President did not know in November 1985 that arms were being shipped to Iran." *Id.* at 24. The Independent Counsel argues that, because no one at the meeting "corrected the Attorney General," *id.,* when he stated that the President may not have had prior knowledge of some aspects of the HAWK shipment, the participants somehow tacitly entered into a conspiracy to hide the President's knowledge of the transaction. *Id.* at 543-45.

All the contemporaneous notes and other documents relating to the meeting reveal, however, that it was convened *not* to discuss how to cope with the 1985 arms transactions and their legality, but rather to discuss how to deal with individuals in Iran in light of the public disclosures of the arms shipments to Iran and how to respond to other countries in the Middle East in light of these disclosures. The reference by Attorney General Meese to the President's knowledge of the shipment may have been a reference to the CIA's involvement in the transaction, or may have referred to other aspects of the event. But it was clearly a digression caused by a question from Chief of Staff Regan, which took no more than a few moments in the course of a two-hour meeting. And the Independent Counsel fails to mention anywhere in his Report that not a single participant in the November 24, 1986 meeting has ever acknowledged or even suggested that the meeting resulted in a conspiracy or cover-up in any way, shape or form.

The Independent Counsel has relied heavily, but selectively,[37] on the various notes of participants in the key meeting to construct a theory that distorts their content and blows a single brief exchange wholly out of proportion. *See, e.g., Final Report*, Vol. I, at 543. Indeed, had any of the targets of his investigation so badly distorted the events and evidence of a transaction, they would have been indicted by Mr. Walsh for obstructing his investigation, false statements, conspiracy or worse, and surely slandered in his Final Report.

For example, presumably to add drama to his argument that Attorney General Meese was the focal point for a cover-up that began when he made his statement at the November 24 meeting, the Independent Counsel quotes a note made by Charles Hill, an assistant to Secretary of State Shultz, based on a "read out" from Secretary Shultz following the meeting. According to the Final Report, the note reflects that "Shultz, who had expected Meese to report fully on his weekend inquiry, said Meese had 's[ai]d nothing' at the meeting." *Id*. But another note of the same "read out" by Secretary Shultz written by a different aide, Nicholas Platt, is more complete and far more revealing on this point. It states that "Meese said practically nothing [at] all by way of describing our policy toward Iran." Nov. 24, 1986 Platt

---

[37] Although the Independent Counsel bases some of his most explosive charges on these notes, he inexplicably fails to include transcripts of the notes as part of or an appendix to the Report.

Note. *That* was the principal focus of the meeting -- the Administration's "policy toward Iran" in light of public disclosures of the arms sales and the foreign policy ramifications of the disclosures. Mr. Meese, of course, had little or no involvement in the 1985 or 1986 arms shipments and would not be expected to be a principal source of future foreign policy toward Iran or other middle eastern countries.

According to the Hill notes, Admiral Poindexter was the first to speak and he articulated the objectives of the Iran initiative as being the encouragement of a "new kind of Iran," to "end [the] war," to "discourage terrorism," and to get the "hostage[s] out." Nov. 24, 1986 Hill Note. Mr. Regan's notes of the meeting likewise state at the outset that Admiral Poindexter "outlined [the] four main objectives of our Iranian initiative in 1985," Nov. 24, 1986 Regan Note, as do Mr. Weinberger's notes.[38]

These notes all agree that Admiral Poindexter's initial comments were followed by a detailed discussion of the United States' "intelligence system for Iran," *see, e.g.,* Nov. 24, 1986 Regan Note, including an assessment of intelligence assets by CIA Director Casey and CIA official George Cave.[39] Mr. Regan's notes dwell at length on this topic, which consumes five full pages out of the ten and one-half pages of handwritten notes that he took at the meeting. *See* Nov. 24, 1986 Regan Notes.

Once the intelligence update was completed, Admiral Poindexter "opened discussion" about the purpose for the meeting: The two "[t]hings to be decided[:] . . . 1) [Whether to] [s]end an emissary to Mid East to explain what we were doing"; and "2) How to proceed with this channel which is still open." Nov. 24, 1986 Regan Note; *see also* Nov. 24, 1986 Platt Note (Admiral Poindexter opened by saying "let's

---

[38]   Mr. Weinberger's notes, similar to Mr. Hill's, state the "4 objectives" as "more moderate govt in Iran," "End Iran-Iraq war," "Stop terrorism in Iran & mid East," and "get hostages back." Nov. 24, 1986 Weinberger Note.

[39]   *See also* Nov. 24, 1986 Hill Note ("Then Casey gave assessment of CIA assets."); Nov. 24, 1986 Platt Note ("Casey & Cave gave assessment").

make some decisions."); Nov. 24, 1986 Weinberger Note (listing same "[t]wo decisions for Pres" that were to be debated). As Mr. Hill's notes of Mr. Shultz's "read out" put it, Admiral Poindexter said that the meeting "[i]s all about our policy toward Iran, how we [are] right and will keep going." Nov. 24, 1986 Hill Note.

According to the various notes, President Reagan stated that he continued to believe that it had been necessary and appropriate to seek out a relationship with moderate Iranian factions.[40] President Reagan expressed the view that the effort to establish a "new base" in Iran had been "reasonably successful" but that the "press exposure has botched that."[41] President Reagan also suggested that we should send an "emissary" to our "Mid East friends" to explain the Iran initiative, *see* Nov. 24, 1986 Regan Note, and observed that the amount of arms involved in the Iranian initiative was exceedingly small when compared with the amounts sold to both Iran and Iraq by other countries.[42]

Thus, the "[t]hrust of [the] meeting was we [were] right" and "how to proceed," Nov. 24, 1986 Platt Note, *not* an exhaustive recapitulation of Attorney General Meese's conclusions and findings following his brief weekend effort to collect the facts regarding past events. Indeed, if it had been such a meeting, it is ridiculous to think that the Attorney General would not have reported on his discovery of the possible diversion of funds to the Contras -- a fact that he *did* disclose in a press conference the very next day. A "lengthy presentation" from the Attorney General simply was not on the agenda, despite the Independent Counsel's inexcusably

---

[40] *See, e.g.,* Nov. 24, 1986 Regan Note; Nov. 24, 1986 Weinberger Note; Nov. 24, 1986 Platt Note.

[41] Nov. 24, 1986 Weinberger Note; *see also* Nov. 24, 1986 Regan Note; Nov. 24, 1986 Platt Note.

[42] *See, e.g.,* Nov. 24, 1986 Weinberger Note (noting that President said that "we sold them 12 million of arms but other countries total about 9-1/2 billion for Iran -- 35 [billion] for Iraq."); *see also* Nov. 24, 1986 Platt Note; Nov. 24, 1986 Regan Note.

misleading statements to the contrary, *see, e.g.*, *Final Report*, Vol. I, at 543, as the
contemporaneous notes clearly demonstrate.

      It was the United States' past and future policy toward Iran and the
Middle East that was the subject of debate and discussion and clearly the main topic of
the meeting, according to the only sources the Independent Counsel cites. Moreover,
had the Independent Counsel not been so consumed with scouring minutia to
manufacture a cover-up, he could have looked in the public record of the Iran-Contra
Congressional Hearings to verify this fact. Indeed, a November 21, 1986
memorandum from Admiral Poindexter to President Reagan, reprinted as an exhibit to
Donald Regan's congressional testimony, explicitly outlines the agenda for the
November 24 senior advisers meeting in a way that closely tracks the notes of the
meeting. *See* Regan Testimony, *in Iran-Contra Congressional Hearings*, 100-10,
Exhibit DTR-51, at 425. In the first section entitled "PURPOSE," the memoranda
states: "To review the situation in Iran and discuss how best to reinvigorate our policy
in the Middle East and Persian Gulf." *Id*. The memorandum then elaborates:

> The disclosure of the Iran initiative has exacerbated the
> leadership struggle in Tehran and damaged our influence in
> the Middle East and Persian Gulf. To assess the
> consequences of this situation, and what we can do to
> restore our position, our discussion will open with a detailed
> briefing on the internal situation in Iran. George Cave,
> CIA's premier expert on Iran (who accompanied Bud to
> Tehran and participated in other meetings with the Iranians),
> will provide the group with an intelligence briefing based on
> our most recent contacts. Cave will depart at the conclusion
> of his presentation.
>
> In the follow-up discussion, it is essential that we reach a
> consensus on how to proceed in our efforts with Iran. Of
> even greater significance is the need to marshal bureaucratic
> resources -- notably the State Department -- to explain the
> rationale for our initiative and to dispatch a special emissary
> to key posts. The mission of the emissary (perhaps the Vice

> President with Under Secretary Armacost) would be to
> explain not only the strategic rationale for our action, but
> also to place the initiative in the context of our broader
> regional objectives . . . .

Thus, the public record reveals that the meeting was not at all what the Independent

Counsel asserts it to be. It is difficult to overstate the level of distortion that the

Independent Counsel has introduced into his analysis of this meeting without examining

the dozens of ways in which his characterizations and conclusions are inaccurate and

misleading.

At the meeting President Reagan repeatedly stated that he viewed the

Iranian initiative as the correct policy and the best way to open up channels to moderate

groups in Iran and pave the way for a positive relationship with the future post-

Khomeini Iran. *See, e.g.,* Nov. 24, 1986 Regan Note. He declared that he did *not*

view it as "arms for hostages." *Id.* Secretary of State Shultz and Secretary of Defense

Weinberger both reiterated their strong disagreement with the policy and argued that it

should be terminated. *See, e.g.,* Nov. 24, 1986 Weinberger Note (depicting policy

arguments of President Reagan, Secretary Shultz and Secretary Weinberger); *see also*

Nov. 24, 1986 Platt Note ("Cap [Weinberger] talked for a long time"); Nov. 24, 1986

Regan Note (depicting arguments of President and both Secretaries Weinberger and

Shultz).

Far from revealing the beginnings of a subtle silent plot to "cover-up" the

President's views, knowledge or activities, the notes of the November 24, 1986

meeting show that President Reagan was unwilling to mislead the American people or

to "apologize" for foreign policy decisions that he recognized carried risks but believed

were "the right thing." Nov. 24, 1986 Weinberger Note. President Reagan said he

was "not that good an actor" to pretend that he did not condone the policy. *See id.*; *see*

also Nov. 24, 1986 Regan Note.

The Independent Counsel turns a blind eye to the clear picture that emerges when the notes that he cites are read from beginning to end and considered together as a whole. He focuses instead only on out-of-context extracts of partially illegible notes concerning one brief exchange during the middle of this lengthy policy debate when Donald Regan interjected the question, "Did we object to Israeli[s] sending HAWKs shipment . . . to Iran?" *See* Nov. 24, 1986 Weinberger Note.[43] Attorney General Meese, who was *not* presiding over the meeting, admittedly had *no* personal knowledge regarding the President's contemporaneous knowledge of the 1985 HAWK shipment or the December 1985 Finding, and had said little if anything up to that point in the meeting. He apparently responded that the HAWK shipment, or perhaps the CIA's involvement in it, may have been "[n]ot legal because no finding. President was not informed." Nov. 24, 1986 Weinberger Note; *see also* Nov. 24, 1986 Regan Note (Attorney General Meese said, "May be a violation of law if arms shipped w/o a finding. But Pres did not know.").[44] But that response, which may have

---

[43] It also should be noted that the Independent Counsel misleadingly intersperses inherently incomplete notes concerning what happened at the meeting with discussions of what Charles Hill, Secretary Shultz's note-taker -- who did not attend the meeting -- "hypothesized" regarding Attorney General Meese's motives based on Mr. Hill's subjective, second-hand interpretations of what Secretary Shultz had told him. *See, e.g., Final Report*, Vol. I, at 543. Such highly unreliable musings by Mr. Hill would not be admissible in court because such second-hand speculation is inherently suspect and misleading. Such idle speculation would not be taken seriously by anyone interested in determining the facts of Iran-Contra and are flatly contradicted by any reasonable and thorough review of the objective record. No responsible prosecutor would use such material to indict, in evidence, in a trial, or in a damning report. Their use by Independent Counsel Walsh to draw fanciful conclusions is reprehensible under any standard.

[44] The Attorney General's purported statement followed his weekend-long investigation during which he heard sharply differing accounts regarding the knowledge U.S. officials had of the HAWK shipment before it occurred. Although Secretary Schultz had made statements to the Attorney General on Saturday, November 22, indicating that U.S. officials, including President Reagan, had contemporaneous knowledge of the HAWK shipment, Lt. Col. North had told the Attorney General on Sunday, November 23, that U.S. officials had been told before the shipment only that it contained "oil-drilling equipment." *See* Meese Testimony, *in Iran-Contra Congressional Hearings*, 100-9, at 242; Testimony of Charles J. Cooper [hereinafter Cooper Testimony], *in Iran-Contra*

[Footnote continued on next page]

referred to the shipment itself or the CIA participation,[45] or the absence of a finding, which *was* supplied a few weeks after the shipment, was obviously based on an incomplete investigation and, perhaps, a casual response to a tangential question. Some of those present may have known that the President knew of the shipment in advance, others did not. Most did not know of the CIA participation. Few knew of the retroactive finding. Under no circumstances could this exchange, in this context, have been an invitation to a conspiracy to "cover-up" wrongdoing by the Administration. Indeed, if the President did *not* know about the HAWK shipment, then he could not have made a finding and the shipments may have triggered greater concerns over their legality. The most commonly accepted view regarding the legality of the 1985 HAWK shipment rests on Presidential approval. But none of the participants could possibly have known what the others knew or did not know or what would have been the most "favorable" version for the Administration. That is not how conspiracies are created. The theory is preposterous.

[Footnote continued from previous page]

Congressional Hearings, 100-6, at 261. Lt. Col. North's account was consistent with that of Mr. McFarlane, who had told the Attorney General earlier in the weekend that "he did not know that there were HAWKs on the plane until substantially after the November transfer." Cooper Testimony, in *Iran-Contra Congressional Hearings*, 100-6, at 255; Meese Testimony, *in Iran-Contra Congressional Hearings*, 100-9, at 228.

45   In fact, Donald Regan testified in Congress that, while the President was informed of the HAWK shipment in November 1985, "the President did not know that the CIA was involved in the November 1985 HAWK shipments." Regan Testimony, *in Iran-Contra Congressional Hearings*, 100-10, at 105; *id.* at 67 ("MR. COURTER: Did President Reagan know . . . about . . . the CIA involvement or cooperation with [the HAWK shipment]? MR. REGAN: No. At least in my presence, it was never told to the President that the CIA in any way was responsible for any part of that transaction."). McFarlane testified to similar effect. *See* McFarlane Testimony, *in Iran-Contra Congressional Hearings*, 100-2, at 261 ("MR. STOKES: Did the President also know that the CIA would play a role in the shipment? MR. MCFARLANE: No, sir, nor did I at the time."). And the Independent Counsel likewise concludes that President Reagan "was informed of and approved in" the HAWK shipment, *Final Report*, Vol. I, at 453, but that "[t]here was no evidence that the President knew in advance that the CIA was going to participate in the HAWK transaction," *id.* at 456.

The Independent Counsel argues that Attorney General Meese's statement must have been a hint to the others at the meeting to conceal the President's knowledge of the HAWK shipment because "no one corrected Meese." *Final Report*, Vol. I, at 542. However, Mr. Meese's extraneous comments concerning his understanding of the specifics of the HAWK shipment were not directly pertinent to the main topic of the meeting. It is perfectly understandable and altogether reasonable that the other participants in the meeting -- who were engaged in tense arguments regarding the foreign policy goals of the United States in the Middle East -- would not have felt it necessary or appropriate to digress in that context into a debate about whether the President did or did not know about the arms shipments or particular aspects of them. And, of course, the only person besides the President who had relatively complete knowledge on the subject was Mr. McFarlane, who was not even present.

There were eight people at the November 24 meeting. It defies common sense that a conspiracy of silence could be orchestrated among eight people, some of whom took and preserved notes of the meeting, on the basis of an uncontradicted, arguably confusing, statement by a single person and the failure by others to contradict him. All of those persons would have to have understood, implicitly, that they were being invited to adhere to Mr. Meese's response, whatever it might have meant to each of them individually, despite contrary evidence, and without *any* discussion of such a plan. And, for the conspiracy to have worked, each would have had to have believed not only that every other person in the room understood Mr. Meese's remarkably oblique signal, but accepted and agreed to adhere to it.

If a conspiracy was to be planned, it would have made much more sense to discuss what was being planned -- and *not to take notes of the discussion*. In fact, of course, no participant in that meeting who had knowledge inconsistent with Mr. Meese's response ever kept it from any investigators, so that if the invitation to

82

conspire was understood by the participants, not a single one of them ever accepted the invitation.[46]

It is particularly irresponsible for the Independent Counsel to predicate his cover-up theory on the fleeting Regan-Meese exchange when the notes reflect that it was sandwiched between the President's repeated statements -- which were consistent with his public statements and statements to investigating bodies both before and after the meeting -- accepting full responsibility for the Iran arms shipments and affirmatively rejecting even the suggestion that he should distance himself from the policy and blame it on his subordinates. According to Secretary Weinberger's notes, the President ended the meeting by saying flatly that he would not "throw[ ] anyone to the wolves" or "go before [the] American people and say 'I apologize' . . . [because] I don't think we did wrong." Nov. 24, 1986 Weinberger Note.

In short, the contemporaneous notes demonstrate that the November 24, 1986 meeting between the President and his senior advisers did not remotely resemble the Independent Counsel's insidious, biased and inaccurate portrayal of the meeting in

---

[46]   The Independent Counsel contends that the details of the November 24, 1986 meeting remained secret and, therefore, the "cover-up" continued until the Independent Counsel "uncovered" the Weinberger and Regan notes of the meeting in 1992. *See, e.g., Final Report*, Vol. I, at 545. However, the Independent Counsel admits that "Hill's notes of Shultz's recollections immediately after the meeting," were produced to the Congressional Committees conducting the Iran-Contra inquiry in 1987. *Id.* at 543. The Independent Counsel cites repeatedly to these very same notes to construct his cover-up/conspiracy theory, *id.* at 543-45, contending that they "show that Shultz and his aides were concerned that the White House was presenting an inaccurate account of the November 1985 shipment," *id.* at 543. Moreover, as the Independent Counsel also concedes, Edwin Meese, who purportedly masterminded the cover-up strategy, also produced his notes of the November 24 meeting to the Congressional Committees in July 1987 and "Meese's notes reflect Regan's question about the HAWK shipment and Poindexter's initial response" that "before December 7, 1985, McFarlane handled the Iran arms sales 'all alone' with 'no documentation.'" *Id.* at 542-43; *see* Meese Testimony, *in Iran-Contra Congressional Hearings*, 100-9, Exhibit EM-49, at 1429-30 (reprinting Meese's November 24 notes).

Given these early disclosures to Congress in 1987, which now form a cornerstone of the Independent Counsel's cover-up theory, it is absurd for the Independent Counsel to contend that there was a five-year conspiracy thereafter to conceal either the November 24 meeting or the President's knowledge of the 1985 HAWK shipment.

his Final Report. Rather than beginning a cover-up, the meeting ended with a forceful statement by President Reagan that he would not sacrifice his principles on the altar of political expediency.

D.   The Independent Counsel's Analysis Of Handwritten Notes From November 1986 Does Not Support His Theory Of A "Cover-Up"

As additional support for his argument that President Reagan "permitted the creation of a false account of the Iran arms sales to be disseminated to members of Congress and the American people," *Final Report*, Vol. I, at 445, the Independent Counsel attempts to find support in "[p]reviously withheld notes" of a November 12, 1986 meeting between the members of the Administration, including the President, and congressional leaders, which Mr. Walsh first reviewed in 1992. *Id*. at 446. But these notes hardly constitute the bombshell that the Independent Counsel makes them out to be. Indeed, the alleged chief villain of Mr. Walsh's conspiracy plot, Edwin Meese, produced his notes of the November 12 meeting to Congress *in July 1987* and these notes subsequently became part of the public record, *see* Meese Testimony, *in Iran-Contra Congressional Hearings*, 100-9, Exhibit EM-21, at 1271-73 (reprinting Meese's November 12 notes), a fact that the Independent Counsel unaccountably fails to mention when analyzing these notes and smearing individuals with his spurious cover-up allegation. *See, e.g., Final Report*, Vol. I, at 528; *see also id*. at 459-60. And the most that Independent Counsel can do in his analysis of the November 12 meeting notes is complain that "[t]he references to the 1985 phase of the initiative are oblique." *See id*. at 459-60. But both Admiral Poindexter and Mr. Regan indicated in multiple briefings to the press over the course of the next two days that the President had approved an Israeli shipment in 1985, refuting the idea that information concerning the 1985 shipments was being intentionally kept from Congress and the public.

Indeed, the Final Report itself concedes that both Admiral Poindexter and Mr. Regan disclosed to reporters on November 13, 1986, just hours prior to the President's Address to the Nation, that in 1985 the United States "had condoned a shipment of arms by Israel to Iran and had replenished it." *Id.* at 460-61 (quoting Regan, Grand Jury, 2/26/88, p. 41). The following day, Mr. Regan again explicitly confirmed during a press briefing intended to amplify and elaborate on the President's Address that the United States had "condoned" "a shipment of arms to Iran from another country" during the summer of 1985. *See* Question and Answer Session with Chief of Staff Donald T. Regan, Internal Transcript, Office of The White House Press Secretary, at 3-5 (1:12 p.m. EST, Nov. 14, 1986). Mr. Regan conceded that that shipment occurred before the January 1986 Finding and said that he was "telescoping into a couple of minutes' conversation hours of lengthy discussions, conversations and negotiations that took place over a period of months in the summer of '85 and on." *Id.* at 3.

While Mr. Regan did not specify whether the shipment involved HAWKs or TOWs, the fact is that he disclosed to the press on November 14, 1986 that the President had authorized shipments of arms to Iran in 1985 -- the very point that the Independent Counsel now claims seven years later was the object of a cover-up.

In an on-the-record press briefing later in the day on November 14, Admiral Poindexter went even further in an exchange with a reporter that completely undermines the Independent Counsel's entire "cover-up" argument:

> Q   A senior official said in the White House yesterday that there was a shipment in the summer of '85 that was condoned by this administration, did not come directly from the United States. The official would not name the country. Now, if there was such a shipment --
>
> ADMIRAL POINDEXTER: And that amount is included in what the President said last night.

Q   All right. If there was such a shipment, what does the word condone mean?

ADMIRAL POINDEXTER: It means that it was *authorized* within the context of this project.

Q   But the President had not signed his January '86 order. How was it authorized?

ADMIRAL POINDEXTER: *It -- it was authorized verbally.*

Q   *By the President?*

ADMIRAL POINDEXTER: *By the President.*[47]

The Independent Counsel also repeatedly cites the handwritten notes of Mr. Regan and others concerning a November 10, 1986 meeting between President Reagan and his top advisers. But these notes add nothing new to the Iran-Contra inquiry and certainly do not prove a "cover-up." Indeed, Mr. Regan's notes of the November 10, 1986 meeting, which the Independent Counsel quotes and cites extensively, were turned over to the Congressional Committees *in July 1987. See* Regan Testimony, *in Iran-Contra Congressional Hearings*, 100-10, Exhibit DTR-41A, at 379. The notes concerning the November 10 meeting of Deputy National Security Adviser Alton Keel and the Weinberger "Memorandum for the Record," also cited by

---

[47]   Press Briefing by Admiral John Poindexter, Internal Transcript, Office of The White House Press Secretary, at 5 (3:23 p.m. EST, Nov. 14, 1986) (emphasis added). While President Reagan did make a statement in a November 19, 1986 press conference erroneously suggesting that there had been no shipments by Israel to Iran in 1985 which the United States had condoned, *see* The President's News Conference, 22 Weekly Comp. Pres. Doc. 1587 (Nov. 19, 1986), he immediately thereafter issued a statement clarifying the issue and acknowledging that "[t]here was a third country involved in our secret project with Iran." *See* Statement By The President, 22 Weekly Comp. Pres. Doc. 1591 (Nov. 19, 1986). In a March 19, 1987 press conference President Reagan explicitly confirmed and endorsed the Tower Commission's finding that he had "verbally" authorized the 1985 shipments. *See* The President's News Conference, 23 Weekly Comp. Pres. Doc. 273, 274 (Mar. 19, 1987).

the Independent Counsel, also were produced to Congress and are contained in publicly available materials. *See id.*, Exhibit DTR-41, at 370; Weinberger Testimony, *in Iran-Contra Congressional Hearings*, 100-10, Exhibit CWW-28, at 578.

The Independent Counsel criticizes Admiral Poindexter's briefing concerning the Iranian initiative during the November 10 meeting as incomplete, and darkly construes the meeting as a precursor to a conspiracy to conceal the 1985 arms sales.[48] However, Mr. Regan's notes reveal that Admiral Poindexter disclosed during the meeting that the United States had replenished the 500 TOWs that were sold to Iran by Israel in 1985, *see* Nov. 10, 1986 Regan Note, and Admiral Poindexter told the media only three days later that the President had *approved* the transfer *and* the replenishment of the TOWs. Even looking through the wildly distorted lens of the Independent Counsel seven years later, it is difficult to see how the November 10 meeting could reasonably be viewed as a basis for concluding that the President or anyone else in his Administration intentionally set out to deceive "Congress and the American people" about the 1985 arms sales.[49]

The Independent Counsel's critique of the swiftness and completeness of disclosures in the early days of November 1986 overlooks another crucial factor. The

---

[48]   To the extent that Admiral Poindexter's November 10 presentation was inaccurate, it was certainly not the Independent Counsel who first discovered and inquired about this subject. Mr. Regan was closely questioned during his congressional testimony concerning Admiral Poindexter's statements and explicitly acknowledged the very inaccuracies that the Independent Counsel now points to as new and shocking revelations. *See* Regan Testimony, *in Iran-Contra Congressional Hearings*, 100-10, at 22-23.

[49]   While the Independent Counsel contends, almost feverishly, that the November 22, 1986 notes of Charles Hill concerning Attorney General Meese's interview of Secretary of State Shultz show that Mr. Meese was laying the groundwork for a cover-up, the notes actually demonstrate precisely the opposite. According to the Hill notes, Secretary Shultz stated that he viewed the Iranian initiative as "a *mistake*, a terrible one. But done for honorable purposes as [the] [President] saw it. Secret but not covered up. . . [O]ur [President's] stock in trade is being straight." Nov. 22, 1986 Hill Note (emphasis in original). Mr. Meese agreed, stating that "We have to get facts so *he* knows facts. And *no* cover-up." *Id.* (emphasis in original).

President, while wanting to make a full public disclosure, was deeply concerned with the safety of the hostages. Thus, according to Mr. Regan's notes of the November 10 meeting, the President declared, "We should put out [a] statement [to] show we do want to get [the] hostages back, that Iranian contacts were for long range, won't deal with terrorists, nor ransom. But cannot get into a q & a [regarding the] hostages so as not to endanger them."[50] The President firmly reiterated this same point later in the meeting: "No further speculation or answers so as not to endanger hostages."[51]

As a result of concern for the safety and return of the hostages, the Administration did modulate its tones during the early days following the first public disclosure of the Iranian initiative on November 3, 1986. But even the Independent Counsel has recognized that "[r]ight or wrong, the President's determination that secrecy was necessary to protect the hostages from murder was a matter for him to decide. Certainly, it was not a frivolous concern, nor was his view of his constitutional powers and responsibilities." *Final Report,* Vol. I, at 453.[52] And the story of the Iran-Contra initiatives was fully and exhaustively told to the Tower Commission, Congress and the American people once talks with the Iranians finally broke off and the risks to the hostages had subsided.

---

50   Nov. 10, 1986 Regan Note; *see also* Regan Testimony, *in Iran-Contra Congressional Hearings*, 100-10, at 22; *id.* at 112; Reagan, *An American Life* at 528 ("I've proposed and our message will be: 'We can't and won't answer any questions on this subject because to do so will endanger the lives of those we are trying to help.'") (quoting Nov. 7, 1986 diary entry).

51   Nov. 10, 1986 Regan Note. Mr. Regan's notes from later that afternoon reflect that information had indicated that the release of the hostages might still be secured, and also confirm that the Administration was concerned that disclosure to Congress and the public had to be balanced against this possibility. *See id.*

52   As discussed in detail *infra* pages 104-09, the President had a statutory and constitutional obligation to protect the lives of the American hostages.

E. It Would Have Made No Sense To Conceal The President's Knowledge Of The 1985 Arms Shipments

The Independent Counsel's "cover-up" theory also does not make any sense because the President's contemporaneous knowledge and approval *supported* the legality of the 1985 arms shipments. As discussed *infra* pages 96-109, the legality of the 1985 arms shipments was strengthened if the President was aware of them and gave his approval. The Attorney General, the Assistant Attorney General and the CIA General Counsel found that the transactions were completely legal, relying in part on the President's involvement. Thus, it would have been counter-productive to try to "cover-up" the President's knowledge or approval of these transactions since they would have been *less* defensible legally if President Reagan had *not* had knowledge of them.

II

FROM THE OUTSET PRESIDENT REAGAN ACCEPTED FULL RESPONSIBILITY FOR THE ACTIVITIES OF THE IRANIAN AND NICARAGUAN INITIATIVES THAT HE AUTHORIZED; THE INDEPENDENT COUNSEL'S "SCAPEGOAT" THEORY IS WITHOUT FOUNDATION

The Independent Counsel also has used his Final Report and its frivolous cover-up hypothesis as an attempt to revive the "scapegoat," or "fall guy," theory that was first advanced six years ago on behalf of Lt. Col. North in the congressional hearings, but was thereafter uniformly rejected by everyone who examined the evidence, including the Independent Counsel. According to the Independent Counsel, the purported "cover-up" instigated at the November 24, 1986 senior advisers meeting was the predominant component of a related "strategy to make National Security Council staff members McFarlane, Poindexter and North the scapegoats whose sacrifice would protect the Reagan Administration in its final two years." *Final Report*,

Vol. I, at xi. However, the Independent Counsel's "scapegoat" theory falls thoroughly apart upon analysis.

The President took full responsibility for Iran-Contra. He refused to walk away from the Iranian initiative or blame his subordinates for actions that he had endorsed. The President gave an Address to the Nation from the Oval Office on November 13, 1986, in which he said that he had authorized arms shipments to Iran, explained the foreign policy rationale of that action, and repeated his own view that the arms shipments were not "ransom" but rather one component of an effort to fulfill the dual objectives of opening a promising channel to Iran and freeing the hostages.[53] The President explicitly acknowledged that the Iran initiative dated back to the summer of 1985, stating that "[f]or 18 months now we have had underway a secret diplomatic initiative to Iran."[54] The President declared that "I authorized the transfer of [arms] to Iran."[55]

The Independent Counsel faults the former President for not spelling out in greater detail in his Address the precise nature of each and every shipment to Iran. For example, he states accusingly that "[t]he President was silent about the 1985 Israeli shipments of U.S. arms to Iran." *Final Report*, Vol. I, at 460. But the President was not attempting in this address to lay out all the details of the covert operation. He did not say when *any* of the arms shipments occurred. Moreover, as discussed above, Admiral Poindexter and Mr. Regan disclosed in press briefings before and after the Address that the President had approved an Israeli shipment to Iran in 1985. And the President made it clear that the overall policy had his imprimatur. He also sought,

---

53   *See* The President's Address To The Nation, 22 Weekly Comp. Pres. Doc. 1559
      (Nov. 13, 1986).

54   *Id.*

55   *Id.*

unsuccessfully, to explain what he perceived then and to this day believes is a misperception of the policy as an "arms for hostages" exchange. As President Reagan wrote in his diary the day before his Address, he "'want[ed] to go public personally and tell the people the truth.'" Reagan, *An American Life* at 528 (quoting diary entry). President Reagan fully recognizes that the policy has been understood as an exchange for hostages, as some of his advisers had predicted. But that does not alter his conviction that that was not his intention.

Nor did President Reagan seek to shift responsibility to the NSC staff for decisions relative to the Contras. When Attorney General Meese first disclosed the so-called "diversion memo" reflecting that funds for the arms sales had been diverted to the Contras, the President appeared personally with the Attorney General at a press conference to disclose discovery of the diversion.[56] And he telephoned Lt. Col. North on November 25, 1986, to offer his sympathy and support.[57] Whatever the wisdom of the President's policies (which may have saved thousands of lives and staved off communist expansion in Central America) and whatever the prudence of contacting Lt. Col. North before knowing the full extent of his activities, these were not the actions of a President seeking to shift responsibility away from himself or to let others take the blame for his actions. In his 16 years as Governor of California and President of the United States, President Reagan has never failed to accept responsibility for his own decisions. Not even his harshest critics, except for the lonely example of Independent

---

[56] *See* National Security Council and Implementation of United States Policy Toward Iran; Remarks Announcing A Review Of The Council's Role And Procedures, 22 Weekly Comp. Pres. Doc. 1604 (Nov. 25, 1986); Transcript of Attorney General Meese's News Conference of Nov. 25, 1986, *reprinted in Iran-Contra Congressional Hearings*, 100-9, Exhibit EM-54, at 1456.

[57] This telephone call was immediately reported in the press. *See, e.g.,* Ignatius, *Reagan Phoned Lt. Col. North With Gratitude*, Wash. Post, Nov. 27, 1986, at A1.

Counsel Walsh, have ever accused President Reagan of that type of conduct. It is completely outside his character.

The Independent Counsel's only "proof" of the scapegoat theory is utterly unreliable and squarely conflicts with direct, overwhelming evidence to the contrary. For example, the Independent Counsel cites the double hearsay grand jury testimony of Oliver North's assistant Robert Earl concerning the November 25, 1986 telephone call between President Reagan and Lt. Col. North. "According to Earl, North told [Earl and another NSC staff member] that President Reagan had called him to express his regret at North's firing and said that the President told North that it was important that Reagan 'not know.' Earl inferred from this statement that North had been cast in a scapegoat's role with the President's knowledge." *Final Report*, Vol. I, at 29; *see also id.* at 465. The problem with Mr. Walsh's reliance on this statement is that Lt. Col. North's purported statement to his assistant is not true, and Mr. Walsh knows it. *Id.* at 465. Even Lt. Col. North acknowledges that he had no such conversation with President Reagan. Indeed, Lt. Col. North has testified that the President said, "*I just didn't know.*" *See* Testimony of Oliver L. North, *in Iran-Contra Congressional Report*, App. B, Vol. 20, at 479 (emphasis added).[58]

In his criminal trial, North asserted a "higher-authorization" defense and sought to call President Reagan as a witness in order to prove that the President did, in fact, "know," and authorized North's activities, including his alleged efforts to conceal the Iran-Contra matters from public disclosure. But he and his lawyers were not able to offer a shred of evidence to support the theory. Indeed, Federal District Judge Gerhard Gesell, who presided over the *North* trial, flatly rejected the argument and quashed the subpoena:

---

[58]   Lt. Col. North's secretary Fawn Hall also testified in Congress that North told her that the President said "[I] just didn't know." Testimony of Fawn Hall, *in Iran-Contra Congressional Hearings*, 100-5, at 502.

The written record has been exhausted in this regard. *The trial record presently contains no proof that defendant North ever received any authorization from President Reagan to engage in the illegal conduct alleged, either directly or indirectly, orally or in writing.* No such authorization to any obstruction or false statement count has been identified in materials submitted to the Court by the defense either in CIPA [Classified Information Procedures Act] proceedings or on the public record. Additionally, the Court has examined President Reagan's responses to extensive interrogatories furnished by him under oath to the grand jury as well as references (filed herewith under seal) to portions of Mr. Reagan's personal diary developed by Independent Counsel during the investigatory stages of this matter. *Nothing there even remotely supports an authorization claim.*[59]

In fact, the Independent Counsel's scapegoat theory is nothing more than a recycled version of the "fall guy plan" about which Lt. Col. North testified during the congressional hearings in 1987. Lt. Col. North told Congress that "[a]s far back as the early spring of 1984, . . . he and [CIA] Director Casey had discussed a 'fall guy plan,'" in which Lt. Col. North would "'take the fall' in the event of public disclosure" of the Iran and Contra initiatives. *See Iran-Contra Congressional Report* at 291. But Congress rejected Lt. Col. North's testimony "attributing knowledge and statements to Casey after Casey's death . . . , particularly insofar as such testimony . . . tends to exculpate North." *Id.* at 291 n.*.

It is ironic that two of the persons whom the Independent Counsel identifies as "scapegoats" deny the theory themselves. Admiral Poindexter testified in Congress that he "'was not a party to any plan to make Colonel North or to make me, for that matter, a scapegoat'." *Id.* at 291. And Mr. "McFarlane flatly denied that any

---

[59] *United States* v. *North*, 713 F. Supp. at 1450 (emphasis added). Interestingly, the Independent Counsel *never* subpoenaed President Reagan. He saved his allegations for his Final Report.

'fall guy plan' ever existed." *Id*. Congress concluded that "[t]here is *no* evidence that the President was aware of or condoned the 'fall guy' plan." *Id*. (emphasis added).

But the "scapegoat" theory is necessary to the Independent Counsel to explain why he was unable to prove or develop any evidence to support his "conspiracy/cover-up/wrongdoing-at-the-highest-levels-of-government" theory. Therefore, without evidence or even a plausible theory, the Independent Counsel goes on to argue that "[i]n an important sense, this [scapegoat] strategy succeeded," because the Independent Counsel "discovered much of the best evidence of the cover-up in the final year of the active investigation, too late for most prosecutions." *Final Report*, Vol. I, at xi. But the purported "new evidence" upon which the Independent Counsel seeks to predicate the scapegoat theory consists only of the handwritten notes and testimony concerning the November 24 meeting and the alleged conspiracy to hide the President's knowledge of the 1985 Iranian arms shipments by "diverting" the Nation's attention to Lt. Col. North and Admiral Poindexter and the diversion. But none of that makes any sense, as has already been thoroughly demonstrated. The Final Report contains virtually nothing of substance that was not known at the end of the congressional investigation in 1987. And revelation of the Contra diversion hardly took attention away from the President or deflected the focus of Congress, the Tower Commission, the Independent Counsel or the American people. Rather, it intensified the glare of the spotlight on the entire Iran-Contra affair, including the issue of when the President knew of and approved the 1985 arms shipments to Iran. Therefore, nothing that President Reagan did forced attention on his subordinates beyond the natural consequences of their own actions.

The "scapegoat" theory therefore is reduced to nothing except an eleventh hour excuse for the Independent Counsel for his failure to prove theories for which there is no evidence.

III

PRESIDENT REAGAN ACTED IN FULL COMPLIANCE WITH THE LAWS AND EXECUTIVE BRANCH POLICIES IN CONNECTION WITH THE IRANIAN ARMS SALES

The Independent Counsel repeatedly seeks to convey the impression that "high-ranking Administration officials violated laws and executive orders" in carrying out the Iranian initiative. *See, e.g., Final Report*, Vol. I, at ix. He specifically contends that the arms sales "contravened United States Government policy and *may* have violated the Arms Export Control Act." *Id.* (emphasis added). More broadly, he asserts that "the Iran . . . operations . . . violated United States policy and law." *Id.* at xi.

The Independent Counsel uses every rhetorical linguistic device available to encourage his readers to believe that President Reagan was directly responsible for illegal activity during the Iranian initiative: "[H]e *set the stage* for the illegal activities of others . . . in authorizing the sale of arms to Iran . . . . The President's *disregard for civil laws* enacted to limit presidential actions abroad . . . *created a climate* in which [Government officials] felt *emboldened* to circumvent such laws." *Id.* at xiii (emphasis added). And, "President Reagan's decision in 1985 to authorize the sale of arms to Iran . . . *opened the way* for . . . the diversion." *Id.* (emphasis added). But these words and phrases are employed precisely because the Independent Counsel lacks any evidence for his conclusions. His empty, unproven and unprovable assertions are among the most egregious and irresponsible segments of Mr. Walsh's Report.

As discussed below, the Iranian arms shipments were a legally justified means by which President Reagan sought to pursue a policy of establishing contacts with moderate elements in Iran and effectuating the release of the American hostages. The arms sales were lawful actions undertaken to fulfill the President's statutory and constitutional duty to protect the lives and liberty of Americans held captive overseas.

95

**A.   The Arms Shipments Were Authorized Under The National
        Security Act And The Economy Act And Were Not Prohibited
        By The Arms Export Control Act**

The Independent Counsel asserts that "[t]here was no way in which

President Reagan's action [in approving the arms sales] could be squared with the Arms

Export Control Act (AECA)." *Final Report*, Vol. I, at 453. However, the

Independent Counsel makes this assertion without any explanation for his conclusion.

It is therefore understandable that his conclusions would be misguided and misleading.

The AECA is one of the laws that regulate the sale and transfer of U.S.

military arms for export to foreign countries. *See* 22 U.S.C. §§ 2751, *et seq.* But the

AECA is not the only statute under which U.S. arms exports may be legally authorized.

As the Office of Legal Counsel of the Department of Justice concluded, "[a]lthough

both statutes [*i.e.*, the AECA and the Foreign Assistance Act of 1961 ("FAA")]

establish comprehensive regulatory schemes in the areas of military assistance and

military sales, they do not purport to constitute the sole and exclusive authority under

which the executive branch may transfer weapons to foreign nations." Charles J.

Cooper, Assistant Attorney General, *Memorandum for the Attorney General Re: Legal

Authority for Recent Covert Arms Transfers to Iran* 1 (Dec. 17, 1986) [hereinafter

Cooper, *Legal Authority*], *reprinted in Iran-Contra Congressional Hearings*, 100-6, at

630.

Well before the Iranian initiative, both the Department of State and the

Department of Justice had determined that arms exports may be authorized outside the

scope of the AECA. In 1981, the Legal Adviser to the Secretary of State concluded:

> It seems clear that Congress has not regarded the FAA and
> the AECA as an exclusive body of law fully occupying the
> field with respect to U.S. arms transfers.

Davis R. Robinson, Legal Adviser, Dep't of State, *Memorandum of Law on Legal

Authority for the Transfer of Arms Incidental to Intelligence Collection* 5 (Oct. 2,

1981). Attorney General William French Smith concurred in this conclusion and wrote

to CIA Director Casey:

> We have been advised by the State Department's Legal
> Adviser that the Foreign Assistance Act and the Arms
> Export Control Act were not intended, and have not been
> applied, by Congress to be the exclusive means for sales of
> U.S. weapons to foreign countries and that the President
> may approve a transfer outside the context of those statutes.

Letter from Attorney General William French Smith to William J. Casey, Director of

Central Intelligence (Oct. 5, 1981), *reprinted in Iran-Contra Congressional Hearings,*

100-10, Exhibit CWW-1, at 502.

Attorney General Smith concluded that arms sales intended "to achieve a

significant intelligence objective" could be authorized pursuant to the National Security

Act ("NSA"). *See id.* This opinion later served as a basis for the conclusion of

Attorney General Meese that the Iranian arms sales were authorized under the NSA.

See Cooper, *Legal Authority* at 18, *reprinted in Iran-Contra Congressional Hearings*

100-6, at 647; *see supra* pages 52-53.

Under the NSA, the NSC is assigned certain explicitly defined functions,

but is also empowered to "perform[ ] such other functions as the President may direct."

50 U.S.C. § 402. The NSA also provides that

> it shall be the duty of the [CIA], under the direction of the
> [NSC] . . . to perform such other functions and duties
> related to intelligence affecting the national security as the
> [NSC] may from time to time direct.

50 U.S.C. § 403. Among the activities undertaken by the NSC and CIA under these

provisions is "the discretion to transfer arms to foreign recipients in the course of

intelligence or intelligence-related activities." Cooper, *Legal Authority* at 2, *reprinted*

in Iran-Contra Congressional Hearings, 100-6, at 631.

Indeed, Congress specifically recognized that intelligence agencies may ship arms pursuant to the NSA. In the Intelligence Authorization Act for Fiscal Year 1986, which amended the NSA, Congress provided:

> Sec. 503. (a)(1). The transfer of a defense article or defense service exceeding $1,000,000 in value by an intelligence agency to a recipient outside that agency shall be considered a significant anticipated intelligence activity for the purpose of section 501 of this Act.
>
> (2)   Paragraph (1) does not apply if --
>
> (A)   The transfer is being made to a department, agency, or other entity of the United States (so long as there will not be a subsequent retransfer of the defense articles on defense services outside the United States Government in conjunction with an intelligence or intelligence-related activity); or
>
> (B)   *the transfer--(i) is being made pursuant to authorities contained in part II of the Foreign Assistance Act of 1961, [or] the Arms Export Control Act . . . .*

50 U.S.C. § 415 (emphasis added). This legislative provision was an "unambiguous recognition that the executive possesses . . . discretion [to ship arms] *apart from* the Foreign Assistance Act and the Arms Export Control Act." Cooper, *Legal Authority* at 3-4, *reprinted in Iran-Contra Congressional Hearings*, 100-6, at 632-33. The reference to arms sales under the AECA as an exception to "[t]he transfer of a defense article" under the NSA "manifestly implied" that arms sales under the NSA are not subject to the terms of the AECA. *Id.*

Under the NSA, a covert action such as an arms transfer is permitted if the President determines that the action would "affect" the national security. 50 U.S.C. § 403(d)(5). Also, if the CIA is involved, the Hughes-Ryan Amendment required a presidential "finding" that the operation is "important to the national security of the United States." 22 U.S.C. § 2422.

Attorney General Meese and Assistant Attorney General Charles J. Cooper concluded that the arms sales were legal based in part on the conclusion that President Reagan had approved those sales as part of an intelligence activities undertaken pursuant to the NSA. *See* Charles J. Cooper, Assistant Attorney General, Office of Legal Counsel, *Memorandum for the Attorney General Re: Statutes Relevant to Recent Actions with respect to Iran* (Nov. 14, 1986), *reprinted in Iran-Contra Congressional Hearings*, 100-6, Exhibit CJC-2, at 515-20; Cooper, *Legal Authority*, *reprinted in Iran-Contra Congressional Hearings*, 100-6, at 630-47. The record firmly supports this conclusion. It is not disputed that President Reagan approved of the arms shipments in 1985 and 1986. Indeed, the Independent Counsel goes to some lengths to insist that the President approved these transactions. The President believed that the shipments affected and were vitally important to the Nation's security interest. The President orally authorized and assented in the Summer and Fall of 1985 to the TOW and HAWK shipments of that year. Also, Admiral Poindexter testified and the Congressional Committees found that in December 1985, President Reagan signed a written Finding approving the CIA's involvement in the November 1985 HAWK shipment. In January 1986 he signed a written Finding authorizing the arms sales that were carried out later that year. And he continued to express his approval for the arms shipments during the course of 1986.

The Independent Counsel criticizes the 1985 arms sales on the ground that those sales were orally approved by President Reagan and not the subject of a written Finding issued in advance of the sales. Yet, there was nothing in the NSA or Hughes-Ryan Amendment at that time requiring the President's approval to be in writing. The Assistant Attorney General noted that "[o]ur conclusion, that Hughes-Ryan findings may take the form of an oral authorization for a particular operation, agrees with previous opinions by Attorney General [Griffin] Bell, by [the Justice Department Office of Legal Counsel], and by the Legal Adviser at the Department of State." Cooper,

Legal Authority at 12 (footnotes and citations omitted), *reprinted in Iran-Contra Congressional Hearings*, 100-6, at 641. Indeed, Congress implicitly recognized that a written Finding was not required by later repealing Hughes-Ryan and amending the NSA to mandate that in the future a Finding be in writing. *See Intelligence Authorization Act for Fiscal Year 1991*, Pub. L. No. 102-88, 105 Stat. 429, 441-42 (1991).

Nor was the President's oral authorization precluded by any Executive Order, as is suggested by the Independent Counsel. "[S]ince such an order was issued within the discretion of the President, it could be rescinded or modified by him if he believed such action appropriate." Meese, *With Reagan* at 268. "Activities authorized by the President cannot 'violate' an executive order in any legally meaningful sense, especially in a case where no private rights are involved, because his authorization creates a valid modification of, or exception to, the executive order." Cooper, *Legal Authority* at 14, *reprinted in Iran-Contra Congressional Hearings*, 100-6, at 643.

There is little doubt that the facts of the 1986 arms sales fit within the paradigm of a covert action authorized under the NSA. The operations, conducted directly by the United States, involved the CIA's purchase of weapons from the Department of Defense under the Economy Act[60] for sale to the Iranians. The President approved these operations in reliance upon the legal opinion of Attorney General Meese and then-CIA General Counsel, now Judge, Stanley Sporkin, that the arms shipments could be authorized under NSA and the Economy Act. *See* Meese Testimony, *in Iran-Contra Congressional Hearings*, 100-9, at 205-09; Sporkin Testimony, *in Iran-Contra Congressional Hearings*, 100-6, at 149-52; Exhibits SS-13, SS-16, *in Iran-Contra Congressional Hearings*, 100-6, at 452-53, 456-59.

---

60   The Economy Act permits the CIA to purchase military arms from the DOD under
      certain terms. *See* 31 U.S.C. § 1535.

Although Israel played a role in the 1985 arms transfers, those shipments also fit within the definition of a U.S. covert operation authorized under the NSA. Israel's involvement in the 1985 arms transfers did not change what was essentially an American-directed operation. The evidence shows that Israel made the 1985 arms shipments only after having been assured that President Reagan had given his general approval for the transactions and had agreed to replace the arms sent to Iran. As Assistant Attorney General Cooper concluded:

> [I]t is apparent that the real nature of the [1985] transaction
> was a bilateral sale between the United States and Iran, with
> Israel serving solely as a conduit or facilitator in the
> execution of that sale.

Cooper, *Legal Authority* at 16-17, *reprinted in Iran-Contra Congressional Hearings*, 100-6, at 646-47 (footnote omitted). The Independent Counsel offers no reasoned analysis to refute this conclusion.

Moreover, even though the AECA is inapplicable, the 1985 arms shipments nevertheless met the "substantive purposes" of the AECA, as the Minority Report of the Congressional Committees found. Under the AECA, the President's approval was required for shipments of U.S.-origin weapons from a foreign country, such as Israel, to a third party or another country. The 1985 arms shipments met this requirement because, according to Mr. McFarlane's testimony, Israel obtained the President's general approval before any shipment occurred. Also, under the AECA, Congress did not need to be notified unless the arms shipment was valued at $14 million or more in acquisition costs. Neither the TOW nor the HAWK shipments reached this level. And other retransfer restrictions of the AECA arguably did not apply to the 1985 arms shipments:

> The retransfer restrictions of the AECA . . . were
> intended to cover situations in which the transferring
> country, rather than the United States, is the sole source of
> the retransfer request. The laws seek to ensure that such

101

retransfers foster the national security interests of the United
States. But in the case of the Iran arms sales, the Israeli
shipments were made with the agreement of American
authorities, and Israel was promised and later was given
substantially identical replacements. Clearly, the Iran arms
sales were premised on U.S. views about America's own
national security interests. In short, the substantive
purposes of the AECA . . . were met.

Iran-Contra Congressional Report at 540 (minority report).

The Independent Counsel does not at all address any of these legal points,
undoubtedly because it is easier to pronounce conclusions without researching the law
and explaining one's conclusions. But it is an irresponsible process for any prosecutor,
especially one with the authority vested in Mr. Walsh.

B.   Delayed Notification Of Congress Was Legally Permissible

Both the AECA and the NSA contain provisions directing the President to
notify Congress of activities undertaken pursuant to those statutes. *See* 22 U.S.C.
§§ 2753(f)(2), 2776(a), 2776(b)(1); 50 U.S.C. § 413. The Independent Counsel
appears to maintain that the arms shipments were unlawful because Congress was not
notified within 30 days after the end of each quarter in which the shipments occurred.
See Final Report, Vol. I, at 453-54.

It has long been accepted, however, that in certain circumstances the
President must have discretion to delay notification of Congress to protect the secrecy
of a covert operation, particularly one in which the lives of American citizens are at
stake. For example, President Carter delayed congressional notification for three
months concerning an operation to smuggle Americans out of the Canadian embassy in
Tehran, and in two other operations related to the Iranian hostage crisis Congress was
not notified for six months. *See H.R. 1013, H.R. 1371, and Other Proposals which
Address the Issue of Affording Prior Notice of Covert Actions to the Congress:
Hearings Before the Subcomm. on Legislation of the House Permanent Select Comm.*

on Intelligence, 100th Cong., 1st Sess. 46 (1987) (testimony of Admiral Stansfield Turner).[61]

Indeed, Congress recognized in the NSA that the notification requirement of the Act was subject to the President's constitutional authority to protect national security:

> To the extent consistent with all applicable authorities and duties, including those conferred by the Constitution upon the executive and legislative branches of the Government, and to the extent consistent with due regard for the protection from unauthorized disclosure of classified information and information relating to intelligence sources and methods, . . . [the congressional intelligence committees are to be kept informed of various intelligence activities].

50 U.S.C. § 413. The legislative history of the NSA also confirms that delayed notification of Congress is permissible. *See Iran-Contra Congressional Report* at 544-45 (minority report) (quoting statements of Members of Congress). In short, as Judge Sporkin put it, it is "Hornbook law" that the NSA "recognizes there will be times when . . . there will be nonnotification" of Congress. Sporkin Testimony, *in Iran-Contra Congressional Hearings*, 100-6, at 195.

The Attorney General concluded that, pursuant to the President's constitutional authority and discretion, notification of Congress was appropriately delayed until the hostages were released. *See* Meese Testimony, *in Iran-Contra Congressional Hearings*, 100-9, at 205-09. The CIA General Counsel and lawyers at the Department of Defense concurred in this conclusion. *See* Sporkin Testimony, *in*

---

61   Certain missions involving the national security must be kept secret, even from Members of Congress, in order for those missions to succeed. *See* Turner, *The Constitution and the Iran-Contra Affair: Was Congress the Real Lawbreaker?*, 11 Hous. J. Int'l L. 83, 101 (1988) (citing examples in U.S. history where Congress was not notified about certain national security measures and observing that "[a] key reason for limiting the participation of the Senate and House of Representatives in the business of foreign affairs was the Founding Fathers' belief that legislative bodies were not good at keeping secrets").

Iran-Contra Congressional Hearings, 100-6, at 151-52. The President determined that absolute secrecy was necessary to protect the lives of the hostages as well as those individuals in Iran who were in contact with U.S. officials. The President was entitled to rely on the legal opinion of his Attorney General and other government legal experts that the President's reasons for delayed notification were legally justified.

Even the Independent Counsel ultimately, albeit grudgingly, recognizes that "[r]ight or wrong, the President's determination that secrecy was necessary to protect the hostages from murder was a matter for him to decide. Certainly, it was not a frivolous concern, nor was his view of his constitutional powers and responsibilities." *Final Report*, Vol. I, at 454.

C.   The Arms Shipments Should Be Considered In Light Of The 1868 Hostage Act

President Reagan's power to authorize the arms sales as part of a plan to effectuate the release of the hostages should also be considered in light of the Hostage Act of 1868, 22 U.S.C. § 1732, a statute that the Independent Counsel fails even to discuss in his Final Report. On its face, the Hostage Act gives the President broad discretion and power to bring about the release of Americans held hostage abroad. The statute provides that "the President shall use such means, not amounting to acts of war, as he may think *necessary and proper* to obtain or effectuate the release." *Id.* (emphasis added).[62] "The phrase 'necessary and proper' is, of course, borrowed from

_____

62   At the time of the arms shipments, the Hostage Act provided:

> Whenever it is made known to the President that any citizen of the United States has been unjustly deprived of his liberty by or under the authority of any foreign government, it shall be the duty of the President forthwith to demand of that government the reasons of such imprisonment; and if it appears to be wrongful and in violation of the rights of American citizenship, the President shall forthwith demand the release of such citizen, and

[Footnote continued on next page]

the Constitution, and has been construed as providing very broad discretionary powers for legitimate ends." 5 Op. Off. Legal Counsel 13 (1981) (citing U.S. Const. art. I, § 8, cl. 18; *McCulloch* v. *Maryland*, 17 U.S. (4 Wheat) 316 (1819)), *available on Westlaw*. Indeed, the President's "necessary and proper" powers under the Hostage Act arguably could have been construed at the time of the arms shipments to include even the authority to take certain action abroad that would otherwise not be authorized under U.S. laws. Congress recognized this when it amended the Hostage Act in 1989 to add the words "and not otherwise prohibited by law" to limit the President's powers under the statute. *See* Pub. L. No. 101-222, § 9, 103 Stat. 1892, 1900 (1989) (amending Hostage Act to read, in pertinent part, that "the President shall use such means not amounting to acts of war *and not otherwise prohibited by law*, as he may think necessary and proper to obtain or effectuate the release") (emphasis added).

The legislative history of the Hostage Act also suggests a broad scope for the President's powers under the Act:

> Proponents of the bill recognized that it placed a "loose discretion" in the President's hands, [Cong. Globe, 40th Cong., 2d Sess.], at 4238 [(1868)] (Sen. Stewart), but argued that "[s]omething must be intrusted to the Executive" and that *"[t]he President ought to have the power to do what the exigencies of the case require to rescue [a] citizen from imprisonment."* *Id.*, at 4233, 4357 (Sen. Williams).

Footnote continued from previous page]

> if the release so demanded is unreasonably delayed or refused, it appears to be wrongful and in violation of the rights of American citizenship, *the President shall use such means, not amounting to acts of war, as he may think necessary and proper to obtain or effectuate the release*; and all the facts and proceedings relative thereto shall as soon as practicable be communicated by the President to Congress.

22 U.S.C. § 1732 (emphasis added).

Dames & Moore v. *Regan*, 453 U.S. 654, 678 (1981) (emphasis added). Senator

Williams, draftsman of the language eventually enacted as the Hostage Act, observed:

> "If you propose any remedy at all, you must invest the
> Executive with some discretion, so that he may apply the
> remedy to a case as it may arise. As to England or France
> he might adopt one policy to relieve a citizen imprisoned by
> either one of those countries; as to the Barbary powers, he
> might adopt another policy; as to the islands of the ocean,
> another. With different countries that have different systems
> of government he might adopt different means." Cong.
> Globe, 40th Cong., 2d Sess., 4359 (1868).

Dames & Moore, 453 U.S. at 677.

The Supreme Court has recognized the President's authority to act

pursuant to the Hostage Act to protect the safety of American citizens abroad. The

Court first noted the protections afforded American citizens under this statute in

Johnson v. *Eisentrager*, 339 U.S. 763, 770 & n.4 (1950), and later relied upon the Act

as a basis for upholding President Kennedy's ban on travel of American citizens to

Cuba, *see Zemel* v. *Rusk*, 381 U.S. 1, 15 & n.16 (1965). Also, after President Carter

negotiated an agreement with Iran to free Americans held hostage in the U.S. embassy

in Tehran, the Court generally relied upon the Hostage Act in addressing whether the

President had congressional authorization to enter into the agreement, which included a

provision suspending the legal claims of U.S. nationals against Iran. *See Dames &*

Moore, 453 U.S. at 677. Although the Court concluded that the Hostage Act did not

constitute "specific authorization of the President's action suspending claims," *id.*, it

nevertheless found the statute "highly relevant in the looser sense of indicating

congressional acceptance of a *broad* scope for executive action in circumstances such as

those presented in [the] case," *id.* (emphasis added).[63]

---

[63] The United States Court of Appeals for the D.C. Circuit upheld a regulation issued on
November 13, 1979, by the Attorney General at the direction of President Carter that
required Iranian college and graduate students to provide information as to residence or
maintenance of non-immigrant status to U.S. officials. Citing the Hostage Act, one judge
on the court observed:

[Footnote continued on next page]

Thus, the Hostage Act is relevant to any legal analysis of the Iranian initiative, which involved actions directly connected with the freeing of Americans held hostage abroad. Indeed, it has been argued that the Hostage Act alone provided President Reagan with sufficient authority to pursue the Iranian initiative. *See* Silverberg, *The Separation of Powers and Control of the CIA's Covert Operation*, 68 Tex. L. Rev. 575, 589 (1990) ("[W]hen President Reagan decided to provide arms to Iran . . . , he was arguably executing his statutory duty under the 1868 Hostages [sic] Act."); Fein, *The Constitution and Covert Action*, 11 Hous. J. Int'l L. 53, 64 (1988) ("President Reagan's covert arms transactions and overtures to factions within Khomeini's Iran thus furthered section 1732 [of the Hostage Act]; indeed, Reagan's actions effectuated the release of three American hostages."). The Independent Counsel's sweeping assertions of illegality of the arms shipments without a detailed and persuasive analysis of the relevant legal authorities is irresponsible. If such an analysis exists, it should have been tendered. If not, the Independent Counsel has been derelict in his duties, but he has not even attempted to put forth his own legal reasoning.

[Footnote continued from previous page]

> In the situation with which we are here dealing, the President's power is at its zenith -- right up to the brink of war and he does act pursuant to the "express authorization" of Congress. . . .
>
> This direction [of the Hostage Act] to the President by Congress is unequivocal. It completely supports every act and order that he has taken to free the United States hostages. No further scrutiny of his acts is required or necessary.

Narenji v. *Civiletti*, 617 F.2d 745, 753 (D.C. Cir.) (MacKinnon, J., concurring), *cert. denied*, 446 U.S. 957 (1980).

D.   The Arms Shipments Should Be Considered In Light Of The President's Constitutional Authority To Conduct Foreign Affairs And To Protect American Citizens Abroad

The Independent Counsel's claims of illegality are also seriously undermined in light of the President's constitutional authority to conduct our Nation's foreign affairs and more specifically to take action that protects the safety and lives of American citizens in foreign countries. The President has "plenary and exclusive power . . . as the *sole* organ of the federal government in the field of international relations -- *a power which does not require as a basis for its exercise an act of Congress.*" *United States* v. *Curtiss-Wright Export Corp.*, 299 U.S. 304, 320 (1936) (emphasis added).[64]

Among the powers of the President in the area of foreign affairs is the discretion to initiate measures to protect the safety of American citizens abroad. As Supreme Court Justice Samuel Nelson, presiding over a federal circuit court, observed in 1860:

> As the executive head of the nation, the president is made the only legitimate organ of the general government, to open and carry on correspondence or negotiations with foreign nations, in matters concerning the interests of the country or of its citizens. It is to him, also, the citizens abroad must look for protection of person and of property, and for the faithful execution of the laws existing and intended for their protection. For this purpose, the whole executive power is placed in his hands, under the constitution, and the laws passed in pursuance thereof; . . . .
>
> Now, as it respects the interposition of the executive abroad, for the protection of the lives or property of the citizen, the duty must, of necessity, rest in the discretion of

---

[64]   *See also Curtiss-Wright*, 299 U.S. at 319 ("In this vast external realm [of foreign affairs], with its important, complicated, delicate and manifold problems, the President alone has the power to speak or listen as a representative of the nation.") (citing remarks of John Marshall as a member of the House of Representatives defending President John Adams's order to extradite a British fugitive).

the president. Acts of lawless violence, or of threatened violence to the citizen or his property, cannot be anticipated and provided for; and the protection, to be effectual or of any avail, may, not infrequently, require the most prompt and decided action. Under our system of government, the citizen abroad is as much entitled to protection as the citizen at home. The great object and duty of the government is the protection of the lives, liberty, and property of the people composing it, whether abroad or at home; and any government failing in the accomplishment of the object, or the performance of the duty, is not worth preserving.

Durand v. *Holland*, 8 F. Cas. 111 (C.C. S.D.N.Y. 1860) (No. 4,186).

Under the Constitution, the President is entrusted with the authority to take appropriate action to protect the lives and liberty of Americans in foreign countries. *See, e.g.,* Charles J. Cooper, Assistant Attorney General, Office of Legal Counsel, *Memorandum for the Attorney General Re: The President's Compliance with the "Timely Notification" Requirement of Section 501(b) of the National Security Act* 14 (Dec. 17, 1986), *reprinted in Iran-Contra Congressional Hearings,* 100-6, Exhibit CJC-21, at 615 ("[T]he Supreme Court has repeatedly intimated that the President has inherent authority to protect Americans and their property abroad by whatever means, short of war, he may find necessary."). President Reagan believed that it was his duty as commander-in-chief to respond in a lawful and prudent, yet forceful, manner to bring about the release of the hostages. *See* Reagan, *An American Life* at 492 ("As president, as far as I was concerned, I had the duty to get those Americans home."); *id.* at 513 ("It was the president's *duty* to get them home. I didn't want to rest or stop exploring any possible avenue until they were home safe with their families.") (emphasis in original).

E. No Criminal Laws Were Implicated By President Reagan's Actions With Respect To The Iranian Arms Sales

There is no basis for suggesting that any of President Reagan's actions with respect to the arms shipments to Iran involved "criminal" violations of the law. If the arms sales violated any laws, which they did not, they did not violate any criminal laws. Neither the Arms Export Control Act nor any other law remotely relevant to the arms sales carried any criminal sanction. Neither Congress nor the Independent Counsel has ever contended otherwise.

The Independent Counsel nonetheless alludes to a peculiar legal theory that he apparently considered advancing that would have asserted that senior Reagan Administration officials, including former President Reagan, engaged in a _criminal_ conspiracy to violate _civil_ laws that purported to restrict the President's foreign policy powers and to regulate arms sales and covert operations. _See Final Report_, Vol. I, at 454-56. But the Independent Counsel admits that "prosecution [based on such a theory] would not have been appropriate." _Id_. Indeed, it would have been utterly frivolous. The only authority under federal law for holding a person liable for criminal conspiracy is 18 U.S.C. § 371, which simply makes it a separate criminal offense to enter into an agreement to violate the criminal laws or to "defraud the United States." As the Independent Counsel himself concedes, "such a charge . . . hardly applied to the President's initial decision to proceed with the arms sales to Iran," _Final Report_, Vol. I, at 456, and "a President relying upon an opinion of the attorney general . . . could hardly be said to be conspiring to defraud the United States," _id_. at 455.

F.   **The Arms Shipments Were Consistent With President Reagan's Policy Decision To Develop Relations With Moderate Factions In Iran**

The Independent Counsel contends that the arms sales to Iran were in violation of U.S. policy. The Independent Counsel forgets, however, that, except in the form of legislation for which Congress has primary responsibility, it is the President who sets policy. The Independent Counsel apparently believes that publicly articulated policy must be maintained rigidly, without exception by the President, even in the face of exigent circumstances. But in the real world, the President may find it necessary, even vital, to deviate from generalized policy positions. Such an action is not a "violation" of a policy, but a change in or an exception to it.

The Iranian initiative was not necessarily even a change in or exception to U.S. policy. President Reagan testified that the arms shipped to Iran were intended to be sold to individuals in Iran who did not support terrorism but were in communication with the Hizbollah terrorists who held the American hostages. *See* Reagan Depo. at 18-19. President Reagan viewed the shipments not as an exchange of arms for hostages, but rather as a mechanism for establishing a relationship with moderates in Iran who might someday take the reins of the Iranian government away from the Ayatollah Khomeini. These neutral third parties, in turn, were to show their good faith by assisting the United States in its attempt to achieve another exceedingly important foreign policy objective of the President -- obtaining release of the hostages. *Id.* President Reagan explained the shipments with this analogy:

> [I]f I had a child kidnapped and held for ransom, and if I knew of someone who had perhaps the ability to get that child back, it wouldn't be dealing with kidnappers to ask that individual to do that. And it would be perfectly fitting for me to reward that individual for doing this. So, that was my position with regard to what they were asking and what they were doing.

Id. at 19; *see also* Cannon, *President Reagan* at 631 (quoting interview with President Reagan in which the former president used the above analogy). Thus, the former President did not view the arms shipments as inconsistent with the U.S. policy of not dealing with terrorists because those shipments were not intended for terrorists.

The Independent Counsel, and others, may choose to disagree with the President's judgments, or to second guess them after the fact. The President has never flinched from the reality that a President must make difficult choices and not all of them will succeed equally. However, the American people overwhelmingly elected President Reagan to make these choices -- and to take responsibility for them. The

Independent Counsel has no such mandate from the American people or from the Court
that appointed him to critique the wisdom of those decisions or to prepare an elaborate
official report setting forth his personal views as to their success or failure. That is a
matter for history and the American people. It is not the role of an independent
counsel.

The independent counsel statute was not enacted to create a policy
ombudsman to deliver foreign policy views. His job is the investigation and
prosecution of crimes. Only an exaggerated sense of his own importance has led the
Iran-Contra Independent Counsel down this unauthorized path.

The President's decisions were within his legal authority, and the
Independent Counsel has not made a case to the contrary. Having failed to do so, the
Independent Counsel exhausted his legitimate and authorized powers and
responsibilities. His other comments carry no more weight than those of any other
citizen.

IV

THE INDEPENDENT COUNSEL'S INNUENDO THAT PRESIDENT REAGAN HAD KNOWLEDGE OF THE DIVERSION IS FRIVOLOUS AND IS COMPLETELY LACKING IN ANY EVIDENTIARY SUPPORT

President Reagan has stated consistently and categorically that he had no
knowledge of the diversion of funds from the sale of arms to Iran to assist the
Nicaraguan Contras. "The President denied unequivocally that he was aware of the
diversion of funds from the proceeds of the Iran arms sales, or that he authorized it."
Final Report, Vol. I, at 447. He made this statement when he announced the
appointment of the Tower Commission, *see* President's Special Review Board for the
National Security Council, 22 Weekly Comp. Pres. Doc. 1610-11 (Dec. 1, 1986); he
repeated it in his interview with the Tower Commission, *Tower Commission Report* at

B-91; he stated it under oath in answers to the Independent Counsel's grand jury inquiries; *see* President's Answers to Grand Jury Interrogatories, Answer Nos. 34, 36-42; he stated it again under oath in the Poindexter trial, Reagan Depo. at 155-57; and he has reiterated that position again and again. *See Final Report*, Vol. I, at 447 n.12 ("The President denied knowledge of the diversion to the Tower Commission, in his sworn Grand Jury Interrogatories, in his testimony in *Poindexter*, and in numerous public statements following the disclosure of diversion."). No one has supplied any evidence to the contrary and *no* investigation by Congress, the Tower Commission, the Independent Counsel, or the press has revealed any information that contradicted the President's clear and unequivocal position.

The Independent Counsel admits that he found "[n]o *direct* evidence . . . that the President authorized or was informed of the profiteering on the Iran arms sales or of the diversion of proceeds to aid the contras." *Id.* at 446 (emphasis added). But there is *no* credible evidence of any sort, *direct or indirect*, in the Report that is inconsistent with President Reagan's position. In fact, on another page in the Report, the Independent Counsel acknowledges that he found "*no* credible evidence that the President authorized or was aware of the diversion of profits from the Iran arms sales to assist the contras." *Id.* at 443 (emphasis added).

Notwithstanding the absence of any basis for impugning the accuracy or integrity of the President's clear and consistent position regarding the diversion, the Independent Counsel has chosen to include in his Report hints, innuendoes, and gross and utterly unfounded speculation that the President must have known about the diversion. For example, the Independent Counsel refers to the "ignorance of the 'diversion' *asserted* by President Reagan." *Id.* at xi (emphasis added). Or, the Independent Counsel "*could not prove* that Reagan authorized or was aware of the diversion," *id.* at xiii (emphasis added), or "*could not prove* the contrary" of the President's denials, *id.* at 447 (emphasis added). While there are a number of

113

examples in the Report of implications without foundation by the Independent Counsel
that the President did not tell the truth, the most blatant and irresponsible distortion
may be found in Chapter 27, where the Independent Counsel imagines that:

> it was doubtful that President Reagan would tolerate the
> successive Iranian affronts during 1986 unless he knew
> that the arms sales continued to supply funds to the
> contras to bridge the gap before the anticipated
> congressional appropriations became effective.

Id. at 446.

This preposterous assertion is unsupported by a shred of real evidence.
The Independent Counsel admits that "[o]nly Poindexter could supply direct evidence"
of such knowledge by the President, "and he denied passing on this information." *Id.*
Thus, there is no evidence at all to support the Independent Counsel's speculation, and
all the affirmative evidence, *i.e.*, testimony by every Administration witness, is to the
contrary. For example, White House Chief of Staff Donald Regan "testified that the
President was 'shocked'" when he learned about the diversion on November 24, 1986.
See id. at 447. Yet the Independent Counsel attempts to turn on its head the lack of
evidence contradicting the President, including any documentary evidence, with the
innuendo that "[t]he wide destruction of records by North eliminated any possible
documentary proof" regarding the President's knowledge of the diversion. *Id.* at 446.
In fact, if there had been documentary proof of the President's involvement, it is
extremely unlikely that Lt. Col. North's limited efforts to destroy documents would
have "eliminated any possible documentary proof" or testimony by any of the many
persons who would necessarily have shared and known about the President's
knowledge.

The Independent Counsel also repeats, although he has relegated it to a
footnote, Admiral Poindexter's peculiar and unfounded speculation that "the President
would have approved [the diversion] had it been presented to him." *Id.* at n.7.

However, President Reagan has repeatedly stated that he would never have condoned violations of the law, and neither Admiral Poindexter nor the Independent Counsel nor anyone else has ever presented any evidence that President Reagan "would have approved" the diversion.

The Independent Counsel does make a passing reference in the same footnote to Lt. Col. North's testimony that "he believed that the President had authorized the diversion." *Id.* However, this supposition by Col. North has never been supported by any evidence. It is the rankest of speculation, and the Independent Counsel obviously cannot and does not give that testimony much credence because he has stated that Col. North's "veracity is subject to serious question." *Id.* at xvi. In fact, when questioned by the Attorney General about the diversion in November of 1986, Lt. Col. North said that the "only persons in Government who knew about the diversion were McFarlane, Poindexter and himself." *Id.* at 212.

The Independent Counsel's effort to challenge President Reagan's statement that he was unaware of the diversion is not based on any evidence. It is irresponsible and unprofessional.

V

PRESIDENT REAGAN COMPLIED WITH ALL LAWS AND EXECUTIVE BRANCH POLICIES RELATING TO CONTRA FUNDING AND ASSISTANCE, AND HE DIRECTED HIS SUBORDINATES TO DO SO AS WELL

The Independent Counsel asserts that "high-ranking Administration officials violated laws and executive orders" with respect to the Nicaraguan initiative. *Final Report*, Vol. I, at ix. He contends that "the provision and coordination of support to the contras violated the Boland Amendment ban on aid to military activities in Nicaragua," *id.* at x, and that "the contra operations . . . violated United States policy and law," *id.* at xi.

This is yet another of countless occasions on which the Independent Counsel has used rhetorical language intended to convey an impression that is contradicted by overwhelming evidence. There is no legitimate basis for charging that President Reagan is directly responsible for the alleged violations of the Boland Amendment. Thus, innuendo and sophistry is used in the place of evidence. According to the Independent Counsel, "President Reagan's directive to McFarlane to keep the contras alive 'body and soul' was viewed . . . as an *invitation to break the law*." *Id.* at xiv (emphasis added).

It is outrageous and an abuse of the Independent Counsel's prosecutorial authority to make such unfounded allegations in his Final Report, especially since he also flatly declares, "There is *no evidence* that McFarlane or *any* NSC staff member raised concerns to the President that his policy directives were causing them to undertake actions that might be unlawful." *Id.* at 104 (emphasis added). To translate President Reagan's desire to support the Contras "body and soul" into an "invitation to break the law" is to engage in the most irresponsible and abusive behavior. Rather than direct his subordinates to break the law, President Reagan's repeated and consistent directive was for his Administration to follow the law and abide by the Boland restrictions.

President Reagan did not authorize or condone any activities in violation of the Boland Amendments. As the President has written, "[f]rom the outset of our program of covert operations in Central America, my instructions were that everything we did must be done legally." Reagan, *An American Life* at 476-77.[65] He "repeatedly insisted that whatever we did had to be within the law, and [he] always assumed that [his] instructions were followed." *Id.* at 485. While the President was unwavering in

---

[65]   *See, e.g., Final Report,* Vol. I, at 452 (The President "issued generalized instructions to his subordinates that they stay within the law.")

his support for the Contras, his activities were limited to those found by the Attorney General to be in compliance with the Boland Amendment. The Independent Counsel has no evidence to contradict the President in this regard.

Moreover, the scope and application of the Boland Amendments were vague, and perhaps deliberately so.[66] The Tower Commission recognized that the Nicaraguan initiative was undertaken in "a highly ambiguous legal environment." *Tower Commission Report* at III-21. Nevertheless, there was and is a substantial body of law supporting the conclusion that all of the activities authorized by President Reagan complied with the requirements of the Boland ban.

Independent Counsel Walsh's assertions of Boland Amendment violations are predicated on erroneous assumptions and fallacious or incomplete reasoning. For example, the Independent Counsel concluded that the NSC, which conducted many of the operations criticized in the Report, was prohibited by the Boland Amendment from coordinating assistance to the Contras. However, the assumption necessary to that conclusion -- that the NSC was an agency covered by the Boland restriction -- was far from clear and probably erroneous.[67] Certainly Congress failed to make that conclusion clear and it surely would have done so had it wished.

---

[66] *See, e.g.*, Note, *Beyond Institutional Competence: Congressional Efforts to Legislate United States Foreign Policy Toward Nicaragua -- The Boland Amendments*, 54 Brooklyn L. Rev. 131, 151 (1988) [hereinafter Note, *Beyond Institutional Competence*] ("The scope of activity prohibited by the Boland amendments is not self-evident. This ambiguity is especially acute when the activities permitted under the ambit of intelligence-gathering are considered. Moreover, to which government entities the amendments apply is equally vague.").

[67] The President's Intelligence Oversight Board undertook a legal analysis of the Boland amendment and concluded that it did not apply to the NSC. *See* President's Intelligence Oversight Board, *Memorandum Re: Allegations Concerning a Boland Amendment Violation by the National Security Council* (Sept. 12, 1985), *reprinted in Iran-Contra Congressional Hearings*, 100-5, Exhibit BGS-9, at 1158-64; Sciaroni, *The Theory and Practice of Executive Branch Intelligence Oversight*, 12 Harv. J.L. & Pub. Pol'y 397, 417-19 (1989) (discussing the process by which memorandum was prepared).

Several statutes containing the Boland Amendment were in effect at

various times when the NSC activities at issue occurred. The pertinent language of the

Amendment provided that no

> funds available to the Central Intelligence Agency, the
> Department of Defense, or *any other Agency or entity of the*
> *United States involved in intelligence activities* may be
> obligated or expended for the purpose or which would have
> the effect of supporting, directly or indirectly, military or
> paramilitary operations in Nicaragua by any nation, group,
> organization, movement, or individual.[68]

Thus, the Boland ban applied only to the CIA, the DOD and agencies "involved in

intelligence activities."

The statutory context indicates that the NSC was not considered to be an

intelligence agency. The Intelligence Authorization Act of 1985 -- which contained

Boland Amendment language[69] -- did not include the NSC on the list of the United

States government entities engaged in intelligence.[70] Moreover, legislative history

---

[68]   Intelligence Authorization Act for Fiscal Year 1984, Pub. L. No. 98-215, § 108, 97
Stat. 1473, 1475 (1983) (emphasis added); Temporary Continuing Appropriations Act,
Pub. L. No. 98-441, § 106(c), 98 Stat. 1699, 1700-01 (1984) (emphasis added);
Department of Defense Appropriations Act for Fiscal Year 1985, Pub. L. No. 98-473,
§ 8066(a), 98 Stat. 1837, 1935 (1984) (emphasis added); Further Continuing
Appropriations Act of 1985, Pub. L. No. 99-190, § 8050, 99 Stat. 1185, 1211 (1985)
(emphasis added); *see also* Continuing Appropriations for Fiscal Year 1987, Pub. L. No.
99-591, § 209(c), 100 Stat. 3341-301 (1986).

[69]

> No funds authorized to be appropriated by this Act or by the
> Intelligence Authorization Act for fiscal year 1984 (Public Law
> 98-215) may be obligated or expended for the purpose or which
> would have the effect of supporting, directly or indirectly,
> military or paramilitary operations in Nicaragua by any nation,
> group, organization, movement, or individual, except to the
> extent provided and under the terms and conditions specified by
> House Joint Resolution 648, making continuing appropriations
> for fiscal year 1985, and for other purposes, as enacted.

Pub. L. No. 98-618, § 801, 98 Stat. 3298, 3304 (1984).

[70]   *See* Pub. L. No. 98-618, § 101, 98 Stat. 3298 (1984); *see also* Intelligence
Authorization Act for Fiscal Year 1984, Pub. L. No. 98-215, § 101, 97 Stat. 1473 (1983)
(omitting NSC from list of intelligence agencies).

suggests that the NSC was not among the entities considered by Congress to be part of the intelligence community. *See* Note, *Beyond Institutional Competence*, at 157-58 ("Given the legislative silence on NSC participation, the fact that the NSC receives its funding from executive branch appropriations, and its conspicuous absence on all the lists purporting to detail the elements of the intelligence community, it is unlikely that Congress had the NSC in mind when enacting the Boland amendments.") (citations and footnotes omitted).[71]

The Independent Counsel also appears erroneously to assume that the President's involvement in encouraging private individuals and third countries to contribute to the Nicaraguan Democratic Resistance violated the Boland Amendments. Private or third-country funding for the Contras did not violate the Boland Amendments, as evidenced by the language of that statute -- which on its face forbids only the use of funds appropriated by Congress -- as well as the legislative history.[72]

---

[71] *See, e.g.*, 131 Cong. Rec. H5902 (July 18, 1985 daily ed.) (remarks of Rep. Stokes) (listing several agencies falling within the category of "intelligence activities" without mentioning the NSC).

[72] Congress was aware of private funding for the Contras, as evidenced by the following remarks made by the sponsor of the Boland Amendments:

> But the Contras, who haven't received $1 from the U.S. Government for more than [one] year, are doing just fine.
>
> They continue their military operations in Nicaragua and, they have increased their numbers.
>
> *They have done this with funds provided by private groups, mostly from the United States.*
>
> Those funds have helped purchase weapons, ammunition, food, clothing, medicine -- everything the Contras have needed to maintain themselves as an army in the field.

131 Cong. Rec. H4118 (June 12, 1985 daily ed.) (remarks of Rep. Boland) (emphasis added). When legislation was introduced that would have made it illegal to provide "private assistance for military or paramilitary operations . . . if the Congress has prohibited the use of covert assistance for such operations" and which would have had "[t]he immeidate impact . . . [of] prohibit[ing] private assistance to the Contras in

[Footnote continued on next page]

Nor was the President or any Executive Branch official barred from encouraging private contributors or foreign governments to provide financial assistance to the Contras. *See id.* at 168. In fact, Congress explicitly authorized the Department of State to solicit humanitarian assistance for the Contras from foreign governments. *See* Intelligence Authorization Act for Fiscal Year 1986, Pub. L. No. 99-169, § 105(b)(2), 99 Stat. 1002, 1003 (1985). And both the Majority and Minority reports of the Congressional Committees investigating Iran-Contra recognized that the President had constitutional authority to encourage third countries and private citizens to provide financial assistance to the Nicaraguan resistance. *See Iran-Contra Congressional Report* at 414, 501-02. It is unlikely that any statute purporting to limit the President's powers in this regard would have been constitutional. *See, e.g.,* Turner, *The Constitution and the Iran-Contra Affair: Was Congress the Real Lawbreaker?*, 11 Hous. J. Int'l L. 83, 119 (1988); *see also Final Report*, Vol. I, at 452 ("[D]iplomatic intercourse with the heads of foreign states is an essential presidential function. Even statutory restrictions in this field may be questionable.").

Thus, the assertion by the Independent Counsel that President Reagan somehow "set the stage for the illegal activities of others by encouraging . . . support of the contras" (*id.* at xiii) is completely unfounded. While it is certainly true that President Reagan continued to support the Contras and encouraged foreign countries and private citizens to provide financial aid to them during the periods when Congress cut off certain funding, the President's actions were fully consistent with the legal restrictions of the Boland Amendments and the President's instructions to his subordinates were to comply fully with that statute.

[Footnote continued from previous page]

Nicaragua," 131 Cong. Rec. H1208 (Mar. 19, 1985 daily ed.) (remarks by Rep. Levine), it was defeated.

CONCLUSION

After an almost seven-year investigation, the Independent Counsel's Final Report makes it clear that President Reagan did not violate any law. But the Report nonetheless engages in unwarranted and irresponsible criticism of the Reagan Administration's policies and asserts that they somehow facilitated or condoned criminal activities. That conclusion is simply wrong. The President pursued the Iranian and Nicaraguan initiatives with honest and legitimate motives, in the sincerely held belief that his actions were warranted and necessary to the national interest, regardless of the political risks to him personally.

The President's support of the Nicaraguan Democratic Resistance and other groups opposing communism throughout the world contributed to the downfall of that ideology, and the President makes no apologies for doing everything he lawfully could to support the resistance movement.

While the Iranian initiative remains a controversial subject, the President believes that his ultimate goals -- to establish dialogue with moderate Iranians and to pursue third-party channels for freeing the hostages -- were worthwhile.

President Ronald W. Reagan's determined and steadfast fight against communism and its growth will be judged by history as a vital turning point in the Twentieth Century. Had his leadership been less forceful and unwavering, the condition of global affairs when he took office in 1981 may well have continued its steady and frightening decline. The potential tragedies at the beginning of the 1980's of thermonuclear war or a world dominated by totalitarian communism were not only averted, they were overcome.

But these are matters for historians and political scientists, not prosecutors, to judge. The final message of Iran-Contra is that certain government policies and opportunities may have been distorted or abused. But President Reagan and his Administration responded immediately, properly and lawfully to the first signs of problems, and the incident should now be placed in its proper historical perspective.

Donald T. Regan

IN THE UNITED STATES COURT OF APPEALS
FOR THE DISTRICT OF COLUMBIA CIRCUIT

Division for the Purpose of
Appointing Independent Counsels

Ethics in Government Act of 1978, As Amended

In re: Oliver North, et al.

Division No. 86-6

(Under Seal)

MOTION OF DONALD T. REGAN WITH RESPECT TO PROCEDURES GOVERNING THE FINAL REPORT OF INDEPENDENT COUNSEL LAWRENCE E. WALSH

Donald T. Regan files this motion to address the procedures to be followed with respect to the Final Report of Iran-Contra Independent Counsel Lawrence E. Walsh ("Final Report" or "Report").

In connection with the Independent Counsel's Final Report and any responses thereto by persons named in such Report, this Court is required to make such orders "as are appropriate to protect the rights of [such] individuals." 28 U.S.C. § 595(b)(3) (1983).[1] Donald T. Regan accordingly respectfully requests that the Court enter the following orders:

(1)   an order approving non-service on Independent Counsel Walsh of Donald T. Regan's Response to the Final Report;

---

[1]   All citations herein are to the 1983 version of the independent counsel statute, which generally governs Independent Counsel Walsh's investigation. *See* 28 U.S.C. § 591 (1988) (note explaining effective dates).

(2)   an order permitting Donald T. Regan to withdraw
his Response to the Final Report that he is submitting
concurrently herewith and to prepare and submit a substitute
or alternative response if the Court orders the Independent
Counsel to withhold or limit publication of any portion of
the Final Report as originally submitted by the Independent
Counsel or otherwise determines to restrict public release of
the Report; and

(3)   an order granting Donald T. Regan seven days
notice prior to the release of any version or portion of the
Final Report and/or Donald T. Regan's Response to the
Final Report to the public, Congress or any other person or
entity.

DISCUSSION

1.   In the event the Court orders any limitation on the publication of
the Final Report, in whole or in part, Donald T. Regan should be afforded the
opportunity to withdraw his Response to the Final Report and to submit a response
addressed to that which will be published as the Final Report. It would be consistent
with the statute (28 U.S.C. § 595(b)(3) (1983)) for this Court to order that Donald T.
Regan be permitted to protect his rights by responding to the Final Report, as
published.

2.   Donald T. Regan has not served his Response to the Final Report
on Independent Counsel. In the absence of authority to respond for the record, the
Independent Counsel has no need for service. The Independent Counsel has no such
authority as confirmed by this Court's opinion and order, filed December 1, 1993, at
page 9:

> Our reading of section 594(h) does not include any authority
> for the Independent Counsel to amend the report during or

after the time set by the division for "comments or factual information" by the individual named. 28 U.S.C. § 594(h)(2).

Further, any order by this Court limiting publication, in whole or in part, of the Final Report, may change the circumstances concerning Donald T. Regan's response. His current response refers to matters included in the Final Report which Mr. Regan has urged should be barred from publication. The Independent Counsel should not be permitted to review those portions of Donald T. Regan's current response which address portions of the Final Report that will be barred from publication. Until this Court rules on what, if any, portion of the Final Report will be published, it is premature to serve the Independent Counsel with a copy of Mr. Regan's current Response to the Final Report.

3. The Court should order that Donald T. Regan be given notice seven days in advance of the release to the public of any portion of the Final Report and/or his Response to the Final Report. Such notice is necessary and appropriate to allow Donald T. Regan and his counsel and other aides to examine the portions, if any, to be publicly disseminated, and to prepare to address and respond to public reports and discussion. The Court may take judicial notice that the release of any portion of the Final Report or the Response to the Final Report will be the subject of immediate and intense media interest. The press will focus on the most provocative and controversial allegations in the Report. Unless an individual against whom allegations are made can respond instantaneously and succinctly to such material, the opportunity to do so effectively is lost. Irreparable damage to reputations can be minimized, albeit not avoided, only by thorough and concentrated anticipation and preparation. Seven days notice prior to public release would be a minimal and reasonable accommodation.

In addition, such notice is necessary to enable Donald T. Regan to consider whether to seek judicial reconsideration or review of any decision of this Court concerning public release of the Report.

CONCLUSION

The orders sought by this motion are reasonable and appropriate. Donald T. Regan's Response to the Final Report should not be published outside the Court until it is determined what portions of the Final Report, if any, will be published. If the Final Report is published in any form or substance different from that submitted August 4, 1993, it is imperative that Donald T. Regan be permitted an opportunity to withdraw his current Response and submit a Response to the Final Report, as published. If the Court orders publication of the Final Report, reasonable advance notice to Donald T. Regan would be needed to allow him and his counsel to prepare to respond to the press and other inquiries that will follow publication of the Final Report and his Response to the Final Report.

Dated: December 3, 1993

Respectfully submitted,

JOHN A. MINTZ
GIBSON, DUNN & CRUTCHER
1050 Connecticut Avenue, N.W.
Washington, D.C. 20036-5306
(202) 955-8587

Attorney for Donald T. Regan

WL933370.009 /1+

IN THE UNITED STATES COURT OF APPEALS
FOR THE DISTRICT OF COLUMBIA CIRCUIT

Division for the Purpose of
Appointing Independent Counsels

Ethics in Government Act of 1978, As Amended

In re: Oliver North, et al.

Division No. 86-6

(Under Seal)

CERTIFICATE OF SERVICE

I hereby certify that a copy of the following was served this 3rd day of December, 1993, by hand delivery to Independent Counsel Lawrence E. Walsh, Esq., Office of Independent Counsel, One Columbus Circle, N.E., Suite G-320, Washington, D.C. 20544:

1.   Motion of Donald T. Regan With Respect To Procedures Governing The Final Report Of Independent Counsel Lawrence E. Walsh.

John A. Mintz

GIBSON, DUNN & CRUTCHER
LAWYERS
1050 CONNECTICUT AVENUE, N.W.
WASHINGTON, D.C. 20036-5300

(202) 955-8500
TELEX: 892501 GIBTRASK WSH
FACSIMILE: (202) 467-0539

December 6, 1993

JAS. A. GIBSON, 1852-1922
W. E. DUNN, 1861-1925
ALBERT CRUTCHER, 1860-1931

LOS ANGELES
333 SOUTH GRAND AVENUE
LOS ANGELES, CALIFORNIA 90071-3197

CENTURY CITY
2029 CENTURY PARK EAST
LOS ANGELES, CALIFORNIA 90067-3026

ORANGE COUNTY
800 NEWPORT CENTER DRIVE
NEWPORT BEACH, CALIFORNIA 92660-6395

SACRAMENTO
400 CAPITOL MALL
SACRAMENTO, CALIFORNIA 95814

SAN DIEGO
750 B STREET
SAN DIEGO, CALIFORNIA 92101-4605

SAN FRANCISCO
ONE MONTGOMERY STREET, TELESIS TOWER
SAN FRANCISCO, CALIFORNIA 94104-4505

SAN JOSE
50 WEST SAN FERNANDO STREET
SAN JOSE, CALIFORNIA 95113

SEATTLE
999 THIRD AVENUE
SEATTLE, WASHINGTON 98104-7089

WRITER'S DIRECT DIAL NUMBER

NEW YORK
200 PARK AVENUE
NEW YORK, NEW YORK 10166-0193

DALLAS
1717 MAIN STREET
DALLAS, TEXAS 75201-4605

DENVER
1801 CALIFORNIA STREET
DENVER, COLORADO 80202-2694

BRUSSELS
AVENUE LOUISE 222
B-1050 BRUSSELS, BELGIUM

PARIS
104 AVENUE RAYMOND POINCARÉ
75116 PARIS, FRANCE

LONDON
30/35 PALL MALL
LONDON SW1Y 5LP

HONG KONG
8 CONNAUGHT PLACE
HONG KONG

TOKYO
1-1-3 MARUNOUCHI, CHIYODA-KU
TOKYO 100, JAPAN

AFFILIATED SAUDI ARABIA OFFICE
CHAMBER OF COMMERCE BUILDING
P.O. BOX 15870
RIYADH 11454, SAUDI ARABIA

OUR FILE NUMBER

RECEIVED
DEC 06 1993
CLERK OF THE UNITED
STATES COURT OF APPEALS

(202) 955-8587

T 75224-00005

Ron H. Garvin, Clerk
United States Court of Appeals
for the District of Columbia Circuit
333 Constitution Avenue, N.W.
United States Courthouse, Fifth Floor
Washington, DC 20001-2866

        Re: In re: Oliver North, et al.
             Division No. 86-6
             (Under Seal)

Dear Mr. Garvin:

        On December 3, 1993, I filed a Response of Donald T.
Regan to Final Report of the Independent Counsel for
Iran/Contra Matters. Inadvertently, the Table of Contents
page bears three erroneous page references.

        Enclosed is a correct Table of Contents page. For
the convenience of the Court, please replace the existing page
in the original and four copies submitted, with this corrected
page. Thank you for this assistance. Please accept my
apology for the error.

                              Sincerely,

                              John A. Mintz /jtf)

                              John A. Mintz

JAM/jtf
Enclosure
cc: T75224-00005

TABLE OF CONTENTS

IN THE UNITED STATES COURT OF APPEALS
FOR THE DISTRICT OF COLUMBIA CIRCUIT

United States Court of Appeals
For the District of Columbia Circuit

Division for the Purpose of
Appointing Independent Counsels

Ethics in Government Act of 1978, As Amended

FILED DEC 0 3 1993

RON GARVIN
CLERK

In re: Oliver North, et al.

Division No. 86-6

(Under Seal)

RESPONSE OF DONALD T. REGAN
TO FINAL REPORT OF THE
INDEPENDENT COUNSEL FOR IRAN/CONTRA MATTERS

Donald T. Regan submits the attached response to the Final Report of the
Independent Counsel for Iran/Contra Matters.

December 3, 1993

Respectfully submitted,

JOHN A. MINTZ
GIBSON, DUNN & CRUTCHER
1050 Connecticut Avenue, N.W.
Washington, D.C. 20036-5306
(202) 955-8587

Attorney for Donald T. Regan

UNITED STATES COURT OF APPEALS
FOR THE DISTRICT OF COLUMBIA CIRCUIT

Division for the Purpose of

United States Court of Appeals
For the District of Columbia Circuit

Appointing Independent Counsel

FILED DEC 0 3 1993

Division No. 86-6

RON GARVIN
CLERK

RESPONSE OF DONALD T. REGAN
TO FINAL REPORT OF THE
INDEPENDENT COUNSEL FOR
IRAN/CONTRA MATTERS

John A. Mintz

GIBSON, DUNN & CRUTCHER

Attorney for Donald T. Regan

December 3, 1993

Washington, D.C.

TABLE OF CONTENTS

**RESPONSE OF DONALD T. REGAN
TO FINAL REPORT OF THE INDEPENDENT COUNSEL
FOR IRAN/CONTRA MATTERS**

In compliance with the Order of the United States Court of Appeals for the District of Columbia Circuit, Division for the Purpose of Appointing Independent Counsel, in <u>In Re: Oliver L. North, et al.</u>, Division No. 86-6, Donald T. Regan is submitting comments and factual information to inform the Court and for possible inclusion as an appendix to the Final Report of Independent Counsel Walsh.

I.   **RESPONSE OF DONALD T. REGAN CONCERNING THE MATERIALS INCLUDED IN THE FINAL REPORT**

A.   **Grand Jury Transcripts Used Improperly**

Having personally reviewed those portions of the Final Report made available to him, Mr. Regan's initial comment is that the Report unjustifiably is abusive of him and others who responded to invitations to testify before the Grand Jury under the Rule that such testimony may be given freely because the record is maintained in secrecy. Not only were passages of his Grand Jury testimony quoted at length in the text, but the portions presented to him for review also contained quoted statements given by others before the Grand Jury. Mr. Regan objects to this subversion of the Grand Jury process, and urges the Court to bar publication of all quotations from or summaries of secret Grand Jury testimony.

B.   **Improper Inclusion of Speculation, Assumption and Innuendo**

In regard to the specific allegations in the Final Report, it appears that Mr. Regan is the target of speculation, assumption, and innuendo crafted into the Final Report by the Independent Counsel, which goes far beyond reporting the facts found and the

evidence establishing the facts. Mr. Regan would urge the Court to
bar publication of all text in the Final Report that presents the
Independent Counsel's biases of belief or allows him to color his
Final Report with unproven conclusions.

II.   **RESPONSES OF DONALD T. REGAN CONCERNING THE SUBSTANCE
      OF THE FINAL REPORT AS IT REFERS TO DONALD T. REGAN**

A.   **Summary of Facts Concerning Donald T. Regan**

Donald T. Regan was Chief of Staff for President Ronald
Reagan from February 5, 1985 through February 27, 1987. On
November 4, 1986, he first learned of press reports of possible
sales of arms to Iran by the United States. Having had general
knowledge of the history of the sales of HAWKs and TOWs to Iran
during 1985 and 1986, he recognized that there was substance behind
the news item and the press would pursue the story. By November 5,
1986, he was arguing for complete disclosure.[1] On November 13,
1986, President Reagan gave an address to the nation in which he
described the arms shipments to Iran and declared that he authorized
the transfer of arms to Iran. In press briefings on November 13,
1986, prior to the President's address and following it, on
November 14, 1986, Mr. Regan confirmed that the United States "had
condoned a shipment of arms by Israel to Iran and had replenished
it."[2]

Further, in response to the following question from the
press on November 14, 1986, Mr. Regan gave the following answer:

---

[1]Mr. Regan gave this information to the Office of Independent
Counsel during formal interview July 14, 1987.

[2]Regan Grand Jury testimony, February 26, 1988, p. 41, quoted in
Independent Counsel Final Report, at pp. 460-461.

Q: "So what you said is, we said we would not
object. This was before the President, in
January of 1986, signed an order lifting for our
purposes his own embargo?"

A: Mr. Regan: "That is correct."[3]

Subsequently, Mr. Regan answered questions fully and

without immunity or claim of privilege as follows:

December 16, 1986 Testimony, Senate Select
Committee on Intelligence

December 18, 1986 Testimony, House Select
Committee on Intelligence

January 7, 1987 Interview by President's
Special Review Board (Tower Board)

March 3, 1987 Deposition, Senate Select
Committee on Secret Military Assistance to Iran
and the Nicaraguan Opposition

July 14, 1987 Interview by Associate Counsels
Chris Todd, Louise Radin, Paul Friedman, Office
of Independent Counsel and Mike Foster, FBI
Special Agent assigned to Office of Independent
Counsel

July 15, 1987 Deposition, House Select
Committee to Investigate Covert Arms
Transactions with Iran

July 30; 31, 1987 Testimony, Joint Hearings,
Senate and House Select Committees

February 3, 1988 Testimony, Federal Grand Jury

February 26, 1988 Testimony, Federal Grand Jury

May 18, 1988 Interview by Judge Walsh

June 15, 1988 Interview by Judge Walsh

---

[3]The White House, Office of the Press Secretary, Internal
Transcript. Question and Answer Session with Chief of Staff
Donald T. Regan. November 14, 1986, 1:12 p.m. EST, at page 5.

March 6, 1991 Interview by Chris Mixter,
Associate Counsel, Office of Independent Counsel
and Mike Foster, FBI Special Agent assigned to
Office of Independent Counsel

January 9, 1992 Interview/document review by
Thomas Baker, Associate Counsel, Office of
Independent Counsel

May 8, 1992 Testimony, Federal Grand Jury

August 12, 1992 Testimony, Federal Grand Jury

December 8, 1992 Interview by James Brosnahan,
Associate Counsel, Office of Independent Counsel

It is in this context of cooperation and candor on the
part of Donald T. Regan that the references to Mr. Regan in the
Final Report should be reviewed.

B.   **Allegation that High Ranking Officials Violated
      Laws and Executive Orders**

The Final Report states:

The investigations and prosecutions have shown

that high-ranking Administration officials

violated laws and executive orders in the

Iran/Contra matter.[4]

Though not named specifically in this declaration,
Mr. Regan submits that it should not be published in its present
form under the authority of the Court because the language unfairly
and without cause harms his reputation as he was among the highest
ranking of administration officials during the time.

C.   **Allegation That Donald T. Regan Withheld
      Information**

The Final Report declares:

_____

[4]Final Report, p. ix.

The Office of Independent Counsel obtained
evidence that Secretaries Weinberger and Shultz
and White House Chief of Staff Donald T. Regan
among others, held back information that would
have helped Congress obtain a much clearer view
of the scope of the Iran/Contra matter.
Contemporaneous notes of Regan and Weinberger,
and those dictated by Shultz, were withheld
until they were obtained by Independent Counsel
in 1991 and 1992.[5]

Mr. Regan did not hold back information. Originals of his
notes had been submitted for White House files, where they might
have been reviewed by Independent Counsel. In his Final Report,
Independent Counsel admitted that "Regarding Regan's notes,
Independent Counsel believed that primary responsibility for
production rested with the White House. Regan produced copies of
his notes when they were subpoenaed."[6] Further, when Independent
Counsel did inquire about copies of his notes, Mr. Regan immediately
agreed and allowed Independent Counsel to review his private office
files. That review was conducted on January 9, 1992 by two
attorneys on behalf of the Independent Counsel. They requested
copies of some documents and only reviewed others at Mr. Regan's
office. The copies requested were delivered immediately to
Independent Counsel. Subsequently, Independent Counsel requested
Mr. Regan to provide copies of the notes that had been reviewed but

---

[5] Final Report, p. xiii.

[6] Final Report, p. 523.

copies not requested on January 9, 1992. Such later-requested copies were delivered to Independent Counsel by letter dated May 4, 1992.

D. **Allegation That Donald T. Regan Made Admissions Only After Repeated Questioning**

The Final Report states that " . . . White House Chief of Staff Regan . . . and others admitted to greater or more specific knowledge only after repeated questioning by Independent Counsel and when confronted with evidence contradicting their earlier statements."[7]

In regard to Mr. Regan's cooperation, this statement by Independent Counsel is not true. Mr. Regan was fully responsive to the inquiries made when interviewed personally by Judge Walsh and during interviews and testimony requested by lawyers representing Judge Walsh. Like any witness, Mr. Regan's recollections as to specific details of events occurring years ago may have been refreshed, but there was no instance in which he "admitted to greater or more specific knowledge only after repeated questioning . . . and when confronted with evidence contradicting . . . earlier statements."

E. **Allegation That Donald T. Regan Attempted To Rearrange The Record**

The Final Report states that " . . . Regan . . . and other senior Administration officials in November 1986 undertook to "rearrange the record, . . . in an effort to protect the President and themselves from accusations of possible violations of law."[8]

---

[7]Final Report, part II, p. 29.

[8]Final Report, Part IX, p. 444.

Mr. Regan did not undertake to rearrange the record for any purpose. As documented above, he advocated complete disclosure of the record.

F.   Allegation That There Was A Possibility of Indictment of Donald T. Regan

The Final Report explains, "Because of the large number of persons investigated, those discussed in individual sections of this report are limited to those as to whom there was a possibility of indictment."[9]   Chapter 30 of the Final Report is an individual section entitled "Donald T. Regan". This labeling of Mr. Regan stands in vivid contrast to the representations made to him by Independent Counsel, throughout the investigation, that he was not a subject or target of investigation for whom indictment was a possibility, but that he was being called upon to furnish information as a witness only.[10]

Mr. Regan responded in good faith reliance upon the representations made by Independent Counsel and never anticipated that his cooperation and candor regarding his recollections of events could be characterized as Independent Counsel has colored them in the Final Report.

G.   Allegation That Donald T. Regan Helped Choreograph A Cover-up

Chapter 30 of the Final Report says that in regard to Mr. Regan, "The question was whether Regan, in concert with the President's other top advisers, helped choreograph a cover-up by

---

[9]Final Report, Executive Summary, p. xvi.

[10]The representations were made orally and finally were confirmed in writing in a letter dated July 27, 1992 from Independent Counsel, copy attached as Exhibit 1.

agreeing to a false version of the arms sales to obscure legally
questionable activity."[11] The Report declares:

> Evidence of the apparent November 1986 cover-up
> of the President's knowledge and approval of the
> November 1985 HAWK missile shipment - - and
> Regan's participation in it - - was not
> developed by Independent Counsel until 1992 when
> he obtained previously withheld notes from
> Weinberger and Regan indicating that Meese
> appeared to have spearheaded an effort among top
> officials to falsely deny Presidential awareness
> of the HAWK transaction. When Regan in 1992 was
> questioned about these events, he was
> forthcoming and candid in his responses. In
> addition, when Independent Counsel late in 1992
> subpoenaed additional notes from Regan, he
> cooperated.[12]

Mr. Regan did not participate in any cover-up. As stated
by the Independent Counsel, when Mr. Regan was asked about the
events, he was "forthcoming and candid."

> Further, the Independent Counsel stated:
> Regan's testimony on the November 1985 HAWK
> missile shipment to Iran has been consistent,
> acknowledging that McFarlane briefed the

---

[11] Final Report, p. 505.

[12] Ibid.

President in Geneva on the HAWKS shipment as it
was about to take place.

The Independent Counsel's footnote 90 declared:
Since his earliest testimony before the SSCI on
December 16, 1986, Regan repeatedly stated that
McFarlane briefed the President during the
November 1985 Geneva summit on a shipment of
arms from Israel to Iran via a European country
. . .

In an apparent contradiction with other
Administration officials who early on maintained
that President Reagan didn't learn about the
true cargo of the November 1985 HAWK shipment
until 1986, Regan told SSCI that a meeting in
the White House residence of the principals on
December 7, 1985, involved "much discussion
about the shipment of those HAWK missiles."
(Regan, SSCI Testimony, 12/16/86, p. 20.) Regan
in his Select Committees deposition of July 15,
1987, recalled there was talk at the meeting of
a need for a Finding if the initiative
proceeded, but he didn't recall anyone saying
one was already drafted. (Regan Select
Committees Deposition, 7/15/87, pp. 15-16.)[13]

Mr. Regan did not withhold any notes. The Independent
Counsel's complaint that it was not until 1992 that he developed

---

[13] Final Report, p. 519.

evidence of Mr. Regan's participation in "the apparent November 1986 cover-up of the President's knowledge and approval of the November 1985 HAWK missile shipment" is not persuasive in view of the ample resources committed to his investigation and the numerous occasions Mr. Regan was questioned.   Further evidence that Mr. Regan was not a participant in any such cover-up is the effort made by Mr. Regan to clarify the facts concerning the November 1985 HAWK shipment. By letter of January 13, 1989[14] (well within the statute of limitations after November 1986 and even within the statute as to November 1985) the Independent Counsel was advised as follows:

Dear Judge Walsh:

    Enclosed is an article from page one of The Washington Post for Sunday, January 8, 1989 captioned, "Walsh Weighs More Charges in Iran Probe."

    The article declares that you are examining statements of Administration officials to determine whether charges are warranted for misleading or obstructing Congress or perjury. The article asserts that " . . . many individuals told apparently false or incomplete stories of the November 1985 shipment to the Tower Commission and the Congressional Iran-Contra Committee." The assertion in the article is then followed by examples, among which is an allegation that Donald T. Regan told the Tower Commission, "Certainly there was nothing said to the President in advance [about the November 1985 shipment], at least not in my hearing, where it was said now may we ship missiles to Iran through Israel. That was not asked of the President." This statement was contrasted with Mr. Regan's statement in his recent book that he recalled a McFarlane briefing of the President of the 1985 Hawk shipment days before it took place.

    For clarity, please refer to the transcript of Mr. Regan's interview by the Tower Board, at page 14, copy enclosed. The full paragraph from which the partial quote in the article was taken clearly shows not only that Mr. Regan was referring to whether the President was asked for authority to ship missiles, but also that Mr. Regan told the Tower Board that the President was told to expect that missiles would be transshipped through Israel into Iran.

---

[14] Letter, January 13, 1989, from John A. Mintz to The Honorable Lawrence E. Walsh, copy attached at Exhibit 2.

Contrary to the appearance suggested by the incomplete quotation in the Post article, the passage cited from Mr. Regan's book is entirely consistent with the full text of his Tower Board interview, and he did not mislead anyone.

Later, in the Post article, it is alleged that Mr. Regan was present on February 11, 1987 when the President met with the Tower Board, and that Mr. Regan did not say anything when the President said he did not remember anything about a call-back of Hawks. Again, the Post article falsely suggests that Mr. Regan misled the Tower Board by his silence. In fact, Mr. Regan was not present at that session.

While I am confident that you would detect the errors in the Post article, this letter is intended to place in your records a clear statement that Donald T. Regan testified honestly and candidly on every occasion, and he was not involved in any misconduct, as alleged in the article.

If you have any questions regarding any statements by Mr. Regan, please call me.

Sincerely,

John A. Mintz

The reply from Independent Counsel[15], dated January 24, 1989, was as follows:

Dear Mr. Mintz:

This is in response to your letter of January 13, 1989. We appreciate your effort to draw the attention of this Office to the full text of Donald T. Regan's interview before the Tower Board on January 7, 1987. Please be assured that this Office is in possession of the full transcript of Mr. Regan's interview and has reviewed that transcript in its entirety.

Sincerely,

Louise R. Radin
Associate Counsel

Clearly, Mr. Regan was not participating in a cover-up of Presidential knowledge when he testified before the Tower Board

---

[15] Letter, January 24, 1989, from Louise R. Radin, Associate Counsel, to John A. Mintz, Esq., copy attached at Exhibit 3.

during 1987, describing the briefing of the President as to the
November 1985 shipment of HAWKs and he was not withholding anything
when he held himself available to explain his statements as
indicated by the invitation, in the January 13, 1989 letter, to the
Independent Counsel to call if he had any questions. Further, the
Independent Counsel could have deduced from Mr. Regan's book, <u>For</u>
<u>the Record</u>, published in 1988 (within the statute of limitations)
that Mr. Regan's published recollection of McFarlane briefing the
President concerning the 1985 HAWK shipment, days before it took
place, was incompatible with any notion of a cover-up of facts by
Mr. Regan.

> Mr. Regan wrote:
>
> During the Geneva summit, Bud McFarlane had
> told the President the details of a plan to sell
> eighty HAWK antiaircraft missiles to Iran
> through the Israelis. It was a complicated
> operation: the Israelis would deliver the
> missiles from their own stockpile to a secret
> destination in Portugal. There they would be
> loaded aboard three transport planes and flown
> to Tabriz. As soon as the first plane was
> airborne, word would be flashed to the Iranians
> by clandestine means and the Iranians would tell
> the terrorists who were holding the five U.S.
> citizens hostage in Lebanon to release them.
> The plane would not land and no missiles would
> be delivered until all five Americans had been
> handed over to the American Embassy in Beirut.

Later on, the United States would give the
Israelis eighty new Hawk missiles to replace the
ones they had delivered to the Iranians; forty
additional Hawks would be given to the Iranians
in a separate transaction. In return the
Iranians would guarantee that no more American
hostages would be taken by terrorists. The swap
of the Hawks for the hostages was scheduled to
happen on Thursday, November 21, 1985. The
transaction was not described in those blunt
terms to the President, Shultz, or me. Reagan
clung to the belief that he was not paying
ransom but merely rewarding an intermediary for
services rendered. . . .

McFarlane's conversation with Reagan took
place before lunch on the first day of the
summit, Tuesday, November 19, ...

Only the President had the authority to
tell McFarlane not to do what he was proposing
to do, and the President - once again saying yes
by not saying no - did not do that. It would
not be surprising if McFarlane gained the
impression that he was being given unspoken
approval to proceed in the hope of getting our
people out of captivity.[16]

---

[16] Regan, <u>For the Record</u> (1988), pp. 319, 320, 321.

H.   Allegation That Donald T. Regan Was Forced to Resign

The Independent Counsel wrote:

Donald T. Regan was Chief of Staff February 1985

to February 1987. He was forced to resign

because he was unable to contain the continuing

political damage being done to President Reagan

by public exposure of the Iran/Contra matters.[17]

The reasons for Mr. Regan's resignation as Chief of Staff

are far more complex than the Independent Counsel's statement would

admit. The details are presented in Chapter 19 of Mr. Regan's book

For the Record.

I.   Innuendo Suggesting that Donald T. Regan Attempted To Orchestrate A Story And Was Engaged In Obstruction

The Independent Counsel employed innuendo unfairly to

abuse Mr. Regan's reputation when he wrote that he had no "usable

evidence"[18] that Mr. Regan was attempting to orchestrate a story or

that he was helping Meese to do it. In the same way, the

Independent Counsel wrote that he had no "direct evidence" of

obstruction[19] by Mr. Regan.

In Mr. Regan's knowledge of these events, he is not aware

of any evidence that he attempted to orchestrate a story or engage

in any obstruction and he did neither. The Independent Counsel's

innuendo is inappropriate and should be barred from publication.

---

[17] Final Report, p. 505.

[18] Final Report, p. 523.

[19] Ibid.

III. CONCLUSION

The abuses by the Independent Counsel in his Final Report should cause concern to the Court that its sponsorship of the public issuance of the Final Report would entangle the Court in the Independent Counsel's scheme to bypass the rules and harm Mr. Regan and others by hyperbole, when he lacked evidence sufficient to support any recognizable charge.

Mr. Regan offers these comments to suggest to the Court that in its review of the Final Report the Independent Counsel has submitted, the Court should consider authorizing publication only of incontrovertible facts supported by specific evidence or the Court should not allow any publication of the Independent Counsel's Final Report.

WL933340.014 /13+

TAB – 1

OFFICE OF INDEPENDENT COUNSEL
555 THIRTEENTH STREET, N.W.
SUITE 701 WEST
WASHINGTON, D.C. 20004
(202) 383-8940

July 27, 1992

BY FAX: (202) 467-0539

Mr. John Mintz, Esq.
Gibson, Dunn & Crutcher
1050 Connecticut Avenue, N.W.
Washington, D.C. 20036-5306

Re: Donald T. Regan

Dear Mr. Mintz:

    I write to confirm our telephone conversations of
this morning. As we discussed, this Office requests
testimony by your client, Mr. Regan, before a Federal Grand
Jury on Friday, August 7, 1992, at 1:00 p.m. The Grand Jury
meets in Grand Jury Room No. 1 on the Third Floor of the
United States Courthouse, Third Street and Constitution
Avenue, N.W., Washington, D.C. You stated that a subpoena
will not be required to obtain Mr. Regan's testimony.

    In conjunction with this appearance, please be
advised that Mr. Regan's status is "witness." He is not a
"subject" or a "target" of the Grand Jury's investigation as
those terms are defined in the United States Attorney's
Manual.

    Please call me if you have an questions concerning
this matter. Thank you for your continuing cooperation.

                       Very truly yours,

                       LAWRENCE E. WALSH
                       Independent Counsel

By:
                       John Q. Barrett
                       Associate Counsel
                       (202) 383-5479

Original by first class mail.

Received 11 48 / TB 7-27-92

TAB - 2

GIBSON, DUNN & CRUTCHER
LAWYERS
1050 CONNECTICUT AVENUE, N.W.
WASHINGTON, D.C. 20036-5303

(202) 955-8500
TELEX: 892501 GIBTRASK WSH
TELECOPIER: (202) 467-0539

January 13, 1989

HAND DELIVERY

LOS ANGELES
333 SOUTH GRAND AVENUE
LOS ANGELES, CALIFORNIA 90071-3197

CENTURY CITY
2029 CENTURY PARK EAST
LOS ANGELES, CALIFORNIA 90067-3026

NEWPORT BEACH
800 NEWPORT CENTER DRIVE
NEWPORT BEACH, CALIFORNIA 92660-6395

SACRAMENTO
1010 F STREET
SACRAMENTO, CALIFORNIA 95814-0826

SAN DIEGO
600 B STREET
SAN DIEGO, CALIFORNIA 92101-4520

SAN FRANCISCO
ONE MONTGOMERY STREET, TELESIS TOWER
SAN FRANCISCO, CALIFORNIA 94104-4505

SAN JOSE
ONE ALMADEN BOULEVARD
SAN JOSE, CALIFORNIA 95113-2267

SEATTLE
701 FIFTH AVENUE
SEATTLE, WASHINGTON 98104-7089

WRITER'S DIRECT DIAL NUMBER

JAS. A. GIBSON 1852-1922
W. E. DUNN 1861-1925
ALBERT CRUTCHER 1860-1931

NEW YORK
200 PARK AVENUE
NEW YORK, NEW YORK 10166-010

DALLAS
1700 PACIFIC AVENUE
DALLAS, TEXAS 75201-4618

DENVER
1801 CALIFORNIA STREET
DENVER, COLORADO 80202-265

EUROPE
04 AVENUE RAYMOND POINCAR
75116 PARIS, FRANCE

LONDON
30/35 PALL MALL
LONDON SW1Y 5LP

HONG KONG
1 DUDDELL STREET
HONG KONG

TOKYO
1-1-3 MARUNOUCHI CHIYODA-KU
TOKYO 100 JAPAN

AFFILIATED SAUDI ARABIA OFFIC
CHAMBER OF COMMERCE BUILDIN
P.O. BOX 15870
RIYADH 11454, SAUDI ARABIA

OUR FILE NUMBER

(202) 955-8587

G75224-0000-

The Honorable Lawrence E. Walsh
Independent Counsel
Office of Independent Counsel
555 13th Street, N.W.
Suite 701 West
Washington, D.C. 20005

Dear Judge Walsh:

Enclosed is an article from page one of The Washington Post for Sunday, January 8, 1989 captioned, "Walsh Weighs More Charges in Iran Probe."

The article declares that you are examining statements of Administration officials to determine whether charges are warranted for misleading or obstructing Congress or perjury. The article asserts that " . . . many individuals told apparently false or incomplete stories of the November 1985 shipment to the Tower Commission and the Congressional Iran-Contra Committee." The assertion in the article is then followed by examples, among which is an allegation that Donald T. Regan told the Tower Commission, "Certainly there was nothing said to the President in advance [about the November 1985 shipment], at least not in my hearing, where it was said now may we ship missiles to Iran through Israel. That was not asked of the President." This statement was contrasted with

The Honorable Lawrence E. Walsh
January 13, 1989
Page 2

Mr. Regan's statement in his recent book that he recalled a
McFarlane briefing of the President of the 1985 Hawk shipment
days before it took place.

        For clarity, please refer to the transcript of
Mr. Regan's interview by the Tower Board, at page 14, copy
enclosed. The full paragraph from which the partial quote in
the article was taken clearly shows not only that Mr. Regan was
referring to whether the President was asked for authority to
ship missiles, but also that Mr. Regan told the Tower Board
that the President was told to expect that missiles would be
transshipped through Israel into Iran.

        Contrary to the appearance suggested by the incomplete
quotation in the Post article, the passage cited from
Mr. Regan's book is entirely consistent with the full text of
his Tower Board interview, and he did not mislead anyone.

        Later, in the Post article, it is alleged that
Mr. Regan was present on February 11, 1987 when the President
met with the Tower Board, and that Mr. Regan did not say
anything when the President said he did not remember anything
about a call-back of Hawks. Again, the Post article falsely
suggests that Mr. Regan misled the Tower Board by his silence.
In fact, Mr. Regan was not present at that session.

        While I am confident that you would detect the errors
in the Post article, this letter is intended to place in your
records a clear statement that Donald T. Regan testified
honestly and candidly on every occasion, and he was not
involved in any misconduct, as alleged in the article.

        If you have any questions regarding any statements by
Mr. Regan, please call me.

                                        Sincerely,

                                        [signature: John A. Mintz]

                                        John A. Mintz

JAM:jtf
Enclosures
cc: Donald T. Regan

UNCLASSIFIED
~~TOP SECRET~~ T 8 000018 14

1 new on the hostages? Anything going on? What about that

2 Iran connection? Anything going on there?

3 So that I could assume that Bud would think

4 there was a sense of urgency here to the extent that the

5 President was concerned about this and wanted something

6 done. He had suggested it. It was his initiative.

7 Something would have to break or not break here, you

8 know. He could assume, I suppose, that the President

9 wanted this. He hadn't raised Cain about the Israeli

10 shipment, so a second try might not be out of order.

11 I can only surmise that. Certainly there was

12 nothing said to the President in advance, at least in my

13 hearing, where it was said, now may we ship missiles to

14 Iran through Israel. That was not asked of the

15 President. The President, however, was told, as I say,

16 on the margins of his briefings for the Gorbachev meeting

17 to expect that there is going to be a shipment of arms

18 coming ███████████████ missiles, transshipped through

19 Israel into Iran, and the hostages will come out.

20 Now, the December meeting got to be more formal

21 because McMahon, among others, raised the question of,

22 you know, what the hell are we doing here. Arms are

23 being sent. Where is the formal authority? You know,

24 what are we doing here? Is this going to be policy?

25 And, as a result of that meeting and people

Walsh Weighs More Charges In Iran Probe

Conflicting Testimony Given on Arms Sale

By Walter Pincus
Washington Post Staff Writer

The Iran-contra investigation headed by independent counsel Lawrence E. Walsh is examining whether conflicting statements made by a number of administration officials to the Tower commission and congressional committees about a key U.S. arms shipment to Iran warrant charges of misleading or obstructing Congress, or perhaps perjury.

Former White House aide Oliver L. North has been charged with creating a false record of the shipment of 18 U.S.-made Hawk anti-aircraft missiles by Israel to Iran with the assistance of the Central Intelligence Agency. Former national security adviser John M. Poindexter has also been indicted on charges of misleading Congress on the shipment.

But testimony recorded in the voluminous public record of the Iran-contra affair indicates that there may have been a broader pattern of deception by the White House, CIA and other administration officials.

Statements on the November 1985 shipment by a number of individuals, from President Reagan and his former chief of staff, Donald T. Regan, on down to CIA operations officers, contradict depositions from other witnesses and documentary evidence produced by various investigations. Together, they indicate that an organized, White House-directed cover-up of this particular shipment took place in the weeks after the arms-for-hostages dealings were first disclosed.

The November 1985 shipment has been the least-publicized of the secret arms sales to Iran. It was scheduled to be the first installment of a total of 80 missiles that were being sold by Israel to Iran, with White House approval, in a covert scheme to free four U.S. hostages

See HAWKS, A14, Col. 1

The Washington Post, Sunday, January 8, 1989

HAWKS, From A1

held by pro-Iranian extremists in Lebanon. Although the scheme ultimately failed, it laid the groundwork for direct U.S. shipments to Iran in 1986.

But the 1985 shipment is the one that may create the most legal problems for those involved and, according to knowledgable sources, could lead to additional indictments.

Any new Walsh indictments would come from a grand jury that for the past several months has been examining the extensive body of Iran-contra information that has now accumulated, including testimony, documents and published accounts. Even without new indictments, however, the events of that November are headed for a hearing in court in connection with this count of the indictment against North.

When the White House first referred publicly to the November 1985 shipment, one year after it had taken place, then-Attorney General Edwin Meese III said the transfer of the U.S.-made Hawks by Israel—prohibited at the time both by administration policy and by arms export laws—took place without presidential approval and without knowledge that missiles were involved. After Washington learned that arms had been shipped, Meese said, the administration demanded they be returned.

That story is apparently false.

The records now indicate that the Hawk shipment was not a runaway operation, as originally described by Meese and later by the president and others. Instead it emerges as a coordinated but flawed covert effort by a team of present or former Israeli officials, an Iranian intermediary and officials in the Iranian prime minister's office, White House aides and d[...] of officials at the CIA, State De[...] ment and Pentagon to satisfy North described as Reagan's c[...] to have the U.S. hostages hon Thanksgiving 1985.

North was so deeply involv[...] the operation that he arrange Church of England emmissary ry Waite to go to Beirut just b[...] the scheduled November arms ment so he could take credit fo release of any hostages. That was made known to North's then-national security adviser dexter, who passed it on to [...] CIA Director William J. Casey Casey's deputy, John N. McM[...] on Nov. 14, 1985, according t[...] records.

The records also indicate th[...] year later, in mid-November when the first disclosures of a for-hostages were rocking the ministration, White House offi began to cover up this partic[...] shipment. A Justice Departr official, Charles J. Cooper, in a supported by Pentagon officials. warned Meese that the Hawk [...] ment may have violated U.S. la[...]

Thereafter, many individuals apparently false or incomplete ries of the November 1985 [...] ment to the Tower commission the congressional Iran-contra c[...] mittees.

The review of documents, timony and other materials sh[...] that:

■ President Reagan received a[...] minute briefing on the 1985 H[...] shipment days before it took p[...] from then-national security adv Robert C. McFarlane. The pr[...] dent and his staff were in Genev[...] the time for a summit meeting, Regan and Secretary of S[...]

THE WASHINGTON POST

More Indictments Possible in Iran-Arms Probe

George P. Shultz were present. In his book, "For the Record," Regan said he recalled that briefing "vividly because I have never before experienced anything like it."

McFarlane, according to Regan, described how Hawk missiles would be carried from Israel to Lisbon, then transferred to other planes and flown to Iran as the order was given for the American hostages to be released. "McFarlane's description of the operation was difficult to follow because of the many bizarre elements involved," Regan wrote.

But 15 months after it took place, and before his book was released, Regan told the Tower commission, "certainly there was nothing said to the president in advance [about the November 1985 shipment], at least in my hearing, where it was said, now may we ship missiles to Iran through Israel. That was not asked of the president."

■ On Nov. 24, 1985, a CIA-owned, St. Lucia Airways Boeing 707 secretly carrying the 18 Hawks flew from Tel Aviv to Cyprus. (The Lisbon stop had been eliminated after the Portuguese government refused to cooperate.) The plane then took off again and crossed into Iranian airspace from Turkey with its Colombian pilot ready to give the agreed-upon code words: "I am coming for Mustafa."

The plane landed at 1:42 a.m., Nov. 25, 1985, at Tehran's airport. After a 30-minute wait, a civilian armed with a machine gun arrived and told the pilot that he expected four more flights from Tel Aviv, but that the crew should not tell the Iranians unloading the cargo where they had come from.

Hours after the Hawk shipment arrived in Tehran, Reagan was told about it by Poindexter at his regular, morning, national security briefing, according to notes of the meeting. Reagan was also told that hostages were expected to be released.

It took over 14 hours for an Iranian military unit to unload the Hawks. Meanwhile, the crew rested at a hotel in Tehran. Once the missiles were unloaded, the plane was towed to the civilian side of the airport, refueled, and took off for West Germany late on the afternoon of Nov. 25.

However, no hostages were released. The Iranian intermediary in the deal, Manucher Ghorbanifar, called his Washington contact, National Security Council consultant Michael Ledeen, and complained that when the Iranians opened the crates of the first 18 Israeli missiles, they found they were an obsolete model Hawk and carried Israeli markings. Ledeen, later that same day, passed the message on to Poindexter.

A day later, Poindexter told North, according to North's notes, that the president wanted the shipments to go on with newer Hawks being delivered and with an American supervising.

However, 14 months later, when he appeared before the Tower commission on Jan. 16, 1987, the president said, according to the commission's report, "he did not remember how the November shipment came about. The president said he objected to the shipment and that, as a result of that objection, the shipment was returned to Israel.

"In his second meeting with the board on Feb. 11, 1987," the report continues, "the president stated that both he and Regan agreed that they cannot remember any meeting or conversation in general about a

Hawk shipment. The president said he did not remember anything about a call-back of the Hawks." Regan was present at this session and did not say anything, according to Tower commission sources.

■ On Nov. 25, 1985, when CIA Deputy Director McMahon learned that an agency proprietary had been involved with a shipment to Iran, he ordered the operations division to provide a briefing to then-agency general counsel Stanley Sporkin to determine if a presidential intelligence order, called a "finding," was required to keep it within the law.

Two CIA operations officers who had been involved in arranging for the 1985 flight to Tehran briefed Sporkin and his deputy, J. Edwin Dietel, about the shipment on the afternoon of Nov. 25, 1985, the day the plane left Tehran. Sporkin and Dietel then met with another CIA lawyer whose notes of that meeting, as well as Sporkin's, show they were told that the plane had delivered missiles.

A year later, Sporkin, Dietel and the third lawyer, Bernard Makowska, all testified to administration and congressional investigators that they had been told there were missiles aboard the plane. The two CIA operatives who briefed them, however, insisted to these same investigators that they only knew the plane was carrying oil drilling or farm equipment.

■ A struggle took place within the CIA over Casey's initial testimony to Congress on the Iran arms shipments. The original CIA chronology of the November 1985 events, drafted by the agency's operations division for those preparing Casey's statement and dated Nov. 19, 1986, described the cargo as missiles. Nonetheless, the draft testimony prepared under the direction of CIA deputy director Robert M. Gates for delivery by Casey two days later, said that the agency did not know there were missiles aboard the plane.

On the eve of Casey's Nov. 21 congressional appearance, CIA lawyer Makowska turned up documents to support Sporkin's and his own position that they had been told by the operations officers that there were missiles on the plane. Casey's testimony was amended but still did not disclose the true details.

TAB – 3

OFFICE OF INDEPENDENT COUNSEL
SUITE 701 WEST
555 THIRTEENTH STREET, N.W.
WASHINGTON, D.C. 20004
(202) 383-8940

January 24, 1989

<u>BY HAND</u>

John A. Mintz, Esq.
Gibson, Dunn & Crutcher
1050 Connecticut Avenue, N.W.
Washington, D.C. 20036

Dear Mr. Mintz:

This is in response to your letter of January 13, 1989. We appreciate your effort to draw the attention of this Office to the full text of Donald T. Regan's interview before the Tower Board on January 7, 1987. Please be assured that this Office is in possession of the full transcript of Mr. Regan's interview and has reviewed that transcript in its entirety.

Sincerely,

Louise R. Radin
Associate Counsel

Glenn A. Robinette

26 November 1993

United States Court of Appeals
District of Columbia Circuit
United States Courthouse
333 Constituion Avenue, NW
Washington, DC 20001-2886

Attention: Ron Garvin, Clerk

Ref: Corrections to the Independent Counsel's Final Report

In my review and knowledge of my actions in Ref Report, I wish to make the following corrections:

Chapter 9, page 176, titled <u>North Security Fence</u>

1. No one - neither <u>I</u> nor anyone else - installed a "Security Fence." Protective security work was done primarily in the residence and included work on a remote locking mechanism for the vehicle entrance gate onto the property.

2. Robinette "<u>became involved in a variety of operations for the Enterprise</u>." This statement regarding "Enterprise" is in error and not true. <u>I</u> never heard the work "Enterprise" used at anytime nor did <u>I</u> know anything about any "Enterprise" operations, activities, personnel, administration or funding. I was given infrequent, unschedulded work on various types of assignments specifically requested by and directly paid by Richard Secord.

Glenn A. Robinette

3265 Arcadia Place, NW
Washington, DC 20015

Maj. Gen. Richard V. Secord, USAF, Ret.

RICHARD V. SECORD
7927 JONES BRANCH DRIVE
SUITE 600 SOUTH
MCLEAN, VA 22102

Dec 20, 1993

Mr Garvin:

Enclosed please find the corrected
letter. There was a computer error in
the original document. Request you destroy
the original.

Thank you very much for calling the error to my
attention.

Sincerely,

R.V. Secord

Encl

AMERICAN RECOVERY CORPORATION

7927 JONES BRANCH DRIVE

SUITE 400 WEST

MCLEAN, VA 22102

Mr. Ron Garvin   December 1, 1993

Clerk of the Court

United States Court of Appeals

For the District of Columbia Circuit

Ref: Independent Counsel Final Report

Dear Mr. Garvin:

Pursuant to 28 U.S.C. 594 (h) I forward herewith comments, analysis
and facts regarding those very limited portions of Independent Counsel
(IC) Lawrence Walsh's "Final Report" which I have been permitted to
read.

On Sept 7, 1993 I petitioned the court for permission to read the entire
report, but the request was denied by order of November 22, 1993.
This denial vitiates the intentions of Congress.   And I find myself
forced to rebut fragments of what purports to be a comprehensive
story.   Nonetheless, I request this letter be prominently included, as
required by law, as a part of the "Final Report".

IC investigations can become witch hunts as the "Ethics in Government
Act" legislative history forecasts.   IC Walsh's travails fulfill this fear
beyond any expectations.   I append to this letter a litany of distortions,
false official statements, fabrications and outright lies perpetrated by
the IC.   Considering that I had access to only a small part of the report,
this listing is damning beyond imagination.

However, one should not be surprised given the tortuous seven year
trail of this IC.   In fact, I knew Lawrence Walsh to be liar when he
testified before Judge Gessell in a <u>Kastigar</u> hearing in June 1988.   Two
months before this hearing Walsh told me (in the presence of
witnesses) that he "...had watched my testimony in Congress and was
very impressed."   When I started expressing amazement and when his
aides gave him sharp looks he said, "Except when you talked about the
money."   This of course was a joke since Albert Hakim's ledgers
(secured through a grant of immunity) were the first substantive
issues in my Congressional interrogation and were the focus of the

page 2, ltr to Mr Garvin

entire hearing. Incredibly, Walsh denied, under oath, having seen any of this. He took this position to avoid being "tainted" and losing his indictment. He is a liar!

Walsh's lies and distortions and abuses continued for years, but now he finally places himself in the bull's eye. When this report is sent to Congress history will expose this man for •the limelight seeking, self aggrandizing, disgracefully invidious scoundrel that he is.

It is nothing short of astonishing that Walsh could be permitted to cause the expenditure of over $100 million of taxpayer's money (Wall Street Journal and other press reports) while occupying ridiculously expensive offices, falsifying travel and per diem vouchers, evading D.C. taxes and supervising an out of control investigation. His merry band even managed to lose (in an airport) numerous sensitive, code word classified documents. Walsh's adventures would make a good comic opera were they not so tragic for his victims.

The fact that it took the IC four years to decide that the top of the Reagan Administration was immersed in Iran/Contra is a sick joke, especially when I made the story clear in hundreds of transcribed pages of OIC interviews. In fact, just last year one of Walsh's associate attorneys, Mr. Reid Weingarten, told me that I was "always the North star" for their investigation. Apparently even the North star was an insufficient vector for Mr. Walsh's errant crusade.

The IC attempts, through the vehicle of this "Final Report", to justify his bewildering years of grandstanding and ostentatious living--all in the name of the rule of law. Thus this wild compendium of false statements. When this report is forwarded Mr. Walsh should be prosecuted for making false statements to Congress.

Additionally, it is my view that the Special Division of the Court which appointed Mr. Walsh shares his culpability. It bends the mind when one considers the Court took no action to reel in Walsh after years of malfeasance and misfeasance. Therefore, it comes as no shock that the U.S. Senate recently took action to at least prevent future IC defamatory acts disguised as "Final Reports".

page 3, ltr to Mr. Garvin

Lawrence Walsh's egregious behavior has brought new meaning to the term "prosecutorial misconduct". It is therefore fitting and necessary under the law for this correspondence to be made part of the "Final Report" I pray the Court will so order.

Sincerely,

R.V. Secord
Major General, USAF(Ret)

Appendix Attached(8 pages)

APPENDIX

The reader may wish to consult the book, "Honored and Betrayed," Secord and Wurts, Wiley & Sons, N.Y., 1992 in order to gain an understanding of the context and basic issues regarding the Iran/Contra affair. As anyone can see from the following examples of a very limited part of the IC Final Report, IC Walsh has issued a major piece of history revised to comport with his public relations agenda.

The following are but a small number of the grossly inaccurate statements and assertions extracted from the limited portions of Walsh's "Final Report" which Secord was permitted to read.

ALLEGATION:
On page 15 the IC states that, "Secord mistakenly said he needed no help." This in regard to a meeting with the CIA in 1985.

FACT:
Secord made no such statement. In fact the meeting was for the purpose of soliciting help. The IC well knows this fact.

ALLEGATION:
On page 17 the IC says (about a Dec 1985 meeting in London) "Mcfarlane spoke of political goals" while Ghorbanifar talked only of arms shipments.

FACT:
Secord was present in the meeting. Both parties talked at length about politics, hostages and arms transfers. This fundamental miscasting of the scenario reveals the IC bias and/or ignorance. Worse, the Office of Independent Counsel (OIC) interviews with Secord (all transcribed) and Secord's Congressional testimony fully describe this crucial meeting.

ALLEGATION:
On page 18 the IC states, "CIA would buy from DOD, and, after payment, transfer the weapons to Secord as its agent to transfer them to Iran."

FACT:
Secord was not an agent of the government and the IC knows it. Only recently has such an absurd theory been raised by the IC. Never during all the criminal cases springing from Iran/Contra did the IC describe Secord as an agent. In fact in the two Clair George trials and in the Clines trial the IC repeatedly referred to Secord as a "third party' or as the "commercial cutout". This of course ("third party") is the language of the Jan. 17, 1986 Presidential Finding which authorized the Iran initiative. The IC

1

is deliberately deceitful here.

ALLEGATION:
Starting on page 20 in a section titled 'THE DIVERSION', the IC shows certain financial data pertaining to the Enterprise. The IC repeatedly alleges a diversion of U.S. government funds.

FACT:
In this section and throughout the report the IC asserts a "diversion", i.e., a misappropriation of government funds. All such charges were dismissed by the Courts with prejudice. There has never been any evidence of a "diversion". Funds were sent to the Contras from the Enterprise solely because of decisions made by Secord. This is an unrebutted fact and clear evidence of the IC's deceit. Moreover, the IC is guilty here of making false official statements.

ALLEGATION:
On page 22 the IC states Secord left a meeting in Frankfurt, Germany with the "Second Channel" (Iranian) officials after learning of the Hasenfus shootdown in Nicaragua. The IC also describes a Da'wa prisoner exchange as part of the 9 point plan.

FACT:
Secord did not leave Frankfurt after learning of the shootdown--North did. Secord instead remained until during the following day when agreement was reached on a 9 point plan. The 9 point plan clearly did not include a Da'wa prisoner swap or release provision. It did include some diplomatic overtures from Iran to Kuwait which would have been difficult to achieve but in everyone's interest. Again the IC's version of even basic events in the Iran/Contra affair is intentionally distorted. This very meeting was the subject of numerous questions and answers involving Secord and others during the Congressional and IC investigations. The record is clear and Walsh tries to fog it.

ALLEGATION:
Starting on page 23 the IC describes the drafting of a Nov 1986 White House memorandum for use by DCI Casey in testimony before the Congressional Intelligence Committees.

FACT:
The description of the evolution of the drafting of this memo, particularly as it relates to the events of the preceding year, 1985, is inaccurate and misleading. It does not mention Secord's participation and walkout, nor does it accurately describe Mcfarlane's role. All the circumstances surrounding this important chapter of the Iran/Contra affair were completely described by Secord during the Congressional and IC investigations and

corroborated by witnesses, e.g., Howard Teicher. It is beyond belief that this episode would be distorted by the IC in view of the extensive, overlapping testimony on the subject.

ALLEGATION:
In Chapter 2, p.105 the IC states "...it was clear from the earliest stages of OIC's investigation that North had working control of the Secord-Hakim covert-action Enterprise." Similar statements start on page 133.

FACT:
As the IC well knows, North did not exercise control. The IC asserts this point in a desperate effort to show an "agency" arrangement on the part of Secord. There are numerous examples of Secord non-concurring with North and refusing to take action or undertake changes. A good example occurred in Sept 1986 when North, in a message document which the IC has in its possession, directed the abandonment of the flying unit in El Salvador. Secord refused in writing and took a completely different course of action. Again, the IC is well aware of these facts, but he chooses to fabricate his own story since the truth does not suit his purposes.

ALLEGATION:
On page 106 the IC states that the worst impact of the severance of the defendants (Poindexter, North, Secord,Hakim) was the delay it imposed on the IC's investigation and trial schedule. "This put off for a year the completion of the Poindexter, Secord and Hakim cases and the opportunity to question him(sic) which was essential to the investigation."

FACT:
Secord answered the OIC's questions in enormous detail during 1987 and 1988. The IC's excuse for failing to see the forest because of the trees does not wash. It is another fabrication and a smoke screen as the IC tries to improve his image.

ALLEGATION:
On pages 161, 163, 168, 171 and 172 the IC repeatedly restates his "agent" claim regarding Secord and Hakim. He also reasserts "diversion", "theft of government funds" and going "...great lengths to conceal this income", all in the context of illegality.

FACT:
No diversion or theft of government funds has ever been proven and all such charges were dismissed by the Courts. The IC smears and unconscionably misrepresents the facts. Virtually every detail connected with the Enterprise funds was examined by the OIC and

3

Congress. No actionable case for "diversion" could be made by the IC and so he hid behind the excuse of classified material restrictions while continuing to cry "diversion". The IC conveniently fails to state why he did not avail himself of the Classified Information Procedures Act for relief when dealing with Secord. Mr. Walsh lost this diversion issue in the Courts, and he cannot admit defeat. Walsh again chooses to distort the truth and use smear tactics.

ALLEGATION:
In Chapter 12, "United States Efforts to Recover The Enterprise Funds", the IC states on page 185 that Counts 1 & 2 of the original indictment in March 1988 (Poindexter, North, Secord, Hakim) "...was sufficient to prove (to the Swiss government) that a fraud on the U.S. Government had occurred."

FACT:
The IC does not state that these charges were dismissed with prejudice in the U.S. Courts nor does he state that the Swiss Ministry of Police and Justice rejected the IC's claim after years of wrangling The IC seems incapable of rendering a high fidelity description of this sorry litany of IC lies. The truth has no meaning for Mr. Walsh, and he obviously has contempt for the American concept of innocent until proven guilty.

ALLEGATION:
In Chapter 17, "U.S. v. Clair George" on pages 233-245, the IC addresses the two Clair George trials. Here he mentions only "Secord's role as a financial intermediary" in the Iran initiative.

FACT:
The IC generally avoids discussing Secord's testimony in these trials as a prosecution repeat as a prosecution witness. In actuality the IC repeatedly referred to Secord in these trials as a business man, a commercial cutout, the third party or the financial intermediary. He tries here in Chapter 17 to finesse the issue knowing that his own prosecutors statements at trial destroy his "agency" theory. As is usual a close reading of the IC's story reveals consistent duplicity and outright lying.

ALLEGATION:
In Chapter 26, page 326, the IC infers Secord misled or covered up regarding North's presence and the substance of meetings on April 20, 1986 in El Salvador, e.g., "A more complete account of Secord's trip to El Salvador emerged in his appearance before the Grand Jury in January 1991."

FACT:
Secord talked at length in Congressional testimony and in OIC interviews in 1987/88 regarding these well documented meetings. All of Secord's statements proved to be truthful and helpful to the

investigators. The OIC interviews covered all participants including Ambassador Corr and the subject matter of the meetings. Again, the IC uses innuendo to continue the smear job so obvious in this report. The truth seems foreign to Mr. Walsh.

ALLEGATION:
The IC states on page 157 that Secord and Hakim early on grafted the business interests "...onto the policy goals of the Reagan Administration."

FACT:
The record is clear. The Administration contacted Secord in 1984 and his involvement in Iran/Contra evolved in many sequential steps over the ensuing 2 1/2 years. All Iran/Contra observers know this fact. Every step of the way is recorded in Congressional testimony and in OIC interviews--all transcribed. The IC's accusation is fantastical and deliberately defaming.

ALLEGATION:
On page 158 Richard Secord and Albert Hakim are described as business partners (in 1984) "...in weapons related ventures."

FACT:
Secord and Hakim ran a business, Stanford Technology Trading Group International, starting in 1983. The firm never involved itself "in weapons ventures" until the onset of what became known as Iran/Contra. This is well known to the IC and represents yet another attempt to darken Secord's reputation through the use of fabrications.

ALLEGATION:
On page 158 the IC states "...Secord and Hakim pleaded guilty to profit-related crimes."

FACT:
Secord pleaded guilty to making a false statement to Congressional investigators regarding North's fence. He did not plead guilty to anything else, especially a "profit-related crime". The IC above all others knows this. This is another false statement by the IC.

ALLEGATION:
On page 159 the IC states with respect to Secord and Hakim's Enterprise operations, "one of their purposes was to avoid the payment of income taxes."

FACT:
No such allegation was ever raised and no questions directed at Secord by the IC regarding this matter. In dozens of hours of interviews comprising hundreds of transcript pages the subject was never explored. This is another outrageous, totally unsupported

fabrication--a false statement.

ALlEGATION:
Starting on page 165 a section begins entitled "The Enterprise Tries To Sell It's Contra-Resupply Operation To The CIA.

FACT:
In the ensuing IC report paragraphs there is no evidence advanced regarding any such effort, and the report does not even mention Secord's extensive testimony on the subject. The fact is that Secord directed that the operation be given free to CIA, and this testimony has been corroborated by Secord's employee, Robert Dutton and by then Assistant Secretary of Defense Armitage. This is a clear cut smear job by the IC and again false statements.

ALLEGATION:
On page 172 the IC states, "cash payments to Secord in 1985 and 1986 totaled approximately $1,037,000... for unknown purposes".

FACT:
Secord testified extensively regarding the refunds to the Israelis, payment to Ghorbahnifer and operational expenses which required cash. None of this has ever been rebutted and the IC well knows it. In fact, Mr. Zucker (the IC's immunized witness) confirmed Secord's story.

ALLEGATION:
On page 180, discussing events in 1986, the IC states, "Secord took the lead. He arranged for a $16,000.00 security system to be installed at North's home...".

FACT:
Until now even the IC never suggested that Secord stepped out with an initiative and "arranged for a $16,000.00 security system". The events surrounding North's security system are well known to the IC. There is not one shred of evidence, including especially Glen Robinette's testimony, to suggest that Secord started this project. The IC again sings a false song and with the clear intention of defaming Secord.

ALLEGATION:
On page 173 the IC states "... he lied when he claimed he acted as a volunteer for the benefit of the United States...". Further on page 173 "... (he) lied to Congress about illegal gratuities provided to North".

FACT:
Secord never used such language before to Congress or in OIC interviews. The fact is Secord pleaded guilty to making a false statement to <u>Congressional investigators</u>, not to Congress. Moreover the IC well knows this to be a contrived scenario to get their "pound of flesh". The IC has in his possession Glen

Robinette's 1986 income tax return which reflects the money given to him by Secord (allegedly for North's fence) as ordinary income, i.e., Robinette paid for North's fence, not Secord. The IC has known this throughout the relevant periods of time. The IC here is libelous and himself a liar.

ALLEGATION:
On page 174 the IC states Haskel delivered an unknown amount of cash to Secord's home on Nov 17, 1986 and Secord claimed it went for operations. However, the IC states, "none of the operatives received significant amounts of cash from Secord after the Oct 5 shootdown."

FACT:
As the IC well knows, large amounts of cash were sent to the Contra project after Oct 5. Over $200,000.00 was issued by Secord through Rafael Quintero to pay for Contra relief. Additionally, $7,000.00 was given to Hasenfus's wife, Sally Jean, in Miami, in late Oct 1986, by Mr. Piowaty (the funds came from Secord). All these facts have been recorded in sworn statements. Moreover, the IC never raised this matter as a serious issue during dozens of hours of interviews with Secord, all of which sessions were recorded and transcribed. Again, this is a blatantly obvious smear attempt and a false statement.

ALLEGATION:
On page 175 the IC asserts "... testimony (Secord's) is blatantly false regarding his personal finances." Also on this page the IC states "In addition, Secord and Hakim established for North and his family a $200.000.00 Swiss investment fund."

FACT:
Secord's testimony to Congress was straight forward, without immunity and painfully accurate regarding his finances. Additionally, the IC's own witness, Mr. Zucker, stated under oath that he did not know whether Secord was aware of the accounting line set up by himself and Hakim regarding North. Thus again there is not one scintilla of evidence to support the IC's assertions. He again makes false statements.

ALLEGATION:
On page 176 the IC states that "Secord also provided cash to North. In Sept 1985, North purchased a vehicle for $9,500.00 shortly after Secord gave North $3,000.00 according to Secord's handwritten notes."

FACT:
As the IC is well aware, the $3,000.00 was part of the money given by Secord to two DEA agents by way of North. The money reimbursed them for expenses incurred in Europe related to U.S. hostages being held in Lebanon. This reimbursement has been attested to by the agents during the IC's investigation and during the Congressional

7

investigation. The IC's distortion of these well proven facts is nothing short of outrageous.

ALLEGATION:
On pages 174-178 the IC describes 8 indictment charges. The IC again and again describes Secord as a perjurer.

FACT:
All these charges were dismissed with prejudice pursuant to a plea bargain in 1989. None of these allegations were proved nor could they have been. Here again the IC, with no proof, engages deliberately in character assassination. Again, Walsh ignores basic American concepts of justice.

George P. Shultz

WILMER, CUTLER & PICKERING

2445 M STREET, N. W.

WASHINGTON, D. C. 20037-1420

—

TELEPHONE (202) 663-6000

FACSIMILE (202) 835-0819,

429-9893, 429-4930, 293-5929

TELEX 440239 WCPI UI

JEFFREY McFADDEN

DIRECT LINE (202)

663-6329

RECEIVED

DEC 03 1993

CLERK OF THE UNITED
STATES COURT OF APPEALS

4 CARLTON GARDENS
LONDON

TELEX 8813918 WCP LDN

RUE DE LA LOI 15 WETSTRAAT
B-1040 BRUSSELS
TELEPHONE 011 (322) 231-0903
FACSIMILE 011 (322) 230-4322

December 3, 1993

BY HAND

Ms. Juanita Mathies
Clerk
United States Court of Appeals
  for the District of Columbia Circuit
333 Constitution Avenue, N.W., Room 5409
Washington, D.C. 20001

Re: <u>In re Oliver L. North, et al., Division No. 86-6</u>

Dear Ms. Mathies:

Please find enclosed for filing with the Division for the Purpose of Appointing Independent Counsels an original and four copies of the Response of George P. Shultz to the Final Report of Independent Counsel Lawrence E. Walsh. We respectfully request that this Response remain under seal until such time as the Division releases the Independent Counsel's Final Report and the Appendix thereto.

As noted in our Response, we also respectfully request that the Response be included in its entirety in the Appendix to the entire Report as provided for under the Independent Counsel Statute, 28 U.S.C. § 594(h)(2).

Thank you for your assistance. Please let me know if you have any questions.

Sincerely,

Jeffrey E. McFadden

Enclosure

United States Court of Appeals
For the District of Columbia Circuit

RESPONSE OF GEORGE P. SHULTZ
TO THE FINAL REPORT OF INDEPENDENT COUNSEL LAWRENCE E. WALSH FILED 5 1993

RON GARVIN
CLERK

As counsel to former Secretary of State George P.
Shultz and on his behalf, we respectfully submit the following
response to Independent Counsel Lawrence E. Walsh's Final Report
on the Iran/Contra matter (the "Report"). We make this
submission pursuant to the provisions of the Independent Counsel
Statute, specifically, 28 U.S.C. § 594 (h) (2).

The Report correctly identifies Secretary Shultz as the
single senior official in the Reagan Administration who
consistently opposed arms-for-hostages deals with Iran. It
credits him and his staff with foiling the efforts of other
Administration officials to cover up aspects of the Iranian arms
initiative and with being the first to inform Congress of what
had happened. It also recognizes that it was the Secretary's
opposition that finally defeated the efforts of other officials
to continue the arms-for-hostages negotiations.

However, the Report also concludes that Secretary
Shultz held back information pertinent to the arms-for-hostages
initiative. It states that the Independent Counsel considered
indicting Secretary Shultz for allegedly testifying falsely to
congressional committees in 1986 and 1987, but decided not to do
so because the Independent Counsel did not believe he could prove
such a charge "beyond a reasonable doubt."

- 2 -

    We strongly object to these statements. The testimony
in question is the very testimony that helped to bring the arms-
for-hostages initiative to an end. It was given on the
Secretary's own initiative. Its primary purposes were to alert
Congress to what had happened to date and to block the ongoing
efforts of other government officials to keep arms-for-hostages
initiatives alive. Coupled with the Secretary's other actions,
it accomplished those purposes. Yet the Report implies that in
the Independent Counsel's view, this same testimony had been
incorrect and misleading. As we show below, the Report itself
contains conclusive proof that any such charge is baseless and
that the Secretary did not hold back any relevant information of
which he was aware. This portion of the Report is an unwarranted
attack on a faithful public servant who tried to prevent the
arms-for-hostages debacle from its outset, who took the
initiative to disclose to Congress the full story as he knew it,
and who finally succeeded in bringing it to a halt.

    We take equal exception to the Report's implicit
suggestion that the Secretary played some part in an alleged
Cabinet-level conspiracy in November 1986 to conceal the fact
that President Reagan had known of a November 1985 arms shipment,
made before a legally required Presidential finding had been
signed and transmitted to the congressional intelligence
committees. In fact, it was the Secretary who, in November 1986,
contemporaneously informed Attorney General Meese of the

- 3 -

President's knowledge and who, only three weeks later, on
December 16, also informed the Senate Select Committee on
Intelligence ("SSCI") of the same fact.

STATEMENT OF FACTS

During the period from mid-1985 to December 1986,
certain members and staff of President Ronald Reagan's National
Security Council ("NSC") were exploring the possibility of
selling arms to Iran with the goal, among other things, of
securing the release of American hostages held in Beirut. The
Secretary consistently opposed such a policy and expressed his
opposition to both the President and to members of the NSC and
its staff. But his view was largely disregarded, and the arms-
for-hostages transactions went forward. Although conceived and
executed as covert operations, they were revealed to the public
on November 3, 1986, in a Lebanese magazine.

From the first public revelations of the Iran-Contra
scandal until the present, the Secretary has consistently and
willingly assisted investigators (including the Independent
Counsel) in their efforts to uncover the pertinent facts. He
directed that everything available in the Department of State be
pulled together so that he could see what he had known and when
and what actions he had taken. During these various

- 4 -

investigations, the Secretary also directed that all relevant
materials, including the personal notes of his Executive
Assistant (Charles Hill), be made available to all investigators.
The Secretary testified repeatedly before congressional
committees and gave a series of long and candid interviews to the
Independent Counsel.

After the revelations in November 1986, the Secretary
argued strongly for full, prompt, and complete disclosure of the
facts relating to the Iran arms sales and the Contra diversion.
This commitment to full public disclosure brought him almost
immediately into conflict with others in the Administration. For
example, soon after the arms transactions were revealed, the
Secretary made his case for full disclosure to Vice Admiral John
Poindexter, then the President's National Security Adviser.
Admiral Poindexter objected, stating "I do not believe that now
is the time to give the facts to the public."[1] The Secretary
later refused, despite Admiral Poindexter's urging, to join the
Vice President, the Secretary of Defense, and the Director of the
Central Intelligence Agency ("CIA"), among others, in signing off
on a press release stating that there was unanimous Cabinet
support of what amounted to the arms-for-hostages policy. Later,
on November 20, 1986, the Department's legal adviser (Judge

---

[1]   Report of the Congressional Committees Investigating
the Iran-Contra Affair, H.R. Rep. No. 433, S. Rep. No. 216, 100th
Cong., 1st Sess., at 293 (1987) (hereinafter "Joint Committee
Report").

- 5 -

Abraham Sofaer), with the Secretary's approval, used Mr. Hill's
notes to head off false testimony that CIA Director William Casey
was scheduled to give to Congress the following day. These and
other initiatives by the Secretary to forestall any "cover-up" of
the facts by Administration officials were fully disclosed during
his congressional testimony in 1986-1987 and interviews by the
Independent Counsel.

On November 21, 1986, President Reagan instructed
Attorney General Edwin Meese to undertake a preliminary
investigation. On November 22, 1986, the Secretary was
interviewed by the Attorney General. The Secretary disclosed in
detail during that interview what he was able to recall at that
time about the arms shipments, including a comment to him by the
President just two days earlier that the President knew of the
November 1985 arms shipment.

To facilitate cooperation with the Attorney General's
preliminary investigation, the Department of State issued a
blanket directive to its personnel on November 29, 1986,
instructing them to cooperate fully with the Federal Bureau of
Investigation ("FBI") and other investigative agencies. The
directive ordered that all relevant materials be produced for
review and use by the investigative agencies. At the Secretary's
direction, the Department's Office of the Legal Adviser ("OLA")
assumed the coordinating responsibility for the Department's

- 6 -

production of materials and liaison with the two FBI agents
initially assigned late in November 1986 to gather information
from the Department.

As part of this commitment to full cooperation with
investigative efforts, the Secretary directed that the
confidential handwritten notes of his Executive Assistant,
Charles Hill, be made available as required. These were Mr.
Hill's notes. Mr. Hill, a career Foreign Service officer, took
extensive notes of daily Department events, including his
meetings with the Secretary, meetings both inside and outside the
Department attended by the Secretary, and telephone conversations
with Department and other officials. Mr. Hill participated in
some of these meetings and conversations and received debriefings
from the Secretary as to other meetings and conversations.

Investigators first saw the Hill notes during the
preliminary investigation when the Attorney General and Assistant
Attorney General Charles Cooper interviewed the Secretary and Mr.
Hill on November 22, 1986 and in a second interview between Mr.
Cooper and Mr. Hill on November 24. During this interview, Mr.
Hill referred often to his notes and, when Mr. Cooper requested a
copy of a particular note, Mr. Hill readily provided it.

The Secretary relied on Mr. Hill's review of these
notes in his efforts to reconstruct the historical record of his

- 7 -

knowledge regarding these events and in his interview by the
Attorney General and his subsequent congressional testimony.

The Independent Counsel's charge that these notes were
somehow withheld is totally without foundation. Their existence
was obvious to all, and even visible to some, of the
investigators. The "excerpts" were from a large body of notes.
These notes were always available and, when requested by the
Independent Counsel, were provided to him. The Independent
Counsel then reviewed, according to his Report, some 22,000 pages
of notes. If the Independent Counsel had asked for the notes in
their entirety earlier, they would have been provided. They were
not withheld. Their existence was well known.

In addition to responding to specific FBI requests, the
OLA made available to congressional staff and the Independent
Counsel several compilations of notes that Mr. Hill had assembled
for Department purposes. These included a notebook that Mr. Hill
had put together to assist the Secretary in preparing for
upcoming congressional testimony and another notebook of notes
from the "post-revelation period" of November and December 1986.
These latter notes document the Secretary's efforts during this
period to bring the arms-for-hostages operation to a close and to
cooperate with investigators in making it public.

Based on his desire to see the facts of the Iran/Contra
affair brought to light and his commitment to bringing the

- 8 -

ongoing arms sales to a halt, the Secretary in late 1986 and in
early 1987 testified repeatedly on the subject, beginning on
December 8, 1986, before an open session of the House Foreign
Affairs Committee. On December 13 and 14, the Secretary learned
of new information about the content of dealings of NSC and CIA
staff members with representatives of Iran. On December 15, he
informed President Reagan, Vice President Bush, Chief of Staff
Regan, and NSC Adviser Keel that "we have an obligation to pass
this information on to Congress. It is explosive." He let
everyone know that he had asked to testify before the SSCI the
next day, December 16. He set out at this hearing all of what he
could recall of the arms dealings with Iran. He informed the
Committee of his concern that the White House and the CIA were
not abiding by the President's decision to transfer the
responsibility for all hostage negotiations to the Department of
State and were continuing arms-for-hostages talks behind the
Department's back. The Secretary also testified before a closed
session of the House Foreign Affairs Committee on January 21,
1987.

Although the specific content of each appearance
obviously varied to some extent, the Secretary consistently
sought to inform the committees of what he could personally
recall regarding the NSC plan to sell arms to Iran, his strongly
expressed opposition to such a policy, his conversations with the
President on the subject, his Department's exclusion in 1985-86

- 9 -

from many aspects of the matter because of his disagreement with
the policy, and his efforts to bring about both full public
disclosure of the relevant facts and to bring the operation to a
halt.

On the day that the alleged diversion of funds from
arms sales became public, November 25, the President appointed a
three-member board, chaired by former Senator John Tower, to
investigate the affair. The Tower Board received testimony from
a wide range of people -- including the Secretary on January 22,
1987 -- and, on February 26, 1987, issued its report. The report
focused almost exclusively on the conduct of NSC members and
staff and those outside the government who worked with them in
the arms deals and diversion of profits. The report stressed
throughout that the Secretary had opposed the arms transactions
whenever and in whatever context they were raised.[2/] In its
conclusion, it noted that the Department of State had been
sidestepped in the formulation and implementation of the Iran
arms policy.

Over the next six years, the Secretary was interviewed
by the Independent Counsel and/or his staff attorneys six times.
In none of these interviews did the Secretary make any attempt to

---

[2/]   See, e.g., Report of the President's Special Review
Board, III-4, III-7, III-8, III-10, III-12 (Feb. 26, 1987).

- 10 -

limit the scope of the interrogation or withhold information from investigators.

Early in January 1987, the Senate Select Committee on Secret Military Assistance to Iran and the Nicaraguan Opposition and the House of Representatives Select Committee to Investigate Covert Arms Transactions with Iran (collectively the "Joint Committee") was established to investigate the Iran/Contra Affair. The Joint Committee held hearings throughout the Summer of 1987. The Secretary appeared before the Committee on July 23 and 24, giving testimony completely consistent with his earlier testimony before other congressional committees and his interviews with the Independent Counsel.

On November 17, 1987 the Joint Committee published its report. Like the Tower Board, the Joint Committee noted that the Secretary had vigorously opposed the arms sales operation and that he and his Department had fully cooperated with investigators.[3] Thus by November 1987, in addition to three interviews with the Secretary and open access to State Department documents (the same documents to which the committees had access), the Independent Counsel had before him the considered judgments of both the Tower Board and the Joint Committee after their investigations. Both reports, although varying in

---

[3]   See, e.g., Joint Committee Report at 165-69, 178, 181, 193, 209, 229, 262-63, 285, 293-301, 305, 309.

- 11 -

emphasis, noted the Secretary's role in opposing the arms sales
at issue and in promoting full disclosure and cooperation with
investigators.

* * * *

The actions and events described above, recounted in
detail in numerous sections of the Independent Counsel's Report,
lead to one irrefutable conclusion: it was Secretary Shultz,
virtually alone among the senior Reagan Administration officials,
who brought a halt to the Iranian arms initiative and defeated
the efforts of some Administration colleagues to cover up the
facts. Given the voluminous evidence leading to this conclusion,
the Report's suggestions that Secretary Shultz may have given
materially false testimony to Congress, and that he may have been
part of a Cabinet-level conspiracy to conceal the extent of the
President's knowledge, are baseless and unwarranted.

1.   The report acknowledges that the two elements
essential to any criminal prosecution -- motive and criminal
intent -- could not be satisfied with respect to the Secretary's
conduct. It concedes that his "admirable role" in November 1986

> makes the misstatements in Shultz's testimony
> difficult to understand. Unlike the false
> testimony of Poindexter, Casey, and
> Weinberger, the misstatements in Shultz's
> testimony do not fit neatly into the
> framework of protecting the President.

(Report at 345.) But this concession is grudging at best.   The
Report cites no evidence -- and there is none -- supporting a

- 12 -

motive or a criminal intent to make any misstatement. This is
particularly so given that the Secretary's testimony before the
SSCI, the testimony the Independent Counsel now criticizes, was
the first detailed public statement by any Administration
official disclosing and criticizing the arms-for-hostages
activities. This testimony was given on the Secretary's own
initiative and eventually -- coupled with his other efforts and
actions -- resulted in stopping the efforts of other officials to
keep the arms-for-hostages operation going.

    2.   The gravamen of the Independent Counsel's charge
is that although the Secretary testified about various occasions
when he had learned of, and had vigorously objected to, arms-for-
hostages activities, he did not mention other occasions when he
allegedly learned of additional arms-for-hostages activities.
The Report suggests that these omissions were deliberate. It
seeks to support this suggestion by citing notes kept by two of
the Secretary's aides -- Charles Hill and Nicholas Platt -- which
refer to arms-for-hostages information received by the Secretary
or other State Department officials that the Secretary did not
mention in his testimony. This suggestion is completely
unwarranted.

    3.   While these Hill and Platt notes do report on
arms-for-hostages information not mentioned in the Secretary's
testimony, much of this information varied in quality from rumor

- 13 -

to hearsay, and its omission did not materially alter the main
thrust of the Secretary's testimony.[4]

The Secretary did not refer in his congressional
testimony to an episode of a planned arms sale in late May 1986
or to a similar brief and aborted effort of which he was informed
on February 11, 1986. He had not remembered them, and his
executive assistant, Charlie Hill, had not found references to
them in his review of notes he had taken. They were located when
the Independent Counsel's office subsequently went through all of
Hill's voluminous notes (22,000 pages), spending far more time
doing so than Hill was able to take from his ongoing operational
duties. The Independent Counsel also found a note in the files
of Defense Secretary Caspar Weinberger referring to a
conversation he had with the Secretary on May 13, 1986, in which
Weinberger told about a possible arms sale to Iran. The
Secretary did not recall this conversation, and had never seen
Weinberger's note, so its contents were not reflected in his
testimony either. These incidents do not change the picture
presented of his consistent opposition to the arms-for-hostages
efforts and the fragmentary nature of his knowledge of what those
on the NSC staff and in the CIA were doing.

---

[4]   The Report also cites a number of notes taken by others
that the Secretary had never seen when he prepared for and gave
his SSCI testimony: notes made by State Department officials
Arnold Raphel, Christopher Ross, and Kenneth Quinn, as well as
several notes made by Secretary Weinberger.

- 14 -

4.   The Report also accepts that the Secretary's testimony was fully consistent with all the notes he had been shown in the process of preparing for his testimony. The Report acknowledges that the contemporaneous Hill notes for November and December 1986 and for 1987 included extensive notes on precisely how Secretary Shultz and his staff prepared for his 1986-87 testimony and that nothing in these notes suggests the Secretary was aware of any other information that he consciously decided to leave out of his testimony. Specifically, the Report states,

> However difficult it may be to believe that
> Shultz could forget events that troubled him
> so deeply, it was significant that none of
> the contemporaneous notes created in November
> and December 1986 suggest that Shultz in fact
> remembered more or different information than
> that to which he testified.

(Report at 372.)

5.   This concession also contradicts the Independent Counsel's unjustified conclusion that in later interviews with the Independent Counsel Staff, the Secretary attempted to "blame Sofaer and the Office of Legal Adviser for Shultz's erroneous testimony," because the Secretary "had reason to know what Hill's notes would contain." (Report at 347.) As the Report itself admits, the Hill notes the Secretary saw before he testified were fully consistent with his testimony. The December 1986 notes relating to the preparation for his testimony show him as telling his staff that the "basic strategy about getting material into the hands of the investigators and the public is the best way to

- 15 -

get this behind us."   (<u>See</u> Hill and Platt notes dated 12/4/86 and

12/6/86; Sofaer note dated 12/4/86.) Moreover, the Secretary has

never blamed Sofaer or attempted to "blame Sofaer" or his office

for any omissions in the Secretary's testimony. The Secretary

believed then and believes now that Judge Sofaer and his office

performed their roles thoroughly and with complete integrity.

      6.   Finally, the Report recognizes that when

interviewed by the Independent Counsel in February 1992 and shown

the Hill, Platt, and other notes relating to earlier events not

covered in his 1986-87 testimony, the Secretary expressly

disclaimed any intention to conceal these events, and said that

if he had been given those notes before his 1986-87 testimony, he

would have included references to the information they described

in his statement to the Committee. Again, these additions would

not have altered the basic thrust of his testimony.

      7.   Because the Report itself acknowledges all of

these facts, it is a serious distortion for the Report to suggest

that the Secretary gave incorrect and misleading testimony for

which he was not prosecuted only because a charge of falsity

could not have been proven "beyond a reasonable doubt." The

truth is that any such charge stands totally <u>disproved</u> by the

other findings of the Report. The testimony reflected fully the

information available to the Secretary at that time.

- 16 -

8.   The Report's oblique references to the Secretary's
possible role in an alleged Cabinet-level conspiracy in November
1986, based on his failure to contradict Attorney General Meese
at the November 24, 1986, National Security Planning Group
meeting, are also wholly unjustified. While repeatedly noting
that no one present at the meeting corrected the Attorney
General's statement regarding the President's asserted lack of
knowledge of the November 1985 shipment of HAWK missiles, the
Report fails to point out that the bulk of the meeting was taken
up, not with the promised presentation of the Attorney General's
investigation to date, but rather with a lengthy presentation by
Admiral Poindexter and William Casey aimed at keeping the arms
initiative alive. The Report further fails to note that the
Secretary was the only person present who vehemently took issue
with Poindexter's and Casey's efforts to keep the initiative
alive, to the considerable displeasure of the President and
others present, and that the Secretary left the meeting early and
was not present when the Attorney General allegedly asked if
anyone had anything to add. The Report fails to note in this
section that, at the very time of this meeting, Director of the
CIA Casey and Vice President Bush and others were urging the
President to "get rid of Shultz" because he was "not on board."

9.   Given the "admirable role" of the Secretary
discussed above, the Report's suggestion that there had been a
short-lived Cabinet-level conspiracy in November of 1986 to

- 17 -

protect the President, if justified as to anyone, should have
excluded the Secretary from any charge of having participated,
and should have acknowledged his actions to foil any such
efforts.   Indeed, it was Secretary Shultz who first informed
Attorney General Meese that the President said he knew of the
November 1985 HAWK shipment -- the fact the alleged conspiracy is
purported to have tried to conceal. And it was also the
Secretary who -- only three weeks after the November 24
"conspiratorial" meeting -- expressly informed the Senate Select
Committee on Intelligence on December 16 of Mr. McFarlane's
report to the Secretary in November 1985 that the President had
approved the HAWK shipment.

                                        * * * *

- 18 -

Secretary Shultz and his counsel respectfully request that the foregoing response be included in its entirety in the Appendix to the Final Report as provided for under the Independent Counsel Statute, 28 U.S.C. § 594 (h) (2).

WILMER, CUTLER & PICKERING

by _____
Lloyd N. Cutler

Counsel for George P. Shultz

Thelma Stubbs Smith

Cadwalader, Wickersham & Taft

1333 New Hampshire Ave., N. W.

Washington, D. C. 20036

Telephone: (202) 862-2200

100 MAIDEN LANE
NEW YORK, N.Y. 10038
TEL: (212) 504-6000
FAX: (212) 504-6666

360 SOUTH FIGUEROA STREET
LOS ANGELES, CA 90017
TEL: (213) 955-4600
FAX: (213) 955-4666

FAX: (202) 862-2400
TWX: 710-822-1934

PALM BEACH, FLA 33480
TEL: (407) 655-9500
FAX: (407) 655-9508

Raymond Banoun
(202) 862-2426

RECEIVED
DEC 0 2 1993
CLERK OF THE UNITED
STATES COURT OF APPEALS

December 2, 1993

VIA HAND DELIVERY

Ron H. Garvin, Clerk
United States Court of Appeals
District of Columbia Circuit
333 Constitution Avenue, N.W.
United States Courthouse, Fifth Floor
Washington, D.C. 20001-2866

> Re: Oliver L. North, <u>et al.</u>
> (Thelma Stubbs Smith)
> Division No. 86-6

Dear Mr. Garvin:

Please accept for filing, under seal in the above-captioned matter, the enclosed **Response of Thelma Stubbs Smith** to the Independent Counsel's Final Report.

Sincerely,

Raymond Banoun

RB:mw

Enclosure

Our Third Century
Founded 1792

**UNITED STATES COURT OF APPEALS
FOR THE DISTRICT OF COLUMBIA CIRCUIT**

United States Court of Appeals
For the District of Columbia Circuit

**Division for the Purpose of Appointing
Independent Counsels**

FILED DEC 0 2 1993

RON GARVIN
CLERK

In Re: Oliver L. North, <u>et al</u>.)
         (Thelma Stubbs Smith)   )
)
 	
	Division No. 86-6
	(Under Seal)

RESPONSE OF THELMA STUBBS SMITH
TO THE INDEPENDENT COUNSEL'S FINAL REPORT

Thelma Stubbs Smith, through undersigned counsel, respectfully submits the instant response to the Final Report of Lawrence E. Walsh, the Independent Counsel appointed by this Court to investigate the so-called Iran-Contra matter. Mr. Walsh filed his Final Report pursuant to 28 U.S.C. § 594(h)(1)(B) on August 5, 1993. Thereafter, Mrs. Smith was notified by this Court that she may submit to the Clerk of the Court by December 3, 1993, any written comments that she requests be included as an appendix to the Report.

BACKGROUND

The Final Report issued by the Office of Independent Counsel Lawrence E. Walsh (hereinafter "OIC") unfairly attacks the credibility of Mrs. Smith and cannot be permitted to remain uncontroverted. Prior to her retirement in 1989, Mrs. Smith had a distinguished career as a civil servant, which spanned some thirty-seven years. During those almost four decades, Mrs. Smith served as an executive secretary for seven Secretaries of Defense, including Caspar Weinberger, and six Assistant Secretaries for International Security Affairs. As a dedicated public servant, she faithfully and honorably served both Republican and Democratic administrations. Indeed, she held high-level security clearances and always acted in a manner beyond reproach.

During the OIC's investigation of former Secretary Weinberger, which ultimately resulted in the return of an indictment, Mrs. Smith submitted to voluntary interviews by the OIC on two occasions. She also testified before the grand jury. To suggest, as does Mr. Walsh in his Final Report, that Mrs. Smith made any intentional misstatement to the OIC during those interviews to which she voluntarily consented, and which she attended without benefit of counsel, is totally without evidentiary support and irresponsible. This demeaning attack by the OIC, however, is but the latest example of the unfair manner in which Mr. Walsh and his staff have treated Mrs. Smith and others throughout the course of their investigation. Indeed, these false accusations by the OIC highlight the vindictive and petty manner in which it has conducted itself and brings into question its entire Report.

DISCUSSION

The Independent Counsel's dissatisfaction with Mrs. Smith stems from her March 5, 1992 interview which OIC investigators conducted at her home. This was the first time that Mrs. Smith had ever been approached by anyone from the OIC. During the course of the interview, which her husband was able to hear in detail from the next room, Mrs. Smith was asked whether she was aware that Secretary Weinberger had maintained handwritten notes during his tenure as Secretary of Defense. At the time, the investigators showed Mrs. Smith samples of the notes to which they were referring. Both Mrs. Smith and her husband specifically recall that she told the investigators that she was aware of the existence of these handwritten notes. Notwithstanding her statements, the agents subsequently prepared a report which incorrectly reflected that Mrs. Smith had stated that she was unaware that Secretary Weinberger had maintained the type of handwritten notes she had been shown. It is this inaccurate interview report which forms the basis for the OIC's allegation that Mrs. Smith had been somewhat untruthful at the time of her first interview by the investigators.

It is unfortunate that the Independent Counsel has seen fit to deny Mrs. Smith access to the investigators' notes and reports, and the notes of OIC staff members who conducted a second interview of Mrs. Smith two weeks later. During that second interview, Mrs. Smith reiterated her earlier statement that Secretary Weinberger had maintained handwritten notes. Thus, an honest civil servant who has never been charged with any offense, and who has served her country with distinction for almost four decades, has to defend her reputation while being denied the very due process rights routinely extended to convicted felons. This lack of fundamental fairness reflects this Independent Counsel's decision to attack anyone whom he perceived did not testify in the manner that he desired, and to reject all precepts of appropriate prosecutorial conduct. The content of the Report (two volumes) shows the length to which this Independent Counsel has gone to publicly smear individuals he was unable to charge because he lacked any evidence, or indeed, which no reasonable and even-handed prosecutor would have ever even contemplated accusing.

For example, on March 23, 1992, Mrs. Smith was voluntarily interviewed a second time by several attorneys and investigators from the OIC. The Final Report, however, states that Mrs. Smith's second interview occurred over one month later, on April 28, 1992 -- the day before she executed an affidavit at the request of Secretary Weinberger's attorneys in which she again acknowledged the existence of his handwritten notes. This obvious misstatement of fact by the Independent Counsel evidently was intended to convey the false impression that Mrs. Smith had executed this affidavit the day after her interview, and somehow bolster the Independent Counsel's weak and meritless accusations. In fact, as noted above, Mrs. Smith's interview with the OIC took place well over a month before she executed her affidavit of April 29, 1992. More importantly, the statement in her affidavit regarding Secretary Weinberger's handwritten notes was fully consistent with what she told the OIC during the first two interviews.

Another example of the OIC's prosecutorial abuses occurred during Mrs. Smith's appearance before the grand jury. Specifically, on May 8, 1992, Mrs. Smith voluntarily appeared and testified before a Grand Jury of the United States District Court for the District of Columbia. By that time, she had retained the undersigned counsel to represent her. In the grand jury, Associate Independent Counsel Thomas Baker, who had been present at Mrs. Smith's March 23 interview, accused her of not having been truthful when she had been interviewed by the OIC investigators on March 5. Mrs. Smith, who had never before been subjected to a grand jury setting, was shocked by Mr. Baker's accusation and sought to explain that the investigators' report did not accurately reflect her March 5 interview. Indeed, during a break prior to the conclusion of her testimony, Mrs. Smith and the undersigned counsel confronted Mr. Baker and questioned him about his improper attempt to mischaracterize Mrs. Smith's earlier statement to the OIC. Mr. Baker had no response and merely shrugged his shoulders. Although shaken by this unfounded attack on her integrity, Mrs. Smith continued to insist on her recollection of the notes.

Immediately following her grand jury appearance, counsel wrote to Mr. Baker to demand that his inaccurate representations to the grand jury be clarified and that the grand jurors be made aware that Mrs. Smith had, during each of her prior interviews on March 5 and March 23, consistently told OIC staff members that she had been aware that Secretary Weinberger maintained handwritten notes. See Exhibit A. Mr. Baker never responded to this letter.

On Tuesday, June 9, 1992, Mr. Baker called the undersigned to schedule another grand jury appearance for Mrs. Smith during that same week. Although Mrs. Smith tried to accommodate Mr. Baker, an illness to an out-of-town member of her family rendered her unavailable to testify on less than forty-eight hours notice. Thus, counsel advised Mr. Baker that Mrs. Smith would be unable to appear before the Grand Jury as he had requested. During that telephone call, Mr. Baker sought permission to interview Mrs. Smith without the presence of her counsel. Mr. Baker was told in clear terms that he was not authorized to do so. Notwithstanding this admonition, Mr. Baker dispatched an OIC investigator to Mrs. Smith's home at 8:00 a.m. on June 12, in an effort to interview her without her counsel's knowledge or presence. Fortunately, Mr. Smith responded to the investigator and Mrs. Smith was not located. See Exhibit B. Not surprisingly, the Independent Counsel omits any reference in the Final Report to this violation of legal ethics by a member of his staff.

In December 1992, after Secretary Weinberger had been indicted, the OIC submitted, in connection with certain pre-trial evidentiary motions, affidavits from the investigators who had interviewed Mrs. Smith on March 5, 1992. These affidavits stated that Mrs. Smith had claimed no knowledge that Secretary Weinberger had maintained handwritten notes. These assertions by the OIC appeared in the <u>Washington Post</u> [Exhibit C] and were a source of great personal embarrassment to Mrs. Smith, as they publicly called into question her honesty and integrity. In an effort to correct the record, the undersigned forwarded a letter to the Independent Counsel which reiterated once again that on March 5 and March 23, Mrs. Smith had told OIC investigators that she had been aware of the existence of Secretary Weinberger's handwritten notes. <u>See</u> Exhibit D. At no time, prior to the issuance of the Final Report, did Mr. Walsh or Mr. Baker respond to the above correspondence or otherwise attempt to refute the facts stated therein.[1]

CONCLUSION

The Independent Counsel's allegations against Mrs. Smith are baseless and irresponsible. We, therefore, request that all references to Mrs. Smith be deleted from the Final Report, or in the alternative, that this submission, with exhibits, be included as an appendix to that Report.

---

[1]   Despite her repeated consistent statements and testimony, the Independent Counsel also suggests that Mrs. Smith may have made a "deliberately false" statement to a co-worker over six years ago concerning Secretary Weinberger's handwritten notes. The basis of this suggestion is what the Independent Counsel concedes are vague alleged statements by the co-worker. We have not been provided with these statements. However, the Independent Counsel in his Report conceded that there were apparent credibility problems regarding this co-worker's testimony. Viewed in this light, Mr. Walsh's accusation is another gratuitous and unfair attack on the reputation of an honest and truthful civil servant with an impeccable thirty-seven-year career of government service.

Respectfully submitted,

Raymond Banoun
D.C. Bar No. 100107
Cadwalader, Wickersham & Taft
1333 New Hampshire Avenue, N.W.
Washington, D.C. 20036
(202) 862-2200

CERTIFICATE OF SERVICE

I hereby certify that on the 2nd day of December, 1993, a copy of the foregoing Response of Thelma Stubbs Smith to the Independent Counsel's Final Report was served by first class mail, postage pre-paid, upon the Office of Independent Counsel Lawrence E. Walsh, One Columbus Circle, N.E., Suite G-320, Washington, D.C.   20544.

Harold Damelin

ATTACHMENT – A

Cadwalader, Wickersham & Taft

1333 New Hampshire Ave., N. W.

Washington, D. C. 20036

Telephone: (202) 862-2200

_____

FAX: (202) 862-2400

TWX: 710-822-1934

100 MAIDEN LANE
NEW YORK, N.Y. 10038
TEL: (212) 504-6000
FAX: (212) 504-6666

660 SOUTH FIGUEROA STREET
LOS ANGELES, CA 90017
TEL: (213) 955-4600
FAX: (213) 955-4666

440 ROYAL PALM WAY
PALM BEACH, FLA 33480
TEL: (407) 655-9500
FAX: (407) 655-9508

Raymond Banoun
(202) 862-2426

May 8, 1992

<u>BY FACSIMILE AND HAND DELIVERY</u>

Thomas E. Baker, Esquire
Associate Counsel
Office of Independent Counsel
555 - 13th Street, N.W.
Suite 701 West
Washington, D.C.   20004

Dear Mr. Baker:

I am writing regarding the appearance of my client, Thelma Stubbs Smith, this morning, before a Grand Jury of the United States District Court for the District of Columbia. During that appearance, you showed her a report prepared by the FBI agents who interviewed her at her home on March 5, 1992, which stated that she had told them she was unaware whether Secretary Caspar Weinberger maintained handwritten notes. You then inquired why it was that she later stated at paragraph 5 of her affidavit of April 29, 1992 that:

> I was aware that Secretary Weinberger kept a pad on his desk on which he scribbled notes reflecting the date, time and other references to telephone calls and meetings.

I was surprised, as was my client, by the suggestion made to the Grand Jury that her statements regarding Secretary Weinberger's notes were inconsistent. As you may be aware, during the March 5 interview, the agents told my client that Secretary Weinberger maintained handwritten notes on small pieces

Thomas E. Baker, Esquire
May 8, 1992
Page 2

of paper, asked her if she had ever observed these notes, and
showed her some of the notes. Ms. Smith replied to the agents
that she had in fact noticed these notes on Secretary
Weinberger's desk and that the notes generally included the time
and place of meetings and telephone calls, the participants, and
other general remarks. She also informed the agents that she
assumed that Secretary Weinberger maintained these notes for
future use if he were to decide to write a book.

In addition, on March 23, 1992, Ms. Smith met with you
and a colleague from your office, and several FBI agents and
repeated the same statements regarding the notes as she had told
the agents on March 5.

Accordingly, I was concerned by any suggestion to the
Grand Jury that somehow my client's recollection of the notes was
of more recent vintage. As we are all aware, for many reasons,
including inability to keep up with a witness, reports of agents
do not always accurately reflect a witness' statement.

I would appreciate it if this letter were placed on the
Grand Jury record so that the jurors are aware of the content of
the communications which my client had with the agents and with
your office.

Sincerely,

RB:dt

ATTACHMENT – B

Cadwalader, Wickersham & Taft

1333 New Hampshire Ave., N. W.

Washington, D. C. 20036

Telephone: (202) 862-2200

100 MAIDEN LANE
NEW YORK, N.Y. 10038
TEL: (212) 504-6000
FAX: (212) 504-6666

660 SOUTH FIGUEROA STREET
LOS ANGELES, CA 90017
TEL: (213) 955-4600
FAX: (213) 955-4666

FAX: (202) 862-2400
TWX: 710-822-1934

440 ROYAL PALM WAY
PALM BEACH, FLA 33480
TEL: (407) 655-8500
FAX: (407) 655-9508

Raymond Banoun
(202) 862-2426

June 12, 1992

BY HAND DELIVERY

Thomas E. Baker, Esquire
Associate Counsel
Office of the Independent Counsel
555 - 13th Street, N.W.
Suite 701 West
Washington, D.C.   20004

Dear Mr. Baker:

As you well know, I represent Thelma Stubbs Smith. I represented her at her last Grand Jury appearance on May 8, 1992 and you elicited that fact from her in the Grand Jury.

Notwithstanding the fact that you knew that she was represented by counsel, and that I had told you on June 12 that I would not permit an interview outside my presence, you sent one of your investigators to her home this morning in order to interview her. That is inappropriate. Your investigator told Mr. Smith that his wife's attorney had been uncooperative. That is totally incorrect.

On May 8, 1992, my client appeared in the Grand Jury on two days notice, without even the benefit of a subpoena, in order to accommodate you because you had represented that the term of your Grand Jury was about to expire. That is nothing short of full cooperation.

As I previously mentioned to you, I will be on vacation beginning June 15 until June 30. I will be in my office on the afternoon of July 1. Therefore, I will not be available to accompany Mrs. Smith to a Grand Jury appearance or to an interview before that time. If you wish to schedule an appearance or a meeting at any time thereafter, we will do our best to accommodate you. As I am sure you recall, it was only on Tuesday, June 9, that you called me to seek her appearance before the Grand Jury. It is not unreasonable to expect that attorneys

Our Third Century
Founded 1792

Cadwalader, Wickersham & Taft

Thomas E. Baker, Esquire
June 12, 1992
Page 2

may have vacation plans in the summer and typically such plans
are accommodated.

Further, in light of the manner in which my client has
been dealt with, my client has informed me that unless she is
provided with a full immunity order under 18 U.S.C. § 6002, she
will invoke the protections afforded her by the Constitution.

In the meantime, in order to accommodate you, we will
accept a subpoena addressed to our client for any date after
July 1. If you wish to serve it directly on her, you may do so,
but you may not ask her any questions.

Sincerely,

RB:dt

ATTACHMENT – C

A4 Friday, December 18, 1992

Weinberger Case Lawyers Trade Pretrial Charges

Former Aide's Affidavit Focus of Dispute

By George Lardner Jr.
and Walter Pincus
Washington Post Staff Writers

In the Iran-contra case against former defense secretary Caspar W. Weinberger, his lawyers and prosecutors accused each other last night of unethical and unprincipled conduct in connection with pretrial pleadings.

The charges stemmed from a motion by Weinberger's lawyers contending that the prosecution made misrepresentations to a grand jury about statements by one of Weinberger's former secretaries at the Pentagon.

To bolster their assertion, defense lawyers submitted an affidavit made by the secretary's husband and accusing an FBI agent attached to the office of independent counsel Lawrence E. Walsh of making a skewed interview report, which the agent later blamed on "politics."

Walsh's office fired back last evening with a motion assailing the allegations as "scurrilous." The prosecution said that both FBI agents who interviewed the secretary denied the husband's allegations "in their entirety."

The dispute is expected to come up today at what was already shaping up as a contentious pretrial hearing before U.S. District Judge Thomas F. Hogan. Weinberger's lawyers also are demanding that the prosecution turn over all records of a mock trial of Weinberger that it conducted last weekend.

In their motion concerning the FBI report, defense lawyers Robert S. Bennett and Carl S. Rauh argued they were entitled to bring it up as part of an effort to impeach four members of Walsh's office who are expected to be called as prosecution witnesses. Weinberger is scheduled to go on trial Jan. 5 on four charges of perjury and lying about the Iran-contra affair and about notes he kept as it unfolded.

According to the disputed affidavit, Edwin E. Smith said his wife, Thelma, a former Weinberger secretary, told the FBI agents in an interview last March that Weinberger kept notes of his meetings and phone calls, but this was left out of the FBI report of the interview. When Thelma Smith appeared before a grand jury last May, her husband said, one of the prosecutors "seemed to accuse her of lying" for

> *Weinberger is expected to go on trial Jan. 5 on four charges of perjury in connection with the Iran-contra affair.*

failing to inform the FBI about the notes.

Edwin Smith said in the affidavit that the FBI agent, when asked about the omission, "replied with words to the effect that sometimes 'politics' enters into such proceedings."

The prosecution accused defense counsel of being bent on "ad hominem attacks on this office, without regard to the truth." Bennett said he stood by his representations and said "it is Walsh and his staff that have violated legal ethics and common decency."

ATTACHMENT – D

Cadwalader, Wickersham & Taft

1333 New Hampshire Ave., N. W.

Washington, D. C. 20036

Telephone: (202) 862-2200

100 MAIDEN LANE
NEW YORK, N.Y. 10038
TEL: (212) 504-6000
FAX: (212) 504-6666

660 SOUTH FIGUEROA STREET
LOS ANGELES, CA 90017
TEL: (213) 955-4600
FAX: (213) 955-4666

FAX: (202) 862-2400
TWX: 710-822-1934

440 ROYAL PALM WAY
PALM BEACH, FLA 33480
TEL: (407) 655-9500
FAX: (407) 655-9508

Raymond Banoun
(202) 862-2426

December 18, 1992

HAND DELIVERED

Lawrence E. Walsh, Esq.
Independent Counsel
555 - 13th Street, N.W.
Suite 701 West
Washington, D.C. 20004

Dear Judge Walsh:

I am writing to you regarding your Office's most recent accusations against my clients Thelma and Edwin Smith contained in this morning's edition of the <u>Washington</u> <u>Post</u> and in the pleading filed by Mr. James J. Brosnahan of your staff on December 17, 1992. I find absolutely outrageous these public attacks on the credibility of witnesses who do not conform their testimony to the desires of your staff. I believe this is demeaning to the Office of the Independent Counsel and also unprofessional.

Prior to her retirement, Mrs. Smith had worked for some thirty-five years for the Department of Defense and served as an executive secretary for seven Secretaries of Defense and six Assistant Secretaries for International Security Affairs, both Republicans and Democrats. To repeatedly suggest, as your Office has over the past ten months, that a career government employee would somehow intentionally misstate facts defies credulity and reflects a lack of sensitivity regarding the role of an impartial, nonpartisan public prosecutor, which was the very purpose of the Independent Counsel.

I have read with interest the affidavits of Messrs. John Sorge and Brian Buckley, which your Office filed yesterday with the United States District Court for the District of Columbia, and find both inherently incredible. Mr. Sorge's statement that when he interviewed Mrs. Smith on March 5. 1992

Our Third Century
Founded 1792

Cadwalader, Wickersham & Taft

Lawrence E. Walsh, Esq.
December 18, 1992
Page 2

she "claims to have had no knowledge of . . . notes and did not recognize the notes [of Secretary Caspar Weinberger] that I had shown to her" is plain incorrect. Not only did Mr. Smith overhear the complete interview of his wife by Mr. Sorge, but also a record of that interview prepared a few days later by Mrs. Smith clearly indicates that she had fully informed your investigators of the existence of these notes. Moreover, some two weeks later, she was interviewed by two members of your staff and repeated her prior statements regarding the existence of Mr. Weinberger's handwritten logs and notes. It is interesting that in your December 17, 1992 pleadings you make no reference to that interview. It is also revealing that Mr. Buckley does not deny that Mrs. Smith mentioned these notes, but merely seeks to support his colleague by asserting, ten months after the interview, that "it would have made quite an impression" on him if she had. It is clear that he has no recollection of the interview.

In addition, Mr. Sorge's statement that when he went to Mrs. Smith's home on June 12, 1992, he merely intended to serve her with a subpoena, is incredulous. When Mr. Smith informed me of Mr. Sorge's visit, within minutes of Mr. Sorge's departure, I called your assistant Thomas Baker to complain that he had sent an investigator to interview Mrs. Smith when he knew that she was represented by counsel. Mr. Baker did not say that the investigator had only sought to serve her with a subpoena. On the contrary, Mr. Baker confirmed that he had sent Mr. Sorge to interview my client because, in his view, I had been uncooperative in scheduling the interview he had requested only two days earlier. Indeed, Mr. Baker insisted that your Office reserved the right to interview anyone without regard to whether they were represented by an attorney.

It is also equally revealing that Mr. Baker did not respond to my letter of June 12, 1992 (appended hereto) in which I repeated what I had earlier discussed with him on the telephone:

> Notwithstanding the fact that you knew that she [Mrs. Smith] was represented by counsel, and that I had told you . . . that I would not permit an interview outside my presence, you sent your investigators to her home this

Cadwalader, Wickersham & Taft

Lawrence E. Walsh, Esq.
December 18, 1992
Page 3

    morning in order to interview her. **That**
is inappropriate. . . .

I have no doubt that if Mr. Baker had only sent Mr. Sorge to
serve a subpoena upon Mrs. Smith, he would have felt compelled to
correct the record. He did not do so because Mr. Sorge's sole
purpose for visiting Mrs. Smith on June 12 was to interview her.

    In addition, since Mr. Baker knew as of May 8, 1992,
when Mrs. Smith appeared before the grand jury, that I
represented her, and since I had agreed to accept any future
service of subpoenas for her, it made no sense for Mr. Baker to
serve her directly on June 12.

    In light of these inaccuracies in the affidavits of
Messrs. Sorge and Buckley, and the existence of contrary
contemporaneous recordings, I submit to you that these affidavits
and your pleadings are not worthy of credibility. Clearly, Mr.
Sorge complained to Mr. Smith about the "politics" of your Office
because at the time he felt a certain kinship with Mr. Smith
because he recognized Mr. Smith as a friend of law enforcement,
who had served on various Advisory Councils to the Fairfax County
Police Department. Now that Mr. Sorge sees his remarks in print
he somehow feels compelled to deny them.

    As a former prosecutor who served as an Assistant
United States Attorney in the District of Columbia for over
thirteen years, including as head of the Fraud Division of that
office, I find demeaning and unbecoming your staff's propensity
to publicly smear citizens. More importantly, in the experience
of any prosecutor, it will neither be the first, nor last time
that an investigator has, intentionally or otherwise, failed to
accurately reflect in his report the complete statement of a
witness, especially where the witness is interviewed without the
benefit of counsel and states something contrary to the wishes of
that investigator.

    Yesterday I agreed, at the request of John Barrett of
your staff, to bring my client to your office on December 22,
1992, so that she could be interviewed once again, this time by
Messrs. Barrett and Brosnahan. However, in view of this
morning's events, Mrs. Smith will no longer accept your Office's
abuse of her rights, or those of her husband, merely because she
has been unable, in good conscience, to mold her testimony to the

Cadwalader, Wickersham & Taft

Lawrence E. Walsh, Esq.
December 18, 1992
Page 4

wishes of your staff.   We will, therefore, not appear on
December 22, 1992.

Sincerely,

cc: John Barrett, Esq.

Cadwalader, Wickersham & Taft

1333 New Hampshire Ave., N.W.

Washington, D.C. 20036

Telephone: (202) 862-2200

100 MAIDEN LANE
NEW YORK, N.Y. 10038
TEL: (212) 504-6000
FAX: (212) 504-6666

660 SOUTH FIGUEROA STREET
LOS ANGELES, CA 90017
TEL: (213) 955-4600
FAX: (213) 955-4666

FAX: (202) 862-2400
TWX: 710-822-1934

440 ROYAL PALM WAY
PALM BEACH, FLA 33480
TEL: (407) 655-9500
FAX: (407) 655-9508

Raymond Banoun
(202) 862-2426

June 12, 1992

BY HAND DELIVERY

Thomas E. Baker, Esquire
Associate Counsel
Office of the Independent Counsel
555 - 13th Street, N.W.
Suite 701 West
Washington, D.C. 20004

Dear Mr. Baker:

As you well know, I represent Thelma Stubbs Smith. I represented her at her last Grand Jury appearance on May 8, 1992 and you elicited that fact from her in the Grand Jury.

Notwithstanding the fact that you knew that she was represented by counsel, and that I had told you on June 12 that I would not permit an interview outside my presence, you sent one of your investigators to her home this morning in order to interview her. That is inappropriate. Your investigator told Mr. Smith that his wife's attorney had been uncooperative. That is totally incorrect.

On May 8, 1992, my client appeared in the Grand Jury on two days notice, without even the benefit of a subpoena, in order to accommodate you because you had represented that the term of your Grand Jury was about to expire. That is nothing short of full cooperation.

As I previously mentioned to you, I will be on vacation beginning June 15 until June 30. I will be in my office on the afternoon of July 1. Therefore, I will not be available to accompany Mrs. Smith to a Grand Jury appearance or to an interview before that time. If you wish to schedule an appearance or a meeting at any time thereafter, we will do our best to accommodate you. As I am sure you recall, it was only on Tuesday, June 9, that you called me to seek her appearance before the Grand Jury. It is not unreasonable to expect that attorneys

Our Third Century
Founded 1792

Cadwalader, Wickersham & Taft

Thomas E. Baker, Esquire
June 12, 1992
Page 2

may have vacation plans in the summer and typically such plans are accommodated.

Further, in light of the manner in which my client has been dealt with, my client has informed me that unless she is provided with a full immunity order under 18 U.S.C. § 6002, she will invoke the protections afforded her by the Constitution.

In the meantime, in order to accommodate you, we will accept a subpoena addressed to our client for any date after July 1. If you wish to serve it directly on her, you may do so, but you may not ask her any questions.

Sincerely,

RB:dt

Abraham D. Sofaer

Hughes Hubbard & Reed

1300 I Street, N.W.

Washington, D.C. 20005-3306

ONE BATTERY PARK PLAZA
NEW YORK, NEW YORK 10004
212-837-6000

47, AVENUE GEORGES MANDEL
75116 PARIS, FRANCE
(1) 44-05-80-00

TELEPHONE: 202-408-3600

TELECOPIER: 202-408-3636

TELEX: 892674

555 SOUTH FLOWER STREET
LOS ANGELES, CALIFORNIA 90071
213-489-5160

801 BRICKELL AVENUE
MIAMI, FLORIDA 33131
305-358-1666

ABRAHAM D. SOFAER
202-408-3700

September 2, 1993

Mr. Ron H. Garvin
Clerk
United States Court of Appeals
Fifth Floor, Room 5409
333 Constitution Avenue, N.W.
Washington, D.C. 20001-2866

Re: <u>**Final Report of Special Prosecutor Walsh**</u>

Dear Mr. Garvin:

Thank you for informing me that I am mentioned in the final report filed by Judge Walsh, and for giving me an opportunity to comment on the report.

1. The Report is incorrect in stating that former Secretary of State George P. Shultz attempted to blame me for errors in testimony due to Mr. Charles Hill's inadequate compliance with the instructions I issued on behalf of the Department to provide the FBI (and other investigators) with a full record of all relevant materials under his control. It is true that Mr. Hill claimed that I had somehow permitted his incomplete submission, and the Report deals accurately with that claim. But Secretary Shultz made no such claim, and advanced no other criticism of me, in any of the materials provided to me for review. Based on my long and close association with Secretary Shultz, and his complete support of my effort to ensure full disclosure, I do not believe that he said anything, anywhere in the Report or otherwise, which could justify the Report's claim. I called Secretary Shultz and asked him if he made any such statement in materials I was not permitted to review; he told me that he did not. Therefore, the statement is unjustified and should be deleted. It could be seen as an effort to suggest that Secretary Shultz did not want the full disclosure which I sought, and that is an untrue suggestion.

DC932420.020

Hughes Hubbard & Reed

Ron Garvin, Esq.
September 2, 1993
Page 2

    2. It is not accurate to say that I was concerned that
Oliver North had "absconded" with the Brunei money. (p.320,
n.38) My concern was that he had diverted the money to other
uses, but not to his own use.

    I would appreciate learning what steps, if any, are taken to
correct these errors.

                              Sincerely yours,

Michael A. Sterlacci

United States Court of Appeals
For the District of Columbia Circuit

FILED DEC 0 2 1993

RON GARVIN
CLERK

December 2, 1993

Mr. Ron Garvin
Clerk
Unites States Court of Appeals
District of Columbia Circuit
Washington, D.C. 20001-2866

Dear Mr. Garvin,

This is in response to your August 9, 1993 letter setting forth an order of the Court authorizing me to review relevant portions of the Independent Counsel's Final Report and "to submit any comment or factual information...for possible inclusion as an appendix to the Final Report."

The following comments are in response to that portion of the Final Report found at Part VIII, p. 441 entitled, "The Department of Defense's Lack of Cooperation with the Office of Independent Counsel's Investigation of Weinberger."

The Office of Independent Counsel (OIC) made more than 100 written and oral requests to the Department of Defense for documents, photos, interviews, inspections and other official information. Many of the requests preceded the 1992 indictment of Caspar Weinberger and were very general in nature. The specific request for originals and/or copies of Garrett's 1987 memoranda to Weinberger and Taft were not produced until after the indictment because they were not discovered by anyone at DOD in response to OIC's generalized requests.   When OIC specifically requested any particularized document, it was located and produced.

Beyond any lack of specificity being a barrier to the production of materials sought by OIC, one needs to view the OIC's production requests in context.   Each request for materials submitted by the OIC was routinely forwarded to the most diverse and inclusive number of DOD components and offices that might have had access to the information sought. DOD has 3.3 million personnel stationed worldwide and, in many instances, all components were the recipients of the numerous requests. Requests from the OIC were sent out verbatim by OGC to avoid any deviation of translation or misunderstanding by the addressees. The responses to each request were then collected by OGC, collated and forwarded in timely fashion to the OIC.

Inquiries began in late 1991 and continued until the December 24, 1992 pardon issued to Caspar Weinberger by President George Bush. Responses to grand jury subpoenas duces tecum and specific requests seeking the precise Garrett document(s) which were located in Mr. Garrett's office, were produced by DOD in a timely fashion. Until the specific request was made for the Garrett document(s) by OIC and forwarded to the Department of the Navy, no personnel in OGC had copies of the document(s) requested or any knowledge of their existence based upon search requests disseminated throughout the entire office. All OIC pre-indictment requests were routinely sent to all offices in the Office of General Counsel because of Mr. Garrett's prior position as General Counsel. Likewise, no other DOD office produced the specific document(s) sought later with specificity by Grand Jury Subpoena until Mr. Garrett's office located the document(s).

Based upon the number of requests sent to DOD and the significant number of DOD offices and personnel asked to produce responses for the OIC, it is unrealistic for the report to suggest that Mr. Sterlacci should have followed up on one request for a 1987 Garrett document that was not located until later identified with particularity by OIC. At that point in time, OIC had already received more than 300,000 documents from DOD in addition to the more than one million documents previously produced by DOD for other Iran-Contra cases (e.g. Oliver North, Poindexter, Fernandez, et al.) and maintained in a secure classified information facility (SCIF) by OIC.

Further, on several occasions before and after the issuance of an indictment, the OIC conducted its own independent investigations and inspections of the entire Weinberger document collection located at the Library of Congress (which would have contained a copy of the Garrett memoranda sought) and at the Federal Records Center, Suitland, Md. which maintains the original copies of all relevant DOD unclassified documents (including all documents involving the former Secretaries of Defense). Also, the OIC communicated directly with and had complete access to volumes of classified documents from the Defense Intelligence Agency covering the entire Weinberger tenure. These independent document searches by OIC were in addition to the numerous interviews of DOD personnel at the Pentagon or before the Grand Jury.

Lastly, since the OIC apparently did not discover the Garrett document by its own investigation, one must ask if the OIC's May, 1992 document request was considered by OIC to be so relevant and important, why it didn't renew its request to OGC for the specific Garrett document until October 1992, a five month hiatus? Moreover, OIC could have chosen to request the document directly from Mr. Lawrence Garrett, since his office ultimately produced the document sent to Mr. Sterlacci's office in response to the specific request. Perhaps a more diligent and effective analysis by OIC of the volumes of documents provided to them would have avoided the Report's claim (in a post-presidential pardon context), that one specific and precise document was not produced by DOD in a timely fashion and therefore hindered its prosecutorial efforts.

The report goes on to state that OIC received an anonymous telephone call on May 21, 1992 suggesting the "investigators look in the office of Deputy General Counsel Michael A. Sterlacci, for information regarding Weinberger. Several of the files produced belatedly by DOD had been stored in Sterlacci's office".

What the anonymous caller did not appear to know was that the General Counsel had specifically designated Sterlacci's office as the central repository for all Iran-Contra documents that were received from DOD components in respose to all OIC requests. This fact was publicized throughout OGC and certainly was known to OIC attorneys and investigators who visited the office on numerous occasions to review records. For OIC to include a footnote in its report implying some furtive motive in the storage of materials specifically kept for them and with their knowledge is very puzzling and raises serious ethical concerns which the court may wish to consider. All documents received by Sterlacci's office were uniformly transferred to the OIC in a timely fashion by written dated responses, copies of which are currently maintained by the DOD Office of General Counsel and can be included as part of the appendix to the OIC report should the Court so desire.

In response to Footnote 311, regarding the scattering of files in different OGC offices before mid-1992 that were subsequesntly located by OGC personnel as part of a routine document retirement to the Federal Records Center, it should be noted that Mr. Sterlacci began his tenure as Assistant General Counsel for DOD on April 6, 1988 and had no responsibility for or knowledge of any documents maintained in OGC offices, including his own staff's files, that were maintained prior to that date. When additional documents were located by another attorney in his own office files, OIC personnel were given immediate notice of their existence and a timely opportunity to inspect and copy any relevant documents. At that time, no one from OIC staff suggested to OGC personnel that any of the documents located were of any import.

OIC's statement that after Weinberger's indictment it discovered that DOD had given Weinberger's defense counsel apparently unsupervised access to documents the OIC had identified as evidence and left, by agreement with DOD, temporarily in DOD custody is mistaken and inaccurate. To my knowledge, documentary evidence discovered by OGC for OIC was never knowingly divulged or produced for Weinberger's counsel. The information given to a legal clerk from Mr. Weinberger's counsel's firm observed by OIC counsel was in response to a distinct and totally separate pre-indictment request for information made by Mr. Weinberger's counsel pursuant to DOD Directive 5405.2, 32 CFR97.2, "Release of Official Information in Litigation and Testimony by DOD Personnel as Witnesses." The legal clerk was unsupervised because he was given a private reading area to review only those documents requested by defense counsel.

(3)

It should be noted that in the pre-indictment and post-indictment timeframes, OIC and Mr. Weinberger's counsel joined issue on the procedures to be used for discovery of DOD documents. The unsettled legal issue concerned the viability of DOD Directive 5405.2 (copy attached) versus Rule 16, Federal Rules of Criminal Procedure. OGC urged both parties to offer a consensus position for DOD to respond to requests by defense counsel for documents or, absent that undertaking, to seek judicial resolution of the matter. Counsel for Weinberger filed with the Court a legal motion and memorandum on the issue, a copy of which was provided to DOD. No written or oral response was ever communicated to DOD by the OIC. Since no additional requests for documents were made by Weinberger's counsel, the legal issue was left unresolved. Subsequently, the DOD Acting General Counsel (by letter noted at report footnote 312) decided that in the post-indictment context, DOD would consult with OIC on future document discovery by Weinberger's counsel.

Lastly, OIC mentions its use of discretion in not committing resources into an investigation of ongoing obstruction by DOD. The simple response to that statement is to note that DOD communications from OIC throughout the Weinberger investigation are replete with statements thanking DOD for its continuing cooperation and efforts in support of OIC. Further, for an office which has spent a reported $35.7 million to date, it strains credulity for OIC to suggest in the report that fiscal responsibility would preclude any legitimate investigation of wrongdoing it perceived by DOD.

Respectfully Submitted,

Michael A. Sterlacci

Michael A. Sterlacci
8228 Toll House Road
Annandale, Virginia 22003
(703) 978-4638

(4)

Department of Defense
DIRECTIVE

July 23, 1985
NUMBER 5405.2 , 32 C.F.R 97.2

GC, DOD

SUBJECT: Release of Official Information in Litigation and Testimony by
DoD Personnel as Witnesses

References: (a) Title 5, United States Code, Sections 301, 552, and 552a
            (b) Title 10, United States Code, Section 133
            (c) DoD Directive 5220.6, "Industrial Personnel Security
                 Clearance Program," December 20, 1976
            (d) DoD 5200.1-R, "Information Security Program Regulation,"
                 August 1982, authorized by DoD Directive 5200.1, June 7, 1982
            (e) DoD Directive 5230.25, "Withholding of Unclassified Technical
                 Data from Public Disclosure," November 6, 1984
            (f) DoD Instruction 7230.7, "User Charges," January 29, 1985
            (g) DoD 5400.7-R, "DoD Freedom of Information Act Program,"
                 December 1980, authorized by DoD Directive 5400.7,
                 March 24, 1980

A. PURPOSE

Under Section 301 reference (a) and reference (b), this Directive establishes policy, assigns responsibilities, and prescribes procedures for the
release of official DoD information in litigation and for testimony by DoD
personnel as witnesses during litigation.

B. APPLICABILITY AND SCOPE

1. This Directive applies to the Office of the Secretary of Defense (OSD),
the Military Departments, the Organization of the Joint Chiefs of Staff (OJCS),
the Unified and Specified Commands, and the Defense Agencies (hereafter referred to as "DoD Components"), and to all personnel of such DoD Components.

2. This Directive does not apply to the release of official information
or testimony by DoD personnel in the following situations:

a. Before courts-martial convened by the authority of the Military
Departments or in administrative proceedings conducted by or on behalf of
a DoD Component;

b. Pursuant to administrative proceedings conducted by or on behalf
of the Equal Employment Opportunity Commission (EEOC) or the Merit Systems
Protection Board (MSPB), or pursuant to a negotiated grievance procedure under
a collective bargaining agreement to which the Government is a party;

c. In response to requests by Federal Government counsel in litigation
conducted on behalf of the United States;

d. As part of the assistance required in accordance with the Defense Industrial Personnel Security Clearance Program under DoD Directive 5220.6 (reference (c)); or

e. Pursuant to disclosure of information to Federal, State, and local prosecuting and law enforcement authorities, in conjunction with an investigation conducted by a DoD criminal investigative organization.

3. This Directive does not supersede or modify existing laws or DoD programs governing the testimony of DoD personnel or the release of official DoD information during grand jury proceedings, the release of official information not involved in litigation, or the release of official information pursuant to the Freedom of Information Act, 5 U.S.C. Section 552 (reference (a)) or the Privacy Act, 5 U.S.C. Section 552a (reference (a)), nor does this Directive preclude treating any written request for agency records that is not in the nature of legal process as a request under the Freedom of Information or Privacy Acts.

4. This Directive is not intended to infringe upon or displace the responsibilities committed to the Department of Justice in conducting litigation on behalf of the United States in appropriate cases.

5. This Directive does not preclude official comment on matters in litigation in appropriate cases.

6. This Directive is intended only to provide guidance for the internal operation of the Department of Defense and is not intended to, does not, and may not be relied upon to create any right or benefit, substantive or procedural, enforceable at law against the United States or the Department of Defense.

C. DEFINITIONS

1. **Demand.** Subpoena, order, or other demand of a court of competent jurisdiction, or other specific authority, for the production, disclosure, or release of official DoD information or for the appearance and testimony of DoD personnel as witnesses.

2. **DoD Personnel.** Present and former U.S. military personnel; Service Academy cadets and midshipmen; and present and former civilian employees of any Component of the Department of Defense, including nonappropriated fund activity employees; non-U.S. nationals who perform services overseas, under the provisions of status of forces agreements, for the United States Armed Forces; and other specific individuals hired through contractual agreements by or on behalf of the Department of Defense.

3. **Litigation.** All pretrial, trial, and post-trial stages of all existing or reasonably anticipated judicial or administrative actions, hearings, investigations, or similar proceedings before civilian courts, commissions, boards (including the Armed Services Board of Contract Appeals), or other tribunals, foreign and domestic. This term includes responses to discovery requests, depositions, and other pretrial proceedings, as well as responses to formal or informal requests by attorneys or others in situations involving litigation.

2

4. <u>Official Information</u>. All information of any kind, however stored, that is in the custody and control of the Department of Defense, relates to information in the custody and control of the Department, or was acquired by DoD personnel as part of their official duties or because of their official status within the Department while such personnel were employed by or on behalf of the Department or on active duty with the United States Armed Forces.

D. <u>POLICY</u>

It is DoD policy that official information should generally be made reasonably available for use in federal and state courts and by other governmental bodies unless the information is classified, privileged, or otherwise protected from public disclosure.

E. <u>RESPONSIBILITIES</u>

1. The <u>General Counsel, Department of Defense</u> (GC, DoD), shall provide general policy and procedural guidance by the issuance of supplemental instructions or specific orders concerning the release of official DoD information in litigation and the testimony of DoD personnel as witnesses during litigation.

2. The <u>Heads of DoD Components</u> shall issue appropriate regulations to implement this Directive and to identify official information that is involved in litigation.

F. <u>PROCEDURES</u>

1. <u>Authority to Act</u>

a. In response to a litigation request or demand for official DoD information or the testimony of DoD personnel as witnesses, the General Counsels of DoD, Navy, and the Defense Agencies; the Judge Advocates General of the Military Departments; and the Chief Legal Advisors to the JCS and the Unified and Specified Commands, with regard to their respective Components, are authorized - after consulting and coordinating with the appropriate Department of Justice litigation attorneys, as required - to determine whether official information originated by the Component may be released in litigation; whether DoD personnel assigned to or affiliated with the Component may be interviewed, contacted, or used as witnesses concerning official DoD information or as expert witnesses; and what, if any, conditions will be imposed upon such release, interview, contact, or testimony. Delegation of this authority, to include the authority to invoke appropriate claims of privilege before any tribunal, is permitted.

b. In the event that a DoD Component receives a litigation request or demand for official information originated by another Component, the receiving Component shall forward the appropriate portions of the request or demand to the originating Component for action in accordance with this Directive. The receiving Component shall also notify the requestor, court, or other authority of its transfer of the request or demand.

c. Notwithstanding the provisions of paragraphs F.1.a. and b., the GC, DoD, in litigation involving terrorism, espionage, nuclear weapons, intelligence means or sources, or otherwise as deemed necessary, may notify Components that GC, DoD, will assume primary responsibility for coordinating all litigation requests and demands for official DoD information or the testimony of DoD personnel, or both; consulting with the Department of Justice, as required; and taking final action on such requests and demands.

2. Factors to Consider. In deciding whether to authorize the release of official DoD information or the testimony of DoD personnel concerning official information (hereafter referred to as "the disclosure") pursuant to paragraph F.1., DoD officials should consider the following types of factors:

a. Whether the request or demand is unduly burdensome or otherwise inappropriate under the applicable court rules;

b. Whether the disclosure, including release in camera, is appropriate under the rules of procedure governing the case or matter in which the request or demand arose;

c. Whether the disclosure would violate a statute, executive order, regulation, or directive;

d. Whether the disclosure, including release in camera, is appropriate or necessary under the relevant substantive law concerning privilege;

e. Whether the disclosure, except when in camera and necessary to assert a claim of privilege, would reveal information properly classified pursuant to the DoD Information Security Program under DoD 5200.1-R (reference (d)), unclassified technical data withheld from public release pursuant to DoD Directive 5230.25 (reference (e)), or other matters exempt from unrestricted disclosure; and,

f. Whether disclosure would interfere with ongoing enforcement proceedings, compromise constitutional rights, reveal the identity of an intelligence source or confidential informant, disclose trade secrets or similarly confidential commercial or financial information, or otherwise be inappropriate under the circumstances.

3. Decisions on Litigation Requests and Demands

a. Subject to paragraph F.3.e., DoD personnel shall not, in response to a litigation request or demand, produce, disclose, release, comment upon, or testify concerning any official DoD information without the prior written approval of the appropriate DoD official designated in paragraph F.1. Oral approval may be granted, but a record of such approval shall be made and retained in accordance with the applicable implementing regulations.

b. If official DoD information is sought, through testimony or otherwise, by a litigation request or demand, the individual seeking such release or testimony must set forth, in writing and with as much specificity as possible, the nature and relevance of the official information sought. Subject to paragraph F.3.e., DoD personnel may only produce, disclose, release, comment upon,

4

Jul 23, 85
5405.2

or testify concerning those matters that were specified in writing and properly approved by the appropriate DoD official designated in paragraph F.1. See United States ex rel. Touhy v. Ragen, 340 U.S. 462 (1951).

c. Whenever a litigation request or demand is made upon DoD personnel for official DoD information or for testimony concerning such information, the personnel upon whom the request or demand was made shall immediately notify the DoD official designated in paragraph F.1. for the Component to which the individual contacted is or, for former personnel, was last assigned. In appropriate cases, the responsible DoD official shall thereupon notify the Department of Justice of the request or demands. After due consultation and coordination with the Department of Justice, as required, the DoD official shall determine whether the individual is required to comply with the request or demand and shall notify the requestor or the court or other authority of the determination reached.

d. If, after DoD personnel have received a litigation request or demand and have in turn notified the appropriate DoD official in accordance with paragraph F.3.c., a response to the request or demand is required before instructions from the responsible official are received, the responible official designated in paragraph F.1. shall furnish the requestor or the court or other authority with a copy of this Directive and applicable implementing Regulations, inform the requestor or the court or other authority that the request or demand is being reviewed, and seek a stay of the request or demand pending a final determination by the Component concerned.

e. If a court of competent jurisdiction or other appropriate authority declines to stay the effect of the request or demand in response to action taken pusuant to paragraph F.3.d., or if such court or other authority orders that the request or demand must be complied with notwithstanding the final decision of the appropriate DoD official, the DoD personnel upon whom the request or demand was made shall notify the responsible DoD official of such ruling or order. If the DoD official determines that no further legal review of or challenge to the court's ruling or order will be sought, the affected DoD personnel shall comply with the request, demand, or order. If directed by the appropriate DoD official, however, the affected DoD personnel shall respectfully decline to comply with the demand. See United States ex rel. Touhy v. Ragen, 340 U.S. 462 (1951).

4. Fees. Consistent with the guidelines in DoD Instruction 7230.7 (reference (f)), the appropriate officials designated in paragraph F.1. are authorized to charge reasonable fees, as established by regulation and to the extent not prohibited by law, to parties seeking, by request or demand, official DoD information not otherwise available under the DoD Freedom of Information Act Program (reference (g)). Such fees, in amounts calculated to reimburse the Government for the expense of providing such information, may include the costs of time expended by DoD employees to process and respond to the request or demand; attorney time for reviewing the request or demand and any information located in response thereto and for related legal work in connection with the request or demand; and expenses generated by materials and equipment used to search for, produce, and copy the responsive information. See Oppenheimer Fund, Inc. v. Sanders, 437 U.S. 340 (1978).

5. **Expert or Opinion Testimony**. DoD personnel shall not provide, with or without compensation, opinion or expert testimony concerning official DoD information, subjects, or activities, except on behalf of the United States or a party represented by the Department of Justice. Upon a showing by the requestor of exceptional need or unique circumstances and that the anticipated testimony will not be adverse to the interests of the Department of Defense or the United States, the appropriate DoD official designated in paragraph F.1. may, in writing, grant special authorization for DoD personnel to appear and testify at no expense to the United States. If, despite the final determination of the responsible DoD official, a court of competent jurisdiction, or other appropriate authority, orders the appearance and expert or opinion testimony of DoD personnel, the personnel shall notify the responsible DoD official of such order. If the DoD official determines that no further legal review of or challenge to the court's order will be sought, the affected DoD personnel shall comply with the order. If directed by the appropriate DoD official, however, the affected DoD personnel shall respectfully decline to comply with the demand. See United States ex rel. Touhy v. Ragen, 340 U.S. 462 (1951).

G. EFFECTIVE DATE AND IMPLEMENTATION

This Directive is effective immediately. Forward two copies of implementing documents to the General Counsel, DoD, within 120 days.

William H. Taft, IV
Deputy Secretary of Defense

Howard Teicher

October 6, 1997

United States Court of Appeals
For the District of Columbia Circuit

FILED OCT 0 6 1993

RON GARVIN
CLERK

Memorandum for the Independent Counsel

From   HOWARD TEICHER

REGARDING Correction to Independent
            Counsel Report

For the record, please note that on page 97, second paragraph, the report states "...McFarlane, accompanied by North, briefed President Reagan, Vice President Bush and Regan on the Tehran mission..." omitting the fact that I also accompanied McFarlane to this Oval Office meeting.

United States Court of Appeals
For the District of Columbia Circuit

FILED OCT 0 6 1993

RON GARVIN
CLERK

IN THE UNITED STATES COURT OF APPEALS
FOR THE DISTRICT OF COLUMBIA CIRCUIT

Division for the Purpose of
Appointing Special Prosecutors
Ethics in Government Act of 1978, as Amended

In Re: *IN RE: Oliver L. North, et al.*
              Teicher Fee Application.   Division No. 86-6

Before: Sentelle, Presiding; Butzner and Sneed, Senior
              Circuit Judges

On July 23, 1993, Howard Teicher applied to the Division for reimbursement of attorneys' fees and costs pursuant to Section 593(f) of The Ethics in Government Act, 28 USC Section 591 *et seq.*, as Amended ("the Act").

On July 29, 1993, The Division issued an Order notifying the Attorney General of the request by Howard Teicher, a subject of the investigation conducted by independent counsel, for an award of attorneys' fees incurred by him during the subject investigation. The Court directed the Attorney General to file a written evaluation of the request for attorneys' fees analyzing for each expense: (A) the sufficiency of the document; (B) the need or justification for the underlying item; and (C) the reasonableness of the amount of money requested.

On September 15, 1993, the Department of Justice ("the Department") filed its written response to the Division. In its response the Department stated, *inter alia*,

> In this case, Howard Teicher, a former member of the National Security Council staff, seeks government reimbursement of about $30,000 in attorneys' fees and expenses under the Ethics in Government Act, 28 U.S.C. Section 593(f). As we now show, his fee application, at least in its current form, must be denied. Teicher is entitled, at most, to a very substantially reduced fee award, if this Court, in its discretion, allows him to file a renewed application that is more appropriately tailored to the Ethics Act's particular requirements and limitations.

Department's Evaluation of Teicher's Fee Request at page 2 (emphasis added).

The Department's response goes on to state that:

> the fee application's main problem is that most of Teicher's fees were incurred in connection with the multiple congressional Iran/Contra investigations, not the Independent Counsel's investigation.

Id., (emphasis added).

However, as the Fee Application makes clear, no problem exists which would preclude the Division from exercising its discretion and awarding Mr. Teicher reimbursement solely for the portion of his attorneys' fees which were incurred because he was a subject of the investigation conducted by the Independent Counsel.

Indeed, throughout his Fee Application, Mr. Teicher repeatedly emphasized that *he has already been reimbursed for a portion of his attorneys' fees and costs* by the Department pursuant to 28 C.F.R. Sections 50.15 and 50.16, as amended, subject to the Civil Division's Administrative Directive on Retention and Payment of Private Counsel. *See* Teicher Fee Application at 3.

Exhibit A to Teicher's Fee Application, is a letter from Stuart M. Gerson, then Assistant Attorney General, Civil Division. In that letter, Mr. Gerson explicitly stated that reimbursement is appropriate for attorney fees incurred by Mr. Teicher in connection with his testimony before the Senate Select Committee on Intelligence, the Senate Select Committee on Secret Military Assistance to Iran and the Nicaraguan Opposition, and the House of Representatives Select Committee to Investigate Covert Arms Transactions With Iran.

> Reimbursement will <u>not</u> be allowed with regard to your testimony before the Tower Commission, the grand jury, and the district court, or for press contacts <u>or other matters not directly associated with your testimony before the congressional committees</u>.

Teicher Fee Application, Exhibit A (emphasis added).

Mr. Teicher <u>does not</u> seek reimbursement under the Act for the same attorneys' fees and costs he incurred in connection with his testimony before the congressional committees. As is clear from his Fee Application, he has already been reimbursed for those legal expenses.

Instead he requests only that the Special Panel exercise its judicial discretion and order that reasonable attorneys' fees and costs be awarded under the Act for attorneys' fees and costs which were incurred because of the investigation conducted by Independent Counsel Lawrence Walsh into the Iran-Contra affair. Mr. Teicher agrees that he is entitled, at most, to a very substantially reduced fee award from the total $30,000 figure determined by the Department to be the amount he is now seeking.

Accordingly, for the reasons set forth in his Fee Application, Howard Teicher submits that he satisfies the requirements of the Act and respectfully requests the Special Panel to exercise its judicial discretion and order that he be awarded reasonable attorneys fees and costs pursuant to Section 593(f) of the Ethics in Government Act, 28 USC Section 591 *et seq.*

At such time, Mr. Teicher and the law firm of Dunnells, Duvall & Porter will be in a position to review his legal bills to determine with specificity, which portion of his total legal costs were attributable to the investigation of the Independent Counsel, and which were attributable to the multiple congressional Iran/Contra investigations. Mr. Teicher will then submit a revised bill to the Special Panel for review by the Department under the criteria set forth in the Act.

Respectfully submitted:

Gayle Radley Teicher, Esq.

4331 Reno Road, N.W.
Washington, D.C. 20008
Telephone: 202-363-6555

United States Court of Appeals
For the District of Columbia Circuit

FILED NOV 0 2 1993

RON GARVIN
CLERK

IN THE UNITED STATES COURT OF APPEALS
FOR THE DISTRICT OF COLUMBIA CIRCUIT

Division For the Purpose of
Appointing Independent Counsels

Ethics in Government Act of 1978, As Amended

IN RE: Oliver L North, et al., Amended Application of
           Howard Teicher For Reimbursement of Attorneys'
           Fees. Division No. 86-6

BEFORE: Sentelle, Presiding, Butzner and Sneed, Senior
           Circuit Judges

Table of Headings

I. MR. TEICHER SEEKS REIMBURSEMENT SOLELY FOR
THOSE LEGAL FEES AND COSTS ATTRIBUTABLE TO THE
INVESTIGATION CONDUCTED BY LAWRENCE WALSH INTO
THE IRAN-CONTRA AFFAIR   P.3

II. MR. TEICHER ASKS THE COURT TO ISSUE A NARROW
RULING WHICH FINDS THAT HE OTHERWISE SATISFIES THE
REQUIREMENTS OF THE ACT AND DIRECTS HIM TO PROVIDE
SUFFICIENT DOCUMENTATION FOR REIMBURSABLE FEES   p.6

III. SECTIONS 594(h)(2) AND 593(f)(1) OF THE ACT
AND THE COURT'S ORDERS OF AUGUST 5, 6 AND SEPTEMBER 24,
1993 SUPPORT THE ASSERTION THAT MR. TEICHER WAS A
"SUBJECT" OF THE INDEPENDENT COUNSEL'S INVESTIGATION   P.8

IV. BOTH THE ORDINARY USAGE OF THE WORD "SUBJECT"
AND SECTION 9-11.150 OF THE DEPARTMENT OF JUSTICE
MANUAL SUPPORT MR. TEICHER'S ASSERTION THAT HE WAS
A SUBJECT BECAUSE ACTIVITIES IN WHICH HE WAS A
CENTRAL PARTICIPANT WENT TO THE CORE OF MR. WALSH'S
INVESTIGATION AND BECAME THE BASIS FOR INDICTMENTS
RETURNED AGAINST OTHER OFFICIALS   P.13

V. MR. TEICHER WAS CLEARLY A "SUBJECT" OF THE
INVESTIGATION BASED ON THE POTENTIAL FOR CRIMINAL
CHARGES OF OBSTRUCTION, AIDING AND ABETTING AND
CO-CONSPIRACY BECAUSE ACTIVITIES IN WHICH HE
PARTICIPATED AND HIS OWN CONDUCT WERE AT ISSUE   P.16

VI. MR. WALSH'S FINAL REPORT REFLECTS THE CENTRALITY
AND SERIOUSNESS OF THE ACTIVITIES, CONDUCT AND EVENTS
IN WHICH MR. TEICHER WAS INVOLVED AS REFLECTED BY IT'S
EXTENSIVE RELIANCE ON HIS NOTES, MEMORANDA AND TESTIMONY   P.18

VII. NOTWITHSTANDING MR. TEICHER'S REASONABLE BELIEF
THAT HE WAS A "SUBJECT" BECAUSE OF CONDUCT AND
ACTIVITIES IN WHICH HE ENGAGED WITH "TARGETS,"
HE TESTIFIED WILLINGLY, COMPLETELY AND TRUTHFULLY   P.21

IN THE UNITED STATES COURT OF APPEALS
FOR THE DISTRICT OF COLUMBIA CIRCUIT
Division For the Purpose of
Appointing Independent Counsels
Ethics in Government Act of 1978, As Amended

IN RE: Oliver L. North, et al., Amended Application of
            Howard Teicher For Reimbursement of Attorneys'
            Fees. Division No. 86-6

BEFORE: Sentelle, Presiding, Butzner and Sneed, Senior
            Circuit Judges

AMENDED FEE APPLICATION

This Application is in response to the Special Panel's
Order of October 4, 1993 which granted Howard Teicher the
opportunity to submit a renewed Application for Attorneys'
Fees pursuant to Section 593(f) of The Ethics in Government
Act, 28 USC Section 591 *et seq.*, ("the Act").

According to the Court's Order, two issues remain
outstanding: the exact amount of attorneys' fees and costs
Mr. Teicher incurred as a result of Independent Counsel
Lawrence Walsh's investigation and whether Mr. Teicher is a
"subject" under the Act.

With respect to the exact amount of attorneys' fees and
costs, this amended Fee Application clarifies that Mr.
Teicher seeks only to be reimbursed under the Act for

attorneys' fees and costs which he incurred as a result of the investigation conducted by Independent Counsel Walsh into the Iran-Contra affair.

With respect to whether Mr. Teicher was a "subject" of the Independent Counsel's investigation into the Iran-Contra affair for purposes of the Ethics in Government Act, Mr. Teicher fully supports this contention by setting forth:

> (1) Sections 594(h)(2) and 593(f)(1) of the Act and the Court's Orders of August 5, 6 and September 24, 1993;

> (2) the facts which demonstrate that even according to the ordinary usage of the word, Mr. Teicher was a "subject" of Mr. Walsh's investigation;

> (3) the policy guidelines set out in Section 9-11.150 of the Department of Justice Manual which make clear that conduct and activities in which Mr. Teicher was a central participant went to the core of the investigation and became the basis for indictments returned against other officials;

> (4) the facts which show that he was exposed to possible indictment based, *inter alia*, on charges of obstruction, aiding and abetting and co-conspiracy because he was a "subject" of the investigation and not a mere witness; and

> (5) the fact that Mr. Walsh's Final Report itself reflects the seriousness of the activities, conduct and events in which Mr. Teicher was centrally involved as reflected by it's extensive reliance on his notes, memoranda and testimony.

I.   MR. TEICHER SEEKS REIMBURSEMENT SOLELY
FOR THOSE LEGAL FEES AND COSTS ATTRIBUTABLE
TO THE INVESTIGATION CONDUCTED BY INDEPENDENT
COUNSEL, LAWRENCE WALSH INTO THE IRAN-CONTRA
AFFAIR

The Ethics in Government Act provides for reimbursement
for attorneys' fees for individuals who satisfy certain
requirements:

> Upon the request of an individual who is the
> subject of an investigation conducted by an
> independent counsel pursuant to this chapter, the
> division of the court may, if no indictment is
> brought against such individual pursuant to that
> investigation, award reimbursement for those
> reasonable attorneys' fees incurred by that
> individual during that investigation which would
> not have been incurred but for the requirements of
> this chapter. The division of the court shall
> notify the Attorney General of any request for
> attorneys' fees under this subsection.

28 USC Section 593(f)(1) (emphasis added).

The Act goes on to provide that:

> The division of the court may direct the
> Attorney General to file a written evaluation of
> any request for attorneys' fees under this
> subsection, analyzing for each expense--
>
> (A) the sufficiency of the documentation;
> (B) the need or justification for the
>   underlying item; and
> (C) the reasonableness of the amount of money
>   requested.

28 USC Section 593(f)(2).

On July 29, 1993, The Division issued an Order notifying the Attorney General of the request by Howard Teicher, a subject of the investigation conducted by independent counsel, for an award of attorneys' fees incurred by him during the subject investigation. The Court directed the Attorney General to file a written evaluation of the request for attorneys' fees.

On September 15, 1993, the Department of Justice ("the Department") filed its written response to the Division. In its response the Department stated, *inter alia,*

> In this case, Howard Teicher, a former member of the National Security Council staff, seeks government reimbursement of about $30,000 in attorneys' fees and expenses under the Ethics in Government Act, 28 U.S.C. Section 593(f). As we now show, his fee application, at least in its current form, must be denied. Teicher is entitled, at most, to a very substantially reduced fee award, if this Court, in its discretion, allows him to file a renewed application that is more appropriately tailored to the Ethics Act's particular requirements and limitations.

Department's Evaluation of Teicher's Fee Request at page 2 (emphasis added).

The Department's response goes on to state that:

> the fee application's main problem is that most of Teicher's fees were incurred in connection with the multiple congressional Iran/Contra investigations, not the Independent Counsel's investigation.

Id., (emphasis added).

On October 6, 1993, Mr. Teicher responded to the Department's evaluation. He repeated his request set forth in his original Fee Application that he be reimbursed <u>solely for the portion of his attorneys' fees which were incurred because he was a subject of the investigation conducted by the Independent Counsel</u>. Mr. Teicher reiterates that he <u>agrees</u> with the Department that he is entitled, at most, to a "*very substantially reduced fee award.*"

As set forth more fully in his original Fee Application, Mr. Teicher has already received partial reimbursement for some of his attorneys' fees and expenses which were incurred as a result of the Iran-Contra affair from the Department in the amount of $13,619.58 pursuant to 28 C.F.R. Sections 50.15 and 50.16, as amended. As set forth fully in the original Fee application, those fees were subject to a cap.

<u>Mr. Teicher did not, however, receive *any* reimbursement from the Department, *partial or otherwise*, for fees incurred as a result of the investigation conducted by the Independent Counsel.</u> Indeed, Mr. Teicher's request for reimbursement for fees attributable to the Independent Counsel was <u>specifically denied</u> by the Department.

Once again, Mr. Teicher emphasizes that he does *not* seek reimbursement under the Act for *any* attorneys' fees and costs which were incurred in connection with his testimony before the congressional committees or elsewhere, but <u>only for those attributable to the investigation conducted by the</u>

Independent Counsel.   Mr. Teicher does not seek
reimbursement under the Act to make up any "shortfall" due
to the Department's cap on fees.

Instead he requests only that the Special Panel
exercise its judicial discretion and order that reasonable
attorneys' fees and costs be awarded under the Act solely
for attorneys' fees and costs which he incurred as a subject
of the investigation conducted by Independent Counsel
Lawrence Walsh.

II.   MR. TEICHER ASKS THE COURT TO ISSUE A NARROW RULING WHICH FINDS THAT HE OTHERWISE SATISFIES THE REQUIREMENTS OF THE ACT AND DIRECTS HIM TO PROVIDE SUFFICIENT DOCUMENTATION FOR REIMBURSABLE FEES

As part of his original Fee Application, Mr. Teicher
submitted copies of all billings which he received from his
attorney's, Robert Bennett and Carl Rauh, former law firm,
Dunnells, Duval & Porter.   However, for a variety of
reasons, some of which are set forth in the original Fee
Application and the attachments thereto, Mr. Teicher has not
received from the firm detailed billing statements which are
limited to the investigation of the Independent Counsel.

Were the Court to exercise its discretion and Order
that Mr. Teicher be reimbursed solely for that portion of
his attorneys' fees and costs attributable to the

6

Independent Counsel, Dunnells, Duval & Porter will thereafter provide sufficient documentation of contemporaneous time records of hours worked and rates claimed which will be submitted by Mr. Teicher for evaluation by the Court. At this point, however, he is without the means to determine with precision which fees and costs are attributable to the Independent Counsel and which are attributable to the other investigations.

For the reasons set forth below and in his applications of July 23 and October 6, 1993 and the attachments thereto, Mr. Teicher submits that he meets the requirements of the Act. He requests the Court to order that he be awarded only such attorneys' fees as were reasonably incurred as a result of the Independent Counsel's investigation.

He respectfully requests the Court to exercise its discretion and issue a narrow Order which: (1) finds that he fully satisfies the requirements of the Act; and (2) permits him to submit a renewed application that conforms to the requirements of the Act by providing documentation which sets forth with precision the dates on which relevant legal work was performed, the nature of the services provided, or the amount of time counsel spent on matters related to the Independent Counsel's investigation.

III. SECTIONS 594(h)(2) AND 593(f)(1) OF THE
ACT AND THE COURT'S ORDERS OF AUGUST 5, 6 AND
SEPTEMBER 24, 1993 SUPPORT THE ASSERTION THAT
MR. TEICHER WAS A "SUBJECT" OF THE
INDEPENDENT COUNSEL'S INVESTIGATION

For the reasons set forth below and in his original Fee
Application and the attachments thereto, Mr. Teicher submits
that he satisfies the requirements of the Act and
respectfully requests the Court to exercise its discretion
and grant him reimbursement for reasonable attorneys' fees
and costs attributable to the investigation of the
Independent Counsel.

As will be factually supported below, Mr. Teicher was
clearly a "subject" of the Independent Counsel's broad
investigation into the Iran-Contra affair. Mr. Teicher asks
the Court to deem him a "subject" in accordance with
Sections 594(h)(2) and 593(f)(1) of the Act and the Court's
Orders of August 5 and 6, 1993 and September 24, 1993. In
addition, this contention is also supported by the policy
guidelines set out in Section 9-11.150 of the Department of
Justice Manual for grand jury witnesses and the facts set
forth below and in his Fee Applications of July 23 and
October 6, 1993 and the attachments thereto.

Section 594(h)(1)(B) of the Act provides:

> [B]efore the termination of the independent
> counsel's office under section 596(b) [28 USC
> Section 596(b)], file a final report with the
> division of the court, setting forth fully and
> completely a description of the work of the
> independent counsel, including the disposition of
> all cases brought, and the reasons for not
> prosecuting any matter within the prosecutorial
> jurisdiction of such independent counsel.

Section 594(h)(2) of the Act provides:

> Disclosure of information in reports. The
> division of the court may release to the Congress,
> the public, or any appropriate person, such
> portions of a report made under this subsection as
> the division of the court considers appropriate.
> The division of the court shall make such orders
> as are appropriate <u>to protect the rights of any</u>
> <u>individual named in such report</u> and to prevent
> undue interference with any pending prosecution.
> The division of the court may make any portion of
> a final report filed under paragraph (1)(B)
> available to any <u>individual named in such report</u>
> <u>for the purposes of receiving within a time limit</u>
> <u>set by the division of the court any comments or</u>
> <u>factual information that such individual may</u>
> <u>submit.</u> Such comments and factual information, in
> whole or in part, may, in the discretion of the
> division of the court, be included as an appendix
> to such final report.

(emphasis added)

On August 9, 1993, Mr. Teicher was sent a letter from

the Clerk of the Court and a copy of an Order filed on

August 5, issued by the Court which authorized Mr. Teicher

or his attorney to examine relevant portions of Mr. Walsh's

Final Report and gave him the right to submit any comment or

factual information for possible inclusion as an appendix.

This August 5th Order was issued under seal. <u>Only</u> <u>individuals</u> "named in such report" were given the opportunity to review the Final Report or received notice from the Court that a Final Report had been filed.

The Order provided that the Clerk:

> shall, for the purposes set forth in 28 U.S.C. Section 594(h)(2), make available the relevant portions of the Final Report, as indicated below . . .to the following individuals named in the Report, or to their attorneys. . . . The Clerk shall advise <u>each named individual of their right</u> <u>under the Act</u> to submit any comment or factual information for possible inclusion as an appendix to the Final Report. . .

(emphasis added)

In a second Order filed on August 6, 1993, the Court ordered that Howard Teicher be added to the list of individuals to whom the Court directed disclosure of the contents of the Final Report.

In an Order filed under seal on September 24, 1993, the Court granted the motion of former President Reagan for an extension of time in which to respond to the Final Report and gave him a 60-day extension of time, to and including December 3, 1993, to make appropriate motions or otherwise respond to the Final Report.

The Court further ordered, on its own motion, that "all parties <u>named in the Final Report</u> who are <u>subject to the</u> <u>Court's Order</u> of August 5, 1993 be granted an extension of time until and including December 3, 1993 to respond to the

Independent Counsel's Final Report." (emphasis added)   Mr. Teicher was granted such an extension.

Although Mr. Teicher does not know who, besides himself, were the other individuals both named in the Final Report and subject to the Court's Order, it is clear from the September 24 Order that former President Ronald Reagan, at least, is one of them.

Besides Mr. Teicher, presumably some of the others who are also listed in the Final Report and <u>subject to the Court's Order</u> include such individuals as: Caspar Weinberger, Robert McFarlane, John Poindexter, Edwin Meese, Donald Regan, George Shultz and Oliver North.

The language of Section 594(h)(2) of the Ethics in Government Act regarding individuals named in the report should be compared to the language regarding subjects in Section 593(f)(1).   <u>Only very selected individuals were subjected to the Court's Order and permitted to review the Final Report and offer comments. Were he not a subject, he would not have been permitted to review the Final Report nor been subject to the Court's Order.</u>

Mr. Teicher submits that pursuant to Section 594(h)(2), the Court's Orders and the facts of the case, he should be deemed a "subject" under the Act. Conduct and activities in which he was a central participant was a basis for investigation, his conduct itself was at issue in the investigation and he was himself exposed to possible indictment for a significant and relevant period of time.

11

The Act provides for reimbursement for attorneys' fees for individuals who satisfy certain requirements:

> Upon the request of <u>an individual who is the subject of an investigation conducted by an independent counsel</u> pursuant to this chapter, the division of the court may, if no indictment is brought against <u>such individual</u> pursuant to that investigation, award reimbursement for those reasonable attorneys' fees incurred by that individual during that investigation which would not have been incurred but for the requirements of this chapter.

28 USC Section 593(f)(1) (emphasis added).

The language of the Act, as set forth in Section 593(f)(1) provides reimbursement for attorneys' fees for "an individual who is the subject of an investigation conducted by an independent counsel". Section 594(h)(2) directs the Court "to protect the rights of any individual named in such report". <u>Mr. Teicher is both named in the report and subject to the Court's Order. Mr. Teicher clearly is an individual subject to Section 594(h)(2) of the Act. Mr. Teicher should be deemed a "subject" by the Court.</u>

Mr. Teicher served Independent Counsel Walsh with a copy of his Fee Application on July 23, 1993. Nevertheless, Mr. Walsh has not contested Mr. Teicher's assertion that he was a subject of his investigation. Nor were repeated telephone calls to Mr. Walsh's office on behalf of Mr. Teicher ever returned.

Mr. Teicher submits that Mr. Walsh has had sufficient opportunity to oppose Mr. Teicher's Fee Application which

12

was filed on July 23 but has chosen not to.   Instead
pursuant to Section 594(h)(2), Mr. Teicher was added to the
list of individuals who were authorized to examine relevant
portions of the Final Report and subject to the Court's
Order.

IV.   BOTH THE ORDINARY USAGE OF THE WORD
"SUBJECT" AND SECTION 9-11.150 OF THE
DEPARTMENT OF JUSTICE MANUAL SUPPORT MR.
TEICHER'S ASSERTION THAT HE WAS A SUBJECT
BECAUSE ACTIVITIES IN WHICH HE WAS A CENTRAL
PARTICIPANT WENT TO THE CORE OF MR. WALSH'S
INVESTIGATION AND BECAME THE BASIS FOR
INDICTMENTS RETURNED AGAINST OTHER OFFICIALS

As factually supported throughout this amended
Application and by the original Fee Application and
attachments thereto, consistent even with the ordinary usage
of the word, Mr. Teicher was most certainly a "subject" of
Mr. Walsh's broad investigation into the Iran-Contra affair
- at least for a significant portion of it.

Under the policy guidelines set out in Section 9-11.150
of the Department of Justice Manual for grand jury
witnesses, a "subject" of an investigation is a person whose
conduct is within the scope of the grand jury's
investigation. A "target" is a person as to whom the
prosecutor or the grand jury has substantial evidence

13

linking him/her to the commission of a crime and who, in the judgment of the prosecutor, is a putative defendant.

Mr. Teicher's own conduct was clearly within the scope of the Independent Counsel's and grand jury's investigation into the Iran-Contra affair. He was centrally involved in activities which became the basis for indictments returned against other officials in the Reagan national security bureaucracy.

At minimum, by virtue of the laws on obstruction, aiding and abetting and co-conspiracy, *inter alia,* it is inconceivable that he was not a subject of the investigation at least until such time as the grand jury and/or the Independent Counsel resolved that he had innocently and lawfully engaged in such activities or conduct.

The Final Report of the Independent Counsel relies extensively on activities in which Mr. Teicher was centrally involved and on his notes, memoranda of conversation and testimony to bolster Mr. Walsh's findings, *inter alia,* that senior members of the Reagan administration misrepresented and tried to cover-up their own and the president's involvement in the Iran initiative by scape-goating members of the staff of the National Security Council (the "NSC").

Significantly, Mr. Walsh relies on Mr. Teicher's contemporaneous notes which recount, *inter alia,* that notwithstanding what was said later, President Reagan's knew in May 1986 that arms were being exchanged for the release of American hostages when he gave orders for the plane

carrying arms to turn around mid-way from Israel to Teheran
if more hostages were not released.   The president gave
these orders at the same time that Howard Teicher, Robert
McFarlane, Oliver North and others were meeting in Teheran
with representatives of the government of Iran.   Mr.
Teicher's notes report this information.

For a significant and relevant time in Mr. Walsh's
investigation, he was a subject, *not* a mere witness nor a
potential witness. As set forth more fully in the original
Fee Application and the attachments thereto, *prior to and
after Mr. Walsh's appointment, White House counsel
specifically declined to advise Mr. Teicher about activities
in which he had engaged as part of his official duties as a
member of the staff of the NSC.*

He retained counsel on December 8, 1986 to defend
himself against possible prosecution only *after* the
president announced on December 2 that he had asked the
Attorney General to apply to the court for the appointment
of an independent counsel.   A significant and relevant
portion of the legal fees and costs were incurred by Mr.
Teicher *after* Mr. Walsh was appointed on December 19 in
defending him against possible prosecution.

Mr. Teicher was centrally involved in the Iran
initiative. Conduct and activities in which he was an
active participant were most definitely within the scope of
Mr. Walsh's investigation and his testimony about what he
knew and what he observed was within the scope of the grand

15

jury's investigation.   He was not a mere witness.   Other individuals were subject to indictment for their participation in the same conduct or activities, which included, *inter alia*, the trip to Iran and the preparation of the chronologies.

Regardless of whether Mr. Teicher was eventually dropped by the Independent Counsel to the level of a "witness," at least until the investigation was fleshed out by the facts, he was a "subject" and meets the standard definition contained in the Department of Justice Manual. In contrast, based on the same conduct, events or activities or arising out of the same events in which Mr. Teicher participated, others were elevated to the level of a "target."

Given the extent of public and private misrepresentation by senior officials of the Reagan administration and others, Mr. Teicher *reasonably believed* that his status could similarly be elevated.

V.   MR. TEICHER WAS CLEARLY A "SUBJECT" OF
THE INVESTIGATION BASED ON THE POTENTIAL FOR
CRIMINAL CHARGES OF OBSTRUCTION, AIDING AND
ABETTING AND CO-CONSPIRACY BECAUSE ACTIVITIES
IN WHICH HE PARTICIPATED AND HIS OWN CONDUCT
WERE AT ISSUE

As is set forth in detail in his original Fee Application and the attachments thereto, Mr. Teicher participated in the secret mission to Teheran by taking detailed notes, preparing memoranda of conversations and engaging in substantive discussions with the Iranians. He returned to Washington and went almost immediately to a meeting in the Oval Office to brief President Reagan, Vice President Bush, Chief of Staff Donald Regan and Admiral John Poindexter, together with Robert McFarlane and Oliver North. He engaged in other discussions with Vice President Bush about the Iran initiative.

After Attorney General Meese went before the public on November 25, 1986 to announce that there had been a diversion of funds to the Nicaraguan Contras, senior members of the Reagan administration and their subordinates began an active campaign of diverting blame to the NSC, falsely accused Mr. Teicher personally, *inter alia,* of being the "architect of the Iran affair," North's "boss," and of being one of the "cowboys" on the NSC staff which had secretly "gone operational" without the knowledge of the president, vice president, chief of staff, secretary of state or secretary of defense.

Mr. Teicher traveled to Teheran with Robert McFarlane and Oliver North, at the direction of Admiral Poindexter <u>all of whom became "targets" of the investigation or putative defendants</u> and whom Mr. Teicher believes were subject to investigation on charges of conspiracy, obstruction and aiding and abetting, *inter alia*. He participated in preparing the chronologies with them and met with other senior administration officials regarding the trip to Iran and the president's initiative. *This conduct was a main focus of the investigation.*

VI. MR. WALSH'S FINAL REPORT REFLECTS THE CENTRALITY AND SERIOUSNESS OF THE ACTIVITIES, CONDUCT AND EVENTS IN WHICH MR. TEICHER WAS INVOLVED AS REFLECTED BY IT'S EXTENSIVE RELIANCE ON HIS NOTES, MEMORANDA AND TESTIMONY

At outset of the Iran-Contra scandal Mr. Teicher was falsely identified by senior members of the Reagan administration and others as Oliver North's "boss" at the NSC and as the "architect" of the Iran affair. It is reasonable to believe that at least for a significant and relevant period of time, Mr. Walsh believed that Mr. Teicher was, in fact, North's superior on the staff of the NSC. Mr. Teicher clearly participated in conduct and activities which were later charged against others in indictments, for at minimum, planning and participating in the trip to Teheran and for the preparation of the chronologies.

Mr. Teicher acted on the reasonable assumption that he had participated in activities which might be considered to be criminal and retained counsel who represented him against potential criminal liability. Given the facts, he did not believe that he was merely a witness. His conduct and activities formed the basis for indictments and charges which were brought against others or which might have been brought against others and went to the heart of the matter.

Indeed Mr. Walsh's Final Report itself reflects the seriousness of the activities, conduct and events in which Mr. Teicher was centrally involved. This is reflected by the Final Report's extensive reliance on Mr. Teicher's notes, memoranda and testimony. Other people became targets, or might have become targets based on the same conduct, activities, events or activities arising out of this conduct. Under the facts of this case, it is inconceivable that Mr. Teicher's status, at least for a substantial and relevant period of time was not that of a subject.

Further, as was set forth more fully above, Mr. Walsh has had the opportunity to contest Mr. Teicher's assertion that he was a subject of Mr. Walsh's investigation into the Iran-Contra affair, but has chosen not to.

Even if Mr. Teicher's status was ultimately downgraded to a witness, and a credible witness, the fact that the Independent Counsel or grand jury later dropped him from "subject" to "witness" should not prevent him from otherwise being reimbursed under the Act for attorneys' fees incurred *while he was a subject*.

Congressional intent in providing for reimbursement for reasonable attorneys' fees and costs in limited cases would not be served if Mr. Teicher were denied the opportunity to be reimbursed for attorneys' fees simply because his activities and conduct were <u>ultimately</u> determined to be innocent and his involvement in criminal acts peripheral. The facts of the case support his assertion that he was a subject.

Mr. Teicher has no knowledge whether the Independent Counsel had substantial evidence linking him to the commission of any crime or whether he became a "target" at any point.

For the reasons set forth above and in his original Fee Application and the attachments thereto, <u>Mr. Teicher submits</u> <u>that he has demonstrated and factually supported the</u> <u>contention that his conduct was clearly within the scope of</u> <u>Mr. Walsh's and the grand jury's investigation into the</u> <u>Iran-Contra affair and that he was a "subject" of the</u> <u>investigation</u>.

Again, Mr. Walsh has had sufficient opportunity to oppose Mr. Teicher's Fee Application which was filed on July 23 but has chosen not to. As is now clear in the Final Report, Mr. Teicher has been absolved of *any* wrong doing, notwithstanding the fact that he was a subject of the investigation.

It is also clear that Mr. Walsh <u>ultimately</u> came to find Mr. Teicher to be credible in that so many of the facts underlying the conclusions of his Final Report come directly from Mr. Teicher's notes, memoranda or testimony.

> **VII. NOTWITHSTANDING MR. TEICHER'S REASONABLE BELIEF THAT HE WAS A "SUBJECT" BECAUSE OF CONDUCT AND ACTIVITIES IN WHICH HE ENGAGED WITH "TARGETS", HE TESTIFIED WILLINGLY, COMPLETELY AND TRUTHFULLY**

Notwithstanding Mr. Teicher's reasonable belief that he was a subject of the investigation because of conduct and activities in which he engaged with others, he testified willingly, completely and truthfully.

<u>His willing cooperation was in marked contrast to many of his colleagues within the national security bureaucracy and senior officials of the Reagan administration who resisted disclosing what they knew or producing notes and memoranda which might prove relevant to the various investigation</u>.

After the Iran initiative became the Iran-Contra scandal, senior officials in the offices of the president, vice president, the Departments of State and Defense and other government agencies, falsely claimed to have had no knowledge of what had transpired.

Apparently, there was a great deal of sudden memory loss. No one seemed to remember anything - except that the allegedly all-powerful NSC staff had "gone operational" and had been running U.S. policy, secretly, for many of the preceding years. Controversial national security decisions had allegedly been made at a "lower level." No one was in charge. All of the key principals, had been "out of the loop," at least according to then Vice President Bush.

Despite President Reagan's professed desire to get all the facts out, and the vice president's stated willingness to "let the chips fall" where they may, even if the "truth hurt," senior members of the Reagan administration ran for cover to avoid becoming embroiled in the controversy and misled members of congress, the Independent Counsel and the media about their knowledge of and involvement in the Iran-Contra affair.

> VIII.   CONGRESS INTENDED THAT AN UNINDICTED
> "SUBJECT" WHO MEETS THE REQUIREMENTS OF THE
> ACT AND WHO INCURS LEGAL EXPENSES, APART FROM
> THOSE INHERENT IN EVERY INDEPENDENT COUNSEL
> INVESTIGATION, SHOULD BE FULLY EXONERATED
> AND HAVE HIS REPUTATION RESTORED

The Independent Counsel mechanism was designed to reach certain goals which included, *inter alia,* <u>affording protection to the reputation of any person subject to</u>

investigation.   In the aftermath of the scandal, Mr.

Teicher's colleagues and superiors in the national security

bureaucracy asserted their constitutional rights while other

government officials acted to deflect attention away from

themselves and onto the NSC staff - as Mr. Walsh's Final

Report *now* makes clear.

During the height of the scandal in late 1986 - early

1987, however, at least one senior official in the Reagan

administration, as part of the effort to scapegoat the NSC

staff,   falsely   asserted,   *inter   alia,*   that   the   Iran

initiative was the result of a plot between the state of

Israel   and   Jews   working   in   the   national   security

bureaucracy, rather than an initiative of the President of

the United States.

Mr. Teicher, who is Jewish, was falsely accused of

being a traitor to his country and a spy for a foreign

government.   Oliver "Buck" Revel, then FBI Associate Deputy

Director   for   Counterintelligence   and   Counterterrorism,

stated *on the record* that this accusation was baseless and

part of a pattern anti-Semitic character assassination which

was taking place.

Mr. Teicher's reputation was substantially harmed by

these efforts and other efforts by senior members of the

Reagan administration to deflect attention away from the

president and themselves by scapegoating the NSC staff.

As set forth in greater detail in his original Fee

Application and the attachments thereto, Mr. Teicher's reputation was also recently attacked during the 1992 presidential campaign by members of the Reagan administration who went on to work in the Bush administration. During the campaign, the media reported that Mr. Teicher had earlier testified that the then vice president was more knowledgeable about the Iran initiative than he now claimed. Mr. Teicher was thrust once again into the public eye and was forced to defend himself against false accusations arising out of his involvement in the Iran affair.

Clearly, however, the public record is still ambiguous and Mr. Teicher's reputation continues to suffer. <u>Congress intended that an unindicted subject who otherwise meets the requirements of the Act who incurs legal expenses apart from those inherent in every Independent Counsel investigation, should be fully exonerated and have his reputation restored</u>.

Mr. Teicher did nothing unlawful or beyond the scope of his official duties. Nevertheless, no matter what else he does in his life, he will always be associated with the Iran affair. He will never regain what he lost, through no fault of his own.

Mr. Teicher welcomes the release of Mr. Walsh's Final Report. After its release, perhaps the record will finally unambiguously indicate that while Mr. Teicher was caught up in the scandal, he did nothing wrong. Perhaps then, finally he will be exonerated and his reputation will be restored.

IX.   MR.   TEICHER   WAS   SUBJECTED   TO   AN
INVESTIGATION   BY   MR.   WALSH   THAT   THE
DEPARTMENT   OF   JUSTICE   WOULD   NOT   HAVE
CONDUCTED   HAD   HE   BEEN   A   PRIVATE   CITIZEN,
SUBJECTED   TO   A   HARSHER   STANDARD   THAN   AN
ORDINARY   CITIZEN   AND   INCURRED   LEGAL   EXPENSES
NO   ORDINARY   CITIZEN   WOULD   HAVE   INCURRED   "BUT
FOR"   THE   REQUIREMENTS   OF   THE   ACT

Under   the   Act   and   the   controlling   case   law,   the
standard for awarding attorneys' fees in Independent Counsel
investigations   requires   proof   that   attorneys'   fees   are
"reasonable," adequately documented and would not have been
incurred "but for" the requirements of the Act.   *In re Meese*
907 F.2d 1192,1196 (D.C. Cir. 1990); *In re Donovan*, 877 F.2d
982, 994 (D.C. Cir. 1989); *In re Olson*, 884 F.2d 1415, 1428
(D.C. Cir. 1989); *In re Sealed Case*, 890 F.2d 451 (D.C. Cir.
1989); *In re Olson/Perry*, 892 F.2d 1073 (D.C. Cir. 1990).

In *In re Meese* 907 F.2d 1192 *supra* at 1196, the Court
stated that the Ethics in Government Act was amended to
allow for reimbursement for attorneys' fees because:

> Congress   learned   that   <u>certain   government
> officials</u> ... had been subjected to investigations
> by independent counsels that the Department of
> Justice would not have conducted had these
> officials been private citizens.... Thus, *these
> officials were· subjected to a harsher standard
> than   ordinary   citizens*   and   incurred   legal

expenses no ordinary citizen would have incurred, *but for* the independent counsel statute. <u>In such cases reasonable attorney fees should be awarded</u>.

H.R. Conf. Rep. No. 452, 100th Cong., 1st Sess. 31 (1987), U.S. Code Cong & Admin. News 1987, pp. 2150, 2197 (emphasis added), as cited in *In re Meese* 907 F.2d 1192 *supra* at 1196.

As is set forth more fully in his original Fee Application and the attachments thereto, Mr. Teicher was subjected to an investigation by Mr. Walsh that the Department of Justice would not have conducted had he been a private citizen. He was subjected to a harsher standard than an ordinary citizen and incurred legal expenses no ordinary citizen would have incurred, but for the requirements of the Act.

Congress intended reimbursement as a safeguard to compensate officials in the event that they incurred extraordinary expenses during a special prosecutor investigation <u>which eventually absolves them of any wrongdoing</u>. See *In re Nofziger*, 925 F. 2d 428 at 444.

Mr. Teicher did not engage in any activities which would have made him a subject or target of an independent criminal investigation by the Department <u>outside of the Act</u>. Mr. Teicher, however, came under suspicion and became a subject of the broad investigation of Independent Counsel Walsh. He was not indicted in connection with this or any other investigation. He would not have been similarly investigated outside of the Act.

With the benefit of counsel and because he was telling the truth, Mr. Teicher was able to resist efforts by senior Reagan administration officials and others to hide their own involvement in the scandal by diverting blame to the NSC staff.   Nevertheless, Mr. Teicher incurred extraordinary expenses defending himself against potential criminal liability which were directly attributable to the investigation of the Independent Counsel based on generalized suspicions arising from Mr. Teicher's participation in President Reagan's initiative to Iran. Mr. Teicher was never indicted.   On the contrary, his testimony, notes and memoranda of conversation are now being used to factually support the Final Report of the Independent Counsel.

In Mr. Teicher's case, the requirements of the Act are satisfied and Congressional intent would be served were the Court to exercise its discretion and order that he be granted reimbursement for attorneys' fees and costs attributable to the investigation of the Independent Counsel

Congressional intent was to grant such fees sparingly to correct an unequal application of the criminal law in cases where the Act subjected covered officials to investigation for criminal offenses for which ordinary citizens would not have been investigated or prosecuted. Such congressional intent is satisfied in Mr. Teicher's case.

In an address to the nation on December 2, 1986, President Reagan announced that he was urging Attorney General Edwin Meese to apply to the court for the appointment of an Independent Counsel to look into allegations of illegality in the sale of arms to Iran and the use of funds from these sales to assist the Contras. The president stated that if illegal acts were undertaken, those who did so would be brought to justice. In a statement made on December 19, 1986, he announced the appointment of Lawrence Walsh to serve as Independent Counsel.

The president promised his complete cooperation and said that he had instructed all members of his administration to cooperate fully with the investigation in order to ensure full and prompt disclosure. Over time and during the course of the investigation by the Independent Counsel, it became evident that Mr. Teicher had done nothing illegal, improper or beyond the scope of his official duties. At all relevant times, Mr. Teicher acted consistently with President Reagan's public pledge and his responsibilities as a public official.

As became clear during the months and years which followed the revelation that President Reagan had sent a special envoy to Teheran to meet with officials of the Iranian government, Mr. Teicher obeyed the letter and spirit of the law in performing his duties as a member of the staff of the National Security Council.

He risked his own life in going to Teheran only because he reasonably believed, based on what he was told by his superiors, that it might be the last opportunity to help save the American hostages. Mr. Teicher acted upon the reasonable belief that his superiors were acting within the course and scope of their authority in directing him to travel to Iran - at the direction of the President of the United States. At all times, Mr. Teicher served his country with honor, courage and distinction. He at least was willing to tell the truth, the whole truth - and share his notes.

Mr. Teicher asks the Special Panel to consider the unique facts presented in this case. He asks the Court to issue a narrow ruling finding that he was a subject of the investigation and otherwise meets the requirements of the Act and Order that he be reimbursed solely for those reasonable attorneys' fees and costs attributable to the investigation of Mr. Walsh. He asks the court to Order that he thereafter be permitted to submit a renewed application that conforms to the requirements of the Act by providing documents which set forth with specificity, exactly which portion of his total legal costs were attributable to the investigation of the Independent Counsel.

For the foregoing reasons, Mr. Teicher respectfully requests the Court to exercise its judicial discretion and order that he be awarded reasonable attorneys' fees and costs pursuant to Section 593(f) of The Ethics in Government Act, 28 USC Section 591 *et seq.*

Respectfully submitted on behalf of Howard Teicher:

Gayle Radley Teicher, Esquire
4331 Reno Road, N.W.
Washington, D.C. 20008

IN THE UNITED STATES COURT OF APPEALS
FOR THE DISTRICT OF COLUMBIA CIRCUIT

Division For the Purpose of
Appointing Independent Counsels
Ethics in Government Act of 1978, As Amended

IN RE: Oliver L. North, et al., Motion by Howard Teicher
            Seeking the Public Release of the Entire Final
            Report of Independent Counsel Lawrence Walsh.
            Division No. 86-6

BEFORE: Sentelle, Presiding, Butzner and Sneed, Senior
            Circuit Judges

MOTION BY HOWARD TEICHER TO REQUEST THAT THE COURT
EXERCISE ITS DISCRETION AND RELEASE TO THE CONGRESS AND
PUBLIC THE ENTIRE FINAL REPORT OF INDEPENDENT COUNSEL
LAWRENCE WALSH, TOGETHER WITH ALL COMMENTS OR FACTUAL
INFORMATION SUBMITTED IN ACCORDANCE WITH 28 U.S.C.
SECTION 594(h)

Howard Teicher, a subject of the above entitled
investigation, respectfully requests the Special Division to
exercise its discretion and release to the Congress and the
public the Final Report of Independent Counsel Lawrence Walsh, *in
its entirety*, together with all comments or factual information
which have been submitted by individuals named in the Report in
accordance with 28 U.S.C. Section 594(h).

Mr. Teicher has learned from reports in the media that some
other subjects of the investigation conducted by Lawrence Walsh
into the Iran-Contra affair have filed motions with the Court to
suppress all or parts of the Final Report. For the reasons set

forth below, he strongly contests any such motions and urges the Court to release the Final Report in its entirety.

Mr. Teicher has already submitted three Fee Applications to the Special Division in support of his request that the Court exercise its judicial discretion and order that reasonable attorneys' fees and costs be awarded to him pursuant to Section 593(f) of the Ethics in Government Act, 28 U.S.C. Section 591 *et. seq.*, (the "Act"). These submissions were filed on July 23, October 6 and November 2, 1993. The Fee Applications and the attachments thereto fully set forth Mr. Teicher's involvement in the Iran affair.

On August 9, 1993, Mr. Teicher was sent a letter from the Clerk of the Court and a copy of an Order filed on August 5, issued by the Court which authorized Mr. Teicher or his attorney to examine relevant portions of Mr. Walsh's Final Report and gave him the right to submit any comment or factual information for possible inclusion as an appendix.

This August 5th Order was issued under seal. <u>Only individuals "named in such report"</u> were given the opportunity to review the Final Report or received notice from the Court that a Final Report had been filed.

The Order provided that the Clerk:

> shall, for the purposes set forth in 28 U.S.C. Section 594(h)(2), make available the relevant portions of the Final Report, as indicated below . . . .to the following individuals named in the Report, or to their attorneys. . . . The Clerk shall advise <u>each named individual of their right under the Act</u> to submit any comment or factual information

> for possible inclusion as an appendix to the
> Final Report. . .

(emphasis added)

In a second Order filed on August 6, 1993, the Court ordered that Howard Teicher be added to the list of individuals to whom the Court directed disclosure of the contents of the Final Report.

In an Order filed under seal on September 24, 1993, the Court granted the motion of former President Reagan for an extension of time in which to respond to the Final Report and gave him a 60-day extension of time, to and including December 3, 1993, to make appropriate motions or otherwise respond to the Final Report.

The Court further ordered, on its own motion, that "all parties named in the Final Report who are subject to the Court's Order of August 5, 1993 be granted an extension of time until and including December 3, 1993 to respond to the Independent Counsel's Final Report." (emphasis added) Mr. Teicher was also granted such an extension. On October 4 he reviewed portions of the Final Report and found them to be accurate. He submitted one brief handwritten comment, correcting a minor omission.

Now Mr. Teicher has learned that the Final Report might not be released, that its release might be further delayed, or that certain sections might be suppressed. Presumably some individuals named in the Report who have been given the opportunity to submit comments or factual information – former senior government officials – may disagree with what was written about them, regardless of the veracity of the Report. Perhaps they are moving to suppress the Final Report on the basis that their reputations will suffer unwarranted harm and they do not want the public to get the impression that one or more of them might have done something improper - if not illegal.

Yet they, like Mr. Teicher, have been given the opportunity under Section 594(h) to submit comments and factual information for inclusion as an appendix to the Final Report. In the aftermath of the scandal, Mr. Teicher's colleagues and superiors in the national security bureaucracy asserted their constitutional rights while other government officials acted to deflect attention away from themselves and onto the NSC staff.

When President George Bush pardoned former Secretary of Defense Caspar Weinberger and others just before the Independent Counsel was to put on its case against Secretary Weinberger for conduct arising out of the Iran-Contra affair, he prevented Mr. Walsh from presenting the issues in the context of a criminal prosecution, leaving only the Final Report as a vehicle to recount the findings of the investigation. By choosing to accept the pardon, Secretary Weinberger willingly relinquished the opportunity to present a vigorous defense of his actions - and his reputation.

Despite President Reagan's professed desire to get all the facts out, and the then vice president's stated willingness to let the chips fall where they may, even if the "truth hurt," senior members of the Reagan administration ran for cover to avoid becoming embroiled in the controversy and misled members of

Congress, the Independent Counsel and the American people about their knowledge of and involvement in the Iran-Contra affair.

Now, when the truth apparently does hurt - they apparently seek to suppress the Final Report. Mr. Teicher submits that it would be manifestly unfair for these senior government officials to now benefit from their earlier misrepresentations and failure to provide relevant notes by prevailing on their motions to suppress all or parts of the Final Report.

The Independent Counsel mechanism was designed to reach certain goals which included, *inter alia,* affording protection to the reputation of any person subject to investigation. Mr. Teicher believes that it is in the public interest for the American people and the Congress to learn the results of Mr. Walsh's investigation and what actually transpired in the Iran-Contra affair.

Mr. Teicher's own life was severely disrupted and his reputation was substantially harmed due to his innocent involvement in the Iran affair and the ruthless efforts by senior officials of the Reagan administration to scapegoat the NSC staff generally and Mr. Teicher in particular. Mr. Teicher's reputation will not be fully restored until the truth is finally told and the Final Report is released.

Mr. Teicher asks that his Fee Applications, together with all attachments thereto be incorporated by reference in support of this Motion. Mr. Teicher also requests that his Fee Applications together with all attachments and this motion be submitted as additional comments to the Final Report and be included as part of the appendix.

WHEREFORE, Mr. Teicher respectfully requests the Special Division to exercise its discretion and release to the Congress and the public the Final Report of Independent Counsel Lawrence Walsh, *in its entirety*, together with all comments or factual information which have been submitted in accordance with 28 U.S.C. Section 594(h).

Respectfully submitted on
behalf of Howard Teicher,

Gayle Radley Teicher, Esq.
4331 Reno Road, N.W.
Washington, D.C. 20038-4221
(202)244-8500

Paul B. Thompson

United States Court of Appeals
For the District of Columbia Circuit

FILED DEC 0 3 1993

RON GARVIN
CLERK

December 3, 1993

Mr. Ron Garvin
Clerk, United States Court of Appeals,
District of Columbia Circuit,
Washington, D.C. 20001

Dear Mr. Garvin,

Your letter of August 9 advised that the United States Court of Appeals for the District of Columbia Circuit, Division for the Purpose of appointing Independent Counsels had issued an order under seal in Division No. 86-6. That order, dated 5 August, specified that Independent Counsel had delivered its Final Report to the Division of the Court and that the contents of the report would not be disclosed to any party without authorization.

Per your letter, the Court authorized me to examine relevant portions of the Final Report under conditions of confidentiality as to the contents of those portions and the fact that a Final Report had been filed.

I have reviewed the portions of the Final Report which were made available to me, and I am hereby submitting comments and factual information for possible inclusion as an appendix.

Sincerely,

Paul B. Thompson

Paul B. Thompson

December 3, 1993

United States Court of Appeals
For the District of Columbia Circuit

FILED DEC 0 3 1993

RON GARVIN
CLERK

UNITED STATES COURT OF APPEALS
FOR THE DISTRICT OF COLUMBIA CIRCUIT

Division for the Purpose of
Appointing Independent Counsels

Ethics in Government Act of 1978, as Amended

In re: Oliver L. North, et al.   Division No. 86-6

Before: Sentelle, Presiding, Butzner and Sneed, Senior Circuit
         Judges

Response to the Independent Counsel's Final Report:

In response to the Court's Order of August 5, 1993, as
extended on September 24, 1993, the following comments and factual
information are forwarded for possible inclusion as an appendix to
the Final Report.

The Final Report contains passages that are prejudicial, and,
in some instances, defamatory in nature due to their numerous
inaccuracies. The opinions expressed in the Report are often based
on uncorroborated theories and statements taken out of context.

The Independent Counsel acknowledges that I was not involved
in the operational details of either the Iran or Contra
initiatives, but then alleges that I became involved in the
criminal activities of others. In fact, my role in the incident
was tangential and was only undertaken in the execution of my
assigned duties as a military assistant to the National Security
Advisor and legal advisor to the NSC staff. I was not party to nor
was I aware of any attempt to conceal or misstate the facts, or any
other alleged misdeeds.

In regard to the Administration's assistance to the Contras,
when I became aware of a Congressional request for White House
documents in August of 1985, I agreed that a thorough search of NSC
files should be conducted similar to other informational searches.
I also directed that a legal memorandum be prepared on the relation
of the Congressional funding restrictions to the Administration's
support of the Contras. I provided professional legal advice on
that issue,   and was not aware of any improprieties or
misrepresentations regarding the policy.

2

In regard to the Iranian initiative, I first began assembling information on its details in early November of 1986 and only learned of its key elements later that month. When I became aware of increasing Congressional and public interest, I personally asked the Attorney General on November 7, 1986, to explain the legal basis for the Presidential action. He assigned a senior Department of Justice official, and I worked closely with him and other Department counsel to resolve the issue.

I was asked to appear before Congressional Committees, the FBI, the Independent Counsel, and the Grand Jury on numerous occasions between March and July of 1987. I did so willingly and without immunity or request for any other form of protection. Altogether I was interviewed twenty three times in sessions ranging from one to six hours. Whenever I became aware of additional information relevant to the investigation, I immediately offered it to the investigators.

It is an abuse of investigatory discretion for the Independent Counsel to selectively present and interpret information in 1993 that he has had in his possession for several years. Even now, I am responding to his conclusions without the benefit of access to the full Report.

I was never indicted, nor was I even provided an opportunity to rebut the Independent Counsel's theories concerning my role in any of this matter. I, therefore, respectfully submit the following comments and factual information pertaining to portions of the Final Report as it is the only recourse available to me.

Paul B. Thompson

RESPONSE TO CHAPTER FOUR OF THE FINAL REPORT

Chapter Four of the Final Report contains numerous factual errors and inaccuracies concerning my limited knowledge of the Reagan Administration's covert action program toward Iran in 1986, and actions taken in support of the anti-Sandinista movement in Nicaragua during 1985 and 1986. I have attempted to respond to those errors and to describe more accurately my role while assigned to the NSC staff.

During his six year investigation, Independent Counsel was not successful in trying to make a case against me. He correctly concludes that I was not involved in the operational details of the Iranian covert action or the Administration's support of the Contra movement in Nicaragua. But, he then tries to show that I became involved in the criminal acts of others.

There is no basis for these allegations; my tangential participation in the alleged improper actions of others was unwitting and due only to the execution of my official duties. Finally, Independent Counsel alleges there are potentially false statements made by me during the course of the investigation in the Spring of 1987. He attempts to establish this by selectively taking many statements out of context and by ignoring other clearly countervailing factors.

The Independent Counsel's goal should be to discover the truth, not to present untested theories. But, how is the truth ever to be arrived at in my case? Over six years have passed since my last official statement in this matter, and no new information has come to light. Independent Counsel determined that there was no basis to prosecute. Yet, now he is making allegations and impugning my reputation when there is no opportunity for rebuttal. A resolution of such inequities can only be attained by using rules of evidence and following established procedures on a fair playing field, where allegations are addressed in a forum in which the same objective individuals hear both sides of the dispute.

By inaccurately describing statements made by me over the course of twenty-three sessions, the Independent Counsel is implying there was a conspiracy to mislead. I was never aware of nor party to such an alleged activity. To the contrary, my sincere attempts to cooperate and explain the intricacies of this situation were unlimited; I stand by every one of them.

In Chapter Four of the Final Report, Independent Counsel selectively presents information which depicts my military duties in 1985 and 1986 in a slanted way in order to support his theories. During that time, I was a professional member of the NSC staff serving in the dual capacity of counsel to the staff and military assistant to the National Security Advisor. Although the National Security Advisor and the Deputy National Security Advisor are part

2

of the President's immediate White House staff and not on the National Security Council staff, they rely on National Security Council staff members to assist them in advising the President.

As counsel to the NSC staff I was responsible for providing advice on the legal aspects of national security issues, and on matters of concern to the NSC in its capacity as a government agency. The NSC legal office provided liaison with the legal offices of the Departments of State, Defense, Justice, Treasury, the CIA, and the White House counsel. With the considerable legal support received from those organizations, it was determined that three staff lawyers for the NSC, an agency of one hundred and fifty individuals, was a sufficient ratio, even by Washington standards.

It was not unprecedented for NSC staff to have multiple duties. My predecessor as General Counsel was also the Executive Secretary of the NSC for two years during his tenure. Prior to serving as General Counsel and military assistant, I was the Assistant General Counsel and Deputy Executive Secretary. And, when I assumed the responsibilities of General Counsel, my previous legal duties were performed by an individual, who also served as the Deputy Executive Secretary. The advantages of this dual function were that it gave the legal department direct access to the central paper flow and most legal issues.

In Chapter Four of the Final Report, Independent Counsel is incorrect on page 137 when he attempts to implicate me in the actions of others, when, in fact, I was not aware of the motive or basis for those acts. My understanding of the Iranian covert action was that the President was acting pursuant to his chief executive authority, on the advice of his senior advisors, including the Attorney General. At no time was I aware of or would I have been party to subversion or usurpation. And, I did not participate in the preparation of false documents, the destruction of any documents, or the misrepresentation of any facts.

The depiction on page 138 of events in Geneva is not accurate. Although I was in the same room with the President, the Secretary of State, and the National Security Advisor during the Geneva Summit on November 18, 1985, I did not participate in their conversation about the purpose for a requested flight of CIA assets via a European country. I was asked by the National Security Advisor to place a call to the Prime Minister of that country, but I was not aware of the purpose for the call nor a party to it.

I did not learn of the reason for the call until 1987 during testimony by Mr. McFarlane and the Secretary of State. I did not know the purpose of the flight or the contents of the aircraft. I kept Mr. McFarlane informed of the status of the attempted telephone call over the next two days, and at one point told him I had learned from LtCol North that the call involved a request for landing permission. Mr. McFarlane expressed surprise that I knew

3

about the landing request, but he added nothing further to my limited knowledge (see Footnote 12). When I talked to Admiral Poindexter during this period, I was not specific about the project because I didn't know anything more about it (page 138). Independent Counsel is confusing my limited knowledge of the event in November of 1985 with what it was in the Spring of 1987.

Contrary to Independent Counsel's conclusions on page 139, I was not aware on November 21, 1986, that Admiral Poindexter had an original Presidential Finding from 1985 in his possession, or of the reasons why he would want to destroy it. I do not know where the Finding had been for the previous year, although I am certain that it was not in my possession. As of November 21, I was unaware of most details of the Iranian covert operation and did not even have a security clearance for the program. I was further unaware of any connection between the Iranian covert operation and the initiative to assist the Contras, or of any attempt to hide or misrepresent the actions of the Administration.

To my knowledge, the President had approved the covert operation toward Iran beginning in January of 1986; and, the actions in support of the Contras were appropriate. In my view, there was an earnest attempt by the White House to respond to Congress, the press, and the public. Several of us were trying to discover and explain the details. I was not aware of an attempt to mislead Congress.

On page 139, the Report inaccurately states that Admiral Poindexter handed me an envelope with three Findings. In fact, the Admiral gave me only one Finding, dated January 17, 1986. Admiral Poindexter knew I only had that one Finding because later that year he sent me a memo from the Department of Defense concerning the Finding with a cover note which read, "put this with the <u>Finding</u>" (Tab A). I kept the January 17 Finding until about November 20, 1986, at which time Admiral Poindexter requested that it be sent to the addressees listed on its cover sheet.

The January 17 Finding was in my custody during this period so I could show it to designated individuals. If I had possessed other Findings bearing on the case, I would have likewise shown them to those individuals.

Independent Counsel implies that I had a December 1985 Finding in my possession by referring to an electronic mail note to me from Admiral Poindexter in which the Admiral asked me to give Mr. Casey a copy of the "very sensitive Finding" (Footnote 22, page 139). The implication is false. In fact, Admiral Poindexter was referring to the January 17, 1986, Finding since Mr. Casey was interested in justifying additional CIA actions taken after January 17. If I had possessed the December 1985 Finding and had thus been able to give it to Mr. Casey, he would not have been concerned about Presidential authorization for the CIA related flight in

4

November 1985.

The account of the destruction of the original December 1985 Finding by Admiral Poindexter on pages 139 and 140 is inaccurate. Contrary to Independent Counsel's opinion, I provided information consistent with my personal knowledge of that event throughout the series of interviews and sworn statements that I participated in during 1987. My final testimony on July 24, 1987, 'that I had not seen the Finding' is virtually identical to that passage cited by Independent Counsel on pages 140 and 141 of the Final Report.

When I learned on June 26, 1987, that Admiral Poindexter may have destroyed the original December 1985 Finding, I immediately requested a meeting with Ms. Judith Hetherton of the Independent Counsel's office; she had asked me to contact her if I had additional information. I informed Ms. Hetherton of that information during a meeting on the afternoon of June 26, 1987, while in the presence of FBI agent Kevin Fryslie.

On page 141, Independent Counsel inaccurately portrays my accounting of the November 21, 1986, conversation with Admiral Poindexter concerning the so called Attorney General's fact finding inquiry. It is misleading to depict the conversation as one in which Admiral Poindexter was informing me that Justice Department personnel were coming to the NSC to gather additional information. At that point, I had already been working with Justice personnel for fourteen days; in fact, I had requested that they be there.

On November 7, 1986, I asked for Department of Justice assistance in explaining the legal basis for the covert operation since I was aware that the Attorney General had initially provided legal advice on the issue to the President. I made the request directly to Mr. Meese in the presence of his assistant, Mr. Ken Cribb. Three days later Mr. Charles Cooper was made available. I spoke frequently with Mr. Cooper between the 11th and the 20th of November and shared with him all of my files, papers, and information. Mr. Meese and Mr. Cooper attended the meeting in Admiral Poindexter's office on November 20 at my suggestion. Admiral Poindexter correctly reflects Mr. Meese's personal knowledge of my role in the ongoing investigation by quoting Mr. Meese as saying his folks "would be contacting me by name," a statement Meese would only have made if he knew of my pre-existing role in the investigation (page 139).

The purpose of Admiral Poindexter's brief conversation with me on November 21 was to tell me he was cooperating with the inquiry and to give me his work files to provide to the Justice Department personnel. Following his earlier meeting that morning with the President and Mr. Meese, Admiral Poindexter apparently decided to share his personal work files. When I noted the folder of work papers, I chided him slightly for not producing it sooner saying they (the Justice Department individuals I had been working with)

5

will be "delighted" to get it--after I had been telling them for the past ten days that we didn't have anything in the front office other than what I already had shared with them.

As reflected in his testimony in May and July of 1987, Admiral Poindexter inaccurately perceived my exclamation at seeing the new files, and apparently thought I was referring to the press' potential reaction to the appearance of additional work files. It is ludicrous for Independent Counsel to suggest on page 141 that Admiral Poindexter's understanding of events is more credible than mine because he said it on national television. Many things are said on national television that are not unassailable. I would have liked the opportunity to testify publicly myself to describe what I am convinced took place.

The legal question at that point regarding the covert operation was whether Presidential authorization existed for the November 1985 shipment, regardless of its contents. Obviously, CIA personnel knew or could have discovered what had been on board the aircraft in November, 1985, had they chosen to do so; but, the legal issue was whether the President had authorized the CIA to carry out the activity.

If Admiral Poindexter had recalled the existence of the signed December 1985 Finding, he could have taken care of CIA's concerns. Without the Finding, it appeared to the CIA that it was being left high and dry without the benefit of Presidential authority for its activities. Apparently Admiral Poindexter sought to avoid embarrassment for the President for what might be perceived as an arms for hostages transaction, when the more serious effect of overlooking the existence of the Finding was the abandonment of the CIA. To fill that void, the Attorney General was proposing that the January 17, 1986, Finding might be applied retroactively to what was essentially an ongoing operation, or alternatively, that perhaps the President could make an "oral" Finding to cover the November 1985 shipment. But it was a void that was difficult and, as it turned out, unnecessary to fill. I did not learn until June 16, 1987, that the signed original Finding had been destroyed. During this period, I had no knowledge that anyone at the NSC or the White House, was destroying or altering official documents.

In regard to Administration activities concerning the Contras, the Independent Counsel tries to find significance in my preliminary, hesitant responses to Committee staff when asked about letters sent from Mr. McFarlane to Congress in 1985. At first, I was surprised during those interviews when investigators asked me about the letters to the Contras and other Central American issues. I had understood the interviews were going to cover Iran related issues (Tab B). When I realized that there was interest in the Contras, I reviewed the files on this issue.

6

In August of 1985, Congress requested information concerning support to the Contras by NSC staff, specifically LtCol North. A normal search was conducted of the NSC files on this subject, and a memo was drafted on the applicability of the recently enacted Boland Amendment to the Department of Defense Authorization Act.

The documents identified by the search were from the NSC official document filing system and were forwarded to Mr. McFarlane. It was not NSC policy to give official documents to anyone outside the agency. In this instance, it would not have been possible without the consent of the President in the event he chose to exercise executive privilege. Instead, Mr. McFarlane endeavored to answer the inquiry, drawing on information in the documents.

The NSC legal memo raised the question of whether the Boland Amendment provisions applied to the NSC staff. (tab C) There was a basis to advocate that the NSC staff was not subject to the Amendment's restrictions. In fact, the NSC was fiscally incapable of violating the prohibition; its total annual appropriation was under five million dollars, most of which went to office and salary costs. However, Mr. McFarlane determined that there had been no violation of the Amendment by NSC personnel and that a legal challenge to the legislation was not relevant.

Any comments made to Mr. Sciaroni were based on this determination by Mr. McFarlane and assurances by LtCol North. (Footnote 74, page 145) I told Mr. Sciaroni about the NSC legal memo pertaining to the Boland Amendment, explained that Mr. McFarlane had determined there had been no violation, and gave access to NSC documents during the meeting. Mr. Sciaroni also had the opportunity to meet with LtCol North and any other member of the NSC staff at his desire.

During this period, Mr. McFarlane asked my advice on the conditions under which documents could be modified. I explained the legal requirement to safeguard official records. I also forwarded a comprehensive legal memorandum on the treatment of records by the NSC staff to Mr. McFarlane on October 28, 1985. (Tab D)

I further advised Mr. McFarlane in writing during this period that the Contra documents in his custody were the property of the President and not subject to his (McFarlane's) disposition. The Independent Counsel misconstrues my memo by implying that I was suggesting to Mr. McFarlane that he not show the documents to Congressman Barnes who had requested to see them. The purpose of the memo to Mr. McFarlane is apparent on its face--to advise him that the documents were not subject to his disposition since they were permanent documents, and possibly subject to executive privilege. I also showed the documents at this time to the White House Counsel.

7

I did not attend the meeting with Congressman Barnes, but I do know that the same documents I had given Mr. McFarlane were on his coffee table when the Congressman arrived. The documents were then returned to me to give them to LtCol North. I returned them to their rightful custodian, the NSC Director of Information Policy.

A Congressional request for Contra related documents was made again in the Spring of 1986. This time LtCol North was made available to meet with Members and staff of the House Permanent Select Committee on Intelligence. Admiral Poindexter also sent a letter to the Committee similar to the one sent by Mr. McFarlane in 1985. It was my understanding that the letter and the North meeting legitimately reflected the situation.

On page 145 Independent Counsel incorrectly states that I was not available to assist him in describing the destruction of the December 1985 Finding. As noted above, I informed Ms. Hetherton on June 26, 1987, of my knowledge, and also did so at many subsequent meetings with representatives from the Office of the Independent Counsel.

On page 145, there is an inaccurate reference to the purpose of a meeting I attended at the request of the House Permanent Select Committee on Intelligence. Mr. Sable from the NSC legislative office is relied on by the Independent Counsel as stating the purpose of the meeting was to talk about Contra activities. In fact, the reason for the meeting was to discuss disinformation (Tab E). The Independent Counsel unfairly implies that I would misstate the reason for meeting with Congressional Members or staff when I fully recognize the Congressional requirement to receive timely and accurate information from the Executive Branch.

Contrary to the allegation by the Independent Counsel on page 145, I have at no time made false statements or obstructed justice. To the contrary, I have been cooperative at all times, never asking for immunity or other protection. I have met on numerous occasions, often at my own expense with investigators, trying to sort out the details of this incident. During the past six years, I have had twenty-three sessions with the Independent Counsel, Grand Jury, FBI, and Congressional Committees.

The Independent Counsel inaccurately describes the purpose of my meeting with him on January 3, 1991, as a "voluntary" interview. In fact, I called Mr. Gillen of the Office of Independent Counsel in December of 1990 and requested the meeting. It was unclear to me why my situation could not be resolved since there had been no new information since 1987. Unlike in the Navy, where the prosecution is obligated to resolve situations in a timely fashion, there is no provision to force the Independent Counsel to clarify one's status--even when interminable delays are prejudicial. In my case, my naval career and personal life have

8

been put in jeopardy as a result of the Independent Counsel's abuse of discretion.

Mr. Gillen agreed to a meeting on January 3, 1991. At the meeting, Mr. Gillen refused to discuss specific details, stating only that he had lingering "concerns", and made inference to conflicting statements from Admiral Poindexter. I then stated that a trial might be the only forum to resolve the issues since it would force him to substantiate his "concerns". In some respects, it would have been preferable to the open ended tactic in which I have had to wait for years to even learn of the allegations. I did indicate that I would endeavor to meet with Admiral Poindexter to determine the basis for his recollection.

On page 146, Independent Counsel notes that I was informed through counsel in the Spring of 1991 that I was now a target of the investigation and that I was invited to appear before a Grand Jury. Upon advice of counsel, I declined the invitation; I felt it was important to discuss this issue with Admiral Poindexter before testifying and wanted to wait until that occurred.

My attempts to meet with Admiral Poindexter were unsuccessful between January 1991 and December 1992. After charges against him were dismissed, I finally talked with Admiral Poindexter and learned that his recollection was indeed imprecise. He did not recall giving me the December 1985 Finding along with the January 17, 1986, Finding; but, instead, he thought he might have given it to me sometime in the Spring of 1986 at Mr. Casey's request so that I could show it to Mr. Gates, who had recently become the Deputy Director of CIA. If this were the case, then surely Mr. Gates or I would have recalled such an event, and it would have had a bearing on the Casey testimony preparation meetings Mr. Gates and I both attended on November 20, 1986. I certainly would have had the Finding in my possession during November, 1986, to share with Mr. Cooper and others.

Once I had this clarification from Admiral Poindexter, as well as an exculpatory polygraph on this issue (Tab F), I immediately contacted Mr. Gillen on December 12, 1992, and again asked for a meeting. He agreed to meet in early January, 1993, two years after my last meeting with him. However, when I called in early January, he had changed his mind and adamantly refused to meet. By this time, the President had given pardons to some individuals in the case, and Mr. Gillen refused to talk with me further, telling me to take up the matter with the Court of Appeals.

9

Response to Miscellaneous References Within the Final Report

The following comments are in response to references to me in several locations throughout the Report. In each instance where my name appeared in a sentence or paragraph, that page was made available. Since the full text of the chapter or passage was not provided, I have responded to the best of my ability.

On page 19, the Final Report incorrectly places me at a meeting on January 20 in the White House situation room. I did not attend that meeting. In fact, I did not have a security clearance for the covert action program which was apparently the subject of the meeting; I was also not involved in or cognizant of the subsequent operational details of the operation.

I did meet on January 20 with three senior individuals from the CIA to show them the January 17, 1986, Finding authorizing the covert operation. That Finding had been given to me shortly after the President signed it on the morning of 17 January 1986. I kept the Finding in my safe and showed it on occasion to individuals, who needed to know of the President's policy directive on this issue. Beyond knowing of the existence and legal rationale for the Finding, I was not included in the operational details of the program.

The reference to me on page 22 of the Report is misleading. It implies that Admiral Poindexter discussed with me sometime in October of 1986 the concerns of Mr. Casey and Mr. Gates that proceeds from the sale of arms to Iran may have gone to support the Contras. Admiral Poindexter never talked to me about an October meeting he had with Mr. Casey and Mr. Gates; and, he never told me about the diversion of funds from the Iranian initiative until after he resigned on November 25, 1986.

The description on page 23 of a meeting which I attended on November 20, 1986, contains several inaccuracies. The passage incorrectly describes the purpose of the meeting. Mr. Casey was to testify the following day before the Intelligence Committees concerning the Iranian covert operation. At the same time, Admiral Poindexter was to meet in the White House with those Members of the Committees who wished to discuss the policy aspects of the initiative. This was consistent with the CIA Director's role to appear before the proper oversight Committees and explain his agency's participation in an operation. It was also practice for the National Security Advisor (who was not in a confirmed position and whose advice to the President was often subject to the protection of executive privilege) to meet with Members of Congress and respond to their questions.

The purpose of the meeting on November 20 was, therefore, for Mr. Casey and Admiral Poindexter to review Mr. Casey's intended testimony. This proved to be difficult in one area where there was

10

disagreement: whether there had been presidential authorization for the use of CIA assets in November of 1985 in support of an activity that was for other than intelligence gathering. (Whenever the CIA engages in such activities, it is required that it have Presidential approval and that it report the activity to appropriate oversight Committees.)

Mr. Casey wanted to testify that the use of CIA assets in November of 1985 had been at the direction of the White House, whereas LtCol North wanted the CIA to take sole responsibility for the activity. The CIA was reluctant to report an act for which it did not have authorization from the President.

Contrary to the Independent Counsel's opinion, legal issues involving the 1985 shipments did not dominate the discussion. As noted above, the only difference of opinion was between Mr. Casey and LtCol North as to whether the White House, meaning the President, had directed the CIA to use its assets to facilitate the earlier shipment to Iran. I had told Mr. Cooper about the meeting. He and I agreed the Attorney General should attend. I had been working with Mr. Cooper for several days, trying to collect facts bearing on the covert operation. By this point, we had become aware of most of the details of the Iranian initiative after January 17, 1986, which were carried out as a result of a Finding signed on that date. We were not clear about events in 1985 to which Mr. Casey and LtCol North were making reference.

The legal issue involving the November 1985 shipment was whether it could be covered by the January 17, 1986, Finding--not the actual contents of the shipment. Whether the shipment was weapons or some other material, Presidential authority would still be required for the CIA to engage in such activity; and, at that point many of us were unaware of the existence of that authority. Hence, the disagreement between North and Casey was whether the CIA had acted with Presidential authority or, if for some highly unlikely reason, it might have acted on its own. Had we known about the earlier December 1985 Finding, then there would not have been disagreement concerning the testimony. The legal discussion considered the possibility of an oral approval by the President, or the possible applicability of the January 17, 1986, Finding.

The reference on page 24 to me concerning Admiral Poindexter's destruction of the only known signed copy of the 1985 Finding is incorrect. Admiral Poindexter apparently had the Finding in his own work files. I did not collect it, nor did I know of its existence.

The reference on page 29 of the Report describing my participation as a witness in the investigation is misleading. I was very cooperative and forthcoming at all times throughout the investigation. From the very beginning I made myself available and continued to do so, often at my own expense, when I was reassigned

11

to duty stations out of the Washington DC area. I testified under oath on four occasions before staff of Congressional Committees, and three times before the Grand Jury. In addition, I met with representatives of the FBI on two occasions, the Office of Independent Counsel on twelve occasions, and Congressional Committees on two occasions for a total of twenty-three sessions, each lasting from one to six hours. Throughout my appearances I never sought immunity or other protection, and would have refused it if offered. I was never called as a witness in any of the trials. As I learned additional information about the matter from publications, subsequent testimony, and reports of trials, I continued to inform the Independent Counsel.

The reference on page 115 of the Final Report to LtCol North's testimony concerning my knowledge of his actions is misleading. North may have known that he was making a false assertion regarding Casey's testimony, but I certainly did not know it. To the contrary, I had attended the meeting to learn about the proposed testimony and had arranged for both Mr. Meese and Mr. Cooper to be there. We were trying to learn the operational details of the covert operation and determine whether the January 17, 1986, Finding applied to it. LtCol North is incorrect in his assumption that others at the meeting such as Cooper, Meese, and I, were aware that his version of the draft testimony was false. He is hinting at a conspiracy of silence by those attending the meeting--an assumption on his part that is totally unfounded.

Footnote 40 on page 116 of the Report is potentially misleading in that it implies that I might have been aware of the contents of documents removed by LtCol North from his office and later returned to me by his attorney. The items given to me by North's counsel were immediately handed over in their wrapped condition to the NSC custodian of documents for proper disposition. I did not review the papers and was unaware of their content.

The reference on page 117 of the Report concerning the timing of Independent's Counsel's knowledge of the existence of the December 1985 Finding is factually inaccurate. I provided information on this issue several times during 1987, and told the Independent Counsel's office about it, as requested. As soon as I learned of the fate of the original December 1985 Finding on June 16, 1987, I called Ms. Hetherton of the Independent Counsel's office and requested a meeting with her. Later that same day, I informed her of my knowledge in the presence of FBI agent Kevin Fryslie. On many occasions after that I also discussed the matter with other members of the Independent Counsel staff. Independent Counsel's statement on page 117 of the Report that the information (from North's testimony) caused him to question me and consider bringing charges based on that information is contradicted by the information in his own possession since June 16, 1987.

The reference on page 130 of the Report to North's testimony

12

that he may have seen the signed Finding in my safe on November 26, 1985 is factually inaccurate. I did not have custody, nor was I aware of the Finding. Furthermore, if North had seen the Finding, then he should have volunteered his knowledge of its existence at the November 20, 1986, meeting on Casey's Testimony. Whether or not North was being disingenuous at that meeting by trying to push the responsibility for the CIA November 1985 activity to a person outside the White House or the US Government, it was neither necessary nor prudent if he had really seen a Finding in which the President had authorized the activity.

The references on pages 214 and 315 of the Report are misleading in that they imply that Admiral Poindexter may have discussed with me the diversion of funds from the Iranian covert operation to other covert projects. Admiral Poindexter never discussed the matter with me, and did not inform me of the diversion until after his resignation on November 25, 1986.

There are numerous references (Pages 320, 510, 526, 529, 531, 532, 533, 535, 536, and 547) to a meeting of agency general counsel on November 18, and to the roles of other counsel generally. Many of these are taken out of context by the Independent Counsel in an effort to support a theory of obstruction on my part. In other cases, individual counsel have misstated my role based on their own narrow exposure to the situation. The role of counsel throughout this incident illustrates the selective use of legal counsel by top level decision makers.

The first time I became aware of the existence of a covert operation toward Iran was on January 16, 1986. At that time, the Attorney General and the CIA General Counsel were providing legal advice to the President's senior advisors on a proposed Finding to be signed by the President. The January 17, 1986, Finding was given to me for the first time later that day, and I kept it in my safe until the following November at which time it was sent to the addressees listed on the cover sheet.

When I asked the CIA General Counsel about the unusual aspect of withholding notification of the Finding's contents from Congress, he explained that it would be the legal interpretation of the statute to do so until the sensitive part of the covert operation was complete.

The operation then proceeded as a CIA covert activity until the following November when it appeared that the program would become public and compromised. At that time, on November 7, I asked the Attorney General, in the presence of his assistant, Ken Cribb, if he could make available the Department of Justice file containing a memo on the legal justification for the Finding. I also asked for a point of contact from the Department to work with as the Administration responded to increased congressional and public interest in the issue. Mr. Cribb called back on November 10

13

with the name of Chuck Cooper, an Assistant Attorney General. I then worked with Mr. Cooper on a very frequent basis, sharing with him all information that I had gathered on the covert operation. I also invited him to attend all meetings of which I was aware.

Unfortunately, a similar arrangement was not possible with Peter Wallison. Even though he was understandably eager to assist, neither Admiral Poindexter nor Ed Meese included him in their meetings—in spite of my request to them on his behalf. The Chief of Staff could have included him, but apparently chose not to do so. For example, on November 12, the President briefed Congressional leaders. Several senior White House staff were present, including the Press Secretary and the Congressional Liaison Officer. Although he had the same line relationship to the Chief of Staff as the others, Peter Wallison was not invited to attend.

Contrary to Wallison's account, I initially called the meeting of agency General Counsel on November 18. The meeting was scheduled to be held in the White House Situation Room, but the location was changed at the last moment in deference to Wallison's position as the de facto senior counsel of the group. I also requested that the legal advisor to the Chairman of the Joint Chiefs of Staff be included at the meeting. The group of general counsel would meet on a fairly regular basis to discuss national security legal issues and to then provide advice to their respective agency heads. The normal procedure was for the counsel with the most information about the issue to present it to the group. After discussion, there would be consensus as to what the collective legal advice should be and who would draft the necessary documentation.

The purpose for the meeting on November 18 was to inform agency counsel of the legal aspects of the Presidential Finding, specifically the rationale for the arms transfers to Iran. I attempted to explain the basis for the January 17, 1986, Finding, and then asked the CIA General Counsel to provide additional details. I then turned to Mr. Cooper to explain the legal justification for the transfers, based on the Department of Justice memorandum.

It is surprising to see Mr. Doherty's description of the meeting on page 320 in which he states that I implied that the transaction constituted a CIA operation. It was my understanding that a covert activity authorized by the President using CIA assets is in fact a CIA operation. (When I showed the Finding to the three senior CIA officials on January 20, it was so they could have their agency execute it.) I have further learned by reading this Report that at the time of the November 18 meeting, Mr. Doherty knew of the existence of the earlier December 1985 Finding, and that, according to information he received from his predecessor, it might have been located in North's safe. (footnote 53 on page 320)

14

Mr. Doherty did not share this information with the rest of us at the meeting.

Certain counsel at the November 18 meeting make issue of the fact that I appeared to withhold information. This is inaccurate. The purpose of the meeting was to discuss the legal rationale behind the covert operation. As the senior legal officer in the Executive Branch, the Attorney General was already providing advice to the President on this matter. I was surprised and concerned at the meeting when it became apparent that none of the counsel had been briefed by their own agency heads--not in January of 1986 when the Finding was signed, not during 1986 when arms shipments were being made of which other senior members of their agencies were clearly aware, and not in November of 1986 when the covert operation became public. When the Secretary of State returned from the Geneva Summit in November 1985, he apparently did not tell his legal advisor of the CIA shipment via a European country. Two months later, both the Secretary of State and the Secretary of Defense were aware of the January 17, 1986, Finding bearing on the same subject, and apparently voiced opposition to it. However, neither saw fit to inform their senior legal advisors and seek clarification as to the covert initiative's basis in law.

During the period between the November 18 meeting and November 20, I attempted to provide liaison between individuals such as Cooper and Wallison, on the one hand, who were genuinely trying to resolve important concerns, and, members of the NSC staff, on the other hand, who clearly knew much more that I did. By late evening of November 20, I finally suggested that Mr. Cooper talk directly with Admiral Poindexter when it became too difficult to act as a liaison for individuals, who were pursuing different goals.

TAB – A

PT 2.

UNCLASSIFIED

N 9897

Paul,

3/12/26

Put these with the

firing

JP

(1353)

T108

UNCLASSIFIED

EXHIBIT JMP-7

UNCLASSIFIED

OFFICE OF THE SECRETARY OF DEFENSE

WASHINGTON, D C 20301

N 9899

12 March 1986

John

MEMORANDUM FOR VICE ADMIRAL POINDEXTER

    The attached memorandum from the Director of the Army Staff
is self-explanatory. It reflects the unease of the Army General
Counsel's office over the transfer of items with which you are
familiar. As you know, we have been handling this program on a
very close hold basis, and the Army has been told nothing with
respect to destination. Per guidance received from NSC, the Army
has been told that they have no responsibility for Congressional
notification. The Army has also been told that whatever notifi-
cations are to be made will be taken care of at the appropriate
time by the appropriate agency and that the Attorney General has
provided an opinion that supports this position.

    The Secretary asked that I make you aware of the Army's
concerns in the event you wish to advise the DCI or the Attorney
General.

Colin L. Powell
Major General, USA
Senior Military Assistant
   to the Secretary of Defense

Declassified 29 June 1987
under E.O. 12356
by B. National Security Council

UNCLASSIFIED

DEPARTMENT OF THE ARMY
OFFICE OF THE CHIEF OF STAFF
WASHINGTON D C 20310

N ̄ 9900

7 MAR 1993

DACS-ZD

MEMORANDUM FOR THE MILITARY ASSISTANT TO THE SECRETARY OF DEFENSE

SUBJECT: Congressional Notification of Significant Intelligence
Activities (U)

1. (TS/NOFORN) On 18 January 1986, the Army responded to a verbal
tasking from your office to provide 1,000 TOW missiles to the
Central Intelligence Agency with a contingency for 3,509 more at a
later date. The first 1,000 missiles were delivered on
14 February 1986 to the CIA.

2. (TS/NOFORN) This request for support circumvented the normal
██████████ System for reasons of security, yet the support
exceeded the $1 million threshold established in the FY86
Intelligence Authorization Bill for reporting to Congress as a
"significant intelligence activity." Funds in excess of $3.5
million were provided by the CIA to reimburse the Army for the
first 1,000 missiles. Billing and payment will occur within 60
days, or when all missiles are delivered, whichever is shorter.
The Agency expects to complete the project within 60 days.

3. (TS/NOFORN) SECDEF memorandum of 13 June 1983, subject: DoD
Support ██████████████████████ (S), establishes responsibility
for notification of Congress of DoD support to the Agency with the
Deputy Under Secretary of Defense for Policy. It also confirms
that primary responsibility resides with the Director, Central
Intelligence. In the case of the TOW missiles, the Army
understanding on responsibilities for notification conforms with
your June 1983 memorandum.

4. (TS/NOFORN) This memo is to assure understanding of statutory
requirements should this issue be raised by one of the
Congressional intelligence committees in the future.

(1356)

Partially Declassified/Released on 29 June 1987
under provisions of E.O. 12356
by C. Reger, National Security Council

ARTHUR E. BROWN, JR.
Lieutenant General, GS
Director of the Army Staff

CLASSIFIED BY: DASP
DECLASSIFY ON: OADR   UNCLASSIFIED NOFORN

TAB – B

U.S. HOUSE OF REPRESENTATIVES

SELECT COMMITTEE TO INVESTIGATE
COVERT ARMS TRANSACTIONS WITH IRAN
UNITED STATES CAPITOL
WASHINGTON, DC 20515
(202) 225-7902

February 25, 1987

Mr. Alan C. Raul
Associate Counsel to the President
Old Executive Office Building
Room 115
Washington, D.C. 20500

Re: <u>Depositions of NSC Personnel</u>

Dear Mr. Raul:

As we discussed on the telephone on February 24, 1987, you have agreed to help the House Select Committee to Investigate Covert Arms Transactions with Iran ("the Committee") to arrange depositions of present and former White House personnel.

The depositions will be taken in Executive Session of the Committee. The only persons present would be any member of the Committee, persons on the Committee staff, the witness, and the attorney for the witness. Except in very unusual circumstances, the depositions would be taken in the Committee's offices or other rooms in the Capitol.

The following is a list of the persons whom the Committee seeks to depose. The names are placed on the list in roughly the sequence in which we would like to take the depositions. I would like to start taking deposition testimony on or around March 4, 1987.

        1.) Craig P. Coy
        2.) Robert L. Earle
        3.) Alton G. Keel
        4.) Paul B. Thompson
        5.) Howard J. Teicher
        6.) James R. Stark

I anticipate that I will expand this list over the next several days. Thank you for your help in this matter.

Very truly yours,

W. Neil Eggleston
Deputy Chief Counsel

TAB – C

NATIONAL SECURITY COUNCIL
WASHINGTON, D.C. 20506

August 23, 1985

INFORMATION

MEMORANDUM FOR W. ROBERT PEARSON

FROM: J. R. SCHARFEN ᐯᏒS

SUBJECT: The 1984 Boland Amendment

Summation:

-- The legislative intent of the Amendment is to end funding in support of paramilitary operations in Nicaragua.

-- Diplomatic and intelligence gathering contacts with Contras are authorized.

-- The Amendment does not define or identify agencies "involved in intelligence activities."

-- The Administration contends the contacts with the Contras are legal under the Amendment.

Legislative History (Pages 1-2):

-- 1982 Boland Amendment prohibition on use of public funds for purpose of overthrowing the Nicaraguan government. (P.L.97-377).

-- 1983 $24 million cap for FY84 on use of public funds for support of paramilitary operations in Nicaragua. (P.L.98-212 and 98-215).

-- 1984 Boland Amendment full prohibition on use of public funds for support of paramilitary operations in Nicaragua subject to possible release of $14 million if the President submits a request after February 28, 1985 and Congress approves by joint resolution. (P.L.98-473 and 98-618).

Legislative Intent (Pages 2-4):

-- The legislative intent of the Amendment is to end public funding for support of paramilitary operations in Nicaragua.

-- The Amendment permits intelligence gathering and diplomatic contacts with the Contras.

-- Agencies "involved in intelligence activities" are not identified or defined.

Reagan Administration's Position (Pages 4-5):

-- Amendment is bad foreign policy.

-- Administration contacts with Contras are legal under the Boland Amendment.

Attachment: P.L. 98-473

TAB – D

October 28, 1985

<u>ACTION</u>

MEMORANDUM FOR ROBERT C. MCFARLANE

FROM: PAUL B. THOMPSON

SUBJECT: NSC Staff Memo

Attached at Tab I is a memo to the staff defining, in general
terms, official records, and reminding the staff of their legal
ethical obligations not to destroy any official record. At Tab
II is a memo regarding maintenance and disclosure of records.

<u>RECOMMENDATION</u>

That you sign the memo at Tab I.

    Approve_____   Disapprove_____

Attachments
Tab I   McFarlane memo to Staff
Tab II   Memo regarding records
         Tab A   Civil Action No. 83-1138 - <u>BNA v. U.S. Department
                  of Justice</u>
         Tab B   5 U.S.C § 552 - FOIA
         Tab C   FOIA Update, Fall '84
         Tab D   FOIA Update, Winter '84
         Tab E   Civil Action No. 82-0929 & 82-2569 - <u>Daw, Lohnes
                  and Albertson v. Presidential Commission on
                  Broadcasting to Cuba</u>
         Tab F   Presidential Records Act
         Tab G   Federal Records Act

MEMORANDUM FOR NSC STAFF

FROM: ROBERT C. MCFARLANE

SUBJECT: Legal Obligations in Preserving Official Documents

In view of the turnover in our staff members, I believe it is
appropriate to remind you of our legal and ethical obligations in
maintaining official documents. This is particularly timely
because some of you have not had prior Federal service and may be
unaware of your responsibilities in this area.

The Presidential Records Act and the Federal Records Act provide
that official documents are the property of the United States
government and must be protected and preserved as such. Only
with the approval of the Archivist of the United States may
official records be legally destroyed. Criminal penalties attach
to any unlawful removal or destruction of Federal records. As
Federal employees, we also have a legal responsibility to inform
responsible officials of actual or threatened unlawful loss or
removal of official records.

Under the Federal Records Act, any documentary material, regardless of physical form or characteristics, made or received by the
NSC either under Federal law or in connection with the transaction of public businesss is an official record. Once a system
number is assigned to a document, it may not be destroyed without
approval. However, the Secretariat may legally destroy extra
copies of records you may have preserved for your convenience.
Such working copies are specifically excluded from the legal
definition of records.

You may of course, legally do what you please with your wholly
personal papers, subject to the contraints imposed by their
security classification. However, it is important to keep in
mind that personal papers are narrowly defined. Personal papers
are materials, including personal correspondence, journals,
diaries, and their functional equivalents, which are neither
developed in connection with nor used during the transaction of
official government business. For example, an evening diary
which refers to government business, but is not used or made
during government transactions, is a personal paper. You must
keep your personal papers segregated from official documents.

If you have any question regarding the maintenance or disposition
of files you should ask the Secretariat for guidance. You are to
follow any guidance received from the Secretariat concerning the
maintenance or disposal of your records.

I ask that you bear in mind your legal and ethical duties to
safeguard Federal records.

INFORMATION

MEMORANDUM FOR ROBERT C. MCFARLANE

FROM: PAUL B. THOMPSON

SUBJECT: Records

Three Federal statutes affect the NSC's duties regarding the
maintenance and disclosure of records; the Federal Records Act
(FRA), the Freedom of Information Act (FOIA) and the Presidential
Records Act (PRA).

FEDERAL RECORDS ACT (FRA)

The FRA requires Federal agencies to maintain a minimum record of
its activities by prohibiting through criminal sanctions the
removal or destruction of "Federal Records". 44 U.S.C. § 3301
defines "Federal Records" to include:

> ...all books, papers, maps, photographs, machine
> readable materials, or other documentary materials,
> regardless of physical form or characteristics,
> made or received by an agency of the United States
> Government under Federal law or in connection with
> the transaction of public business and preserved or
> appropriate for preservation by that agency or its
> legitimate successor as evidence of the organization,
> functions, policies, decisions, procedures, operations,
> or other activities of the Government or because of the
> informational value of data in them. Library and museum
> material made or acquired and preserved solely for refer-
> ence only for convenience of reference, and stocks of
> publications and of processed documents are not included.

Note the language "or appropriate for preservation". This gives
an agency some flexibility in defining a record when it makes its
record management policy. For example, a legitimate standard for
an agency to use in determining whether a document is a Federal
record for FRA purposes is whether it was transmitted from one
staff member to another or kept exclusively by a lone member.
Extra copies of documents and personal papers are not Federal
records under the FRA.

FPMR 101-11.202-2(d) provides a legal definition of personal
papers and prescribes standards for their maintenance:

2

Papers of a private or nonofficial character which pertain
only to an individual's personal affairs that are kept in
the office of a Federal official will be clearly designated
by him as nonofficial and will at all times be filed
separately from the official records of his office. In
cases where matters requiring the transaction of official
business are received in private personal correspondence,
the portion of such correspondence that pertains to official
business will be extracted and made a part of the official
files....

PRESIDENTIAL RECORDS ACT (PRA)

The PRA provides that Presidential Records are the property of
the Federal government and must be preserved. 44 U.S.C. § 220
1(2) defines Presidential records to include:

> [D]ocumentary materials, or any reasonably segregable
> portion thereof, created or received by the President, his
> immediate staff, or a unit or individual of the Executive
> Office of the President whose function is to advise and
> assist the President, in the course of conducting activities
> which relate to or have an effect upon the carrying out of
> the constitutional, statutory, or other official or
> ceremonial duties of the President. Such term-- ...

> (B) does not include any documentary materials that are (i)
> official records of an agency (as defined in section 552 (e)
> of title 5, United States Code [5 USCS § 552 (e)]);

The exception referred to in (B) above is a reference to the
FOIA which defines the term 'agency' as including any executive
department, including the EOP. By the terms of the PRA, records
may not be both "Presidential" and "official records of an
agency". The PRA excludes personal papers and extra copies of
documents from the definitions of presidential records.

44 U.S.C. § 220 1(3) defines personal papers as:

> "The term 'personal records' means all documentary
> materials, or any reasonably segregable portion therof, of a
> purely private or nonpublic character which do not relate to
> or have an effect upon the carrying out of the consti-
> tutional, statutory, or other official or ceremonial duties
> of the President. Such term includes-
>> "(A) diaries, journal, or other personal notes
>> serving as the functional equivalent of a diary
>> or journal which are not prepared or utilized for, or
>> circulated or communicated in the course of,
>> transacting Government business;

3

The PRA does not leave the same room for discretion by an agency in defining a Presidential record as allowed by the FRA in defining Federal records.

FREEDOM OF INFORMATION ACT (FOIA)

In contrast to the FRA, FOIA does not require an agency to create or obtain a record. Since the FRA permits the destruction of "non-record material" at the discretion of an agency or agency employee, documents will be available under FOIA solely based on whether an employee chose to keep a non-FRA document. See BNA v. U.S. Department of Justice, No. 83-1138, slip op. at 19-20 (D.C. Cir. Aug. 31, 1984) (Tab A). Thus, logically, an agency should not apply the narrow FRA definition of Federal records when responding to a FOIA request. The agency must search those documents on hand whether they fit the FRA definition of Federal records or not. And although an agency employee could have destroyed a document legally under FRA before the FOIA request was received, he may not do so once the agency receives the FOIA request. (There is, however, a contrary case which supports a more narrow search for just FRA type documents. See Dow, Lohnes below).

Through the FOIA applies only to "agency records" the act never defines what an agency record is. 44 U.S.C. § 2201 (Tab B). As a result, case law has had to define FOIA's applicability to various requested material. Courts use the personal record analysis to uphold agencies decisions to withold documents under the FOIA.

In the BNA case the court held that telephone message slips were personal records and not subject to the FOIA. The court justified the decision on the grounds that (1) the slips contained "no substantive information" (2) they were not used by anyone other than the person called and (3) there might not be a way for the official to segregate personal from business calls. See "FOIA UPDATE", U.S. Department of Justice, Vol. V, No. 4, Fall 1984, at 3-4 (Tab C). The same court held appointment calendars were personal records of officials and thus outside of FOIA because (1) the calendars were created for the personal convenience of the individual officials so they could organize both their personal and business appointments, (2) although there was some access to the calendars to determine the officials availability, they were not distributed to other employees, and (3) the agnecy had not exercised control over the documents, such as requiring the employee to maintain calendars. The court in BNA clearly stated a document created within an agency cannot be regarded as "personal" merely on the ground that its author is free to dispose of it at his personal discretion (as he could

4

under the FRA). _Id._ at 4. The _BNA_ court did hold "daily agendas" were "agency records" where (1) they were created expressly to facilitate the agency's daily activities, (2) were in fact circulated to the staff for a business purpose, and (3) though they contained a mix of personal and business references, the personal matters were easily segregated. _Id._ at 3-4.

The _BNA_ court concluded that determining whether a document is a personal record must be made on a case by case basis. The following factors are relevant to the personal record/agency record determination:

> Creation - Was the document created by an agency employee on agency time, with agency materials, at agency expense? (If not, then it very likely is not an "agency record," on that basis alone.)

> Content - Does the document contain "substantive" information? (If not, then it very likely is not an "agency record," on that basis alone.) Does it contain personal as well as official business information?

> Purpose - Was the document created solely for an individual employee's personnel convenience? Alternatively, to what extent was it created to facilitate agency business?

> Distribution - Was the document distributed to anyone else for any reason, such as for a business purpose? How wide was the circulation?

> Use - To what extent did the document's author actually use it to conduct agency business? Did others use it?

> Disposition - Was the document's author free to dispose of it at his personal discretion? What was the actual disposal practice?

> Control - Has the agency attempted to exercise "institutional control" over the document through applicable maintenance or disposition regulations? Did it do so by requiring the document to be created in the first place?

> Segregation - Is there any practical way to segregate out any personal information in the document from official business information?

> Revision - Was the document revised or updated after the fact for record-keeping purposes?

_Id._ at 3.

5

CONGRESSIONAL REQUESTS

Department of Justice FOIA policy distinguishes between requests made by the House of Congress as a whole (including through its committee structure) and requests from individual members of Congress. "FOIA UPDATE," U.S. Department of Justice, Winter 1984 Vol. V, No. 1, at 3-4 (Tab D). Even where a FOIA request is made by a Member acting in his or her official capacity, it is not a "Congressional" request unless it is made by a committee or sub-comittee chairman, or otherwise under the full and express authority of a committee or subcommittee. Id.

A lone member who requests documents from an agency is treated as a normal person under FOIA. Consequently, the FOIA exceptions such as the National Security exception may be invoked to withold the documents. Whereas if the Congress acts on behalf of a Committee it is exempt from the execeptions that apply to individuals.

FOIA "is not authority to withold information from Congress." 5 U.S.C. § 552 (c). The FOIA explicitly exempts Congress under section C. Id. However, an agency may refer to the President who may invoke executive privilege and refuse to disclose requested information to the Congress.

EXECUTIVE PRIVILEGE AND NSC RECORD SEARCHES

The NSC maintains at least two separate sets of files, one for institutional records used in discharging the agency's responsibilities under the National Security Act and one for documents received or generated by or on behalf of the President in NSC's capacity as advisor to the President. The court in Dow, Lohnes upheld the NSC's view that the latter documents are Presidential and not agency documents. Dow, Lohnes & Albertson v. Presidential Commission on Broadcasting to Cuba No. 82-0929, slip op. at 2-5 (D.D.C. Sept. 28, 1984) (Tab E). This allows the NSC to respond to document requests by searching just the institutional files and not the Presidential files. This is justified by the fact the NSC's non-institutional files which are kept separately from NSC agency records are not property subject to the free disposition of the agency. The Dow, Lohnes court held that the "NSC properly limited its search efforts to its institutional records, and ... has conducted an adequated search." Id. at 4.

Once documents are properly labelled Presidential, executive privilege can be invoked to protect the confidentiality of communications between the President and those who advise and assist him in the performance of his duties. See U.S. v Nixon 418 U.S. 683, 705-705 (1973). Although the privilege is

6

qualified, it is strongest when used to protect military, diplomatic or National Security secrets. This privilege applies to communications made in shaping policies and making decisions.

TAB – E

LEE H. HAMILTON, INDIANA, CHAIRMAN

LOUIS STOKES, OHIO
DAVE McCURDY, OKLAHOMA
ANTHONY C. BEILENSON, CALIFORNIA
ROBERT W. KASTENMEIER, WISCONSIN
DAN DANIEL, VIRGINIA
ROBERT A. ROE, NEW JERSEY
GEORGE E. BROWN, JR., CALIFORNIA
MATTHEW F. McHUGH, NEW YORK
BERNARD J. DWYER, NEW JERSEY
BOB STUMP, ARIZONA
ANDY IRELAND, FLORIDA
HENRY J. HYDE, ILLINOIS
DICK CHENEY, WYOMING
BOB LIVINGSTON, LOUISIANA
BOB McEWEN, OHIO

THOMAS K. LATIMER, STAFF DIRECTOR
MICHAEL J. O'NEIL, CHIEF COUNSEL
STEVEN K. BERRY, ASSOCIATE COUNSEL

U.S. HOUSE OF REPRESENTATIVES

PERMANENT SELECT COMMITTEE
ON INTELLIGENCE
WASHINGTON, DC 20515

ROOM H-405, U.S. CAPITOL
(202) 225-4121

October 9, 1986

Vice Admiral John M. Poindexter, USN
Assistant to the President for
   National Security Affairs
The White House
Washington, D. C.   20500

Dear Admiral Poindexter:

Thank you for providing two members of your staff, Paul Thompson and
Ron Sable, to brief the Committee concerning the Washington Post stories on
Libyan disinformation. They helped the Committee reach a better understanding
of what actually occurred in August of this year.

Mr. Thompson emphasized to the Committee that the final National Security
Decision Directive signed by the President contained no mention of
disinformation. He also referred to several working papers - including those
of State (dated August 6, 1986) and CIA, and a memorandum you wrote to the
President - used to prepare for the National Security Planning Group meeting
of August 14 - and an August 7, 1986 National Security Council memorandum on
Chad. The Committee would like to review these documents in order to gain an
understanding of what was considered and then rejected as Administration
policy.

With particular reference to the NSDD, you should be aware that the
classified annex to the FY 87 Intelligence Authorization Act states that the
text of NSDDs which have a bearing on intelligence policy ought to be provided
to the intelligence committees.

Your further cooperation and understanding in this matter will be greatly
appreciated.

With best wishes, I am

Sincerely yours,

Lee H. Hamilton
Chairman

SECRET   Unclassified

TAB – F

 DIVERSIFIED DETECTION SERVICES, INC.

2740 Chain Bridge Road. Vienna, Virginia 22181
703-941-9113

April 29, 1991

Mr. Joseph E. diGenova
Attorney at Law
1200 New Hampshire Avenue, N.W.
Suite 200
Washington, D.C. 20036

Dear Mr. DiGenova:

At your request, Mr. Paul B. Thompson, 202 3rd Street, N.E., Washington, D.C. 20002 was administered a polygraph examination in my office at 2740 Chain Bridge Road, Vienna, Virginia 22181 on April 26, 1991.

The purpose of this examination was to determine whether or not Mr. Thompson was truthful when he denied having in his possession between December 5, 1985 and November 20, 1986 the 1985 finding, better known as the Arms for Hostages document, if he had suggested to Admiral Poindexter on November 21, 1986 the 1985 finding should be destroyed and finally if he had ever by himself or with anyone destroyed knowingly and intentionally any document related to the Iran Contra Affair.

In the pre-test interview, the following relevant questions were developed, reduced to writing and reviewed with Mr. Thompson and his responses were as follows.

#3. Did you to your knowledge have in your possession between December 5, 1985 and November 20, 1986 the 1985 finding?

RESPONSE: No

#5. Did Admiral Poindexter give to you at anytime prior to November 21, 1986 the so called 1985 finding?

RESPONSE: No

#8. Did you say or suggest to Admiral Poindexter on November 21, 1986 that the 1985 finding should be destroyed?

RESPONSE: No

#9   Did you ever at any time knowingly and intentionally
     destroy by yourself or with any other person any document
     related to the Iran Contra Affair?

     RESPONSE: No

Mr. Thompson was administered a MGQT type examination. Four
polygrams were administered including a stem test. After careful
analysis of the polygrams, it is my opinion Mr. Thompson was
truthful in his responses to the relevant questions.

                         Sincerely,

                         James L. Wilt
                         Polygraph Examiner
                         Virginia State License #27

Samuel J. Watson, III

LAW OFFICES

STEIN, MITCHELL & MEZINES
1100 CONNECTICUT AVENUE, NORTHWEST
WASHINGTON, D. C. 20036

BASIL J. MEZINES
GLENN A. MITCHELL
JACOB A. STEIN
GERARD E. MITCHELL
ROBERT F. MUSE
DAVID U. FIERST
RICHARD A. BUSSEY
PATRICK A. MALONE
ROBERT L. BREDHOFF
CHRISTOPHER H. MITCHELL
GEORGE A. TOBIN
SHARON M. JOHNSTON
JOAN D. MEZINES

OF COUNSEL
GEORGE ANTHONY FISHER

TELEPHONE: (202) 737-7777
TELECOPIER: (202) 296-8312

United States Court of Appeals
For the District of Columbia Circuit

FILED SEP 3 0 1993

RON GARVIN
CLERK

September 30, 1993

HAND DELIVERED

Ron Garvin
CLERK
United States Court of Appeals for the
   District of Columbia Circuit
United States Courthouse
333 Constitution Avenue, N.W.
Washington, D.C. 20001-2866

Dear Mr. Garvin:

   I, as attorney for Samuel J. Watson III submit the following:

   1.   We thank you for the opportunity to examine those portions of the Final Report recently submitted to the United States Court of Appeals for the District of Columbia, Division for the Purpose of Appointing Independent Counsels that are relevant to my client, Samuel J. Watson III. We were allowed to see the following pages of the report: pages 43, 44, 443, 444, 485, 486, and 489 to 503. The following comments are based on that viewing.

   2.   I submit the following comments on Mr. Watson's behalf and ask that they be included in their entirety in the Final Report when it is prepared and published.

   3.   The report omits any statement concerning Mr. Watson's military career which led to his selection in November 1985 as Deputy Assistant to the Vice President for National Security Affairs. I give in summary fashion his military career because it shows he was involved in no activity that would have given him an understanding of the alleged events which the Independent Counsel assumes he understood and joined in.

   Samuel J. Watson III was commissioned a Second Lieutenant of

STEIN, MITCHELL & MEZINES

September 20, 1993

Page 2

Infantry from Lafayette College in 1961. He served in Germany as an infantry platoon leader, and was with the 3rd Battalion, 187th Airborne Infantry of the 11th Air Assault Division at Fort Benning which pioneered air mobility and airborne tactics for later use in Vietnam. He went to Vietnam in 1965 with 1st Air Cavalry Division in an airborne infantry battalion; and transferred to 1st Brigade of 101st Airborne Division (serving in the Brigade S-3 (Operations) section, and the 2nd Battalion, 327 Airborne Infantry as a company commander) till late 1966. He taught at the Ranger School and returned to the 3rd Brigade of the 101st Airborne Division where he was the Brigade S-4 (Logistics) officer in 1968, and was with the 2nd Battalion, 506th Airborne Infantry in 1969 in the A Shau Valley and at Firebase Airborne. He led the last U.S. troops out of the Valley. After receiving a Masters degree in International Affairs from The George Washington University he taught U.S. national strategy and decision-making, and arms control at the United States Army Command and General Staff College. He worked on the SALT II nuclear negotiations between the United States and the Soviets, was a policy officer in the State Department's Bureau of European Affairs, was Chief of Staff of Reagan-Bush Transition team at CIA and then Special Assistant to CIA Director, and then on the START talks. From 1985-1989 he was Deputy Assistant to the Vice President for National Security Affairs. From 1989 until 1992 he was a Senior Fellow and Deputy Director of the Strategic Concepts Development Center of the Institute for National Strategic Studies of the National Defense University. He retired a Colonel. He was awarded the Purple Heart, Soldier's Medal, four Bronze Star Medals, four Air Medals, three Defense Superior Service Medals, two Army Commendation Medals, the Combat Infantryman's Badge, Ranger Tab, Pathfinder Badge and Master Parachutist Badge, and, seven campaign stars for Vietnam service.

4.   It is self evident from what is set forth above that prior to his appointment by Vice President Bush he was involved with infantry, combat, training, education, and arms control. He had a very short tour of duty with the CIA which generally involved managing a team of advisors, assisting in the transition from President Carter to President Reagan. It did not involve itself with covert operations.

Mr. Watson deeply resents the assertion, accusation and assumption that he was aware

September 20, 1993

Page 3

---

of alleged unlawful activity in his work with Vice President Bush, or that he sought to conceal what he knew, or withheld documents, or engaged in or conspired to commit "acts of concealment." His background makes it obvious that Vice President Bush did not select Mr. Watson because of any prior involvement in Latin American or covert intelligence activities. Mr. Watson's record shows that anyone interested in a person who could be manipulated to commit wrongful acts certainly would not have selected Mr. Watson. Such conduct is completely foreign to anything he did before his appointment. He was brought on by and assisted people who had been in place long before him. The pace of the office was such that his learning process was day-to-day and on-the-job. He found himself in totally new areas of responsibility. Even a person educated or experienced in Latin American or covert intelligence operations would find the pace hectic and sometimes baffling. Mr. Watson's responsibilities to Vice President Bush were parallel to those held by eight to ten full time NSC staff persons in areas such as Europe, the Soviet Union, NATO, tactical and strategic nuclear arms control, chemical arms control, verification, military programs, continuity of government, Latin America, Canada, Mexico, and nuclear strategy. The White House pace rarely afforded one the luxury of retrospection, contemplation, or consideration that illegal behavior might be occurring in the sly. This is especially so if a decision were made by others to keep illegality secret and to deny the Office of the Vice President awareness or access to it.

Mr. Watson's own background had been among those who dealt fairly with him and he dealt fairly with them.

The Independent Counsel chose to look upon Mr. Watson as someone withholding information important in some way to the investigation of a White House activity. The full details were never given to Mr. Watson, and yet the Independent Counsel expected Mr. Watson to grasp them from the first day he arrived in November 1985. Statements by the Independent Counsel that Mr. Watson withheld information, withheld documents which were not in his possession but rather in the possession of the White House, or engaged in "acts of concealment," are disingenuous and border on the dishonest and cowardly.

What triggered the decision to make Mr. Watson the subject of scrutiny? The answer turns on an event which Mr. Walsh and his associates decided was of cosmic significance but in reality was a momentary, inconsequential event among thousands of others. It now appears that the interruption of his and his families' personal life and his professional career for some seven years is tied to the Independent Counsel's fallacious logic of whether or not Mr. Watson ever used the words "resupply of the Contras."

Mr. Walsh assumes that if Mr. Watson said those words it corroborates Mr. Walsh's unwarranted belief that Mr. Watson, Mr. Gregg, and Vice President Bush must have been part of a conspiracy to commit illegal acts. Therefore, Mr. Walsh demanded Mr. Watson, one, concede that he used the words "resupply of the Contras;" and, two, he implicate himself in the

STEIN, MITCHELL & MEZINES

September 20, 1993

Page 4

_____

"plot."

Whether or not Mr. Watson did in fact use those words can only be answered by Mr. Watson's best recollection which is that he didn't use those words. Even if they were used it was to convey a thought divorced from any knowledge of illegal activity. If the words were used they were consistent with the United States Government's policy which was that the administration felt morally compelled, and legally justified (by Act of Congress) in giving humanitarian aid to the Contras in Nicaragua. Mr. Watson could find no fault with the idea that humanitarian aid was appropriate.

His determination that such aid was appropriate was not based on any legalistic analysis. He is not a lawyer. He recalls seeking no legal advice concerning this issue. Mr. Watson assumed the honesty of those in the White House.

In interrogations concerning the use of these words the point was made over and over that he should "come clean" and spend a weekend or two with Independent Counsel telling them "all." The point was also made that he should have known what was going on around him. The fact of the matter is that as he looks back it is clear that he was not aware of all that was going on around him. Mr. Watson does not suggest by this comment that he is pointing a finger at anyone. It is just that so many disconnected events made up his day that it was close to impossible on a day-to-day basis to organize and draw the inferences Independent Counsel demanded of him. Great pressure was put upon him to go beyond his recollection. It would have been dishonorable to do so and Mr. Watson refused to do so.

And now let me get into the details which relate to what is in the report.

Part IX, "Investigations of the White House," Chapter 29, "Donald P. Gregg," page 491:

Mr. Watson joined the Office of the Vice President in early November 1985. This is relevant as concerns events, notebook entries, letters or memos prepared before that time which Mr. Watson was unaware of until well after the events in question.

In early November 1985 as he joined the White House staff the Vice President asked Mr. Watson to be his principle staff support for Latin American issues. Mr. Watson was not an expert on Latin American affairs. Nonetheless, Mr. Watson accepted this responsibility when requested to do so by the Vice President.

Concerning the scheduling memorandum prepared by Mrs. Phyllis M. Byrne requesting a meeting with the Vice President for Mr. Felix Rodriguez, the Independent Counsel's report would be far more accurate and even balanced had it stated:

STEIN, MITCHELL & MEZINES

September 20, 1993

Page 5

"While Mrs. Byrne strongly asserted that Mr. Watson gave her the phrase "resupply of the Contras," she moved away from her absolute certainty in the first sworn testimony taken from her (Congressional testimony, June 16, 1987). Mr. Watson disputes her assertion (though he agrees he gave her a phrase describing Rodriguez as "a counter-insurgency expert from El Salvador").

It is most unusual that the Independent Counsel has chosen to rely on Mrs. Byrne's absolute recollection of the origin of the phrase "resupply of the Contras," and chosen to ignore her vacillation as to whether Mr. Watson gave her that phrase in her very first testimony (see her Congressional testimony transcript, June 16, 1987, pages 11-13). Notably, in the closing moments of that testimony she modified her absolute statements that Mr. Watson had given her the words concerning resupply of the Contras instead saying she thought she recalled he had.

The report would have been even more accurate and complete had it said that Mr. Watson did not know that Mr. Rodriguez had made such a request until asked by Mrs. Byrne how to describe Mr. Rodriguez, and that Mrs. Byrne testified that she had the phone conversation with Mr. Rodriguez concerning the requested meeting, that she discussed the meeting with Mr. Gregg before beginning to prepare the request, and that then she penned in Mr. Gregg's initials (as she later did on the Briefing Memorandum for the May 1, 1986 meeting).

The Independent Counsel ignored Mrs. Byrne's close and long relationship with Mr. Rodriguez, her extensive phone calls with him, and her willingness to supply Mr. Rodriguez with Vice Presidential mementos (e.g., cuff links, tie bars) until Mr. Watson objected. The Independent Counsel failed to grasp the difference between being able to describe someone (Mr. Rodriguez -- as a "counter-insurgency expert from El Salvador), and being able to describe the purpose of a meeting.

In many cases, memories of events often differ, human nature causes each of us to see and hear things differently, to assign different meanings, and to remember and recall them differently, if at all, and the human mind often tends to blot out unpleasant experiences. The undersigned has found that more contemporaneous recollections of events are more reliable and accurate. The Independent Counsel himself points out this very problem in his report on page - 43.

Mr. Watson believes that any discussions in Winter and Spring 1986 in the Office of the Vice President concerned supply of humanitarian aid to the Nicaraguan Freedom Fighters, not supplies in the context of the Boland Amendment prohibition on military assistance and lethal supplies. The December 1985 State Department cable which the Independent Counsel finds so

September 20, 1993

Page 6

damning refers to the Congressionally authorized supply of humanitarian aid and foodstuffs to the Nicaraguan Contras. That there was a crisis about these supplies in December 1985 was a matter which was entirely proper for Mr. Watson to point out to Mr. Gregg. While a "secret" operation, it was neither covert nor illegal as the Independent Counsel in his rush to find blame faultily implies.

Counsel ignored the other plausible and time context explanations of the phrase "resupply of the Contras" Mr. Watson offered in his various testimonies.

Finally, though my client disputes Mrs. Byrne's and the Independent Counsel's absolute assertions that he provided the phrase "resupply of the Contras," (he has testified that he does not believe he gave the phrase to her) there would have been nothing wrong with discussing that issue, or proposing it for discussion with the Vice President. He pointed this out in his Grand Jury testimony.

For the phrase "resupply of the Contras" to appear in a memo to the Vice President, or for the purposes of scheduling a meeting for him was entirely legal, except for the Independent Counsel's apparent believe that discussions on this issue within the Office of the Vice President were somehow banned, improper, or illegal, or discussions should not include issues on which the Vice President might have to cast a deciding vote in the United States Senate. There would have been nothing wrong with discussing "resupply of the Contras" (even though it was not discussed in the May 1, 1986 meeting), nor to hear the views of Mr. Rodriguez, a "counter-insurgency expert from El Salvador." Perhaps my client did not phrase the above in elegant enough terms for the Independent Counsel to grasp the simplicity of this logic.

Concerning notes which the Independent Counsel wants to blame Mr. Watson for withholding until 1991, Mr. Watson had no role and was not consulted on any White House decisions to withhold his notes. Mr. Watson provided everything he had to the proper White House officials in a timely fashion in late 1986 or early 1987 pursuant to the request by Congressman Lee Hamilton or others. Later, when the Independent Counsel subpoenaed other materials (home phone records, Economist pocket diaries, etc) Mr. Watson was scrupulous and prompt in his response.

It is disingenuous and malicious for the Independent Counsel to asperse Mr. Watson and label his immunized testimony in repeated appearances before the second Grand Jury (1991-1992) as "futile" for failing to recall events five or more years past. That the Counsel was unable to coerce false testimony or testimony to their liking from Mr. Watson is a tribute not a damnation.

As for the "acts of concealment," the Independent Counsel, after almost seven years of

STEIN, MITCHELL & MEZINES

September 20, 1993

Page 7

---

examination and study, still fails to appreciate the context of how the White House works. The White House staff is paid to assess information before rendering it or to advise based on it, to the President and Vice President. Senior United States government officials had surveyed their organizations and thought they were correct in stating the Hasenfus airplane had no connection to the US government. We now know this was wrong, and their statements were wrong. But, for the Independent Counsel to now impose his naive view of the modern White House as a new standard for criminal investigation and prosecution is ludicrous. For him to consider criminal charges against Mr. Watson for not speaking up when there was only one source is preposterous. On October 5, 1986 when the Hasenfus event occurred Mr. Watson had been absent from and out of contact with the White House for almost three weeks. Mr. Watson is not aware that there were any formal or informal meetings or telephone conference calls to assess the Hasenfus shootdown or to decide on public statements.

Conclusion by the Independent Counsel, pages 500-503:

Mr. Watson believes, as he has said since 1986, that he was unaware of the illegal White House-directed supply of military assistance and lethal supplies to the Contras, and that he was excluded from the central issues relating to the Contras and Nicaragua and the 1985 and 1986 RIG meetings. This view is borne out by the Independent Counsel's conclusion, e.g.,

> "There was no credible evidence obtained that the Vice President or any member of his staff directed or actively participated in the contra-resupply effort that existed during the Boland Amendment prohibition on military aid to the Contras. To the contrary, the Office of the Vice President's staff was largely excluded from RIG meetings where contra matters were discussed and during which, particularly in Summer 1986, North openly discussed operational details of his contra efforts. During 1985 and 1986, when Abrams, Fiers and North met to discuss Central American matters too sensitive for the RIG, no evidence that the OVP staff was included or even informed of their discussions. ...."

Mr. Watson had nothing to gain by altering or concealing his recollections. The implication left by the Independent Counsel of Mr. Watson's role is entirely at odds and inconsistent with how colleagues knew Colonel Watson throughout his military, combat and government service.

And so, it seems to me and Mr. Watson that the Independent Counsel's efforts to link him to the behavior and decisions in the National Security Council exemplify unfair use of the Independent Counsel's unlimited power. It violates the fairness of our American sense of right and wrong and the decent ways in which Americans feel its citizens would treat one another.

STEIN, MITCHELL & MEZINES

September 20, 1993

Page 8

_____

And then, it was not for illegal acts themselves that the Independent Counsel sought Mr. Watson but rather his inability to understand or appreciate the acts of others, his inability years later to remember events as the Independent Counsel wished him to. For the Independent Counsel to cause such disturbances in one's life and disrupt a promising career is at odds with what is good about our country.

Sincerely yours,

Jacob A. Stein

Caspar W. Weinberger

SKADDEN, ARPS, SLATE, MEAGHER & FLOM

1440 NEW YORK AVENUE, N.W.

WASHINGTON, D.C. 20005-2107

FAX: (202) 393-5760

DIRECT DIAL
(202) 371- 7403

(202) 371-7000

United States Court of Appeals
For the District of Columbia Circuit

FILED DEC 0 3 1993

RON GARVIN
CLERK

BOSTON
CHICAGO
LOS ANGELES
NEW YORK
SAN FRANCISCO
WILMINGTON

BEIJING
BRUSSELS
BUDAPEST
FRANKFURT
HONG KONG
LONDON
MOSCOW
PARIS
PRAGUE
SYDNEY
TOKYO
TORONTO

December 3, 1993

BY HAND-DELIVERY

Marilyn Sargent, Esq.
Chief Deputy Clerk
United States Court of Appeals for
  the District of Columbia Circuit
Washington, D.C. 20001-2866

               Re: Response of Caspar W. Weinberger to
                    Final Report

Dear Ms. Sargent:

          Enclosed are an original and three copies of
Caspar Weinberger's response to Mr. Walsh's Final Report
which was filed on August 5, 1993.

                              Sincerely,

                              Roberto Iraola

Enclosure

United States Court of Appeals
For the District of Columbia Circuit

FILED DEC 0 3 1993

RON GARVIN
CLERK

RESPONSE OF CASPAR W. WEINBERGER TO THE FINAL REPORT

By: Skadden, Arps, Slate, Meagher & Flom
December 3, 1993

TABLE OF CONTENTS

UNITED STATES COURT OF APPEALS
FOR THE DISTRICT OF COLUMBIA CIRCUIT

Division for the Purpose of Appointing
Independent Counsels

In Re: Oliver L. North, et al.   )   Division No. 86-6
)   (Under Seal)
)
)

RESPONSE OF CASPAR W.
WEINBERGER TO THE FINAL REPORT

On August 5, 1993, Lawrence E. Walsh, the Independent

Counsel appointed by this Court on December 19, 1986, filed his

Final Report pursuant to 28 U.S.C. § 594(h)(1)(B). That same

day, this Court entered an order making available portions of the

Final Report to a number of persons named therein stating that

"each such individual shall, not later than October 4, 1993,

submit to the Clerk of the Court . . . any written comments or

factual information that they request be included as an Appendix

to said Report."[1] Thereafter, on September 24, 1993, the Court

extended the time for filing any motions or responses to December

---

[1]   Order of Division for the Purpose of Appointing
Independent Counsels (August 5, 1993) at 2. Mr.
Weinberger was not named in the August 5, 1993, order. On
August 6, however, the Court entered another order iden-
tifying him as one who "should be added to the list of
individuals in the prior order of the Court." Order of
Division for the Purpose of Appointing Independent Coun-
sels (August 6, 1993) at 1.

3, 1993.[2] Caspar W. Weinberger, through undersigned counsel,
hereby submits the following response to the allegations made
against him in the Final Report.

I. BACKGROUND

As is well known, Mr. Weinberger was one of the most
vigorous opponents of the initiative to trade arms clandestinely
to Iran in exchange for American held hostages in Lebanon by
groups sympathetic to Iran (the "Iran initiative"). Mr.
Weinberger cooperated fully with all investigations of the Iran-
Contra matter, including those conducted by the Tower Commission,
the Joint Select Committees of Congress and the Independent
Counsel. His prosecution by Mr. Walsh on a five-count indictment
alleging obstruction of Congress, perjury and false statements
was nothing short of a gross abuse of the prosecutorial power by
an independent counsel who needed to rehabilitate his image after
an abysmal five and a half year investigation which cost taxpayers over $35 million.

Mr. Weinberger was innocent of all charges filed
against him. He had no motive to lie about the Iran-Contra
matter or his notes. To the contrary, the notes demonstrate the
vigor of his opposition to the Iran initiative. Indeed, there
can be no argument that Mr. Weinberger intended to hide his notes

---

[2]　　Order of Division for the Purpose of Appointing
Independent Counsels (September 24, 1993) at 1.

because he deposited them at the Library of Congress and made them available to Mr. Walsh.

In addition, Mr. Weinberger passed, with flying colors, a rigorous lie detector test on the very issues which formed the basis of the indictment. Many well-respected Americans also executed affidavits which were submitted to Mr. Walsh attesting to Mr. Weinberger's honesty and integrity, and supporting his innocence. One such notable example was General Colin Powell, the former Chairman of the Joint Chiefs of Staff who worked closely with Mr. Weinberger on a daily basis as his senior military assistant. Most telling, perhaps, was the joint letter to Mr. Weinberger's counsel by Senators Warren B. Rudman and Daniel K. Inouye, the former Co-Chairmen of the Senate Select Committee investigating the Iran-Contra matter before which Mr. Weinberger was charged with lying. In their letter, Senators Rudman and Inouye stated: "It is inconceivable to us that [Secretary Weinberger] would intentionally mislead or lie to Congress."[3]

Finally, Mr. Weinberger was the last witness to give public testimony on these issues and he and those who assisted him in preparing for his testimony before Congress were aware of

---

[3] Letter from Warren B. Rudman and Daniel K. Inouye to Robert S. Bennett dated April 29, 1992, at 2 appended hereto as Attachment A.

the allegations on the public record. Put another way, the Select Committees were fully cognizant of the facts relating to the Iran-Contra matter by the time Mr. Weinberger testified. Therefore, it simply would have been irrational for him to commit perjury regarding events about which Congress was fully aware, as Mr. Walsh alleged in his indictment.

In light of this record and the numerous abuses by Mr. Walsh and the members of his office in the course of their seemingly endless investigation of Iran-Contra, President George Bush, on December 24, 1992, granted Mr. Weinberger "a full, complete, and unconditional pardon . . . for all offenses charged or prosecuted by Independent Counsel Lawrence E. Walsh or other members of his office, or committed by . . . [Mr. Weinberger] and within the jurisdiction of that office."[4] The district court thereafter dismissed the charges against Mr. Weinberger with prejudice.

II. THE FINAL REPORT

A. General Observations

Notwithstanding former President Bush's pardon almost 12 months ago, and the district court's subsequent dismissal of the charges against him, Mr. Weinberger still confronts a segment of a lengthy report written by Mr. Walsh that asserts he

---

[4]   Grant of Executive Clemency dated December 24, 1992, at 3.

committed various criminal offenses. The very fact that Mr. Weinberger must respond to this report represents, as further described below, the final chapter in a long line of prosecutorial abuses by Mr. Walsh and his staff.

A reading of those portions of the report which were made available to counsel reveals that Mr. Walsh has transformed his statutory reporting requirement under 28 U.S.C. § 594(h)(1)(B) into a massive effort to rewrite history and resurrect his and his office's reputation, all at enormous taxpayer expense.[5] Of course, in this context, Mr. Walsh is free from the constraints that foiled his other efforts, namely, the rule of law administered by a court in which his purported "facts" would be subject to cross-examination by an adversary.

Not surprisingly, in his Final Report, Mr. Walsh questions President Bush's constitutional prerogative to exercise his pardon power,[6] while gratuitously concluding that there was insufficient evidence "the pardon was secured by corruption."[7] He also seemingly relitigates the district court's repeated dismissals of charges that Mr. Weinberger withheld his notes from

---

[5] It was estimated that Mr. Walsh expended more than one million dollars from May 1993 to August 1993. York, "The Final (Pay) Days of Lawrence Walsh," The Wall Street Journal, Aug. 11, 1993 at A8.

[6] Final Report at 48.

[7] Id.

Congress,[8] asserts that Mr. Weinberger was guilty of the offenses charged,[9] and alleges a conspiracy among high-level Reagan Administration officials to cover-up the Iran-Contra matter.[10] Part VIII of the Report contains a section titled "The Government's Case Against Weinberger" which purports to describe, in detail, particular documents and the expected testimony of witnesses the Office of Independent Counsel ("OIC") intended to present at trial.[11] As promised by Mr. Walsh during his interview with Scott Spencer for the cover story of the July 4, 1993 issue of the New York Times Magazine, the Report contains, as Mr. Walsh put it, "things we were not able to prove."[12]

A prosecutor, of course, should not use his position and resources as a forum to present his side of a case that never goes to trial. The Final Report does just that. Mr. Walsh's one-sided and bitter presentation, however, does not withstand scrutiny when one considers the record. It also flies in the face of a venerable legal concept that Mr. Walsh acknowledged

---

[8] Id. at 415 & n.100 & 102.

[9] Id. at 415-30.

[10] Id. at xi, 456-60, 480-83, 526-27.

[11] Id. at 415-30.

[12] Spencer "Lawrence Walsh's Last Battle," The New York Times Magazine, (July 4, 1993) at 33.

previously but now ignores: "Anglo-American law places its faith in proof of facts, and not in speculation."[13]

B. The Allegations In The Indictment

At the time of the pardon, there were four counts pending against Mr. Weinberger as a result of the indictment filed against him on June 16, 1992.[14] Specifically, count II alleged that Mr. Weinberger made a false statement during his June 17, 1987 deposition before the House Select Committee investigating the Iran-Contra matter regarding his recollection of payments by Saudi Arabia to the Contras. Counts III and IV alleged that Mr. Weinberger committed perjury in his Congressional testimony on July 31, 1987 with regard to (i) his knowledge of a shipment of 18 HAWK missiles to Iran in November 1985 and (ii) his memory of whether "replenishment" of Israeli arms supplies was "an issue." Count V alleged that during an interview on October 10, 1990, Mr. Weinberger made false statements to the OIC concerning his note-taking practices.

These allegations -- essentially premised on purported discrepancies between Mr. Weinberger's testimony in 1987 about

---

[13]   Second Interim Report, December 11, 1989 at 48.

[14]   The first count of the indictment charging obstruction of Congress was dismissed by the district court for failure to state an offense. For ease of reference, we retain throughout this response the numeration of the counts as they appeared in the original indictment.

events in 1985 and daily jottings regarding the events about which he testified -- were baseless. The OIC would not have been able to establish that Mr. Weinberger had any <u>intent</u> to lie to Congress or the OIC.

     With respect to Mr. Weinberger's testimony before Congress -- counts II, III and IV -- Mr. Weinberger simply did not lie or commit perjury. A number of factors support this conclusion. First, despite Mr. Walsh's microscopic and tortured analysis, the fact of the matter is that the notes do not contradict Mr. Weinberger's testimony. Second, counts II and III charge Mr. Weinberger with crimes for asserting that he had no "memory" of events that took place almost two years prior to his testimony. Neither the notes nor any other documents or testimony would have provided evidence to the contrary. Third, with respect to count III, while Mr. Weinberger testified that he was aware of proposals to send arms to Iran in exchange for the release of American hostages held in Lebanon, he had never been advised that 18 HAWK missiles were to be sent or had been delivered to Iran, and the OIC would have been unable to prove otherwise.[15] Fourth, Mr. Weinberger was the last witness to testify on

---

[15] Mr. Walsh states in his report that "[b]eginning in late September 1985 and continuing through the end of 1986, Weinberger also received a sizeable quantity of highly classified intelligence reports regarding the Iran initiative. These intelligence reports provided detailed
                                         (continued...)

these issues. At that time, the Select Committees were fully

cognizant of the facts and circumstances surrounding the Iran-

Contra matter. Therefore, it would have been irrational for Mr.

Weinberger to commit perjury regarding events about which Con-

gress was fully aware.

It is noteworthy that the former Chairman and Vice-

Chairman of the Senate Select Committee, Senators Rudman and

Inouye, stated for the record that

---

[15] (...continued)
information regarding the pricing and delivery of missiles sold to Iran and the release of American hostages
in Lebanon." Final Report at 415 (footnote omitted). As
Mr. Walsh is well aware, these "highly classified intelligence reports," which were the subject of hearings
under the Classified Information Procedures Act, contained garbled and confusing information regarding arms
and hostages. Thus, Mr. Weinberger noted in an entry
dated September 20, 1985: "Saw Colin Powell - re strange
[intelligence reports] about our hostages - the [Irani-
ans] seem to think they are getting arms." Weeks later,
on October 3, 1985, Mr. Weinberger noted again: "Colin
Powell in office - with [intelligence reports] about
Iranians claiming arms transfers by us for return of
prisoners." The contention that Mr. Weinberger received
intelligence reports in 1985 that "provided detailed
information" regarding arms and hostages is misleading
because these reports were not deemed reliable. Of
course, since these intelligence reports were made available to the OIC in its investigation of Oliver North and
others, if Mr. Walsh really deemed them proof that Mr.
Weinberger perjured himself when he discussed his knowledge of the HAWK shipment he would not have waited five
years to charge Mr. Weinberger. The fact of the matter
is that the OIC had these "intelligence reports" with
"detailed information" for five years and did nothing
about them. Now, in his attempt to rewrite history, Mr.
Walsh presents them as further "proof" that Mr.
Weinberger was aware of the HAWK shipment in 1985.

While Secretary Weinberger testified that he did not have contemporaneous knowledge of the 1985 arms shipment to Iran through Israel, he indicated that his recollection of dates was not as good as it once was and that he had difficulty sorting out what he knew at any particular time from what he had learned later. We were aware that his recollection as to the state of his knowledge in the fall of 1985 might have been imperfect as he had a poor recollection as to certain documents. <u>We were also aware that Secretary Weinberger received intelligence reports concerning the Iranian initiative which contained suggestions that shipments might be taking place in the Fall of 1985. What was important to us, however, was not the date on which the Secretary knew or could have inferred from other information that arms shipments might have taken place, on which the testimony and evidence was murky, but the adamant position that the Secretary consistently took with the President in opposing sales to Iran on which the testimony was incontrovertible</u>. The fact that his advice, like that of Secretary Shultz, was overridden by the President and rejected by the National Security Advisor was a key finding of our investigation and was described in our report.[16]

The significance of a letter such as this cannot be understated. After all, these were the Chairman and Vice-Chairman of the Senate Committee before whom Mr. Weinberger allegedly had perjured himself stating in clear and unambiguous terms that when Mr. Weinberger knew about shipments or replenishment of such shipments was not material. What was important was the "adamant position that the Secretary consistently took with the President in opposing sales to Iran on which the testimony was incontrovertible." The Senators also stated that "[b]ased upon our dealings with him over the years, we know Secretary Weinberger to be

---

[16]   Attachment A (emphasis added).

a man of the highest integrity and honor. It is inconceivable to
us that he would intentionally mislead or lie to Congress."[17] Mr.
Walsh, however, was not impressed by what the heads of the
Committee had to say. After investigating this matter for over
six years, he was determined to try in a court of law the politically controversial Reagan Administration policy to sell arms to
Iran in exchange for the release of American hostages, as well as
an alleged conspiracy to cover up this policy which he believed
was hatched in November 1986.[18]

In the hopes of buttressing the record in support of
the declination of any contemplated prosecution, Mr. Weinberger
underwent a rigorous polygraph examination conducted by Paul K.
Minor, who served as the Federal Bureau of Investigation's
Polygraph Program Coordinator and Chief Polygraph Examiner from
1978 to 1987. Specifically, Mr. Minor asked Secretary Weinberger

---

[17]   Id.

[18]   Mr. Walsh's obsession with Iran-Contra enjoys some
literary parallels. As Herman Melville recounted over
one hundred years ago in his masterpiece Moby Dick:

> All that most maddens and torments; all that
> stirs up the lees of things; all truth with
> malice in it; all that cracks the sinews and
> cakes the brain; all the subtle demonisms of
> life and thought; all evil, to crazy Ahab, were
> visibly personified, and made practically as-
> sailable in Moby Dick.

Iran-Contra, it appears, visibly personified the great
white whale for Mr. Walsh.

11

the following questions: (1) Did you ever intentionally withhold diary notes from any governmental entity?; (2) Did you deliberately mislead any governmental entity, including the Office of Independent Counsel, about your diary notes?; (3) Did you knowingly engage in a cover-up with senior Administration officials in the fall of 1986 or in 1987 regarding Ronald Reagan's participation in the Iran-Contra matter?; (4) During your June 1987 deposition, did you deliberately lie to the House Select Committee Counsel about the existence of your diary notes?; and (5) Did you deliberately mislead any governmental entity regarding your knowledge of the transfer of arms to Iran from August to November 1985? Mr. Weinberger answered no to each of these questions. Mr. Minor concluded that "[t]here was no indication of deception to any relevant question and . . . Mr. Weinberger truthfully answered each of the . . . questions."[19]

Finally, with respect to count V, Mr. Walsh is well aware that his office was given unimpeded access to Mr. Weinberger's records regarding the Iran-Contra matter. As the

---

[19] A copy of Mr. Minor's resume and the report he prepared containing the results of the polygraph examination are appended hereto as Attachment B. Although Mr. Walsh asked at least one witness interviewed by his office whether he would be willing to undergo a polygraph examination, thereby suggesting that he considered such an examination to be of some investigative value, he never requested that Mr. Weinberger undergo any further polygraph examinations.

Final Report acknowledges, Mr. Weinberger's attorney, William P. Rogers, told Associate Independent Counsel Craig A. Gillen on September 13, 1990 that Mr. Weinberger's documents were either in the possession of the Select Committees or at the Library of Congress.[20] Indeed, Mr. Walsh told the Court that there was not "any issue of fact" about this.[21]

Then, during the OIC's October 10, 1990 interview of Mr. Weinberger, the OIC again was directed to the documents at the Library of Congress and told it could have access to them.[22]

---

[20]   Final Report at 412.

[21]   Transcript of Oral Argument (September 10, 1992) at 21.

[22]   See id. at 21. As Mr. Walsh notes in his Final Report, the OIC's account of that meeting "is based upon the FBI Record of Interview, also referred to as a '302'." Id. at 412 n.87. Mr. Walsh further states: "Weinberger and his counsel were permitted to review the FBI agent's October 10, 1990, interview report when they returned to the Office of Independent Counsel for another interview on December 3, 1990. Both Weinberger and his counsel complimented the report's accuracy and thoroughness and contrasted it favorably with the report of the 1988 interview, which had suggested he was an avid note-taker." Id. at 413. (footnote omitted). The report of that interview demonstrates clearly that Mr. Walsh is adept at rewriting history. Specifically, the report of the December 1990 interview states in part:

> Rogers and Weinberger were advised of the identities of Bever, Mark and Steele, after which they each were given a copy of a FD-302 reflecting an interview with Weinberger on October 10, 1990 by Special Agent Michael S. Foster.

                                              (continued...)

13

Shortly after the interview, Associate Independent Counsel Thomas D. Bever wrote Mr. Rogers to advise him that they had "contacted the Library of Congress in order to review the papers [Mr.

22(...continued)

Once they had finished reading the FD-302, Rogers and Weinberger were advised by Bever that the interview today would deal with [classified], vice presidential knowledge, and what meetings the Vice President attended.

At this time, Rogers interrupted stating he wanted to comment regarding a point made on page 7 of Weinberger's interview of October 10, 1990. This page has a significant paragraph referencing an allegation that Weinberger has withheld some of his notes. Rogers asked if the Office of Independent Counsel were ready to discuss and deal with this.

Bever responded that the OIC is not planning to nor needs to talk about this paragraph today. Specifically, the discussion today is about intelligence [classified] with the First Channel and the Second Channel, but will primarily deal with the First Channel.

The report of this interview makes no mention of Messrs. Rogers and Weinberger praising the accuracy of the report of the October 10 interview. To the contrary, the report states that Mr. Bever (who declined defense counsel's request for an interview) did not permit Mr. Rogers or Mr. Weinberger to make any further comments concerning the October 10 report after Mr. Rogers asserted that he wanted to comment on the allegation that Mr. Weinberger had withheld his notes. As reflected in the December 1990 report, Bever wished to discuss only "vice presidential knowledge."

14

Weinberger] donated to the Library."[23]   The Library had informed

the OIC that Mr. Weinberger's written permission was required and

therefore, "[g]iven the cooperative nature" of their prior

meeting, Mr. Bever requested such permission.[24]   A few days later,

on November 8, 1990, Mr. Weinberger executed a formal authoriza-

tion permitting the OIC to inspect and "obtain copies of such

notes and documents related to the Iran/Contra matter."[25]   Thus,

it defies reason to allege that Mr. Weinberger lied to Mr. Walsh

about the existence of his notes during his interview which

served as the basis of count V, when prior to the interview, he

had advised the OIC that all his Iran-Contra papers were with the

Select Committees or the Library of Congress, and after the

interview, he granted Mr. Walsh unimpeded access to all such records.[26]

---

[23]   Letter from Thomas D. Bever to William P. Rogers
dated October 30, 1990. Mr. Bever participated in the
October 10, 1990, interview. He subsequently was identified by the OIC as a potential government witness and declined defense counsel's request for an interview.
Letter from Thomas D. Bever to Carl S. Rauh dated September 22, 1992.

[24]   Letter from Thomas D. Bever to William P. Rogers
dated October 30, 1990.

[25]   A copy of Mr. Weinberger's letter to John Haynes
dated November 8, 1990 is appended hereto as Attachment
C.

[26]   The Final Report also mentions that there were
photographs of Mr. Weinberger and his notes. Specifically, Mr. Walsh states in his Report at page 420:

(continued...)

Mr. Walsh alleges in his Report that "[a]fter mistakenly searching for relevant documents in the classified section of
the Weinberger collection at the Library of Congress, OIC in late
1991 discovered in the unclassified section approximately 7,000
pages of handwritten notes by Weinberger, including nearly 1,700
from the 1985-1986 Iran/Contra period."[27] He also maintains that

---

[26](...continued)

> Weinberger personally packed his
> diary notes as he was preparing to
> leave office in November 1987. On
> that day, Roger Sandler, a freelance
> photographer, was present to take
> photos for a magazine profile of
> Weinberger. These photos show Wein-
> berger handling large stacks of his
> diary notes, neatly bundled together
> with binder clips and rubber bands.

What Mr. Walsh fails to mention, however, is that
these photographs (see Mr. Sandler's affidavit found at
Attachment D), which were intended for national publication, were provided to Mr. Walsh by counsel for Mr.
Weinberger. The Department of Defense did not have any
copies of these photographs. Mr. Walsh did not discover
these photographs in the bowels of the Department of
Defense. To the contrary, they were presented to Mr.
Walsh as exculpatory evidence demonstrating that Mr.
Weinberger had no intent to hide or secrete his notes.
Mr. Walsh, unfortunately, never understood that it would
have been irrational for Mr. Weinberger to withhold his
notes intentionally in April 1987 (when requests for such
materials were issued by the Joint Select Committees) and
then in November 1987 permit a photographer to take
pictures of his "crime" for all the world to see. Thus,
far from being incriminating, the circumstances surrounding the taking of these photographs provided powerful
exculpatory evidence that simply did not comport with Mr.
Walsh's theory of this matter.

[27]   Final Report at 47 (footnote omitted).

16

"[t]he investigators were directed to the classified subject list in the Library's index to the Weinberger collection. Investigators found no collection of notes among the materials they examined."[28] In a footnote, Mr. Walsh further states: "In what may have been a misunderstanding, the OIC investigators did not believe they were at liberty to examine other parts of the index and therefore did not see the references to diary and meeting notes in the description of unclassified material."[29] These self-serving statements are not credible and border on the ludicrous. Further, Mr. Walsh ignores the conclusive evidence demonstrating their inaccuracy.

Conspicuously absent from Part VII of the Final Report captioned "Officers of the Department of Defense (United States v. Caspar W. Weinberger and Related Investigations)", comprising of thirty-seven pages and three hundred and fourteen footnotes, is the affidavit of Allan Teichroew.[30] Mr. Teichroew was and

---

[28]   Final Report at 413 (footnote omitted).

[29]   Id. at 413 n.92.

[30]   This affidavit, as well as those of Colin L. Powell (former Chairman of the Joint Chiefs of Staff), William H. Taft IV (former Unites States Ambassador to NATO), John E. Haynes (Twentieth Century Political Historian in the Manuscript Division of the Library of Congress), Donald S. Jones (retired Vice Admiral of the U.S. Navy), Lawrence H. Garrett, III (former General Counsel at the Department of Defense), Edward J. Shapiro (former Assistant General Counsel at the Department of Defense),
(continued...)

continues to be the Assistant Head for Processing of the Prepara-

tion Section of the Manuscript Division at the Library of Con-

gress.

According to Mr. Teichroew, on November 20, 1990 --

less than two weeks after Mr. Weinberger had granted the OIC

permission to review "notes or other documents" and "to obtain

copies of such notes and documents related to the Iran/Contra

matter," attorneys from the OIC, including Mr. Gregory Mark,

visited the Library of Congress to review the Weinberger papers.[31]

Mr. Teichroew reviewed a register or "Finding Aid" with Mr. Mark

which documented the organization of the papers. For approxi-

mately 15 to 20 minutes, Mr. Teichroew explained the use of the

Finding Aid to the OIC attorneys.[32] Specifically, he advised the

attorneys that the Finding Aid contained a series description, a

scope and content note, and a more detailed container listing,

---

[30](...continued)
Thelma Stubbs Smith (former private secretary to Secretary Weinberger), Lieutenant General Gordon E. Fornell
(former Senior Military Assistant to Secretary
Weinberger), and Roger Sandler (a freelance photojournalist), were submitted to Mr. Walsh during pre-indictment
discussions in support of various arguments -- all to no
avail. They are all appended as Attachment D.

[31]   Affidavit of Allan Teichroew dated April 16, 1992 at
3.

[32]   Id. at 4.

with specific reference to the Department of Defense series.[33]

All of these make reference to diary notes.[34]

---

[33]   Id.

[34]   For example, the scope and content note's second
paragraph found at page 4 of the Finding Aid states in
part: "Included in the [Weinberger] papers are appointment books, <u>diary notes and other jottings</u>[.]" (emphasis
added). The scope and content note's seventh paragraph
at page 5 of the Finding Aid describes the Department of
Defense files. It reads in part as follows:

> Department of Defense files in these papers
> begin with transition material documenting the
> Reagan Administration's first steps in military
> leadership. Other series from this period
> include appointment records and <u>diary notes</u>, a
> private file of miscellaneous correspondence,
> and a large group of subject files. Notable
> among the appointment data is a special catego-
> ry of White House, cabinet, and other important
> <u>meeting notes</u> containing the Defense
> Secretary's <u>handwritten jottings</u> and sometimes
> those of Reagan and Vice President George Bush.
> (emphasis added).

The next paragraph explains that subjects in the Department of Defense files include "U.S. - Soviet nuclear
weapons discussions, the invasion of Grenada, the
Falklands War, various crisis in Lebanon, American policy
toward Nicaragua, relations with NATO, U.S. attacks on
Libya, terrorism, <u>and the Iran-Contra affair</u>." (emphasis
added).

On page 12 of the Finding Aid, there is a two-page
description of the Department of Defense series of the
Weinberger papers. Boxes 576-592 are described as "Appointment and Diary Files, 1980-87," which in turn are
described as including "Appointment books, <u>diary notes</u>,
activity logs, social calendars, telephone call sheets,
and handwritten notes kept by Weinberger of White House,
cabinet, and other important meetings he attended while
Secretary of Defense." (emphasis added). Finally, page

(continued...)

The contention that Mr. Weinberger did not give the OIC
permission to review the unclassified portion of his collection
or intended to mislead the OIC is, as the record demonstrates,
nothing more than a figment of Mr. Walsh's imagination -- a vivid
and engaging one obsessed with the detection of sophisticated
conspiracies at the highest levels of government. Mr.
Weinberger's written authorization permitting the OIC to inspect
and "obtain copies of . . . notes and documents related to the
Iran/Contra matter" did not make any distinction between unclassified and classified material. Evidently, when Mr. Mark first
went to the Library of Congress, he focused solely on classified
material.[35] In order to have determined what container to select

---

[34] (...continued)
84 of the Finding Aid, which contains a more detailed
container listing of Department of Defense related papers, indicates that "diary notes" for the years 1980 to
1987 are included in the series.

[35]   See Attachment C to Teichroew affidavit. Mr. Walsh
asserts in his Report that "[w]hen OIC investigators returned to the Library of Congress in November 1991, they
reviewed the entire index and found thousands of pages of
diary and meeting notes that Weinberger had created as
secretary of defense. These notes, which contained
highly classified information, had been stored in the
unclassified section of the Weinberger collection."
Report at 413 (emphasis original; footnote omitted).
This statement is misleading insofar as it suggests that
one year earlier investigators had not been permitted to
review the register containing unclassified information
which identified diary notes as part of the collection.
Furthermore, the register contains a three page description captioned "Classified Items Removed." There is a
                                        (continued...)

from Mr. Weinberger's collection, however, he must have used the

Finding Aid, the organization of which was explained to him by

Mr. Teichroew. Inexplicably, he declined to ask for notes

clearly described as part of the collection.[36]

On November 30, 1990, when Mr. Mark visited the Library

a second time, he reviewed top secret material.[37] Prior to

selecting particular containers in the collection with this

material, however, he was given access to the Finding Aid.

Again, Mr. Mark did not ask for any notes.

It was not until November 1991 -- one year after Mr.

Weinberger granted the OIC permission to review his documents --

that the OIC requested Mr. Weinberger's notes during his tenure

as Secretary of Defense. They were made available to the OIC.

Months later, Mr. Weinberger was rewarded for his cooperation by

the return of a five-count indictment. Contrary to the impres-

---

[35] (...continued)
reference at page three of that list to certain appointment and diary files which had been removed because they
were classified. The investigators, which it appears
were obsessed with the review of classified material,
apparently also overlooked the reference to "classified"
diary files on this list.

[36]   Mr. Mark was one of three lawyers from the OIC
present during the October 10, 1990 interview. One would
assume that armed with the knowledge that Mr. Weinberger
allegedly had withheld his notes, he would have looked
for references to notes in the Finding Aid to the collection.

[37]   See Attachment C to Teichroew affidavit.

21

sion created by Mr. Walsh in his Final Report, however, it was
not any action by Mr. Weinberger that precluded "discovery" of
the notes. Rather, it was the sloppiness and carelessness of the
OIC that resulted in its not having the notes until November
1991.[38]

III. THE OIC'S PROSECUTORIAL ABUSES

The prosecution of Caspar W. Weinberger must be considered against the backdrop of Mr. Walsh's flagrant abuses of his
prosecutorial powers. As noted previously, after having spent
over five years and in excess of $35 million dollars investigat-
ing Iran-Contra, Mr. Walsh needed to justify his dismal prosecutorial record. He was driven by the belief that the Reagan
Administration had broken the law by selling arms for hostages
and that Administration officials knowingly had engaged in a
cover-up of this decision in November 1986. After the failure of
his major prosecutions, Secretary Weinberger was the only vehicle
left by which Mr. Walsh could present his thesis.[39]

---

[38]   This, after all, was the same office which reportedly lost a suitcase of classified documents after dropping
it off "at a curb-side check in" at an airport following
its interview of former President Reagan. Johnston,
"Federal Agents Investigating Loss of Iran-Contra Papers," The New York Times (Oct. 10, 1992) at 6.

[39]   One of the myths fostered by Mr. Walsh was that the
prosecution of Secretary Weinberger would expose a conspiracy by officials in the highest levels of government.
That is to say, while the indictment contained five
                                        (continued...)

Mr. Walsh's abuse of the prosecutorial power vested in

his office manifested itself prior to the return of the indict-

ment against Mr. Weinberger in June 1992 in his use of the grand

jury.   After the indictment was returned, Mr. Walsh's abuses

continued unabated.   Some of the more notable ones which are

recounted below entailed: (i) a disregard for discovery obliga-

tions; (ii) comments to the press; (iii) an attempt to have a

lawyer who was a witness to one of the charges try the case; (iv)

the "mock" trial of Mr. Weinberger; (v) the politically motivated

second indictment; and (vi) improper fiscal practices.   When

considered together, these abuses reveal Mr. Walsh's zealousness

---

[39] (...continued)
specific and narrow charges against Mr. Weinberger, it
was replete with surplusage insinuating a conspiracy on
the part of former Presidents Bush and Reagan, as well as
other high officials within the Reagan Administration.

In response, Judge Thomas F. Hogan, to whom this
case was assigned, made clear that this prosecution would
not serve as a forum for Mr. Walsh to present his thesis.
For example, at the very outset, when Mr. Weinberger was
arraigned, Judge Hogan observed that while "the indictment itself [wa]s rather lengthy . . . the complexity of
the charges . . . did not seem . . . to be that involved." Transcript of Arraignment (June 19, 1992) at 3.
Subsequently, when ruling on the defense's motion to
strike this surplusage, Judge Hogan expressed "concer[n]
that the indictment rea[d] like a charge of conspiracy,
although no conspiracy [wa]s charged" and stated that
absent a "real relationship" to the charges, evidence of
these other "allegations" would not be admissible.
Memorandum Opinion and Pretrial Order No. 6 (September
29, 1992) at 13.

23

and poor judgment. Additionally, they demonstrate that Mr. Walsh perceived himself and members of his staff as exempt from the guidelines that bind other prosecutors and the laws applicable to other government officials.

A. Use Of Grand Jury To Intimidate Witnesses

On March 30, 1992, after several years of believing himself to be a cooperating witness, Mr. Weinberger received a target letter inviting him to testify before the grand jury.[40] Following counsel's advice, Mr. Weinberger declined the invitation. With counsel's assistance, however, Mr. Weinberger continued to cooperate with the OIC's investigation. Counsel met several times with Mr. Walsh and members of his staff in an attempt to convince the OIC that a prosecution of Mr. Weinberger was unwarranted and would result in a miscarriage of justice.

In preparing for the meetings with Mr. Walsh, counsel for Mr. Weinberger, who unlike Mr. Walsh had not been investigating Iran-Contra for close to six years, needed to gather the

---

[40] Prior to this invitation, Mr. Weinberger had been interviewed by the OIC and/or the FBI on five occasions. He also had testified about matters relating to Iran-Contra before the Senate Select Committee on Intelligence, the House Permanent Select Committee on Intelligence, the President's Special Review Board (Tower Commission), the House Committee on Foreign Affairs, the Senate Select Committee on Secret Military Assistance to Iran and the Nicaraguan Opposition, and the House Select Committee to Investigate Covert Arms Transactions with Iran.

24

facts and learn as much information as possible. This logically

entailed interviewing present and former employees at the Depart-

ment of Defense and the Library of Congress, as well as obtaining

documents from those entities. Throughout this investigative

process, it gradually became clear that the OIC had a different

view of the type of access defense counsel was entitled to

regarding witnesses and documents.

The extent to which the OIC was willing to interfere

with counsel's defense efforts reached a climax when, prior to a

meeting with Mr. Walsh and members of his staff in early June

1992, counsel learned that Department of Defense employees had

been subpoenaed to appear before the grand jury and been command-

ed to produce documents relating not to Iran-Contra but to their

communications with the defense. Shocked by this flagrant abuse

of the grand jury process, counsel wrote Mr. Walsh:

> To subpoena witnesses to appear before the
> grand jury to answer questions and produce documents
> about their contacts with us has the effect of chilling
> our access to these witnesses. As we are certain you
> are aware, the District of Columbia Circuit has ruled
> that witnesses "are the property of neither the prose-
> cution nor the defense." Gregory v. Unites States, 369
> F.2d 185, 188 (D.C. Cir. 1966), cert. denied, 396 U.S.
> 865 (1969).

> Here, serving grand jury subpoenas on witnesses
> who have elected to share information with us so that they
> can testify about their communications with us is not much
> different than if you had instructed the witnesses not to
> speak with us unless members of your staff were present.
> The effect on the witnesses, in either instance, is the
> same. Not surprisingly, at least one witness has indicated

25

that the receipt of a subpoena has had a chilling effect on his dealing with us. Thus, by this conduct, your office appears to be engaging in what the court in Gregory proscribed -- the "suppression of the means by which the defense [can] obtain evidence." Id. at 189. The message is clear - if you give any assistance to Mr. Weinberger's counsel - you will be subpoenaed to the grand jury or . . . will be told you are a "subject" of the investigation.[41]

On June 10, 1992, Mr. Gillen responded on behalf of Mr. Walsh asserting that the OIC was not interested in blocking counsel's access to witnesses but that was "a different matter than the issue of whether Department of Defense employees provided [defense counsel] . . . document requests issued by this Office to the Department of Defense in the course of a criminal

---

[41]   Letter from Robert S. Bennett and Carl S. Rauh to Lawrence E. Walsh dated June 1, 1992 at 1-2. Counsel concluded the letter by stating:

> Finally, we must tell you in all candor that we are surprised at this conduct. We have engaged in a meaningful dialogue in the last several weeks about the merits of a possible prosecution of Mr. Weinberger. Naturally, to address your concerns, members of our staff have sought to obtain documents and interviewed witnesses. We simply do not see how else we could have made our various presentations to you. These unfair tactics are most troubling since, as we mentioned to you during one of our initial meetings, we have elected not to withhold any information from you and instead to disclose fully the merits of our defense.

investigation."[42] Mr. Gillen further asserted that he believed

such "document requests would be treated as confidential" and

that he was "not aware that . . . formal requests were filed" for

copies of such documents, specifically a letter by the OIC to the

Department of Defense dated May 27, 1992.[43]

As Mr. Walsh is aware, on June 19, after the return of

the indictment, counsel responded to Mr. Gillen's earlier letter

stating:

> I am in receipt of your letter dated June 10,
> 1992. In that letter, you assert that "based upon
> conversations with Department of Defense representa-
> tives," you believed that "your document requests would
> be treated as confidential." You also state that you
> "are not aware that . . . formal requests were filed"
> by us for copies of such documents, specifically a
> letter by your office to the Department of Defense
> dated May 27, 1992.
>
> Michael Sterlacci, the Deputy General Counsel
> of the Department of Defense ("DoD"), has advised us
> that he is not aware of any express or implied agree-
> ment between the Office of Independent Counsel and DoD
> regarding DoD's production, if it elects to do so, of
> document requests made by your office. Indeed, I
> understand that Mr. Sterlacci has advised you of the
> same.

---

[42]   Letter from Craig A. Gillen to Robert S. Bennett
dated June 10, 1992 at 1.

[43]   In his Final Report, Mr. Walsh, who never discussed
this matter with counsel but delegated it to Mr. Gillen,
asserts that "[d]uring the investigation, the OIC discovered that DoD officials had faxed to Weinberger's counsel
copies of at least one OIC document request to DoD, which
the OIC regarded as confidential." Final Report at 442.

With respect to your statement about our alleged failure to file a "formal request" prior to receiving a copy of your May 27, 1992 letter to DoD, let me correct the record. On April 14, 1992 -- six weeks before your letter -- we made a written request to DoD for access to document requests generated by your office. As we have previously advised you, all we want is a level playing field. Government agencies and personnel are not the personal property of the Independent Counsel. They are available to both sides.[44]

Mr. Walsh never responded to this letter perhaps because he could not accept the basic proposition that witnesses -- much less those that were employed by the Department of Defense -- were not the property of the OIC.

---

[44] Letter from Robert S. Bennett to Craig Gillen dated June 19, 1992 at 1. In his characteristic fashion, Mr. Walsh irresponsibly maligns former Deputy General Counsel Michael Sterlacci by stating that several "files produced belatedly by DoD had been stored in Sterlacci's office" and that the "OIC received an anonymous telephone call on May 21, 1992, suggesting that investigators look in the office of Deputy General Counsel Michael A. Sterlacci for information regarding Weinberger." Final Report at 441 (footnote omitted). Counsel is not aware whether Mr. Sterlacci will be afforded an opportunity to read this reference about him in Mr. Walsh's report. What counsel can say, however, is that after Mr. Walsh intimidated the Department of Defense and dissuaded it from cooperating with counsel, this matter was brought to the court's attention. At that time, defense counsel advised the court: "We had the full cooperation of the Department of Defense. Mr. Michael Sterlacci, an attorney in the General Counsel's Office there, who I highly compliment, said that he would treat the Office of Independent Counsel and provide them with all information that they requested and he would provide Mr. Weinberger and his defense team with all information they requested." Transcript of Status Hearing (November 24, 1992) at 11. Apparently unable to forgive Mr. Sterlacci for giving the defense equal consideration, Mr. Walsh takes a cheap shot at him in his Final Report.

B. Improper Public Comments On The Pending Case

On June 19, 1992, only days after the return of the five-count indictment against Mr. Weinberger, Mr. Walsh appeared on the television program "Nightline." During that appearance, Mr. Walsh explained how "as long as [the OIC] continue[d] to work up toward the center of responsibility, it [wa]s very difficult to give a good reason for stopping" the investigation of Iran-Contra.[45] Mr. Walsh further stated that "[w]ithin the terms of the indictment . . . it [wa]s apparent that the center of interest as to a part of the investigation were certain White House meetings in the fall of 1986 . . . which had to do with activities by high government officials in the fall of 1985."[46] Lastly, Mr. Walsh recounted how he and Mr. Gillen gave the matter of Mr. Weinberger's prosecution "extended discussion" and, in terms of a possible plea, they did the best they could "confronted with the circumstances that we were."[47]

After this appearance, counsel wrote Mr. Walsh asserting that it was inappropriate for him "to appear on national television to discuss this matter and defend [his] actions

---

[45]   ABC News *Nightline*, Air Date June 23, 1992, Transcript at 1.

[46]   *Id*. at 2.

[47]   *Id*. at 3.

29

regarding it."[48] Counsel further noted: "As a former Federal judge, you should appreciate that public statements by the prosecutor may impact on a fair trial."[49]

Nevertheless, Mr. Walsh continued making public comments. Less than a week after his national appearance on television, Mr. Walsh submitted his Third Interim Report to Congress. In that report, he stated that his office was now attempting to determine "whether officials at the highest level of government, acting individually or in concert, sought to obstruct official inquiries into the Iran Initiative . . . by withholding notes, documents and other information, by lying, and by supplying a false account of the 1985 arms sales from Israeli stocks and their replenishment by the United States."[50] Mr. Walsh further commented that his "continuing investigation was fueled by newly discovered documents, including the personal notes of key officials, CIA cables and tapes, and other records previously withheld from Independent Counsel and other investigating bodies."[51]

Again, counsel wrote Mr. Walsh to admonish him for issuing "interim reports or any other reports regarding Mr.

---

[48]   Letter from Robert S. Bennett to Lawrence E. Walsh dated June 25, 1992.

[49]   Id.

[50]   Third Interim Report, June 25, 1992 at 1.

[51]   Id. at 6.

Weinberger or the facts alleged in the indictment against him until the case [wa]s resolved in court."[52] Counsel warned Mr. Walsh that the issuance of such reports "prejudic[ed] the right of [Mr. Weinberger] to a fair trial" and requested that:

> If you have any intention of issuing any future reports or making any more public appearances or statements which in any way relate to my client or issues covered by the indictment, please advise me so that I can seek appropriate relief from Judge Hogan.
>
> While I fully realize that you are an Independent Counsel, you are not so independent that you can disregard fair play.[53]

Mr. Walsh responded that he "did not contemplate a further interim report, although the Ethics in Government Act clearly authorizes such measures."[54] This, of course, is not the case at all. The authority to file interim reports is derived from 28 U.S.C. § 595(a)(2), a general Congressional reporting provision. Notwithstanding this Congressional reporting provision, a conscientious independent counsel who had a case pending in court should not discuss any aspect of the case in such a report in a manner that will prejudice the right of the accused

---

[52]   Letter from Robert S. Bennett to Lawrence E. Walsh dated June 26, 1992 at 1.

[53]   Id. at 1-2.

[54]   Letter from Lawrence E. Walsh to Robert S. Bennett dated June 26, 1992.

to a fair trial.[55] Mr. Walsh did not appreciate this fundamental

prosecutorial tenet. In his view -- whether or not an investi-

gation was pending or even if someone had been charged as a

result of that investigation -- there was nothing improper about

referring to that matter.[56]

Even after President Bush's full pardon, Mr. Walsh

continued to make public statements abusing his prosecutorial au-

thority. On national television, he accused President Bush of

"misconduct," and charged that his pardon "completed" the "Iran-

contra coverup."[57] Further, Mr. Walsh falsely alleged that Mr.

Weinberger made an "early and deliberate decision to conceal and

---

[55]   See Department of Justice Manual (hereinafter "Justice Manual"), Title 1, Chapter 7 (1993-2 Supp.).

[56]   Mr. Walsh' abuse of the reporting requirements under
28 U.S.C. § 595(a)(2) was even more flagrant in his
Fourth Interim Report which was filed on February 8,
1993. Unable to accept that the presidential pardon had
put an end to his six-year investigation, Mr. Walsh
attacked President Bush, claiming that he had misused the
pardon power and reverted to his familiar conspiratorial
themes that Mr. Weinberger and others lied to conceal
information about the Iran initiative from Congress and
the American public. This report, which grossly distorted and misrepresented the record, was immediately and
widely reported in the press. It also had the effect of
circumventing the protections afforded to Mr. Weinberger
and others under Section 594(h)(2) which permits individuals named in the Final Report, subject to the Court's
discretion, to submit in response "comments or factual
information."

[57]   "Independent Counsel's Statement on the Pardons,"
New York Times, (Dec. 25, 1992) at A22.

32

withhold his notes" and that those notes "contain[ed] evidence of

a conspiracy among the highest-ranking Reagan administration

officials."[58] Again, Mr. Walsh chose to air his alleged charges

of misconduct against Mr. Weinberger in the press, where his

"evidence" would not be subject to the rule of law.

Mr. Walsh's inappropriate comments as a prosecutor

belie an even more egregious aspect of his conduct: his failure

to understand, appreciate and apply the Department of Justice

policies that guide the exercise of prosecutorial discretion.

The Principles of Federal Prosecution articulate a variety of

factors for federal prosecutors to consider when determining

whether to bring an indictment.[59] In the Final Report, Mr. Walsh

explains the factors that guided his prosecutorial decisions as:

"the seriousness of the crimes, the certainty of the evidence,

the likelihood that the targeted individual could provide valu-

able information to the investigation, and the centrality of the

individual to the Iran/Contra events."[60]

This simplistic list differs dramatically from the

carefully crafted Principles of Federal Prosecution. Indeed,

then Attorney General William Barr was reported to have stated

---

58   <u>Id</u>.

59   Justice Manual, Title 9, Chapter 27.

60   Final Report at 49.

during an interview less than three weeks before the scheduled
trial: "People in this Iran-Contra matter have been prosecuted
for the kind of conduct that would not have been considered
criminal or prosecutable by the Department of Justice, applying
standards that we have applied for decades to every citizen."[61]
Mr. Walsh, however, was a prosecutor not subject to the normal
Department of Justice oversight mechanisms and exhibited disdain
towards policies applicable to Department of Justice prosecutors.

C. Abuse Of The Discovery Process

Well aware of experiences in previous Iran-Contra
prosecutions, where voluminous and wide-ranging discovery requests buried defendants with information that was not exculpatory, and of marginal or no relevance to the OIC's cases-in-chief
or to the preparation of their defenses, counsel's discovery
letter was tailored narrowly to request documents relevant to the
indictment's charges and other allegations against Mr.
Weinberger.[62] Counsel also sought immediate production of excul-

---

[61]   Meddis, "Barr Rips Into Iran-Contra Cases/
Prosecutions Called 'Unfair,'" USA Today (December 17,
1992) at 2A.

[62]   Mr. Walsh states in his Final Report that after Mr.
Weinberger's indictment, the OIC discovered that "DoD
personnel had given Weinberger's counsel apparently unsupervised access to documents the OIC had identified as
evidence and left, by agreement with DoD, temporarily in
DoD custody." Final Report at 442. According to Mr.
Walsh, "[t]his discovery was accidental" and came about
                                        (continued...)

34

patory information under <u>Brady</u> v. <u>Maryland</u>[63] and statements of

government witnesses under the Jencks Act.[64]

Not surprisingly, the court chastised the OIC for its

failure to abide by its obligations to produce <u>Brady</u> and Jencks

material. Specifically, as to <u>Brady</u> material, the court granted

the defense's motion to compel production of exculpatory state-

ments in their entirety rather than the summaries the OIC fur-

nished. Noting that "in this Circuit 'it is clear that the

common practice [was] for the government to produce the documents

---

[62](...continued)
when "[a]n OIC attorney arrived at the Pentagon to take
custody of documents and found that one of Weinberger's
attorneys was photocopying the documents in the OGC's
offices without any visible supervision by DoD personnel." <u>Id</u>. at 443. This conduct, according to Mr. Walsh,
"jeopardized the integrity of original evidence in a
pending criminal case and allowed Weinberger's counsel to
circumvent ordinary discovery procedures." <u>Id</u>. Again,
these passages are reflective of the paranoia under which
Mr. Walsh and members of his office operated. They also
demonstrate Mr. Walsh's unjustified belief that the Department of Defense was a component of his staff. Suffice it to say that counsel's discovery letter to the
OIC, which set forth seventy categories of documents, is
not consistent with any attempt to "circumvent ordinary
discovery procedures." More to the point, no evidence
was placed in "jeopardy" and it was Mr. Walsh's overzealous staff that suffered from a lack of supervision.

[63]   373 U.S. 83 (1963).

[64]   18 U.S.C. § 3500.

35

themselves,'"[65] the court ruled that "[s]ummaries of such testimony w[ould] not suffice to ensure a fair trial in this case."[66]
Moreover, the court stated that "through the course of the
ongoing [Classified Information Procedures Act] hearings, the OIC
ha[d] been put on notice of much of the defendant's case," and
therefore it "caution[ed] the OIC from taking a less than broad
view of what the defendant may believe [wa]s exculpatory."[67]

     Most troubling about Judge Hogan's ruling was the fact
that in this Circuit, the law is clear that a defendant is entitled to the complete text and <u>not</u> a prosecutor's summary of a
witness' exculpatory statement. Indeed, two weeks prior to
November 2, 1992 -- the date the court ordered that exculpatory
material be produced to the defense -- counsel wrote the OIC
specifically stating: "with respect to your obligations under
<u>Brady</u>, we expect to receive complete and unredacted statements of
any witness whose testimony would tend to exculpate Mr.
Weinberger in any fashion."[68] If that were not enough, after the

---

[65]   Memorandum Opinion and Pretrial Order No. 11 (December 11, 1992) at 4 (quoting <u>United States v. Poindexter</u>,
No. 88-0080-01 (D.D.C. March 5, 1990)).

[66]   <u>Id</u>. at 4

[67]   <u>Id</u>.

[68]   Letter from Roberto Iraola to John Q. Barrett dated
October 19, 1992 at 1.

OIC produced summaries on November 2, counsel again wrote the OIC

reiterating:

> we believe that your <u>Brady</u> obligations require production of
> the transcripts of the grand jury testimony of the various
> witnesses for which you have provided summaries, as well as
> the agents' notes or FBI 302 reports reflecting interviews
> with such witnesses, to the extent that such material is
> exculpatory in any fashion. Indeed, we understand that
> Judge Harold H. Greene ordered your office to produce the
> precise exculpatory statements in the case against Mr.
> Poindexter.[69]

Mr. Walsh, however, was not interested in producing exculpatory

evidence in the manner provided by law in this jurisdiction.

Thus, it was only <u>after</u> counsel filed a motion to compel and the

court <u>granted</u> the motion -- less than one month before the start

of the trial -- that the complete text of the exculpatory state-

ments of numerous witnesses were produced.[70]

Similarly, with respect to Jencks statements, the OIC

refused to produce handwritten notes taken by government agents

during interviews of prosecution witnesses. Again, two weeks

prior to the scheduled production of Jencks material on November

---

[69]   Letter from Robert S. Bennett to John Q. Barrett
dated November 4, 1992 at 1.

[70]   Mr. Walsh, who does not appear to be financially accountable to anyone, caused Mr. Weinberger, who is financially accountable for his fees, to incur substantial
legal expenses by his zealous and unreasonable tactics.
These tactics would not have been engaged in by professional prosecutors knowledgeable and willing to follow
Department of Justice guidelines and District of Columbia
law.

2, counsel notified the OIC in writing that he expected to receive "handwritten notes of interviews."[71] When none were produced, counsel wrote the OIC stating he "had expected to receive . . . any handwritten notes of interviews."[72] It required a motion to compel and the intervention of the court for the OIC to understand that it had an obligation to review these materials "to determine whether they [we]re substantially verbatim."[73] The OIC's feeble contention that "[h]andwritten notes of investigation are work product and are not 'statements'"[74] under Jencks was rejected by the court with Judge Hogan voicing "concer[n] that the OIC may be interpreting the Jencks Act more narrowly than the Court rea[d] the Act."[75] Mr. Walsh's unwillingness to provide the defense with notes of interviews of government witnesses which the defense could use to impeach their testimony under the absurd justification that these notes constituted work product demon-

---

[71]   Letter from Roberto Iraola to John Q. Barrett dated October 19, 1992 at 1.

[72]   Letter from Robert S. Bennett to John Q. Barrett dated November 4, 1992 at 2.

[73]   Memorandum Opinion and Pretrial Order No. 11 (December 11, 1992) at 6.

[74]   Letter from George C. Harris to Robert S. Bennett dated November 11, 1992 at 2.

[75]   Memorandum opinion and Pretrial Order No. 11 (December 11, 1992) at 6.

strates, once again, the desperation with which his office viewed this prosecution.[76]

D. The Disqualification Of Craig Gillen

During the course of pre-indictment discussions with Messrs. Walsh and Gillen, it became apparent that the OIC was considering bringing at least one false statements charge against Mr. Weinberger in connection with his unrecorded interview on October 10, 1990. Counsel pointed out at these discussions that Mr. Gillen, the lead prosecutor in the office, would not be able to try the case if this was one of the charges because he was a witness to, and a material participant in, that interview. The OIC repeatedly scorned counsel's view of this matter.

---

[76]   Some abuses were corrected without the court's intervention. For example, during the course of discovery, counsel requested that the OIC provide a collection of "over thirty bound volumes of Mr. Weinberger's public statements during his tenure as Secretary of Defense." See Letter from Roberto Iraola to John Q. Barrett dated December 15, 1992. The OIC advised counsel that it did not possess those volumes. When counsel learned from representatives of the Department of Defense that such volumes had in fact been produced to the OIC, and confronted the OIC with this information, the OIC explained that although it "d[id] not yet possess 'thirty bound volumes' of Mr. Weinberger's public statements" it did "possess copies of fourteen such volumes for calendar years 1981, 1982, and 1987 which [it] ha[d] borrowed from various entities for the duration of this case and promised to return thereafter in good condition." See Letter from John Q. Barrett to Roberto Iraola dated December 17, 1992 (emphasis added). This exchange is illustrative of the sophistry which the OIC used in fulfilling its obligations prior to trial, all of which contributed to delay and increased expense.

On June 19, 1992, following the return of a five-count felony indictment charging obstruction of Congress, perjury and false statements -- the last count based on the October 10, 1990 interview -- Mr. Weinberger was arraigned before Judge Hogan. At that time, Mr. Gillen announced that he would be the lead prosecutor.[77] Counsel alerted the court that the defense would file a motion to disqualify Mr. Gillen because he was "an essential witness" to the last count which alleged that Mr. Weinberger had made false statements during his interview with Mr. Gillen on October 10, 1990.[78] Indeed, Mr. Gillen specifically was named in count V of the indictment as a witness to the alleged false statements. Mr. Gillen's response was: "in our pre-indictment negotiations with Mr. Bennett, he has made his position on my ability to try this case very clear, so his announcement today comes as no surprise, and my announcement to him should come as no surprise, and that is, the standard for disqualification, which is compelling necessity, will not be met by their motion."[79]

Unable to convince Mr. Walsh that Mr. Gillen could not remain in this case with count V in the indictment, the defense filed a motion to disqualify him because his status as an active

---

[77]   Transcript of Arraignment (June 19, 1992) at 3.

[78]   Id.

[79]   Id. at 7-8.

participant and witness to events central to count V would give

the prosecution unfair advantage during trial -- completely unre-

lated to the merits. Since Mr. Gillen was a "player" in those

events his opening statement, for example, would present a

scenario that the jury would be tempted to believe because he was

there. His presentation of evidence and cross-examination would

carry added weight to the jury because he was there. In closing

argument, his oratory would seem more persuasive to the jury

because he was there. Repeatedly, the jury would be tempted to

draw the inference that Mr. Gillen's extra-record knowledge and

apparent recollection of material facts would lend credibility to

the testimony of OIC's witnesses and his arguments.

        In addition, it was necessary to bar Mr. Gillen from

trying the case because the defense was entitled to preserve an

unencumbered right to call him as a witness at trial to secure

his evidence regarding the events underlying count V. Counsel

asserted in the motion to disqualify that the absence of a tape

recording or other transcription of the October 10, 1990 inter-

view would turn the trial of this count into a swearing contest

that likely would require all participants, including Mr. Gillen,

to testify on the hotly disputed issues of what Mr. Weinberger

was asked, said and meant at the time. Moreover, William P.

Rogers, Mr. Weinberger's counsel at the time, had several conver-

sations with OIC personnel, including Mr. Gillen, in the fall of

1990. Those conversations, counsel argued, could be relevant to show what Mr. Weinberger was asked, said and meant during the October 10, 1990 interview. Finally, Mr. Gillen had interviewed Mr. Rogers after Mr. Weinberger had become a focus of the grand jury's investigation.[80]

Unlike any other motion in this litigation, Mr. Walsh personally argued on behalf of the OIC against disqualification of Mr. Gillen. The court was not persuaded by Mr. Walsh's position that the standard for disqualification had not been met. To the contrary, after discussing the viability of certain prophylactic measures that would have to be taken to insure a fair trial if Mr. Gillen were to remain in the case, Judge Hogan ruled:

> [T]he Court is concerned about how opening
> statements, closing arguments, and related
> matters would be handled. The Court is mind-
> ful that even inadvertent error in any of

---

[80] Indeed, as Mr. Rogers pointed out to Mr. Gillen prior to his interview:

I will be glad to communicate with you on this matter as Judge Walsh wishes, even though it would appear that you may be [a] witness your-self to the same events about which you would like to question me. This would suggest that you seek my testimony not for an investigative purpose, but for some trial related purpose, such as preparing the testimony of other wit-nesses or avoiding your own need to testify.

Letter from William P. Rogers to Craig A. Gillen dated May 1, 1992 at 1.

42

these areas could be prejudicial to the defendant and lead to a mistrial at the least.
Accordingly, the Court will not rule on this
motion until after further discussion with
Mr. Gillen at a future pretrial conference.
Unless the Court is satisfied that Mr. Weinberger will not be unduly prejudiced by Mr.
Gillen's involvement in the case, Mr. Gillen
will be disqualified. If the Court determines the proposed prophylactic measures will
not protect Mr. Weinberger from undue prejudice, the OIC will be given the option of
removing Mr. Gillen or dismissing this count
of the indictment. Accordingly, to avoid any
delays in trial should problems arise, the
OIC is advised to have other counsel available to proceed if necessary.[81]

Not surprisingly, at a subsequent status hearing, Mr. Gillen

announced: "In light of the Court's concerns about my participa-

tion in the trial as articulated in the order, we are going to

get alternative trial counsel to try the case."[82]

The unfair advantage in prosecuting a case where the

lead counsel is intimately involved with one of the charges is

obvious. It is not the common practice of the Department of

Justice to charge individuals for making false statements to the

FBI during the course of an interview. It is almost unheard of

---

[81]   Memorandum Opinion and Pretrial Order No. 6 (September 29, 1992) at 12.

[82]   Transcript of Status Hearing (October 9, 1992) at 3.
Mr. Walsh blithely describes in a footnote the controversy created by his attempt to have an attorney -- who was
also a witness -- try the case. He states: "Gillen
withdrew voluntarily from the case on October 9, 1992,
following the District Court's preliminary ruling on this
issue." Final Report at 415 n.101.

43

for a prosecutor to try a case where the alleged false statements were made to him during the interview because prosecutors are not in the business of engaging in swearing contests with witnesses. Moreover, the "exculpatory no" doctrine normally prevents such a charge from succeeding.[83] Mr. Walsh, however, was determined to obtain a conviction at any cost. Department of Justice policies and procedures were not of major concern to him. Again, it took a motion by the defense and the intercession of the court to obtain a level playing field.

E. The Politically Motivated Second Indictment

Another egregious example of Mr. Walsh's overreaching can be found in the return of a single count indictment against Mr. Weinberger -- which the court ruled was barred by the statutes of limitations -- days before the 1992 presidential election. As explained more fully below, this conduct, perhaps like none other, demonstrated that by the fall of 1992, Mr. Walsh was simply out of control.

The first count of the initial indictment, returned against Mr. Weinberger in June 1992, charged him with obstruction

---

[83] This doctrine holds that an individual may not be prosecuted under the false statements statute for statements which are simply negative responses to interrogation by government investigators. See, e.g. United States v. Cogdell, 844 F.2d 179, 182-85 (4th Cir. 1988); United States v. Medina de Perez, 799 F.2d 540 (9th Cir. 1986).

of Congress for his alleged failure to turn over his notes to the
Select Committees in response to their document requests. On
September 29, 1992, however, the court dismissed this count on
the ground that it failed to allege an offense under United
States v. Poindexter, 951 F.2d 369 (D.C. Cir. 1991), cert.
denied, 113 S.Ct. 656 (1992). Instead of curing this pleading,
Mr. Walsh filed a new indictment charging Mr. Weinberger with a
different offense -- one count of making a false statement at the
deposition taken on June 17, 1987. By this time, Mr. Walsh,
after much difficulty, had replaced Mr. Gillen with James
Brosnahan, a prominent San Francisco Democrat who personally had
contributed to the Clinton-Gore Campaign and whose law firm also
had donated over $20,000 to the campaign.[84]

Upon the new indictment's release on October 30, 1992,
the Democratic candidates for President and Vice President
reacted instantaneously, characterizing the indictment as "smok-
ing gun" evidence that President Bush was being untruthful about
his role in the so-called "arms-for-hostages" deal.[85] News
coverage of these events saturated the media during the last

---

[84]   See Hedges, "Target with political baggage," The
Washington Times, (Nov. 19, 1992) at A1.

[85]   See S. Yoachum, "Clinton Swiftly Attacks Bush on
Latest Iran-Contra Disclosure," San Francisco Chronicle
Oct. 31, 1992 at A-5; D. McManus, "Note Says Bush Knew of
Arms, Hostages Swap," Los Angeles Times (Oct. 31, 1992)
at A-1.

45

weekend of the campaign, including multiple articles in The

Washington Post and the lead news stories on all three network

newscasts the evening the indictment was released.[86] That same

evening, President Bush himself was subjected to intense and

---

[86]   See, e.g., W. Pincus and G. Lardner, "Bush Stance,
Iran-Contra Note at Odds," Washington Post (Oct. 31,
1992) at A-1; J. Yang, "Bush Paints Fearsome Halloween
Portrait of Foe: President Sticks to Character Theme,
Deflects Arms-for-Hostages Issue on Wisconsin Train
Trip," Washington Post (Nov. 1, 1992) at A-18; D. Balz,
"Bush, Perot Lash Clinton," Washington Post (Nov. 2,,
1992) at A-1; W. Pincus, "Roots of Bush's Iran Credibili-
ty Gap," Washington Post (Nov. 2, 1992) at A-13; A.
Devroy and W. Pincus, "GOP Calls Release of Weinberger
Papers a Political 'Low Blow'," Washington Post (Nov. 3,
1992) at A-10. See also Transcript of ABC World News To-
night (Oct. 30, 1992) at 1-2; Transcript of CNN Daybreak
(Oct. 31, 1992) at 1; Transcript of CBS Evening News
(Oct. 30, 1992) at 1-3; Transcript of NBC Nightly News
(Oct. 30, 1992) at 1-2. See also R. Pear, "New
Weinberger Notes Contradict Bush Account on Iran Arms
Deal," New York Times (Oct. 31, 1992) at A-1; A.
Rosenthal, "A Battle of the Negatives," New York Times
(Oct. 31, 1992) at A-1; M. Kelly, "Democrat Fights Per-
ception of Bush Gain," New York Times (Oct. 31, 1992) at
A-1; A. Lewis, "Foul Words and False," New York Times
(Nov. 2, 1992) at A-19; Editorial, "George Bush, Caught
in the Loop," New York Times (Nov. 2, 1992) at A-19; W.
Safire, "To Remember After E-Day," New York Times (Nov.
2, 1992) at A-19; D. Johnston, "Casting Doubt on Bush
Account of Iran Arms Deal," New York Times (Nov. 2, 1992)
at A-38. See also D. Rogers, "Bush Confronts Fresh
Evidence on Iran-Contra," Wall Street Journal (Nov. 2,
1992) at A-4. Including the above-cited newspaper accounts, a Nexis search disclosed some 70 articles about
these issues published in American and some foreign
newspapers between Oct. 31 - Nov. 4, 1992. In addition,
this topic was the subject of numerous television news
broadcasts throughout that weekend. See, e.g., Transcript, MacNeil/Lehrer NewsHour, Oct. 30, 1992.

lengthy questioning, on national television, about the indictment and his role in Iran-Contra.[87]

Counsel filed a motion to dismiss the new indictment on the grounds that it was barred by the statute of limitations. Judge Hogan agreed, rejecting the OIC's contention that the indictment was saved by 18 U.S.C. § 3288 which allows new charges to be brought within six months "[w]henever an indictment is dismissed for any error, defect, or irregularity with respect to the grand jury." Noting that the "lack of reported authority indicate[d] to the Court that the Department of Justice ha[d] not used the statute in the manner the OIC now s[ought] to use the statute" and that the OIC "could have sought a grand jury indictment charging both [false statements and obstruction of Congress] when the original indictment was returned, but failed to do so," Judge Hogan ruled that such "failure [could not] be remedied after the statute of limitations ha[d] run by charging [Mr. Weinberger] under a new indictment that substantially amend[ed] the charge."[88] The new indictment, therefore, was dismissed on statute of limitations grounds.

---

[87]   Transcript of Interview with President Bush, *Larry King Live* (October 30, 1992) at 1-4, 11-12.

[88]   Memorandum Opinion and Pretrial Order No. 12 (December 11, 1992) at 6 & n.1.

The filing of this politically controversial charge which was time-barred was unconscionable. In doing so, Mr. Walsh failed to adhere to Department of Justice procedure.[89] Again, it took the intercession of the court to correct the prosecutorial abuses of Mr. Walsh and his staff.

F. The Mock Trial

On December 11-12, 1992, less than a month before the start of Mr. Weinberger's trial, the OIC conducted an unprecedented "mock trial" complete with testimony, exhibits and multiple juries chosen from a cross-section of District of Columbia citizens.[90] According to press reports, the OIC recruited a "scientifically chosen group of 36 mainly black District of Columbia citizens" to sit as mock jurors.[91] For two days, they listened to Mr. Brosnahan and an individual playing defense counsel Robert S. Bennett present opening statements, documentary

---

[89]   At the time of the indictment, there was no reported authority indicating that the Department of Justice ever had sought to use the statute, which had been in effect for over fifty years, as the OIC attempted to do. Id. at 10-11. There is still no reported authority of its doing so.

[90]   See Pincus, "'Mock Trial' of Weinberger Is Staged By Independent Counsel's Prosecutors," Washington Post (Dec. 15, 1992) at A-5; "The Iran-Contra Market Researchers," Washington Times, (Dec. 16, 1992) at G-2.

[91]   Pincus, "'Mock Trial' of Weinberger Is Staged By Independent Counsel's Prosecutors," Washington Post (Dec. 15, 1992) at A-5.

exhibits, and testimony concerning the charges against Mr. Weinberger.[92] The mock trial included persons who acted out the roles of witnesses, and who were cross-examined. An individual impersonating a judge, complete with robe, presided at the "trial." Another individual, dressed in a military uniform, played the part of a member of General Colin Powell's staff. As reported by one of the mock jurors who was outraged by such conduct, Mr. Brosnahan's case included "blownup" versions of "actual handwritten notes" by Mr. Weinberger and others.[93] At the close of the testimony, the mock jurors were divided into three groups, each of which conducted separate, videotaped deliberations.[94]

The use of mock jurors demonstrated, once again, the unusual and costly lengths to which Mr. Walsh was willing to go to secure a conviction against Mr. Weinberger, the unlimited resources he used to pursue that goal, and his repeated deviation of standard Department of Justice procedures. The weekend exercise, which Judge Hogan described as "extravagant",[95] report-

---

[92]   Id.

[93]   Id.

[94]   Id.

[95]   Transcript of Status Hearing (December 18, 1992) at 6.

49

edly cost $52,600.[96] According to press reports, the mock trial was conducted "to familiarize [Mr.] Brosnahan . . . with D.C. juries."[97] The Department of Justice, of course, does not offer prosecutors in the District of Columbia such resources to "familiarize" them with juries before initiating prosecutions. Indeed, a spokesman for then U.S. Attorney Jay B. Stephens was reported to have stated that Mr. Stephens' office "had not staged a mock trial in the approximately 7,000 cases that ha[d] gone to trial in the past five years."[98]

G. Fiscal Abuses

Mr. Walsh's abuses were not limited to his conduct in the grand jury's investigation of Mr. Weinberger or the litigation that ensued following the return of the indictment. Mr. Walsh operated as if he had been given a blank check by the taxpayer to insure his maximum personal comfort over the course of his eternal investigation. This was confirmed by an audit of his office conducted by the Government Accounting Office ("GAO") which concluded that for at least the first two years of his investigation, Mr. Walsh was reimbursed for first-class travel

---

[96] Seper, "Mock trial by Walsh violated hiring rules," The Washington Times, (Dec. 23, 1992) at A1.

[97] See Pincus, "'Mock Trial' of Weinberger Is Staged By Independent Counsel's Prosecutors," Washington Post (Dec. 15, 1992) at A-5.

[98] Id.

without any corroborating certifications or authorizations ever being found.[99] The GAO audit also determined that Mr. Walsh was reimbursed improperly for travel between Washington and his residence in Oklahoma, as well as for transportation between his office and his regal living quarters at the Watergate Hotel in Washington, D.C.[100] Indeed, as far as lodging and meals, the auditors concluded that the total amount of unallowable reimbursement for these categories amounted to $78,000 more than the per diem rate.[101]

As if these abuses were not enough, it was reported that Messrs. Walsh and Gillen failed to pay income taxes to the District of Columbia and were fined by the District of Columbia government.[102] Such repeated, deliberate flaunting of regulations and laws is unbecoming those granted the responsibility to enforce them. Mr. Walsh is indeed fortunate that a Walsh clone was not appointed as special counsel to investigate his fiscal abuses.

---

[99] Financial Audit, Expenditures by Nine Independent Counsels (October 1992) at 18.

[100] Id. at 14-15.

[101] Id. at 16-17.

[102] Hedges, "D.C. Fines Iran-Contra prosecutor over taxes," The Washington Times (Sept. 23, 1992).

IV. CONCLUSION

As demonstrated by the discussion above, Mr. Walsh's abuses, culminating with his unsupported allegations in the Final Report, demand that the Report remain under seal. Alternatively, if the court ultimately elects to make it public, any references to Mr. Weinberger therein should be redacted. This, after all, is a report from the same independent counsel who promised publicly that his Final Report would include "things we were not able to prove."[103] Mr. Walsh, at least in this instance, should be taken at his word. Therefore, since he was not able to prove any of his allegations against Mr. Weinberger, he should not be recompensed with yet another public forum in which to air his unsubstantiated musings.

Mr. Weinberger was accused falsely of crimes he did not commit by an overzealous and unaccountable prosecutor. There-fore, when confronted with the opportunity to enter a plea to a single misdemeanor offense, he declined and stated that "in order to avoid . . . indictment, [he] was not willing to accept an offer by the Office of Independent Counsel to plead to a misde-meanor offense of which [he] was not guilty, nor was [he] willing

---

[103]   Spencer, "Lawrence Walsh's Last Battle," <u>The New York Times Magazine</u>, (July 4, 1993) at 33.

52

to give them statements which were not true about [himself] or
others."[104]

There was no credible evidence that Mr. Weinberger
committed any crime. As the record demonstrates, Mr. Weinberger
had no motive to lie about his notes or the Iran initiative. To
the contrary, the notes demonstrated the vigor of his opposition
to trading arms for hostages. Indeed, there can be no argument
that Mr. Weinberger intended to hide his notes because he deposited them at the Library of Congress and made them fully available to Mr. Walsh and members of his office.

As President Bush recognized in his pardon, "Caspar W.
Weinberger is a true American patriot."[105] He was innocent of all
charges leveled against him and he would have been vindicated
fully at trial. Simply put, Mr. Weinberger's prosecution represented a gross miscarriage of justice perpetrated by an irresponsible prosecutor.

---

[104]   Statement of Caspar W. Weinberger following indictment appended hereto as Attachment E.

[105]   Grant of Executive Clemency dated December 24, 1992
at 1-2.

Respectfully submitted,

SKADDEN, ARPS, SLATE, MEAGHER
& FLOM

By: _____
Robert S. Bennett

By: _____
Carl S. Rauh

By: _____
Roberto Iraola
Benjamin B. Klubes

1440 New York Avenue, N.W.
Washington, D.C. 20005

Counsel for Caspar W.
Weinberger

54

CERTIFICATE OF SERVICE

I hereby certify that on the 3rd day of December, 1993, a copy of the foregoing response was served by first class mail, postage prepaid, upon the Office of Independent Counsel Lawrence E. Walsh located at 1 Columbus Circle, N.E., Suite G320, Washington, D.C.   20544

Roberto Iraola
_____
Roberto Iraola

United States Court of Appeals

For the District of Columbia Circuit

FILED DEC 0 3 1993

RON GARVIN

CLERK

RESPONSE OF CASPAR W. WEINBERGER TO THE FINAL REPORT

ATTACHMENTS

By: Skadden, Arps, Slate, Meagher & Flom

December 3, 1993

TAB – A

ROBERT C BYRD WEST VIRGINIA, CHAIRMAN

DANIEL K. INOUYE, HAWAII
ERNEST F HOLLINGS SOUTH CAROLINA
J BENNETT JOHNSTON LOUISIANA
QUENTIN N BURDICK, NORTH DAKOTA
PATRICK J LEAHY VERMONT
JIM SASSER, TENNESSEE
DENNIS DeCONCINI, ARIZONA
DALE BUMPERS ARKANSAS
FRANK R LAUTENBERG NEW JERSEY
TOM HARKIN IOWA
BARBARA A MIKULSKI MARYLAND
HARRY REID NEVADA
BROCK ADAMS WASHINGTON
WYCHE FOWLER JR GEORGIA
J ROBERT KERREY NEBRASKA

MARK O. HATFIELD, OREGON
TED STEVENS, ALASKA
JAKE GARN, UTAH
THAD COCHRAN, MISSISSIPPI
ROBERT W KASTEN, JR. WISCONSIN
ALFONSE M D'AMATO, NEW YORK
WARREN RUDMAN NEW HAMPSHIRE
ARLEN SPECTER PENNSYLVANIA
PETE V DOMENICI NEW MEXICO
DON NICKLES OKLAHOMA
PHIL GRAMM TEXAS
CHRISTOPHER S BOND MISSOURI
SLADE GORTON WASHINGTON

JAMES H ENGLISH STAFF DIRECTOR
J KEITH KENNEDY MINORITY STAFF DIRECTOR

United States Senate

COMMITTEE ON APPROPRIATIONS
WASHINGTON, DC 20510–6025

April 29, 1992

Robert S. Bennett, Esq.
Skadden, Arps, Slate, Meagher & Flom
1440 New York Avenue, NW
Suite 1100
Washington, D.C.   20005

Dear Mr. Bennett:

You have asked us, as Chairman and Vice Chairman of the Senate Iran-Contra Committee, whether if Secretary of Defense Weinberger learned of arms shipments to Iran in the fall of 1985 as opposed to a later time that would have been material for the Committee's purposes. As Chairman and Vice Chairman of the Committee, we directed and supervised the investigation and defined the issues that had to be addressed.

While Secretary Weinberger testified that he did not have contemporaneous knowledge of the 1985 arms shipment to Iran through Israel, he indicated that his recollection of dates was not as good as it once was and that he had difficulty sorting out what he knew at any particular time from what he had learned later. We were aware that his recollection as to the state of his knowledge in the fall of 1985 might have been imperfect as he had a poor recollection as to certain documents. We were also aware that Secretary Weinberger received intelligence reports concerning the Iranian initiative which contained suggestions that shipments might be taking place in the Fall of 1985. What was important to us, however, was not the date on which the Secretary knew or could have inferred from other information that arms shipments might have taken place, on which the testimony and evidence was murky, but the adamant position that the Secretary consistently took with the President in opposing sales to Iran on which the testimony was incontrovertible. The fact that his advice, like that of Secretary Shultz, was overridden by the President and rejected by the National Security Advisor was a key finding of our investigation and was described in our report.

We confirmed that Secretary Weinberger was opposed to the sales, not only by the testimony of other witnesses such as Admiral Poindexter, Mr. McFarlane, Secretary Shultz and Donald Regan, but from contemporaneous documents, including a PROF note written by North in which William Casey was described as believing that Secretary Weinberger would continue to create "road blocks" to arms sales to Iran. We even elicited testimony from Secretary

Robert Bennett, Esq.
April 29, 1992
Page 2

Shultz that Secretary Weinberger warned the President that the
sales to Iran might be criminal violations. In short, we focused
on Weinberger's staunch opposition to the sales, which was material to our investigation, not on the communications that might have
alerted him to the fact that transfers might have been taking
place earlier than he recalled. Senator Rudman's questioning of
Secretary Weinberger, which we attach, reflects that focus.

Finally, we shall end on a personal note. Our relationship
with Secretary Weinberger is professional and not personal. Based
upon our dealings with him over the years, we know Secretary
Weinberger to be a man of the highest integrity and honor. It is
inconceivable to us that he would intentionally mislead or lie to
Congress.

Sincerely yours,

Daniel K. Inouye
United States Senator

Warren B. Rudman
United States Senator

Attachment

TAB – B

AMERICAN INTERNATIONAL Security Corporation

10805 Main Street • Suite 600 • Fairfax, Virginia 22030
(703) 691-1110

Paul K. Minor
President

POLYGRAPH EXAMINATION REPORT

CLIENT	EXAMINATION DATE	TIME IN	TIME OUT
	05/05/92	9:30	10:40

EXAMINEE NAME	DATE & PLACE OF BIRTH
Caspar W. Weinberger	08/18/17, San Francisco, CA

HOME ADDRESS	SOCIAL SECURITY NUMBER
P.O. Box 159, Mt. Desert, Maine	096-12-1745

PRESENT EMPLOYER & POSITION	CITIZENSHIP/ALIEN REGISTRATION NUMBER
Forbes Magazine	U.S. Citizen

PURPOSE OF EXAMINATION

_____ Pre-employment Screening   __X__ Specific Issue

CONCLUSION

__X__ No Deception   _____ Deception   _____ Inconclusive
Indicated   Indicated   (See Information)

INFORMATION: Prior to the polygraph pre-test interview and examination, the examinee read
and voluntarily signed the consent/waiver form, which with all other examination material,
is retained in our files. Should you need further information, please do not hesitate to
contact our office.

The Office of Independent Counsel is looking into the possibility that
Mr. Caspar W. Weinberger, while serving as Secretary of Defense and
thereafter, deliberately misled government investigative bodies regarding
what is now known as the Iran-Contra matter.

During polygraph testing, the following questions were asked of Mr.
Weinberger which are believed to directly address the issues of concern
to the Office of Independent Counsel:

A) Did you ever intentionally withhold diary notes from any governmental
    entity? (No)
B) Did you deliberately mislead any governmental entity, including the
    Office of Independent Counsel, about your diary notes? (No)
C) Did you knowingly engage in a cover-up with senior Administration
    officials in the fall of 1986 or in 1987 regarding Ronald Reagan's
    participation in the Iran-Contra matter? (No)
D) During your June 1987 deposition, did you deliberately lie to the
    House Select Committee Counsel about the existence of your diary
    notes? (No)
E) Did you deliberately mislead any governmental entity regarding your
    knowledge of the transfer of arms to Iran from August through
    November 1985? (No)

Continued

POLYGRAPH EXAMINATION REPORT CONTINUED: Caspar W. Weinberger

There was no indication of deception to any relevant question and it
is the opinion of the examiner that Mr. Weinberger truthfully answered
each of the above questions.

The examiner used standard polygraph techniques which are taught by the
U.S. Department of Defense Polygraph Institute at Fort McClellan, Alabama,
and by the FBI, at Quantico, VA.

The charts and other documents were reviewed and approved by a second
experienced examiner who concurred with the results.

Paul K. Minor
AISC
Virginia Dept. of Commerce License #1601/574

CURRICULUM VITAE

NAME: Paul K. Minor

BIRTH: December 6, 1940

ADDRESS: American International Security Corporation
           10805 Main Street, Suite 600
           Fairfax, VA   22030

TELEPHONE: (703)691-1110

EMPLOYMENT: President, American International Security
                 Corporation, 1987-Present

              Polygraph Program Coordinator and Chief
                 Polygraph Examiner,
                 Federal Bureau of Investigation
                 1978-1987

              Chief, Polygraph Office, US Army Criminal
                 Investigation Command, 1974-1977

              Criminal Investigator, 1st Region, US Army
                 Criminal Investigation Command, 1973-1974

              Criminal Investigator, 4th CID, Military District
                 of Washington, 1971-1973

              Officer-in-Charge, Honolulu Field Office
                 USACID, 1970-1971

              Criminal Investigator, CID Detachment, 9th
                 Infantry Division, Republic of
                 Vietnam, 1968-1969

              Military Police Corp, US Army, 1962-1968

EDUCATION:

Degree	School	Year	Major
MS	University of Baltimore Baltimore, MD	1979	Crim Justice

EDUCATION (cont):

Degree	School	Year	Major
BA	University of Baltimore	1974	Sociology/ Crim Justice
Graduate	FBI National Academy Quantico, VA	1974	N/A
LLB	LaSalle University Chicago, Illinois	1974	
Graduate	Logistics Mgt. Course	1974	
Graduate	Polygraph Examiner Training, US Army Ft. Gordan, GA (Honor Graduate)	1972	
Graduate	Criminal Investigation Course, US Army Ft. Gordon, GA	1968	
Graduate	Physical Security Supervisers Course	1965	
Graduate	Police Administration Course	1964	
Graduate	7th Army Non-Commissioned Officers Academy	1964	
Graduate	Military Police School	1962	

TEACHING EXPERIENCE:

Associate Professor, Department of Psychology
University of Baltimore   1976-1977
(Graduate Level Senior Polygraph Examiners Course)

Adjunct Faculty Member
Columbia College
Hyattsville, MD   1977-1980
(Police Admin.)

FBI Academy
Quantico, VA   1978-1987

GUEST LECTURER:

US Army Polygraph School

George Washington University

American University

Federal Protective Service Academy

Federal Inter-Agency Polygraph Committee Seminar

American Polygraph Association Seminar

American Association of Police Polygraphists
Annual Seminar

Tennessee Polygraph Association

Northwest Polygraph Association

National Academy of Polygraphists Annual Seminar

Virginia Polygraph Association

Alabama Polygraph Association

Maryland Polygraph Association

Wisconsin Polygraph Association

Colorado Polygraph Association

PROFESSIONAL ASSOCIATIONS:

Association of Federal Investigators

American Polygraph Association
(Past Vice-President, Government)

American Society for Industrial Security

American Association of Police Polygraphists

FBI National Academy Associates

Maryland Polygraph Association (Past President)

National Academy Associates

Virginia Polygraph Association (Past President)

1) EXPERIENCE WITH THE FEDERAL BUREAU OF INVESTIGATION (1978-1987)

Directed, coordinated, and monitored the FBI Polygraph Program.
Exercised technical supervision of and provided investigative
direction for approximately fifty Special Agent Polygraph
Examiners in support of criminal and security investigative
activities throughout the Bureau and in support of investigative
activities of other law enforcement and criminal justice system
agencies. Oversaw the operation of the Unit and was responsible
for objectives consistent with maximum efficiency and economy
of polygraph operations and optimum utilization of manpower
and material assets.

Served as the Bureau's Chief Polygraph Examiner, conducted
polygraph examinations in selected highly important and/or
sensitive investigations and, interrogation of subjects,
victims, witnesses, informants, and assets in criminal and
intelligence cases.

Was responsible for the FBI Polygraph Training program including
issuance and revision of manuals and instructional material
and orientation of newly trained examiners into FBI Field Office
operations. Participated as an instructor in refresher courses
and polygraph seminars. Lectured to new Agents and in-service
Agents regarding the polygraph technique and its utilization
in the Bureau. Personally wrote the curriculum and oversaw
the Advanced Polygraphy Course-a nine semester hour graduate
level course accredited by the University of Virginia.

Was the primary individual responsible for the Bureau's
Polygraph Quality Control Program. In this capacity is
responsible for insuring that examinations conducted by Bureau
Agents are in strict conformance with accepted polygraph
operating procedures and standards.

Had frequent contacts with all divisions of the Bureau relative
to urgent matters, arrangements for special projects, and
personnel matters, and with representatives of the Department
of Justice other government agencies, and foreign governments
concerning polygraph matters. Served as member of the Federal
Interagency Polygraph Committee.

2) EXPERIENCE WITH THE UNITED STATES ARMY CRIMINAL INVESTIGATION
   DIVISION (USACIDC) 1974-1977

Position-Chief, Polygraph Division, US Army Criminal Investigation
Command (USACIDC)

Four years experience in planning, budgeting, developing, and
managing all facets of a centrally controlled polygraph examiners
assigned throughout the world to include quality control exercise
upon each polygraph examination.

Conducted complete quality control upon polygraph examinations
conducted by USACIDC examiners.
Developed and implemented USACIDC polygraph training programs.
Developed and administered equipment procurement and repair programs.
Administered the Polygraph Examiner Internship program.
Recommended the awarding or withdrawal of polygraph certification.
Conducted polygraph examinations of applicants for polygraph training.
Conducted polygraph examinations in cases involving Special Agents,
special interest cases and as directed by Director, Crime Records
Directorate, or the Commanding General, USACIDC.
Budgeted for equipment, training and travel expenses.
Maintained personnel polygraph certification files.
Administered a records management program assuring complete
retreiveability of polygraph examination records.
Maintained polygraph statistics and prepared statistical reports.
Maintained liaison with other agencies regarding polygraph matter.
Assuring current status of all polygraph forms, publications, and
directives.
Lectured on polygraph related matters throughout the world.
Coordinated all polygraph examiner initial assignments and transfers.
Conducting field visits and inspections pertaining to polygraph
activities.
Reviewed requests for polygraph examinations for legal and technical
sufficiency prior to authorizations.
Maintained liaison with all Field Office, District, and Region
Operations Officers to insure their full awareness of current
polygraph policies and to assure that their polygraph requirements
are fully satisfied.

3) MISCELLANEOUS INFORMATION

Associate Professor, Department of Psychology, University of Baltimore
teaching advanced Polygraph techniques and procedures.

1973-Polygraph Coordinator, First Region, USACIDC, coordinating all
polygraph activity in the First Region, which consists of all
Northeastern states through Virginia and West through Iowa. Was
selected for this position, the first of it's kind, from about 55
other USACIDC polygraph examiners, to conduct a pilot program of

centralized control of polygraph resources. During this period polygraph activity in First Region increased more than 300% and otherwise achieved such success that the program was adopted on a USACIDC worldwide basis the following year. This pilot program was conducted with five examiners under my supervision. This is the same program which in 1977 was adopted by the FBI and is still used there today.

1972-Completed polygraph training. Conducted polygraph examinations in the Eastern portion of the United States, on a full time basis supporting nine field offices. Also conducted Physical Security Surveys in Virginia, Maryland and Pennsylvania installations.

1968-71-Special Agent, US Army Criminal Investigation Command with assignments in Vietnam and Hawaii. Conducted Physical Security and Crime Prevention Surveys throughout Hawaii and the Pacific territories.

Principal duty in Hawaii was as Agent-in-Charge of the Honolulu Field Office.

Military Police duty included supervision of the security staff at US Army HQ, Europe and the private residence of the Commander-in-Chief Heidelberg, Germany; as well as duty with the elite Honor Guard of the 529th MP Company that performed throughout Europe.

OTHER:

 1991 - Appointed to the Virginia Governor's Polygraph Advisory Board.

TAB - C

Mr. John Haynes
20th Century Specialist
Library of Congress
Manuscript Division
101 Independence Avenue, S.E.
Rm LM-102
Washington, D.C. 20540

Dear Mr. Haynes:

     Independent Counsel Lawrence E. Walsh seeks access
to notes or other documents produced by or for me in regard
to the Iran/Contra matter during my tenure as Secretary of
the U.S. Department of Defense. It is my understanding that
my written permission is required prior to the Library of
Congress voluntarily providing the Office of Independent
Counsel access to said notes or other documents. I am
willing to grant such permission provided that the access to
and review of my materials be in the presence of my Executive
Assistant Kay Leisz. Accordingly, by this letter, I hereby
grant permission for members of the Office of Independent
Counsel to review my files which are potentially relevant to
its investigation, in order to obtain copies of such notes
and documents related to the Iran/Contra matter for the
period of January 1, 1984 through August 31, 1987, on the
condition that their access to and review of said papers be
in the presence of my Executive Assistant Kay Leisz.

Caspar W. Weinberger

Subscribed and sworn before me this ___8th___ day of
__November__, 1990.

Notary Public

My commission expires: April 14, 1992.

TAB-D

<u>AFFIDAVIT OF EDWARD J. SHAPIRO</u>

I, EDWARD J. SHAPIRO, being duly sworn, do depose and state as follows:

1. I am a partner at the law firm of Latham & Watkins in Washington, D.C. From August 1986 through January 1988, I was Assistant General Counsel (Legal Counsel) of the Department of Defense ("DoD").

2. Sometime after November 1986, then DoD General Counsel Lawrence H. Garrett, III and I agreed that DoD would assemble a group of lawyers to coordinate the response of DoD to the many requests for documents and information that had been and would be directed to DoD in connection with the Iran-Contra matter. Several attorneys and, to the best of my recollection, clerks were detailed to my office from the several military departments for the purpose of collecting and producing documents in response to document requests from various requesters including at least Congress and the Office of Independent Counsel ("OIC"). While I do not recall circumstances surrounding the DoD's response to each individual request, I believe that each request was satisfied to the best of our ability. I managed the lawyers who coordinated the collection and production efforts in 1986-1987. While my best recollection is that I reviewed a relatively small number of documents, I did not generally gather or review the substance of the documents collected and produced.

3. To the best of my knowledge and recollection, no division or subdivision of the DoD was exempted from the document collection process.

4.   I understood at the time (and continue to understand) that then Secretary of Defense Caspar W. Weinberger was aware that various requests for documents and information had been received by DoD. Either Secretary Weinberger personally or Mr. Garrett conveyed to me at the time that Secretary Weinberger's instructions were that DoD should cooperate fully with all requests for documents or information received in connection with the investigation. While I do not recall the precise language used by or attributed to Secretary Weinberger, I generally recall that the substance of his instructions was to give the investigators all of the documents and information that they requested. I do not recall any instruction or statement by Secretary Weinberger or Mr. Garrett that was in any way inconsistent with this instruction. Mr. Garrett also instructed me, and I instructed the lawyers working in my office, to cooperate with the investigations by complying with all requests for documents or information. To the best of my knowledge and understanding these instructions were followed.

5.   The practice and procedure in connection with DoD's efforts to collect documents and information, as best I can recall, was that the lawyers working in my office sent requests and instructions to the various departments and offices within DoD. The departments and offices then conducted their own searches of their files and forwarded responsive documents to the lawyers who had requested them.

6.   To the best of my knowledge and understanding, no lawyer working in my office conducted a physical search for

documents in the immediate Office of the Secretary of Defense. This was in keeping with the general procedure used by the lawyers working on the document requests, as set forth in Paragraph 5 above. I do not know which person or persons within that office conducted searches in response to particular requests, or what particular areas they searched. My general experience in working with the immediate Office of the Secretary of Defense suggests to me that any of his secretaries and/or military assistants may have been involved in such processes. I do not now recall any specific discussion relating to document collection with any of these individuals, however.

7. I do not recall having a concern that DoD was not producing all responsive materials in compliance with particular requests for documents. I do recall generally some concerns being expressed from time to time by individuals outside of DoD about the pace at which DoD made and completed its responses. However, I do not have a specific recollection of any particular concern or discussion relating to this topic.

8. I recall participating in preparing Secretary Weinberger for his July 31 and August 3, 1987 testimony before a Joint Congressional Committee. I recall that at least Mr. Garrett, William Taft (Deputy Secretary of Defense), Richard Armitage (Assistant Secretary of Defense for International Security Affairs), and Lincoln Bloomfield (Mr. Armitage's assistant) also participated in such preparation. I do not have a specific recollection whether or not I met with Secretary Weinberger to participate in preparing him for his June 17, 1987

deposition by Congressional investigators, although I may have participated in such a session. I recall being present at his deposition.

9. The preparation for Secretary Weinberger's Congressional testimony was, based on my knowledge and experience, typical of how attorneys prepare their clients for depositions or testimony. It is my best recollection that during the preparation, Secretary Weinberger used a binder of documents. While I do not recall with certainty, I believe the documents in this binder may have been furnished or identified by Congressional investigators as those likely to be covered during the testimony.

10. I do not recall whether Secretary Weinberger received or reviewed a transcript of his June 17, 1987 deposition testimony prior to his Congressional appearance, referenced in ¶ 8. I do not recall any statements made by Secretary Weinberger during his Congressional testimony preparation that were at odds with his sworn testimony, nor have I learned anything since that would cast doubt on the truthfulness of that testimony.

11. I held discussions with the Library of Congress leading to finalization of the Agreement of Deposit ("Agreement") between Secretary Weinberger and the Library of Congress. My understanding was and is that this Agreement represents a typical arrangement for the deposit of the papers of public figures at the Library of Congress, and to my knowledge was fully consistent with all legal and regulatory requirements.

12.   The Agreement mentions on the first page an attached "schedule" describing certain of Secretary Weinberger's papers to be deposited at the Library of Congress. I do not recall ever seeing such a schedule, nor can I say with any certainty that such a schedule ever actually existed. I did not select or review any of the Weinberger papers to be deposited at the Library of Congress.

13.   I know Secretary Weinberger to be a person of the utmost integrity, honesty and honor. In all of my dealings with him, he has been entirely candid and truthful. I have never seen anything in his conduct, or learned any facts, to lead me to believe that he would knowingly or intentionally withhold relevant materials from Congress or investigators, or deliberately mislead or lie to them about the existence of such materials.

_____
Edward J. Shapiro

Subscribed and sworn before
me this 29ᵗʰ day of April 1992.

_____
Notary Public

My commission expires:___11/14/93___

5

AFFIDAVIT

I, **DONALD S. JONES**, depose and say that

1. I am a retired Vice Admiral in the United
States Navy. I began my career in the United States
military as a naval aviator in 1951. From approximately
April 1982 to August 1983, I served as the Senior Military Assistant to the Deputy Secretary of Defense. In
this capacity, I attended numerous meetings with Secretary of Defense Caspar W. Weinberger. I left that post
to become Commander of the Third Fleet, stationed in
Hawaii. In the summer of 1985, I returned to Washington
as the Deputy Chief of Naval Operations for Plans, Policy, and Operations. At that time, General Colin L.
Powell was the Senior Military Assistant to Secretary
Weinberger.

2. In or about February 1986, I relieved General Powell as the Senior Military Assistant to Secretary
Weinberger. My role in this position was to support
Secretary Weinberger in the carrying out of his many
duties. My responsibilities included managing access to
Secretary Weinberger. I had to assure that Secretary
Weinberger received a balanced range of opinions on the
issues he confronted, had input from those in the Department of Defense whose judgment he most respected, and was

not unnecessarily bothered by those with no legitimate
reason to see him. With the possible exception of direct
communications with other Cabinet-level officials, it
would have been highly unusual -- if indeed it ever occurred -- for any official matter to reach Secretary
Weinberger's attention without first passing through me.

3. I retired from the military in approximately February 1987, after 37 years of service. In March
1991, I moved to Pittsboro, North Carolina, where I currently reside. I still sit on several corporate Boards
of Directors.

4. While working for Secretary Weinberger, I
noticed that he was in the habit of making notations of
events and calls on a small pad. I, and I believe Secretary Weinberger, considered these jottings to be personal
and informal and in the nature of brief diary notes,
rather than official, formal Department of Defense records. Secretary Weinberger never attempted to hide
these diary-type jottings. He wrote them openly. Because I considered them to be personal rather than official, I never reviewed these notes, nor discussed them
with Secretary Weinberger.

5. Although I was Secretary Weinberger's Senior Military Assistant at the time of Attorney General
Edwin Meese's investigation into the Iran-Contra affair,
I do not recall any requests for any documents in connection with that investigation. Standard operating procedures for requests directed to Secretary Weinberger were
very clear. Under these procedures, any request for
documents located in Secretary Weinberger's suite of
offices and under his control would have been forwarded
to me, rather than directly to Secretary Weinberger. I
do not recall receiving such a request in connection with
the Meese investigation.

6. Similarly, any request in connection with
the Tower Commission's investigation calling for documents located in Secretary Weinberger's suite of offices
and under his control would have been forwarded to me.
Such a request would not have gone directly to Secretary
Weinberger. Although I recall reviewing requests from
the Tower Commission, I did not receive any request that
I believed called for the production of Secretary Weinberger's personal diary-type jottings. Likewise, I never
received any requests that called for the production of
any handwritten notes I might have generated relating to
the Iran-Contra affair.

3

7.   Accordingly, although I knew that Secretary
Weinberger retained his daily jottings of events, I never
asked Secretary Weinberger to produce these jottings, nor
to my knowledge -- as the individual who managed access
to Secretary Weinberger -- did anyone else ever ask him
to produce these jottings. At no time was I, or to my
knowledge Secretary Weinberger, contacted by a member of
the Department of Defense's General Counsel's staff, or
by any other attorney, with regard to compliance with the
Tower Commission's requests. Had Secretary Weinberger
ever been asked to produce his informal jottings, I feel
confident that he would have complied fully with this
request.

9.   Based on my experiences with Secretary
Weinberger as Senior Military Assistant to the Deputy
Secretary of Defense and as Secretary Weinberger's Senior
Military Assistant, I know Secretary Weinberger to be a
man of the highest integrity and honesty who strove to
avoid even the appearance of impropriety. I have never
known him to lie about anything, and I find it impossible
to believe that he would have intentionally misled any
investigative body examining the Iran-Contra matter about

4

the existence of his informal jottings if he had understood that they were relevant to any investigation.

Donald S. Jones

DONALD S. JONES

April 25 '92

DATE

Subscribed and sworn before
me this _____ day of April 1992.

Notary Public

My commission expires:

March 26, 92

5

AFFIDAVIT

I, **THELMA STUBBS SMITH**, being duly sworn, do depose and state as follows:

1.   I worked as the Private Secretary to Secretary of Defense Caspar W. Weinberger from 1981 through November 1987. I worked in the Department of Defense for 37 years and have served seven Secretaries of Defense.

2.   My desk was located in the outer office outside of Secretary Weinberger's office. Kay Leisz, Secretary Weinberger's Confidential Assistant, also sat outside his office. Our duties for Secretary Weinberger included typing correspondence, answering his telephone and placing calls for him, scheduling his appointments and keeping his calendar. We also were responsible for placing documents in his In Boxes and removing them from his Out Box.

3.   Secretary Weinberger worked extremely hard. He typically spent approximately 12 hours at the office and then brought two to three briefcases of work home with him each night. Secretary Weinberger had approximately 12 to 13 scheduled appointments each day and received numerous telephone calls each day.

4. Secretary Weinberger had an extremely large desk in his office. To my knowledge, Secretary Weinberger never locked this desk or anything in his office.

5. I was aware that Secretary Weinberger kept a pad on his desk on which he scribbled notes reflecting the date, time and other references to telephone calls and meetings. I considered these to be personal notes. It was my belief that he made these notes to assist him in writing a book.

6. Secretary Weinberger occasionally made margin notes in briefing books. At the conclusion of a meeting, he placed the briefing book in his Out Box. The briefing books then were placed in the Out Box in the outer office by my desk. The Correspondence & Directives Division ("C&D") was responsible for taking the documents from the Out Box and distributing them as appropriate. Accordingly, any notes regarding the Iran-Contra matter that Secretary Weinberger made in briefing books would have been turned over to C&D or the office that prepared the briefing book.

7. Secretary Weinberger on occasion placed small pieces of paper with jottings in his Out Box. Ms. Leisz and I placed these in the safes behind our desks

2

and later put them in an envelope marked "Handwritten Notes" in the office vault. We were not required to save these notes, but did so in the event that Secretary Weinberger should request them. He never asked to see these notes and I do not believe that he was aware that we saved them.

8. When Secretary Weinberger left the Department of Defense in November 1987, I recall that I packed the handwritten notes that I had placed in the vault, together with the appointment calendars and personal items, such as invitations and files on his home, in boxes. I typed a list of 14 boxes of such items. See Attachment A.

9. I understand that Secretary Weinberger refers to the handwritten notes described above in paragraph 5 as "telephone logs." While I do not specifically recall packing these handwritten notes, the index I prepared indicates that one box contained telephone logs for the period 1980 to 1987.

10. It was my understanding that all the documents I packed were to be transferred to the Library of Congress. The index I prepared of these documents is entitled "SECRETARY OF DEFENSE WEINBERGER'S PERSONAL PAPERS FOR TRANSFER TO THE LIBRARY OF CONGRESS." Once

3

the boxes were packed, they were taken by personnel from
C&D.

      11. I do not recall anyone asking me to gather
documents from the Office of the Secretary of Defense
regarding the Iran-Contra matter. Had I received such a
request, I would not have thought of the handwritten
notes described above in paragraphs 5 and 7 both because
I would not have associated these with the Iran-Contra
matter and because I considered these to be simply
handwritten notations, not documents.

      12. I have great esteem for Secretary
Weinberger. He is a person of the highest integrity and
honor and I felt privileged to work for him.

Thelma Stubbs Smith
Thelma Stubbs Smith

Subscribed and sworn before
me this __29th__ day of April 1992.

_____
Notary Public

My commission expires:

__October 14, 1995__

4

ATTACHMENT
A

SECRETARY OF DEFENSE WEINBERGER"S PERSONAL PAPERS
FOR TRANSFER TO THE LIBRARY OF CONGRESS

14 MISCELLANEOUS BOXES

BOX 1 - Box A - Blank Note Pads; Notes From Meetings

BOX 2 - Box B - Old Financial Records

BOX 3 - Box C - Telephone Logs - 1980; 1981-1987

BOX 4 - Box D - Old Financial Statements; Telephone Logs - 1970s

BOX 5 - Box E - Old Bank & Financial Data; Note Pads/Meetings 1981-1982

BOX 6 - Box F - Office Diaries, 1971-1975(July)

BOX 7 -   CWW - Personal Thank Yous - 1981-1986
           CWW - Social Engagements & Calendars - 1981-1982
           Invitations Accepted - 1981-1986

BOX 8 - Desk & Miscellaneous Items
        Personal Clippings - 1980
        Photos/Charts

BOX 9 - Old Insurance Files/Supplies

BOX 10 - CWW - Personal 1981-1986
         CWW - Telephone Call Sheets 1981-1986

BOX 11 - CWW - Personal Red Economist Diaries, 1982-1983-1985-1956
         Schedule Books - Day at A Glance 1981-1986

BOX 12 - CWW - Mixed Clippings

BOX 13 - Logs Kept By Receptionists 1981-1987

BOX 14 - Memos & Notes
         Photographs - Nixon - Bechtel

AFFIDAVIT

I, **ROGER SANDLER**, being duly sworn, do depose and state as follows:

1. I am a freelance photojournalist and have photographed former President Ronald Reagan and numerous other government officials and candidates for office over the years.

2. In November 1987, I was doing a special assignment for a major magazine on Secretary of Defense Caspar W. Weinberger. I believe that the magazine was either <u>Time</u> or <u>Washingtonian</u>, but I do not now specifically recall the name of the magazine.

3. I went to Secretary Weinberger's office at the Pentagon on either his last day or next to last day in office in November 1987 to take photographs of him for publication related to the special assignment described above.

4. I spent approximately one hour taking photographs of Secretary Weinberger in his office. During this time, Secretary Weinberger packed various artifacts, mementos and other personal items located in his office. He described many of these personal items to me during the shoot.

5. I took photographs of Secretary Weinberger

as he packed these items.   Appended hereto as Attachment
A are photocopies of 11 of the photographs I took that
day.

      6.   I very much appreciated that Secretary
Weinberger spent so much time with me during the shoot.
I also appreciated the fact that Secretary Weinberger
allowed me to capture him on film in such an informal,
relaxed way on his last or next to last day in office.

                                        _____
                                        Roger Sandler

                                        29 April 1992
                                        _____
                                        Date

Subscribed and sworn before
me this 29th day of April 1992.

_____
Notary Public

My commission expires:

October 14, 1995
_____

ATTACHMENT
A

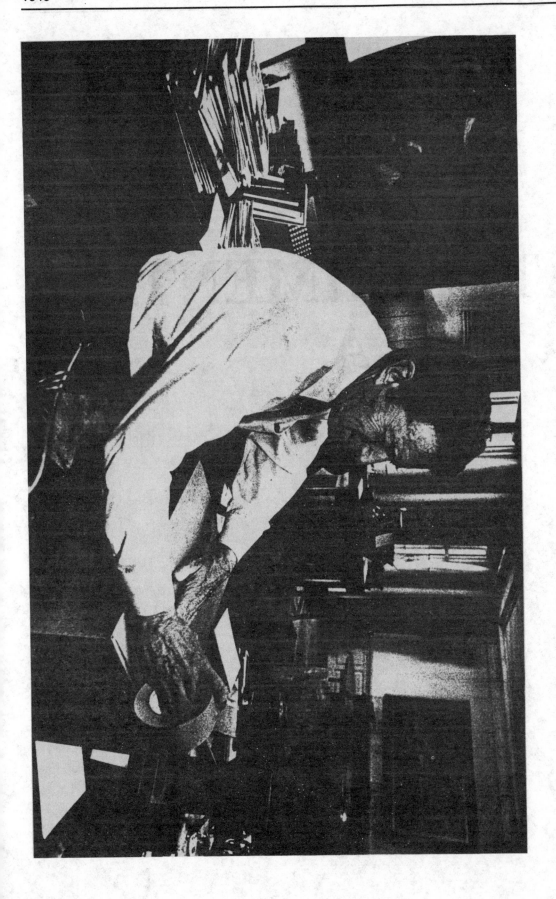

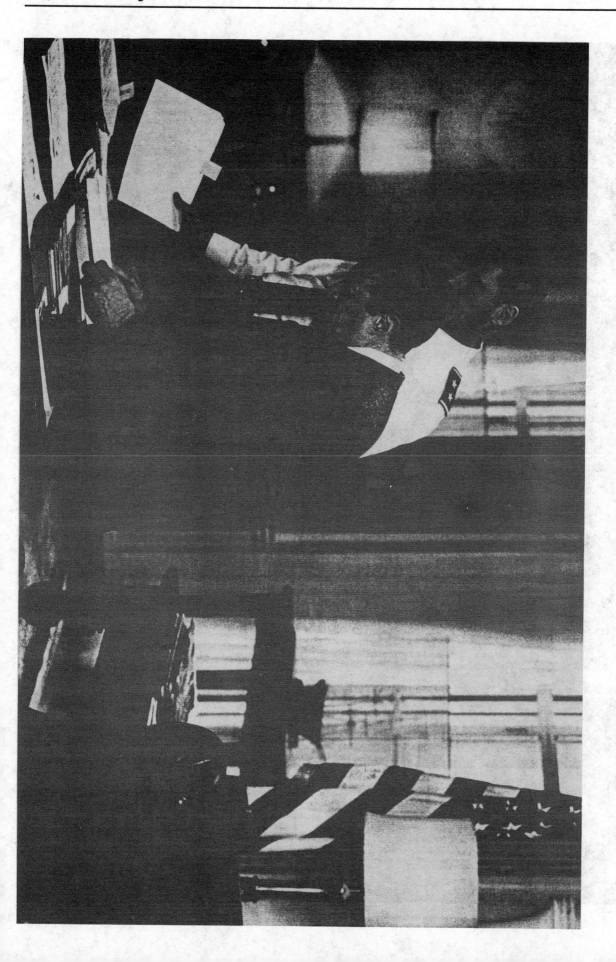

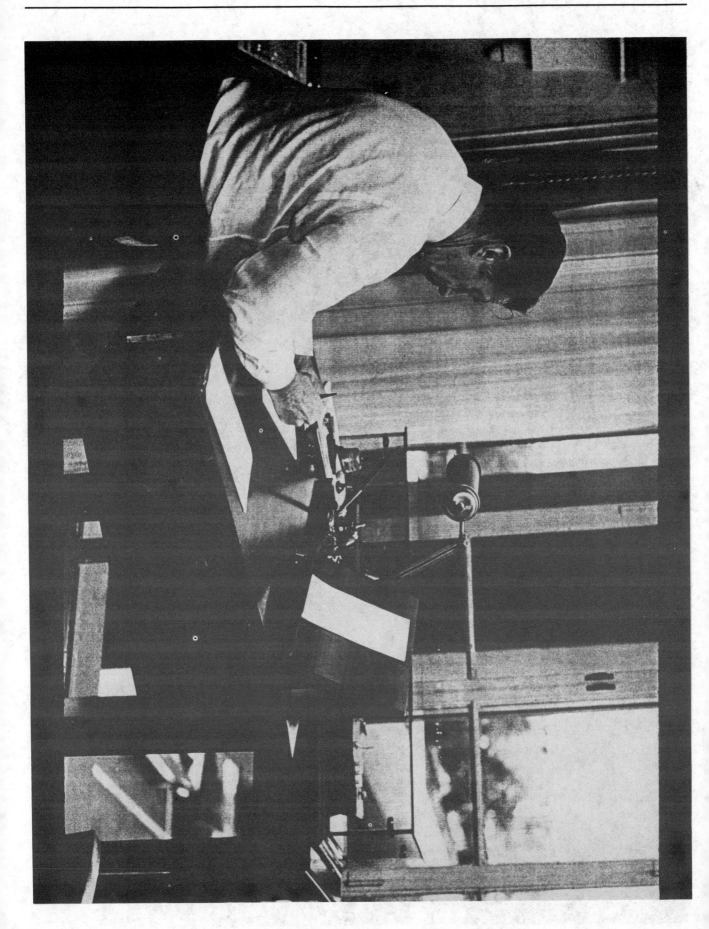

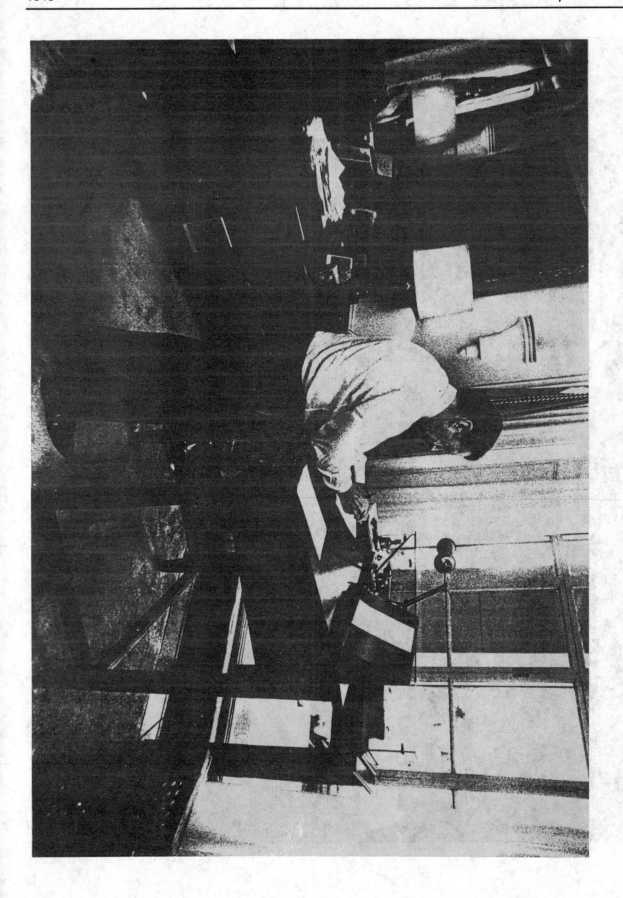

AFFIDAVIT OF LAWRENCE H. GARRETT, III

1. I am currently the Secretary of the Department of the Navy.

2. From early February 1986, until early August 1987, I served as the General Counsel of the Department of Defense ("the Department") under Secretary of Defense Casper W. Weinberger.

3. I first met Secretary Weinberger in the late fall of 1985, when I interviewed for the position of General Counsel. Since that time, I have had numerous opportunities to work with and observe Secretary Weinberger. In my opinion, he is a man of the utmost integrity and has the highest regard for the Constitution and other laws of the United States.

4. On or about November 28, 1986, the Department received a letter addressed to the Secretary from then Attorney General Edwin Meese seeking documents related to or referring to the Iran-Contra affair. The office of the General Counsel was assigned the responsibility to comply and respond to this and all subsequent requests for documents received by the Department. I appointed Assistant General Counsel Edward Shapiro to carry out the aforementioned assignment. Mr. Shapiro put a team together, consisting of attorneys from the office of the General Counsel as well as an attorney from each of the military services, in order

to gather relevant documents and respond to the aforementioned
requests, as well as anticipated requests from various
Governmental agencies.

5.   Mr. Shapiro's office drafted a memorandum
regarding the request, which was sent under my signature to all
offices and components within the Department. Although the
immediate office of the Secretary of Defense was not named as an
addressee of the memorandum, his office would have been covered
organizationally. In normal course, the Executive Secretariat
should have received a copy of the memorandum and arranged for
collection of all relevant documents from the Secretary's suite
of offices. In my experience, it would be highly unusual for a
Secretary of Defense, or other principal officers of the
Department, personally to search his or her office in response to
this or any other document request. Such activity is the
responsibility of, and is normally carried out by, his or her
immediate administrative staff.

6.   Document requests were and are frequent and
numerous within the Department, probably numbering in the
thousands each year. Such requests include Congressional
requests, requests under the Freedom of Information Act (FOIA),
and discovery requests in the many lawsuits in which the
Department or one of its components is a party.

7.   I do not recall discussing with Secretary
Weinberger the specific details of the November 28th request,
or any subsequent request. It is not likely that I would have
discussed requests for information with him other than in

very general terms. I do recall apprising the Secretary from time to time that the Department was receiving such requests. I recall that Secretary Weinberger treated very seriously the requests for documents and factual information concerning the involvement of the Department in the Iran-Contra affair. The Secretary was adamant that the Department cooperate fully and be completely forthcoming with respect to all such requests. We never discussed the possibility of withholding any documents responsive to the many requests received. I am confident that no documents were intentionally withheld.

8. Between November 1986 and the time I left the General Counsel's office in August 1987, the Department received numerous document requests relating to the Iran-Contra investigations. While I do not recall the specific procedures followed concerning each request, I am confident that the Department attempted to comply fully with each such request.

9. On at least two occasions, I assisted in preparing Secretary Weinberger for his testimony before Congress regarding the Iran-Contra affair. To my knowledge, the purpose of the preparation sessions was to refresh Secretary Weinberger's recollection of facts about which he had knowledge and to generally apprise him of the sequence of events which occurred within the Department. To the best of my knowledge and belief, no effort was made to conceal knowledge from the Congress, or any other investigative bodies.

10. I recall that when the Iran-Contra story broke in November/December 1986, Secretary Weinberger expressed his staunch opposition to the selling of arms to Iran; and he expressed his regret that his position on the matter had not been followed. From the time the Department received its first request and throughout my time of service with him, his direction was always the same whenever the subject came up: cooperate fully. Secretary Weinberger was not, in my experience, a "detail person". He dealt in broad policy matters, leaving the execution of his policy decisions to the various agencies and military departments under his authority and control. It was my perception that he knew little, if anything, about the details regarding the manner in which elements of the Department carried out their role in the transfer of arms to Iran.

11. I have been told that Secretary Weinberger maintained personal diary notes that were not produced in response to the various document requests. As I mentioned previously, I did not personally question Secretary Weinberger about the existence of personal notes or diaries. With the benefit of hindsight, he would have been better served had I done so. I do recall that early on in the process I told his secretaries that a document request had been received and asked them whether Secretary Weinberger had any notes regarding the Iran-Contra affair. They said he did not have any such notes. This did not surprise me since it comported with my own observations that Secretary Weinberger did not take notes at meetings that I attended.

12. Secretary Weinberger at all times directed full cooperation and compliance with all of the investigating bodies. I am confident that if I or members of my staff had asked him specifically whether he kept diary notes, he would have provided them so that any relevant portions could be given to the requesting entities.

13. In all of my dealings with Secretary Weinberger, I have never known him intentionally to misrepresent or lie about anything. As with us all, sometimes his memory of past events is not strong. I am absolutely confident that any failure of the Department to produce Secretary Weinberger's diary notes was the result of oversight and not an effort to withhold information. Based upon my knowledge of and experience with him, I am also sure that Secretary Weinberger did not lie to either Congress or the Office of the Independent Counsel about his diary notes. I am confident he did not associate his diary notes with the requests for documents being made of the Department.

14. There is no individual for whom I have higher personal regard as to his honesty and integrity than Secretary Weinberger.

H. LAWRENCE GARRETT, III

Subscribed and sworn before me this 28th day of April, 1992.

Colleen D. Ercole

Notary Public

My Commission Expires:_____

MY COMMISSION
EXPIRES FEB. 28. 1995

AFFIDAVIT

I, **GORDON E. FORNELL**, depose and say that

1. I am a Lieutenant General in the United States Air Force and the Commander of the Air Force Systems Command Electronic Systems Division, headquartered at Hanscom Air Force Base in Massachusetts. I first joined the United States military in 1958. From 1981 to 1985, I was stationed at the Pentagon as the Special Assistant to the Chief of Staff for ICBM modernization. In this capacity, I briefed Secretary of Defense Caspar W. Weinberger on the MX missile approximately once a month. On several occasions, Secretary Weinberger and I testified together before Congress. In 1985, I left the Pentagon to become Commander of the Armament Division, headquartered at Eglin Air Force Base in Florida.

2. In or about January 1987, I became the Senior Military Assistant to Secretary Weinberger. I remained in this position under Secretary of Defense Frank Carlucci until September 30, 1988. As Senior Military Assistant to Secretary Weinberger, I attended every meeting he held in his office at the Pentagon, with the exception of a very few social lunches with personal friends. In addition, I reviewed all official documents

directed to Secretary Weinberger prior to passing them on
to him.

3. During meetings in his office, Secretary
Weinberger would not take notes. Occasionally, when he
was not in meetings, I observed Secretary Weinberger
jotting down notations on a small pad on the corner of
his desk. These jottings would be brief and, as far as I
could tell, contained little more than a few key words.
Because I considered these jottings to be personal, I
never reviewed them. Neither I, Secretary Weinberger,
nor anyone else who worked for Secretary Weinberger
treated these jottings as official, formal Department of
Defense records. In contrast to these jottings or diary
notes, the official schedules and daily logs of Secretary
Weinberger's activities were maintained by the secretaries in the office and were typewritten. Handwritten
instructions from Secretary Weinberger that were treated
as official records were usually typed up by the secretaries, but the secretaries never typed up Secretary
Weinberger's informal diary notes.

4. I do not recall being involved in any re-
quests from Attorney General Edwin Meese or from the
Tower Commission for documents relating to the Iran-
Contra affair. I believe that the Department of Defense

2

had already complied with these requests by the time I became Secretary Weinberger's Senior Military Assistant.

5.   During my tenure as Senior Military Assistant, I believe that I would have seen or otherwise been informed of any requests from any body investigating the Iran-Contra affair for documents from Secretary Weinberger and his immediate staff. I recall at least one such request. Because I believed that the files containing documents responsive to this request were not maintained in Secretary Weinberger's suite of offices, I believe that I instructed Correspondence & Directives (C&D) to provide the requested records. At some point we were asked to provide copies of Secretary Weinberger's schedules and daily logs. The secretaries in our office, Kay Leisz and Thelma Stubbs Smith, accordingly photocopied Secretary Weinberger's typewritten schedules and daily logs. Examples of these schedules and daily logs are attached as Exhibit A and Exhibit B hereto, respectively. Neither I, Secretary Weinberger, nor anyone else on Secretary Weinberger's staff associated this request for documents with Secretary Weinberger's informal jottings.

6.   As the person who reviewed all official documents directed to Secretary Weinberger and who attended all official meetings with Secretary Weinberger at

3

the Pentagon, I am unaware of anyone ever asking Secretary Weinberger to produce his informal jottings to any body investigating the Iran-Contra affair. Had Secretary Weinberger been asked to produce these jottings, I am confident that he would have done so without hesitation.

7. Given the informal, personal nature of Secretary Weinberger's diary-type notes, I never associated them with any request that came to my attention for documents related to the Iran-Contra affair. Similarly, Secretary Weinberger never indicated in any way that he considered these jottings or diary notes to contain information relevant to inquiries into the Iran-Contra affair. When we attempted to reconstruct the sequence of events relating to Iran-Contra in preparation for Secretary Weinberger's testimony before Congress in July and August 1987, Secretary Weinberger never reviewed or even referred to these jottings. It never occurred to me that these jottings might have been useful in helping to reconstruct past events.

8. Secretary Weinberger is an honest man whose character is beyond reproach. I have never known him to lie about anything, and I find it impossible to believe that he would have intentionally misled any investigative body examining the Iran-Contra affair about the existence

4

of his informal jottings or diary notes if he had under-

stood that they were relevant to any investigation.

_____
GORDON E. FORNELL

24 APRIL 1992
DATE

Subscribed and sworn before
me this 24th day of April 1992.

_____
Notary Public

My commission expires:

12 Dec 1997
_____

ATTACHMENT
A

DEPSECDEF TAFT'S SCHEDULE FRIDAY, 1 FEBRUARY 1985	SECDEF WEINBERGER'S SCHEDULE FRIDAY, 1 FEBRUARY 1985
0830 Host Staff Meeting, 3E928	0715 Courier at home
0945- Address Navy Commodores, 1015 4E442 (Cdr Loop escort)	0730 ~~Breakfast at the Brazilian Embassy~~
1030 Mr. Ron Lauder re: Emerging Technologies	0845 <u>Time</u> Magazine Interview
1100 Meeting w/Connie Newman, Chairperson of DACOWITS	0945 Call on Cong Daniel
1200 Adm Burkhalter (Interview)	1015 Call on Cong Price
1230 Lunch	1045 Call on Cong Alexander
1330 CJCS/SecDef Meeting	1115 Call on Cong Foley
1400 To AF Clinic - Immunizations	1200 Family Luncheon Group at the White House
1430 DRB Meeting, 3E928	1330 CJCS, et al
1630 <u>Time</u> Magazine Interview w/Bruce von Voorst & Col Bob O'Brien	1400 Remarks to Staffers of Congressional Budget Cmtes, 5A1070

ATTACHMENT
B

		SECDEF'S CALENDAR		DATE FRIDAY 1 FEBRUARY 1985	
TIME IN	TIME OUT	SECRETARY'S WHEREABOUTS	VISITORS		REMARKS
0845		Arrived on Office			C/CC
0846	0850		Gen Powell		
0850	0906		Graham Allison		
0906	0908		Gen Powell		
0906	0940		Mr. Burch		
0906	0940		TIME Magazine Interview, et al		
0930	0941		Gen Powell		
0939	0940		Mr. Rourke		
	0940	Departed for Capitol Hill			C/CC
1343		Returned to Office			C/CC
1347	1407		Gen Powell		
1350	1405		Gen Vessey		
1350	1405		Adm. Moreau		
	1407	Departed to 5A1070			
1429		Returned to Office			C/CC
1717	1735		Gen Powell		
	1850	Departed to Quarters			C/CC

TELEPHONE CHECK	☑ OFC	☑ WH	☑ NMCC	☐	INITIAL

FORM 16, 1 May 80

AFFIDAVIT OF JOHN E. HAYNES

I, John E. Haynes, do affirm and say:

1. I am the Twentieth Century Political Historian in the Manuscript Division of the Library of Congress ("LOC").

2. As part of my duties, I have been involved in matters related to the papers of former Secretary of Defense Caspar W. Weinberger ("Weinberger papers"), which are deposited at the LOC, although I did not process the collection.

3. The Weinberger papers have been deposited at the LOC pursuant to an Agreement of Deposit that leaves title to the papers with Mr. Weinberger. See Attachment A. In my experience, this type of agreement is common for living public figures who deposit their papers at the LOC.

4. Pursuant to the Agreement of Deposit, access to the Weinberger papers is limited to Mr. Weinberger, LOC staff, and those who have the written permission of Mr. Weinberger. In my experience, such restricted access is common for the papers of public figures still living.

5. A draft register, or "Finding Aid," was prepared by archivists at the LOC who processed Mr. Weinberger's papers. The Finding Aid contains a detailed description of the Weinberger papers and, to my knowledge, was prepared without input from Mr. Weinberger or his staff. The Finding Aid, a portion of which is attached in Attachment B, makes a number of

references to Mr. Weinberger's "diary notes," during his years as Secretary of Defense. The scope and content note of the Finding Aid mentions the diary notes and also states that the Defense Department series of the Weinberger papers contains materials relating to the Iran-Contra affair and other historical events.

6. On or about November 8, 1990, I received a letter from Mr. Weinberger acknowledging that the Office of Independent Counsel ("OIC") had requested "access to notes or other documents produced by or for [him] in regard to the Iran/Contra matter during [his] tenure" as Secretary of Defense, in the LOC's possession, and granting the OIC access to all his papers potentially relevant to the OIC's investigation and "related to the Iran/Contra matter for the period of January 1, 1984 through August 31, 1987." See Attachment C. It was and is my understanding that this grant of permission encompassed OIC access to the "diary notes" referenced above in ¶ 5.

7. Thereafter, on or about November 20, 1990, OIC attorneys visited the LOC to review the Weinberger papers, pursuant to Mr. Weinberger's grant of permission referenced above in ¶ 6. To the best of my recollection, I was present when the senior archivist for the collection, Allan Teichroew, explained to the OIC attorneys how to use the Finding Aid.

2

8. On or about November 26, 1991, the OIC asked to copy certain of the Weinberger papers which, to my understanding, the OIC attorneys had already reviewed. See Attachment D. In my view, the OIC's request for copies of documents appeared to exceed the access which previously had been granted to the OIC by Mr. Weinberger. Therefore, I notified Mr. Weinberger of the OIC's request through his secretary, Kay Leisz.

9. Ms. Leisz subsequently informed me that Mr. Weinberger wished to review the requested documents before they were copied. On or about December 16, 1991, Mr. Weinberger and Ms. Leisz visited the LOC to view the documents. See Attachment E. To my knowledge, Mr. Weinberger had not reviewed these documents prior to December 16, 1991.

10. On or about December 16, 1991, during their visit, I accompanied Mr. Weinberger and Ms. Leisz to a LOC carrel and served them the documents they requested, which the OIC sought to copy.

11. While I was serving documents on or about December 16, 1991, I recall hearing Mr. Weinberger make a comment to the effect that he had been unaware or surprised at something, with reference to the documents he was reviewing. I do not recall his exact words nor do I know to what specifically he referred at the time the comment was made. To

3

the extent I was aware, the comment was casual and did not appear to be one of concern. I do not know to whom Mr. Weinberger directed the comment, and recall hearing no response from anyone in the room.

12. I could not see specifically what Mr. Weinberger was viewing when he made the comment referenced in ¶ 11, and do not know specifically to what he was referring, since by that time I had produced a number of documents in several boxes for him to review. From my subsequent review of LOC call slips prepared on December 16, 1991, and with reference to the Finding Aid, I recall that appointment files, diary notes, official logs, social engagement calendars, telephone call sheets, and meeting notes were among the documents made available for Mr. Weinberger's review at that time. See Attachments B and E.

13. Sometime after Mr. Weinberger's visit to the LOC on or about December 16, 1991, I was informed that he had granted permission to the OIC to copy all of the documents

4

requested. I informed the OIC of this full grant of permission

by letter dated January 6, 1992. <u>See</u> Attachment F.

John E. Haynes
John E. Haynes

**Subscribed and affirmed before me
this 22nd day of April 1992.**

Notary Public

My Commission Expires:

October 14, 1995

ATTACHMENT
A

AGREEMENT OF DEPOSIT

AGREEMENT MADE AS OF THE <u>7th</u> DAY OF <u>August</u>, 19 <u>87</u> between the Library of Congress, Washington, D.C., hereinafter called the Library, and Caspar W. Weinberger, hereinafter called the Depositor, witnesseth:

WHEREAS, the Depositor is desirous of depositing with the Library a collection of his personal papers, more particularly described on the schedule attached hereto, without transferring title to same, and

WHEREAS, the Library desires to accept said materials for custodial care and appropriate service to the public, without obtaining title to same,

NOW THEREFORE, the Library and Depositor mutually agree as follows:

1.   <u>Access and Organization</u>. All of the material in the collection shall be available to the staff of the Library approved by the Depositor, and shall be available to the Depositor for all purposes. The staff of the Library which has been granted access shall use such access to organize the material, and otherwise administer the material. Otherwise, access to the material shall be limited to those with the written permission of the Depositor and any requisite security clearance.

2.   <u>Photoreproduction</u>. Provided they have the express written permission of the Depositor, and subject to any conditions he may impose in such a written expression of

permission, persons granted access to the collection may procure single-copy reproductions of the unclassified, unpublished writings in the collection.

3. <u>Additions and Removals</u>. Such papers as the Depositor may deposit with the Library of Congress in the future will be governed by the terms and conditions of this AGREEMENT OF DEPOSIT. There may be material subject to this AGREEMENT OF DEPOSIT which the Depositor wishes neither to leave on deposit with, nor to give to, the Library. Accordingly, the Depositor may also remove, or cause a representative acting with the Depositor's written authorization to remove, any of the papers deposited hereby from the custody of the Library of Congress at his complete discretion. The Depositor shall notify the Library of Congress upon removal of any material. Upon the removal of any papers, they will no longer be governed by the terms and conditions of this AGREEMENT OF DEPOSIT. All other parts of this AGREEMENT OF DEPOSIT are subordinate and subject to this paragraph 3.

4 <u>Term of Deposit</u>. The collection shall remain in deposit in the Library of Congress for a term of not less than ten years, beginning with the date of deposit; provided, however, that any future gift of all or any part of the collection to the UNITED STATES OF AMERICA, for the benefit of the Library of Congress, shall, upon the effectiveness of the gift instrument, cause the gift to supersede and to terminate the deposit of the property constituting such gift.

In witness whereof, we have hereunto set our hands and seals.

August 26, 1987
Date

Caspar W. Weinberger   (seal)

Aug 7, 1987
Date

Librarian of Congress   (seal)

Attachment

ATTACHMENT
B

LIBRARY OF CONGRESS
MANUSCRIPT DIVISION

The Papers of

CASPAR W. WEINBERGER

The papers of Caspar W. Weinberger (1917-), lawyer, politician, television commentator, newspaper columnist, and cabinet official, were deposited in the Library of Congress from 1981 to 1988.

The status of copyright in the unpublished writings of Caspar W. Weinberger is governed by the Copyright Law of the United States (Title 17, U. S. C.).

Video tapes and audio recordings have been transferred to the appropriate custodial division of the Library of Congress where they are identified as a part of these papers.

The Caspar W. Weinberger Papers are restricted unless written permission is give by Mr. Weinberger. In the case of classified material, requisite security clearances are also necessary. Requests for access are not being entertained at this time.

Photoduplication is allowed only with the written permission of Casper W. Weinberger.

Linear feet of shelf space occupied: 379
Approximate number of items: 370,000

CASPAR W. WEINBERGER PAPERS

Classified Items Removed

Below is the container list of classified material removed from the papers of Caspar W. Weinberger. References are to exact series and folder titles from which the items were taken. The list is for staff use only. Readers will learn from cross reference sheets in the applicable files of the papers whether and why classified material has been removed.

Not described by this list is material from Weinberger's Department of Defense subject file, which is classified in such quantity that the entire subseries has been placed in the security vault. Information regarding the latter can be found in the main register to the Weinberger Papers (boxes 622 to 889) and in the various inventories of the DOD subject file.

Also not described by this list are the classified items themselves. Inventories of the two DOD series represented, the appointment and diary notes file and Weinberger's 1986 chronological file, are instead located at the beginning of each file in the papers. In the case of the 1986 chronological file, they appear as well at the beginning of each monthly segment. Another set has been retained as part of the working index to other Weinberger DOD files kept in the vault.

Weinberger Papers: Classified Items Removed

Container Nos.   Contents

OFFICE OF MANAGEMENT AND BUDGET, 1969-73

1   Subject file, 1969-73
                       Budget
                           Fiscal Year
                               1973
                                   Supplemental items (folder 1)
                       Confidential Statement of Employment and Financial
                           Interests
                       Council of Economic Advisors
                       Defense, Department of
                       Information leaks
                       Office of Economic Opportunity
                       Personnel data book, June 1970
                       Revenue sharing
                           Desk file, 1971 (folder 2)
                       State, Department of
                       Stockpiles (folder 1)
                       Trips
                           June 1971
                       Wage-price freeze
                           Budget reduction
                       White House
                           General (folder 2)

DEPARTMENT OF HEALTH, EDUCATION, AND WELFARE, 1972-75

                   General File, 1972-75
                       Confidential Statement of Employment and Financial
                           Interests
                       Joint Drug Cabinet Committee meeting, 1973
                   Speeches, Trips, and Meetings, 1973-75
                       Speeches
                           Jan. 26-28, 1975
                       Trips
                           Foreign
                               Aug.-Sept. 1973
                                   U.S.S.R. and Poland
                                       General (folder 1)
                               May 3-11, 1974
                                   Australia and New Zealand
                               May 2-9, 1975
                                   Australia and New Zealand
                                       General

Weinberger Papers: Classified Items Removed

Container Nos.   Contents

DEPARTMENT OF DEFENSE, 1980-87

1 &(cont.)

Transition, 1980-81
    Idea suggestions (folder 2)
Appointment and diary file, 1981-87
    White House, cabinet, and other important meeting notes
        Set B (photocopies of originals not in collection)
            1981 (folders 1-2)
            1982 (folder 1)
            1983 (folder 2)
            1984 (folders 1-2)
            1985 (folders 1-2)
            1986 (folder 3)
            1987 (folders 1-3)

2

Chronological File, 1986
    Jan.-May 12 (8 folders)

*3

    May 13-July 22 (8 folders)

*4

    July 23-Sept. 30 (8 folders)

*5

    Oct.-Dec. (8 folders)

CASPAR W. WEINBERGER PAPERS

Classified Portion
Department of Defense: Subject File

The subject file portion of the Department of Defense series in the Weinberger Papers has been removed from general circulation because the bulk of the material consists of classified government documents. The file extends from box 622 to box 890 and is described in the container list of the collection. A dummy sheet indicating the containers' removal has been placed in the physical space on the shelf between boxes 621 and 891.

Preceding the DOD subject file for each year is an index or inventory of the documents for that year. Listed sequentially, in the order of their arrangement, documents are first cited by control number (when there is one) and then by content, date, authorship, etc. Entries are grouped alphabetically by subject as described in the container list of the collection.

Copies of the DOD subject index have also been interfiled among the appropriate topical categories. At the front of folder one of the 1981 Central America file, for example, is the inventory for all the items of all the folders under that title for the year. The interfiled index is of special importance because of annotations indicating the sensitivity of certain classified documents. Separated from the main group of classified material are three categories of items: top secret documents, secret restricted data, and top secret restricted data. As noted on the inventories where they appear, one asterisk indicates removal to a separate location of top secret material, two asterisks for removal of secret restricted data, and three asterisks for removal of top secret restricted data. Staff and readers with permission to use the Weinberger Papers can refer to separate inventories of the three most sensitive categories for information regarding their extent and character.

A third set of DOD subject file indexes consists of a working index used during processing and retained as a master listing of the items' classification. The working index is not for circulation and not part of the collection. It is a reference/processing tool. Noted before each entry on the working index is the current standing of the material cited. A hyphen ("-") next to an entry indicates the material is unclassified. A "d" before the item indicates the material has been declassified according to instructions on the document(s). Other markings signify the following: "c" means confidential; "s" means secret; "frd" means formerly restricted data; "ts" with a red line drawn through means top secret material; "srd" crossed in red means secret restricted data; and "tsrd" boxed in red means top secret restricted data. Red has been used to alert staff quickly to sensitive items removed for special handling.

NB: Most documents listed in the subject file indexes contain more material than is cited. Briefing books, for instance, consist of many items brought together as one unit and listed as a single document. In treating the various classifications which appear within, the procedure followed has been to rate the whole according to the most sensitive part. If even one page of one item is top secret, then the document as a whole has been given a top secret designation. Similarly, if only one item in a packet of correspondence is confidential, the whole packet has nonetheless been described as confidential.

Biographical Note

1917, Aug. 18	Born, San Francisco, CA.
1933	Graduated, San Francisco Polytechnic High School
1938	Graduated, Harvard College
1941	LL.B., Harvard Law School
1941-45	U.S. Army
1942	Married Jane Dalton
1945-47	Law clerk, U.S. Judge William E. Orr
1947-69	Practiced law with firm of Heller, Ehrman, White & McAuliffe (partner, 1959-69)
1952-58	State Assemblyman, California Legislature
1958	Unsuccessful candidate to become Republican nominee for Attorney General of State of California
1959-68	Newspaper columnist on California politics and government Moderator of television program, "Profile: Bay Area," KQED, San Francisco
1960-62	Vice chairman, Republican Central Committee of California
1962-64	Chairman, Republican Central Committee of California
1967-68	Chairman, Commission on California State Government Organization and Economics
1968-69	Director of Finance, State of California

1970	Chairman, Federal Trade Commission
1970-72	Deputy Director, Office of Management and Budget
1972-73	Director, Office of Management and Budget
1973	Counselor to the President for Human Resources
1973-75	Secretary of Health, Education, and Welfare
1975-80	General counsel, vice president, and director, Bechtel Group of Companies
1978-79	Member, State of California Commission on Government Reform
1981-87	Secretary of Defense
1988-	Publisher, <u>Forbes Magazine</u>

Scope and Content Note

The papers of Caspar W. Weinberger span the years 19() to 1987, with the bulk of the items concentrated in the period 1951 to 1987. The collection focuses on his career in California state politics and the federal government, but also includes family papers, files from a private legal practice, and considerable material relating to his work in public television, as a San Francisco Bay Area newspaper columnist, and with the Bechtel Group of Companies as the international construction firm's vice president and general counsel. Featured are lengthy records of his cabinet positions under Presidents Nixon and Ford between 1970 and 1975 and from 1981 to 1987 when he was President Reagan's Secretary of Defense during a period of rapid increase in military expenditures. His earlier Washington posts involved stints as Deputy Director and then Director of the Office of Management and Budget and two years as Secretary of Health, Education, and Welfare before and after the resignation of Richard Nixon following the Watergate scandal. Prior to holding these positions, Weinberger had served briefly as head of the Federal Trade Commission in 1970.

Included in the papers are appointment books, diary notes and other jottings; personal, general, and business correspondence; legislative and political matter; and subject files, financial data, television scripts, newspaper columns, book reviews, texts of speeches, and assorted printed matter. Files related to Weinberger's service as Secretary of Defense consist mainly of photocopied duplicates rather than original items. Most are classified government documents and cannot be served to the general public.

Weinberger's early interest in politics is demonstrated by scrapbooks and other items he kept about national affairs while a student at San Francisco Polytechnic High School in the 1930s. He was a star pupil whose commencement oration on the nobility of politics (texts of which survive among his childhood materials) anticipated his first run for public office as a Republican candidate for the California State Assembly in 1952. He won in a Bay Area contest, and his four consecutive terms in Sacramento are meticulously recorded in legislative files for the period. Noted statewide for his efforts to reorganize California's Alcoholic Control Board, Weinberger competed for a spot on the 1958 GOP ticket as state attorney general but lost in the primary to a more conservative challenger. His files trace some of the ideological and organizational issues involved, shifting subsequently to the crucial years between 1960 and 1964, when as vice chairman and later chairman of the State Republican Central Committee he shepherded the state party through various factional struggles culminating in the ascendance nationally of the so-called Goldwater wing of the GOP. Correspondence from the period foreshadows the Washington administrations of Nixon and Reagan, in that letters and related material concern the pre-presidential careers of both future chief executives and their various California and Sunbelt supporters. Among the more frequent or prominent letter writers are Goodwyn Knight, Robert Finch, John Tower, Barry Goldwater, Nelson Rockefellor, William P. Clark, George Murphy, George Christopher, and William F. Knowland.

Journalism and the news media were Weinberger's second interests, and after leaving the state assembly he began ten years as moderator of "Profile: Bay Area," a public affairs program on San Francisco public television station KQED. The production is fully documented with scripts, correspondence, and

related matter. Also well covered is a syndicated newspaper column he wrote
from 1958 to 1966 titled "California Commentary."

In 1966, then Governor Reagan appointed Weinberger to be California State
Finance Director. Weinberger's papers are thereafter arranged by career
episode, with general and personal correspondence for a given period
congregated under position title. Students of the Nixon White House can turn
first to the FTC segment to trace Weinberger's initial Washington connection,
after which considerable information is available in OMB files on critical
budgetary and fiscal matters for the 1971 to 1973 period. As HEW secretary,
Weinberger grappled with welfare reform, abortion, and affirmative action in
education, issues extensively treated with other topical and policy questions
under the HEW heading. Already during his FTC-OMB appointments, Weinberger
began keeping terse journal notations or diary notes of important events and
meetings. These notes can be used with various White House, cabinet, and
other subject files to glean highlights of his contribution to the Nixon-Ford
presidencies. Themes of significance in addition to topics already mentioned
range from Nixon's 1973 attempt to reorganize the Executive Branch (material
on this is concentrated in a file on Weinberger's ephemeral post as Counselor
of Human Resources), to such ongoing issues as the federal budget deficit,
social security funding, and increased health care costs.

At Bechtel from 1975 to 1980, Weinberger refocused on California and
private business interests. He was still oriented toward national politics,
however, with the goal after the election of Jimmy Carter being the return to
the White House of a Republican administration. To this end, Weinberger
joined the Reagan team well in advance of the former governor's 1980 campaign,
and in the Bechtel files is correspondence and commentary important to the
sweep that took both to Washington. Subjects of interest tend toward
diplomatic and military topics rather than the previous concentration on
domestic affairs, with U.S.-Soviet arms negotiations and the 1979-80 Iranian
hostage crisis among the principal items considered.

Department of Defense files in these papers begin with transition
material documenting the Reagan Administration's first steps in military
leadership. Other series from this period include appointment records and
diary notes, a private file of miscellaneous correspondence, and a large group
of subject files. Notable among the appointment data is a special category of
White House, cabinet, and other important meeting notes containing the Defense
Secretary's handwritten jottings and sometimes those of Reagan and Vice
President George Bush. Writings by his superiors are brief and infrequent but
include choice comments as well as amusing sketches.

The most substantive of the Defense Department materials is an extensive
subject file organized, copied from originals at the Pentagon, and indexed by
his staff. Treated within yearly alphabetical groupings are the great and
small events of world affairs during the 1980s, including information on the
character and opinions of the major individual participants. Among the score
or more incidents and developments covered are U.S.-Soviet nuclear weapons
discussions, the invasion of Grenada, the Falklands War, various crises in
Lebanon, American policy toward Nicaragua, relations with NATO, U.S. attacks
on Libya, terrorism, and the Iran-Contra affair. Budgetary and management
issues are recurring topics as well, especially in relation to OMB Director
David Stockman and leading policy shapers in Congress, while another episode
covered is the aftermath of the March 1981 assassination attempt on President
Reagan. The file as a whole is characterized by documentation of every sort,

much of it classified, including correspondence with world leaders, memoranda
of conversations, memoranda between cabinet and other executive-level
officials, diplomatic and military cables, briefing data, minutes or synopses
of
White House and National Security Council meetings, and reports (political as
well as military) regarding the spectrum of U.S. interests on the
international scene.

Prominent correspondents whose names have not been cited above include
Spiro Agnew, Richard Armitage, Menacham Begin, Frank Carlucci, Peter Lord
Carrington, William J. Casey, William J. Crowe, King Fahad, Indira Gandhi,
Mohamed Abdul Halim Abu Ghazala, Alexander M. Haig, Charles Hernu, Michael
Heseltine, King Hussein, Fred C. Ikle, Helmut Kohl, Yuko Kurihara, Robert
McFarlane, Mohamed Hosni Mubarak, John M. Poindexter, Richard Perle, Colin
Powell, Elliott Richardson, Yitzhak Shamir, Ariel Sharon, Bernard W. Rogers,
George P. Shultz, Giovanni Spadolini, Margaret Thatcher, John Vessey, and
Manfred Woerner,

Description of Series

Container Nos.   Series

1-5   **Family and Childhood Papers, 1910-79.**
                        Correspondence, legal papers, school materials,
                        photographs, early business items, scrapbooks, printed
                        matter, and various miscellany. Organized alphabetically
                        by type or topic of material.

5-12   **Law Office, 1927-55.**
                        Corrrespondence, memoranda, briefs, writs, notes, and
                        other material concerning Weinberger's law practice,
                        mostly from the period 1948-52. Organized alphabetically
                        by case or subject.

13-116   **California State Government, 1951-79.**

    13-92   Legislative Assembly, 1951-58
                                Correspondence, memoranda, bills, notes, charts,
                                lists, legal data, and various printed material
                                pertaining to Weinberger's duties in the California
                                Legislative Assembly from 1952-58. Organized
                                according to session and then by topic, type of
                                material, or name of correspondent.

    93-104   Commissions, 1962-79
                                Correspondence, memoranda, reports, bulletins,
                                minutes of meetings, press material, and related matter
                                concerning Weinberger's chairmanship of the Commission
                                on California State Government Organization and
                                Economics ("Little Hoover Commission") and membership
                                on the State of California Commission on Government
                                Reform. Organized according to commission and
                                alphabetically therein by type or topic of material.

    105-116   State Director of Finance, 1968-69
                                Correspondence, reports, appointment files, diary
                                notes, invitations, speech material, and other files
                                concerning Weinberger's tenure as Director of
                                California State Finance. Organized alphabetically by
                                type or topic of material.

Container Nos.	Series
117-147	**California Politics, 1951-66.**

      117-130

Campaigns, 1951-66
    Correspondence, memoranda, calendars, photographs, financial items, press material, lists, notes, campaign advertisements, speech material, printed matter, and other material relating to various state and national political campaigns in which Weinberger was involved as a candidate or Republican Party official between 1952 and 1966. Organized alphabetically by office sought and chronologically by election therein.

      130-131

Radio Program: "People and Politics," 1959-62
    Correspondence and scripts from a daily radio program Weinberger chaired to explain and promote Republican views on state and national political affairs. Organized according to type of material and chronologically therein.

      132-147

Republican State Central Committee, 1960-64
    Correspondence, memoranda, subject files, speech material, minutes of meetings, and other data documenting Weinberger's tenure as vice chairman and chairman of the Republican State Central Committee. Organized chronologically and then alphabetically by type or topic of material.

148-200   **California Public Affairs, 1957-68.**

      148-167

General Correspondence, 1959-67
    Correspondence and related matter pertaining to Weinberger's activities on behalf of various religious, philanthropic, educational, and other private and public institutions in San Francisco and elsewhere during the period between his duties as state assemblyman and subsequent state and national office. Organized alphabetically by type or topic of material.

      167-180

Newspaper Column: "California Commentary," 1958-66
    Correspondence, drafts and printed copies of columns, and financial and other materials documenting Weinberger's semi-weekly newspaper articles about California state government. Arranged alphabetically by type of material and chronologically within.

Container Nos.   Series

148-200   **California Public Affairs, 1957-68 (continued).**

    180-200   Television Programs, 1959-68
          Correspondence, scripts, lists, and printed matter
relating to public television programs hosted by
Weinberger on station KQED in San Francisco. Topics
were political and social issues affecting California
and the nation. Organized alphabetically by type of
material.

201-216   **Federal Trade Commission, 1970-71.**
          Correspondence, memoranda, appointment files, lists,
articles, Congressional testimony, diary notes, subject
files, invitations, press material, speeches, printed
matter, and miscellaneous data regarding Weinberger's
duties as Chairman of the Federal Trade Commission.
Correspondence includes letters with legislators,
government officials, and the general public. Arranged
alphabetically by topic or type of material.

217-304   **Office of Management and Budget, 1969-73.**

    217-221   Appointment and Diary Files, 1970-72
          Appointment books and diary notes recording
Weinberger's personal and public activities while
Deputy Director and Director of OMB. Arranged
alphabetically by type of material and chronologically
within.

    221-231   Correspondence, 1970-73
          Correspondence with legislators, government
officials, politicians, friends, acquaintances, and the
general public. Includes attached and related matter.
Organized into general and personal files and
alphabetically therein.

    231-293   Subject File, 1969-73
          Correspondence, memoranda , charts, lists, minutes,
of meetings, bulletins, briefing data, bills, press,
material, reports, interviews, invitations, printed
matter, and other miscellaneous material from
Weinberger's tenure at OMB. Alphabetically arranged by
topic or type of material.

Container Nos.	Series

217-304   **Office of Management and Budget, 1969-73 (continued).**

    293-304   **Speech File, 1970-73**
Texts of speeches and related matter regarding
their presentation, including notes, correspondence,
invitations, and programs. Organized chronologically
by date of speech. Miscellaneous background materials
appears at the end of the file and is arranged
alphabetically by subject.

305-470   **Department of Health, Education, and Welfare, 1972-75.**

    305-318   **Appointment and Diary Files, 1973-75**
Appointment books, schedules, and diary notes
recording Weinberger's personal and public activities
while Secretary of HEW. Arranged alphabetically by
type of material and chronologically within.

    318-365   **Correspondence, 1973-75**
Congratulatory, Congressional, general, and
personal correspondence, including attached and
appended material. Arranged alphabetically by name of
correspondent within applicable segments.

    365-405   **Reading File, 1973-75**
Reading file of letters sent. Organized into
departmental and personal segments, each arranged
chronologically, and a secretariat file consisting of
alphabetical and chronological subgroups. The
alphabetical subgroup contains both topical and
personal name files.

    405-426   **General File, 1972-75**
Correspondence, memoranda, reports, briefing
material, minutes of meetings, charts, lists, bills,
invitations, and printed matter concerning the
programs, staff, and operation of HEW. Arranged
alphabetically by type or topic of material.

    427-451   **Subject File, 1972-75**
Correspondence, memoranda, bills, Congressional
testimony, reports, briefing material, press data,
grant files, contracts, charts, lists, printed matter,
and miscellaneous files pertaining to sustantive
functions of HEW. Organized alphabetically into
primary issue categories and arranged alphabetically by
subtopic within. Among the principal categories are
budget issues, civil rights, education, and national
health care.

Container Nos.	Series

305-470   **Department of Health, Education, and Welfare, 1972-75 (continued).**

      451-470   Speeches, Trips, and Meetings, 1973-75
          Correspondence, texts of speeches and talks, trip itineraries, programs, printed matter, and other material relating to Weinberger's appearances, visits, and attendance before and with public groups on behalf of HEW. Organized chronologically within speech, trip, and meeting categories.

471-472   **Counselor to the President for Human Resources, 1973.**
       Correspondence, reports, speeches, meeting material, printed matter, and miscellaneous items relating to President Richard Nixon's assignment of Weinberger as head of a new and short-lived executive office. Arranged alphabetically by subject or type of material.

473-571   **Bechtel Files, 1968-80.**

      473-482   Appointment and Diary Files, 1975-80
          Appointment books, daily schedules, diary notes, and telephone log books recording Weinberger's business, political, and personal activities while general counsel and vice president of the Bechtel Group of Companies. Organized alphabetically according to type of files and chronologically within.

      482-508   General Correspondence, 1976-80
          Correspondence and memoranda with attached and related matter. Arranged chronologically by year and alphabetically by topic or name of person therein.

      508-522   Chronological File, 1975-80
          Letters sent and some correspondence received. Arranged chronologically.

      522-564   Subject File, 1968-80
          Correspondence, memoranda, reports, articles, interviews, invitations, itineraries, minutes of meetings, lists, charts, press material, printed matter, and miscellaneous files concerning Weinbergers's personal, business, and political activities during his career at the Bechtel Group of Companies. Includes related files from his appointments in Washington, D.C., after 1968. Arranged alphabetically by topic or type of material.

Container Nos.	Series

565-571   **Bechtel Files, 1968-80 (continued).**

    565-571   Speech File, 1975-80
        Texts of speeches and related matter regarding their presentation, including notes, correspondence, invitations, and programs. Background and press material precedes chronologically arranged texts.

572-890   **Department of Defense, 1976-87.**

    572-576   Transition Papers, 1980-81
        Correspondence, schedules, briefing material and notes, invitations, reports, topical files, printed matter and miscellaneous items concerning the transition from President Carter and the Reagan administration. Organized alphabetically by topic or type of material.

    576-592   Appointment and Diary Files, 1980-87
        Appointment books, diary notes, activity logs, social calendars, telephone call sheets, and handwritten notes kept by Weinberger of White House, cabinet, and other important meetings he attended while Secretary of Defense. Organized alphabetically by type of file and chronologically within. White House and other important meetings notes are arranged in two sets, the second of which consists of photocopies of originals not in the papers. Included in the latter is an index of the notes compiled and photocopied by Weinberger's staff.

    592-607   Private File, 1976-87
        Correspondence, memoranda, minutes of meetings, invitations, press items, reports, printed matter, and miscellaneous data. Alphabetically arranged by subject or type of material.

    608-621   Chronological File, 1986
        Photocopies and a few originals of outgoing correspondence, memoranda, and related matter for 1986. A complete index of the file, compiled by Weinberger's staff at the Department of Defense, precedes the documents. The index and file are organized chronologically on a monthly basis, and copies of the index for each month are also filed prior to each calendar change. Included in the series are numerous classified items now removed from general use. Items withdrawn have been identified by asterisk(s) next to the document control numbers on the monthly index sheets.

Container Nos.	Series
572-890	Department of Defense, 1976-87 (Continued).

    622-890   Subject File, 1981-87 (Classified).

Photocopies and a few originals of correspondence, memoranda, reports, military orders, budgetary and administrative files, transcripts of high-level conversations, diplomatic exchanges, military cables, technological data, and numerous related files concerning Weinberger's tenure as Secretary of Defense. Organized chronologically by year and alphabetically by subject therein. An index of documents compiled by Weinberger's staff precedes the file for each year. Subject entries are also preceeded by indexes, with the pertinent sheets appearing at the front of the first folder on the topic covered. The entire series has been removed from general use because of its classified contents.

891-946   **Miscellany, 1948-87.**

    891-892   Book Reviews by Weinberger, 1948-80

Writings, correspondence, notes, printed matter, and other materials relating to the preparation and publication of book reviews. Arranged chronologically by appearance of review.

    892-896   Photographs, 1960-87

Positive photographic prints and some negatives, primarily of Weinberger's public life. Organized chronologically.

    897   Teaching File, 1949-61

Correspondence, lecture notes, attendance charts, and miscellaneous items concerning Weinberger's presentations to California Bar Association meetings and college and university classes which he taught in San Francisco.

    897   Steep Ravine, 1961-72

Correspondence, clippings, and miscellaneous material relating to the attempt by Weinberger and others to make Steep Ravine a California State Park.

Container Nos.   Series

891-946   **Miscellany, 1948-87 (Continued).**

   898-946   Printed Matter, 1951-80
                                         Clippings and other printed matter regarding
                                      Weinberger, organized on a monthly or yearly basis.

947   **Oversize, 1934.**
                                      Scrapbook concerning national politics kept by
                                   Weinberger as a child, removed from the family papers
                                   because of its size.

Container Nos.   Contents

Container Nos.   Contents

      DEPARTMENT OF DEFENSE, 1976-81 (Continued)

575
         Transition, 1980-81
           Thank-you letters
             (1 folder)
           Miscellaneous
             (4 folders)

576
             (1 folder)
         Appointment and diary file, 1980-87
           Appointment books
             1981 (2 volumes)

577
             1982 (3 volumes)

578
             1983 (3 volumes)

579
             1984 (3 volumes)
             1985
                (2 volumes)

580
                (1 volume)
             1986
           Diary notes
             Dec. 1980-Mar. 1981 (2 folders)

581
             Apr. 1981-June 1982 (5 folders)

582
             July 1982-Sept. 1983 (5 folders)

583
             Oct. 1983-Dec. 1984 (5 folders)

584
             Jan. 1985-Mar. 1986 (5 folders)

585
             Apr. 1986-Sept. 1987 (6 folders)

586
             Oct. 1987
           Official log of activities
             Jan. 1981-June 1983 (5 folders)

587
             July 1983-June 1986 (6 folders)

588
             July-Dec. 1986
           Social engagements calender (Caspar W. and Jane
             Weinberger)
             1981-86 (6 folders)

589
             1987
           Telephone call sheets, 1981-86 (6 folders)

Container Nos.   Contents

DEPARTMENT OF DEFENSE, 1976-87 (Continued)

590   **Appointment and diary file, 1980-87**
              White House, cabinet, and other important meeting notes
                  Set A (originals)
                      1981-87 and undated (9 folders)

591   Set B (photocopies of originals not in collection)
                      Index, 1981-87
                      1981-84 (9 folders)

592   1985-87 (8 folders)
              Private file, 1976-87
                  American Ditchley Foundation
                      (1 folder)

593   (2 folders)
              Bechtel, 1980-85
              Biographical data
              Boards

594   Bohemian Club (3 folders)
              Churchilliana

595   Clubs
              Correspondence
                  Personal
                      1981-May 1983 (3 folders)

596   June 1983-1985 (4 folders)

597   1986
              Thank-you letters
                  1981-April 1984 (5 folders)

598   May 1984-1985 (4 folders)

599   1986
              Miscellaneous
                  Feb. 1981-Apr. 1983 (4 folders)

600   May 1983-1984 (5 folders)

601   1985-86 (4 folders)
              Council on Foreign Relations
              Duncan, Virginia B.

ATTACHMENT
C

Mr. John Haynes
20th Century Specialist
Library of Congress
Manuscript Division
101 Independence Avenue, S.E.
Rm LM-102
Washington, D.C. 20540

Dear Mr. Haynes:

Independent Counsel Lawrence E. Walsh seeks access
to notes or other documents produced by or for me in regard
to the Iran/Contra matter during my tenure as Secretary of
the U.S. Department of Defense. It is my understanding that
my written permission is required prior to the Library of
Congress voluntarily providing the Office of Independent
Counsel access to said notes or other documents. I am
willing to grant such permission provided that the access to
and review of my materials be in the presence of my Executive
Assistant Kay Leisz. Accordingly, by this letter, I hereby
grant permission for members of the Office of Independent
Counsel to review my files which are potentially relevant to
its investigation, in order to obtain copies of such notes
and documents related to the Iran/Contra matter for the
period of January 1, 1984 through August 31, 1987, on the
condition that their access to and review of said papers be
in the presence of my Executive Assistant Kay Leisz.

Caspar W. Weinberger

Subscribed and sworn before me this _____8th_____ day of
November_____, 1990.

Notary Public

My commission expires: April 14, 1992.

ATTACHMENT
D

**OFFICE OF INDEPENDENT COUNSEL
SUITE 701 WEST
555 THIRTEENTH STREET, N.W.
WASHINGTON, D.C. 20004
(202) 383-8940**

November 26, 1991

<u>BY HAND</u>

Mr. John Haynes
20th Century Specialist
Library of Congress
Manuscript Division
101 Independence Avenue, S.E.
Room LM-102
Washington, D.C. 20540

Dear Mr. Haynes:

In accordance with the procedure agreed upon by former Secretary of Defense Caspar W. Weinberger and the Department of Defense, representatives of this office reviewed certain of Mr. Weinberger's papers at the Library of Congress on November 21, 1991. At that time we completed our review of the papers and submitted to Audrey Wright a list of classified documents, as well as a few documents maintained in the unclassified document repository. I understand that the classified documents will be transferred, following appropriate security procedures, to the Department of Defense. DOD will then review the documents to determine whether copying will be authorized.

In addition to the few unclassified documents just mentioned, we would also like to request copies of the documents in the following files contained in the boxes maintained in the unclassified repository of Mr. Weinberger's papers:

        Box 579:   1985 App't files & diary notes

        Box 580:   1985 App't files & diary notes
                      1986 App't files & diary notes

        Box 584:   January 1985 - March 1986 notes

        Box 584:   March - December 1986 notes

        Box 587:   Official logs from January 1985 - June 1986

Mr. John Haynes
November 26, 1991
Page 2

> Box 588:   Official logs from July - December 1986
>
> Box 589:   Telephone call sheets from 1985 & 1986

As requested by Mr. Weinberger's executive assistant, Ms.
Liesz, we have reviewed our records, and it appears that we
do not already have copies of these documents. Please
provide the copies of the unclassified documents directly to
us.

    Please call me if you have any questions. We
appreciate your cooperation and assistance.

              Very truly yours,

              LAWRENCE E. WALSH
              Independent Counsel

        By: *Thomas E. Baker*
              Thomas E. Baker
              Associate Counsel

cc: Caspar W. Weinberger √
      Michael A. Sterlacci, DOD

ATTACHMENT
E

MANUSCRIPT DIVISION COLLECTION REQUEST

Collection Title:
Weinberger

Container or Reel Numbers:

579   589 —
587   588

Researcher's Name (please print):	Seat Number:
C. Weinberger	

Researcher's Signature:	Date:
John Haynes	12-16-91

For Staff Use Only

Ident. Number: 75883	Location or Micro. Ac. No.:	Staff Initials: JOHN HAYNES	Units Served: 4

86-37 (rev 7/89)

MANUSCRIPT DIVISION COLLECTION REQUEST

Collection Title: Weinberger Collection

Container or Reel Numbers:
580, 581, 582, 583, 584, 585, 586
590, 591, 592, 579, 589, 587, 588

Researcher's Name (please print):	Seat Number:

Researcher's Signature:	Date:
Kay O. Levin	12/16/91

For Staff Use Only

Ident. Number: 75883	Location or Micro. Ac. No.:	Staff Initials: JOHN HAYNES	Units Served: 14

86-37 (rev 7/89)

COLLECTIONS OF THE MANUSCRIPT DIVISION, LIBRARY OF CONGRESS

ATTACHMENT F

THE LIBRARY OF CONGRESS

WASHINGTON, D.C. 20540

MANUSCRIPT DIVISION

January 6, 1992

Dear Mr. Baker:

Mr. Caspar Weinberger has given permission to the Office of Independent Counsel to make copies of all material in those containers in the Caspar W. Weinberger papers you specified in your letter of November 26, 1991 to me: boxes 579, 580, 584, 587, 588, and 589. These boxes do not contain classified material and no other permission is necessary.

The boxes will be available for copying by a representative of the Office of Independent Counsel at the Manuscript Reading Room: 8:30-5:00, Monday through Saturday. A prior appointment is not necessary. Coin-operated copy machines are available in the Manuscript Reading Room. Copying of identified material can also be done by the Library of Congress's Photoduplication Service, but at a higher cost and service may be delayed.

Sincerely yours,

John E. Haynes
20th Century Political
History Specialist

Mr. Thomas E. Baker
Office of Independent Counsel, Suite 701
555 Thirteenth Street NW
Washington DC 20004

AFFIDAVIT

I, COLIN L. POWELL, depose and say that

1. I am currently the Chairman of the Joint
Chiefs of Staff. I was appointed to this position by
President Bush. My term began on October 1, 1989 and I
was reappointed for a second term beginning October 1,
1991. Prior to being named to my present position, I
served as Commander in Chief, Forces Command,
headquartered in Atlanta, Georgia. I also served as
Assistant to the President for National Security Affairs
from December 11, 1987 to January 1989. Prior to that, I
was in command of the V U.S. Corps in Frankfurt, Federal
Republic of Germany.

2. From July 1983 to March 1986, I served as
Senior Military Assistant to Secretary of Defense Caspar
W. Weinberger. I was his chief executive assistant. I
saw virtually all the papers that went in and out of his
office, and consulted with him on a daily basis. I was
the person who largely determined who would or would not
have access to him and it was my responsibility to see to
it that he was fully and properly briefed on all relevant
matters.

3. During the period I worked with Secretary
Weinberger at the Department of Defense, I observed on
his desk a small pad of white paper, approximately 5" x
7". He would jot down on this pad in abbreviated form
various calls and events during the day. I viewed it as
his personal diary which reflected a record of his life.
Knowing Secretary Weinberger as I did and knowing the
routine way he would jot down notes on these pads, it is
entirely possible that it would not have occurred to him
to associate or link these private notes on the 5 x 7
pads with a governmental request for "notes" in the
context of the Iran-Contra matter. I do not believe that
he would have viewed these as official documents. While
I had open access to his office and papers, I never read
the notes on the 5 by 7 pads because I considered them a
private diary.

4. Secretary Weinberger's diary notes were
never dealt with in a secretive way. The pad with his
notations would sit on his desk with the completed pages
turned over. When he completed a pad, it would go into
his desk drawer and he would begin to write on a new pad.

5. Secretary Weinberger was extremely astute
regarding the matters at hand which we were working on.

Once we moved on to other things, his memory for past events was not particularly good. He would forget facts, dates and details. One of my responsibilities was to see to it that his memory was refreshed and that he had all the details and information necessary when he was required to deal with past meetings, conversations and events. In this regard, I often helped prepare him for his Congressional testimony.

6. I believe that Secretary Weinberger was one of the true heroes of the Iran-Contra matter. He was adamantly opposed to the sale of arms to Iran and spoke up forcefully inside the government in an effort to prevent it from occurring. In the last several weeks, I have been asked to review a number of Secretary Weinberger's diary notes by both Independent Counsel and Mr. Weinberger's attorneys. While I have not reviewed them all, the notes I have seen show a person committed to trying to stop the Administration from transferring arms to Iran but who was frustrated in his efforts. I would have discussed the events referred to in the notes with Secretary Weinberger when they were happening. I shared his views and worked closely with him in the effort to defeat a proposal which we both thought was

3

misguided. When his position was rejected and the
President approved the sale of arms to Iran, Secretary
Weinberger asked me to handle the matter for the
Department of Defense ("DoD") and in doing so to minimize
DoD's involvement in the sale of arms to Iran. I did so
until my transfer in March 1986. At all times he
insisted that everything would be done by the book.

   7. Some of the notes I reviewed covered the
fall of 1985. These notes do not suggest to me that
Secretary Weinberger knew, at the time that they were
prepared, that Israel had sent missiles to Iran. I do
not believe that I knew in the fall of 1985 that Israel
had sent missiles to Iran. While I believe we may have
heard about discussions or proposals or suggestions
involving such activities, to the best of my recollection
we did not know that any such activities had actually
been carried out until long after. I also wish to
emphasize that while the Iran-Contra matter has been
given a great deal of attention, it was only a "blip" on
the screen in the Secretary's office during 1985. In the
fall of 1985, neither of us spent a great deal of time on
this issue. It became important much later.

4

8. During all of the years I have known
Secretary Weinberger, I have never known him to lie about
anything. He is a "straight arrow" and one of the most
honest men I have ever known. It is inconceivable to me
that he would lie to Congress or to the Office of
Independent Counsel. Moreover, it is impossible for me
to believe that he would have lied about the existence of
his diary notes had he understood that they were relevant
to what was being asked of him.

COLIN L. POWELL

21 Apr 92
DATE

Subscribed to and sworn to me this 21st
day of April, 1992.

Nancy E Hughes
Notary Public

My commission expires 5 June 1992 .

5

AFFIDAVIT OF ALLAN TEICHROEW

I, Allan Teichroew, do affirm and say:

1.   I am the Assistant Head for Processing of the Preparation Section of the Manuscript Division of the Library of Congress.

2.   In 1987-1988, as part of my responsibilities, I reviewed and processed the papers of former Secretary of Defense Caspar W. Weinberger ("Weinberger papers"). I was a senior archivist at the time. Archivist Connie Cartledge assisted me in this effort. The processed collection of the Weinberger papers currently contains approximately 370,000 items.

3.   The Weinberger papers processed by Ms. Cartledge and me included ninety-nine cartons of unclassified material, which were received by the Library of Congress on or about April 5, 1988. Attachment A to this affidavit is the accession and processing sheet documenting this receipt.

4.   With Ms. Cartledge's assistance, I organized the Weinberger papers and created a register, or "Finding Aid," documenting this organization. The Finding Aid contains a series description, scope and content note, and detailed

container listing of the various series contained within the Weinberger papers. To the best of my ability, the Finding Aid accurately described the Weinberger papers in a fashion that would helpfully assist researchers. Portions of the Finding Aid are contained in Attachment B to this affidavit.

5. I did not consult with either Mr. Weinberger or anyone from his staff about the preparation of the Finding Aid. The Finding Aid is solely the product of the Library of Congress.

6. On page 4 of the Finding Aid, in the scope and content note's second paragraph, it states in part: "Included in the [Weinberger] papers are appointment books, diary notes and other jottings[.]" I wrote the scope and content note and, with input from Ms. Cartledge, coined the term "diary notes" to describe certain handwritten notes on pads of paper, which Ms. Cartledge and I reviewed while processing the Weinberger papers.

7. On page 5 of the Finding Aid, the scope and content note's seventh paragraph describes Department of Defense files. It reads in part as follows:

> Department of Defense files in these papers begin with transition material documenting the Reagan Administration's first steps in military leadership. Other series from this period include appointment records and diary notes, a private file of miscellaneous correspondence, and a large group of subject files.

2

8. On page 5 of the Finding Aid, the scope and content note's eighth paragraph contains a reference that the Defense Department series of the Weinberger papers contains materials related to the Iran-Contra affair, and other historical events.

9. On page 12 of the Finding Aid, there begins a two-page description of the Department of Defense series of the Weinberger papers. Boxes 576-592 are described as "Appointment and Diary Files, 1980-87," which in turn is described as including "Appointment books, diary notes, activity logs, social calendars, telephone call sheets, and handwritten notes kept by Weinberger of White House, cabinet, and other important meetings he attended while Secretary of Defense."

10. The term "diary notes," referenced above in paragraphs 6 and 9, is repeated again on page 84 of the Finding Aid. The entry on page 84 indicates that "diary notes" for the years 1980-1987 are included in the series.

11. On or about November 20, 1990, one or more attorneys from the Office of the Independent Counsel ("OIC"), including, as I recall, Mr. Gregory Mark, visited the Library of Congress to review the Weinberger papers. I understood that Mr. Weinberger had granted permission to the OIC to review his papers held at the Library of Congress, related to the OIC's investigation of the Iran-Contra affair.

3

12. On or about November 20, 1990, I was asked to and did review the Finding Aid with the CIC attorneys, including, as I recall, Mr. Mark. For approximately 15 to 20 minutes, I explained to the OIC attorneys how to use the Finding Aid. I explained to them that the Finding Aid, portions of which are in Attachment B, contained a series description, scope and content note, and a more detailed container listing, with specific reference to the Department of Defense series. This series includes, among other things, the referenced "diary notes."

13. On that date, November 20, 1990, and again on November 30, 1990, I served Mr. Mark of the OIC with boxes containing Weinberger papers. Call slips referencing this service are attached at Attachment C.

14. I am familiar with the fact that access to the Weinberger papers is restricted. In my experience, this not an uncommon treatment for the papers of former public officials.

4

15.   I am familiar with the fact that the Agreement
of Deposit covering the Weinberger papers leaves title to those
papers with Mr. Weinberger.   In my experience, this is a common
arrangement.

Allan Teichroew

Subscribed and affirmed before me this _16_ day of
April, 1992.

Notary Public

My Commission Expires:

My Commission Expires July 18, 1994

ATTACHMENT
A

001	A- 75353

008 $3.a

LIBRARY OF CONGRESS

Manuscript Division

ACCESSIONING AND PROCESSING RECORD

Accession No.: ___19.812___   Date of Receipt: 4-5-88   Accessioner: at/ᵒ
(035#b)

To: 4-13-88   4/14/88
☑ 1. Head, Prep. Section   ☑ 4. Specialist(s):   ☐ 6. Editor
                                  (037)
☑ 2. Assistant Chief 14 Apr 86   M C N W P R L S B H A F   ☐ 7. Head, Prep. Section
☐ 3. Chief   ☑ 5. Head, Prep. Section   ☐ 8. Processor
                                  4-15-88

Main Entry:
(105)   Weinberger, Caspar W.

Form of Material: Papers, 1961-1987. (244)	Item Count: (302#b) Addition, ca. 70,000 items.

Description at Receipt:
(520)   General, personal, and official correspondence, diaries, appointment
books, calendars, chronological files, subject material, financial
data, speeches and related matter, photographs, Dept. of Defense
news digests, books, and printed matter, and miscellaneous files,
chiefly from Weinberger's years as U.S. Secretary of Health,
Education and Welfare, an executive with The Bechtel Corporation,
and as U.S. Secretary of Defense.

Source: Hon. Caspar Weinberger (541#bc) via: U.S. Dept. of Defense	Status: Deposit
	Location: Processing Area 4

Special Remarks and Reminders:
    Includes some <u>classified</u> material.
    Container list accompanied collection now with processors.
    99 cartons.

A06-4-26-88

ATTACHMENT B

LIBRARY OF CONGRESS
MANUSCRIPT DIVISION

The Papers of

CASPAR W. WEINBERGER

The papers of Caspar W. Weinberger (1917-), lawyer, politician, television commentator, newspaper columnist, and cabinet official, were deposited in the Library of Congress from 1981 to 1988.

The status of copyright in the unpublished writings of Caspar W. Weinberger is governed by the Copyright Law of the United States (Title 17, U. S. C.).

Video tapes and audio recordings have been transferred to the appropriate custodial division of the Library of Congress where they are identified as a part of these papers.

The Caspar W. Weinberger Papers are restricted unless written permission is give by Mr. Weinberger. In the case of classified material, requisite security clearances are also necessary. Requests for access are not being entertained at this time.

Photoduplication is allowed only with the written permission of Casper W. Weinberger.

Linear feet of shelf space occupied: 379
Approximate number of items: 370,000

CASPAR W. WEINBERGER PAPERS

Classified Items Removed

Below is the container list of classified material removed from the papers of Caspar W. Weinberger. References are to exact series and folder titles from which the items were taken. The list is for staff use only. Readers will learn from cross reference sheets in the applicable files of the papers whether and why classified material has been removed.

Not described by this list is material from Weinberger's Department of Defense subject file, which is classified in such quantity that the entire subseries has been placed in the security vault. Information regarding the latter can be found in the main register to the Weinberger Papers (boxes 622 to 889) and in the various inventories of the DOD subject file.

Also not described by this list are the classified items themselves. Inventories of the two DOD series represented, the appointment and diary notes file and Weinberger's 1986 chronological file, are instead located at the beginning of each file in the papers. In the case of the 1986 chronological file, they appear as well at the beginning of each monthly segment. Another set has been retained as part of the working index to other Weinberger DOD files kept in the vault.

2

Weinberger Papers: Classified Items Removed

Container Nos.   Contents

OFFICE OF MANAGEMENT AND BUDGET, 1969-73

1   Subject file, 1969-73
                      Budget
                          Fiscal Year
                              1973
                                  Supplemental items (folder 1)
                      Confidential Statement of Employment and Financial
                          Interests
                      Council of Economic Advisors
                      Defense, Department of
                      Information leaks
                      Office of Economic Opportunity
                      Personnel data book, June 1970
                      Revenue sharing
                          Desk file, 1971 (folder 2)
                      State, Department of
                      Stockpiles (folder 1)
                      Trips
                          June 1971
                      Wage-price freeze
                          Budget reduction
                      White House
                          General (folder 2)

        DEPARTMENT OF HEALTH, EDUCATION, AND WELFARE, 1972-75

                  General File, 1972-75
                      Confidential Statement of Employment and Financial
                          Interests
                      Joint Drug Cabinet Committee meeting, 1973
                  Speeches, Trips, and Meetings, 1973-75
                      Speeches
                          Jan. 26-28, 1975
                      Trips
                          Foreign
                              Aug.-Sept. 1973
                                  U.S.S.R. and Poland
                                      General (folder 1)
                              May 3-11, 1974
                                  Australia and New Zealand
                              May 2-9, 1975
                                  Australia and New Zealand
                                      General

Weinberger Papers: Classified Items Removed

Container Nos.   Contents

DEPARTMENT OF DEFENSE, 1980-87

1 (cont.)

Transition, 1980-81
    Idea suggestions (folder 2)
Appointment and diary file, 1981-87
    White House, cabinet, and other important meeting notes
        Set B (photocopies of originals not in collection)
            1981 (folders 1-2)
            1982 (folder 1)
            1983 (folder 2)
            1984 (folders 1-2)
            1985 (folders 1-2)
            1986 (folder 3)
            1987 (folders 1-3)

2

Chronological File, 1986
    Jan.-May 12 (8 folders)

3

    May 13-July 22 (8 folders)

4

    July 23-Sept. 30 (8 folders)

5

    Oct.-Dec. (8 folders)

CASPAR W. WEINBERGER PAPERS

Classified Portion
Department of Defense: Subject File

The subject file portion of the Department of Defense series in the
Weinberger Papers has been removed from general circulation because the bulk
of the material consists of classified government documents. The file extends
from box 622 to box 890 and is described in the container list of the
collection. A dummy sheet indicating the containers' removal has been placed
in the physical space on the shelf between boxes 621 and 891.

Preceding the DOD subject file for each year is an index or inventory of
the documents for that year. Listed sequentially, in the order of their
arrangement, documents are first cited by control number (when there is one)
and then by content, date, authorship, etc. Entries are grouped
alphabetically by subject as described in the container list of the
collection.

Copies of the DOD subject index have also been interfiled among the
appropriate topical categories. At the front of folder one of the 1981
Central America file, for example, is the inventory for all the items of all
the folders under that title for the year. The interfiled index is of
special importance because of annotations indicating the sensitivity of
certain classified documents. Separated from the main group of classified
material are three categories of items: top secret documents, secret
restricted data, and top secret restricted data. As noted on the inventories
where they appear, one asterisk indicates removal to a separate location of
top secret material, two asterisks for removal of secret restricted data, and
three asterisks for removal of top secret restricted data. Staff and readers
with permission to use the Weinberger Papers can refer to separate inventories
of the three most sensitive categories for information regarding their extent
and character.

A third set of DOD subject file indexes consists of a working index used
during processing and retained as a master listing of the items'
classification. The working index is not for circulation and not part of the
collection. It is a reference/processing tool. Noted before each entry on
the working index is the current standing of the material cited. A hyphen
("-") next to an entry indicates the material is unclassified. A "d" before
the item indicates the material has been declassified according to
instructions on the document(s). Other markings signify the following: "c"
means confidential; "s" means secret; "frd" means formerly restricted data;
"ts" with a red line drawn through means top secret material; "srd" crossed in
red means secret restricted data; and "tsrd" boxed in red means top secret
restricted data. Red has been used to alert staff quickly to sensitive items
removed for special handling.

NB: Most documents listed in the subject file indexes contain more
material than is cited. Briefing books, for instance, consist of many items
brought together as one unit and listed as a single document. In treating the
various classifications which appear within, the procedure followed has been

to rate the whole according to the most sensitive part. If even one page of one item is top secret, then the document as a whole has been given a top secret designation. Similarly, if only one item in a packet of correspondence is confidential, the whole packet has nonetheless been described as confidential.

2

Biographical Note

1917, Aug. 18	Born, San Francisco, CA.
1933	Graduated, San Francisco Polytechnic High School
1938	Graduated, Harvard College
1941	LL.B., Harvard Law School
1941-45	U.S. Army
1942	Married Jane Dalton
1945-47	Law clerk, U.S. Judge William E. Orr
1947-69	Practiced law with firm of Heller, Ehrman, White & McAuliffe (partner, 1959-69)
1952-58	State Assemblyman, California Legislature
1958	Unsuccessful candidate to become Republican nominee for Attorney General of State of California
1959-68	Newspaper columnist on California politics and government Moderator of television program, "Profile: Bay Area," KQED, San Francisco
1960-62	Vice chairman, Republican Central Committee of California
1962-64	Chairman, Republican Central Committee of California
1967-68	Chairman, Commission on California State Government Organization and Economics
1968-69	Director of Finance, State of California

3

1970	Chairman, Federal Trade Commission
1970-72	Deputy Director, Office of Management and Budget
1972-73	Director, Office of Management and Budget
1973	Counselor to the President for Human Resources
1973-75	Secretary of Health, Education, and Welfare
1975-80	General counsel, vice president, and director, Bechtel Group of Companies
1978-79	Member, State of California Commission on Government Reform
1981-87	Secretary of Defense
1988-	Publisher, Forbes Magazine

Scope and Content Note

The papers of Caspar W. Weinberger span the years 1919 to 1987, with the bulk of the items concentrated in the period 1951 to 1987. The collection focuses on his career in California state politics and the federal government, but also includes family papers, files from a private legal practice, and considerable material relating to his work in public television, as a San Francisco Bay Area newspaper columnist, and with the Bechtel Group of Companies as the international construction firm's vice president and general counsel. Featured are lengthy records of his cabinet positions under Presidents Nixon and Ford between 1970 and 1975 and from 1981 to 1987 when he was President Reagan's Secretary of Defense during a period of rapid increase in military expenditures. His earlier Washington posts involved stints as Deputy Director and then Director of the Office of Management and Budget and two years as Secretary of Health, Education, and Welfare before and after the resignation of Richard Nixon following the Watergate scandal. Prior to holding these positions, Weinberger had served briefly as head of the Federal Trade Commission in 1970.

Included in the papers are appointment books, diary notes and other jottings; personal, general, and business correspondence; legislative and political matter; and subject files, financial data, television scripts, newspaper columns, book reviews, texts of speeches, and assorted printed matter. Files related to Weinberger's service as Secretary of Defense consist mainly of photocopied duplicates rather than original items. Most are classified government documents and cannot be served to the general public.

Weinberger's early interest in politics is demonstrated by scrapbooks and other items he kept about national affairs while a student at San Francisco Polytechnic High School in the 1930s. He was a star pupil whose commencement oration on the nobility of politics (texts of which survive among his childhood materials) anticipated his first run for public office as a Republican candidate for the California State Assembly in 1952. He won in a Bay Area contest, and his four consecutive terms in Sacramento are meticulously recorded in legislative files for the period. Noted statewide for his efforts to reorganize California's Alcoholic Control Board, Weinberger competed for a spot on the 1958 GOP ticket as state attorney general but lost in the primary to a more conservative challenger. His files trace some of the ideological and organizational issues involved, shifting subsequently to the crucial years between 1960 and 1964, when as vice chairman and later chairman of the State Republican Central Committee he shepherded the state party through various factional struggles culminating in the ascendance nationally of the so-called Goldwater wing of the GOP. Correspondence from the period foreshadows the Washington administrations of Nixon and Reagan, in that letters and related material concern the pre-presidential careers of both future chief executives and their various California and Sunbelt supporters. Among the more frequent or prominent letter writers are Goodwyn Knight, Robert Finch, John Tower, Barry Goldwater, Nelson Rockefellor, William P. Clark, George Murphy, George Christopher, and William F. Knowland.

Journalism and the news media were Weinberger's second interests, and after leaving the state assembly he began ten years as moderator of "Profile: Bay Area," a public affairs program on San Francisco public television station KQED. The production is fully documented with scripts, correspondence, and

related matter. Also well covered is a syndicated newspaper column he wrote
from 1958 to 1966 titled "California Commentary."

In 1966, then Governor Reagan appointed Weinberger to be California State
Finance Director. Weinberger's papers are thereafter arranged by career
episode, with general and personal correspondence for a given period
congregated under position title. Students of the Nixon White House can turn
first to the FTC segment to trace Weinberger's initial Washington connection,
after which considerable information is available in OMB files on critical
budgetary and fiscal matters for the 1971 to 1973 period. As HEW secretary,
Weinberger grappled with welfare reform, abortion, and affirmative action in
education, issues extensively treated with other topical and policy questions
under the HEW heading. Already during his FTC-OMB appointments, Weinberger
began keeping terse journal notations or diary notes of important events and
meetings. These notes can be used with various White House, cabinet, and
other subject files to glean highlights of his contribution to the Nixon-Ford
presidencies. Themes of significance in addition to topics already mentioned
range from Nixon's 1973 attempt to reorganize the Executive Branch (material
on this is concentrated in a file on Weinberger's ephemeral post as Counselor
of Human Resources), to such ongoing issues as the federal budget deficit,
social security funding, and increased health care costs.

At Bechtel from 1975 to 1980, Weinberger refocused on California and
private business interests. He was still oriented toward national politics,
however, with the goal after the election of Jimmy Carter being the return to
the White House of a Republican administration. To this end, Weinberger
joined the Reagan team well in advance of the former governor's 1980 campaign,
and in the Bechtel files is correspondence and commentary important to the
sweep that took both to Washington. Subjects of interest tend toward
diplomatic and military topics rather than the previous concentration on
domestic affairs, with U.S.-Soviet arms negotiations and the 1979-80 Iranian
hostage crisis among the principal items considered.

Department of Defense files in these papers begin with transition
material documenting the Reagan Administration's first steps in military
leadership. Other series from this period include appointment records and
diary notes, a private file of miscellaneous correspondence, and a large group
of subject files. Notable among the appointment data is a special category of
White House, cabinet, and other important meeting notes containing the Defense
Secretary's handwritten jottings and sometimes those of Reagan and Vice
President George Bush. Writings by his superiors are brief and infrequent but
include choice comments as well as amusing sketches.

The most substantive of the Defense Department materials is an extensive
subject file organized, copied from originals at the Pentagon, and indexed by
his staff. Treated within yearly alphabetical groupings are the great and
small events of world affairs during the 1980s, including information on the
character and opinions of the major individual participants. Among the score
or more incidents and developments covered are U.S.-Soviet nuclear weapons
discussions, the invasion of Grenada, the Falklands War, various crises in
Lebanon, American policy toward Nicaragua, relations with NATO, U.S. attacks
on Libya, terrorism, and the Iran-Contra affair. Budgetary and management
issues are recurring topics as well, especially in relation to OMB Director
David Stockman and leading policy shapers in Congress, while another episode
covered is the aftermath of the March 1981 assassination attempt on President
Reagan. The file as a whole is characterized by documentation of every sort,

much of it classified, including correspondence with world leaders, memoranda
of conversations, memoranda between cabinet and other executive-level
officials, diplomatic and military cables, briefing data, minutes or synposes
of
White House and National Security Council meetings, and reports (political as
well as military) regarding the spectrum of U.S. interests on the
international scene.

   Prominent correspondents whose names have not been cited above include
Spiro Agnew, Richard Armitage, Menacham Begin, Frank Carlucci, Peter Lord
Carrington, William J. Casey, William J. Crowe, King Fahad, Indira Gandhi,
Mohamed Abdul Halim Abu Ghazala, Alexander M. Haig, Charles Hernu, Michael
Heseltine, King Hussein, Fred C. Ikle, Helmut Kohl, Yuko Kurihara, Robert
McFarlane, Mohamed Hosni Mubarak, John M. Poindexter, Richard Perle, Colin
Powell, Elliott Richardson, Yitzhak Shamir, Ariel Sharon, Bernard W. Rogers,
George P. Shultz, Giovanni Spadolini, Margaret Thatcher, John Vessey, and
Manfred Woerner,

Description of Series

Container Nos.	Series

1-5   **Family and Childhood Papers, 1910-79.**
Correspondence, legal papers, school materials, photographs, early business items, scrapbooks, printed matter, and various miscellany. Organized alphabetically by type or topic of material.

5-12   **Law Office, 1927-55.**
Corrrespondence, memoranda, briefs, writs, notes, and other material concerning Weinberger's law practice, mostly from the period 1948-52. Organized alphabetically by case or subject.

13-116   **California State Government, 1951-79.**

13-92   Legislative Assembly, 1951-58
Correspondence, memoranda, bills, notes, charts, lists, legal data, and various printed material pertaining to Weinberger's duties in the California Legislative Assembly from 1952-58. Organized according to session and then by topic, type of material, or name of correspondent.

93-104   Commissions, 1962-79
Correspondence, memoranda, reports, bulletins, minutes of meetings, press material, and related matter concerning Weinberger's chairmanship of the Commission on California State Government Organization and Economics ("Little Hoover Commission") and membership on the State of California Commission on Government Reform. Organized according to commission and alphabetically therein by type or topic of material.

105-116   State Director of Finance, 1968-69
Correspondence, reports, appointment files, diary notes, invitations, speech material, and other files concerning Weinberger's tenure as Director of California State Finance. Organized alphabetically by type or topic of material.

S

Container Nos.	Series
117-147	**California Politics, 1951-66.**

117-130   Campaigns, 1951-66
Correspondence, memoranda, calendars, photographs, financial items, press material, lists, notes, campaign advertisements, speech material, printed matter, and other material relating to various state and national political campaigns in which Weinberger was involved as a candidate or Republican Party official between 1952 and 1966. Organized alphabetically by office sought and chronologically by election therein.

130-131   Radio Program: "People and Politics," 1959-62
Correspondence and scripts from a daily radio program Weinberger chaired to explain and promote Republican views on state and national political affairs. Organized according to type of material and chronologically therein.

132-147   Republican State Central Committee, 1960-64
Correspondence, memoranda, subject files, speech material, minutes of meetings, and other data documenting Weinberger's tenure as vice chairman and chairman of the Republican State Central Committee. Organized chronologically and then alphabetically by type or topic of material.

148-200   **California Public Affairs, 1957-68.**

148-167   General Correspondence, 1959-67
Correspondence and related matter pertaining to Weinberger's activities on behalf of various religious, philanthropic, educational, and other private and public institutions in San Francisco and elsewhere during the period between his duties as state assemblyman and subsequent state and national office. Organized alphabetically by type or topic of material.

167-180   Newspaper Column: "California Commentary," 1958-66
Correspondence, drafts and printed copies of columns, and financial and other materials documenting Weinberger's semi-weekly newspaper articles about California state government. Arranged alphabetically by type of material and chronologically within.

9

Container Nos.	Series

148-200   **California Public Affairs, 1957-68 (continued).**

    180-200

Television Programs, 1959-68
    Correspondence, scripts, lists, and printed matter relating to public television programs hosted by Weinberger on station KQED in San Francisco. Topics were political and social issues affecting California and the nation. Organized alphabetically by type of material.

201-216   **Federal Trade Commission, 1970-71.**
    Correspondence, memoranda, appointment files, lists, articles, Congressional testimony, diary notes, subject files, invitations, press material, speeches, printed matter, and miscellaneous data regarding Weinberger's duties as Chairman of the Federal Trade Commission. Correspondence includes letters with legislators, government officials, and the general public. Arranged alphabetically by topic or type of material.

217-304   **Office of Management and Budget, 1969-73.**

    217-221

Appointment and Diary Files, 1970-72
    Appointment books and diary notes recording Weinberger's personal and public activities while Deputy Director and Director of OMB. Arranged alphabetically by type of material and chronologically within.

    221-231

Correspondence, 1970-73
    Correspondence with legislators, government officials, politicians, friends, acquaintances, and the general public. Includes attached and related matter. Organized into general and personal files and alphabetically therein.

    231-293

Subject File, 1969-73
    Correspondence, memoranda , charts, lists, minutes, of meetings, bulletins, briefing data, bills, press, material, reports, interviews, invitations, printed matter, and other miscellaneous material from Weinberger's tenure at OMB. Alphabetically arranged by topic or type of material.

10

Container Nos.	Series

217-304   **Office of Management and Budget, 1969-73 (continued).**

    293-304   Speech File, 1970-73
          Texts of speeches and related matter regarding
their presentation, including notes, correspondence,
invitations, and programs. Organized chronologically
by date of speech. Miscellaneous background materials
appears at the end of the file and is arranged
alphabetically by subject.

305-470   **Department of Health, Education, and Welfare, 1972-75.**

    305-318   Appointment and Diary Files, 1973-75
          Appointment books, schedules, and diary notes
recording Weinberger's personal and public activities
while Secretary of HEW. Arranged alphabetically by
type of material and chronologically within.

    318-365   Correspondence, 1973-75
          Congratulatory, Congressional, general, and
personal correspondence, including attached and
appended material. Arranged alphabetically by name of
correspondent within applicable segments.

    365-405   Reading File, 1973-75
          Reading file of letters sent. Organized into
departmental and personal segments, each arranged
chronologically, and a secretariat file consisting of
alphabetical and chronological subgroups. The
alphabetical subgroup contains both topical and
personal name files.

    405-426   General File, 1972-75
          Correspondence, memoranda, reports, briefing
material, minutes of meetings, charts, lists, bills,
invitations, and printed matter concerning the
programs, staff, and operation of HEW. Arranged
alphabetically by type or topic of material.

    427-451   Subject File, 1972-75
          Correspondence, memoranda, bills, Congressional
testimony, reports, briefing material, press data,
grant files, contracts, charts, lists, printed matter,
and miscellaneous files pertaining to sustantive
functions of HEW. Organized alphabetically into
primary issue categories and arranged alphabetically by
subtopic within. Among the principal categories are
budget issues, civil rights, education, and national
health care.

Container Nos.	Series
305-470	**Department of Health, Education, and Welfare, 1972-75 (continued).**

12

Container Nos.	Series

565-571   **Bechtel Files, 1968-80 (continued).**

   565-571   Speech File, 1975-80
      Texts of speeches and related matter regarding their
presentation, including notes, correspondence,
invitations, and programs. Background and press
material precedes chronologically arranged texts.

572-890   **Department of Defense, 1976-87.**

   572-576   Transition Papers, 1980-81
      Correspondence, schedules, briefing material and
notes, invitations, reports, topical files, printed
matter and miscellaneous items concerning the
transition from President Carter and the Reagan
administration. Organized alphabetically by topic or
type of material.

   576-592   Appointment and Diary Files, 1980-87
      Appointment books, diary notes, activity logs,
social calendars, telephone call sheets, and
handwritten notes kept by Weinberger of White House,
cabinet, and other important meetings he attended while
Secretary of Defense. Organized alphabetically by
type of file and chronologically within. White
House and other important meetings notes are
arranged in two sets, the second of which consists of
photocopies of originals not in the papers. Included
in the latter is an index of the notes compiled and
photocopied by Weinberger's staff.

   592-607   Private File, 1976-87
      Correspondence, memoranda, minutes of meetings,
invitations, press items, reports, printed matter, and
miscellaneous data. Alphabetically arranged by subject
or type of material.

   608-621   Chronological File, 1986
      Photocopies and a few originals of outgoing
correspondence, memoranda, and related matter for
1986. A complete index of the file, compiled by
Weinberger's staff at the Department of Defense,
precedes the documents. The index and file are
organized chronologically on a monthly basis, and
copies of the index for each month are also filed
prior to each calendar change. Included in the series
are numerous classified items now removed from general
use. Items withdrawn have been identified by
asterisk(s) next to the document control numbers on
the monthly index sheets.

13

Container Nos.	Series
572–890	**Department of Defense, 1976–87 (Continued).**

622–890 Subject File, 1981–87 (Classified).
Photocopies and a few originals of correspondence, memoranda, reports, military orders, budgetary and administrative files, transcripts of high-level conversations, diplomatic exchanges, military cables, technological data, and numerous related files concerning Weinberger's tenure as Secretary of Defense. Organized chronologically by year and alphabetically by subject therein. An index of documents compiled by Weinberger's staff precedes the file for each year. Subject entries are also preceeded by indexes, with the pertinent sheets appearing at the front of the first folder on the topic covered. The entire series has been removed from general use because of its classified contents.

891–946   **Miscellany, 1948–87.**

891–892 Book Reviews by Weinberger, 1948–80
Writings, correspondence, notes, printed matter, and other materials relating to the preparation and publication of book reviews. Arranged chronologically by appearance of review.

892–896 Photographs, 1960–87
Positive photographic prints and some negatives, primarily of Weinberger's public life. Organized chronologically.

897 Teaching File, 1949–61
Correspondence, lecture notes, attendance charts, and miscellaneous items concerning Weinberger's presentations to California Bar Association meetings and college and university classes which he taught in San Francisco.

897 Steep Ravine, 1961–72
Correspondence, clippings, and miscellaneous material relating to the attempt by Weinberger and others to make Steep Ravine a California State Park.

Container Nos.   Series

891-946   **Miscellany, 1948-87 (Continued).**

  898-946   Printed Matter, 1951-80
                          Clippings and other printed matter regarding
                          Weinberger, organized on a monthly or yearly basis.

947   **Oversize, 1934.**
                          Scrapbook concerning national politics kept by
                          Weinberger as a child, removed from the family papers
                          because of its size.

83

Container Nos.	Contents

BECHTEL FILES, 1968–80 (Continued)

564   **Subject file, 1968–80**
     Miscellaneous
    Speech file, 1975–80
     General background material
      1975–76 (4 folders)

565   1977–80 (2 folders)
     Press material, 1975–76 (2 folders)

566   Speeches
      Aug. 24, 1975–June 5, 1976 (10 folders)

567   June 10, 1976–Feb. 11, 1977 (15 folders)

568   Feb. 23–Sept. 19, 1977 (10 folders)

569   Oct. 13, 1977–Dec. 12, 1978 (14 folders)

570   Jan. 17–Sept. 13, 1979 (16 folders)

571   Sept. 24, 1979–Nov. 18, 1980 (15 folders)

DEPARTMENT OF DEFENSE, 1976–87

572   **Transition papers, 1980–81**
     Confirmation material
      Notebook for Congressional hearing, Dec. 19, 1980
       (2 folders)
      Miscellaneous (2 folders)
     Daily schedule
     Foreign Policy Advisory Group
     Idea suggestions
      (1 folder)

573   (2 folders)
     Inaugural matters
     Invitations accepted
     Office of Management and Budget position paper
     Personal matters
     Referrals

574   Spending Control Task Force
     Spending reduction recommendations (3 folders)
     Thank-you letters
      (1 folder)

8.

Container Nos.	Contents

DEPARTMENT OF DEFENSE, 1976–81 (Continued)

575
    Transition, 1980–81
      Thank-you letters
        (1 folder)
      Miscellaneous
        (4 folders)

576
        (1 folder)
    Appointment and diary file, 1980–87
      Appointment books
        1981 (2 volumes)

577
        1982 (3 volumes)

578
        1983 (3 volumes)

579
        1984 (3 volumes)
        1985
          (2 volumes)

580
          (1 volume)
        1986
      Diary notes
        Dec. 1980–Mar. 1981 (2 folders)

581
        Apr. 1981–June 1982 (5 folders)

582
        July 1982–Sept. 1983 (5 folders)

583
        Oct. 1983–Dec. 1984 (5 folders)

584
        Jan. 1985–Mar. 1986 (5 folders)
        } TO FC

585
        Apr. 1986–Sept. 1987 (6 folders)
        Apr 1986 – Dec 1986

586
        Oct. 1987
        (3 folders) → TO FC
      Official log of activities
        Jan. 1981–June 1983 (5 folders)

587
        July 1983–June 1986 (6 folders)

588
        July–Dec. 1986
      Social engagements calender (Caspar W. and Jane
        Weinberger)
          1981–86 (6 folders)

589
          1987
      Telephone call sheets, 1981–86 (6 folders)

85

Container Nos.   Contents

DEPARTMENT OF DEFENSE, 1976-87 (Continued)

590   **Appointment and diary file, 1980-87**
                 White House, cabinet, and other important meeting notes
                     Set A (originals)
                         1981-87 and undated (9 folders)

591   Set B (photocopies of originals not in collection)
                             Index, 1981-87
                             1981-84 (9 folders)

592   1985-87 (8 folders)
             Private file, 1976-87
                 American Ditchley Foundation
                     (1 folder)

593   (2 folders)
                 Bechtel, 1980-85
                 Biographical data
                 Boards

594   Bohemian Club (3 folders)
                 Churchilliana

595   Clubs
                 Correspondence
                     Personal
                         1981-May 1983 (3 folders)

596   June 1983-1985 (4 folders)

597   1986
                     Thank-you letters
                         1981-April 1984 (5 folders)

598   May 1984-1985 (4 folders)

599   1986
                     Miscellaneous
                         Feb. 1981-Apr. 1983 (4 folders)

600   May 1983-1984 (5 folders)

601   1985-86 (4 folders)
                 Council on Foreign Relations
                 Duncan, Virginia B.

ATTACHMENT C

MANUSCRIPT DIVISION COLLECTION REQUEST

Collection Title: Weinberger, Caspar

Container or Reel Numbers:

#622, 669, 719, 799, 840, 765, 885

Researcher's Name (please print): Gregory Mark	Seat Number:
Researcher's Signature:	Date: 11/2/90

For Staff Use Only

Ident. Number: 75883	Location or Micro. Ac. No.:	Staff Initials:	Units Served: 7

86-37 (rev 7/89)

MANUSCRIPT DIVISION COLLECTION REQUEST

Collection Title: Weinberger Caspar

Container or Reel Numbers:

TS21 - Iran & Israel
Honduras, Central America

TS22- Nicaragua

Researcher's Name (please print): Gregory A Mark	Seat Number:
Researcher's Signature:	Date: 11/30/90

For Staff Use Only

Ident. Number: 75883	Location or Micro. Ac. No.: vault	Staff Initials:	Units Served: 2

86-37 (rev 7/89)

MANUSCRIPT DIVISION COLLECTION REQUEST

Collection Title: Weinberger, Caspar

Container or Reel Numbers:

TS23   TS24
Iran   Israel

Researcher's Name (please print): Gregory A Mark	Seat Number:
Researcher's Signature:	Date: 11-30-90

For Staff Use Only

Ident. Number:	Location or Micro. Ac. No.:	Staff Initials:	Units Served: 2

86-37 (rev 7/89)

AFFIDAVIT

I, WILLIAM H. TAFT, IV, being duly sworn, do depose and state as follows:

1. I am the United States Ambassador to NATO and have served in that position since 1989. From 1984 - 1987, I was the Deputy Secretary of Defense under Secretary of Defense Caspar W. Weinberger. From 1981 - 1984 I served under him as General Counsel of the Department of Defense. I also served in government with Secretary Weinberger at the Office of Management and Budget as his executive assistant from 1970 - 1973 and as his executive assistant while he was Secretary of the Department of Health, Education and Welfare from 1973 - 1975.

2. In my capacity as Deputy Secretary of Defense, I worked closely with Mr. Weinberger. We routinely discussed important policy matters and kept each other fully informed of such matters.

3. I did not learn until the fall of 1986 through media accounts that Israel had sold American-supplied arms to Iran in the fall of 1985. Based on my personal and professional relationship with Mr. Weinberger, I feel certain that had he been aware of the Israeli shipments to Iran prior to the fall of 1986, he would have informed me in the course of our discussions of the American shipments to Iran which occurred in the first part of 1986.

1

4. I am aware that documents indicate that I
was present at a meeting on October 4, 1985, with CIA
Director William Casey, his Assistant John McMahon and
Secretary Weinberger. I have reviewed Secretary
Weinberger's diary notes for October 4, 1985, which
reflect a breakfast meeting with Messrs. Casey, McMahon
and me. See Attachment A. The notes state: "Ollie
North's negot. with Iranians - Told them no U.S. arms to
be sold or given to Iran." While I do not recall this
meeting, this statement reflects Secretary Weinberger's
consistent position which was to oppose any transfer of
arms to Iran.

5. I also have been advised that according to
Noel Koch, who was a Deputy Assistant Secretary of Defense
under Richard Armitage, Mr. Koch attended a meeting in
January 1986 with Secretary Weinberger and me. Mr. Koch
reportedly asked during the meeting whether anyone would
go to jail as a result of the decision to send American
arms to Iran. I do not recall any discussions of criminal
liability regarding the sale of arms to Iran which had
been approved by the President.

2

6.   I do not recall anyone at any meeting ever suggesting that direct U.S. sales of weapons to Iran should be authorized because this was merely an extension of the policy of allowing Israel to sell American-made weapons to Iran.

7.   I recall that Secretary Weinberger may have raised questions surrounding the legality of the sale of arms to Iran after he learned in January 1986 that the President had directed such sales in the future. At all times, Secretary Weinberger was adamantly opposed to the policy of selling arms to Iran and sought to delay implementation of that policy by raising all possible objections that could be made. However, Mr. Weinberger was not responsible for giving legal advice on these matters as this was the responsibility of the Attorney General of the United States.

8.   In January 1986, after the President directed the sale of arms to Iran in the future, Secretary Weinberger delayed implementation of this policy for approximately two weeks because of his staunch opposition to the policy.

9.   At the time that Congress began investigating the Iran-Contra matter, and throughout various other investigations of this matter, I recommended that the Department of Defense fully cooperate with all investigations.   It also was Secretary Weinberger's steadfast and unwavering position that the Department of Defense fully cooperate with the investigative bodies and provide all documents requested.   It was our view at the Department of Defense that we had opposed the policy of selling arms to Iran and that we would cooperate fully with all investigations.   I firmly believe that the Department of Defense, including Secretary Weinberger, cooperated fully with all investigations concerning the Iran-Contra matter.

10.   Based upon my close working relationship with Secretary Weinberger, including my knowledge of his demanding schedule and work practices, I can state that he would not have searched his files personally for documents responsive to requests.   Instead, he would have relied on his assistants to handle such matters.   In fact, in responding to requests for documents from my files, I made files available for others to conduct the document review.

4

11. I have known Secretary Weinberger for approximately 20 years. I know Secretary Weinberger to be a person of the highest integrity and honor who has served the United States for nearly four decades. Secretary Weinberger is a man of his word.

William H. Taft, IV

Subscribed and sworn before me this 14th day of April 1992.

Notary Public

THOMAS J. TIERNAN
Consul of United States
of America

My commission expires:

N/A

TAB-E

STATEMENT OF CASPAR WEINBERGER

I am deeply troubled and angry at this unfair and unjust indictment. A terrible injustice has been done to my family and to me.

I vigorously opposed the transfer and sale of arms to Iran and fought it at every turn inside the Administration. As everyone knows, I strongly disagreed with President Reagan on this issue.

I fully cooperated with every aspect of the investigations conducted by Congress and the Office of Independent Counsel. I even gave the Office of Independent Counsel access to all the papers they requested which have been at the Library of Congress for many years. At no time did I ever knowingly misrepresent the facts or deceive Congress or anyone else.

In order to avoid this indictment, I was not willing to accept an offer by the Office of Independent Counsel to plea to a misdemeanor offense of which I was not guilty, nor was I willing to give them statements which were not true about myself or others. I would not give false testimony nor would I enter a false plea. Because of this refusal, which to me is a matter of

conscience, I have now been charged with multiple
felonies.

The decision to indict me is a grotesque
distortion of the prosecutorial power and a moral and
legal outrage.

I am innocent and will fight this injustice to
the end with the assistance of my counsel, Robert Bennett
and Carl Rauh.

Because this matter is now in the Courts, I am
told by my attorneys that I should have no further public
comment until the matter is finally resolved.

For that reason, I am sorry to say I will not
be able to follow my usual practice and answer your
questions. Thank you for your attention.

2
○

ISBN 0-16-043009-7

9 780160 430091

90000